D1590840

OXFORD STUDIES IN
SOCIAL AND CULTURAL ANTHROPOLOGY

NUER PROPHETS

OXFORD STUDIES IN SOCIAL AND CULTURAL ANTHROPOLOGY

Oxford Studies in Social and Cultural Anthropology represents the work of authors, new and established, which will set the criteria of excellence in ethnographic description and innovation in analysis. The series serves as an essential source of information about the world and the discipline.

OTHER TITLES IN THIS SERIES

Organizing Jainism in India and England
Marcus Banks

Society and Exchange in Nias
Andrew Beatty

The Culture of Coincidence:
Accident and Absolute Liability in Huli
Laurence Goldman

The Female Bridegroom: A Comparative Study of Life-Crisis Rituals in South India and Sri Lanka
Anthony Good

Of Mixed Blood: Kinship and History in Peruvian Amazonia
Peter Gow

Exchange in Oceania: A Graph Theoretic Analysis
Per Hage and Frank Harary

Knowledge and Secrecy in an Aboriginal Religion: Yolngu of North-East Arnhem Land
Ian Keen

The Interpretation of Caste
Declan Quigley

The Arabesk Debate: Music and Musicians in Modern Turkey
Martin Stokes

NUER PROPHETS

A History of Prophecy from the
Upper Nile in the Nineteenth and
Twentieth Centuries

DOUGLAS H. JOHNSON

CLARENDON PRESS · OXFORD
1994

Oxford University Press, Walton Street, Oxford OX2 6DP
Oxford New York Toronto
Delhi Bombay Calcutta Madras Karachi
Kuala Lumpur Singapore Hong Kong Tokyo
Nairobi Dar es Salaam Cape Town
Melbourne Auckland Madrid
and associated companies in
Berlin Ibadan

Oxford is a trade mark of Oxford University Press

Published in the United States
by Oxford University Press Inc., New York

British Library Cataloguing in Publication Data
Data available

Library of Congress Cataloging in Publication Data
Johnson, Douglas Hamilton, 1949–
Nuer prophets: a history of prophecy from the Upper Nile in the nineteenth and twentieth centuries/Douglas H. Johnson.
—(Oxford studies in social and cultural anthropology)
Includes bibliographical references and index.
1. Nuer (African people)—Religious life. 2. Prophecy History—19th century. 3. Prophecy—History—20th century. 4. Prophets—Sudan—History—19th century. 5. Sudan—Religion. 6. Prophets—Sudan—History—20th century. I. Title II. Series.
BL2480.N7J64 1994 299'.685—dc20 93-22152
ISBN 0-19-827907-8

1 3 5 7 9 10 8 6 4 2

Typeset by Best-set Typesetter Ltd., Hong Kong
Printed in Great Britain
on acid-free paper by
Biddles Ltd, Guildford and King's Lynn

FOREWORD

NUER, and the neighbouring Dinka, are emblematic peoples in social anthropology. Apart from their personal qualities (attractively stereotyped as tough individualists, bloody-minded renouncers of government), the studies of them by Evans-Pritchard and by Godfrey Lienhardt are a corpus which explores the social organization and spiritual life of stateless people in the southern Sudan. The people and the books together stand for the immensely important proposition that, to paraphrase Professor Gellner, anarchy can lead to solidarity: Hobbes was wrong, and social order does not always and necessarily depend on the existence of state's men.

The books themselves are emblematic of a particular and successful strand of social anthropology. In their different ways they invited readers to perceive a structure of social relations underlying the variety of everyday life. The structure was essentially one of loyalty, of continuities of support, and its form was given by a series of variations on the themes of kinship and descent. The particular brilliance of those works was to show how the structure underlay political, economic, and spiritual activity. The result was a significant development of social anthropology, in addition to their crucially important contribution to political philosophy.

Dr Johnson's work combines the expertises of anthropology and history, and is complementary to that corpus. For some of the earlier work, given its purpose of elucidating a structure of relations, was notably abstract: the day-to-day improvisations on the themes were not always in the foreground. So, to imagine normal everyday life, readers had to emphasize what was under-emphasized in the texts, and to muddy the elegance of the patterns with rather few instances of real people doing real things on specified days. Dr Johnson's book, the fine result of twenty years of fieldwork, archival research, and practical intervention, takes prophets as the key to Nuer political and spiritual organization. By exploring the careers of Nuer and Dinka prophets, of failed prophets, and their relations with other Nuer and Dinka, and with representatives of the governments of Sudan, he has produced a most remarkable work. Prophets were a particular manifestation of spirituality, and one of the many virtues of Dr Johnson's work is that he places prophets in the general context of 'mantic'—his neutral and inclusive term—activity. They were part and parcel of Nuer political and religious understanding and experience. But Dr Johnson also shows how many British administrators put the prophets in the same category as the Muslim religious and political leaders of the Sudan, who had supported the Mahdi and defeated General Gordon. Dr Johnson explores both Nilotic and Imperial personnel—their careers, aspirations, and expectations; places them within an account of the structure of relations of Nuer and British social organization, and then explains the outcome of the clash between them: it is a subtle and nuanced historical anthropology.

Evans-Pritchard urged anthropologists to become historians. He thought they were more likely to succeed when they studied 'more civilized' people, partly because the historical records were more complete. In fact, it is probably fair to say that the work in the Mediterranean countries by his younger colleagues and students, which he supported and which he expected to produce the new connubium, was disappointing. It is quite otherwise with this book. Dr Johnson's meticulous work in the archives of the administration benefits from his easy familiarity with the country and ecology of Nuerland, and it is integrated with other sources. On the one hand, the administrators wrote memoirs and reminiscences of their service; some based works of fiction on their experience. On the other hand Nuer preserved records of events. Some of these, work by Nuer and Dinka historians and sociologists, are in print. Others are oral: men remembered what their fathers and grandfathers had told them. It is one of the most impressive beauties of this book that Dr Johnson has not simply characterized these transmitted biographies as legends or traditions, but has dissected them for the information they contain. Some is explanatory but uncorroborated; some fits neatly with what administrators filed. The most striking example perhaps is his reconstruction of both sides of General Gordon's conversation with Nuaar Mer in 1874 (p. 131): a restoration of an event to something like its original complexity and uncertainty. The prophets and others also composed songs which boasted of their success and threatened rivals with defeat: widely diffused, they are a source that Dr Johnson again uses judiciously to reconstruct the ambiguities of the past. He also draws upon material which anthropologists have conventionally classified as myth. His reasons for doing so are that although the narratives are often patently implausible in their detail they none the less influenced the actions of Nuer who knew them; they were consequential because they affected people's strategies and tactics, and are in this sense part of a historical explanation.

The result of this careful and scrupulous deployment of different kinds of records of the past—archives, literature, autobiography, oral biography, oral literature, myth—is without any doubt the most successful attempt yet to marry anthropology and history: the combination of narratives and structure illuminates each. It gives added pleasure that the work concerns a less 'civilized' people, and is a substantial enhancement of our understanding of the subjects of Evans-Pritchard's major works.

John Davis
Professor of Social Anthropology, University of Oxford

PREFACE

In August 1991, while I was making a survey of the Pibor River for the World Food Programme's relief operation in the Southern Sudan, a Nuer veteran of the Sudan People's Liberation Army showed me one of his most valued possessions: a battered copy of Evans-Pritchard's *Nuer Religion*. He had served in the Anyanya guerrilla army of the Sudan's first civil war and had been absorbed into the national army after the Addis Ababa peace agreement in 1972. He had been one of the original Bor mutineers in May 1983, was wounded, captured, and lost a leg. After he was released from prison, at the request of the Sudan government's Nuer allies, he returned to his home area. There he became active in the mediation efforts which eventually brought about a merger between the mainly Nuer pro-government Anyanya II and the anti-government SPLA which included Nuer, Dinka, and others. In recognition of his contribution to the movement the commander of the SPLA, John Garang (a Twic Dinka), gave him a copy of *Nuer Religion*, telling him that it was about the Nuer prophet Ngundeng and contained 'the history of our people which has never been written'. The veteran could not read English but, having heard of my first visit to Ngundeng's Mound in 1975, he brought the book to me, thinking that I had written it.

This was but one of many encounters that year in which the topic of Ngundeng was raised by people whom I had never previously met but who knew of my long-standing interest in the nineteenth-century prophet. I arrived in Nasir in June to help organize the international relief effort for the thousands of Sudanese who were fleeing into the area after the evacuation of the refugee camps in Ethiopia. I was surprised to discover how many of those I spoke to had heard of my visits to Ngundeng's Mound some sixteen years before. The two most frequent questions I was asked in the early days of the emergency were: 'When are relief supplies coming?' and 'When is your book on Ngundeng coming out?' (to neither question could I give a satisfactory answer). The interest in Ngundeng increased throughout the year as his old prophecies foretelling the war were reinterpreted as predicting the coming of peace. It was not just the Nuer who took an interest in this speculation: for the first time since Guek Ngundeng had been ridiculed in *Punch* in 1927, the name of a Nuer prophet appeared in the British press.[1] So disturbing was the invocation of Ngundeng in the political struggle within the SPLA that one influential Sudanese politician warned that these 'folk tales ought really to be confined to anthropological and historical studies at academic institutions

[1] 'Tribal Hatreds Fuel Sudan's War of Rebels', *Sunday Telegraph*, 26 Jan. 1992, p. 18.

rather than being given the time of day by Southern leaders'.[2] Less than a year later the exploits of a new prophet, Wut Nyang, not only appeared in the international press, but were broadcast on the BBC World Service.

I relate these stories to give readers some idea of the continuing power that Ngundeng's prophecies have in the Southern Sudan, as well as to illustrate how the study of prophets must include the study of prophecy. They also demonstrate the difficulty in declaring a terminal date for this study. This book is concerned primarily with events between 1870 and 1988. The events of 1991–2 do not require an alteration in the analysis of those years, but they do require their own explanation. I can only hope that what I have written will make it possible for readers to make sense of future manifestations of prophecy in the Upper Nile as well as understand past and present appearances. For this reason I feel that a comprehensive approach to the topic is both academically and historically justified—whatever demands this places on present and future readers—for the historical record is as important as current interpretation.

This book has grown out of my original doctoral research in the 1970s as well as later research in the 1980s. I offer it primarily as a contribution to African religious history and the social history of the Southern Sudan; and secondarily as an addition to the Africanist interpretation of British imperial history, Nilotic studies, and Nuer ethnography. It is best to make this declaration at the outset, for any book on the Nuer is likely to be misapprehended either as a 'tribally' based study of only local interest, or as a theoretical discussion of the work of Sir Edward Evans-Pritchard. My interest in Evans-Pritchard flowed naturally from my original interest in the peoples of the Southern Sudan, rather than the other way around. A study of Nuer history, and specifically of Nuer prophets, was first suggested to me within months of the end of the first Sudanese civil war by a Nuer, the late Stephen Ciec Lam, whose own family had been intimately connected with the lives of several prophets. I hope that this case-study in Sudanese history may help readers to understand better the complex past of the Sudan, the region of the Southern Sudan, the Nilotic heartland, and the Nuer people.

The study of prophets and prophecy is essentially historical, and as such can illuminate both contemporary concerns and indigenous historiography. The anthropological treatment of African prophets outside the Christian and Muslim traditions has, on the whole, been socio-functional, focusing on the role of the prophet within a social structure experiencing crisis or 'rapid social change'. Africanist historians have tended to borrow their models of African religion from anthropologists and have discussed prophets almost exclusively in relation to millenarian or proto-nationalist movements. The prophet as crisis leader is a familiar model. Evans-Pritchard adapted it from Robertson

[2] *Sudan Democratic Gazette*, 20 (Jan. 1992), 2.

Smith's Old Testament studies to fit the modern Nuer. It forms an essential part of Weber's studies of ancient Judaism and charismatic authority. Yet historians face considerable problems when applying this sociological model to historical cases. By focusing on prophetic figures and prophetic times as nodal points in history after which all things change, the historian obscures both processes of change and continuities of which prophets might be a part. Prophets become both cause and effect; what preceded them is, by implication, not as important to know as what followed them. The old order, by this definition, must have been 'in crisis' to produce a prophet; it must have failed.

I have offered elsewhere a critique of the crisis theory of prophets, especially as applied to African cases.[3] In this study I wish to re-emphasize the prophet's fundamental involvement in issues concerning the moral community, and to demonstrate the value—even the necessity—of studying prophets and prophecy through the parallel methods of biography and historiography. The biography of any thinker must show the development of an individual's thought, not in the abstract, but in a personal sense. A prophet's message is not delivered fully formed, though it may be remembered as such. It is developed and elucidated through dialogue, debate, and the analysis of events. The task of historians is to provide some chronology of sayings, some context for the formation of prophecy, rather than merely to sample their contents, 'as customs-officers gauge a cargo', to use W. G. Collingwood's image. As biographers, historians must adopt a profounder approach, working like a geologist puzzling over some inversion of strata who, 'on accurately plotting it out upon his map or model, sees the fitness and necessity of the phenomenon; so, with the biographical scheme understood, the discrepancies and difficulties . . . fall into their place and explain themselves'.[4] The study of prophecy, the record and interpretation of a prophet's message, must, in its turn, be historiographical; it must analyse how the understanding of prophecy changes each time prophecy is made manifest. Here Maurice Bloch's analogy for the historical study of ritual is apt: 'It is rather as if instead of understanding the nature of particles by looking at their apparent structure one analyses them by looking at their trajectory and dispersal in an accelerator.'[5] The historical trajectory of prophecy becomes one of our main objects of study.

To make a full study of prophets we must study both the lives of prophets and the life of prophecy. We must analyse, through a variety of sources and biographical detail, what the prophets did, what they tried to do, and the impact of their own times on their careers. In studying the life of prophecy we

[3] Johnson and Anderson (1994).

[4] W. G. Collingwood, *The Life and Work of John Ruskin* (London, 1893), ii. 5.

[5] M. Bloch, *From Blessing to Violence: History and Ideology in the Circumcision Ritual of the Merina of Madagascar* (Cambridge, 1986), 183.

must analyse the effect the prophets' words and messages had on their own society, and on others, during their lives and after. In this we must study how any society apprehends what it considers the truth, and how it expects to apprehend the truth. In documenting the shifts in such apprehension we trace the outline of religious change.

Robin Lane Fox's study of the late pagan and early Christian Mediterranean world has shown how such changes can be documented from scraps and fragments of mundane and routine oracles. The peoples of the classical world expected to see, hear, and converse with their gods; they expected to be able to put questions to them at oracle shrines and learn their answers. Christianity co-opted pagan religious language, pagan oracles, and pagan epiphanies. Christians explained the experience of communion with the divine in a different way, but often using the same language. The new explanation produced a different public expectation; with the new expectation there came a different personal experience of the divine; an early example of what Godfrey Lienhardt, in his study of the Christian use of Dinka religious language, calls 'linguistic parallax'.[6]

This book examines changes in expectation and meaning in a Nilotic religion through the development of the prophetic idiom among the Nuer. It makes use of remembered prophetic songs, differing perspectives reflected in oral historical testimony, and the almost epigraphic quality of contemporary colonial texts to reconstruct the lives of the prophets and the life of prophecy. The first section explores the colonial context of the written sources concerning the prophets (Chapter 1), and in doing so seeks to identify the ideology behind the political (and usually negative) interpretation of prophets in those sources. It then goes on to reconstruct Nilotic ideas of the moral community and the religious idioms on which the first Nuer prophets drew in the nineteenth century (Chapter 2). The second section, the core of the book, is arranged around the biographical study of the major prophets. We begin with the first two great nineteenth-century prophets, Ngundeng and Deng Laka (Chapters 3 and 4), who became the archetypes for many later prophets. They fashioned a new idiom out of the combination of religious ideas and experiences to be found on the eastern frontier of Nuer society. Ngundeng appears as an inspirational prophet while Deng Laka was altogether more pragmatic. The characteristics of prophecy at this time became defined within the expanding Nilotic community in which both men lived, free from the direct interference of, but not entirely untouched by, competing states in the region. We then follow their twentieth-century successors (especially their sons, Guek Ngundeng and Dual Diu) and examine the development of prophecy during a period when the pervasive presence of government steadily

[6] Robin Lane Fox, *Pagans and Christians in the Mediterranean World from the Second Century A.D. to the Conversion of Constantine* (London, 1986); R. G. Lienhardt, 'The Dinka and Catholicism', in J. Davis (ed.), *Religious Organization and Religious Experience* (London, 1982).

limited and refined the definition of permissible prophetic activity (Chapters 5 and 6). Chapter 7, which concludes this section, examines the later introduction of the prophetic idiom to the Nuer homeland in the west and the impact of the colonial government on Western Nuer prophets in the 1920s and 1930s. This period is of added importance because the direct observations of Nuer spiritual activity contained in the ethnographies of Evans-Pritchard and Fr. Crazzolara come mainly from the Western Nuer during this phase of colonial intervention. Chapters 8 and 9 in our final section look at the trajectory of prophecy in recent times, how prophets have conformed to the expectations aroused by specific prophetic traditions and are still engaged with issues of peace and war, and how what earlier prophets said and did is now very much part of the present.

In applying critical tests to both indigenous and colonial sources I am running counter to the current mainstream in the historiography of the Sudan's Condominium period, where the essential accuracy of official sources is often implicitly assumed, and where personality is given greater weight in historical explanation than politics or policy. The confrontation between the Condominium government and the Nuer prophets in the 1920s was more than just a clash of personalities. It came at a pivotal point in the colonial history of the Southern Sudan and was emblematic of the relations between the government and the non-Muslim peoples it ruled. The 'Nuer problem' was solved by applying those policies of segregation and isolation which were soon applied to the whole of the Southern Sudan in relation to the rest of the country. The official rationale for this local policy was that it was forced on government as a response to Nuer truculence and aggression. Yet those prophets who actively collaborated with government faced exile and gaol, just as did those who resisted. The official interpretation became embedded as much in ethnographic accounts of the Nuer as in Condominium historiography. It is only by studying in detail the colonial experience of particular Sudanese peoples like the Nuer that historians will eventually be able to readjust the biases inherent in colonial sources and make a definitive statement about the character of the Anglo-Egyptian period and the consequences of its administration of the Sudan.

Our reassessment of the character of Condominium rule is forced upon us in part by our assessment of the Nuer experience. This leads us inevitably to Evans-Pritchard's ethnography. In this book I, of course, take issue with Evans-Pritchard on many points, but in a very profound way this study would have been impossible without his writing, which not only interprets Nuer society brilliantly but now serves as a significant historical source in itself. I see my research as building on his work, and it is from him that I take many of my points of departure. There is now a large, and still growing, class of secondary studies concerned with theoretical discussions of Evans-Pritchard's Nuer trilogy. None is based on a systematic and comprehensive analysis of primary materials, and inevitably these historical reconstructions and explanations suffer from the limitations of their sources. In attempting to define a new starting-point for the historical study of Nilotic peoples I have thought it best to confine my use of ethnographic reference to studies based on primary field experience, leaving to one side, for the time being, commentary and reinterpretation.

The Nuer have been afflicted by state-generated violence throughout much of the twentieth century, and this has often been the context of field research in their homeland. Evans-Pritchard began his field-work during the final stages of military pacification. My first period of field-work, in 1975–6, took place in the uneasy and often disturbed peace which followed the end of the first Sudanese civil war in 1972. My subsequent field visits in 1981–3 coincided with the build-up to the second civil war, and my work was abruptly halted by the outbreak of war in 1983. My visits to the field in 1990 and 1991 were made while employed in the United Nations relief operation and were concerned almost entirely with the consequences of ongoing civil strife. It is no wonder that prophetic pronouncements on peace and war have taken on a new poignancy and an added urgency to many Nuer, their neighbours, and those concerned with their welfare.

Finally, I make no apology for the detail presented in this study, nor for the frequent references to unfamiliar persons, peoples, and places. It is only through encounter that the unfamiliar becomes familiar. Too often the peoples of the Southern Sudan—the Nuer especially—have been generalized into abstraction. Readers who wish to understand the Southern Sudan must be willing to assimilate the detail, and I hope that this book will be a useful guide to help them do so.

D.H.J.

Oxford
1992

ACKNOWLEDGEMENTS

A STUDY so long in the making owes much to the help of many friends, and I must mention at least a few. In my earlier research in Khartoum I received kind assistance and encouragement from Professor Yusuf Fadl Hassan, Dr Muhammad Ibrahim Abu Salim, Dr Peter Garretson, Bona Malwal, and the late Dr Abbas Ibrahim Muhammad Ali. In Upper Nile Province many officials gave of their time and knowledge, and in addition to those mentioned as sources I am especially indebted to the province commissioners, first the late Peter Gatkuoth Gual, and then Philip Obang and Joshua Dei Wal; the deputy commissioners Venansio Loro, Samuel Ater Dak, and David Koak; and assistant commissioner John Wicjaal Buom. Other officials include Cuol Rambang, Justin Yak, Michael Mario, Reath Cuol, Timothy Tot, Daniel Diu, Lazarus Lei, and James Bol Kalmal. I owe a special thanks to those Nuer friends who became willing collaborators, in particular the late Stephen Ciec Lam, but also Stephen With Cakuen, Francis Gai, and the late Bertram Both Peat. I am especially indebted to my assistants Gabriel Gai Riam, Simon Kuny Puoc, and Philip Diu Deng. I was also given much help and support from many of my colleagues in the Regional Ministry of Culture and Information in Juba.

Part of my research was funded in 1982 by a Fulbright-Hayes research grant. I was able to begin writing this book while College Fellow at St Aidan's College, Durham University, in 1987. I am particularly indebted to the late Mrs Kay Coriat and to Mrs Jean Eastwood for permission to publish their husbands' photographs, and Dr Peter Garretson for permission to reproduce his photograph of Gony Yut. Terese Svoboda has very kindly granted permission to quote from her Nuer song translations in *Cleaned the Crocodile's Teeth* (1985). My thanks also to Jonathan Cape for permission to quote from M. Fausset's *Pilate Pasha*, and to Mrs J. H. R. Shaw for permission to quote from the diary of her father G. A. Heinekey.

Scholarly advice has come from many persons, but especially from my former supervisors Christopher Ehret and Terry Ranger, and from Richard Gray, Richard Hill, Godfrey Lienhardt, P. P. Howell, David Anderson, Gabriel Giet Jal, Sharon Hutchinson, and the late Peter Lienhardt. Philip Lyon Roussel, Stephen Abraham Yar, Terese Svoboda, and the late John Winder all shared their knowledge of the Nuer with me.

It is to my family that my greatest debt is owed: to my mother Frances Chapman, who shared at a distance the vicissitudes of all my field research, and who died before the final manuscript was published; to my wife Wendy James, whose own work has set an inspiring standard, and to whom this acknowledgement of critical interest and assistance is long overdue; and to my children Fiona and Roger, who might be forgiven the impression that adult conversation oscillates entirely between the topics of 'the government' and 'the Sudan'.

IN MEMORIAM

W. MacLean Johnson
Frances Clausen Chapman

CONTENTS

List of Figures xvi
List of Maps xvii
Note on Orthography xviii
Abbreviations and Glossary xix

PART I: PRELUDE

1. 'The Hammer of the Kujurs': Government, Ethnography, and Nilotic Religions 3
2. DENG and Aiwel: Elements of the Prophetic Idiom and Definition of the Moral Community 35

PART II: PROPHETS

3. Ngundeng: Prophetic Inspiration on the Eastern Frontier 73
4. Deng Laka: A Pragmatic Prophet 126
5. Guek Ngundeng and the Minor Prophets: Divinity Dispersed 164
6. Dual Diu and the Continuity of a Prophetic Tradition 204
7. Prophetic Rivalries in the Western Homeland 242

PART III: PROPHECY

8. Prophetic Traditions in Peace and War 289
9. The Life of Prophecy 327

APPENDICES

1. Nilotic Populations 357
2. Nuer Divisions 360
3. Nuer Age-Sets 362

Sources and References 364
Index 381

FIGURES

Facing page 1: Ngundeng's Mound, *c.*1924 (Coriat) xxii

1. Ngundeng's Mound, 1902 (Crispin) 89
2. The Tree of Good Things, Ngundeng's Mound, 1975 107
3. Diagram of Ngundeng's Mound 107
4. Ngundeng's baton 108
5. Matit Kal at Deng Laka's grave, Dor, 1976 162
6. Ngundeng's Mound after demolition, 1928 (Coriat) 196
7. Car Koryom under arrest, 1928 (Eastwood) 196
8. 'I will lay down the point of the Mound, the fig-tree will bend in the middle.' Guek's body, hanging from the Tree of Bad Things, 1929 (Coriat) 200
9. Dual Diu, *c.*1924 (Coriat) 212
10. Dual Diu's return, 1955 (from a sketch in NRO UNP 1/28/218) 235
11. Diagram of Dual Diu's homestead and grave, 1976 239
12. Nyup Dak (widow of Lam Liew) and Riei Pok, the prophet of GÄR, clear the ground around the shrine to Nyanwir at Dual Diu's grave, 1976 240
13. Gaaluak Nyagh, *c.*1925 (from Fergusson, *The Story of Fergie Bey*) 255
14. Gony Yut, in leopard-skin, Mogogh Conference, 1975 (Garretson) 310
15. Wyld, Coriat, and Tunnicliffe (OC police) with Ngundeng's relics (spear, pipe, drum, sack, shrine-stick, and barbless fish-spear), 1929 (Coriat) 318
16. Ngundeng's Mound, 1990 345

MAPS

1. Upper Nile Province, 1910–1976, showing province boundaries and administrative outposts 19
2. Ecological regions and Nilotic peoples in the Southern Sudan 39
3. Lou and Jikany territory in the late nineteenth and early twentieth centuries 80
4. Gaawar and southern Dinka territory 129
5. The Nuer–Dinka border, 1910–1936 171
6. Western Nuer territory 246

NOTE ON ORTHOGRAPHY

THERE are a number of systems of orthography for the Nuer and Dinka languages currently in use in the Sudan, mainly derived from those developed by different Christian missions. In the transcription of songs and phrases I employ a system used by many literate Nuer, which would be immediately recognizable by them, however unsatisfactory it may appear to professional linguists. 'C' is written rather than 'ch' or 'sh', but 'ŋ' is written for 'ng' only when transcribing songs or whole sentences. In the spelling of personal names I have in a few cases dispensed with the genitive so that non-Nuer speakers will easily recognize the names of divinities or follow genealogies; e.g. Ngundeng, rather than Ngundeang (or ŋundeaŋ), and Dual Diu, rather than Dual Diau. In writing the names of many persons who were alive when I did my field-work, I have adopted the spellings they personally used, whatever the inconsistencies with other transcriptions. I have mainly followed Evans-Pritchard's spelling of section and tribal names. The writing of place-names presents more problems, as there is little consensus in various geographical sources. In writing Arabic geographical names I use the same formula employed in Howell, Lock, and Cobb, *The Jonglei Canal*, which gives the simplest and most common transcription (Bahr el-Jebel, Bahr el-Zeraf, etc.). The names of towns and district headquarters are also given in their standardized form (Malakal, Nasir, Fashoda, etc.). Nilotic place-names are mostly unrecognizable on modern maps, having been first Anglicized, and then Arabicized; thus Pangak has become Fangak, and ultimately Fanjak. Fully accurate transcriptions would in many cases increase the difficulty in locating places on the Sudan survey maps (which are my main source). I have tried to render names as close to their current pronunciation as possible, while retaining the use of initial 'f' and 'p' as they most commonly appear (though they are largely interchangeable). For similar reasons I also retain the prefix 'a' for those Dinka place-names in territory now occupied by Nuer (Ajuong, Ayod). This compromise may lack true consistency, but it will at least enable the non-specialist reader to recognize names of places when cross-checking them in other sources.

ABBREVIATIONS AND GLOSSARY

ADC	assistant district commissioner
AMC	Archivio Storico della Congregazione dei Missionari Comboniani, Rome
BD	Bor District
BGP	Bahr el-Ghazal Province
cieng	(Nuer) a territorial or social unit of indeterminate size, applied to the family homestead, lineage segment, clan, or tribal territory
Civsec	civil secretary's files, NRO
CND	Central Nuer District
Coriat MSS	Papers of Percy Coriat, MSS Afr. s.1684 Rhodes House, Oxford
Dakhlia	Department of Interior files, NRO
DC	district commissioner
dura	(Arab.) sorghum
ED, END	Eastern District, Eastern Nuer District
ENRC	Eastern Nuer Rural Council
GGR	[governor-general's report] *Reports on the Finance, Administration, and Condition of the Sudan*
Intel	Intelligence Department files, NRO
JAH	*Journal of African History*
jallaba	(Arab.) merchant
JASO	*Journal of the Anthropological Society of Oxford*
JIT 1954	Jonglei Investigation Team, *The Equatorial Nile Project and its Effects on the Anglo-Egyptian Sudan* (Khartoum, 1954), 4 vols.
JRAI	*Journal of the Royal Anthropological Institute*
khor	(Arab.) seasonal watercourse
L.E. (£E)	Egyptian pound, currency of the Sudan until 1956, roughly equivalent to £1. 0*s*. 6*d*.
LND	Lou Nuer District
luak	(Nilotic) cattle byre, barn
MP	Mongalla Province
MPMIR	Mongalla Province Monthly Intelligence Report
NRO	National Records Office, Khartoum
OC	officer commanding
PPH MSS	Papers of P. P. Howell, SAD
PRO	Public Records Office, Kew
SAD	Sudan Archive, University of Durham
SCR	strictly confidential report
SDIT 1954	*Natural Resources and Development Potential in the Southern Provinces of the Sudan: A Preliminary Report by the Southern Development Investigation Team, 1954* (London: Sudan Government, 1955)
SIR	*Sudan Intelligence Report* (1898–1920)
SMIR	*Sudan Monthly Intelligence Report* (1921–8)

SMR	*Sudan Monthly Report*, NS (1929–)
SNR	*Sudan Notes and Records*
SRO	Southern Records Office, Juba
TD	Torit District
toic	(Nilotic) seasonally flooded pastureland
UNP	Upper Nile Province
UNPMD	Upper Nile Province Monthly Diary
zariba	(Arab., pl. *zarā'ib*) thorn hedge enclosure, fortified camp
ZV, ZVD, ZVR	Zeraf Valley, Zeraf Valley District, Zeraf Valley Region

Ngundeng's Mound, *c.*1924 (Coriat)

PART I
PRELUDE

What was the meaning of the mocking of the prophets?
(G. K. Chesterton, *The Napoleon of Notting Hill*)

1

'The Hammer of the Kujurs': Government, Ethnography, and Nilotic Religions

In January 1906 the Lou Nuer prophet Ngundeng Bong died. One of his sons, Garang Ngundeng, later described to me his father's final day:

> He came and spent a day here, at Wunkuel, at the pool of Nyangkor Nhial, where his wife's brother Thiengjiok was. When he talked he went to the dance place and said to the people, 'You people, when I go, you will never find my footprints.' A man named Jiek said, 'Ngundeng, what is wrong? Why should your footprints not be found?' [Ngundeng] said, 'That is true, my father's brother, you will never find them.' He left the dance and Jiek followed him, saying, 'Please kill a cow [as a sacrifice].'

A beast was slaughtered and divided up. A few visitors gathered at Ngundeng's cattle byre to get their share of meat, milk, and porridge. Ngundeng lay inside the byre, propped up against the pile of ashes in the hearth. Garang Ngundeng, then still an uninitiated boy, brought in the milk, but the gourd was too heavy for him to handle and one of the visitors poured the milk into the porridge. Ngundeng stirred it, gave some to the dogs and the rest to his guests, eating none himself, but eating some of the cooked meat from the ox he had just sacrificed. Then one of the visitors, a man from Eastern Jikany named Gang Wan, announced that he was leaving that day to go south to Rumjok territory to settle in the broad, well-watered pastures of the Lang section. Ngundeng, who was still lying down, asked him if he had first spoken with the elders of Lang. Gang Wan answered 'no' as each elder was named. Finally, Ngundeng burst out,

> 'My friend, how can I cross the border to the territory of Lang? That land belongs to the Lang section, I have nothing to say about it. My friend, do not ask me, for I have nothing to do with that land of Lang. That land belongs to Lang.' He was very bitter. Gang Wan was afraid and kept quiet, with his head bowed.

But even though Ngundeng was annoyed at Gang Wan's decision to leave him, and to settle in Lang without first approaching the elders there, he slaughtered two goats before Gang Wan left, and gave him meat and milk to sustain him on his journey.

Garang and others then went to a nearby hamlet. The next morning

Garang was awoken and told that his father had died. Two men smeared ashes over Ngundeng's special bulls, the black Carlel and the white Tutbor. Garang and a sister milked two cows, but the rest of the cattle were not milked that morning. Everybody, including Ngundeng's wives, ran from their houses to where Ngundeng had died. He was buried inside his own byre by his elder sons Reath and Bor. Garang arrived at his father's place after the burial.

When I came I was told to go and bring Dok Kuok, Yiec Jok, Bol Toang, and Nyak Nguol [Lou elders during Ngundeng's time]. I found Dok and Bol Toang conversing. When I told them of Ngundeng's death Dok said, 'If Ngundeng is dead, I will not go there.' So we came, the rest of us. We walked throughout the night, and that day was his mourning ceremony. That was how he died.[1]

Within a few weeks of this the prophet's family was visited by the senior inspector of Upper Nile Province, Captain H. D. E. O'Sullivan. No British official had visited Ngundeng's village since 1902, when Major Blewitt led an armed column into Lou Nuer country, burned the village, and looted the ivory around Ngundeng's shrine. Ngundeng (or Dengkur, as he was known to outsiders) had remained aloof since that time. When reports of Ngundeng's final illness reached the province capital Kodok that January Captain O'Sullivan was sent with a small escort to make 'Deng Kur declare, if he was not really dead, and if dead to take such steps as would prevent the selection of a new head chief'. He found Ngundeng's family naturally apprehensive about the intentions of the 'Turuk' (or Turk, as the government was known), but also nervous about the threatening actions of Thie Ruea, one of Ngundeng's rivals. They confirmed Ngundeng's death but declined to identify his grave. After an extended tour of Lou country O'Sullivan reported back to his governor:

Corroborated information—Deng Kur died of lung disease . . . Probable reason for not wishing to disclose grave, fear of any kind of desecration. That he was much beloved as well as feared by all. Very just, always helped poor, never allowed killing; but hated the 'red-man', and was preaching revenge on the Turk (the day he fell ill) this year.[2]

This was the closest any government official ever came to that most famous of all Nuer prophets. It was also the most favourable report on him to be written by any administrator for years to come. During the last years of his life Ngundeng suffered from a universally bad press. He was described as 'a mere magician, who excels in pretension to the art of sorcery, communes with spirits, and fancies he can control the elements'. After he died the province governor noted in his annual report, despite the paragraph quoted above,

[1] Garang Ngundeng L1.2. All interviews are listed by name of informant and number of interview, as given in the list of oral sources and interviews.

[2] H. D. E. O'Sullivan, 'Lau Nuers', 14 Mar. 1906, NRO Dakhlia I 112/13/87.

'Fearing him living, Deng Kur's people did not appear to mourn him when dead.'[3]

These two accounts of Ngundeng's death, one by his son, and one by a British administrator, represent the two very different ways that Ngundeng, and all other Nuer prophets, were evaluated. On the one hand, people were attracted to the prophets by their generosity and fairness; those around them took note of everything they did and said and consulted them on many matters; though consulted the prophets were not always listened to, and it was frequently only after their deaths that people realized the full force of the truth of their words (here, Ngundeng's prediction of his own death). On the other hand, administrators were concerned only with the prophets as potential allies or enemies. Of all that the prophets said or did, of all that others said about them, it was those words revealing their attitude towards government which received most attention. Everything else was subordinated to this most crucial administrative question. The record of the government's preoccupation with responses to itself was later translated as a record of the prophets' preoccupation with government. Herein lies the origin of the image of the prophet as warrior and resistance leader, which not only dominated administrative reports but has continued to influence academic writing.

This chapter examines the evolution of external descriptions of the Nuer prophets. We will summarize the history of contact between the Nuer and the colonial government, examining in particular those government attitudes towards religion and religious leaders in the Sudan which helped to shape the ethnographic and historical interpretations of the Nuer prophets. This is an essential prelude to disentangling the official interpretation of events from other facts about those events which can be found in the written and oral record. Once we know clearly why administrators perceived the Nuer and the prophets as they did, we can more easily try to reconstruct how the Nuer prophets perceived themselves, the societies they were in, and the government that hovered menacingly on their horizon or intervened so forcefully in their lives.

The British officers who led the Anglo-Egyptian army in the overthrow of the Mahdist state and the reconquest of the Sudan in 1898 already perceived the Nuer as a warrior race.[4] The military nature of early administration, involving as it did the demand for submission from peoples in territories formerly claimed by Egypt but who had remained independent of Mahdist control, ensured that most early encounters between government and Southern Sudanese peoples would be dominated by confrontation and conflict. Although the Nuer were not the first to resist, they were among the first to be attacked. Despite the fact that no organized bodies of Nuer fought

[3] Matthews (1905: 151; 1906: 727).

[4] Gleichen (1898: 121); Johnson (1981: 512; 1989*b*: 131–2).

government troops until 1910 (and then only in response to gross injustice by a local police officer), they were identified as hostile and warlike from the very start. In the catalogue of Nuer truculence administrators later produced, provocation was rarely considered.

Thus Sir Harold MacMichael, civil secretary from 1926 to 1934 and the Sudan government's first unofficial historian, listed various operations against the Nuer, both great and small, beginning in 1902 and ending in 1929. There was 'a small and fruitless expedition' against 'the Nuer witchdoctor Mut Dung ("Deng Kur")'; troops were sent 'against the Nuer for attacking the police post at Duk Fadiat' in 1910; those operations 'were extended to the Gaweir (Nuer)' in 1911; a further patrol ('which achieved little') in 1913 because of 'the truculent attitude of the Gaweir', and an abortive attempt the same year to occupy Gaajak Nuer country; more 'usual trouble' with the Nuer in 1914; 'unrest and intertribal fighting continued without interruption' in Upper Nile throughout 1916; troops were sent into Nuer country again in 1917; there were 'minor operations' against the Nuer in 1919–20; more intertribal quarrels between Dinka and Nuer around Lake No in 1923; action 'against Garluark, the recalcitrant chief of the Nuong Nuer' in 1924, despite which the Nuong 'misbehaved themselves' again in 1925. All of this proved that 'the Nuer remained truculent and incorrigible, and year by year one section or another indulged in an orgy of atrocities . . . The witchdoctors and the young "braves" ruled the roost, and the chiefs had little authority.' The small government retaliatory patrols had varying success and contributed to a game which, he contended, was not unpopular with the Nuer themselves. It was their understanding (according to MacMichael) that while they looted the Dinka in the spring and summer, the government looted them in winter. 'Their own action was obviously justifiable by ancient custom; that of the government caused no particular resentment or surprise.' The comprehensive measures of the 'Nuer Settlement' of 1928–9 at last rounded up 'the recalcitrant element' and opened Nuer country to various 'civilizing influences'.[5]

In MacMichael's summary Nuer actions are simplified to mechanical laws of behaviour. Hostilities are presented as initiated by the Nuer, stemming from their irreconcilably aggressive attitude towards their neighbours and the government. Their resistance was organized by 'witch-doctors' (also called by the colloquial Arabic *kujur*, a pejorative term administrators applied indiscriminately to priests, prophets, and magicians). This is, in fact, how historians who base their accounts on government records have generally analysed this period of punitive patrols and pacification campaigns. Whether the Nuer are presented approvingly as heroic resisters to colonialism, or their actions are described neutrally, their hostility and resentment are treated as

[5] MacMichael (1934: 101–2, 175–7, 180–2).

objective facts confronting administration.[6] Specific patrols and campaigns will be discussed in detail in the following chapters, and the Nuer version of events and interpretation of their conflict with the government will be given there. Here we will analyse how the structure of colonial rule in the Sudan itself contributed to this sequence of violent confrontations. In particular we will discuss the military imperative which so often propelled the early administration of the Southern Sudan.

Britain rested its claim to the Sudan on the reassertion of Egyptian sovereignty over its former territories. This was its strongest international legal argument, but with France, Belgium, Italy, and imperial Ethiopia already in occupation of parts of the old Egyptian empire, the Anglo-Egyptian government of the Sudan had to reinforce its theoretical position with 'effective occupation' on the ground. After the Battle of Omdurman on 2 September 1898 there was a rush to the furthest edges of the old Egyptian Sudan to establish a *de facto* presence along its former borders. Thus, after isolating the French at Fashoda on the White Nile, troops reoccupied the old Egyptian posts at Nasir on the Sobat and Bor on the Bahr el-Jebel, forestalling any future Abyssinian or Belgian advances. It was as if the outline of the country was to be drawn first, leaving the interior to be shaded in later.[7]

The occupation of the interior of the Sudan proceeded from fixed administrative points outwards into the rural areas. Military patrols traversed the country seeking, and often obtaining, formal submission to the new government from tribal leaders. The early administrative centres of the Southern Sudan were located along the main rivers, which linked them to the headquarters at Khartoum. Movement into the interior was hampered by the seasonal constraints of the Upper Nile, when waterlogging of the clay plains during the rainy season impeded the movements of armed columns. Thus for many years administration of the Nuer and other peoples of the flood zone followed a transhumant pattern, mirroring that of the Nilotic pastoralists themselves. During the dry season the government left the rivers and moved into the plains as the Nuer did the opposite, moving from their villages to the khors (seasonal watercourses) and the river banks. In the rains the government withdrew once again to the rivers, while the Nuer withdrew to the interior of the plains. Though contact between government and the Nuer increased over the years, this pattern never really changed. Continuity of administration was maintained through the seasons only in the last two decades of British rule, when self-administering Nuer courts were created and small outposts were manned year-round by Sudanese police.

Discontinuity in administration was a constant problem during the first

[6] Collins (1971: 180–4, 195–203, 217–18); Warburg (1971: 139); Hassan Ahmed Ibrahim (1985*a*: 81; 1985*b*: 595); Daly (1986: 145–8).

[7] For diplomacy surrounding the Nile Basin see Sanderson (1965: chs. 14–17). For the occupation of the Sudan's borders see Sandes (1937: chs. 9, 17).

thirty years of imperial rule in the Upper Nile. There has been a tendency in both administrative and historical writing to describe the development of administration in the rural Sudan broadly as an uninterrupted evolutionary process. Government arrives in an area, it sets down roots, it grows and spreads, it blooms. It was scarcely ever checked or diverted; it did not disappear in one place to reappear in another. This impression may represent the experience of administrators, who saw a continuity in their life's work even as they were transferred from district to district. It does not necessarily correspond to the experience of the Sudanese, and especially not that of the Nilotic pastoralists of the Upper Nile. Posts were suddenly opened and just as suddenly closed. An inspector was assigned to a district and then was called away for other duties, or retransferred to the army, or was invalided out. His replacements came in rapid succession or did not come at all. An obstacle of policy or an absence of resources diverted the course of the administration's normal transhumant movements. Local alliances were made by one official and subsequently forgotten by another. Most Nilotic pastoralists experienced an episodic administration until the 1930s. This affected their perception of the reliability, permanence, and strength of government.

Just as crucial in forming official perceptions which governed action was the structural amnesia of administration. It would be difficult to claim that government policy towards the Nuer much before 1935 was based on accumulated experience. There were too many points at which administrative amnesia set in and broke the continuity of contact. The periodic shifting of personnel and abandoning of headquarters meant that information was most often passed on via an official oral tradition which was largely unconnected to the records inspectors were required to write, and file clerks required to keep, and which often did survive long after the British had left. The frequent, sudden, turnover of province personnel meant that even the oral history network was sometimes broken. Those in the province during World War I confessed to little knowledge of what their predecessors had done. The generation of the 1920s knew virtually nothing of what had happened before 1919. It was only with the publication of Evans-Pritchard's early ethnography on the Nuer in the widely distributed *Sudan Notes and Records* in the 1930s that administrators acquired an accessible written point of reference as a standard of comparison for their own experience. The 1930s became the decade of revelation. The period before 1930 receded further and further as an administrative *jahiliyya*—'age of ignorance'—about which less and less was reliably known. Most of the continuity in Nuer administration was provided by the Nuer themselves, not only in the person of their chiefs, who served under many administrators, but in their individual and collective memories, which spanned the pre-colonial and colonial periods.

The discontinuity of administration was a product, in part, of the fitful transition from military to civilian rule. The administration of the Southern

Sudan during the first two decades of this century was overwhelmingly military. Almost all administrators were soldiers seconded from the Egyptian army (the first civilian administrator was sent to Upper Nile Province in 1907, but there was no civilian governor until 1919). British officers occupied the ranks of governor and inspector, while Egyptian and Sudanese officers were appointed to the lower ranks of *ma'mur*, sub-*ma'mur*, and police officer. Soldiers of the Sudanese battalions of the Egyptian army occupied the outposts and were gradually replaced by police, who were themselves mostly recruited from the army and retained a military organization. Most of the soldiers, and therefore most of the police, were ex-slave soldiers impressed into the Egyptian army during the nineteenth century. Many were Dinka or Shilluk; only a few were Nuer.[8]

The reliance on soldiers in administration was an unavoidable necessity, but it created a number of problems in policy-making and implementation. The military influence of this period left its mark on administrative structures and on an approach to administration which placed great emphasis on submission and obedience from native leaders and their peoples, the demonstration of government strength as a matter of prestige, the precedence of security over justice, and the search for native chains of command through which to govern.

Submission was, of course, the first objective in the occupation of the Sudan, a necessary preliminary to administration. Submission had to be demonstrated in a tangible way and reinforced by repeated signs of obedience, as in the payment of taxes or the acceptance of legal judgments. There was a tension between demanding obedience for its own sake and seeking to persuade the people to accept government through the provision of services in return, which derived from the tension inherent between military and civil administration. The protagonists of each approach were not strictly divided between the military and civilian camps of the political service; soldiers were among the first to advocate a truly civil administration and a civilian governor was responsible for the last and most elaborate punitive campaign in 1929. But the internal momentum of local military and strategic considerations continually undermined tentative moves in the direction of civil authority. Policy in Nuer administration from 1902 to 1927 fluctuated in emphasis between demonstrations of force on the one hand, and nurturing a native judicial system on the other, as the main forms of exerting government control.[9] The advocates of civil administration alternated with the proponents of military control. Civil administration was most favoured by the governors Matthews (1902–10), Stigand (1916–19), and Struvé (1919–26), while military force was most marked under Blewitt (1900–2), O'Sullivan (1910–11), Woodward (1911–16), and Willis (1926–31).

[8] Johnson (1989*a*: 79–81; 1991*b*).
[9] Johnson (1982*a*: 195–8; 1986*a*: 62–70).

Major Arthur Blewitt was the commander of the first Anglo-Egyptian military campaign against the Nuer, an incursion into Lou Nuer country in 1902. It was a campaign undertaken with the dual purpose of supporting the government's allies among the Dinka of the Sobat and Khor Fulluth and undermining the power of the Lou prophet Ngundeng. It was instigated by Dinka complaints (which we will see were false) of constant harassment and raiding by Ngundeng and his people. Blewitt summoned Ngundeng to submit and pay tax, or be punished. When there was no reply the Lou villages were burned, their cattle seized, and Ngundeng's shrine desecrated. Blewitt was convinced that Ngundeng had 'lost all prestige' by these actions and advocated a continuation of the policy of patrols traversing Nuer country.[10]

There was no immediate tangible gain from this unilateral declaration of hostilities. Blewitt's general approach to administration did not find favour in Khartoum, where he was considered an inefficient, self-serving careerist.[11] Shortly after his expedition he was transferred to the north and replaced by Major G. E. Matthews, another soldier, but a man of a completely different temperament who was more hesitant about committing the government to military action and expenditure. Matthews criticized his predecessor's regime, specifically questioning the value of the military patrol, writing that

> The Government has undoubtedly lost rather than gained ground, owing to the unfortunate results obtained by the expedition to Dinkur [*sic*] in April last when the inhabitants fled before the Government troops and returned to find their villages burnt and cattle vanished, without having realized the force which had effected these removals.[12]

Matthews's administration was marked by a reduction in the reliance on armed force and by an attempt to enter directly into the judicial life of the people, regulating their internal and external affairs by involvement in litigation and arbitration. Inspectors toured their districts accompanied by only a few police, rather than by platoons of soldiers. They were encouraged to hear cattle cases and settle disputes using a mixture of customary law (where known) and the Sudan Penal Code. It was Matthews's hope that his inspectors would 'give interpretation to British honesty' and demonstrate the government's pacific intentions through the righting of wrongs and the return of stolen property. He wished to win over the Nuer (especially the Lou) by ensuring that justice was seen to be done and giving wide publicity to those cases where the government found in favour of Nuer against Dinka. He personally restored to the Lou in 1906 cattle and hostages taken by the government's Dinka allies in 1902.[13] Thus it was that he also sent his

[10] Blewitt (1902), quoted in Johnson (1982*b*: 123–5).

[11] C. Fergusson to Wingate, Khartoum, 23 June 1902, SAD 272/4/77–8; Sanderson and Sanderson (1981: 36); Daly (1986: 75–6).

[12] Matthews (1902: 346).

[13] Johnson (1991*b*; 1986*a*: 63–6); Matthews (1906: 727).

senior inspectors to contact the most influential prophets—successfully with the Gaawar prophet Deng Laka in 1905, unsuccessfully with Ngundeng in 1906—and Matthews himself visited Deng Laka in his own village shortly before the latter's death in 1907.

Matthews was oppressed by the scant resources available to his Cinderella province and his letters and reports often make dispiriting reading. His style of administration had few admirers among his later subordinates. The demands on inspectors were great, the results of judicial intervention often ambiguous, progress was slow, and considerable patience was required. Only K. C. P. Struvé, the first civilian to join the province administration and Matthews's last senior inspector, was favourably influenced by Matthews's methods and worked along similar principles during his own tenure as governor after World War I. Matthews's immediate successors, Captains O'Sullivan and Woodward, adopted a simpler, more direct, more aggressive policy of armed tribute-collecting patrols, which gave administrators something tangible to achieve and report.

Matthews had stressed that the payment of tribute in cattle by the Nuer was to follow, not precede, the establishment of a system of justice. O'Sullivan proposed the reverse. He employed the army as tribute collectors on a series of regular patrols through Nuer country with the intention of strengthening administrative control over the people, maintaining security, and opening up trade routes. Province revenue was thus increased by enforcing the payment of cattle in tax, but the main motivation of the system was to force the Nuer to obey and respect the government. The Nuer were reluctant to give up their cattle, especially as government involvement in the arbitration of disputes declined under the new system. Active resistance to tribute patrols increased from 1913 throughout the years of World War I.[14] O'Sullivan left the province shortly after instituting this policy. It was left to his successor, Captain F. W. Woodward (acting governor 1911–13, governor 1913–16), to defend the policy when Khartoum expressed some doubts about the rising level of violence which followed its introduction. In 1913 J. J. Asser, the acting commander-in-chief of the Egyptian army, wrote to Woodward from Khartoum, 'I cannot help thinking of the time it took us to gain the confidence of the Nuers south of the Sobat owing to our war-like attitude in the time of Blewitt Bey. Moreover, it seems scarcely reasonable to expect people to pay a tax when you have done absolutely nothing for them.'[15]

But administrative amnesia had already set in; the events of 1902 were too distant to be recalled in 1913. Woodward retorted:

> I am not aware of the details of Blewitt Bey's expedition and the reasons for same against the Nuers, but I was an Inspector in the Sobat Valley during the Governorship of Ma[t]thews Pasha when the method of procedure was visiting the Nuers with a

[14] GGR 1910, 92–4; Johnson (1982*a*: 195; 1986*a*: 66–7).

[15] 'Extract from Colonel Asser's Inspection Report, 1913', NRO UNP 1/12/101.

small escort of police, listening to cases, giving decisions which could not be insisted upon, making presents to chiefs and receiving nothing in exchange except promises to pay tribute the following year which were never fulfilled. My predecessor took up a totally different line and insisted on a tribute by means of patrols; this at once made administration easier and the tribesman understood that he was under Government . . . it has not been customary to administer first and demand tribute later.[16]

There was both passive and active resistance to the payment of tribute among the Lak, Thiang, Gaawar, Lou, and Eastern Jikany Nuer between 1913 and 1919 (the Western Nuer then came under the jurisdiction of the Bahr el-Ghazal and Nuba Mountains provinces and were not yet administered). There was outright fighting between government troops and the Gaawar during the years 1913–17, and a decline in the tribute collected from all peoples throughout most of the years of World War I. Nuer resistance was inspired only in part by a desire to protect their herds; it also followed on the realization that the government offered very little in return for payment in cattle. When the government failed to protect the Nuer from Anuak raiding in 1911–14, the Lou and Jikany ceased to pay tribute and took up arms against the Anuak themselves. Further south the Gaawar found themselves increasingly in conflict with government representatives over their border with the Nyareweng and Ghol Dinka, and this, too, contributed to confrontation, which the government defined as rebellion.[17]

The Nuer–Dinka border was complicated by the fact that for administrative convenience the governnment had made the provincial boundary between Upper Nile and Mongalla coincident with a tribal boundary between the Nuer and Dinka. The administrations of the two provinces soon found themselves in conflict any time there was a movement or dispute across the notional border. The original agreement had been negotiated in 1909–10 by K. C. P. Struvé, R. C. R. Owen (governor of Mongalla Province), Deng Laka's son Macar Diu, and a number of Dinka and Lou leaders. Problems immediately arose when the Lou were ordered to move out of Mongalla into Upper Nile. The Mongalla Province *ma'mur* at Duk Fadiat (a Dinka police officer) refused to hear a Lou complaint against the Dinka because they were no longer under the jurisdiction of his province. But he did confiscate cattle from the Lou at the request of the Dinka, in the process of which one Nuer was killed by police. When neither province took action on behalf of the relatives of the murdered man, a group of Lou attacked the police post at Duk Fadiat, nearly overwhelming it before being repulsed. The governors of each province took the side of their own people, Upper Nile blaming the incident on the Dinka, and Mongalla blaming the Nuer. This first border incident was a foretaste of

[16] F. W. Woodward to civil secretary, 28 Oct. 1913, NRO UNP 1/12/101.
[17] Johnson (1982*a*: 195–6).

things to come. Even minor disputes between the two peoples became major issues dividing the two provinces. It was almost impossible for the two administrations to settle cross-border problems of outstanding marriage-payments and cattle-thefts. In the absence of any effective administrative system of arbitration, both peoples increasingly resorted to self-help to restore the cattle each thought was owed to them. With Upper Nile Province forcibly taking cattle in tribute on one side of the border, and Mongalla Province defending the Dinka on the other, the Nuer perceived the government as pro-Dinka. The crisis came in 1916 when a Lou raiding party annihilated a party of soldiers who came to the aid of the Dinka in Bor District. This forced the government to escalate its military activities and launch a full-scale military expedition against the Lou the following year.[18]

It was the perceived Nuer threat to peoples already under administration which frequently impelled government to take action against the Nuer. Thus either rumoured or reported raiding led to the campaigns of 1902 against Ngundeng (on behalf of the Khor Fulluth Dinka), 1917 against the Lou and Gaawar (on behalf of the Mongalla Province Dinka), and 1919–20 against the Eastern Jikany (on behalf of the Meban). Those peoples who had submitted to the government naturally received a more favourable hearing than those who had not; there was thus a structural bias in favour of administered subjects in their complaints against the Nuer. We will see in subsequent chapters that the government frequently revised its opinion of Nuer culpability once contact was made, but before that happened the momentum of military action often overrode all other considerations. Blewitt decided to attack Ngundeng and burn Lou villages on the advice of the Dinka accompanying him.[19] An even clearer case of the pressure from allies can be found in the 1917 patrol against the Lou.

While the expedition's main body of troops traversed Lou country, another column patrolled the Gaawar–Lou border to prevent the escape of refugees. Mongalla Province wanted this column also to attack the Gaawar as punishment for earlier raids on the Dinka. Upper Nile Province was anxious not to distrub the Gaawar, with whom it had tried to improve relations the previous year. The governor insisted that the column restrict its activities to Lou escapees. Khartoum accordingly ordered the army not to raid the Gaawar and their prophet Dual Diu, unless attacked first. The diary of one officer attached to the column reveals how the expectations of accompanying Dinka predisposed the army to attacking Dual.

Monday March 5th . . . Dwal Diu, who at present we are not allowed to destroy unless he shows signs of open hostility, although he will do all he can expect to help the Lau Nuers if he can. Of course if he shows the least sign of open hostility he gets smashed.

[18] Ibid. 191–8. See below, Chs. 5 and 6.
[19] Blewitt (1902), reprinted in Johnson (1982*b*: 125).

Rather hope he does as I think from a military point of view better for this column. All our carriers expect him to be attacked by government as it is his men who have always raided them & taken their cattle!

Tuesday. March 6th Reports came back to me from Scouts lot of cattle & people in front. Of course these were Gaweir Nuers whom we could not molest unless they showed signs of open hostility but of course they didn't. Dinkas with column very surprised & disappointed that we did not take their cattle . . . Head man of Dinkas with us can't understand why we don't punish Gaweir Nuers as it is from them they have always suffered & not so much from the Lau Section of Nuers . . . It is a hopeless position for the O. C. Column, as his hands are tied & there is no doubt Sheik[h] Dwal Diu should be severely punished for his past behaviour.

When, finally, four days later it was reported that some of Dual's men had fired on two Dinka messengers, orders were given for the column to capture Dual. 'I don't suppose he will come in quietly, so I expect there will be a scrap which means Gaweir Nuers will be punished which I think is only right & will mightily please Dinkas.'[20] So, the Gaawar were included in the military operations, even though they had had nothing to do with the raid which provoked the campaign in the first place.

The cycle of violence, once begun, was difficult to break. By 1916 officials in Upper Nile Province began to question the value of their administrative system. The inspector of the Zeraf District, responsible for the Gaawar, described the method of adminstration there:

To put concisely it is this—Once a year (Jan. or Feb.) the Inspector of the Zeraf Valley accompanied by an escort (this year it consisted of 30 Slavery Police mounted on mules and 5 police) makes a tour through his District collecting practically by force a tribute amounting to some 300 head of cattle, realising when sold perhaps L.E. 700 to L.E. 800. This takes a month and during the remainder of the year no representative of the Government goes near these people except perhaps it be for punitive purposes. . . . The present system has now been in practice for many years and I consider a change is necessary . . . I maintain that no attempt has yet been made to administer these natives. For you cannot call the yearly tour which I have already described, administration.[21]

The inspector of the Sobat Valley at Nasir, Major C. H. Stigand, who was soon to become governor of the province, wrote in a similar vein about his own experiences.

The Policy, which has been adopted here, of collecting a tax without attempting any administration appears to me unjust and worse than that unsound also. Such a policy has always required a large Military force to uphold and has always resulted, sooner or later, in arousing the hostility of the people so governed . . . it contains within itself the

[20] G. A. Heinekey, 'Diary of Patrol 33 against Lau Nuers', Heinekey MSS.

[21] E. D. Bally, 'Appreciation of the Present Method of Administration Employed in the Zeraf District, Upper Nile Province', 8 Mar. 1916, SRO UNP SCR 14.

seeds of its own failure. It utterly neglects the fostering of a native organization and chain of responsibility, and the interesting of the natives themselves in their own Government, by which methods alone a large body may be controlled by an insignificant minority. It claims a tax whilst failing to construct the machinery by which it may be collected in an orderly and just manner.

Yet while everyone, from the governor-general and the civil secretary on down, agreed that such a policy should be stopped, military necessity made it impossible to do so. 'I should like to recommend that the Inspector should disassociate himself entirely from the position of authorised cattle snatcher,' Stigand concluded. 'I am afraid that this is not possible at present. Any serious relaxation of this programme would be interpreted as weakness and encourage further opposition.'[22] The opposition the government had engendered had first to be overcome. This required sufficient force to maintain prestige and impress the Nuer with the government's strength. There were to be two more substantial military campaigns—the Lou in 1917 and the Jikany in 1919–20—before Stigand's more systematic approach to administration could be tried.

It was left to Struvé to try it. He succeeded Stigand in 1919 and began the transition from military to civil administration, following the ambiguous political results of the ambitious, but expensive, campaign of 1919–20. He had been doubtful about the value of tribute patrols before World War I, and was even less convinced as governor that 'sending an inspector round the country with a small patrol collecting cattle can be called administration at all', and wished to institute a more comprehensive system within the interior. But Khartoum's financial constraints inhibited his experiments, and an early request for motor cars with which to supply the newly opened district headquarters at Ayod was turned down. Similarly Khartoum vetoed his proposal to call a moratorium on tribute collection during the entire year of 1923, in order to allow his district commissioners time to devise a new scheme for tribal organization and administration. The old system had to remain in place while a new system was introduced piecemeal.[23]

Despite Khartoum's restrictions, there was a change in administrative theory which coincided with Struvé's own approach. The Milner Commission of 1919–20 advocated decentralization in the Sudan and 'the employment, wherever possible, of native agencies for the simple administrative needs of the country'. This statement was consistent with the evolution of

[22] C. H. Stigand, 'Report on Sobat Valley Nuer', May 1916, NRO UNP 1/12/101. See also: civil secretary [Lee Stack] to governor-general, 28 Mar. 1916, and governor-general to civil secretary, 31 Mar. 1916, both in SRO UNP SCR 14.

[23] Governor UNP to civil secretary, 12 Sept. 1920, SRO UNP SCR 14.A.5; governor UNP to civil secretary, 2 Dec. 1922, and civil secretary to governor Malakal, 18 Dec. 1922, both in NRO Civsec 1/2/6; Intelligence Dept., 'Note on Military Action and Administration in Nuer Country', 23 Nov. 1927, NRO Dakhlia I 112/13/87.

administrative thinking within the Sudan, and in fact was derived in part from submissions made to the Commission by members of the Sudan government. It became formal policy by 1921, and throughout the rural Sudan administrators sought to build formalized structures of 'tribal organization' compatible with the devolutionary principles of native administration. The powers of rural leaders—nomad sheikhs in the north and chiefs in the south—were gradually given legal definition. Inspectors were renamed 'district commissioners' in 1922 and were expected to supervise the work of the chiefs and native courts in their districts. In the southern provinces this meant a further move away from the military confrontations which had characterized the first two decades of administration, in favour of an increased acceptance of and reliance on customary law in governing rural areas. But the very diversity of Southern Sudanese societies meant that there could be no uniform structure of native administration. It was up to each province, and indeed each district, to discover structures most suitable to its own situation. In the Upper Nile Struvé gave his district commissioners considerable latitude in devising their own organizations.[24]

The real change for the Nuer came about not so much through the refinement of administrative theory, as through the appointment of district commissioners who eventually became conversant in Nuer. John Lee served briefly in the Zeraf Valley before being posted to Nasir in 1921, and Percy Coriat was sent to Ayod in 1922, where he spent the entire rainy season (an unusual and unrepeated experiment in Nuer administration). That both men were able to make direct contact with individual Nuer rather than rely on police or army interpreters did much to overcome Nuer suspicion, and also gave the government far more reliable information on which to base decisions.

Between 1920 and 1926 overt government pressure on the Nuer diminished. As district commissioners and police appeared more regularly in the rural areas, the external threat to Nuer livelihood and security declined. Administrators discovered who were the accepted Nuer leaders and incorporated them into the structure of district administration as it was being built. Taxes were reformed and spread more evenly throughout the sections, and the chiefs and local police became responsible for collection. The army was less and less in evidence and was progressively withdrawn from the districts. Informal courts were set up to settle disputes, and the Nuer leaders showed themselves increasingly willing to accept government mediation in their conflicts with neighbouring peoples, such as the Dinka. Compared with the pre-war era, the early 1920s was not a time of growing colonial domination or stricter controls. If anything, Nuer leaders were beginning to experience greater influence in their dealings with government officials.[25]

[24] MacMichael (1934: 145), quoting the Milner Report; Daly (1986: 360–79); Collins (1983: 53–60); Johnson (1986*a*: 67–8).

[25] Johnson (1986*a*: 67–71; 1991*b*).

There was, however, an inherent contradiction in the principle of devolution as practised in the Sudan which was to undermine this improvement in Nuer–government relations. Administration was to proceed through native institutions and customs, but only those institutions which were deemed useful and only those customs which were not repugnant to British ideas of justice and humanity. Governing through custom did countenance both intervention and invention. Law was subject to a British assessment of 'reasonableness', tribal organization could be restructured or invented to conform to administrative ideas of hierarchy and chain of command.[26] Any break in the continuity of administrative thinking could redirect development along different lines, especially in this formative period. Such a break and redirection did occur in Upper Nile Province in 1926 when Struvé retired and was replaced by C. A. Willis, the former director of intelligence in Khartoum.

The policy of devolution (only rarely called indirect rule in contemporary official documents in the Sudan) was both broad and vague, as befits a simple theology, and as such was used to justify a wide variety of styles of administration. Struvé had been an apostle of a gradual process of co-opting native leaders and regulating their activities, a gradualness in part imposed on him by lack of finances. His successor, Willis, was an interventionist. As director of intelligence he had tried to assume a general role in guiding native affairs and native administration throughout the Sudan. His conduct alienated many of his colleagues, and his failure to anticipate the 1924 mutiny in Khartoum led to his removal from the central government. His transfer to one of the least developed provinces in the country was humiliating. While Khartoum seemed willing to compensate him with an allocation of greater resources than had been given to Struvé, Willis was not allowed the freedom of action he had once enjoyed in Khartoum. His approach to the administration of his province can be seen as being motivated by resentment of his treatment and a desire to vindicate his reputation.[27]

The principle of organizing native chiefs into courts to try cases by customary law, and the raising of bodies of 'chiefs' police' from among the people themselves to assist the chiefs in enforcing their decisions, was established policy under Struvé but had yet to be uniformly implemented in all districts.[28] Willis wanted to accelerate the pace of implementation of these policies, but he also wanted to expand the range of government projects and soon outlined a comprehensive plan for road-building, public health, and the development of an administrative clerical staff, all of which required additional money, personnel, and administrative regulations. Most of his proposals (except for the road) were rejected by the civil secretary, MacMichael, between April and June 1927 as being too expensive, or as expanding local

[26] Makec (1988: 26–30); Johnson (1986*a*: 68).

[27] Daly (1980: 34–6; 1986: 276–8, 400–1); Johnson (1979: 8; 1985*a*: 132–4; 1993*a*).

[28] Johnson (1986*a*: 69–70; 1991*b*).

government bureaucracy at the expense of rural administration.[29] It was shortly after these rejections that Willis began warning Khartoum of an imminent Nuer insurrection which would require a scale of expenditure and implementation of projects similar to those which had just been turned down.

The evidence concerning the Nuer rising will be analysed in Chapters 5 and 6. Here we consider those factors that led to a return of the military imperative in Nuer administration. The personalities of the administrators in the 1920s, the emphasis which policy then placed on tribal discipline and reorganization, and the Sudan government's general suspicion of religious leaders combined to produce a final confrontation.

Rationalizing administrative theory in the early 1920s was accompanied by a rationalization of administrative boundaries. All the Nuer, along with many of their neighbours, were to be brought together under one administrative system in one province. Thus the contentious tribal/province border area of Duk Fadiat and Duk Fayuil was transferred from Mongalla Province to Upper Nile early in 1926. The whole of the Western Nuer, along with some of their immediate Dinka neighbours, were scheduled for transfer from Bahr el-Ghazal to Upper Nile in 1928. This brought not only all Nuer districts, but all Nuer district commissioners, under one governor. Their very different methods of administration came under Willis's scrutiny and criticism. He managed to alienate not only his own Nuer expert, Coriat, but the incoming district commissioner from Bahr el-Ghazal, Captain V. H. Fergusson, who had governed the Western Nuer since 1921. At the same time he approved highly of Major J. W. G. Wyld, district commissioner of the Dinka at Duk Fayuil, and often preferred Wyld's judgement on Nuer administration to Coriat's.[30]

Major Wyld was a former regular army officer with experience in irregular warfare gained during World War I in the Near East and in the Russian civil war. Struvé had found him 'rather brilliant' but also impetuous. 'Under a military style of Government he might be something of a fire-eater, and too prone to force the pace', Struvé had advised Willis before leaving the province. 'I sometimes think he chafes a little under the restraint of a chief who has himself got past that stage and seen the futility of it.'[31] But Willis liked his style (while disapproving of his spelling, said to be a legacy from his father, then Merton Professor of English Language and Literature in the University of Oxford). Impatient to reorganize the province his way, Willis was glad of a subordinate who seemed as keen to establish discipline and order as he was himself. Wyld's task in Mongalla Province had been different from those in the Upper Nile districts. He was attempting to invent tribes out of a diverse group of refugees who had abandoned their lands to the slavers and

[29] Johnson (1985*a*: 133); Collins (1983: 120–3).
[30] Johnson (1993*a*; 1985*a*: 136–7); Fergusson (1930: 236–7, 277, 283–6).
[31] K. C. P. Struvé, 'Handing Over Notes 1926', SAD 212/9.

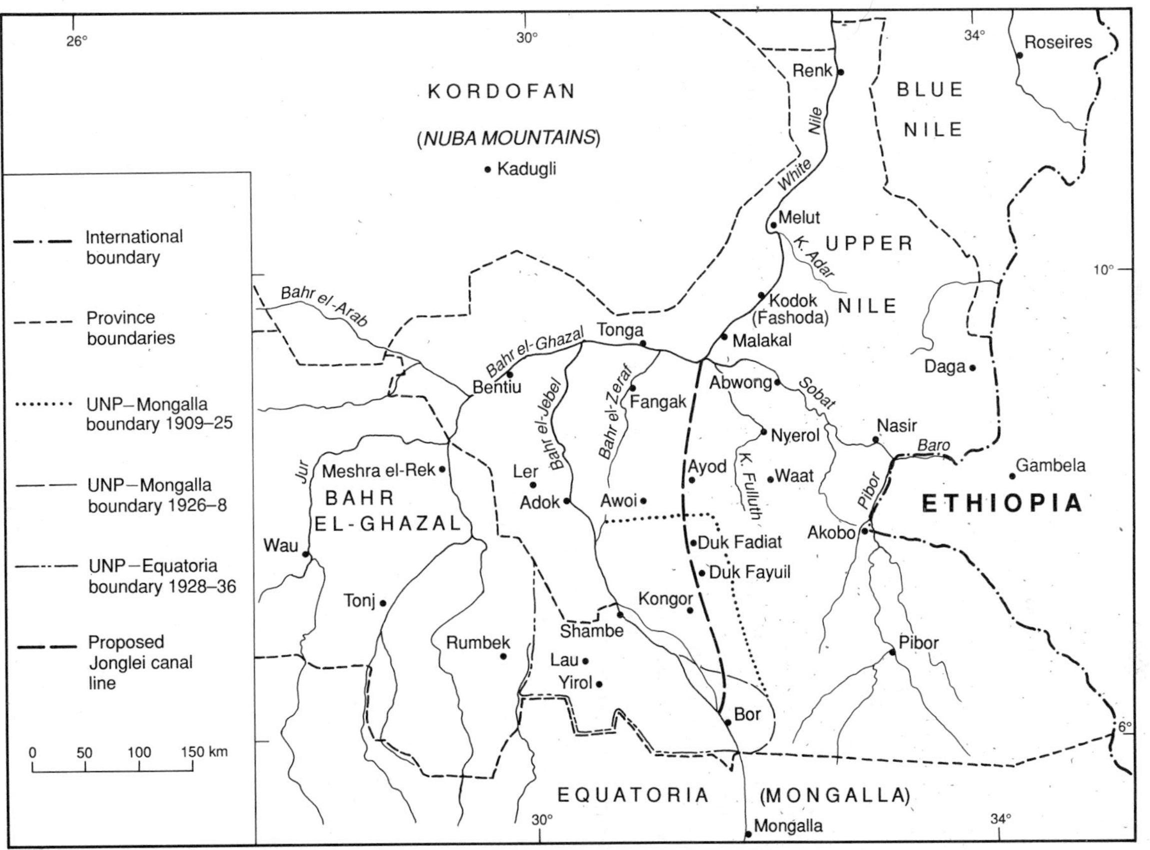

Map 1. Upper Nile Province, 1910–1976, showing province boundaries and administrative outposts

the Nuer during the previous century. He thus had the opportunity not only to tailor a tribal structure to the specifications of native administration, but also to create a new office of chief. Willis approved entirely of such innovation. He himself was dissatisfied with the lack of acceptable chiefly authority among the Nilotic pastoralists of his province and proposed to create a new class of chief, patterned after that type found in 'the more organised and less individualistic peoples both north and south', who could both issue and enforce orders. This required the introduction of 'tribal discipline', by which the peoples of the region got in the habit of carrying out orders through work on government projects, such as road-building.[32]

Wyld identified the Nuer across his district frontier as the main obstacle to his work. It was not just that they used to raid his Dinka; it was that they attracted great numbers of Dinka who preferred to live among the Nuer rather than under the new chiefs Wyld wished to support. Wyld was committed to 'preserving Dinka integrity' and ultimately saw 'the hopeless state of intermixture' between the tribes as undermining his attempts to redefine the peoples and redraw tribal boundaries.[33] In this Wyld ran counter to previous administrative opinion. As early as 1913 an Upper Nile Province inspector had declared that 'to imagine that Nuers and Dinkas on each side of the boundary live in a constant state of war is quite contrary to the facts'.[34] Towards the end of World War I the inspector from Bor in Mongalla Province, one of Major Wyld's predecessors, confirmed this from his own observations.

> So long as a firm administration on the spot, and therefore easily accessible to the natives, holds the balance and redresses grievances, the tendency of the Nuers and Dinkas, who are closely allied in customs, both tribal and personal, is to fuse with one another. This has always occurred in the past in [between] the intervals of fighting. To support the idea of a tribal boundary is merely to strive to keep open a sore which would otherwise tend, with proper treatment, to heal itself.[35]

It was precisely to encourage such healing that Struvé had secured the transfer of the border region to his province. But the new theory of native administration could be, and was, used to justify Wyld's principle of separation; thus undercutting entirely the thrust of Struvé's earlier policy.[36]

Wyld had been restrained by Struvé; Willis now found himself restrained by Khartoum's refusal to grant funds and approve new administrative schemes.

[32] C. Armine Willis, 20 Apr. 1928, Nasir END 1.F.1, vol. i; C. A. Willis, 'Native Administration among the Nuer', 28 July 1927, NRO UNP 1/44/329; Willis, 'Memorandum "B"', 9 Mar. 1928, NRO UNP 1/5/27.

[33] J. W. G. Wyld, 'Report on the Duk Raid', 10 Dec. 1928, NRO Civsec 5/3/12.

[34] G. B. Wauhope to governor, UNP, 22 Apr. 1913, NRO UNP 1/12/101.

[35] J. Stevenson-Hamilton, inspector Bor, to governor MP, 14 Sept. 1918, Malakal UNP SCR 14.A.

[36] Johnson (1982*a*: 198–200).

Khartoum, however, had to take seriously any reports of possible unrest and threats to internal security. Wyld was convinced that the Nuer were a permanent threat to security; Willis had failed once before to detect a revolt, and he now gave every indication of a man intent on retrieving his reputation. He accepted Wyld's evidence of a conspiracy of Lou Nuer 'witch-doctors' (or 'kujurs') and forwarded it to Khartoum to support his request for military assistance to enforce his administrative policies. The suppression of the conspiracy was administratively convenient, as he admitted after receiving Khartoum's approval for a military campaign.

I have received reports which go to confirm the probable rising of Gwek Wonding [son of Ngundeng], as I had anticipated . . . In many ways however it gives an opportunity to start the 'native administration' with a definite demonstration of what is to happen to those natives who refuse to recognise the chiefs' and the Government's authority.[37]

Wyld, too, saw the campaign as an undisguised blessing, writing shortly after operations had begun,

In former reports I have suggested the desireability [*sic*] of collecting Dinka elements interspersed amongst the Lau Shens [*ciengs*].

The Nuer dissafective [*sic*] this year will in my opinion have done much to facilitate this process when operations have been brought to a successful conclusion.[38]

The officials in Khartoum periodically tried to qualify their commitment to the use of troops, but Willis and Wyld repeatedly forced the pace. The governor-general, Sir John Maffey, ordered that operations should not begin until Coriat, due back from leave in November, had a chance to report on the real state of disaffection in his district. If he found that a rising was being planned, the RAF would be used to overawe the Nuer into submission (a proposal which responded to pressure from London to expand the role of the air force in imperial defence). Coriat reported after touring his district that the matter could be cleared up with a full squadron of mounted police, 'but Willis said they could'nt [*sic*] be spared from other District duties, so the General had to decide on the Army being brought in'.[39] The RAF only dispersed the Lou, who sought refuge with other Nuer, including the Gaawar. Willis took this opportunity to extend operations to the Gaawar, Wyld's main enemies. Though in fact the Gaawar had been on good terms with the government since 1918, particularly because of the personal friendship between Coriat and the Gaawar prophet Dual Diu, Willis wrote of them, 'The Gaweir really want a sending through; they are full of rifles and have been distinctly saucy

[37] 'Extract from a Letter from Mr. Willis to Sir John Maffey', *c.*Sept. 1927, NRO Civsec 5/2/10.

[38] 'Extract from Report of District Commissioner Bor and Duk', 29 Dec. 1927, NRO UNP 1/4/27.

[39] Maffey 19 Nov. 1927, NRO Civsec 5/2/10 and UNP 1/5/27; Coriat (1927); Coriat to wife, undated [*c.*Mar. 1928], quoted in Johnson (1993*a*). For RAF see Killingray (1984).

before but not quite to the point of needing serious attention. If they now harbour all the Kujur, they must learn better.' In approving plans for a march through Gaawar country the civil secretary refused to sanction military operations other than those forced on the troops *en route*. But Wyld brought with him some 300 Dinka 'friendlies' and insisted on sending the troops in a sweep through Dual Diu's village. Shortly after that the Gaawar attacked the Dinka and a government police post in retaliation.[40]

The Nuer reaction to events initiated by the government was taken as proof of their innate hostility to government. The assassination of Captain Fergusson in the Bahr el-Ghazal in December 1927 was at first misattributed to a Western Nuer prophet, and seemed to confirm Willis's general point (see Chapter 7). It was Wyld who proposed the details of a comprehensive programme which involved the concentration of Lou and Gaawar into restricted areas while troops swept the country dealing with recalcitrants, the creation of a tribal boundary and no man's land between Nuer and Dinka, and the repatriation of Dinka living north of the boundary to the area south of it to form a compact Dinka population capable of resisting future Nuer incursions. Willis adopted this as the essence of his own 'Nuer Settlement', which was designed to 'establish proper discipline and control and preclude further disturbance of peace'. To Wyld's plan were added his own earlier proposals to expand communications and other government services. Presented now as a necessary security measure to ensure the peace, Khartoum approved some of the projects and allocated the funds it had earlier denied him.[41]

The 'Nuer Settlement' ended with the death or exile of the Lou and Gaawar prophets, and was the prelude to a progressive secularization of Nuer office-holders in native administration. The momentum of the military imperative which we have discussed above may have been generated by a combination of administrative policy and personalities, but this alone was not sufficient to convince Khartoum of a real danger of rebellion. It was the threat of a religious rising organized by the 'witch-doctors' or 'kujurs' which caused the greatest alarm and persuaded officials in Khartoum to sanction war, even when they suspected Willis's motives. Whatever motives may have lain behind the 'Nuer Settlement', the Nuer prophets were the justification for military action and the official target of government retribution. It was the culmination of a long struggle in which the government alternately tried to suppress and to co-opt prophets, a struggle which was directed by the Sudan government's concern with legitimate leadership and its suspicion of unorthodox religious leaders.

The early seasonal patrols which penetrated the interior demanding

[40] Willis to MacMichael, 16 Jan. 1928, and civil secretary to governor Malakal, 31 Jan. 1928, both in NRO Civsec 5/2/11. See also Ch. 6.

[41] Wyld, 'Report on the Duk Raid'; Willis, 'Nuer Settlement 1929', 28 June 1929, NRO Civsec 1/3/8.

submission from the inhabitants could not employ the same arguments of legitimacy which Britain and Egypt had employed in international circles. Since the old Turco-Egyptian regime was associated with slave-raiding and extortionate taxation, British officers, even while commanding soldiers recruited by that regime, were at pains to dissociate themselves from the earlier period and emphasize that they represented a new government different from that of the old 'Turks'. But by not invoking loyalty once offered to the former government, the new government had difficulty evoking any loyalty at all. The quickest way to establish the legitimacy of government rule was to co-opt the existing legitimacy of tribal leaders. If there was a hierarchy of leadership with an established procedure of succession, the co-optation of that structure allowed the government to intervene in the succession to secure the election or appointment of a 'loyal' contender. As in other parts of colonial Africa many leaders in office at the time of conquest were deposed by the government and replaced by their kinsmen, who at least acknowledged a duty owed to the government who supported them.

When the government entered the Southern Sudan it fully expected to find the same range of 'meks' (kings), 'sultans', 'sheikhs', and 'omdas' it had found in the north, and these titles were employed even after most administrators were aware of their inappropriateness. Only among the Shilluk and the Azande did they find lines of authority of the type which could be co-opted from the top down, and by so doing secure the submission of an entire group of people through the subordination of their leaders. Elsewhere lines of authority were less clear or conducted less power. Here the questions of 'legitimacy' and 'loyalty' became confused, for loyalty to the government did not always carry legitimacy with it, and 'disloyal' leaders were not always illegitimate in the eyes of their people. The government ultimately claimed to be the defender of tradition and custom, but not all of its allies were so traditional. Some who attained great power through manipulating government support did not always follow customary ways, as seen, for instance, in the cases of Ali al-Tom of the Kababish Arabs or Deng Majok of the Ngok Dinka.[42] The delineation of tribal societies in the Sudan was very much a twentieth-century activity, with the government attempting to redefine legitimacy at the same time that it upheld custom. Nowhere was this more evident than with the Nuer. Though some of the more perceptive officials privately acknowledged the contradiction of their own position, the thrust of government policy was to define the prophets as illegitimate usurpers of chiefly authority, and create a hierarchy of chiefs which was fully subordinated to the external authority of administration.[43]

Hostility to the prophets was not derived only from nineteenth-century

[42] Asad (1970: 158–72); Deng (1986: esp. chs. 5–8).
[43] Johnson (1986*a*: 67–72; 1989*b*: 231–4).

stereotypes of African religious figures, though certainly Schweinfurth's patronizing and critical description of a Dinka 'Cogyoor' in the 1860s was widely read by administrators.[44] It was part of a general hostility to any form of prophetic, millennial, or ecstatic religion; a fear of the uncontrolled emotional force of religious ecstasy or fanaticism which could lead to either personal breaches of the peace or political revolt. Muhammad Ahmad al-Mahdi had been a *sufi* mystic before overthrowing the Turco-Egyptian regime, and during the first seventeen years of Anglo-Egyptian rule not a year passed without the government taking action against a real or threatened religious revolt by *sufi faqis* (holy men), new *mahdis*, or *nabi ʿisas* (prophet Jesuses) in the Northern Sudan. Thus Lord Cromer announced as early as January 1899 the government's policy towards unorthodox Muslim movements. The *faqis* of the old brotherhoods were not to be allowed to resume their teaching. Such *faqis* had 'lived on the superstitious ignorance of the people, were one of the curses of the Soudan, and were responsible in a great measure for the rebellion', he claimed. Their private mosques and shrines 'cannot be allowed to be re-established, as they generally formed centres of unorthodox fanaticism'. A Board of Ulema (religious teachers) was established in 1901 to strengthen orthodoxy and to counter the influence of 'the numerous heretical Moslem sects of which the Sudan had ever been a hot-bed'.[45]

Orthodoxy was thus equated with legitimacy, and fanaticism with rebellion and usurpation. The equation was not confined to the Muslim north. In the south the 'witchdoctors, *shamans* or rainmakers' were compared with such 'fanatics' as 'the *mahdi* or *nebi ʿIsa*' of the north, and the Nuer prophets were at first described as 'Mahdis', 'Khalifas', and 'fakirs'.[46] The restrictions proposed by Cromer for the *sufi* mystics were frequently transferred to anyone called a 'kujur' in the south: numerous 'kujurs' there were identified as ringleaders of rebellions against the chiefs or the government; they were arrested or exiled; their shrines were demolished or desecrated; even the grave of one old 'witch-doctor' was dug up and his remains burned to destroy their 'magical' influence.[47] The attitude of officials towards religion was strikingly portrayed in that much neglected novel *Pilate Pasha*, set in the 1920s but written in the 1930s, from an intimate knowledge of administrators' personal conversations. An old hand instructs a newcomer to a composite province:

[44] Schweinfurth (1874: i. 331–2).

[45] Warburg (1971: 95–108), quoting 'Viscount Cromer's Speech to the Sheikhs and Notables of the Soudan at Omdurman', 4 Jan. 1899 (p. 95), and Adeny to Baylis, 21 Jan. 1902 (p. 96).

[46] MacMichael (1934: 96); Johnson (1981: 514); Blewitt (1902); Wilson (1903*b*: 9); Gordon (1903: 12); *SIR* 106 (May 1903), 3; Cooke (1935: 224).

[47] Woodward (1911: 246); *SIR* 236 (Mar. 1914), 5; 255 (Oct. 1915), 3; 288 (July 1918), 3; 291 (Oct. 1918), 3; 309 (Apr. 1920), 4; 329 (Dec. 1921), 3.

'you speak as if religion and excitement and trouble were the same things,' objected Garland.

'So they are .... you may be sure if there is any trouble religion is at the bottom of it.... The Sudan is a big country... and contains all sorts of races and climates... And whatever sample has a try at making history, religion is at the bottom of it. It may be a witch-doctor among the bareskins farther east, or a fiki dreaming in the tents of the Beduin in the north, but each and all must have a go at the Hukuma [government]. Then the police call in the soldiers, there is a patrol, and it isn't all over till somebody is hanged.... So now you have the Golden Rule for dealing with Mahdis!' exclaimed Terrilow with enormous emphasis. '"Catch them young and hang them early", and you might also add, "scatter their ashes to the winds."'[48]

The analogy of the Mahdiyya was carried a further step in the assumption that, just as the Mahdi had usurped legitimate authority and had destroyed the power of rural tribal leaders, so, too, had the 'kujurs' usurped the authority of the hypothetical southern chief. The absence of any obvious executive figure among the Nuer was explained by reference to the activities of the prophets. There *had* been chiefs in the past, but the 'kujurs' had undermined their position and shoved them into the background. Since the prophets had arisen in the last quarter of the nineteenth century, the analogy with the Mahdi was reinforced. For many years there was a search to find members of the real chiefly families who could replace the prophets.[49] Given the government's overriding preoccupation with co-opting legitimacy, its fundamental hostility towards any inspired religious figure wielding political authority or influence, and its sustained attempt from the earliest years of this century to find an alternative to the prophets, any structural hostility between the Nuer prophets and the government was generated from within the structure of the Sudan government itself.

Any person labelled a 'kujur' was automatically identified as potentially uncontrollable and subversive. But the term was so widely used as to embrace almost any slightly odd person, from a certifiable madman to a Dinka spear-master. Their outward behaviour appeared to place them all in the same class. When Matthews and Struvé met Deng Laka in 1907, Matthews wrote that he 'approached us by a series of mysterious circlings, looking in any direction but our own, and, having finally halted in front of us, he hastily divested himself of a leather apron and waved it in our faces'. This seemed similar to the type of 'kujur' of whom Struvé later complained, who came 'making uncouth noises and dancing towards you with his spear, which at times has been thrown: when the Nuers are satisfied that this has not impressed you, they make excuses that he is only a madman.' Officials were eager to diminish the influence of 'kujurs' in any way they could. Thus at one place on his 1906 tour of Lou country O'Sullivan 'tested the power of a Kodgur here, by

[48] Fausset (1939: 30, 33). [49] Johnson (1981: 514–15).

laughing at him before all the people, and telling him he was a very ordinary man, and the people followed suit and began "kicking the dog who was down"'.[50]

There were a number of magicians and lesser prophets among the Nuer who imitated the great prophets in manner and dress. It was, perhaps, difficult for administrators to distinguish between them on their fleeting visits to Nuer country. But in substantial matters officials found that they often had to suppress their instinctive reactions and reach some compromise with the influential prophets if government was to make any entry into Nuer life. They realized early on that their only options in regard to Ngundeng were to reconcile or remove him,[51] but they did not then have the capacity to remove Ngundeng or any other prophet. They made determined efforts to meet with and win over Deng Laka and one of Ngundeng's Jikany disciples. Struvé, who met Deng Laka, later continued this policy in the 1920s. Thus friendly overtures were made to Ngundeng's son Guek, and the government's official dealings with Dual Diu were reinforced by Coriat's additional ties of personal friendship.

This policy was expedient rather than permanent. It was always hoped that at some future date the 'chiefs' could regain their rightful position and take over from the 'kujurs'. Thus, Captain Fergusson recognized the authority of Western Nuer prophets but hoped 'gradually to induce the people to take their cases before their chiefs instead of the "kujurs"'.[52] H. C. Jackson, the senior inspector of Upper Nile Province who first contacted Guek in 1921, also concluded that the 'kujurs' and witch-doctors were the only persons with power among the Lou and 'decided that faute de mieux the Govt had better employ these people and try and win them over to the Govt[']s point of view rather than appoint some nincompoop who could not stand up to the Kujur'. Yet he also declared that 'these reactionary witchdoctors are as much a curse in the South Sudan as the illiterate fiki is in the North. They stand for all that is retrograde, they hate progress.'[53] This contradiction in attitudes had to be resolved once there was an acceleration in the construction of a hierarchy of recognized chiefs, to whom limited judicial and administrative powers were being devolved. It was not a question of how to accommodate one or two well-disposed prophets within the new structure; it was a question of whether they could be accommodated at all. This was the issue Willis forced at the very beginning of his administration.

In his correspondence with Khartoum Willis declared that the entire success of native administration among the Nuer depended on the removal of

[50] Matthews (1907); Struvé, quoted in O'Sullivan (1910: 414); O'Sullivan, 'Lau Nuers'.

[51] Gordon (1903: 12).

[52] Fergusson (1921*a*); id. 'Visit to the Nuong Nuers', 6 Mar. 1921, NRO Civsec 1/2/5; and id. in Jackson (1923: 107).

[53] Jackson: to Butts, 15 Nov. 1927, NRO Civsec 5/2/10 (1923: 91).

the 'kujurs'. He claimed that this had been proven in the Bahr el-Ghazal where 'the persistently obstructive attitude of certain Kujurs (rain makers and jujumen)' had necessitated the use of troops. The death of most 'kujurs' in battle made possible 'the development of the Chiefs' authority, and the establishment of a Tribal discipline' among the Western Nuer 'that surpasses anything to be found elsewhere among the Nuer'. He then concluded:

> the influence of the Kujur is anti-government and has to be broken if the Government chiefs are to execute their proper authority. The Kujur are comparable to the 'hedge fikis' of the Northern Sudan . . . their position and wealth depend on keeping the people ignorant and frightened of their supposed supernatural powers; and in the nature of things they must be reactionary and opposed to a policy of progress such as the Government proposes . . . on the elimination of the Kujurs, the Chiefs can acquire and use authority over their people.[54]

This argument was advanced before there was any substantial evidence against Guek, and certainly none against Dual Diu. It was, in fact, first proposed by Major Wyld.[55] Guek's guilt of subversion was adduced from 'the nature of things'. This natural and anticipated reaction was itself adduced by analogy with other religious and magical disturbances (the two were constantly conflated in the administrative mind). There had been the magical associations, or 'secret societies', of the Azande which were proscribed by the Unlawful Societies and Witchcraft Ordinance in 1919, but which subsequently appeared among the Jur-Beli of Rumbek in 1921; the Yakan or 'Allah Water' cult in Equatoria Province and northern Uganda, which was associated in administrators' minds with the appearance of a 'holy lake' among the Atuot, also in 1921; the spread of the magic root *matthiang goh* among the Jur-Beli and Dinka of Rumbek District; and the 'rebellion' of the Dinka prophet Arianhdit in 1922. Each had seemed capable of attracting followers across social and even international boundaries, and was all the more subversive for that. Though there was no direct connection between these different movements and events, administrators constantly tried to find one, attributing a Dinka origin to Yakan, and searching for cultic similarities between the Zande societies, *matthiang goh*, and even the Nuer prophets.[56]

This 'rising' of Arianhdit, the Abiem Dinka spear-master of the Pariath clan, was a precedent for action against the Nuer prophets, and revealed a similar pattern of government suspicion and hostility. Arianhdit's desire for peace is documented in the offical record, but his attempt to create peace without reference to the government was interpreted as rebellion. Born Bol Yol, he became a prophet towards the end of World War I when the Abiem

[54] Governor UNP to civil secretary, 6 Aug. 1927, NRO Civsec 57/2/8.

[55] Wyld to Willis, 5 Aug. 1927, NRO UNP 1/44/329.

[56] Johnson (1991*a*); Driberg (1931); Middleton (1963); Fergusson (1922: 163–6; 1923*a*: 112–14); 'Bahr el-Ghazal Province Intelligence Report', Jan. 1923, NRO Intel 2/27/217; Willis (1928: 203).

Dinka, living near the borders of Darfur and Kordofan, were in a turbulent state, affected in part by the recent collapse of Ali Dinar's sultanate. Bol Yol was possessed by both his clan-divinity DENG PIOL ('DENG clouds') and ARIANHDIT, 'Ariath the Great', the founder of his clan. His divinity manifested itself by giving him the power of life and death but also became known 'in the truth of his words'. It was as a peacemaker that Arianhdit made his name. As he later stated, 'Dinka were in war, they loot[ed] cattle from each other and Sultans were timid and appealed to me for compromise.' He was able to persuade raiders to return their cattle, and feuding sections to compose their differences; he prevented fights between the Dinka and Arabs, and rebuked young warriors for fighting. His influence grew as his success in peacemaking grew, and his success became the ultimate proof that he was a man of Divinity. He was able to settle feuds among peoples as distant as the Rek and Agar Dinka, and attracted supplicants from the Shilluk-Luo. It was this last aspect which first appealed to, and then alarmed, the government. His peacemaking successes were reported, as also was his desire to live peacefully with the government—but at a distance. By refusing to meet with any representative of the government he demonstrated to administrators that 'either he distrusts the Government or that he is hostile'. When emissaries purporting to come from Arianhdit began to appear in different parts of Bahr el-Ghazal Province preaching a variety of causes, including rejection of the government, it appeared that his only possible reason for uniting the Dinka was to raise a rebellion. Many of these emissaries were soon proved to be bogus, using the prophet's popularity for their own ends, but the government was encouraged in its fears by a number of Dinka chiefs who found their people moving off to the prophet. When an Arab merchant also reported that Arianhdit was being advised by an old Dinka formerly imprisoned by General Gordon, fears of an anti-government movement increased. Arianhdit's appearance coincided with the 'holy lake' of the Atuot and Agar and the discovery of 'secret societies' among the Jur-Beli, so government apprehension was at its height. An attack on a government police post by warriors who either disobeyed Arianhdit, or were not even his own followers, led to Arianhdit's arrest and banishment to Khartoum.[57]

[57] Lienhardt (1961: 48, 76–7, 156–7; 1958: 131); *SMIR* 323 (June 1921), 6–7; 324 (July 1921), 5; 326 (Sept. 1921), 5–6; 328 (Nov. 1921), 7; 329 (Dec. 1921), 4; 332 (Mar. 1921), 7; acting governor BGP to DC Eastern District, 30 Nov. 1921, NRO BGP 1/3/14; Fergusson to governor BGP, 12 Nov. 1921, NRO BGP 1/2/8; governor BGP to OC Patrol 101, 12 Jan. 1922, 'Dirar Ali—Statement By', 13 Nov. 1921, governor BGP to civil secretary, 24 Nov. 1921, 14 Mar. 1922, 13 Apr. 1922; and 'Statement of Bol Yol', all in NRO Intel 1/20/109. See also Majok (1984: 111–26), where the only evidence of Arianhdit's planned resistance comes from government sources, but where Dinka oral sources stress his peaceful mission. The rapid circulation of propaganda derived from a prophet, but spread by agents of which he had no knowledge, for purposes he did not share, has parallels in the Ghost Dance of the 1890s (Lesser 1978: ch. 2, esp. p. 57).

The years during and immediately after World War I had increased the Sudan government's sensitivity to external subversion and the movement of ideas, but this sensitivity was sharpened by the new theories of native administration. If the diverse peoples of the Sudan were to be administered according to their own custom, that custom had to be protected against contamination from other sources of custom or law. This was the logic behind the 'Closed Districts' policy applied to most districts of the southern provinces, as well as to some rural areas of the northern Sudan. A variety of 'foreign' influences were seen as disruptive of tribal discipline.[58] Islam and mission Christianity were the most frequently cited, but vigilance extended to foreign native customs. Thus the Zande secret societies were condemned because of their Congolese origin, and because they spread beyond the Azande to other peoples. One of Willis's most influential ethnographic falsifications was his assertion that the Nuer prophets represented a 'foreign' cult, and were perverters of the Dinka 'Cult of Deng' who had imported it to the Nuer and even Shilluk.[59] This became administrative orthodoxy for many years.

The suppression of such 'alien' prophets may have been presented as an administrative necessity by a governor who craved an expansion of his executive authority, but there were limits beyond which the governor-general and the civil secretary would not be pushed. If Willis played upon generalized fears of fanatic religious rebellions, both Sir John Maffey and Harold MacMichael were also aware that a ruthless and indiscriminate suppression was likely to produce the very resistance it was intended to forestall. Maffey rejected Willis's early request for autonomous authority to eliminate all 'kujurs'. He instructed that the governor be reminded that he had to accommodate himself to primitive mentality.

> He must seek to use the forces which control and influence the tribal mind. If he proclaims himself as the Hammer of the Kujurs he will stir up serious trouble. He must remember that 'The blood of the martyrs is the seed of the Church', and I should like him to read 'Edwin Smith's "Golden Stool"' if he has not already done so. . . . I am perfectly prepared to deal strongly with hostile Kujurs. Equaly I am anxious to see them find a place in native administration to which their influence entitiles them. Tactful handling will bring many of them on the side of the angels.[60]

It was already becoming evident that the blanket use of the words 'kujur' and witch-doctor was clouding the government's understanding of tribal society and obstructing its search for administrative chiefs. It was in this spirit that the civil secretary, MacMichael, asked what there was 'in the beliefs of

[58] Sanderson and Sanderson (1981: 120, 182, 423).

[59] Johnson (1985*a*).

[60] Civil secretary to governor UNP, 28 Apr. 1928, NRO Civsec 36/2/4 and SRO UNP 66.E.2.

the people which, so to speak' gave the 'kujurs' 'a warrant' and enabled them to 'obtain all the power & respect' they had.[61] It was this which led to Evans-Pritchard's employment on a study of the Nuer which was to extend over six years, from 1930 to 1936.

Evans-Pritchard brought a scholarly precision in terminology which the amateur scholars of the Sudan administration sorely needed. In his first description of prophets and other religious functionaries among the Nuer he warned:

> This term 'witchdoctor' does duty for a number of totally distinct magical and religious specialists with separate ritual and social functions. It has been commonly applied by Europeans to land-experts, cattle-experts, various other experts controlling departments of nature, diviners, magicians of various kinds, experts who derive their offices from totemic filiation, physicians who heal the sick, sorcerers who cause sickness, persons possessed by spirits, persons who exorcise them, prophets and so on. Attention to terminology related to religion and magic among a people like the Nuer is not inspired by pedantic love of classification alone but is an essential preliminary to understanding the institutions with which they are linked. To heap together all the people who seemed to do 'odd' things is disastrous to ethnological description and to good administration alike.[62]

Evans-Pritchard effectively banished the words witch-doctor and 'kujur' from the vocabulary of British administrators of the Nuer, but they were reluctant to accept the term of prophet he introduced for the Nuer *guk*, frequently writing it only between inverted commas. They were more interested in the advice he could give them on other, more secular, figures around whom administration could be built. Evans-Pritchard had to conduct his research within the context of government suppression of the prophets, and the forcible (though temporary) separation of the Lou and Gaawar Nuer from the Nyareweng, Ghol, and Luac Dinka. This limited any direct investigation of religious matters. His analysis of Nuer religion had to await the completion of more practical studies of ecology, kinship, political organization, and social structure. Whereas his earlier publications were either subsidized by the Sudan government or appeared in *Sudan Notes and Records*, his writings on Nuer religion, an interest which developed after he left the Sudan, appeared in more purely academic journals.[63]

The conditions of his research, and the needs of his administrative audience (with their interest in pragmatic ethnography), did influence Evans-Pritchard's presentation of Nuer society. He accepted, for instance, the established version of Nuer aggression and hostility towards the Dinka and government, which he incorporated into his analysis of the segmentary system

[61] Minute page, NRO Civsec 36/2/4.
[62] Evans-Pritchard (1935: 54–5).
[63] Johnson (1982*c*: 244).

of Nuer lineages.[64] But he did recognize that the moral relations between the peoples of the Southern Sudan and the government were of fundamental importance.[65] His presentation of the Nuer prophets as political leaders stemmed directly from this recognition.

Evans-Pritchard could not carry out sustained inquiries into the lives of the Nuer prophets. They were either dead, in hiding, or in exile. But he did have an interpretative model of prophetic action in the work of the Old Testament scholar W. Robertson Smith. Robertson Smith presented the prophets of Israel as confronting the great empires of their day in periods of national, and even world, crisis. 'The prophet was not an ordinary preacher;' he wrote of Isaiah, 'his voice was mainly heard in great political crises, and in uneventful times he might well be silent for years.' It was in 'the greatness of the crisis' that Isaiah expanded 'the prophetic horizon'.[66] Here was a parallel to the recent situation of the Nuer as they, too, confronted the most powerful empire of the day.

Evans-Pritchard integrated this model of crisis into his structural analysis of Nuer society, asserting that:

> The only activities of prophets which can truly be called tribal were their initiation of raids against the Dinka and their rallying of opposition to Arab and European aggression, and it is in these actions that we see their structural significance and account for their emergence and the growth of their influence.

Of the recent government pacification campaigns which ended in the death and exile of so many prophets he suggested, 'As we understand the situation, the prophets were inevitably opposed to the Government because it was this opposition among the people which led to their emergence and was personified in them.'[67]

This analysis was accepted by British administrators from the mid-1930s on. F. D. Corfield, Evans-Pritchard's friend who was also later the author of the official report on Mau Mau in Kenya, wrote from Nasir in 1935 that

> crisis in the life of a nation may bring out a man of exceptional influence and it is not unreasonable to suppose that Ngundeng became famous because he happended to pit himself against the Government and the a[d]vent of the Government was undobutedly the greatest crisis that the Nuer had yet experienced.[68]

P. P. Howell, writing in the shadow of his academic and administrative predecessors, declared that Ngundeng 'was thrown up like some dictator, in a time of great adversity, when the Nuer were facing the threat of foreign

[64] Johnson (1981: 517–22); James (1990*b*).

[65] Evans-Pritchard (1938*b*: 76).

[66] Robertson Smith (1897: 294–5, 331).

[67] Evans-Pritchard (1940*a*: 188–9).

[68] F. D. Corfield, 'Note on the Origin of Native Authority among the Nuer with Particular Reference to the Jekany Dor', 1935, NRO UNP 1/51/4.

invasion, first by the Dervish and later by the present government', and that he became a symbol 'of co-ordinated tribal resistance to foreign aggression'.[69] It was essentially a secular interpretation of a religious figure, which adminstrators accepted as compatible with both their secularization of Nuer administration and their belief that the prophets were either foreign imports or aberrations in Nuer political life. Their removal during the Nuer Settlement, wrote Coriat's successor among the Lou, Captain Alban, 'left us with the normal tribal elements'. The prophets were found to be 'excrescences, even if large excrescences, on the Nuer tribal body', concluded Coriat's successor among the Gaawar, John Winder, 'and to build on them was proved to be building on false foundations'.[70] Evans-Pritchard's original analogy with the prophets of Israel may not have been intended to reassure administrators—it certainly did not suggest that the prophets were foreign to the Nuer—but it did reinforce the administrators' conclusion that the appearance of prophets, as an emergency response to alien governments, had little to do with the lasting and fundamental values of Nuer society.

Those prophets who survived the Nuer Settlement lived under regular surveillance but were unmolested as long as they confined themselves to a rigidly defined set of religious and ritual activities. As administrative fear of these later prophets decreased, so the crimes of the earlier prophets were magnified in official histories. Evans-Pritchard's identification of the prophets as resistance leaders inspired administrators to embroider the official record with details not found in contemporary documents. Thus, by 1946 it was being said that the 1902 patrol marched 'to the famous pyramid where a fair fight took place', though there had been no fight at Ngundeng's shrine. So, too, the history of the 1917 patrol was rewritten in a draft handbook for Upper Nile which declared that the Lou Nuer, 'under the influence of the great witch doctor Wendung the builder of the pyramid, attacked the Government post at Ajak and killed a mamour and many Dinkas'. Guek's downfall was explained in various ways. The same handbook stated that during 1927 'administration under Mr Coriat was making good progress when Gwek Wendeng afraid of losing his paramount authority among the Lau decided to defy the Government'. Another official attributed that outbreak of hostilities to the 'threat to public security' posed by the 'ceaseless war between a Gaweir/Lau Nuer alliance and a Nyarraweng/Ghol Dinka alliance' throughout the 1920s. The final official word was published in the report of the Jonglei Investigation Team, just before the departure of the British:

> Matters came to a head in 1928 when the District Commissioner of Western Nuer District was assassinated by the Nuong Nuer and in Lau Nuer country Gwek

[69] Howell (1948*b*: 53).

[70] A. H. Alban, 'Note on the Indigenous Basis of the Present Administrative System', 26 June 1935, SRO UNP 32.B.1; J. Winder, 'Note on the Evolution of Policy in Regards to Chiefs Sub-Chiefs & Headmen', Nasir END 1.F.1 and 2, vol. i.

Ngundeng, a 'Prophet' of wide repute, showed open defiance of the government. In the same year, the Gaweir Nuer and some Lau, led by Dwal Diu (son of another 'Prophet'), fell upon the Nyareweng Dinka across the border and attacked the government post at Duk Faiwil. Reprisals followed in the form of military operations, supported by aircraft, which were known as the 'Nuer Settlement', and the Nuer learnt a lesson which they have not forgotten. The means have been justified by the end, since there was no lasting resentment and the Nuer responded whole-heartedly to the period of pacification which followed. From a suspicious and intractable people they quickly became what they are now; still proud, still essentially independent in spirit, but friendly and on the whole progressive in their outlook.[71]

We will see in the following chapters that a number of contemporary documents giving the lie to these latter-day reconstructions survived in government offices in the Sudan long past the period of British administration. An official history true to its own sources could have presented a fundamentally different interpretation of historical events. But the mythology surrounding the Nuer is so entrenched that even later historians have overlooked evidence in the documents to present a picture of the prophets consistent with the caricature which emerged towards the end of the Condominium period. Prophets are still described as 'emergency leaders', as organizers of resistance whose conscious intention was to forge stronger political ties in the face of 'a direct challenge to their entire social and political structure', but who achieved only 'an ephemeral unity' before being swept aside by British machine-guns, or as 'symbols of the tribe' whose 'main political function had been to lead cattle raids against neighbouring tribes'.[72]

If the fallibility of official amnesia is to be overcome, if the Nuer perception and understanding of their own past is to be retrieved from the mythologizing of generations of administrators, then Nuer testimony must be faithfully reported. The Nuer memory may even be more reliable than that of alien administrators. Over fifty years ago one governor was struck by the close attention Nuer chiefs paid to all that was said in the annual meetings he used to attend. 'I have formed a habit of keeping notes of these addresses,' he recorded, 'and on returning to a District in the following year I find they remember accurately all that passed at the last meeting.'[73] We may not expect to find verbatim reports of conversations that took place over a hundred years ago in Nuer testimony recorded today, but we can expect to find something of the essence of what was said, and what was understood, as well as, perhaps, what was misunderstood.

Garang Ngundeng died a few months after recording those memories of his

[71] R. E. Lyth, 'Short Summary of the Recent History of the Murlee, Lau Nuer and Anuak Tribes', 16 Mar. 1946, NRO UNP 1/44/329; 'Upper Nile Province Handbook', Chs. 1 and 2, 1948, NRO UNP 1/44/328; J. S. R. Duncan, DC Central Nuer, to governor UNP, 25 Oct. 1949 SRO UNP 66.B.5/4; JIT 1954: i. 208.

[72] Sanderson and Sanderson (1981: 6); Collins (1971: 218; 1975: 41–2); Daly (1986: 145).

[73] A. G. Pawson in UNPMD May 1933, SRO BD 57.C.1.

father's death which begin this chapter. He was decrepit but not senile when he spoke; his reminiscence was full of the details of what he heard around him on a day seventy years earlier. Clearly he did not tell, and could not remember, all that had happened to him on that one day, but he told enough to give us an idea of what it was like to live in the household of a prophet at the beginning of this century. It is from similar testimony, corroborated at points by contemporary documents often overlooked by administrators and historians, that the following study is constructed. It is only in this way that we can hope to get closer to understanding what the Nuer prophets said and did in their own time, as well as how they are understood now.

2

DENG and Aiwel: Elements of the Prophetic Idiom and Definition of the Moral Community

Mantic figures and the moral community—environmental and historical patterns—spiritual centres in the flood region—Nuer movement and occupation of the east—social and religious idioms of the Nilotic community—free-divinities

Mantic figures and the moral community

In this chapter we will examine the broader Nilotic heritage, on which the Nuer have drawn, in order to trace changes in expectation (if not meaning) as the prophetic idiom developed out of the experience of the nineteenth century. We will want to identify those aspects of spiritual activity and power on which the prophets based their own authority, and which acted as precedents for prophetic activity. Here, to avoid the generalities inherent in the terminology of spirit possession, we can profitably revive Nora Chadwick's use of the term 'mantic' in her thoughtful, but now neglected, book *Poetry and Prophecy*. Mantic activity refers to the acquisition, cultivation, and declaration of knowledge; knowledge of the commonly unknown present and past, as well as of the future.[1] Chadwick adapted this Greek cousin of 'prophetic' to avoid the common confusion which equates prophecy exclusively with prediction, and to focus attention on the intellectual and artistic qualities of mantic persons—seers, shamans, and prophets. We will want to look at the forms of mantic activity among the Nilotes and the Nuer before the appearance of the first known Nuer prophets, especially in association with affliction, healing, the control of natural and social events, and uncovering the truth both about individuals and about society.

Mantic activity among the Nilotes is intimately associated with defining and sustaining a moral community, and the Nuer prophets were particularly identified with this concern. We must therefore broadly examine Nilotic definitions of the moral community. At the same time we must understand that the composition of Nilotic communities was constantly changing

[1] Chadwick (1952: pp. xiii–xiv).

throughout the nineteenth century (and very likely in many preceding ones), producing corresponding redefinitions of the moral community. For this reason our understanding of those definitions must proceed from an understanding of historical developments among the Sudanese Nilotic peoples, the processes by which Nilotic societies have merged with or have separated from each other.

Environmental and historical patterns

We know from historical linguistics that the Nuer have formed a distinct part of the group of Western Nilotic-speaking peoples for some centuries,[2] yet in many ways the people we now call Nuer, and the distinctive features which characterize modern Nuer society, are a product of the nineteenth century. For the purposes of this study it is not important to establish either the territorial origin of the Western Nilotic-speaking peoples, or the time-depth of their differentiation into specific languages and societies. Instead we will assume what has been suggested by historical linguistics and partially confirmed by archaeology: that by the beginning of the eighteenth century, a period touched on by indigenous historical traditions, much of the area of the Upper Nile Basin had long been settled by related groups of Nilotic-speaking peoples who, though varying in social structure and political organization, shared considerably in material culture, social values, and religious ideas.[3] The historical traditions which have been the object of the greatest study do not represent the ultimate origins of peoples, but instead refer to the formation of more recent political systems or prominent political groups. They make important statements about political and social processes, and in that respect can be understood as the distillation of extended historical experience.[4] They also often refer to specific events and individuals of recent date, and so can be used in the construction of chronological history. In this chapter we will explore themes contained in the myths and historical traditions of Nilotic peoples as a prelude to the historical investigation of the lives of the Nuer prophets. We will look at the impact of ecology on social organization and social values and examine common ideas about spiritual power: its importance to life and well-being, the danger it poses to those who must approach it, the necessity of controlling and containing it through shrines and regulating the transmission of spiritual authority in society over time. We will then give a summary of the history of the Nuer movement from their western homeland to new lands east of the main channel of the Nile, before discussing the main elements of the social and religious idioms of Nilotic society, and the

[2] McLaughlin (1967: 13–27); Ehret *et al.* (1975: 85–112); Ehret (1982: 19–48); David (1982: 78–103).

[3] Ehret (1982); David (1982); Robertshaw (1987: 177–89).

[4] See esp. R. G. Lienhardt (1975: 213–37).

way in which the Nuer occupation of new territories began to change those idioms.

The occupation of the Upper Nile Basin by Nilotic-speaking pastoralists, their differentiation from each other, their movements, and their economic activities have taken place against the background of a progressive drying out of the region over millennia. Both long-term and short-term pulsations in the climate of northern Africa have been influential in the adoption of pastoralism and the dispersal of pastoralists throughout the region. Because the general trend of desiccation has been punctuated by a succession of wetter and drier periods, the general movements of pastoralists have been neither unilinear nor unidirectional. Territory which was abandoned during one phase may have been reoccupied in a later phase. In any historical period there have been shifts in the availability of water, vegetation, and flood-free land, all of which have affected patterns of human settlement. The linguistic evidence suggests that there has been a considerable overlaying of peoples and languages, rather than a succession of population displacements. In this respect the most recent movements of Western Nilotic societies must be recognized as modern representations of a far older pattern.[5]

The area of the Sudan currently inhabited by Western Nilotic-speaking pastoralists contains a number of land types subject to different patterns of rainfall and river flooding. The territory now occupied by the Shilluk and Northern Dinka falls within the central rainlands zone of the Sudan, with mainly clay soils of relatively good fertility, but with cultivation limited by rainfall levels of 440–750 mm. annually. Further south the flood region covers most of what is now administratively called Upper Nile and Bahr el-Ghazal. Here the land is flat, heavy clay soil, of high fertility, and with only a few outcroppings of slightly higher, sandier soil. Because of the structure of the soil and the lack of slope to the land, this area is subjected to severe seasonal river and rain flooding which limits its use for cultivation. The western edge of the flood region is bounded by the ironstone plateau, a well-drained area suitable for permanent habitation, but with shallow soil of low fertility. The variety of grasslands found in the flood region provide modern pastoralists with different types of grazing throughout the dry season, but this requires constant movement to take advantage of the irregular availability of water and the life-cycles of different grasses. Similar types of soils and grasses are found throughout the flood region, but in substantially different combinations to constitute distinct ecological zones or sub-zones. The most valued grasses are those found in the seasonally river-flooded grasslands, the *toic*, which are exposed late in the dry season as the flood waters recede. All communities, therefore, try to ensure access to some form of *toic*, wherever their wet season

[5] Gowlett (1988: 27–45); Ehret (1974; 1982); David (1982); Johnson (1986*c*: 131–44; 1988*c*: 211–24).

settlements may be. While movement can be general throughout the region in the dry season, the permanent population is restricted by the availability of flood-free land during the wet season. That availability is affected by the levels of the major rivers as well as by fluctuations in annual rainfall. Any long-term rise in the main rivers and expansion of the permanent swamp can thus significantly alter the land available for settlement, cultivation, and grazing. The loss of any one type of land has meant that individuals, families, or whole groups must search for new areas in which to settle or to graze. The settlements in more favoured areas have thus been constantly reinforced by emigrants from periodically less-favoured regions. Those areas which have consistently been able to support the largest populations have been those which combine large stretches of permanently habitable land with access to flood-fed seasonal grazing. These include the ridges on both banks of the upper White Nile and lower Sobat, and the transitional belt between the flood zone and the eastern edge of the ironstone plateau.[6]

Permanent settlement within the flood region is problematic. There are sandy ridges bordering the seasonal watercourses west of the Bahr el-Jebel; larger ridges also on the northern and eastern sides of the Zeraf Island parallel to the White Nile and Bahr el-Zeraf; a further series of low ridges and knolls to the east, running parallel to the Bahr el-Jebel and Bahr el-Zeraf; and parts of the eastern plains to the south (and immediately north-east) of the Sobat which are subject only to rain flooding, but which are also exceedingly dry in the dry season. The areas closest to the rivers are most vulnerable to sustained rises in water levels, which have occurred frequently in the past, while the plains are susceptible to periods of prolonged drought. Alternating periods of high rivers and low rainfall have in the past (as now) caused an oscillation of movement between the river edges and the drier plains. For this reason there has been constant movement into, out of, and through the flood region.[7]

Spiritual centres in the flood region

Movement of peoples and reinforcement of settlements from south to north along the banks of the White Nile, and west to east along the Sobat, are indicated in the historical traditions of the Lwo-speaking Shilluk and Anuak. The details of clan and other traditions suggest processes of amalgamation, rather than the mass migration often assumed. Similarly, established Dinka communities along the White Nile and within Bahr el-Ghazal were frequently

[6] For land types: SDIT 1954: 35–6, 61, 74, 81–2, 90–2; JIT 1954: i. ch. 2; Howell, Lock, and Cobb (1988: chs. 7–10, 12, and 13). For importance of micro-relief see Mawson (1989: 38–42). For populations: Appendix 1 below. For transhumant patterns: Evans-Pritchard (1940*a*: ch. 2); Lienhardt (1958); Mohamed Osman el Sammani (1984: ch. 4).

[7] Johnson (1986*c*, 1988*d*, 1990).

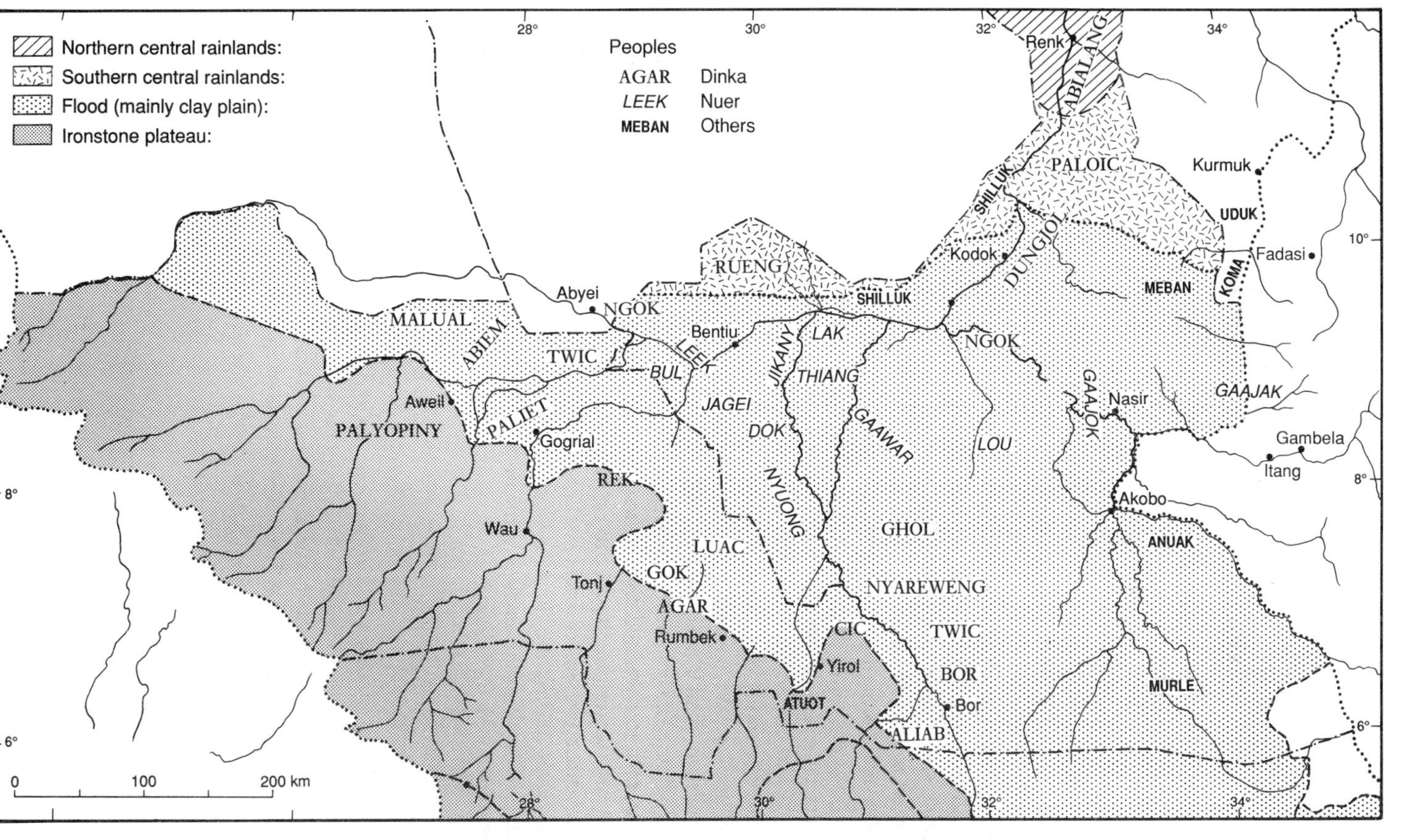

Map 2. Ecological regions and Nilotic peoples in the Southern Sudan

Source: Based on SDIT 1954.

reinforced by immigrants from a Dinka heartland east of the Bahr el-Jebel. Newcomers and older settlers had to form and reform themselves around established, or newly established, figures of authority whose permanence was evoked by reference to the transmission of spiritual power, often linked to a fixed, central site. Among the Shilluk the person of the king (*reth*) and the site of his royal capital, Fashoda, became the centres of focus for the kingdom and for new peoples brought into association with it. Periodically the royal enclosure at Aturwic within Fashoda became the focal point of royal ritual when the ancestral and national divinity Nyikang was brought to confront each new king there. In a similar way shrines among the Eastern Dinka and spear-masters among other Dinka have served as spiritual focuses around which different elements of society combined.[8]

The most important Dinka shrines east of the Bahr el-Jebel were Luang Deng and Puom (or Luang) Aiwel. Each is associated with one of the two central figures in Dinka religion: Deng and Aiwel. Luang Deng was built as a homestead with huts and byres dedicated to each member of the family group of Dinka ancestral divinities: Deng, his father Garang, his mother Abuk, his maternal uncle Pajok, Deng's wife Arek, Pajok's mother Kerciek, and Pajok's wife Nyancar.[9] Many of these divinities later appeared as free-divinities among the Nuer.

Deng is said to have constructed his main byre—the central shrine—to contain all bad thoughts and bad things. He continues to be approached through the master of the clan-divinity (*beny yath*), the custodian of the shrine. Modern members of the shrine-master's family employ the language of seizure in describing how Deng chooses a new master in each generation. The Nuer-speaking son of a recent shrine-master used the Nuer term for prophet, *guk kuoth*, to describe the *beny yath*.[10] This may be a modern adaptation of the Nuer idiom. Earlier sources indicate that, though Deng may have resided in the person of the custodian, he communicated through dreams rather than speaking directly through the mouth of the shrine-master, as Nuer divinities do through their prophets.[11] Still, the similarity in mantic activity is strong enough for people close to both the prophets and the custodians to make the comparison, and we can suggest the likelihood that the shrine-masters were prototypes for the prophets. They represented a controlled form of activity by a single divinity, which became general after the control of that shrine was broken. Individuals came (and still come) to the shrine-master for personal consultation about illness and misfortune. There were regular sacrifices and

[8] Johnson (1990).

[9] Howell (1961: 99).

[10] Wan Deng D1; also Leek Deng Malual and Malual Amol D3 described their priestly ancestors as seized by Deng.

[11] DC Bor and Duk District to governor UNP, 13 May 1931, SRO UNP 66.B.11; Seligman and Seligman (1932: 181).

ceremonies for general well-being at Luang Deng in the past, and it is possible that all relevant sections of Dinka were represented and participated. DENG is known for giving rain, *deng* also being the Dinka word for rain. ABUK, too, is associated with water, especially with floods. There were, and still are, general sacrifices at the shrine for cultivation and rain.[12]

DENG is a divinity who is also thought of as an ancestor. Aiwel Longar is another ancestor of particular importance, being the first and archetypical spear-master. Myths about him are known throughout Dinka country. In the east he is linked with Luang Deng and with Puom Aiwel; in the west he is linked only with the ancestors of the current lines of spear-masters. The example of his shrine and the motifs of his myth were a significant influence on Nuer prophets in the nineteenth century.

The story of Aiwel's birth to a childless, and in most versions an old and barren, woman is commonly told among the Dinka. The Eastern Dinka identify Aiwel's father as a Power (*jok*), who is sometimes described as 'one by himself'. His mother gave birth to Aiwel after being impregnated by the Power in the river. Aiwel is sometimes said to have been born with a full set of teeth (something also claimed for the divinity DENG), an augury of religious power. He was either a precocious or an abnormal child who, in some versions, was mistreated because of his kinless status but who could at an early age kill through his word alone. As an adult Aiwel (also known by his ox-name Longar) demonstrated his spiritual strength in many ways, sometimes by providing life-saving water when people were suffering from thirst, and at other times killing or endangering those with whom he lived.[13] He thus represents the danger of real spiritual power, which can be creative and destructive in turn. He is regarded ambivalently by those in the myth (and by those who now tell the myths) as the source of life and well-being, but potentially also as a withholder of life; therefore the archetype of the unpredictable and oppressive ruler.

Most versions of the myth describe how this spiritual power was curbed or contained. In the widely known western and northern versions Aiwel stabs the people in the head with a fishing-spear as they try to follow him across a river. He is stopped by the ancestors of the various spear-master clans, abetted by a woman from Aiwel's own family (a wife or a daughter) who instructs them how they may cross the river. The new spear-masters then receive from Aiwel their clan divinities (especially RING, Flesh), the power to curse, and the power to pray and to invoke the fishing-spear, which becomes the symbol of their office.[14] In the southern (i.e. Nyareweng, Rut, Luac, and Bor) versions

[12] Cuol Dual G13.2, Wan Deng D1; Howell (1945*b*: 322; 1961: 101).

[13] Lienhardt (1961: 172, 188–92); Ibrahim Bedri (1939: 125–8); O'Sullivan (1908: 15). For DENG, see Seligman and Seligman (1932: 148).

[14] Lienhardt (1961: 173–87); Ibrahim Bedri (1939: 128–9); Deng (1980: 37–8, 209–10, 229–32, 253–5).

Divinity intervenes and neutralizes Aiwel, who is then approached through a shrine built over his grave. In one Aiwel is expelled from Luang Deng because of a dispute with the Sun and flees to the place now known as Puom (a raised part of a river bank). To avoid the Sun Aiwel hides in his byre, coming out only at night. The Sun appeals to the Moon, who spears Aiwel through the head and body with a fishing-spear, transfixing him to the ground. Aiwel is not killed, but his people come and bury him alive—some say at his own instruction—by constructing a huge mound over him, a mound which the Nuer now call Puom Aiwel or Puom Longar, but which some Dinka also still call Luang Aiwel, the byre of Aiwel Longar. The mound was large, but it did not cover the fishing-spear, whose shaft protruded from the apex. Another common story is that Aiwel used to build his byre out of living people, and it is for this reason that once the Moon speared him his people came and raised a mound over him. The byre of living people is echoed in other stories of the building of the mound after Aiwel's death, in which live persons formed the scaffolding around the byre during its construction as it was raised higher and higher.[15]

The eastern and western versions of the myth of Aiwel (which have been analysed most carefully by Godfrey Lienhardt) have common features in representing Aiwel as both a life-giver and a death-dealer. Aiwel denied his followers life, 'which was in his power to give', by directly endangering them in some way. It is through the intervention of women—women of Aiwel's own family in the west, the Moon, a female figure, in the east—that Aiwel's 'killing power is counteracted, and his "life" becomes available to others'. His spiritual power is thus controlled and made accessible to others through the persons of the new spear-masters in the west and north, and through the new shrine built above his grave in the east. The story of Aiwel's death is not just an explanation of the origin of various clan-divinities (such as Flesh and Rain) among certain groups of Dinka; it is the story of the foundation of a shrine by which spiritual power was contained, and through which it could be approached.[16]

The process of containing spiritual power in the act of making it accessible to a wider community helps to create a moral community. This is illustrated in the parallel case of Luang Mayual of the Agar Dinka, as analysed by A. N. M. Mawson. The first Agar spear-master also made his byre out of the bodies of living persons. He was then buried alive, and his shrine became a place where people were assured regular access to life. Periodic participation in rebuilding this shrine was one way of assuring collective access. The shrine in the myth was quite literally a bringing together of people; just as the physical shrine

[15] Lienhardt (1961: 189); Ibrahim Bedri (1948: 47); Wan Deng EHJP-9; Howell (1948*b*: 52–3); Johnson (1990).

[16] Lienhardt (1961: ch. 5, esp. pp. 194–6, 199).

periodically regathers people around it. In this way, Mawson explains, the mythical and current shrines become 'condensed images of society, condensed images of the moral and political communities with which and through which people lived'.[17] Such periodic communal rites at central shrines are occasions when the moral community is reaffirmed, and even redefined. This is true at the installation of the Shilluk king; we will see that it was also true for the building and maintenance of Ngundeng's Mound.

The ambivalent nature of such power is emphasized above: it is neither totally benign nor entirely predictable, but it is absolutely necessary for the maintenance and continuation of life. It must be sought at the same time that it is kept at a distance; its vitality must be preserved, its transmission in society regulated, its accessibility to all mediated, but its danger must be controlled. Just as the first spear-master was both a life-giver and a death-dealer, so his successors have the power to bless and to curse.[18] The presence and continuity of spiritual power is secured through shrines or through figures of spiritual authority, but the community at large must negotiate access to the beneficent and life-giving properties of this power. In addition to communal rites, this is most often done through women, and they represent, either in myth or in actual life, a further way by which the danger inherent in the representative of Divinity or spiritual power is moderated or overcome. The role of women or female figures in the Aiwel myths has already been mentioned, and the spear-master clans, the descendants of Aiwel, are frequently referred to as *wen dyor* (also *din dyor* or *men dyor*), 'sons of women'. Among the Western Dinka the best way 'to harness for oneself the life-giving powers of the masters of the fishing-spear is through a woman who will relate one to them'. It is the daughters and sisters of spear-masters who link them to the rest of the community, and the spear-master clans stand as maternal uncles in relation to the other lineages grouped around them.[19] We will see a repetition of this mediating role of women and maternal kin in the lives of some of the main Nuer prophets.

Taken together the myths of DENG and Aiwel represent a development in the apprehension of spiritual power and the transmission of spiritual authority, which is bound up with the migration and reinforcement of Dinka settlements throughout the Upper Nile region. The founding of spear-master clans is associated with a northward and westward movement of Dinka communities out of a southern Dinka homeland into the White Nile and Bahr el-Ghazal regions. The settlements on the Duk ridge are explained by reference to Aiwel himself. The Western Dinka associate their own recent movements with Aiwel, and to them Puom Aiwel is supposed to be the mound on which

[17] Mawson (1989: 102–17, 131, 230).
[18] R. G. Lienhardt (1975) on the same qualities attributed to Nilotic kings.
[19] Lienhardt (1961: 108, 200, 214; 1955: 25–42); Ibrahim Bedri (1948: 42).

Aiwel himself stood as he speared those who tried to follow him across the river. It is important to note, however, that neither Aiwel nor the spear-masters are credited with founding the earliest remembered Dinka settlements. The Dinka occupation of the western edge of the flood zone has recently been described as a gradual settlement over several generations, rather than a mass invasion. According to Western Dinka political theory, which is based on both historical and recent experience, political groups spread over larger territory as they increase in size, segmenting as they grow. Segments move away from the parent body as they become larger, claiming their own pastures and wet season camps to satisfy their expanding needs. These new settlements in turn attract later settlers, the latest of which are often relegated to marginal areas not dominated by the earlier settlers. The newcomers tend to move off in search of better sites once their own numbers increase to the point where they are capable of surviving on their own. These movements are most usually organized around spear-masters, who thus become the nuclei around which Dinka groups form and re-form.[20]

This pattern of movement discernible for the Dinka, and the new and old idioms of spiritual authority associated with it, can be traced also in Nuer movements during the nineteenth century. We will see below how many groups of Nuer moved out of marginal land to seek new territories in the east; and how in their process of movement they either adopted new mobile focuses of spiritual power, or grouped themselves around both old and new spiritual centres in the lands they came to occupy.

Nuer movement and occupation of the east

Evans-Pritchard presents a generalized account of Nuer movement out of their homeland. As a model of an essentially aggressive migration, organized for warfare, and propelled by feuds, it still dominates the lines of inquiry followed in much secondary anthropological literature. It cites no specific historical instances, and it is based equally on the impressions of nineteenth-century travellers and the angry assertions of self-pride by a recently defeated people in the mid-twentieth century. The image of the Nuer as militarily invincible and the Dinka as perpetually defeated is contradicted by documentary evidence and the historical traditions of both groups of people. The description of Nuer migration as one long campaign of conquest is not sustained by my research on the Gaawar nor by Gabriel Jal's research on the Jikany (both of which will be outlined below). There was a more complex pattern of dislocation, opportunity, and redistribution of population, consistent with earlier patterns already described.[21]

20 Stubbs and Morrison (1938: 251); Lienhardt (1958: 114–16); Johnson (1990).
21 Evans-Pritchard (1940*a*: 126–35); Johnson (1981: 518–20; 1982*a*: 184–91); Jal (1987).

The focal point for the Nuer prior to their settlement in the east was a tamarind tree (*koat*) at the village of Koat-Liec in the historical Nuer homeland west of the Bahr el-Jebel. All Nuer groups, except the Jikany, claim to have originated beneath this tree. It burned down in about 1918, but the site is still sacred and is still the focus for sacrificial activity on behalf of all Nuer (see Chapter 8 below). The tree is a communal symbol, a symbol of communities past, present, and even future. In a sense trees 'create' communities by gathering people under them, and they represent the community in many myths throughout the region.[22]

It is as a symbol of social and genealogical incorporation that the tree figures in most Nuer myths. In their most generalized form these myths account for the appearance of the Nuer, the Dinka, and other peoples with whom the Nuer have come into contact. More specifically they give an account of the relationship between Nuer descent groups, or clans. Most Nuer clans claim descent from the two brothers Gee and Aak, either directly or by incorporation. The Jagei of the west and the Jinaca of the Lou are represented as direct descendants of Gee. The ancestors of many other clans, however, appear independently, either falling directly from the tree or from the sky near it, and join one or other of the two broad divisions of the Nuer by adoption or marriage into the family of one of the two brothers. Thus the founding ancestors of the Jimem lineage of earth-masters and the two main Gaawar clans, the Jakar and Ganwar (or Gaawar), were all brought in and attached in some way to the original community surrounding the tree. The incorporation of foreigners into the Nuer lineage system thus appears to be a long-established practice, pre-dating the nineteenth-century eastern expansion.[23]

The fragmentation of Nuer society through feuds is also a feature of myth. The division between the brothers Gee and Aak, their physical separation by a watercourse, and fighting across that divide are recalled as the beginning of the process of intersectional feuding which has been a constant feature of Nuer social life. Feuds have often been referred to as factors in the dispersal and settlement of the Nuer on both banks of the Bahr el-Jebel.[24] Some of the most frequent causes of sectional friction have been conflicts over rights to pasturage and dry land for settlement, both of which are affected by floods. The Western Nuer area, with its limited stretches of elevated land, its dense network of intersecting watercourses, and its proximity to the low banks of both the Bahr el-Jebel and the Bahr el-Ghazal, is particularly susceptible to flooding when the river level rises or the main channel shifts through blocks of

[22] Santandrea (1968: 110, 114–15, 160–1); Titherington (1927: 171); Lienhardt (1961: 36); Evans-Pritchard (1940*b*: 33); James (1979: 68–74).

[23] Jackson (1923: 70–3); Fergusson (1921*b*: 148–50); Evans-Pritchard (1933: 34; 1934: 41; 1940*a*: 212–13, 230–1, 238; 1956: 83); Crazzolara (1953: 8–11, 66–7).

[24] Jackson (1923: 72); Diu Garadin G4; Evans-Pritchard (1940*a*: 33–4, 209).

matted vegetation (*sudd*). When the river spills into previously dry areas, or when the swamps to the west and south merge into each other (as often happens in years of high rain or high river), then communities are brought into increased competition over depleted resources. Land pressure can occur when population increases, or when the area of usable land decreases, or when both happen together. Access to available land must be negotiated through political and kinship networks. This is crucial in deciding whether groups stay or leave. An excess of population to usable land seems to have been the principal initial cause of the Nuer migrations.[25]

At the end of the nineteenth century the French colonial officer Charles Michel noted that the Nuer occupied the right bank of the Baro River only after it had been abandoned by the Anuak in the face of a Mahdist attack. Michel asked whether this was analogous to the way the Nuer had earlier secured possession of the Sobat itself.[26] With some modifications, we can answer yes. The Nuer did take some territory directly through raiding, but their settlements were secured more through seizing land previously abandoned because of floods, feuds, or raids by other peoples. Once the Nuer occupied it, such land was also resettled by the Dinka and Anuak peoples who had earlier left it. This fact is repeatedly mentioned in twentieth-century administrative reports, in the ethnography, and in the testimony of the peoples who inhabit the area today. The process will be summarized in this chapter, but further examples will be found in succeeding chapters.

We have already mentioned that the highest population densities are usually to be found where large stretches of flood-free land are found adjacent to seasonal river-flooded pastures, in particular along the White Nile ridges and the eastern rim of the ironstone plateau, and that movement into and out of the main area of the flood zone has been a constant feature of the Nilotic way of life. This provides the context of Nuer movement and explains, in part, its direction towards the Dinka of the Sobat and the eastern plains. The Dinka population of the White Nile and the ironstone rim at the beginning of the nineteenth century appears to have been both large and strong. The White Nile Dinka frequently fought the Shilluk and the kingdom of Sennar in the late eighteenth century and spread their settlements east and north-east, to territory south of the Blue Nile now occupied by the Koma and Nuer. Dinka immigrants from the south, fleeing floods, feuds, or crop failures in the flood zone, continued to reinforce the Northern Dinka settlements. War with the Shilluk sometimes forced the Dinka to abandon riverside settlements directly opposite Fashoda, but their power along the river was broken only in the 1860s, after some forty years of sustained raiding and warfare by the Turco-Egyptian army and their nomad Arab allies. Throughout this period the Dinka

[25] JIT 1954: i. 10–15, 207–8; Evans-Pritchard (1940*a*: 64, 111); Coriat (1931*a*).
[26] Michel (1901: 308–9).

were known to external observers as determined, persistent, and able fighters, who succumbed only to the repeated attacks of politically more powerful and better-armed assailants.[27]

The Dinka of the Bahr el-Ghazal region were spared similar assaults until the second half of the nineteenth century. Their size relative to the Western Nuer was likely to have been in proportions similar to those in the mid-twentieth century (see Appendix 1), possibly greater, given that the Western Dinka suffered more from the late nineteenth-century wars in the Southern Sudan than did the Nuer. The Western Nuer were able to take some territory adjacent to the Bahr el-Jebel formerly belonging to the Dinka south of them during the 1840s, but there is no evidence to show that the Nuer made any sustainable advances into Dinka territory to the west. On the contrary, an entire age-set of the Jikany, initiated at the beginning of the nineteenth century, was virtually annihilated in war with the Western Dinka, and this was one reason why the Jikany looked for safer lands to the east. Elsewhere hostilities were often contained by exchanges and intermarriage, as between the Jikany Nuer and the Rueng Dinka in the north, and the Nyuong Nuer and the Agar, Cic, and Angai Dinka in the south. The pattern of Western Nuer and Western Dinka raiding in the nineteenth, as in the twentieth century (see Chapter 7), appears to have done no more than periodically alter the configuration of sectionally owned pastures, with the Dinka giving up some of their *toic* to the Nuer while retaining their hold on that larger area of wet season grazing which lies close to their villages.[28]

By the end of the first quarter of the nineteenth century there were large Dinka populations in the north and west. The north continued to attract newcomers from that part of the flood zone bounded by the Bahr el-Jebel, Sobat, and Pibor, while in the west some sections of Twic, Luac, Ghol and Angai Dinka were forced to move because of feuds and bad grazing and were resettling in the east. The possibility that western immigrants were able to occupy some territory temporarily abandoned by Eastern Dinka communities is suggested by more recent events. At the beginning of this century the balance of riverside grazing shifted between the Aliab Dinka (on the west

[27] O'Fahey and Spaulding (1974: 63); Massaia (1974: 208); Beltrame (1974: 242); Corfield (1938: 138); Selim Bimbachi (1842: 23–5); Werne (1849: i. 147); T. A. Maclaglen, 'Dunjol Dinka', 1931, SRO UNP 66.A.4; J. W. G. Wyld, 'Report and Notes on Bor-Duk District'. Nov. 1930, NRO Civsec 57/2/8; Ibrahim Bedri (1948: 40, 42); Petherick (1861: 345, 348, 357); Hill (1959: 108–9); Bartoli (1970: 7–8, 34–5); Brun-Rollet (1855: 90–1); Lejean (1865: 15, 60); Poncet and Poncet (1937: 21); Schweinfurth (1874: i. 71–2, 83); Baker (1875: i. 70); Wilson (1903*a*: 16–17); Mercer (1971: 424–6).

[28] For Western Nuer in the 19th century: Fergusson (1921*b*: 150, 154–5); Selim Bimbachi (1842); Thibaut (1856: 84); Brun-Rollet (1855: 111, 147); Poncet and Poncet (1937: 46–50); 'Extract from Western Nuer Monthly Diary for January, 1934', Nasir END 66.A.1; JIT 1954: i. 237. For Jikany: Jok Jang and Gai Ruea Jk1.1; Jal (1987: 383); B. J. Chatterton, 'Jekaing Nuer & Rueng Dinka', 1933, SRO UNP 66.A.4. For distribution of Bahr el-Ghazal grazing, SDIT 1954 99.

bank) and the Bor Dinka (on the east), when the Aliab appropriated Bor pastures for their own large herds after Bor cattle had been decimated by disease. The pattern of west–east movement which began early in the nineteenth century thus seems to have been impelled by both dislocation in the west and opportunity in the east.[29]

Accounts of Gaawar, Lou, Thiang, Lak, and Jikany Nuer movements across the river suggest a similar combination of reasons. The Gaawar came because of floods in their homeland; the Jinaca of the Lou feuded and split off from the Jinaca of the Rengyan; the Thiang and Lak followed the Lou because the river was low enough to cross; and the Jikany were beset by floods and split internally in a leadership dispute. The Gaawar and Lou occupied the Zeraf Island in the 1820s, while the Jikany migration began later, in *c.*1827–30, at the beginning of the reign of the Shilluk king Awin but during or soon after the first Turco-Egyptian raid on the Dinka of the Sobat in 1827. The Gaawar and Lou settlement of the east bank of the Bahr el-Jebel originally involved no fighting with the Ngok and Luac Dinka on the Zeraf Island. The Lou had to fight the Ngok after being defeated in a feud with the Lak and Thiang, and the Gaawar attacked the Luac only when they were once again flooded out of their own settlements.[30] We will look at the movements of the Gaawar and the Jikany in some detail.

The Gaawar very clearly recall that their exodus out of the west was caused by water, not war. One testimony presents the Gaawar as relegated to marginal, flood-prone land. This is consistent with the myths of the origin of the Gaawar ancestors as latecomers to the main Nuer community. When asked why the Gaawar left their land one informant stated:

> It was because of floods. The Gaawar used to fight with another section there, on the other [western] side. The land of those people was good, but the land of Gaawar was bad. In one of the fights a very good Gaawar man was killed by that section. That section said they would pay compensation with cattle, but the Gaawar refused. The Gaawar said that their man should be compensated for with land. They wanted land, and not cattle. . . . The leader of that section agreed to the compensation and told his people to give the Gaawar the land that they wanted. So the Gaawar came to that land. Then the leader of those people who had given the land to the Gaawar cursed them. He cursed the Gaawar, saying 'You will always have floods.' That is why we, the Gaawar, have always been chased by floods. That area was taken by floods, so the people moved to another place called Bel. When floods took Bel people came to [A]dok. Then from Dok people came to Ager [on the Zeraf Island]. When people came to Dok the people crossed the river—the Bar went to [A]juong and the Radh to Pakuem.[31]

[29] Wyld, 'Report and Notes on Bor-Duk District'; Cuol Yoal EHJP-1, Marol Ater and Macol Dier EHJP-10; Archdeacon Shaw to DC Nuer and Dinka (Southern Area), 7 Aug. 1928. SRO BD 66.B.2.

[30] For Shilluk regnal dates see Johnson (1992*b*) and Jal (1987: 28–40).

[31] Kulang Majok EHJP-7.

Other Gaawar confirm this search for dry land, especially during the time of Buogh Kerpeil, a member of the Yilbith age-set who led the Gaawar onto the Zeraf Island.[32] The early part of the nineteenth century, but especially the 1820s, appears to have been a time of declining precipitation in the land of the Nile headwaters, producing generally low rivers, punctuated by high floods. *Sudd* blocks and clogged channels from low rivers altered the distribution of water along sections of the Bahr el-Jebel and Bahr el-Zeraf so that some areas, such as Adok, Ajuong, and Pacier (see Map 4), became waterlogged and swampy for considerable periods of time, while others along the east bank of the Bahr el-Jebel became drier. The independent testimony of Gaawar and Dinka suggests a succession of local floods during this period which seriously altered settlement patterns. The Thoi, Luac, Rut and Ghol Dinka all claim that floods forced them to abandon their villages close to the river and relocate along the already populous Duk ridge *before* the Nuer arrived. Even the shrine of Luang Deng was temporarily abandoned at this time. The Gaawar remember that they were driven further east towards Pakuem (near Puom Aiwel) when the level of the Bahr el-Jebel rose, flooding that low-lying land in which they lived. The Lou, Lak, and Thiang were similarly affected, and the Lak and Thiang combined to oust the Lou, who then invaded the Ngok Dinka on the north-eastern ridges of the Zeraf Island. The Luac relate that they had plenty of cattle and grain at Pakuem, and that the Gaawar attacked because they were hungry, having no crops of their own. This is consistent with Gaawar memories of being flooded out of their land. The Luac were driven from Pakuem, but the Gaawar also later occupied areas previously abandoned to the flood which the Dinka had not yet reclaimed.[33]

We know from travellers' accounts that Gaawar raided the Luac, Ric, and Angai Dinka annually throughout the 1850s, but that throughout the 1860s the Luac and Gaawar were still to be found on both banks of the Bahr el-Zeraf.[34] The battle at Pakuem was the only battle in which the two halves of the Gaawar, Radh and Bar, combined to fight the Dinka. After that individual Gaawar groups occupied territory on their own.[35] Given what we now know about the environmental conditions of the Bahr el-Zeraf at this time, we can see that the annual raids of the Gaawar were specific to this time and place, not part of a grand pattern or strategy of Nuer conquest. During the decades of the 1860s and 1870s, as we shall see in Chapter 4, Gaawar and Dinka settlements between the Bahr el-Zeraf and the Duk ridge lived mixed together in varying forms of alliance or hostility. Gaawar society grew by attracting many incomers, especially from the west. By the early 1860s there

[32] JIT 1954: i. 207–8; Diu Garadin G4, Mar Kutien G5, Cuol Macar, Ruot Rom, Gai Thung EHJP-4.

[33] Johnson (1988*a*: 183–4, 1992*b*); Cuol Kai A6, Cuol Yoal and Piot Yak EJHP-1, Wan Deng EHJP-9.

[34] Lejean (1865: 68, 81); Poncet and Poncet (1937: 46, 57, 118); Marno (1873: 130–3).

[35] Coriat (1923).

was regular contact with the Western Nuer who crossed the Bahr el-Jebel to exchange their cattle for Gaawar grain. Individuals came to settle, and groups such as the Jaloh split, some remaining in the west, and others becoming part of the Bar Gaawar.[36]

The myth about the origin of Kar and War, the ancestors of the Jakar and Ganwar clans, is told in many forms. All emphasize Kar's role as the first to descend from heaven, and as the one who either enticed War down or persuaded him to stay. Some also give the ancestors of the Jaloh and Kuec, associated with the modern Gaawar, a role in uniting the two brothers.[37] The following version of the myth of Kar and War was told to me by Diu Garadin, a member of the Yaal age-set initiated at the turn of this century. His own grandfather was a Nyuong Nuer who came east shortly after the Gaawar settled along the Bahr el-Zeraf. As a child and young man Diu was part of that later movement of the Bar Gaawar which brought them to the Duk ridge. His relation of the myth incorporated his own, his family's, and many another Gaawar's personal experiences of piecemeal migration and settlement.

At first people came from the west in the sky of Divinity. They came down one by one. Kar came first and was followed by Kuec, and Loh came down too. Their brother War remained in the sky. They came and stayed in a place called Koat-Liec. Kar said, 'Our brother is in the sky, we have to trick him to come down. We have to kill a cow and roast the meat. There is a tamarind tree which starts in the ground and goes up to the sky. When he smells the meat he will come by this tamarind tree.' So they roasted all the meat. [Kar] said, 'He will come soon, let us go away because he likes meat very much.'

War came down and found the meat and ate it, then he went away to hide himself. The rain rained that day. They came and found his footprints and they understood that he had come. Kar decided to cut the tree that goes to the sky, because if he left it, War would come and eat and go straight to the sky. When he came he ate and he went to the tree and found that the tree was cut down. He said, 'They have tricked me.'

Loh and Kuec were already down. They tried to find him but they could not get him. He hid himself. Then Kuec went fishing and Loh went after the cattle with Kuec's dog. The dog smelt the man. When Loh came where he was he asked him, 'Are you the one?' He brought him out. By the evening he went to the cattle-camp. Kuec claimed that the man was found by his dog and Loh said, 'If I did not go, would your dog go?' They quarrelled and fought.

In the beginning it was Kar who brought people down. And then each section went to his cattle camp. [He then listed the descendants of Gee and Aak, with Kar and War as sons of Aak. By the end of the list he had become confused.] Yes, War brought people down. People came to Koat-Liec. This is how people [*naath*] came into existence.

A man named Gatnyal [honorific name for Buogh Kerpeil] said, 'I will go to the other side of the river, because these birds who are crossing the river and come back

[36] Petherick and Petherick (1869: i. 138, 147); Howell (1945*a*: 97).
[37] Evans-Pritchard (1940*a*: 230–1); Coriat (1923).

must have an island to stay on.' People crossed the river and came to a place called Pawarjak. This is how we crossed the river. They stayed there. Dinka were in a place called Pakuem and War. The Nuer decided to go and attack them. So they captured their cattle and came to these places Pakuem and War. Dok, Kuec, Jaloh remained on the other side of the river [Bahr el-Jebel]. All the Gaawar crossed the river, even those who were foreigners [*rol*] came with Gaawar. Gatnyal was the one who brought people to Pawarjak, near the river.

When the Dinka were defeated in Pakuem, Gatnyal and his people came to their places. People were coming bit by bit. They came and settled in Wau and Nyot [on the Zeraf Island]. Dinka were on the other side of the river [Zeraf], they again were defeated and came to Luak Kuoth [Luang Deng], Woi, Pacier and Rupciengdol, too. Again they were attacked by Nuer and came to this place, Duk. Do you get me my son? DIU [Deng Laka] was the one who brought us here.[38]

Just as Nuer society in the west was created through the amalgamation of diverse elements around the tree, so, too, was modern Gaawar society in the east created around those leaders who brought the people into new lands. There is a progression from Kar and War to Buogh Kerpeil to Deng Laka. Just as the ancestors came down the tree 'one by one', so people crossed the river 'bit by bit'. Even the finding of War in the *toic* has echoes in the way the Dinka refugees Nuaar Mer and Deng Laka were later found in the bush. This version of a standard myth is a distillation of Gaawar historical experience.

The Jikany Nuer do not claim to originate at the tree of Koat-Liec. Rather, their ancestor Kir was found floating in a gourd by a Dinka near the confluence of the Bahr el-Jebel and Bahr el-Ghazal. As the myth is usually told among the Western Jikany, who currently live north of the Bahr el-Ghazal close to the Rueng Dinka, it explains their relationship to the Rueng and Ngok Dinka, and later their relationship through intermarriage to other groups of Nuer. As the myth is currently told among the Eastern Jikany, who live north and south of the Sobat, it links them with the Anuak, whose former territory they now occupy. In the Eastern Jikany versions Kir is an Anuak who comes floating down the Sobat. Thus the Jikany migration east of the Nile is presented as a return to the original home of their founding ancestor.[39]

Kir's foreign origin indicates that the Jikany were newcomers in the Nuer homeland, at least as a lately formed autonomous group along the northern fringe of the central settlement area, where the Bahr el-Ghazal and Bahr el-Jebel rivers meet to form the White Nile. This is an area intersected by a number of watercourses and is susceptible to flooding not only in years of

[38] Diu Garadin G4. Other versions mention cutting the rope and War's greediness for meat, Kulang Majok EHJP-7.

[39] For versions linking Kir with the Dinka: Stigand (1919: 224–5); Jackson (1923: 75, 179); J. F. Tiernay, 'Legendary History of the Jikaing', 1931, SRO UNP 66.A.6/4; Chatterton, 'Jekaing Nuer & Rueng Dinka', 1933, SRO UNP 66.A.4; Evans-Pritchard (1933: 36); Crazzolara (1951: 151–2). For version linking Kir with the Anuak: Jal (1987: 15–16). For similar Anuak myths see Evans-Pritchard (1940*b*: 31–3, 77).

high Bahr el-Jebel floods, but in years when a high Sobat pushes back the waters of the White Nile. Dr Gabriel Jal has collected and studied the Jikany historical traditions, and it is his analysis which is summarized here. Some time at the beginning of the nineteenth century, around the time that the Lou and Gaawar crossed to the Zeraf Island, Jikany country south of the Bahr el-Ghazal was habitually flooded. An attempt to move across the river was prohibited by the Bul Nuer, into whose territory the Jikany wished to move. Another barrier to the west was presented by the Western Dinka, who virtually annihilated an entire Jikany age-set (Yoac-nuac) in one battle.[40]

The inability of the Jikany to move into adjacent territories created internal problems, and there were disputes for leadership at this time. Latjor Dingyang, the leader of one of the younger age-sets, proposed to move not west, but east, across the White Nile into Padang Dinka territory north of the Sobat. Latjor secured the support of a woman diviner (*tiet*) as well as the guardian of the spear of WIU, the clan spear of the Gaatgankir clan around whom the rest of the Jikany were grouped. Latjor's migrants were not just Jikany, but included Lou, Rengyan (Jagei), Leek, and Bul Nuer, members of the Jimem, Ganwar and Jakar clans, and even Rueng Dinka. Some came in groups, others as specially recruited individuals. The event which may have initiated both this recruitment and the migration was a civil war in Shilluk country between 1827 and 1830 at the outset of the reign of Awin. Awin hired the Nuer to help him defeat his opponents, but after doing so they looted other Shilluk settlements for cattle before crossing the White Nile into Nyiel Dinka country.[41]

The Jikany struck Nyiel settlements but did not remain in their territory. Their tactic of infiltrating Nyiel camps at night and then attacking at dawn simultaneously from within and without was designed to scatter the Nyiel warriors, leaving cattle, women, and children behind undefended. Taking these the Jikany moved quickly away from the Nile along the Khor Adar and stopped at Malou, in Dungjol Dinka country. Here the Jikany combined with the Dinka to repel a Turco-Egyptian slave-raid, an event which firmly dates the Jikany migration to 1827 or soon after.[42]

The subsequent pattern for Nuer occupation of lands north of the Sobat was set at Malou during the early 1830s. Raids against the Nyiel Dinka had been for quick gain of cattle and captives, not territory. At Malou the Nuer married and exchanged bridewealth with the Padang Dinka around them, especially the Dungjol (which explains the strong ties which still exist between the Dungjol and Eastern Jikany). The settlement at Malou grew with the arrival of newcomers from both the Western Nuer and the Dinka. As the

40 Jal (1987: 32–4, 383).

41 Ibid. 34–8; Bil Peat L12.2, Tut Jiak Gai L21.1, Duop Biciuk Jk2.

42 Jal (1987: 50–7); Bartoli (1970: 7–8).

settlement grew various Nuer began to hive off. This usually occurred during seasonal transhumant movements, and groups did not return to Malou in the rains if they found some other place preferable to live. The Mor Lou crossed the Sobat, joining the Gun Lou at this time. The Padang Dinka themselves began to split up, some staying with the Jikany while others moved off further east. As Malou attracted more and more Nuer from the west, tensions developed within the Nuer community between the old campaigners and the newcomers. Opposition formed against Latjor, especially when he tried to take the relics of Kir from the control of the Gaatgankir clan. The Gaajak split off from the Gaajok, and the Laang section from the Wangkeac. From the late 1830s throughout the 1840s Nuer groups spread throughout the lands east of Malou and south of the Sobat. It was during this period that Nuer raids against Dinka recommenced.[43]

The pattern of settlement and raiding, which Dr Jal clearly describes in his discussion of lineage politics, was again a product of tension between early settlers and newcomers. The initial Gaajak settlement of the far eastern Dinka lands was made possible and even accelerated by marriage with existing independent Dinka settlements. Once this territory had thus been secured for Nuer occupation, new groups of Gaajak followed, and it was these newcomers who initiated the raids against the Padang, driving them further east or north. But since Dinka captured in Nuer raids were subsequently adopted or married into Nuer lineages, and were not reduced to the level of a separate suppressed social stratum, this phase of displacement was followed by the return of many Padang to their old territory, rejoining relatives left behind. But the dominant lineages to which settlers linked themselves were now Nuer, not Dinka.[44]

The Sobat valley saw a succession of droughts during the 1850s and 1860s. Dr Jal has analysed the names of members of the Maker age-set, born in the late 1850s, and finds that many commemorate famine. There are indications in the Blue Nile records of a number of sharp drops in rainfall in the Ethiopian highlands between 1840 and 1860, especially in the late 1850s, which would have affected Sobat levels. The recurrence of drought accelerated the dispersal of Nuer sections into the Anuak territory along the tributaries of the Sobat and Pibor rivers, and intensified Anuak opposition to the Nuer. Earlier Shilluk raids against Nuer settlements close to the mouth of the Sobat also forced the Nuer to keep moving east. This was the time of the unsuccessful Lou and Jikany invasion of the Anuak in Buongjak. Yet, as with the Jikany and Dinka north of the Sobat, many Nuer tried to secure their new settlements by establishing stable relations with the Anuak. Thus the Laang

[43] Jal (1987: 61–9, 84–100).
[44] Ibid. 90–5.

section joined the Lou to invade Buongjak, but lived peacefully with their immediate Anuak neighbours.[45]

The Nuer occupation of the eastern flood zone was affected by external political events. The Shilluk civil war gave Latjor the opportunity to recruit a large force. The Turco-Egyptian assault on the peoples of the White Nile and Sobat eased the Nuer entry in two ways: by weakening potential opposition, but more importantly by giving some groups of people an incentive to seek Nuer assistance and secure their presence, as at Malou. South of the Sobat Dinka communities faced another long-standing threat in the Murle. Murle raids before and during the time of the Nuer entry into the Zeraf Valley are mentioned by the Ghol, Duor, Nyareweng, and Bor Dinka. Dinka communities often did unite together successfully to repel the raiders, but these successes were often bought at a price. When the Duor fled the Murle invasion of Duk Fadiat the Ghol combined with them to eject the Murle from the Duk ridge, but then became the dominant partner in the Ghol–Duor community. The Nyareweng and Padang united to defeat Murle raiders, but disputes over leadership and captured cattle drove them apart and damaged the internal unity of the Nyareweng. It was in the aftermath of the Murle raids that the Lou began to enter Padang territory and raid the Nyareweng.[46]

The Dinka communities were not so much dispersed by the Nuer arrival as redistributed. Some went to settle in new places: the Ngok to the Sobat, those Dungjol and Padang living south of the Sobat joined their kinsmen along the White Nile, and a variety of Dinka from the Bahr el-Zeraf joined others already on the Duk ridge and along the Khor Fulluth. But as with the Padang north of the Sobat, the movement was reversable. There was extensive assimilation, adoption, and intermarriage between the old Dinka communities and the expanding Nuer frontier society, to such an extent that between 50 and 80 per cent of the Eastern Nuer may be of Dinka origin. There has been so much assimilation of Dinka that the Eastern Nuer use of the word for Dinka, *jaang*, does not always have that exclusive and derogatory sense sometimes associated with it. Nuer of different eastern communities call each other *jaang*, and even ancestors from distant Nuer groups are sometimes referred to as *jaang*. In this sense a Dinka is not someone to raid, but a person with whom one might have a potential, or as yet undiscovered, relationship.[47]

[45] Ibid. 106, 130–43; Herring (1979: chart 2.2m, p. 85). Jal suggests that the Maker were born in the 1860s, but if most Maker were 18 years old in 1875 (the date he gives for their initiation) then they would have been born in *c*.1857. For the Shilluk raids see: Thibaut (1856: 48); Werne (1849: ii. 232–46, 279, 292); Duc d'Aumont et de Villequier (1883: 196); Poncet and Poncet (1937: 28); Machell (1896: 34).

[46] Bullen Alier Buttic (1982: 58–9); Marol Ater (Angai), Macol Dier (Duor) EHJP-10, Makor Guot D3.

[47] Evans-Pritchard (1933: 5, 53; 1940*a*: 130, 221–2); Crazzolara (1953: 36, 51–2). Among the Eastern Jikany there is no longer a distinction made between 'Dinka' and later Nuer immigrants; they are all known as 'Dinka' (Hutchinson 1988: 65 n. 1).

The pattern of Nuer migration was similar to previous Nilotic migrations. Its initial motivation was environmental. Specific local conditions along the Bahr el-Jebel, the Bahr el-Ghazal, or the Sobat created difficulties in habitation which in turn contributed to internal tensions and confrontations. The timing and direction of Nuer movement was frequently opportunistic, taking advantage of local changes in river levels and the environmental or political preoccupations of their neighbours. Initial settlements were reinforced by social integration which not only attracted other Nuer, but allowed Dinka and Anuak to regain access to their old territories. The Nuer secured their settlement east of the Nile more by marriage and adoption than by warfare. We cannot speak of a Nuer conquest, but we can speak of a Nuer occupation. Nor can we really describe Nuer history as a process by which the Nuer emerged out of the Dinka and became increasingly differentiated from them. Rather, the direction during the last two centuries has been the other way. The Nuer have been merging with the Eastern Dinka and have come more and more to resemble them. This is particularly evident in an examination of their common social ideas and their changing religious idioms.

Social and religious idioms of the Nilotic community

The Western Nilotic-speaking peoples of the Sudan are closely related, both by their origin and by their subsequent history. The modern Nuer language is almost as close to the Lwo languages of Shilluk and Anuak as it is to Dinka.[48] The patterns of population overlay (rather than displacement) and the history of intermarriage and incorporation suggest that any attempt to identify the 'origin' of discrete ideas among one people and trace their transfer to others would be difficult in the extreme. Evans-Pritchard makes frequent reference to Dinka myths and divinities entering Nuer society, with such identifiable Dinka influences supposedly being greater in the west than in the east. Certainly some divinities, such as DENG or NYIKANG, may be more closely associated with one group of people than another; it may be possible to trace some transfers historically; but given the common pool of social values and religious ideas it is less important to identify routes of transmission than to understand how ideas developed and influenced each other between societies. We will here examine how idioms of religious expression and practice changed meaning as they were applied to different situations and in different

[48] MacLaughlin (1967) compared the vocabulary of the Eastern Jikany, Anuak, and Bor Dinka, calculating the similarities as Nuer–Dinka 42–4%, Nuer–Anuak 37–40%, and Dinka–Anuak 33–7%. The Eastern Jikany would be the furthest from the Bor of any Dinka dialect. His calculation for Nuer and Anuak is too low. My own comparison of 100 word-lists between dialects of Western and Eastern Nuer, Western and Northern Dinka, Shilluk, and Anuak produced the following calculations (making no deductions for common proto-Nilotic vocabulary); Nuer to Shilluk and Anuak 50%, Nuer to Dinka 55.5–58%, Shilluk and Anuak to Dinka 41–42.5%.

contexts by different peoples. It is one of the main features of the lives of the Nuer prophets that they developed a prophetic idiom out of the broader Nilotic religious traditions. It is the purpose of this section to trace the outline of that tradition by examining similar beliefs and practices among the Nuer, Dinka, Atuot, and Lwo-speaking peoples, their ideal of a moral community, and the relationships which exist between the spiritual world and the social order.

The moral community of the Nilotes involves, as Godfrey Lienhardt has explained, 'a willingness to share, give, loan, and accept compensation for wrongs'.[49] This is the opposite of the standard image of the Nuer and Dinka, who most often figure in the Sudanese popular imagination as aggressive warriors, constantly at war with their neighbours and each other. War and feuds have been, and still are, facts of life in the Sudan, and the Nilotes do value individual bravery and communal solidarity in fighting. But the attributes of a warrior, which must be cultivated in order to protect society, can and do impel individuals and entire groups into fighting that goes beyond self-defence. Peace among the Nilotes is highly prized, more especially because it is so difficult to attain. Thus the moral community can be maintained only by an adherence to the values of neighbourliness, and by the willingness to accept mediation of disputes within the community itself. The challenge of the nineteenth century for many Nilotic societies, especially the Nuer, was to define who was included in the moral community and who remained outside it. The definition had to be flexible.

Evans-Pritchard defined the tribe among the Nuer as the largest group to combine in warfare. The tribes themselves segment into sections; the largest he terms primary sections, but these, too, divide into smaller and smaller sections. Each section (*cieng*) is usually associated with a territory of permanent settlement, to which the section gives its name. Local settlements, as well as tribal sections, are made up of agnatic lineages (also called *cieng*), sometimes also having a territorial association. For convenience I will retain Evans-Pritchard's terminology for the major divisions among the Nuer (tribe and section), though not his finer gradations (maximal/minimal and major/minor lineages). In doing so I must stress a distinction which Evans-Pritchard himself made about Nuer kinship, and which has recently been re-emphasized on the reissue of his main kinship study: there is a difference between the discourse of political association and the discourse of kinship.[50] Membership of political/territorial groups is based on residence, and kinship itself is not simply lineage membership based on descent. The principles of political segmentation cannot be transposed to describe the processes of kinship affiliation. We will see throughout this study that Nuer actions cannot be

[49] R. G. Lienhardt (1975: 218).

[50] Evans-Pritchard (1940*a*: 5–6 and ch. 4; 1951: 23); James (1990*a*: p. xiii).

explained by simple reference to the forces of 'segmentary opposition'. Local patterns of kinship affiliation altered the composition of political units, causing a redefinition of moral communities, and affecting internal and external patterns of confrontation and co-operation.

Among most groups of Nuer and Dinka permanent rights to the use of territory (settlement, pastures) are usually traced through agnatic ties. Expanding Nuer settlements incorporate newcomers by establishing either real or fictive links with the dominant lineage. With foreign Nuer it may be by tracing a link to a female ancestor. Captured foreigners (Dinka and Anuak) had the clan spear of their captors invoked over them, and were later formally adopted as full members of the lineage. Among the Western Dinka territory is shared out between lineages of individual agnatic groups who have come into temporary association with each other. But neither the tribe (however genealogically or territorially defined), nor its lineages, nor the large villages which compose them, are exclusive groups of agnates, but a mixture of intermarried neighbours and families.[51]

Two complementary, but sometimes also conflicting, principles of behaviour operate in such mixed settlements. The greatest demands are placed on the closest kin; therefore the greatest potential for competition and rivalry exists between groups of agnates. Between kin linked by a maternal tie, however, the ideal relationship is one of tenderness, affection, and easy companionship. The maternal uncle is a support to his sister's son, and among the Nuer, Dinka, Anuak, and Shilluk it is to his mother's brother's people that a man will turn in times of trouble, and especially in times of dispute with his agnatic kin. Men linked through women—a sister, daughter, mother, or grandmother—ideally live in amity and peace. The presence of maternal kin can help to stabilize relations between groups, but there is also an inherent conflict between loyalties owed to paternal and maternal kin. A settlement can be pulled apart by a major quarrel, and it is at such times that agnatic loyalties forcefully assert themselves, polarizing segments despite the ideal relationship which should exist between them. Yet one's mother's brothers are entitled to support and protection, and to fight them is shameful. This is one reason why a quarrel can lead to the breaking up and dispersal of a group rather than to prolonged fighting.[52]

The maintenance of the moral community depends on its members adhering to basic social values, but also on the ability of mediators and peacemakers within the society, 'be they priests or others' (as Godfrey Lienhardt has observed), to promote 'a spirit of generosity and magnanimity which makes peace through their mediation possible'. The ideal Nilotic leader

[51] Evans-Pritchard (1940*a*: 142, 221–2; 1950; 1951: ch. 1); Jal (1987: 51); R. G. Lienhardt (1958: 126–8; 1975: 219).

[52] Evans-Pritchard (1940*a*: 209; 1951: 157–8, 162–7); R. G. Lienhardt (1961: 129; 1958: 119; 1955: 29–42; 1975: 219–20).

is both generous and hospitable, attracting many persons and predisposing them to accept his intervention. He must be even-tempered and be able to listen and persuade others to behave peacefully by reason and eloquence. The emphasis on words is important. It is not just the quality of speaking which is involved, but the quality of listening. Among the Nuer the ideal of leadership is expressed in the spokesman (*ruic*), whose virtues are best conveyed by our own notion of the 'statesman'. The spokesman of the people (*ruic naadh*) is a concept, an ideal, rather than an institution or office. The spokesman must put into words the feelings of his own people, must represent them to others, but he can do this only by listening to what they say. Mere facility with words is not enough to be persuasive, and a Nuer leader must be persuasive above all things.[53]

The power of words is found in only a few. In theory the most effective mediators are those who have the divinity Flesh (RING) in their bodies and it is this divinity which gives their words force. These persons perform what can broadly be described as priestly duties. They are the Dinka master of the fishing-spear (*beny bith*, pl. *bany*), the Atuot owner of Flesh (*gwan riang*), and the Nuer earth-master (*kuaar muon*, pl. *kuar*), whose emblem of office is the leopard-skin (*tuac*). The religious idiom of Flesh which inspires them all is expressed in different ways. Aiwel gave the Dinka spear-masters Flesh as their special clan-divinity. Among the Eastern Dinka Flesh is associated with Fire (*mac*), and Blood (*riem*), and the Northern Dinka masters are in fact known as *bany riem*. Flesh is incarnate in the masters' bodies; it 'awakens' in them at sacrifices where it is invoked; it inspires them to know and speak the truth (to speak 'what is (becomes) true'). Through the spear-masters Flesh illuminates the way for the rest of Dinka society. Not only does it mediate between human beings and Divinity, it can be invoked against the malign spiritual influences of witches and magicians.[54] Flesh has similar properties among the Atuot, a people related to both the Dinka and Nuer. There Flesh is the 'eldest' of heavenly powers, associated with breath and life, and has affinities with female symbols of fertility and procreation. It 'fills' or 'covers' its agents, giving their words (especially their curses) a special potency, so that they can bring about a deed by simply speaking it. Among the Nuer the sacerdotal power of both the earth-master and the man of cattle (*wut ghok*) is derived from the divinity of Flesh (*kuoth rieng*). It descended from Gee through successive generations. Both the earth-master and the man of cattle invoke it, among other divinities, at sacrifices. Both have the power to curse. The man of cattle's words affect the welfare of cattle; the earth-master's words have specific power over the land, but also have a divine sanction behind them when they are employed as

[53] Quotation from R. G. Lienhardt (1975: 218); Deng (1986) is an exposition of the qualities of Nilotic leadership; Burton (1987: 85); Howell (1954: 30–2). Lewis (1951: 77–84) presents an over-formalized spokesman, which is not consistent with Nuer statements to me.

[54] Lienhardt (1961: 135–46, 172, 227–30).

a threat against anyone obstructing the rightful course of the master's peacemaking function. As with families of Dinka spear-masters or Atuot owners of Flesh, the divinity Flesh does not appear in all members of the families of Nuer masters. It is a hereditary and inherent virtue implicit in all men of such lineages, active in some, strong in only a few, and manifest in the deeds and, above all, the words of the masters.[55]

The importance of the divinity Flesh among Nuer masters seems to have been underestimated in the ethnography. It is significant of some recent change that both Atuot and Nuer have declared that the peacemaking and judicial roles of those inspired by Flesh declined with the creation of the more secular administrative system of courts under the British.[56] The secularizing trend which had started before Evans-Pritchard's field-work did affect what he was able to observe. In this respect it may have led him to propose a dichotomy between 'priest' and 'prophet' among the Nuer which is not, in fact, so clear cut. While Crazzolara translates *kuaar* as 'master', and Howell as 'expert', Evans-Pritchard identifies the *kuaar* as a 'priest' who represents men to Divinity by invoking the divinity of *his* flesh, contrasting with the prophet who, inspired by a divinity, represents Divinity to men.[57] Testimony of the importance of Flesh among the Dinka, but more especially among the Atuot, gives credence to the Nuer assertion of its greater importance among the Nuer in the recent past.[58] The earth-masters, by invoking Flesh, do what the Dinka spear-masters and the Atuot owners of Flesh do; they represent Divinity (through *their* divinity) to the people at the same time that they invoke that divinity on behalf of the people. It is this similarity in the beliefs about Flesh which enables us to equate the Dinka *beny* with the Nuer *kuaar* (an equation older Nuer make themselves), and translate the latter as 'master'.

Mediators and peacemakers are, in essence, life-givers, and in this respect share some attributes of Divinity. The first spear-master, Aiwel, is also the archetypical Dinka man of Divinity (*ran nhialic*), by which later men of Divinity, such as Arianhdit, are judged. Aiwel, as we shall also see, was the prophet Ngundeng's chosen model. In what circumstances, we should ask, does Divinity intervene so strongly in the affairs of human beings, and when do human beings seek such an intervention?

In his study of Dinka religion Godfrey Lienhardt adopted the terms Divinity, clan-divinities, free-divinities, (earthly) Powers, and emblems where

[55] Burton (1987: 84–7). In standard Nuer orthography it would be *guan rieng*, *rieng* being the genitive of *ring*, and *riang* being 'satisfaction' or 'repletion'. I retain Dr Burton's spelling here to emphasize that it is a different development of the concept. For earth-masters and men of cattle see Evans-Pritchard (1935: 40, 49–51; 1940*a*: 152–5, 172–6; 1956: 109–10, 113–14, 167–8, 192, 291–301); and Kiggen (1948: 275).

[56] Burton (1987: 84–5); Ruot Rom EHJP-4.

[57] Crazzolara (1953: 13, 75); Howell (1954: 213 n. 1); Evans-Pritchard (1956: 299–300, 304).

[58] Garang Ngundeng L1.3, Gatkal Ngundeng L3.3, Cuol Macar, Ruot Rom, Gai Thung EHJP-4.

Evans-Pritchard for the Nuer used God, Spirit, sky spirits (spirits of the above), earth spirits (spirits of the below), and totems. The former terminology seems to me better suited for dealing with the common features of Nilotic religious life than the latter. I will therefore employ the terms hitherto associated with Dinka divinities and Powers throughout this study.

Divinity in nature is ubiquitous. It is like the wind and the air, and it falls in the rain. The cluster of related words which describe Divinity in Sudanese Nilotic societies repeatedly invokes these associations with sky and rain. In Dinka, Nuer, and Atuot *nhial* means 'the sky' or 'above'. Divinity in Dinka is *nhialic*, 'in the sky', and rain (a child of *nhialic*) is *deng*. *Nhial* in Atuot can also be translated as God or 'a revelation of God'. *Kwoth* in Atuot is both rain and the spirit or Power associated with rain; rain in Shilluk, Anuak, and other Lwo languages is *koth*. In Nuer Divinity is *koth* or *kuoth*, *kuoth nhial* is Divinity above (in the sky), and *nhial* is both sky and rain. The descent of Divinity is evoked by its association with rain, and for Divinity to appear in society and influence the affairs of men and women it must descend and establish a specific relationship with a person. The smallness and powerlessness of human beings below in relation to Divinity above is further evoked in Nuer, Dinka, and Atuot by the image of the tiny black ant (*cuk*, *acuk*).[59]

Divinity here below, divinity in society, is also described in the different Nilotic languages by related terms or in related ways. The most all-embracing term, and the one most generally used, is *jok*. *Jok*, or Power, among the Dinka includes Divinity (*nhialic*), clan- and free-divinities (*yeeth*, sing. *yath*), and the earth Powers (*jong piny*) of magical substances (*wal*). *Jok* (or *juok*) among the Lwo-speaking peoples describes ancestral ghosts, the hereditary power of chiefs, priests, and diviners, the involuntary power of a witch, Powers which afflict or protect men, Powers which inhabit magical substances (*yath*), and diseases and epidemics. Among the Atuot Powers (*jao*, sing. *jok*) are divided into Powers of the sky (*jao nhial*) and earthly Powers (*jao piny*), which guide diviners or inhabit magical substances (*wal*) recently imported from the Jur-Beli or the Dinka. Among the Nuer *jok* is applied in a more restricted range to epidemics, ghosts (*jook*, sing. *joagh*), and possibly to some magical substances among the Western Nuer. Divinities and Powers alike are described as *kuuth* (sing. *kuoth*). But the Nuer make the same distinction between the above and below which is implicit among the Dinka and explicit among the Atuot, dividing all spiritual manifestations between divinities of the above (*kuuth nhial*) and earthly Powers (*kuuth piny*). The earthly Powers include clan-divinities, tutelary Powers, Powers of magical substances (*wal*), talking Powers

[59] Evans-Pritchard (1935: 45; 1956: 10); Crazzolara (1953: 61, 94–5, 162); Kiggen (1948: 147, 162); Lienhardt (1961); Nebel (1979: 145, 177, 187); Heasty (1937: 88); Tunnicliffe (1932); Simeoni (1978: 108); Burton (1981: 57, 76–7, 148).

found in fetish bundles (*kulang*, pl. *kulaang* or *kulangni*), and what Evans-Pritchard calls nature sprites (*bieli*, sing. *biel*).[60]

Evans-Pritchard claims that the division between divinities of the above and earthly Powers among the Nuer is recent, and that originally the Nuer knew only *kuoth* and the *colwic* spirits, the spirits of persons struck by lightning and taken by *kuoth*.[61] The division into the above and the below, according to his account, came about only when free-divinities (*kuuth nhial*) began seizing prophets, and magical substances (*kuuth piny*) entered the land. We will test that by looking at *biel* and *ring*, and at the types of mantic activity which are known to have pre-dated prophets.

The *bieli* have been classed in the ethnography as a separate kind of earthly Power. They can be bought and sold like magic; they can seize persons and speak through them like a free-divinity or a talking fetish; they are associated with light and with mainly natural objects such as trees, rivers, stones, grass, red cobras, but also cattle-pegs; they appear in association with some lineages of mantic persons such as the man of cattle and the water-master.[62] They seem to have more creative and tutelary attributes than normally associated with earthly Powers.

Biel was known before the recent free-divinities. Among the Western Nuer it is said that *biel* was known before TENY, MAANI, and DENG appeared; that it is unlike the types of magic which came from the Dinka; and that in fact it 'is the divinity which created people'. *Biel* seems to have been associated with the clan-divinities of the earth-master, man of cattle, and other mantic persons; it was also associated with the tutelary Powers of other clans. But when the prophets of the new free-divinities came, 'we left all those things which we used to do'. *Biel* has now been assimilated as a divinity of the above, though a small one; as a child of divinity (*gatkuoth*), the son of TENY, MAANI, DENG, and DIU, even though it preceded them. In keeping with the changing idiom, people can be seized by *biel* and become known as owner of *biel* (*guan bila*), but this does not give them the same abilities as the new *guan kuoth*, the prophets.[63]

Because of its creative function *biel* is sometimes assimilated to the free-divinities. Among the Gaawar I was told that everybody is born with their own *biel*. It represents each person's defining characteristic; one might almost call it a personal *genius*.[64] Other Nuer confirmed its creative power, especially in

[60] Lienhardt (1961: 28–32, 65); P'Bitek (1971: 111–13, 130–3, table); Ocholla-Ayayo (1976: chs. 7 and 8); Hofmayr (1925: 187, 193, 209–10); Santandrea (1948: 182–3); Burton (1981: ch. 4; 1987: 83–4); Evans-Pritchard (1937: 224; 1938*a*: 64–5; 1956: 60, 63, 97); Crazzolara (1953: 62, 134, 142–3, 184–6).

[61] Evans-Pritchard (1956: 29).

[62] Ibid. 63, 97–9, 113, 136–7; Crazzolara (1953: 136–7, 142, 157, 211); Howell (1953: 86).

[63] Biel Tip Gai Dkl.

[64] Matit Kal G9.4. The term 'genius' is adopted from James (1988), but without implying an equivalence with the Uduk *k̲ashira/*.

the begetting of persons and cattle. Its influence is confined to the homestead, and for that reason it could also be called an earthly Power, because it is here on earth. The son of a famous Western Nuer man of cattle explained that since *biel* is found here on the ground, it is like an earthly Power. It is neither a divinity of the above nor an earthly Power as currently understood, though clearly it is like both. *Biel* is inherited by men of cattle, similar to, but not the same as Flesh.[65] Flesh, too, has sometimes been described by Western Nuer as like either a divinity above or a Power below.

Among the Atuot there is a similar division between Powers of the above and below, between those that originate with God (or Divinity), and those which are active in the lives of the people. It is the strength and relative importance of the Powers which seems to distinguish the different levels. Flesh is classified as a heavenly Power, and the owner of Flesh and the owner of Divinity (*gwan nhial*) seem to be the same. *Abiel* is an earthly Power, but one of the oldest. *Abiel* was the first earthly Power to afflict people, but it was also the first Power to help a person see other Powers that troubled people. It was thus the first Power used by diviners.[66] Even though Flesh is found inside a person, its creative function in bringing and preserving life and well-being places it among the Powers of the above, while *abiel* remains firmly attached to people below.

The Atuot example helps to clarify the seemingly contradictory statements about *biel* and Flesh reported among the Nuer. The categories of above and below refer to function rather than hierarchy. What is creative is by analogy associated with Divinity above. What is merely protective, instructive, or afflictive in human affairs remains below. Thus for the Nuer *biel* and Flesh are like Divinity above in their creative attributes, but are like lower Powers in so far as they are restricted to individuals or certain lineages.

It is thus that tutelary divinities or Powers of other mantic persons are also described as earthly Powers. These are found among that large category of persons known as owners of a divinity (*guan kuoth*). The *guan kuoth* include persons whose abilities are derived through a tutelary relationship with a divinity, modern prophets, and the earth-masters and men of cattle.[67] Those who operate in association with a tutelary divinity sometimes have that divinity explicitly named, as with the owner of the dura-bird divinity (*guan kuoth keca*) and the owner of the crocodile divinity (*guan kuoth nyanga*), whose divinities enable them to perform rites to protect crops from the dura-bird or persons from crocodiles. More often these mantic persons are identified by the emblem of the divinities, and the divinity itself is implied rather than stated. Thus the *guan kuoth nyanga* is sometimes referred to as the owner of the

65 Thomas Riek Nguot A13.

66 Burton (1981: 76–90; 1987: 83, 88–9). The initial 'a' is a typical Dinka prefix.

67 Evans-Pritchard (1956: 44–5, 303) excludes the latter two.

fishing-trap (*guan thoi*), and the fighting expert (*ngul*) is also known as the owner of the spear-shaft or owner of the spear (*guan tang* or *guan muot*). The owner of grass (*guan juaini*) or owner of the fishing-spear (*guan biedh*) sacrifices and invokes his divinity to bless pastures and rivers before people go to graze each wet season. The owner of the woman's sleeping mat (*guan yiika*), now more commonly called the *kuaar yiika*, invokes the divinity of 'the sleeping mat itself' (*kuoth yiika puonde*) when treating women who have miscarried. It is only recently, and under the influence of the British administration who popularized the term *kuaar* as denoting a chief or office-holder, that all these various *guan kuoth* have been called *kuar*.[68]

These tutelary divinities are the clan-divinities of specific lineages. Clan-divinities are known among the Dinka as 'Powers which are related to people'. They are common to all members of the clan, no matter how widely scattered. They may be represented by small mud shrines in a homestead, or by the forked shrine-stick (*ghoro* in Dinka, *riek* in Nuer) that can be carried anywhere. Clan-divinities symbolize 'the power and moral demands of agnatic kinship', and in that sense are central to, and focus the attention of, different segments of society.[69] The individual clan-divinities of the lineages of mantic persons are given a wider application when invoked at sacrifices and rites at specific times (before a raid, before going to pasture, before crossing a stream, before planting) to assist a specific enterprise. Thus named divinities associated with specific persons are habitually invoked on behalf of a larger community.

Clan-divinities may belong to all members of a clan, and some tutelary divinities may belong to all members of the lineages of mantic experts, but there are other divinities which can be acquired and become associated with an individual or a family. Such divinities can be brought in by marriage, and husbands and children can be troubled by, and therefore come to respect, the clan-divinities of their wives' or mothers' lineages. These may be remembered for a generation or two, then forgotten, and perhaps remembered again by a later generation. The accumulation of divinities can be represented by specific shrines in homesteads (often cattle-pegs where sacrifices take place), but also by the dedication of cattle to them. The accumulation of new divinities can be likened to the proliferation of clan spears among the Western Dinka during the process of political segmentation and migration. Some of these new divinities may be forgotten after a short period, but the range of known divinities and Powers is forever expanding. In the nineteenth century especially, as Nuer society assimilated an increasing number of adopted

[68] Evans-Pritchard (1956: 60, 67, 71, 97, 243, 290, 303); Crazzolara (1953: 137). For the *kuar* see Howell (1953: 87; 1954: 212–15). For *guan juaini* see Jal (1987: 72). For a fuller discussion of the above see Johnson (1980: 133–9).

[69] R. G. Lienhardt (1961: 30–1; 1975: 219).

foreigners and foreign wives, exposure to a wide variety of other clan- and tutelary divinities increased.[70]

The acquisition of divinities or Powers can bring new abilities. They can give a person limited control over the emblems of their divinities (crocodiles, cobras, etc.), or they are invoked to protect the individual or family. Powers are often associated with illness, and a person who has been so afflicted is often then able to treat the illness in others.[71] Diviners (*tiit*, sing. *tiet* in Nuer and Atuot, *tyet* in Dinka), too, acquire the ability of divination. Divination and healing are techniques which must be learned (throwing cowries or pebbles, massaging parts of the body, performing specific rites for hunting), but there is usually also an association with a tutelary divinity or Power. Both Evans-Pritchard and Howell argue that no specific spiritual manifestation is involved in divination, but all Nuer I questioned confirmed that the diviner is aided by some sort of divinity. This is also true of diviners among the Dinka, Atuot, and Lwo-speaking peoples. Shilluk diviners work in conjunction with a *jok*, as their title *ajuogo* indicates. Atuot diviners have a *jok* inside them to help them see the *jok* inside afflicted persons. They acquire their *jok* either through affliction themselves, or through induction by another diviner. Among the Nuer living east of the Nile today there are hereditary diviners who are said to come from adopted families of Dinka diviners.[72]

This summary of Nilotic tutelary divinities helps to establish the range of mantic activity that might have existed among the Nuer before the prophets came to prominence. It shows us the way in which Divinity, in different manifestations, is seen to establish a link with individual social groups as well as with individuals in society, and through them becomes more widely available to all. It also shows that close association with a divinity or Power changes the internal character of a person. Those to whom spiritual ability is granted have their internal natures changed, however slightly. This is explicitly recognized by the Dinka, who speak of renowned men of Divinity on the model of Aiwel as 'creators' (*aciek*). They are vehicles of Divinity whose very inner beings are different.[73] But others, too, are changed inside, and this gives them the ability to control what others cannot control, to see what others cannot see, to know the truth, to speak what is, or what becomes, true. Even the witch, the person with the 'evil eye' (*peth*) who can kill involuntarily just by looking, is different inside from ordinary people. Thus it is that the Nuer

[70] Evans-Pritchard (1956: ch. 3, also pp. 38, 48, 57, 114, 162, 206, 209, 220, 222); Crazzolara (1953: 149, 157, 165); Lienhardt (1961: 254–61).

[71] American Mission (1932); Crazzolara (1953: 138); Evans-Pritchard (1956: 34, 44).

[72] Evans-Pritchard (1956: 88, 95–6, 225); Howell (1945: 98–9; 1954: 212, 217); Crazzolara (1953: 135); Lienhardt (1961: 68, 71–3); Ibrahim Bedri (1948: 44–5); Burton (1987: 83, 89–91); Seligman and Seligman (1932: 188); P'Bitek (1971: table).

[73] Lienhardt (1961: 52, 74, 170). See also Evans-Pritchard (1956: 34, 44) on temporary and permanent possession.

prophet, too, is 'scraped out' and becomes a sack or vessel of divinity, a *guk kuoth*, filled rather more completely than the other *guan kuoth*.

Spiritual power can be manipulated in many ways. Persons with a special relationship with a divinity—whether Flesh, another clan-divinity, or a personal divinity—can invoke (*lam*) it at a sacrifice or other rite. It can be invoked to heal or protect, but spiritual strength can be used to harm. The curse of the spear-master and the earth-master is used as the ultimate sanction against persons disrupting social harmony. Others can curse as well. Many myths refer to conditional curses of the ancestors, the curse which will be fulfilled in the future if any of their descendants disobey certain injunctions. This type of curse resembles most closely the later ability of prophets to bring about things in the distant future merely by speaking them. The *muot* sacrifice, too, by which dogs or goats are sacrificed and buried to bring about the death of someone else, can be performed by an earth-master, but it can also be performed by anyone wanting vengeance. It is not considered the same as the modern use of magic to kill—theoretically it works only against a guilty party—but it is clearly similar. Thus there do seem to be precedents for the types of activity for which the prophets, and their less welcome counterparts the magicians, later became famous.

Free-divinities

Both Nuer and Dinka claim that free-divinities, the divinities who seized persons and spoke through their mouths, appeared in the late nineteenth century,[74] producing a new form of mantic activity. New types of magic, motivated by Powers who afflicted persons and sometimes spoke through them, also began to appear then, though their rapid spread within various Nilotic communities is more recent. The appearance of free-divinities, like the rise of the prophets, has often been linked by scholars to the nineteenth-century invasion of the Southern Sudan by the Turco-Egyptian government, ivory and slave merchants, the Mahdists, and European imperial powers. The wars of the nineteenth century did have a disrupting effect, and the organization of trade routes linking a network of fortified commercial centres (*zariba*, pl. *zara'ib*) did assist the proliferation of free-divinities and the spread of magic, but these do not by themselves explain the phenomena. The appearance of prophets and new types of magicians among the Nuer was largely a consequence of the Nuer occupation of the eastern lands.

Local communities among various Nilotic societies are organized around the dominant lineages of 'original settlers', those who occupied the territory first, or who by their position of dominance take precedence over other lineages. Among the Nuer and the Shilluk the same word, *diel*, is used for

[74] Lienhardt (1961: 163–4, 169); Evans-Pritchard (1956: 29).

such lineages. Among the Western Dinka the lineages of the spear-masters are supposed to be the 'original settlers' or 'owners' of a territory. The Dinka spear-master lineages are maternally linked to the other commoner (*kic*) clans of the territory, and are usually classed as mother's brothers to the dominant commoner clan. Thus the spear-master's rôle as peacemaker is reinforced both by the code of behaviour expected between mother's brothers and sister's sons, and by alliance with another powerful kin-group whose support in disputes can usually be counted on.[75] The dominant lineages of the Western Nuer are not the same as the earth-master lineages. The earth-masters are supposed to come from neutral lineages if their mediation between opposing segments is to be effective. The relatively large lineages of masters in the west do provide the earth-master with support during disputes, but there are fewer such lineages among those Nuer who went east. Among the eastern Jikany something akin to the Dinka structure exists whereby the Maleak earth-masters are classed as maternal uncles to the Gaajak, but elsewhere in the east masters from other lineages are widely scattered and are linked to their communities through a variety of kinship ties.[76]

The new settlements of the Jikany and Lou were organized around the old dominant lineages of the Gaatgankir and Jinaca. The dominant lineages of the Gaawar, Lak, and Thiang migrations seem to have come into being through initiating the migrations and becoming, in fact, the 'original settlers' in their new territories. The lack of masters remained a problem. The creation of masters 'by hand' (*tetde*), the investing of mediating power in a commoner or foreigner by a master or by the community, seems to have become a regular feature of Nuer life after the major migrations began. The Thiang on the Zeraf Island made an Anuak into their earth-master, and it is from him that all current masters are derived. Some dominant lineages also provided masters, as, for instance, did the Gaatgankir. The best-known case is among the Gaawar, when the leader of their migration, Buogh Kerpeil, was raised up to the sky by other elders, who gave him a gourd of milk to drink, into which each had placed spittle as a form of blessing.[77]

Only the Gaatgankir validated their position by reference to their founding ancestor Kir. None of the other new earth-master lineages seemed to try to justify themselves by establishing a link with any ancestral Nuer master. But there were Dinka available to provide that sort of legitimacy, not only for the earth-master lineages, but for the 'original settler' (*diel*) lineages. The incorporation of Dinka into the dominant lineages of the Gaawar and Lou after crossing the river was quite deliberate. The *diel* were owners of the land as leaders of the original settlers. In leading a society which contained both

[75] Lienhardt (1958: 113–14, 119–20; 1961: 9).
[76] Evans-Pritchard (1935: 45–8; 1956: 292–3).
[77] Evans-Pritchard (1935: 46–8; 1956: 293); Lewis (1951: 81–2); Howell (1954: 29–30); Cuol Kai A6.

newcomers and older inhabitants, the claim to ownership, to being 'original', could be validated only by including some of the real original settlers. In the generation after occupation adopted Dinka earth-masters became prominent among the Lou and Gaawar. The two best known, Yuot Nyakong and Nuaar Mer, were members of dominant lineages as well as earth-masters. Their being *diel* and Dinka at the same time was reconciled by the Nuer who claimed that they came from Dinka 'earth-master' lineages, a recognition of their being the real owners of the land.

Whether these men were in fact Dinka spear-masters is not important to establish at this point. They were among many Dinka who brought with them into Nuer society new clan-divinities and emblems to respect or invoke. Invoking Dinka divinities became common in Nuer society, as did the appearance of those divinities outside their original territory. The breaking of the territorial cohesion of Eastern Dinka groups by the Nuer occupation, the unravelling of the kin network, seems to have contributed to the uncontrolled appearance of previously controlled Dinka divinities. The best known all seem to have come from Luang Deng.

Luang Deng was briefly abandoned to floods and the Gaawar, but DENG reappeared elsewhere. One Ngok Dinka woman, Awin Wut, visited the abandoned shrine on her own and was seized by the divinity DENG. When she returned to her village on the Sobat she built a replica Luang Deng, which continued to operate as a shrine well into the twentieth century. Some Rut Dinka of the shrine-master family fled the Gaawar and settled among the Nyareweng. They, too, built another shrine to DENG, with a shrine-master from among their own number. The behaviour of DENG in the nineteenth century was repeated by the Bor Dinka clan-divinity Lirpiou in the twentieth. When the caretaker of the spear was imprisoned in the late 1940s for conspiracy to murder, and the sacred spear of Lirpiou itself was confiscated and taken to Khartoum, the clan-divinity, no longer being confined to one place, object, or person, began to seize and speak through persons all over Bor Dinka territory. It was not only DENG who replicated itself in this way. GARANG, ABUK, and PAJOK have since become the most common free-divinities among both the Dinka and the Nuer.[78]

The Dinka word for free-divinity is the same as for clan-divinity, *yath*, and both are known as 'Powers which are related to people'. The best-known free-divinities bear the same names as clan-divinities known in the east. Free-divinities first appeared among the Western Dinka at about the same time as they did among the Nuer, but in those tribes, such as the Twic and Rueng, who are closest to the Nuer and who had some ties with Eastern Dinka groups.[79] The releasing of the clan-divinities from the control of

[78] P. P. Howell to John Longe, 29 Mar. 1944, SAD 642/10/12; Deng Macot D3; *SMR* 191 (Jan.–Feb. 1946), 7; Evans-Pritchard (1956: 241 n. 2).

[79] Lienhardt (1961: 30–1, 104, 163, 169).

Luang Deng can account for part of this, but other disturbances were affecting Dinka and, to a lesser extent, Nuer society at this time.

Slave-raiding on a commercial scale inside the Southern Sudan began in the 1840s and expanded from the Bahr el-Jebel into the Bahr el-Ghazal and other territories throughout the 1850s and 1860s. Numerous Dinka were captured, dislocated, and moved along the caravan routes to fortified camps at Bor, Rumbek, Meshra el-Rek, Wau, and other places. Many stayed at these camps as slaves, while others were exported north. Captured slaves, forcibly removed from their home territories, were cut off from their relatives, their clan-divinities, and their cattle. The loss of cattle meant that not only did they no longer have their 'walking shrines', dedicated to various divinities, but they could no longer participate in communal sacrifices to their divinities. It seems that some re-established contact with their divinities, or their divinities with them, through dramatic forms of spirit seizure. Not only do we have accounts of Dinka mantic activity in the *zara'ib* of the Bahr el-Gahzal by the late 1860s, we also know of the growth of spirit cults, such as the *zar*, throughout slave and ex-slave communities in the northern Sudan and Egypt from this time on. One Dinka ex-slave, Salim Wilson, seems to have been led to Christ and the Holy Spirit while seeking to reconnect himself with his clan-divinity.[80]

It was not, as we have seen, just in the slave camps where seizure began to take place, nor was it just among those taken as slaves. The dislocation caused by raiding—whether by the Nuer, other Dinka, or the army and slavers—was widespread and even those not captured could find themselves separated from their families. The experience of a young Dinka man travelling at some distance from his home in the late 1940s, which Godfrey Lienhardt records, offers a glimpse of what may have been a widespread occurrence in the late nineteenth century. Separated from his family at the time his father died the young man was seized several times by an unknown Power. Though the people around him tried to get the Power to speak its name and explain why it was troubling the boy so, it never did. Only when the young man returned home and made several sacrifices was his mind laid to rest and the seizures stopped.[81]

Illness is often diagnosed as an affliction by a Power, and different illnesses, and different Powers, require their own medicine. Among the Nuer and the Dinka medicine takes its name, *wal*, from the fact that its various types are made of plants (*wal*). Some old medicines, such as 'pollution' medicine (*wal nueera*) and incest medicine (*wal ruali*), used to be administered for ailments attributed to spiritual pollution. Contact with new peoples brought contact

[80] Schweinfurth (1874: i. 306, 331–2); Johnson (1988*b*: 174–9). For *zar*: Lewis (1971: 214–15); Fakhouri (1968: 49); Zenkovsky (1950: 70–1); Messing (1958: 125); Trimingham (1949: 176); Seligman and Seligman (1932: 15–16).

[81] Lienhardt (1961: 57–62).

with new medicines, new forms of magic; such contact may have even stimulated the need for personal protective medicines. As the Nuer moved into new lands they often found powerful forms of magic associated with the original inhabitants. Thus it is that many of the most renowned magicians of the Lou and Gaawar claimed to have first obtained their magic from either the Dinka or some other early inhabitants of the country in which they settled. Magic that could kill may have been known earlier than the mid-nineteenth century, but the private use of dangerous magic for personal ends certainly seems to have increased from the late nineteenth century on. The most potent form, *kulang*, a magic root whose motivating Power speaks through those who own it and demands sacrifices of goats and other gifts, seems to have appeared among the Gaawar and Lou only in the 1890s, after the prophets had become well established.[82] Magicians are known by the magic they possess, such as owner of magic (*guan wal*) or owner of a fetish (*guan kulang*), and the Powers residing in the magic are spoken of as earthly Powers.

Some of the most powerful new magic came from the Azande and the Jur-Beli of the Bahr el-Ghazal, peoples with a reputation for using poisons and incantations to kill their enemies. The experience of the Agar Dinka, the Atuot, and the Western Nuer is that magic entered their countries from further west, and for the rest of the Nuer in the twentieth century the Bahr el-Ghazal was certainly known as a source of new magic.[83] It is by this analogy that Evans-Pritchard has also suggested that free-divinities first entered the Nuer from the west, since his experience was that free-divinities were more active among the Western Nuer than in the east.[84] When he did his field-work the prophets of the east were suppressed, dead, or in hiding, and free-divinities had been temporarily silenced. The same conditions did not prevail among the Western Nuer, where some prophets continued to function as government chiefs. Free-divinities and new earthly Powers originally arose from within the new society the Nuer were creating, no matter how they were later reinforced.

Nuer society east of the Nile experienced accelerated political fragmentation as a result of movement, settlement, and incorporation of large numbers of new people. Eastern Dinka society was dislocated by the Nuer occupation of their land. This was going on by the time new military and commercial forces from the north began to intrude into the Southern Sudan. The Nuer community east of the Bahr el-Zeraf was highly mixed with the Dinka. Bilingualism in Dinka and Nuer was still found in many communities early in the twentieth century.[85] Dinka clan-divinities were entering Nuer

[82] Evans-Pritchard (1935: 72; 1956: 99).

[83] Ghawi (1924: 78–80); Evans-Pritchard (1956: 99); Lienhardt (1961: 64); Burton (1981: 90).

[84] Evans-Pritchard (1953: 56–7).

[85] H. D. E. O'Sullivan, 'Lau Nuers', 14 Mar. 1906, NRO Dakhlia I 112/13/87; Woodward (1907: 6); J. L. F. Tweedie to governor UNP, 28 Jan. 1914, SRO UNP 14.1.

families; other Dinka divinities were being freed from the control under which they had formerly operated. The similarities in social ideals which the Nuer and Dinka both held were strengthened by this forced propinquity. Though initial relations between the Dinka and the incoming Nuer were often violent, the need for internal peace was certainly understood by all. As more Nuer were born to Dinka mothers, so more Nuer had Dinka maternal uncles, and the definition of who was to be included in the moral community perforce had to expand.

It is the Dinka experience that a true man of Divinity 'creates for people the experience of peace between men', and one manifestation of that is the ability to persuade segments of society over a wide area to compose their feuds.[86] Divinity is inherent in the masters of both the Dinka and the Nuer, and it is through them that Divinity transcends the political fragmentation of society. It is understandable, then, that Divinity did begin to appear in the new Nuer-Dinka community, and did begin to transcend political segmentation when the existing masters could not. The first divinity to do so was DENG, a divinity already centrally established in the worship of the peoples of the area, already known for its life-giving properties, already associated with the cool rainy season, and with the peace coolness evokes. There is evidence that DENG was already known to the Nuer of the west, just as it was known to the southern Shilluk, who included a number of Dinka.[87] The name Ngundeng, 'gift of DENG', is given by Western Nuer to a child born after his mother ceases menstruating. The Lou claim that their prophet Ngundeng, a member of the Thut age-set, was born in the west. The name appears rarely, but it also occurs as the name of the father of one of Ngundeng's Thiang Nuer contemporaries and age-mates, Balang Ngundeng. DENG was neither completely foreign nor unknown; it had begun to bestow its gifts on the Nuer before they left home.

[86] Lienhardt (1961: 157–8).
[87] Hofmayr (1925: 426).

PART II
PROPHETS

Let two prophets, or three, speak while the rest weigh their words; and if a revelation comes to someone else who is sitting by, the speaker should stop speaking. You can all prophesy, but one at a time, then all will learn something and all receive encouragement. The prophetic spirit is to be under the prophets' control, for God is a God not of disorder but of peace.

(New Jerusalem Bible, 1 Cor. 14: 29–33)

3

Ngundeng: Prophetic Inspiration on the Eastern Frontier

Ngundeng's birth and seizure—Ngundeng the earth-master; DENG and the gift of life—Ngundeng's Mound: Aiwel Longar and the primacy of DENG—spiritual and political propaganda: the composition of Ngundeng's songs—Ngundeng and the construction of peace—Ngundeng and the north—Ngundeng's legacy

Ngundeng Bong is generally considered to have been the first prophet. As one of his posthumous sons put it: 'Divinity who created people, it was here. The great Divinity [*kuoth dit*] who created all the lands, they knew it. They knew only it. In the past they did not know any divinity in the world who made men mad. The divinity who seizes a man came to be known with Ngundeng.'[1] The only mantic persons (*guan kuoth*), one grandson declared, were the masters and magicians: 'In the past the Nuer had no real *guan kuoth* like those who fell here. The *guan kuoth* they had were the *kuar tuac* [earth-masters], who strengthened themselves with magic, and the *kuar ghok* [cattle-masters], who strengthened themselves with magic.'[2]

There were precedents of seizures in mantic activity; this much we can infer from the internal evidence contained within the stories about Ngundeng's seizure by the divinity DENG. Ngundeng was not, as we have explained in Chapter 2, the first 'owner of a divinity' among the Nuer. He also may not have been the first to speak with the voice of a divinity. But he was the first to bring together the ideas of Divinity and spiritual behaviour associated with Aiwel, DENG, and the Nuer earth-masters. More than anyone else, Ngundeng created a new role, the 'vessel of divinity' (*guk kuoth*). All the early prophets fashioned their own role to suit the context of their community, but none had such an influence on the idea of the prophet in Nuer society as Ngundeng.

The details of Ngundeng's life come from many sources, exclusively oral. Ngundeng had no direct dealings with the Anglo-Egyptian government, so even those contemporary documents which mention him are based on hearsay. My own field research on Ngundeng is biased towards the life story

[1] Macar Ngundeng L2.
[2] Gatkek Bol Ngundeng L7.2.

of the prophet as told by his family. Yet I have been able to draw on the perceptions of others: opponents as well as friends of Ngundeng, Mor and Gun Lou, Jikany and Gaawar Nuer, and various Dinka. The family's testimony contains evidence of the way Ngundeng wished to be received. The testimony of others enables us to discover how he is remembered.

Ngundeng's birth and seizure

Ngundeng Bong was born into a family of Gaaleak earth-masters living among the Jikany at the end of the 1830s. His father, Bong Can, came from the Bul Nuer area on the Bahr el-Ghazal to settle near a sister who had married into a Maleak family among the Gaajok. Bong was welcomed as an earth-master, especially after his brother-in-law's death. Bong's nephew personally handed his father's leopard-skin over to Bong. Bong later died fighting the Dinka.[3]

The position of earth-master among the Jikany was somewhat different from that in the west. The Jikany, being a mixture of foreign groups, have no earth-master lineages of their own (the dominant clan, the Gaatgankir, provide the guardians of the clan spear of WIU). The masters of the Eastern Jikany are all Gaaleak, originally from Bul. There were relatively few of them and there was very little competition between them. The same can be said for the Lou, where many masters came via the Jikany. One effect of this scarcity of masters was that there was competition for, rather than between, earth-masters in Lou and Jikany. Their influence was more limited than in the west, since they came from small lineages who could not count on the support of a large and powerful kin-group. Their powers of mediation thus rested more on their individual abilities as arbiters than on the mobilization of public pressure through relatives.[4]

Competition between masters thus did not greatly influence Ngundeng's early career, but the need to overcome the limitations of the master's position in the social structure of the east, and the need to increase his spiritual strength, were of greater importance. In his creation of a more powerful spiritual authority among the Eastern Nuer, Ngundeng stressed many attributes of Divinity represented in the Dinka myth of Aiwel, the first spear-master and the archetypical man of Divinity. The emblems and symbols of Divinity were introduced over many years, but the ideas concerning a man of Divinity are clearly expressed in the story of Ngundeng's birth as now told by his family.

The facts of Ngundeng's parentage, the incidents of his seizure by a divinity, and his madness while living among the Jikany are widely known

[3] Dhieyier Bol Ngundeng L6.1 and L6.4, Macar Ngundeng L2, Gatkek Bol Ngundeng L7.2, Appendix 3 for Jikany age-set dates.

[4] See Howell (1954: 28).

among both the Lou and Jikany. Other stories concerning his birth and childhood, which closely resemble the Aiwel myth, are not well known in the land where he grew up. They are told mainly by Ngundeng's descendants, and this suggests that it was Ngundeng himself who grafted elements of the Aiwel myth on to his biography. He emulated Aiwel in other ways throughout his life.

The agreed historical facts of Ngundeng's birth are that his mother Nyayiel, of the dominant Leng section of the Gun Lou, was betrothed to Hoth Can, Bong's half-brother, but married Bong after Hoth was killed by lightning. Bong had a number of children by other wives, but Ngundeng was Nyayiel's only child. It is claimed that Ngundeng was born late in his parents' marriage, after his mother was past menopause. His name, 'Gift of DENG', does suggest that he was born after a period of barrenness. There are a number of gynaecological problems in the villages of the Southern Sudan where undernourishment is a seasonal fact of life, and it is not uncommon for relatively young women to experience an interruption in menstruation which may be mistaken for early menopause. The divinity DENG is widely associated with fertility and the curing of barrenness.

Whether the circumstances of Ngundeng's birth later suggested the Aiwel parallels to him is not our concern here. The story which is now told states that Nyayiel stayed with Bong for many years until she was old and white-haired, whereupon Bong told her to return to her parents' home. No bridewealth was reclaimed; therefore they were not divorced. She stayed with her kin until one night she was disturbed by a visitation:[5]

> Something came by night and said to Nyayiel, 'You, Nyayiel, you must go back to your home.' Nyayiel told it, 'Why must I return to my home?' It said, 'You go. You will give birth to a child.' Nyayiel told it, 'How can I give birth to a child, when I have become old and have no monthly bleeding?' It told her, 'Go back. The child you are going to bear will be given a name from here. When you give birth, he will be called 'Ngundeng', like the gift [*muc*] which is given to a person.' 'Truly?' It said to her, 'Go!'

Nyayiel returned to Bong and told him what she had heard. They slept together one night only, but Nyayiel conceived. No one could believe she was pregnant; they assumed her swelling abdomen was some disease which would kill her. She carried the child for twelve months, and when she cried out in her labour pains, people said,

> 'Why does Nyayiel call people? If it is death, let her die.' They did not know it was a child. Those hard-hearted people said, 'We will go and see her.' They came. The child was born. Other people heard that Nyayiel gave birth to a child. Then people ran saying, 'Nyayiel gave birth! Is that really a child?' When that was over they saw it was born with all its teeth: the lower teeth and the upper teeth. They said, 'Nyayiel gave

[5] This summary is based on Deng Bor Ngundeng L5.1, Dhieyier Bol Ngundeng L6.1 (quotations), Gatkek Bol Ngundeng L7.1, Bil Peat L12.1.

> birth to a child which has never been seen before', because all its teeth were there, and it was her first time. It surprised people greatly.

Some say that Ngundeng spoke to his mother at birth, and that he crawled off into the bush when he was only an infant but then returned on his own. He was also left-handed. These elements are also found in the Aiwel myth. Aiwel's mother was barren and past menopause when she gave birth through the intervention of a power. The infant displayed a number of remarkably developed abilities impossible for a child its age. Aiwel's birth and early childhood were a prelude to more remarkable spiritual manifestations when he grew up. Ngundeng's later appropriation of the myth reinforced aspects of his prophecy and ideas about the nature of his divinity which would have been well understood in societies as mixed with the Dinka as were the Lou and Jikany. It is primarily on the basis of this adoption of the Aiwel myth that a British administrator later wrote that 'we may assume also that his apprenticeship as a Wizard was served under a Dinka master'.[6] As in the Aiwel myth, this story of Ngundeng's birth establishes that the transmission of Divinity is to be traced through Ngundeng's mother, and not through his patriline. There is no connection between the circumstances of Hoth Can's death and Ngundeng's later seizure (and those of the family whom I asked seemed surprised I should try to draw such a link). In fact, though Ngundeng would normally have been known as Ngundeng Hoth, after the man for whom his mother was married, he was always known as Ngundeng Bong, after his *genitor*. Divinity intervened twice to bring his parents together to produce Ngundeng.

If we assume, more on the evidence of his name than on this story, that there was something unusual about Ngundeng's birth, we can begin to understand how Ngundeng himself may have developed the idea that he had a personal association with Divinity. A child born in certain peculiar circumstances is said to have Strength (*buom*) which can be dangerous to those around it. A child born after an interruption in its mother's menstruation is known as *muok* and will have Strength. Similarly, a child who is either born with some teeth, or whose upper teeth come in first, has Strength. A left-handed child also has Strength, but this is regarded more as a peculiarity than a defect and is scarcely dangerous. All these abnormalities are attributed to the intervention of some divinity or Power, and this may have later predisposed Ngundeng to mantic seizures.

Ngundeng's childhood is also associated with strange happenings, most of which are cited as precedents for his later behaviour. His infant sojourn in the bush was clearly a prelude to his solitary wanderings as an adult. He is also supposed to have avoided fighting other boys, and was taunted as a coward. One bully was so persistent that Ngundeng finally announced mysteriously

[6] Coriat (1939: 222).

that if the boy wanted a fight, he would find something that would fight him. The boy suddenly died. This, too, foreshadowed Ngundeng's later condemnation of fighting, his refusal to fight when provoked, and his ability to kill with words.

The real importance of these stories lies not in any biographical facts they may contain. Stories of Ngundeng's childhood are now told to show how Divinity, though not yet active and as yet unannounced, was already inherent in Ngundeng; that 'Divinity itself was already hiding in his body' (*ci kuoth rɔ co tɔu tɛkɛ ɛn rɛy puonydɛ ɛnɔ*), and that 'when our father was created, he was created a man of Divinity' (*ca cakɛ ran kuoth*).[7] Not all Lou accept this. Tut Jiak Gai, a Mor Lou member of the Dang-gonga age-set, who met and spoke to Ngundeng and was blessed by him, was unaware of any miraculous birth. 'He was born like us', he claimed, 'then later he got his divinity when he became a grown man.'[8] But for the family, the circumstances of Ngundeng's birth set him apart from all other prophets who came after him. One grandson explicitly stated: 'Some say that Ngundeng's divinity began later. It did not begin later, it was born with him. He was created with divinity. He did not become mad like other prophets [*gook*]. He came with it during his childhood.'[9]

Ngundeng's childhood was spent among the Jikany soon after they crossed the Nile. Many of the family agree that Ngundeng was born in Western Nuer, and it would seem that Bong joined the Jikany after the initial migration, but while they were still in Malou.[10] This period, lasting until about 1845, was, as we have already seen, a period of internal tensions between the old campaigners and the newcomers who followed them to Malou, and between the Gaatgankir and Latjor. These tensions ultimately led to divisions and further migrations, with the Gaajak and Gaajok splitting. The Wangkeac and Laang sections of the Gaajok came into conflict, the Laang finally leaving to raid the Dinka and settling south of the Sobat. Living among the Wangkeac Ngundeng would have observed the divisive tendencies then splitting Nuer society apart by the time he was initiated into the Thut age-set in *c.*1855.

Ngundeng's early manhood coincided with a time of drought and scarcity along the Sobat. Raids against some Anuak increased, but there were attempts to settle peacefully alongside nearby Anuak communities. The Laang section respected their near Anuak neighbours but also joined the combined Lou–Jikany expedition to the Buongjak area between the Pibor and Agwei rivers in the 1860s. Nuer raiding into Buongjak was witnessed by Debono as early as 1855, but the main invasion probably took place later. Buongjak, with its abundance of water, was especially attractive to the Lou who now found

[7] Macar Ngundeng L2, Deng Bor Ngundeng L5.1.
[8] Tut Jiak Gai L21.1. [9] Gatkek Bol Ngundeng L7.1.
[10] Dhieyier Bol Ngundeng L6.1, Gatkek Bol Ngundeng L7.2.

themselves living on a seasonally dry plain. They were led by a man of cattle named Beac Colieth, and Jikany joined this invading force either as individuals or as whole sections. The invasion was a disaster. The Anuak retreated, drawing the Nuer further into their territory, until the Nuer herds were decimated by tse-tse fly, and the Nuer themselves were struck by smallpox and died in large numbers. The Nuer sections dispersed and retreated to their old homes.[11] It was a stark choice for the Lou to stay or return, and Beac Colieth at first refused to leave:

Smallpox finished people at Buongjak, so they wanted to return home. The man known as Beac Col said they should not return home. If they returned, he should be carried with his head pointing to the bush, away from home. So he was carried. When he was asked what this meant, he said that a divinity would come to their place.[12]

The rootlessness of this period is mentioned in the family account of Ngundeng's seizure:

People were roaming about in the bush. There was no home in which to settle. People went to Gaajak and people went to a place called Buongjak. The divinity caught him while he was walking. The young men, the old men, and the other people who were walking with him, they said, 'What makes Ngundeng stupid [*dor*]?' Some said it was a divinity, and some said he was a fool. Nobody spoke with him.[13]

Ngundeng was seized after the failure of the Buongjak campaign. The precise location of his seizure is in some doubt. Thorow and Weibel, both in Gaajak territory, are mentioned.[14] By now he was married to three wives. As an earth-master he should have commanded some respect, but his peculiar behaviour and extraordinary statements were unacceptable. He claimed to be seized by an unnamed divinity and tried to get people to listen to him, but 'when his divinity then spoke, people denied it [saying], "Divinity is above [*kuoth ɛ nhial*]."'[15] Ngundeng had few relatives to support him: his father and a sister had been killed by Dinka, and a half-brother had already gone to the Lou. He felt, so his family now says, both isolated and rejected.

Ngundeng's peculiar behaviour included wandering alone in the bush, fasting for long periods, drinking nothing but water, and eating human faeces. He avoided speaking or arguing with people. It is for this reason that no one treated him seriously when he began talking about his divinity. Moving from Thorow to Weibel (now Weideang) he built a small mound shrine but

[11] Jal (1987: 130–43); Evans-Pritchard (1940*a*: 60, 132; 1940*b*: 10); Debono (1860: 351). Evans-Pritchard dated the invasion to 1870–80. Debono's contemporary account and Jal's recalculation of Jikany age-sets prove that this must have happened no later than the 1860s.

[12] Bil Peat L12.2. See Lewis (1951: 80), on Beac being 'carried back protesting'.

[13] Dhieyier Bol Ngundeng L6.1.

[14] Cuol Thijoak L10.1, Tut Jiak Gai L21.1, Nyang Kuac Agok L15.3.

[15] Gai Ruea Jk1.3.

abandoned it when he decided to settle among the Lou. He passed through Kuanylualthoan, near present-day Nasir, and then tried to cross the river by canoe, accompanied by his wives, two children, and his cattle. This was Laang territory, a section then at enmity with the Wangkeac. They mocked him as 'the fool of Wangkeac', called him a liar, beat him, broke his bead necklace, threw his shrine-stick and his leopard-skins in the river, and took off with some of his cattle.[16] Ngundeng's father's link with the Jikany lay through his sister, who had married a Jikany man. The Jikany were thus Ngundeng's father's sister's sons (*gaatwac*), and relations with them, unlike those with paternal kin, are supposed to be easy and friendly in Nuer society. First ignored, and then abused, Ngundeng expressed shock at this treatment, saying, 'Why do my father's sister's sons treat me like this? Even if I were a fool, should they take my things by force and throw them into the river?'[17] Ngundeng's personal experiences echo what we now know of the state of increased feuding within Gaajak and Gaajok society at that time.[18] His decision to go to the Lou and seek out his maternal uncles is typical of many Nuer men who find themselves in conflict with other relatives, for the bond between a man and his mother's brothers is particularly strong and tender.[19]

Ngundeng's descendants now claim another reason for his departure. His apparent madness, a grandson has said, was intended by Divinity to attract attention, because 'Divinity wants to be recognized by everybody'. Divinity knew that no one would believe Ngundeng 'if he spoke like us, so he was made mad [*yong*]. In those days Nuer did not believe that an owner of Divinity [*guan kuoth*] spoke truly [*ruac baŋ i thuɔk*], even if he killed people.' But his seizures alienated those he was supposed to attract. Not only were the words of the new divinity ignored, but Ngundeng's position as an earth-master suffered from the ridicule he attracted. Ngundeng, we are now told, hoped for greater recognition elsewhere.[20]

Ngundeng did not go directly to his mother's people but went instead to the Ciec section of the Yoal-Gaadbal at Panyang (now Pul Turuk). These were children of his mother's father (*gaat guan man*). They already had an earth-master, a Dinka named Ruea Kerjiok, whom they feared would return to the Dinka if they let Ngundeng in, so they refused Ngundeng permission to join their cattle camp.

The elders of Ciec section discussed the matter. They said, 'Boys, Ngundeng Bong and Ruea Kerjiok: Ruea Kerjiok is an earth-master, and Ngundeng Bong is an earth-master. Boys, can we have two earth-masters in our camp, can we keep two earth-masters both in Panyang? We will not get rain in our camp if we have two

[16] Gatkek Bol Ngundeng L7.1 and L7.2.
[17] Dhieyier Bol Ngundeng L6.1.
[18] Jal (1987: 90–100).
[19] Evans-Pritchard (1951: 157–8, 162–7).
[20] Gatkek Bol Ngundeng L7.1 and L7.2.

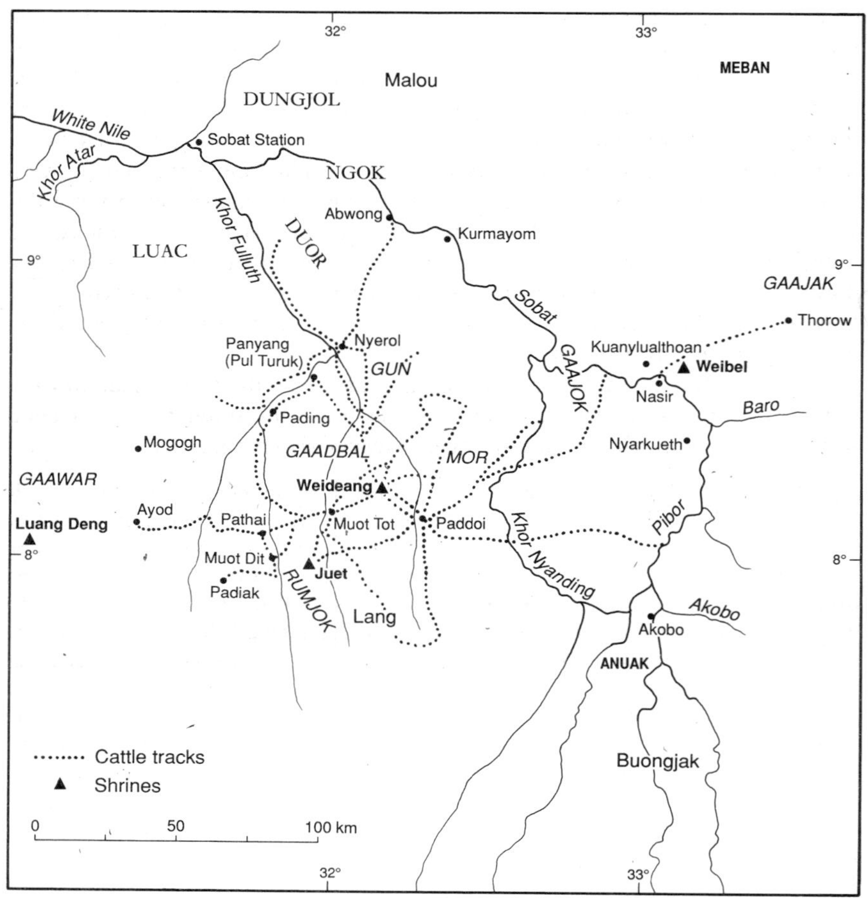

MAP 3. Lou and Jikany territory in the late nineteenth and early twentieth centuries

earth-masters.' They asked, 'How will we solve it?' They said, 'We will do it this way: Ngundeng must go to his grandmother's people. Puol and Yoal sections are one, they are Gaadbal together. Ngundeng will not be sent away, but he must go to his grandmother's people. . . . Now, if we send Ruea Kerjiok away, he is a foreigner and may leave us completely, but Ngundeng will settle with his grandmother's people.

Ngundeng left with a bad grace. His family now claim that he predicted the coming of the 'Turuk' to Panyang and said that though Yoal and Ngundeng would someday be one, none of his family would ever live with them at Panyang. This story accounts for the hostility which later grew between the Ciec section leaders and Ngundeng's family, especially between Kerjiok's grandson Guet Thie, and Ngundeng's son Guek. Ngundeng left for Juet, south-east of Muot Dit, where his mother's section lived.[21]

At Juet Ngundeng settled with the Malual subsection of Puol. He apparently lived a normal life cultivating and tending cattle for two years. Then he was seized and went mad again. The seizure was preceded by an illness which produced partial paralysis. Shortly after he recovered he went mad. As with the previous seizure, Ngundeng would go walking in the bush. He ceased to eat normal food or drink milk, but ate tobacco, mud, grass, and even human faeces. He would collect faeces and dry them in the sun like cow dung, make a small fire with them, and then sit facing the wind while they burned. Ngundeng became very thin, and his hair grew long and matted. As in Jikany, people avoided him.[22]

Ngundeng had at least four wives, having married a Rumjok woman in Lou, and they found his behaviour trying. Nyatot Kun, the mother of his second son Reath, is remembered to have been particularly exasperated.

Ngundeng used to go to the bush by himself, then he would come home. He ate only tobacco and water. When he was satisfied he came home and found that Mother of Reath [Manreath] had gone away, but she left the doorway of her hut open. Ngundeng went into the hut and found some tobacco inside which Mother of Reath had hidden from him because she no longer regarded him as a good man. Mother of Reath returned. When she saw him she said, 'It is you, Ngundeng!' 'It is I, mother of my son', Ngundeng replied, hiding the tobacco with his hand between his thighs. 'You fool who dirties his hand with faeces! Do you come here to take my tobacco? You are no good!' She grabbed the tobacco but caught hold of Ngundeng's testicles, too. She pulled his testicles, and Ngundeng collapsed. 'You have spoiled my tobacco, and you do not bring me anything I can use!' [Ngundeng replied], 'You, mother of my son, Nyatot Kun, wife I married myself, I am no fool. My first wife, where can I find tobacco? Sister, your next child after Reath will be your monthly bleeding [you will no longer give birth]. Reath will beget our children.'[23]

This is the first prediction attributed to Ngundeng during his madness. It may have been as much an expression of his fears as of his intentions. Reath did become his most prolific son, inheriting Ngundeng's youngest wives on his death and becoming the *genitor* of many of Ngundeng's posthumous children.

It was when persons provoked him that Ngundeng's spiritual strength began to reveal itself. While wandering in the bush around Juet, Ngundeng came across some of Malual section sacrificing an ox. Though Ngundeng had not been eating meat, 'Divinity told him to come and eat meat.' So he sat by himself apart from the rest. They noticed 'Nyayiel's fool' and decided to

[21] Ibid. (quotation from L7.1). Bil Peat L12.1 claimed that Ngundeng's sister married into Yoal, but Gatkek says they were *gaatwac*.

[22] Dhieyier Bol Ngundeng L6.1, Deng Bor Ngundeng L5.1, Macar Ngundeng L2, Gatkak Bol Ngundeng L7.1, Bil Peat L12.1.

[23] Gatkek Bol Ngundeng L7.2.

throw him the ribs normally thrown in the bush for WIU. But a man from Ciec section, one of his mother's fathers' children (*gaat guan man*), objected to the ribs being given to a fool. He took them away from Ngundeng.

Ngundeng looked at the man and watched him carefully. His maternal cousin [*gatnar*] rolled the ribs in ash and put them in the fire. Ngundeng turned away from them. He went away. Ngundeng went back to the bush, he went back to his usual place. Ngundeng said, 'This is good.' His maternal cousin took out the meat and ate it. He went to his hut at midday. He took his headrest and slept. In the evening, at the time cattle dung is gathered up, people tried to wake him. They found that man was finished; he was dead. 'Yes', [people said], 'Nyayiel's fool has finished something.'[24]

It was one of Ngundeng's maternal uncles, Ran Pinyien, who finally proposed that a prayer-meeting (*pal*) be organized. The sacrifice of oxen, he said, would cure Ngundeng of his illness, if he were ill, or reveal his divinity, if he were seized. Others dissented, wondering why they should waste cattle on a foolish man. So Ran Pinyien offered to give Ngundeng a white cow first, to see what would happen. Ngundeng drank the cow's milk. Ran Pinyien then sacrificed a reddish-brown patched ox (*makol*), and other sections, too, sacrificed oxen at a prayer-meeting. Ngundeng's aberrant behaviour ceased, he began to eat normal food, and his speech became comprehensible. It was after this prayer-meeting that he announced that he was seized by the divinity DENG.[25]

This prayer-meeting is something of an anachronism in the family accounts. At that time, they claim, no divinity had ever spoken through a man, prayer-meetings were unknown (*thiɛlɛ pal*), and it was Ngundeng who taught people to pray.[26] But clearly there was an expectation that some resolution to his illness could be achieved and something revealed through sacrifice. Ngundeng later taught the people *his* prayers, through his songs, which drew on both Nuer and Dinka religious imagery. This was his innovation. Some may have tried it before him, with less success. Other Lou recall that there were precedents before Ngundeng's divinity spoke. His illness may have been caused by a Power or other spiritual agent. There might also have been other men in Jikany who claimed seizure by a divinity before Ngundeng. If so, they were soon eclipsed by Ngundeng's reputation, and, it is said, Divinity left them for Ngundeng because they did not communicate its words correctly.[27] Once Ngundeng's divinity did speak and was named, it was up to Ngundeng to establish the character and attributes of that divinity through his own words and actions.

[24] Gatkek Bol Ngundeng L7.1.

[25] Dhieyier Bol Ngundeng L6.1, Deng Bor Ngundeng L5.1, Macar Ngundeng L2, Bil Peat L12.1.

[26] Macar Ngundeng L2, Bil Peat L12.1, Dhieyier Bol Ngundeng L6.1.

[27] Cuol Thijoak L10.1.

Ngundeng the earth-master; DENG and the gift of life

Ngundeng claimed to be an earth-master because his natural father, Bong, had assumed the office. In using Bong's name, rather than Hoth's, Ngundeng drew attention to his descent from an active master. We may infer from this that both the office and the function of earth-master were important to him. Certainly mediation in feuds, the power to bless the land to make cultivation abundant, and the power to curse are mentioned by two of his grandsons as being Ngundeng's most significant activities *as an earth-master*.[28] Mediation, blessing, and cursing were also his most important activities as a prophet, involving, as they did, the gift of life. But when Ngundeng arrived among the Lou he was still only a minor earth-master. The most renowned Lou master was a Dinka, Yuot Nyakong.

The Lou were led into their territory by Beac Colieth, a man of cattle. Migration can be most easily organized by a man of cattle as he is responsible for the seasonal movements of herds and cattle camps, and he also opens and closes the age-sets which initiate young men as warriors. Migration is an aspect of division in Nuer society, but permanent settlement requires a degree of co-operation. For this an earth-master is needed, and the Lou had few such masters. They were also newcomers in Dinka territory, usurpers of the Dinka right to their own land.

Yuot Nyakong came from a Dinka family adopted into the Jimem master lineage, coming originally from the east of the Lou but joining Beac Colieth's cattle camp. It appears that both Yuot and his brother Pakol were given leopard-skins by the Lou. As well as being adopted into a Nuer lineage of masters, Yuot is said to have come from a Dinka 'earth-master' family. As a master he was inspired by Flesh, and even today is remembered as a *kuaar rieng*, master of Flesh. This spiritual virtue guided him in knowing and speaking the truth, or, as one man put it, 'When he spoke a thing, it came to be.' In addition to owning two other family tutelary divinities Yuot also had magic.[29]

Yuot was the most influential Lou leader during the early settlement period. He combined a number of qualities the Lou needed in a leader at that time. He came from outside Lou society; thus he was able to maintain that neutrality between the lineages so necessary for mediation. He was a Nuer earth-master who was also accepted as a Dinka 'earth-master'; thus transferring to the Nuer, in his own person, the authority over this newly occupied land which formerly belonged to the Dinka. The Nuer preference

28 Dhieyier Bol Ngundeng L6.1, Gatkek Bol Ngundeng L7.2.

29 Bazett Lewis, 'Kwar Twac's Wut Ghoks etc.', 30 Dec. 1942, in PPH (Private), PPH MSS; Wor Tiäp L18, Lok Jabä L19, Gatkal Ngundeng L3.3, Tut Jiak Gai L21.1 and L21.2, Bil Peat L12.3.

for Dinka 'earth-masters' during this period is marked. There were others among the Lou, such as Ruea Kerjiok, and the Jimem clan itself adopted an entire Dinka section.[30] We will see that the Gaawar, too, incorporated Dinka 'earth-masters' into their own earth-master lineages. The elevation of Dinka to positions of Nuer leadership recognized, at the same time that it facilitated, the large-scale assimilation of Dinka into Nuer society.

When the merchant companies of the Zeraf established themselves on the Sobat sometime in the late 1860s or early 1870s, they used Yuot's brother, Pakol Nyakong, as their agent in transporting cattle and slaves from the Zeraf to the Sobat. Pakol fell out with the slavers after which he was never seen again. The slavers then began to deal directly with Yuot, who is remembered to have assisted the 'Turuk' to collect cattle tribute and raid the Dinka, but, unlike the Gaawar Nuaar Mer, he did not raid other Nuer. Yuot continued to be remembered among the Lou, at least, as a man of great sanctity, and the extensive herd he amassed came mostly from cattle given to him for mediating homicide cases. Partly because of their distance from the rivers, and partly because of Yuot's activities, the Lou were less affected by the slavers than the Gaawar. There was not the same proliferation of internal feuds as followed Nuaar Mer's collaboration.[31]

Ngundeng left the Jikany before the Egyptian outpost of Nasir was established in 1874, and his arrival among the Lou appears to have pre-dated the coming of the slavers to Pul Turuk (as Panyang became known). He was living in Juet during the time Yuot dealt with the merchants and their soldiers. He was also in Juet when Yuot was lured into Dinka country by the Nyareweng, held for ransom, and then killed even after the ransom cattle were paid. Ngundeng was then becoming known as a man of Divinity and is said to have warned Yuot not to visit the Dinka. Yuot's death occurred after the departure of the merchant companies from the Bahr el-Zeraf in 1874 and may have been vengeance for his assisting the slavers against the Dinka. Though he was killed by the Nyareweng, other Dinka seem to have been in on the plot, just as they were involved in raids against the Lou at this time. Yuot was killed, so the Lou claim, in a manner resembling the sacrifice of an ox through suffocation. As spears could not pierce his body, sticks were shoved through his orifices until he died. Yuot's body was dismembered, and pieces of it were boiled and buried in a *muot* ceremony aimed against the Lou (see above p. 65). Then followed a period of raids, which resulted in a series of Dinka defeats. The Lou attacked the Nyareweng separately, but it was Ngundeng who organized the most successful defence against Dinka

[30] Evans-Pritchard (1934: 22–3).

[31] Wor Tiäp L18, Lok Jabä L19, Tut Jiak Gai L21.1, Bil Peat L12.1; *SIR* 113 (Dec. 1903), 2; Lewis, 'Kwar Twac's Wut Ghoks etc.'

aggression, and it is Ngundeng who is credited with bringing this period of violence to an end.[32]

The Lou were attacked toward the end of 1878 by a coalition of Dinka and Gaawar, led by a Dinka stranger named Deng Cier who claimed to be a prophet of DENG. Deng Cier was as much a challenge to established local authorities (such as the Luaŋ Deng shrine-master and Nuaar Mer) as to the Lou. Ngundeng, who had announced his seizure by DENG only a few years previously, first avoided a fight but then arranged an ambush at the Lou cattle camps around Pading on the Khor Fulluth. Lulled into thinking the Lou herds were undefended the raiders were attacked and pushed back into the river, where they were speared like so many fish—an incident with clear resonances of the Aiwel myth. The battle had far-reaching political consequences. Not only did Ngundeng gain wide acceptance as *the* prophet of DENG, but his victory led directly to the rise of Deng Laka, the overthrow of Nuaar Mer among the Gaawar, and the break-up of many Dinka groups.

Victory was attributed to DENG and especially to Ngundeng's sacrifice of an ox at the beginning of the battle. In the past Nuer had fought with the aid of clan-divinities, but DENG was no Nuer clan-divinity. Ngundeng claimed that DENG was a divinity for all people, and with Pading he began to offer proof that this was so. Paradoxically his victory helped to establish Ngundeng's reputation as a peacemaker; for the battle was fought in self-defence and not for gain, and it reinforced (or even introduced) the idea that, through Ngundeng, DENG could control both life and death. It demonstrated the prophet's gift of life, and helped to establish DENG's primacy over all other divinities.[33]

The greatest gift of Divinity is the gift of life, and it was as the creators, protectors, and controllers of life that prophets established themselves as men of Divinity. Through their blessings and prayers they attempted to cure the sick, ensure the fertility of women and cows, and secure the abundance of crops. As the givers of life they could also be the takers of life; their curse was supposed to carry the power of death, and their sacrifices in war could destroy their enemies. Life and death alike are controlled by Divinity, and men of sanctity or men who work with magic are both deemed able to manipulate life and death through the aid of a divinity or a lower Power. But the curse of an earth-master or the spell of a magician generally affects individuals, not whole groups. In providing proof of a stronger ability, one that affected entire communities, the prophets convinced people that their strength was greater than that of either the masters or the magicians. In doing so the prophets

[32] Evans-Pritchard (1935: 57–8); Bil Peat L12.1, Gatkal Ngundeng L3.3, Makor Guot D3. Ngundeng did not organize Lou retaliation against the Nyareweng.

[33] For a full account of the battle see Johnson (1994).

associated themselves with Divinity above; thus stressing the difference between their own divinities and those tutelary divinities and lower Powers invoked by other persons.

Ngundeng is often said to have demonstrated his life-controlling power through his ability to kill. At the first sacrifice to DENG some dogs were supposed to have died after eating the meat of the sacrificial victim. Their bodies were left out in the sun to rot all day, and in the cool of the evening Ngundeng struck each dog's corpse with a bundle of grass, resurrecting them all. Ngundeng was also credited with the power of resurrection at the Battle of Pading,[34] and similar stories are told of other prophets elsewhere, such as Deng Laka among the Gaawar, the prophets of TENY among the Western Nuer, and Ngundeng's modern successor, the Gaajak prophet Bangong Diau.

All successful prophets became known for the ability to kill by word or thought, and Ngundeng was especially famous for this. The deaths of the childhood bully and the maternal cousin who denied him WIU's ribs are often cited as early examples of Ngundeng's ability. After he became a prophet deaths of any enemies or persons who had refused his demands were also attributed to Ngundeng, even if he had not uttered a specific threat. This action is reminiscent of the 'evil eye' or involuntary witchcraft (*peth*), an inherited trait which acts indiscriminately, endowing its owner with the ability to harm or kill merely by looking at a person. *Peth* is also associated with WIU, the clan-divinity of the Gaatgankir of Jikany. Ngundeng frequently invoked WIU in his songs and likened himself to a man with *peth* in the following song which announced:

I ŋundeaŋ ca pɛɛthdɛ bi luäŋ	Ngundeng's *peth* will not weaken
ŋundeaŋ Boŋ ca pɛɛthdɛ bi luäŋ	Ngundeng Bong's *peth* will not weaken
Kuthɛ tony bi wec wuu!	For he blew his pipe, going 'wuu'!
Bi kuaar waŋdɛ böli luak	And the master's eyes lit up in the byre[35]

Though Ngundeng proclaimed his dangerous nature by direct comparison with *peth*, one difference was that while a person with *peth* could not control the harm he did, Ngundeng could. He was able to direct his spiritual strength against specific targets. The Lou have drawn attention to this in another way, by claiming that Ngundeng was able to kill animals at sacrifices merely by shaking his baton (*dang*) or his pipe at them.[36]

The spiritual ability to kill was but one aspect of controlling life, and Ngundeng went beyond those who cursed or conjured by creating life as well. The divinity DENG was already known for its life-giving qualities, being

[34] Gatkek Bol Ngundeng L7.1; Johnson (1994).

[35] Nyang Kuac Agok L15.2. Songs were initially transcribed and translated by Gabriel Gai Riam and Simon Kun Puoc. All final translations have been made in collaboration with Gabriel Gai Riam.

[36] Coriat (1939: 225–6).

associated with rain with its connotations of cool weather, the revival of grass and cattle, the procreation of children, and the end of the deadly dry period. The Nuer already had recourse to DENG to improve the fertility of women. They also came to know DENG through the shrine at Luang Deng, where the divinity was appealed to for grain and for the protection of cultivation through the control of rain and floods. DENG was also known for taking persons into the bush and returning them safely, as it had done with Ngundeng. Ngundeng reinforced these life-giving associations with DENG. He told the Nuer that his divinity came from the direction of the north wind, which brings coolness. The ox-name he adopted after his seizure, Dengkur, is a white ox with black eyes, calling to mind the black and white of rain clouds, and it was by this name that he was commonly known throughout the rest of his life.[37]

Just as DENG is supposed to have made his mother fertile, so Ngundeng gained a reputation for making barren women fruitful. Supplicants would bring an ox, which Ngundeng sacrificed to DENG. He would then anoint the woman's stomach with either butter or his own spittle, both being fluids considered to have life-giving properties. This would be accompanied by a blessing on the child about to be conceived in the form of a prophecy about its character (it would be a good cultivator, it would be talkative, etc.), sometimes even announcing the unborn child's name. Ngundeng was acknowledged as the spiritual father of the children born by his blessing. Such cures were usually administered to individual supplicants, but Ngundeng is further credited with having cured an entire generation of infertile women. The mothers of the Dang-gonga age-set in both Lou and Jikany were supposed to have suffered mass barrenness until they sought Ngundeng's help. He sacrificed a white ox for them all, and children who were born and subsequently marked in the Dang-gonga age-set (*c.*1895) were also known as the children of the white ox. It was by such widespread application of his divinity to individual and personal problems that Ngundeng established and maintained his claim to spiritual primacy both within and beyond Lou society. He treated women from Lou, Jikany, Thiang, Lak, Western Nuer, and Gaawar, even including a wife of the prophet Deng Laka.[38]

Ngundeng gained credit as a provider and protector of life. The ill and the infertile came to him to be cured by his sacrifices. His reputation was also considerably enhanced by his response to the twin epidemics of smallpox and

[37] Lienhardt (1961: 65, 92, 95); Cuol Thijoak L10.1. *Dengkur* does not mean 'The God of War or the Wrathful God' (Coriat 1939: 223). I am not convinced that it is the ox-name of the divinity DENG (Evans-Pritchard 1956: 29).

[38] Evans-Pritchard (1935: 57); Coriat (1939: 223); DC, END, to DC, LND, 22 June 1957, Nasir ENRC SCR 66.A.1; Stigand (1918*a*: 118); Jal (1987: 383–4); Gai Ruea Jk1.3, Macar Ngundeng L2, Simon Mayan Tut L17, Matit Kal G9.2 and G9.3. Stigand and Jal date the sacrifice at about 1877–8. No source I know of suggests that it took place before Pading, so it must have been post-1878.

rinderpest which entered Nuer country from Ethiopia in about 1888–9. He is said to have foreseen these diseases and went out to meet them in the bush, sacrificing dozens of oxen in front of the path of the plagues, leaving them to rot, untouched, and sacrificing more cattle in his village, where the meat of the sacrificial animals was eaten. Both the Jikany and Lou lost many cattle to rinderpest, the older generations dying in the subsequent famine, but the smallpox appears to have been halted and did not afflict the Lou again until the early 1920s. These two related epidemics were extraordinary occurrences, and Ngundeng adopted an extraordinary method of mass sacrifice to meet them. To prevent a recurrence he then built his famous Mound, in which all diseases and bad things were buried (Fig. 1).[39]

In later years British administrators attributed his apparent success to the accuracy of his timing, undertaking sacrifices when the epidemic was already on the wane.[40] Still others were willing to see some scientific method in his madness. One doctor, mistakenly attributing these successes to Ngundeng's son Guek, praised the prophet as 'no mean epidemiologist' who, observing the direction in which the rinderpest epidemic was spreading, created a 'scorched earth' zone between it and the main body of cattle. When smallpox entered the land he banned dances and ordered people to leave their huts and sleep in the open. There was meat available from daily sacrifices, so 'the extra food strengthened their resistance and with the avoidance of normally crowded conditions the smallpox smouldered out'.[41]

Ngundeng's efforts do appear to have helped limit the spread of rinderpest among the Nuer. Ten years later the Lou were observed to have large herds of healthy cattle.[42] Whether Ngundeng controlled these two epidemics by chance or by shrewd observation is beside the point. He is remembered as being successful, and his success is attributed to the spiritual strength of DENG. The memory of his success has certainly grown with time, and the presence of disease and warfare in modern Lou society is frequently explained by reference to the demise of Ngundeng and Guek, and to the destruction of the Mound shrine they built and maintained.

Ngundeng's Mound: Aiwel Longar and the primacy of DENG

Ngundeng is most famous for building a large earth Mound as his central shrine. He called it his *bie* or his *paduil*, two words which modern Lou associate only with Ngundeng's Mound and for which they offer no other meaning (*bie* in fact means the tip of a horn). Though conical in shape, and resembling both Nilotic cattle byres and the tombs (*gubbas*) of northern

[39] Evans-Pritchard (1935: 57; 1956: 225–6 (where this is presented as a habitual practice)).
[40] Alban (1940: 201).
[41] Cruikshank (1962: 85).
[42] Johnson and Pankhurst (1988: 63–4).

FIG. 1. Ngundeng's Mound, 1902 (Crispin; reproduced by permission of Durham University Library); see also Figure 16

Sudanese Muslim saints, it was called a 'pyramid' by British officials, and its significance to the Lou or to Ngundeng was never investigated or explained. There was already a tradition of large fixed shrines in the Upper Nile region, and Ngundeng's Mound continued that tradition. Just as other shrines were political as well as religious centres, so Ngundeng's Mound demonstrated a shift in the political centre of the Nuer immigrants. In building it, Ngundeng drew explicitly on the symbolism of Puom Aiwel and Luang Deng.[43]

The first *bie* Ngundeng built was in Weibel on Khor Wakau. It was a small mound variously called a *bie*, Luak Deng, and Puom Longar. Weibel itself was renamed Weideang (the place of DENG). This small mound was also surmounted by a fishing-spear, which Ngundeng took with him when he left Jikany. After the Battle of Pading Ngundeng returned to Juet and proposed that the Lou move from there to Weibel, where there was more water. The Lou, remembering the natural disasters of the Buongjak campaign, refused. So Ngundeng remained at Juet and began building another Mound there, some say—apparently incorrectly—burying the Dinka spears captured at Pading inside it. At that time the Lou were unenthusiastic about the labour involved in building a large shrine.[44]

Juet is near the southern frontier of Lou country, close to the Dinka but not to other Lou. Ngundeng persuaded a Rumjok man, Gai Mot, to exchange

[43] Johnson (1990).

[44] Gatkek Bol Ngundeng L7.1, Dhieyier Bol Ngundeng L6.1, Garang Ngundeng L1.1, chiefs of *cieng* Yol Jk4.

villages with him, and Ngundeng moved to Keij, a village in the centre of Lou country, in Gun territory but within sight of the first Mor settlements. Ngundeng moved because he wanted to be centrally located, accessible to all people.[45] The move to Keij (also renamed Weideang) came well after the end of the main migratory phase of the Lou. They continued to expand the frontiers of their territory, but they refused to contemplate another large-scale migration. Weideang placed Ngundeng within reach of all the different territorial segments of the Lou; it also placed him nearer to the Jikany while keeping him in touch with the Dinka. It represented the physical centre of the new Nuer community east of Khor Fulluth. It was here that Ngundeng built his last and largest Mound, providing the Eastern Nuer with a spiritual focus of the type they had once had in the tree at Koat-Liec and in the myths surrounding it. The sixty-foot-high Mound became a shrine like Luang Deng (known as Luak Kuoth to the Nuer), and transcended the political divisions within and around Eastern Nuer society. It was a place where the divinity DENG could become available not just to the Nuer, but to all people. Ngundeng's success in creating this centre is revealed in an administrative assessment of his village written within a few weeks of his death. The village was judged the obvious 'diplomatic site' for a government post. It 'is the centre from which all cattle tracks radiate to the summer grazing grounds, and all of the permanent-villages[,] it is within a day's march of many of the main reservoir-ponds on each of the big Khors. . . . It is the centre of the Shens [*ciengs*].'[46]

We do not know the date of Ngundeng's move to Weideang. We do know that the Mound's construction began as a result of the twin epidemics of rinderpest and smallpox which hit the Lou in 1888–9. These were years of drought as well as disease, so we can assume that the building of the Mound, with the stockpiling of food and the organization of labour it involved, began only after the Lou had begun to recover. Tut Jiak Gai, a member of the Dang-gonga age-set whom I interviewed in 1975 and 1976, could not remember when construction began but did remember that it was being built when he was an adolescent and was still being built at the time when his age-set was marked.[47] The building went through different phases, beginning with the preparation of huts and collection of grain for the workforce, laying the foundation with local labour, and adding to the height with labour from other Nuer groups.[48] Percy Coriat, the Nuer-speaking district commissioner who oversaw the demolition of the Mound in 1928, gave this version of how Ngundeng began its construction:

[45] Macar Ngundeng L2, Dhieyier Bol Ngundeng L6.1, Bil Peat L12.1.
[46] H. D. E. O'Sullivan, 'Lau Nuers', 14 Mar. 1906, NRO Dakhlia I 112/13/87.
[47] Tut Jiak Gai L21.1.
[48] Evans-Pritchard (1935: 62–3); Coriat (1939: 223–4).

Wundeng . . . shut himself up in his hut and refused to see or speak with anyone or to partake of food and drink for seven days. He then fell into a trance from which he did not awake until three days and three nights had passed. According to some accounts, he perched himself upon the roof of a cattle hut before falling into a state of insensibility, remaining on the top while vast crowds collected to see the performance. At the end of this period word was passed far and wide summoning all tribesmen of the Nuer clans to a gathering at Keij on the full moon of the month of the saving [harvest]. Story has it that for days the plain of Keij was black with people. Blood feuds were forgotten. Not only from the Lau country but from the Garjak on the Abyssinian border, from the Gaweir on the Zeraf valley from the Nuong of the Jebel river and even from the Bul country north of the Bahr El Ghazal tribesmen foregathered at the behest of Wundeng. On the night of the full moon, in the light of a circle of fires Wundeng gave expression to the commands of the Spirit. Throughout the night he stood shouting exhortations to the assembled warriors. At dawn on the following morning he carried the first load of earth to the site he had chosen for his *Luak Kwoth* (House of God) and thus was begun the building of the Pyramid itself. From that hour until it was completed he supervised and controlled the work of thousands of Nuer. Mud was dug from adjacent pools and khors and carried in baskets to the ground where it was shaped and pounded to the required dimensions. As the mound rose in height, tiers of workers handed up the baskets to others above them. Bulls were brought from all over Nuer land and the meat was divided and eaten by the builders. When there was a shortage of bulls, corn was distributed from the granaries. Day after day the work continued. It is believed that four rain[y] seasons passed before the *Bie Dengkur* (mound of Dengkur) was finished.[49]

Evans-Pritchard's less vivid account of the building of the Mound was based on witnesses contemporary with, and perhaps identical to, Coriat's:

The building of this mound was a gigantic task. It was constructed of wet ashes mixed with baked and unbaked earth, for the material was excavated from two large vacated cattle camps where ashes and other camp debris had grown from year to year and became sodden and agglutinated by many seasons of rain. The workers who built it stood one above the other in tiers from the base of the pyramid, and each handed up materials to the man above him. A low palisade of elephants' tusks was planted round the base of the pyramid, a pile of tusks was buried in the centre of the mound, and one or two protruded from its summit. It does not seem that there was any systematic conscription of labour in the building of the mound but people came voluntarily from all over the countryside to assist and often brought bullocks with them for sacrifices. They would spend three or four nights in one of the temporary grass shelters, which others, since departed to their homes, had put up; and when the food that they had brought with them was finished, they would return to their homes also, and their places would be taken by other pilgrims. The flesh of sacrificed bullocks was divided among the workers and lengthened their supplies. It is said that people brought handfuls of ashes to add to the mound from Gaajok and Gaajak and Gaagwang countries as an act of piety.[50]

[49] Coriat (1939: 224). [50] Evans-Pritchard (1935: 62–3).

These descriptions, more detailed than those gathered in 1975–6 when nearly all who had witnessed the building of the Mound were dead, find general confirmation in contemporary songs and later oral testimony. Garang Ngundeng, the prophet's son born in the 1890s, remembered that the construction of the Mound took four years. Tut Jiak Gai said that the Lou were involved in the work for only two years, after which the Jikany, the Ngok Dinka, and others added to the structure for another three. From others we learn that the work began in the month of *kor* (November–December), after the second harvest and at the beginning of the dry season. The base of the Mound was made from the trunks and branches of trees cut from the woods which covered the site. Ashes were brought from as far away as Jikany to put on top. Ngundeng asked people to come but did not force them; they came willingly because they believed in his divinity and wanted his blessing. Workers were fed in part from their own provisions, and in part from a large plantation of sorghum and maize which Ngundeng cultivated for a considerable distance around the site. Ngundeng maintained this plantation (covering a square mile or more) for the rest of his life, to feed visitors and supplicants.[51]

A number of songs refer to the building of the Mound. This one, addressed to 'Kerdol's children' (the Lou), mentions the Ngok Dinka and the flags of *marol* (the 'Turuk') and may refer to the brief, but brutal, raids on the Sobat mouth by the *ansar* (habitually an army of many flags) during al-Zaki Tamal's Shilluk campaign in 1891–2.

<table>
<tr><td>Bi piny matɛ tɔaŋä luakdä</td><td>All the land will gather to build my byre</td></tr>
<tr><td>Bi ŋa hä gak Gaatkerdol?</td><td>Who will deny me, Kerdol's children?</td></tr>
<tr><td>A luak wuɔw!</td><td>Let the byre shout!</td></tr>
<tr><td>Tɔŋ luak Deŋ</td><td>Build the byre of Deng</td></tr>
<tr><td>ci tuŋ guarɛ mat cia rial</td><td>for the elephants' tusks have been gathered and become shining</td></tr>
<tr><td>Cia ben tɔaŋ Gaatkerdol</td><td>Kerdol's children, you came to build</td></tr>
<tr><td>ɛ ŋa bi ŋa ŋicɔ?</td><td>Will you recognize each other?</td></tr>
<tr><td>Caŋɛ ŋɔk bi mi tɔaŋ</td><td>Even the Ngok will come to build</td></tr>
<tr><td>Cia dual kɛ bɛɛr marɔl</td><td>You who feared marol's flags</td></tr>
<tr><td>Gueth mi de jany ka ram kɛl</td><td>The strength that can remain in one man</td></tr>
<tr><td>Cak lɛ riet ni hɔw</td><td>His power is changing the universe</td></tr>
<tr><td>Joknyal yiɛth tuŋdɛ puar</td><td>The ox Joknyal, who stabs the clouds with his horn[52]</td></tr>
</table>

In another song Ngundeng speaks with the voice of Deng, referring to himself as a hairy man, and pronouncing his shrine to be a place of life:

<table>
<tr><td>Yiɛana wut guori</td><td>I bound a hairy man</td></tr>
<tr><td>Ba naŋ ni luak</td><td>And I will take him to the byre</td></tr>
</table>

51 Garang Ngundeng L1.1, Tut Jiak Gai L21.1, Nyang Kuac Agok L15.5, Gatkal Ngundeng L3.2, Bil Peat L12.1.

52 Nyang Kuac Agok L15.1.

Tɔŋ Dɛŋ luak mɔ Paduil	Deng is building a byre, which is Paduil
Cia guath yiee	It is a place of life
Ba tɔŋ ca Paduil	I will build this Paduil
bi wut luakdɛ yɔŋ	when the man of the byre goes mad[53]

There are references in these songs to Ngundeng's seizure fits and his appeal to many peoples. The Lou will not recognize each other, there will be so many, and, perhaps, they will forget their quarrels; those who feared outsiders will find strength and life at the Mound. It is, or is proclaimed to be, a profound change.

It is difficult to estimate how many persons were involved in the building of the Mound. In addition to those peoples mentioned above, Anuak, Murle, and even Shilluk are said to have come.[54] The Mound was estimated in 1917 to be some fifty feet high with a diameter of about 100 feet, which would give it a volume of 131,250 cubic feet. We do not know the division of labour between those who fetched mud and ash and those who packed it on the Mound, but if each person who brought earth brought only ten cubic feet, then some 13,000 persons would have been involved in fetching alone. The gourds, pots, and baskets used as containers would have held only one or two cubic feet each, 13,000 workers must be taken as a reasonable minimum.

The Mound was frequently referred to as a cattle byre (*luak*), and it did indeed contain a black and white animal of the *ker* configuration, which was buried alive at the outset. A hole was dug, into which the animal was placed and then covered with wood and ashes. Ox horns were found in the middle of the Mound during excavations to blow it up in 1928. The remains of other cattle may have been incorporated in it as it was built. Coriat mentions the sacrifice of a white bull (perhaps a misidentification), and numerous bone fragments can still be seen on the Mound's surface. Ivory, too, was brought to adorn the Mound: a large fence of it surrounded the base, and six tusks (two facing the Gun and four facing the Mor, Jikany, Anuak, and Murle) circled the apex. That the ivory was brought by many supplicants is implied in the first government report on the Mound in 1900, based on hearsay and giving that perverse twist to the evidence typical of so many government accounts of the prophets. It was alleged that Ngundeng's 'village has a fort made of elephant's [*sic*] tusks, taken from Dinkas, Shilluks, and Nuers in various raids. This fact has been corroborated by several independent witnesses interviewed by the Mudir of Fashoda.'[55]

When finished Ngundeng's Mound resembled both Luang Deng and Puom Aiwel. It resembled Luang Deng spiritually, in that all evil was closed up

[53] Cuol Puyu L22.1

[54] Tut Jiak Gai L21.1, Cuol Puyu L22.2, Gatkal Ngundeng L3.1.

[55] Gatkal Ngundeng L3.2; Coriat (1939: 225, 234); Garang Ngundeng L1.2 and L1.3. Quotation from *SIR* 72 (July–Aug. 1900), 2. No ivory was found inside the Mound when it was demolished (McMeekan 1929: 289).

inside it: all evil thoughts and actions, all diseases and epidemics, all magic. Ngundeng told the Lou this, and he frequently referred to the Mound in his songs as *Luak* DENG and *Luak Kuoth*. It resembled Puom Aiwel physically, both as an earth mound, and because (as at Weibel) Ngundeng placed a fishing-spear at its apex. The myths about Aiwel Longar mention that he built his own cattle byre out of the bodies of living men, who stood on each other's shoulders, tier upon tier. Stories about Puom Aiwel describe the human scaffolding surrounding it as it was built higher and higher. The mound built over Aiwel's byre had the haft of a fishing-spear sticking out of the apex. All of this is echoed in the building of Ngundeng's Mound, which is also called *Puom Longar* in Ngundeng's hymns.

The imagery of Aiwel stabbing the people with his fishing-spear was deliberately evoked by Ngundeng's imitation of Puom Aiwel. It was 'Divinity's fishing-spear' (*biedh kuoth*), Tut Jiak Gai said.[56] Garang Ngundeng explained it this way: 'It was put in because of the fishing-spear of Longar. The work that it does when Longar thrust the fishing-spear down, all the people were finished by him. Divinity said that it should be imitated.' Longar, he claimed, had been a prophet; 'long ago Longar was speaking to the world. When he was speaking to the world, he became a prophet [*guk*].' Longar, and no one else, was the precursor to Ngundeng: 'Long ago Longar ruled [*ruac*] his territory. He pierced the people [*naath*] with the fishing-spear, he himself. People who tried to talk with him, he himself pierced them with the fishing-spear. The divinity was repeated when he [Ngundeng] put the fishing-spear in the top of his shrine.' DENG and Aiwel were associated in the stories concerning Luang Deng, but Garang went further and declared that the divinity BUK, the mother of DENG, was also the mother of Longar, whom she conceived when she was penetrated by water.[57] It was Ngundeng's innovation to combine the two Dinka figures—one a clan-divinity, and the other the original spear-master—not only in one shrine, but in one person. In one of Ngundeng's songs DENG announces himself as a new divinity:

ɛ ba ku nyurɛ kɛ laat gaatka dial	Let me sit while all my children talk
Lapä kuoth mi göl	I am a different divinity
Lapä kuoth gaanka dial	I am a divinity for all my children

But he then goes on to declare his affinity with Longar, saying:

Tɔaŋä puɔm Loŋar	I will build Puom Longar
Taakɔ kar, kɔnɛ ŋundeaŋ	We are related, Ngundeng and I
Taakɔ kar	We are related[58]

[56] Tut Jiak Gai L21.2.
[57] Garang Ngundeng L1.3.
[58] Nyang Kuac Agok L15.1.

The Aiwel imagery is repeated in the stories now told about Ngundeng's victory at Pading.[59] This appropriation of Aiwel was important in Ngundeng's career as a peacemaker. It reinforced his role as a mediator not only among the Nuer, but among the Dinka. In also appropriating the divinity DENG, Ngundeng attempted to regulate spiritual activity throughout the Eastern Nuer community. Both in his Mound and in his hymns he declared the primacy and ubiquity of DENG.

Evans-Pritchard published a hymn to DENG, originally taken down in Dinka by Godfrey Lienhardt in the early 1950s. In it DENG warns:

> A man avoiding DENG
> Will find DENG in front.
> On the right he will find DENG,
> On the left he will find DENG,
> Behind him he will find DENG.

Compare this with the following Ngundeng song, sung in Nuer:

Bar ran rɔdɛ ci gak kɛ Dɛŋ	Somebody fled for he quarrelled with DENG
Mi wii nhiam bi nɛɛn ni Dɛŋ	If you go ahead you will see DENG
Ka luonyi jɔk bi jek ni Dɛŋ	And if you go back you will find DENG
Ram böth Dɛŋ bi Dɛŋ we jek nhiam	He who precedes DENG will find DENG in front
Mi wii liɛc bi Dɛŋ ku nɛɛn kɔru	You will see DENG if you look back[60]

It is likely that some of Ngundeng's hymns to DENG, as well as some of Deng Laka's hymns, were based on the Dinka songs sung at Luang Deng. Ngundeng is not known to have visited the shrine himself, but there was contact and, at least at the beginning of his career, he sent cattle to the shrine. His ox-name, Dengkur, was conferred upon him by the caretaker of the day, Deng Aguer.[61] In this way the shrine recognized Ngundeng's autonomy. There was mutual co-optation between the old shrine and the new prophet. The new centre of DENG was a transplant, not a rival.

Ngundeng's reputation as a prophet grew with each reported success: victory at Pading, curing the mothers of the Dang-gonga age-set, combating the epidemics of rinderpest and smallpox. As it grew he was able to regulate the appearance of divinities among the Lou and Jikany by co-opting other prophets, diviners, and even magicians, as his *dayiemni*, or disciples. The *dayiemni* were seized by divinities of their own, but subordinated to the divinity of a major prophet. Crazzolara describes the *dayiemni* as a class of spirit, but this I think gives the wrong emphasis. The divinities of the *dayiemni*

[59] Johnson (1994).

[60] Evans-Pritchard (1956: 47); Cuol Puyu L22.1.

[61] Wan Deng D1. Bullen Alier Buttic was told by the custodian of Luang Deng, Raak Yaak, in 1957 that Deng Aguer had given Ngundeng this ox-name.

usually are active only in the presence of the divinity of a prophet, and then they sing his praises and his songs. Their seizures are stimulated by the prophet's seizure.[62]

Ngundeng had *dayiemni* very early in his career; the brothers Thijok and Riek Dul, known as the prophets DHOL and GUIC-GUIC, were with him at Pading. They maintained an autonomy of their own, living on the border between the Lou and Gaawar, but other, later *dayiemni* were more Ngundeng's own creation. Ngundeng referred to these persons somewhat disparagingly in one of his songs as *yiom-yiomni*, tassels on the horns of a bull.[63] Sometimes men came to Ngundeng after having announced the names of their own divinities, but it was Ngundeng who provided the final confirmation of seizure and pronounced the new divinity's name. After Ngundeng built his Mound he attracted more hopeful *dayiemni*. Tut Jiak Gai, who witnessed some of these comings and goings, commented: 'All those divinities came to the Mound. They were recognized when DENG was seized. All the prophets [*gook*] came, and each divinity was introduced as such and such a divinity, and each prophet was introduced as such and such a divinity when he came here to the Mound.'[64] The divinities were said to reside in the Mound. When Ngundeng was seized and began to sing, they would re-enter the *dayiemni* and sing, too. Ngundeng also sent his *dayiemni* on errands. He was like a chief, one of his sons later stated, using the modern structures of rural administration as an illustration, and his *dayiemni* were his police.[65] The lesser divinities which accumulated around Ngundeng included a number of older and well-known names. There was a *dayiem* seized by BIEL. Another was seized by CAK, 'creator', and was retained at the Mound to help cure barren women. Yet another was seized by PAJOK. Ngundeng announced that this PAJOK was the maternal uncle of DENG; thus following the kinship classification employed at Luang Deng. A small shrine to PAJOK was built near the Mound.[66]

It is said that Ngundeng collected diviners and magicians together and made them his *dayiemni*. Ngundeng had no quarrel with diviners who did not join him and continued on their own way in their own places,[67] but he waged a consistent campaign against magicians, insisting that they bury their magic in the Mound.[68] He denounced magicians in his songs and accused some pretended prophets of conjuring, using *tueth*, the Dinka word:

[62] Crazzolara (1953: 159). 'Dayim' is recorded as a free-divinity among the Bor Dinka, see Shaw (1915: 20).
[63] Kulang Majok G6.6.
[64] Tut Jiak Gai L21.2.
[65] Macar Ngundeng L2.
[66] Ibid., Garang Ngundeng L1.3, Tut Jiak Gai L21.2.
[67] David Koak A2, Garang Ngundeng L1.3.
[68] Gatkal Ngundeng L3.2.

A lɛ gook rɔ lɛ tueth	Prophets who conjure
A lɛ rɔ lɛ gör kä wal	And those who search for magic
Wutni bä kɛ näk ɛnaak	I will kill them all[69]

When the Lou were reluctant to give up their magic he mocked them, saying, 'Lift up your hands, Kuol's sons, they smell,' accusing them of so fouling their hands with magic that they were no longer fit to be lifted in prayer. It was partly the secret use of magic that Ngundeng abhorred, and he stressed the difference between his divinity and the secret use of magic:

Ba kɛ yiee gai wei wuol cat	I came with a good breath
La ŋɛr ku lokɛ	And I reject secret things
Ci ŋɛr cuyɛ	I am tired of these secrets
Ci DEŊ a DEŊ	DENG has become DENG
Wa ji ŋuot Kuol	If I kill you Kuol [Lou]
Ci DEŊ a DEŊ	DENG has become DENG[70]

He could not suppress magic entirely, and he seems to have distinguished between magic and medicine. Like a medieval cathedral, Ngundeng's Mound attracted all sorts of hawkers, including those with some sort of medicine to sell. One man, a Luac Dinka named Akuei Biel, had a type of medicine called *abiel* which could make barren women conceive. He mixed fresh dung ashes with the churned milk of a newly calved cow. He took this mixture to the Mound where lots of people were gathered. He would pray there, like anyone else, but he would also find out who the childless women were. He would give these women a small spoonful, and if they conceived and gave birth later, he would collect from one to three cows in payment. He became very rich, and married six wives himself.[71] This sort of curative medicine Ngundeng apparently did not object to, nor did he seem to resent the competition it presented. In fact when one of his wives, Nyaduong, was without child, despite all Ngundeng could do, he asked the Dinka to bring something from their own country to help her. They brought a frog (*guek*), which Ngundeng had made into a stew and gave to Nyaduong to eat. She did conceive after that, and gave birth to a son, who was named Guek to commemorate the cure.[72]

The more dangerous types of magic, the fetishes (*kulangni*) and those which killed secretly, Ngundeng did try to suppress. The fetishes seem to have arrived among the Lou in the 1890s, just before Ngundeng built his Mound. He even exiled his eldest son Riam when Riam purchased a fetish and began singing songs in praise of it.[73] Despite Ngundeng's dire warnings and the reputation of his divinity, not all magicians feared him. Lam

[69] Nyang Kuac Agok L15.1. [70] Cuol Puyu L22.2.

[71] Philip Diu Deng A8.2.

[72] Evans-Pritchard (1935: 60); Bil Peat L12.1 and L12.2, Deng Bor Ngundeng L5.2.

[73] Gatkek Bol Ngundeng L7.2. O'Sullivan, 'Lau Nuers', mentioned Ngundeng's quarrel with Riam but did not state its cause.

Tutthiang, a Rumjok man of cattle, inherited *kulang maluth* from his father and used it to kill enemies. He refused Ngundeng's general summons to help build the Mound and bury his magic there. He once did accompany his relatives when they brought his dying brother-in-law to Ngundeng for treatment, but the man died just as Ngundeng placed him in 'the pool of bad things'. Enraged, Lam struck Ngundeng, declaring 'This thing of yours lies! This thing of yours is not a divinity!' Ngundeng had to restrain his own followers from attacking Lam, but he cursed Lam, predicting that he and his family would be swallowed up by the foreigners who were then appearing in the land.[74] Lam settled close to the Nyareweng Dinka, but he outlived both Ngundeng and his son Guek. His own son Mayan Lam was government interpreter during the Nuer Settlement of 1929 and was present at Guek's demise. Not all of Ngundeng's curses or predictions were to be feared.

There were territorial limits to Ngundeng's strength when combating magicians, but he managed to expel them to the very limits of Lou country and beyond. Magicians were able to function mainly by keeping their distance. Riam Ngundeng went to the Gaajak. Lam Tutthiang resided on the Nyareweng Dinka border. Another renowned magician, Bul Kan, the son of a Dinka, lived close to the Ngok near the Sobat. Nyang Yuot, Yuot Nyakong's son and a renowned earth-master, also kept magic and went to live with the Mor on the expanding eastern frontier of Lou territory.[75]

Ngundeng faced challenges from distant prophets, some of whom laid claim to his own divinity, DENG. After he built his Mound he had considerable success in seeing them off; either exposing them as frauds, or co-opting them as his *dayiemni*, or claiming credit for their appearance. Three of the best-known rivals were Nyakong Bar, Reath Yac, and Duop Thar.

Nyakong Bar was a Gaajak woman who claimed to be seized by WIU. She proposed to build her own Mound among the Gaajak, and enlisted the support of several Gaajak leaders. Ngundeng denounced them all in this song, abusing them with Dinka and Arabic words for 'women' (*tiek* and *marieme*):

Kɛn kuar cuk wi we thei	The masters of the ants have become weak
Ci lɛ ŋuanni tiɛk	Women are better than they
Ci ka ni mariɛmɛ lɛ kɛ lɛ jäl laŋ laŋ	They are like women walking and shivering
Gaati cuorɛ ha kuon	Do not leave me children
A lɛm ni tar tet	Lift up your hands
Palɛ DEŊ kɛ tok	and pray to DENG with laughter
Ram mi wa kɛ dhoc bi liadɛ	A man who takes them seriously will die
jiäk bi goc dak	and not reach good things[76]

[74] Madhir Lam L20, Garang Ngundeng L1.2, Deng Bor Ngundeng L5.1.

[75] For Bul Kan: Evans-Pritchard (1935: 72–3; 1950: 384–5). For Nyang Yuot: P. L. Roussel, 'List of Notables, and Chiefs Now Retired or Dismissed', 2 Nov. 1954, SRO LND 10.A.

[76] Nyang Kuac Agok L15.1, Cuol Puyu L22.2.

Nyakong came to Ngundeng's Mound to assert her claim. Ngundeng told her that if she really had a divinity, she could run up the side of his Mound, as he did. She failed mid-way, her divinity disappearing into the Mound. Ngundeng humiliated her by setting her to grind grain like any other woman and giving her to one of his *dayiemni* to sleep with.[77]

Another Gaajak rival sometimes mentioned along with Nyakong Bar was Reath Yac, who claimed to be seized by DENG. Ngundeng dismissed this in a song which began, 'DENG has become confused on earth and his head was dizzy | DENG was confused among the prophets'. He then ridiculed Reath:

Gook jamuok ci mut kɛ liar rɔ	The bad prophets' spear was turned against them
Ci mut ɛ luac-luac me te kɛ riɛm	The spear became soft with blood . . .
Waa taŋ yiath ba yiɛth ni cieŋ kor	If I stab with the spear-shaft I will stab during war
Waa taŋ yiɛth bi ciekdɛ waak	If I stab with the spear-shaft the woman will cry
Reath Yaac kuoth mi nindien?	'How big is Reath Yac's divinity?'
Bilɛ til ɛ	It is very small

In another song Ngundeng belittled Reath's claims, saying, 'Reath, you claim to be a diviner for nothing.' Ngundeng eventually summoned him to the Mound and set him tests in public which he failed.[78]

Ngundeng's Mound had a drawing power of its own. Before its construction Ngundeng apparently did visit the Gaajak, once to sacrifice a white ox for barren women, and perhaps once or twice to confront rival prophets.[79] But after the Mound was built rivals had to come to him; it was a challenge they could not ignore. Many of Ngundeng's tests involved public humiliation, but he seems to have been content to allow many prophets to continue as his subordinates. Both Nyakong Bar and Reath Yac are sometimes mentioned by Lou as two of Ngundeng's Gaajak *dayiemni*. Ngundeng may have redefined or renamed the divinities they claimed. Certainly he appears to have allowed a number of 'refractions' of DENG to flourish among the Gaajak. Reath Yac's divinity was DENG CIERKOAR, and other Gaajak *dayiemni* represented DENG JAMBIEL, DENG COTKUAI, and DENG NYANGEAR, all of them ox-names of DENG.[80]

Ngundeng did not always confront other prophets or dispute their claims. He sometimes took credit for the appearance of new divinities, and composed songs about them. In due course it was assumed that his songs predicted the arrival of these new prophets. This happened with Duop Thar, a man of the Laang primary section of the Gaajok, who claimed to be seized by the divinity GÖT. The following song is now said to have been composed by Ngundeng

77 Cuol Puyu L22.4, Nyang Kuac Agok L15.5, Gai Ruea Jk1.3.
78 Song from Cuol Puyu L22.1, Gai Ruea Jk1.3.
79 Gai Ruea Jk1.3.
80 Simon Mayan Tut L17.

before Duop was so seized. In it he mentions Wiu, the clan-divinity of the Gaatgankir clan (a divinity associated with the evil eye), and invokes the Thiang spear, the clan spear of the Gaatgankir, but also the clan spear of the Bor clan, to which Duop Thar belonged.

Ci Göt pɛɛn cɛ naath ruony dheŋ	Göt fell and gave the people a star
A Wiu kor kamni hä ran	Wiu of war give me a person
A Wiu be pɛɛn piny	Wiu will fall down
Lapɛ mut thiaŋdɛ	He is our Thiang spear
Döny lec nhial ca ku pɛɛn piny	The one who grows upper teeth, I have fallen down
Lapɛ tör kuoth ca ku pɛɛn	I am the only divinity, I have fallen
Kuoth gaat kiir ca ku pɛɛn	Divinity of Kir's children has fallen
Kuoth pɛɛthä ca ku piny	Divinity of the evil eye, I have come down[81]

Duop Thar may have negotiated his autonomy. He sent cattle to Ngundeng's Mound and was known as one of Ngundeng's *dayiemni* (he is described as Ngundeng's 'khalifa' in an early British report), but he was one of the few *dayiemni* to continue to act as a prophet on his own after Ngundeng's death.[82] Ngundeng is also credited with foretelling Deng Laka's seizure by Diu in a song resembling the one quoted above. There is also a story that Diu first came to a man named Mabior living at Pathai, but that Ngundeng sent word that Diu should go to the Gaawar, after which Deng Laka became a prophet. At no time, however, did Ngundeng ever claim Deng Laka as a *Dayiem*; the significance of the stories and songs about Göt and Diu is that they both refer to autonomous prophets whom Ngundeng could neither completely discredit nor co-opt.

There was a complex political as well as spiritual contest involved in the annunciation of a divinity's name and descent. In remarking on the competition between prophets Evans-Pritchard represents their 'air spirits' as patrons 'of political leaders' whose influence was limited in part by the segmentary social order. It was only in warfare that a prophet could symbolize the unity of a tribe and act as a pivot of federation between adjacent Nuer tribes.[83] This structural emphasis over-simplifies the prophets' political impact. The descent of divinity implies a transcending of political and social boundaries. Acknowledgement of divinities represented at major shrines, such as Luang Deng and Ngundeng's Mound, cut across internal as well as external divisions. Lines of kinship did, however, affect allegiances and recognition: the Lou had more marriage links with the Jikany than with the Gaawar, and the focus of Ngundeng's attention was on Jikany and Lou rivals,

[81] Cuol Puyu L22.1.
[82] Ibid.; Woodward (1907: 7); Johnson (1992*a*).
[83] Evans-Pritchard (1956: 115, 117–18; 1940*a*: 187–9).

rather than rivals further west. In negotiating a certain amount of autonomy with these distant *dayiemni*, Ngundeng also negotiated a recognition of the primacy of DENG. The lesser divinities may thus have been restricted to smaller political segments, but acknowledgement of DENG, and of Ngundeng as the prophet of DENG, was not completely dictated by structural principles.

Spiritual and political propaganda: the composition of Ngundeng's songs

Ngundeng spread his message through hymns and praise-songs, presenting his teachings in this form so that they could be easily remembered and broadcast. His songs contain references to contemporaries and events in his life; the historical circumstances of his prophecies are therefore still known and remembered (though increasingly subject to reinterpretation). The songs provide the most direct evidence of what Ngundeng thought and said, though even so they must be used with care.

In theory all songs were composed ('created') by DENG and revealed to Ngundeng, and through him to his *dayiemni*. Ngundeng's songs were in fact created by many composers, Ngundeng as well as others, and individual authorship is still remembered. But the songs are presented as DENG's words, rather than Ngundeng's. When Ngundeng is mentioned, it is in the third person; the first person is usually reserved for DENG.

Ngundeng claimed to speak directly to DENG and to be the only one to hear what DENG said. There is a story of how, during one of his early seizures, Ngundeng was sleeping in the same hut as a man named Yioi. Yioi heard Ngundeng talking in the night and the next morning asked with whom he had been conversing. Ngundeng replied it was Divinity. Yioi was sceptical, claiming to others that Ngundeng only dreamt of Divinity.[84] But a conversational tone was employed in some songs, such as this one in which DENG and Ngundeng converse in alternate lines, and which would seem to date from late in Ngundeng's life, after 1902 when the Anglo-Egyptian army (the 'gunmen') raided his village:

ŋundeaŋ!	Ngundeng!
'Weu!'	'Yes!'
ŋundeaŋ!	Ngundeng!
'Weu!'	'Yes!'
Kama ji ghɔɔk ti jal kɛ BUK ti	I give you the cattle which belong to BUK
'Guaa cu kɛ ŋun ɛ kɔ kɔan kɔ thuok kɔnɛ rɔlmac'	'Father, do not give them to me, let me finish with the gunmen'
ŋundeaŋ!	Ngundeng!
'Weu!'	'Yes!'
ŋundeaŋ!	Ngundeng!

[84] Cuol Thijoak L10.1.

'Weu!'	'Yes!'
Kama ji ghɔɔk ti jithkiɛn pan-pan ti cie paak	I give you the cattle with ears as large as the fruit of the *paak* tree [*Calotropis procera*]
'Guaa cu kɛ ŋun ɛ kɔ kɔan kɔ thuok kɔnɛ rɔlmac'	'Father, do not give them to me, let me finish with the gunmen'[85]

There are disputes, as well as conversations, recorded in the songs. The most remarkable is the criticism levelled at Ngundeng by a Gaajak man who later became his principal singer. Rambang Thiciot, a lame man nicknamed Ngol Rietni ('the lame man of words'), was a gifted composer who claimed direct inspiration from Divinity for his hymns. When Ngundeng sent for him to visit the Mound, Rambang refused. In this song he disputed DENG's assertion of primacy and invoked Tut Gar, the ox with the spreading horns, an old image of Divinity (*Kuoth*) holding the universe between its horns, against the upstart free-divinity (DENG).

ŋundeaŋ Boŋ jiak ciöl guäi?	Ngundeng Bong, why do you call people for nothing?
Bie ku lɛldi math DEŊ?	DENG, what will you do?
Mɛ caŋ kɛnɛ pai, ram pal bi been	If it is the sun and the moon, he who prays will come
Lɛp cɔtlual yapɛ DEŊ	The tongue of the ox Cotlual denies DENG
Bia lia jek ci jiɛn ba tek pal bi ben	You will find death has gone, I will pray for life to come
Cä be cak lɛ dhɔŋ yɛ	I will tell you first
ɛn lar laarɛ hän Tut Gar	It is I, Tut Gar, who brings news
DEŊBUKɛ thiɛlɛ hä ŋɛr kɛ piny kɛ liw	DENG of BUK, I have no secrets from the whole world

The story now told among the Lou is that Rambang sent messengers to sing this song to Ngundeng, but when they reached Lou territory they forgot the song and had to return to Rambang for reinstruction. They again set off singing this song but were met by one of Ngundeng's *dayiemni* who ordered them to stop singing. They stopped and were led into Ngundeng's presence, where Ngundeng greeted them singing Rambang's composition. In this way he proved that DENG, and not Rambang, was the real creator of the song.[86]

In whatever way the rivalry between the two men was resolved, Rambang was won over. He became Ngundeng's chief bard (*kiid*) and was a frequent visitor to the Mound. His songs (and his authorship) are better known among the Eastern Jikany than Ngundeng's other songs, and in this way Ngundeng managed to spread his own fame among the Gaajak through Rambang, and encouraged them to visit the Mound. Rambang's song denouncing DENG and

[85] Nyang Kuac Agok L15.1.
[86] Nyang Kuac Agok L15.1 and L15.5.

Ngundeng has become part of the body of Ngundeng songs, but he soon composed hymns in praise of DENG. The following is one of the most commonly sung of all. It refers to DENG by the ox-name *kueijiok*, a black and white configuration with a white spot on the head, evoking wisdom. As with the song quoted above, it employs well-known images, this time describing DENG as a herd bull leading the other animals safely through the bush, watched over by a careful herder, Ngundeng.

Tut mi dit DEŊ KUEIJIOK	The great bull, DENG KUEIJOK,
Tut mi jal kɛ gaatkɛ dɔɔr	The bull who walks with his children in the bush
Cuayɛ bath loo gaatka	Be not discouraged my children
Yienɛ kɛ wut mi nɛɛn yɛ	A watchful man is herding you
Wut mi pal caŋ kɛnɛ pai amani cur	A man who prays to the sun and moon, even to the stars
Tut mi dit DEŊ KUEIJIOK	The great bull, DENG KUEIJOK,
Tut mi nɛɛn gaake dɔɔr	The bull who looks after his children in the bush
Cuayɛ gai kɛ thaaiɛ ba rɔ paar	Be not surprised, for he will gather you up without hurrying.
Yieni DEŊ	DENG guards you
Ran mi lok ni jal DEŊ	Someone who refuses to walk with DENG
cɛrɔ bi maat gaatDEŊ	will not gather together with DENG's children
i mɔ rɛlɛ	but will be alone
Ran mi lok ni jal kuoth	Someone who refuses to walk with Divinity
cɛ rɔ bi maat gaatDEŊ	will not gather together with DENG's children
i mɔ rɛlɛ	but will be alone[87]

We can see from the above examples that Ngundeng's hymns did not differ in form from other Nuer hymns. What Ngundeng and his bards did, which may have been distinctive, was to invoke a whole range of free- and clan-divinities in songs devoted to establishing DENG's primacy. The free-divinities TENY, WIU, BUK, and GÖT were frequently mentioned, sometimes individually, sometimes in association with each other. Ngundeng invoked the clan spears of the dominant clans of the Jikany and Lou: *mut WIU*, the spear of the Gaatgankir, and *mut ghama* (spear of the thigh), the spear of the Jinaca. He also invoked the clan-divinity Flesh in a variety of forms, but most often as 'Flesh of the Leak section', Flesh of his Gaaleak clan. A number of tutelary divinities of other lineages (some of which may have been earthly Powers) were also named. In this way Ngundeng brought a whole range of divinities—both old and new—into association with DENG, absorbing the tutelary

[87] Cuol Puyu L22.1.

divinities of clans and lineages just as he co-opted other free-divinities. Their subordination to DENG was sometimes made explicit. When the Jinaca, the 'original settlers' of Lou, were disinclined to listen to Ngundeng he declared, 'your spear of the thigh, to whom did you give it? Your spear of the thigh, it is DENG.'[88]

There was an element of 'party propaganda' in these hymns—to use Fr. Crazzolara's phrase[89]—a declaration of allegiance. But by invoking so many divinities and subordinating them to DENG, Ngundeng was also blurring the distinctions between them. This was an important element in his attempt to construct peace for the wider community, a peace which was frequently threatened by internal divisions and feuding.

Ngundeng and the construction of peace

Ngundeng's origin outside the community of his mother's agnates helped him later to transcend the divisions of that community and may have facilitated the acceptance of his divinity by the Lou. He was not, like the Dinka spear-masters, a 'mother's brother' to the Lou, but he was part of a maternal kin relationship such as exists between Dinka spear-masters and their communities. Ngundeng's position as a 'sister's son' to the Lou reinforced his ability to mediate between Lou factions. According to the customs imposed by such a relationship, he was supposed to live in peace with his mother's brothers. Such an obligation was reciprocal, and these patterns of respect helped Ngundeng in his role as peacemaker, a role inherent in his office as earth-master.

Ngundeng had mediated homicide cases in Jikany, performing the sacrifices which composed feuds and ensuring that compensation cattle were paid. He continued to do this among the Lou. In common with other earth-masters and even respected elders he also instituted preventive measures, such as forbidding young men to carry spears to dances, thus reducing the chances that any fight which might break out would lead to serious injury or death. As a prophet he had additional sanctions which enforced compliance with his mediation. The prophet's reputation for being able to kill by word or thought encouraged persons to attend his summonses. He used his *dayiemni* to bring in defendants. Whenever he received a complaint of cattle-theft or adultery, he would send a *dayiem* with a metal ring to the accused, who was then requested to come to Ngundeng to confess his guilt or make his defence. It was thought that if the person did not do so and was guilty, his disobedience would bring about his death.[90]

[88] Nyang Kuac Agok L15.2.
[89] Crazzolara (1953: 164).
[90] Bil Peat L12.1, Tut Jiak Gai L21.2, Gatkek Bol Ngundeng L7.1, Deng Bor Ngundeng L5.1.

When, despite his injunctions, feuds did break out among the Lou, Ngundeng intervened to try to end them, often resorting to songs of ridicule to try to bring the feuding sections together. In the following song he criticizes three large sections for refusing to heed him: the Rumjok, the Nyarkuac of the Gaadbal, and the Gaaliek of the Mor. He reminds them that each person is powerless in relation to his Mound, no matter how large or bellicose his section.

Hän hoara nathɛ	I wanted to protect the people
Cu kɛla dhoalkä Lɔu	But there is one thing from the Lou that confused me
Dit mi gueth yiou	It is the anger of iron [spears]
Ca bi lɛ teak mat miɛh	I cannot hide it, these gatherings,
Kɔ kɔn gaatnar	my uncles' sons
Diokda yik thilɛ kɔ lany	The shrine and I, there is no refuge
Lany bɛ ramɔ jek goladɛ	Everyone will be found separately
Rumjok cɛ pam ku ŋiɛn	Rumjok put a stone on his head
darɛ ciɛ ni tuŋ	and it becomes a horn
Ca gaatliek de lar ci Nyarkuac	I cannot talk of Gaaliek, Nyarkuac
ɛ duor ci ku tuol	has become somthing worse[91]

Such songs may have helped to mobilize public opinion in favour of mediation. Both Ngundeng and his son Guek were known to have enforced compensation payments between Lou sections and between the Lou and Gaajok.[92] Internal divisions were transcended to a certain extent when opposing sections accepted Ngundeng as the prophet of DENG, and by extension acquiesced in his teachings of peace. To reinforce acquiescence Ngundeng enticed the different sections to his Mound through the universal spiritual appeal of his shrine, and through the collection of cattle and the redistribution of foodstuffs.

Ngundeng's Mound fixed a permanent site through which Divinity could be approached and at which it could appear. The very solidity of the Mound helped to expand Ngundeng's influence beyond his immediate social limits. As with the permanent shrines which preceded it those who came to help build the Mound, and those who brought mud and ashes to maintain it, became part of a moral community and were involved in an activity which was supposed to bring life to them and to their kin. Individuals could come with entirely personal problems, but whole sections would send delegations, and these may have been the times when Ngundeng invoked their divinities and clan spears in his songs. Many of Ngundeng's sacrifices were intended to have a universal effect, ensuring the well-being not just of individuals, or single

[91] Song recorded at the Mound, 22 June 1975. For feuds of the Nyarkuac and Rumjok after Ngundeng's death see Evans-Pritchard (1940*a*: 144–5).

[92] Evans-Pritchard (1940*a*: 145).

sections, or even just of the Lou, but for all the adherents of DENG. 'He built the Mound so that people will sit in one place,' one of his grandsons commented, explaining the Mound's attraction. 'He who heard of it from afar comes to see the byre, and those who had trouble were brought to the byre.'[93]

The Mound was so arranged as to accommodate a large and diverse collection of visitors. There were shady trees to sit under, and two large pools dug on either side of it during construction provided drinking water. The pools were located on the eastern and western sides of the Mound, and each had a large fig-tree growing by it. The eastern pool was the *pul leak*, the pool of Ngundeng's clan, associated with good things, and the western pool was the *pul jiakni*, the Pool of Bad Things, where sick persons were bathed and treated. The trees were known also as *jiath leak* (Fig. 2) and *jiath jiakni*. Close to the Mound Ngundeng had his own huts and byres, some of them keeping his drums (a large and a small one), used at his gatherings (Fig. 3).

There were often large-scale sacrifices at the Mound, and the major divisions of the Lou each had their own sacrificial site. The Mor sacrificed an animal on the way to and one at the Mound. The two main divisions of the Rumjok, Jak (Maiker) and Dak, sacrificed at the Mound: Dak next to Mor and Jak in front of Ngundeng's byre. Gaadbal sacrificed next to the *jiath leak*, while Ngundeng's family sacrificed in front of the byre where the drums and other special items were kept. There was also a spot in the bush some 500 yards north-east of the Mound where cattle were sacrificed to the Vulture (*cuor*). These sacrifices were undertaken for the benefit of all, and the donation of cattle by different groups helped to ensure that any benefits derived from the sacrifices would include them.

Ngundeng bound the different sections to him through their cattle. As there are shared interests in each head of cattle, and as the sacrifice of a beast represents a sacrifice on behalf of those who share those interests, so the donation of cattle to Ngundeng represented far more than individual ownership or the economic potential of each animal. Each animal represented a tacit acceptance of Ngundeng's spiritual claim by the section that donated it. If it was dedicated to a divinity and kept at the Mound, its group was bound to the continuing religious observances at the Mound. If it was sacrificed for the general good, its group was included in the larger community's relationship with Divinity. If it was slaughtered to feed other supplicants who came to the Mound, or given to them to take away to their homesteads, then it indirectly connected the original donors to the other persons who came to the Mound for help. In this way membership in the moral community was constantly reaffirmed and redefined.

Ngundeng's demands for cattle were frequent, and his *dayiemni* scoured the land insisting that they be given cattle for the Mound. Such persistent

[93] Dhieyier Bol Ngundeng L6.1. Cf. Mawson (1989: 103–14).

FIG. 2. The Tree of Good Things, Ngundeng's Mound, 1975

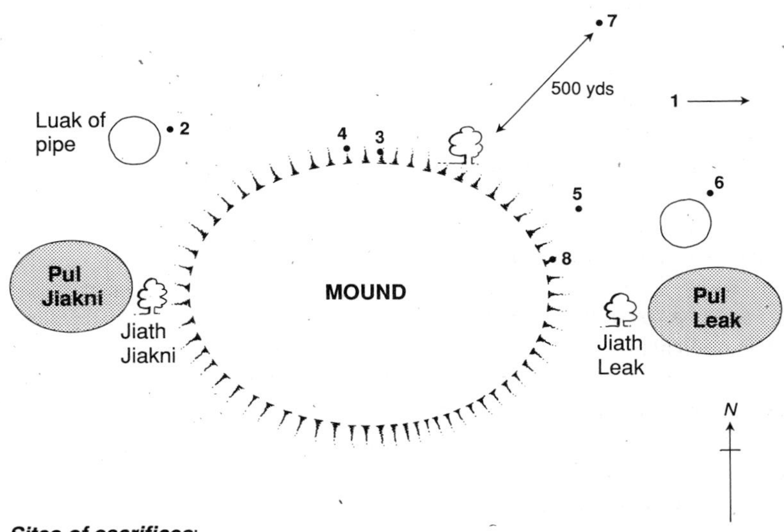

***Sites of sacrifices*:**

1 Mor, on way to Mound
2 Cieng Ngundeng, at luąk of the pipe
3 Mor
4 Cieng Dak
5 Gaadbal
6 Jak, at Ngundeng's luak
7 Cuor (pile of bones marks the site)
8 'Kolkera', the 'entrance' to the Mound

FIG. 3. Diagram of Ngundeng's Mound (not to scale)

FIG. 4. Ngundeng's baton

requests gave the prophet a reputation for greediness, and his *dayiemni* were often suspected of using the prophet's requests to collect cattle on their own behalf. Not surprisingly Ngundeng's demands were sometimes refused. Ngundeng sang bitterly of such rejection, and he reminded those who would refuse him of the symbols and proofs of his spiritual strength: the ox *jokpading* who was sacrificed at the battle of Pading, his ox-name *kur*, the leopard-skins which were the symbols of the master's office, and his baton (Fig. 4), the curved stick with which he killed so many persons at Pading that the vultures came swooping down.

Cu we mɔ biɛtɛ mɔ ku natha nyuän	When I am silent, people think me a fool
Ci hän a nyuän pɛla	I am not a fool, I am wise
Lok ni ruai mi but	I reject continuous words
Ci gaat ka pal yar	For children spoiled the prayer [with their chattering]
Mi wa muoi ni jok padiŋ	But if I mention *jokpading*
Bi cuɔr nyur be luny piny	The vultures will come and sit down
Jok padiŋ moya mi wa kɛ moi kendial	If I repeat *jokpading* many times
Moya kur pith kuacda piny	If I mention *kur* and put down my leopard-skins
Tuothä daŋ kɛ wainom	Then I can clean my baton without interruption[94]

[94] Nyang Kuac Agok L15.2.

The threat was explicitly stated at times, and Ngundeng warned, 'A man who refuses me a cow, I will curse him.'

The threat was mainly spiritual, for it is now said that Ngundeng forbade his *dayiemni* to extract cattle by force. Those who lived some distance from Ngundeng, both territorially and socially, were most likely to refuse. Yioi Binie, the Wangkeac leader living on the Pibor, at first refused to send a cow but then sent a small calf as an insult. He survived, but others who refused died, and their deaths were attributed to Deng. Fear may have motivated some who gave cattle, but those who gave received a reciprocal gift in the form of Ngundeng's blessing. Just as retribution might be long in coming, so might the blessing.

During the building of the Mound Ngundeng called for cattle. The men of the Bul section of Mor refused, since no previous divinity had made such demands. One man, Pet Juol, especially objected. His nephew, Tut Jiak Gai, recalled, 'he said, "Why, if no divinity before has killed cattle, why should Ngundeng kill cattle? Why?"' So no cattle were sent. Then Pet Juol died suddenly at a wedding dance.

Another prophet was consulted and he said, 'He [my uncle] is killed by the prophet of Deng because he would not take a cow to the prophet of Deng.' We were told that we would die. So my mother and I took a small heifer and took it to the prophet of Deng. I went to him in the byre. We went and told him, 'Prophet of Deng, we have come with a cow.' He began singing a song, saying:

Rami penä yaŋ bakɔ lamna lath	Someone who refuses me a cow, we will curse each other
Rami penä wɛaŋ bakɔ lamna lath	Someone who refuses me a cow, we will curse each other
Ruai ɛ luak ker ɛn ruai na jiany	The word is in the byre, the word has not delayed
Nyäl kɛ Wiu	Nyal is with Wiu

He then sang this song:

Ram ci kɔn gueth cɛ de lɛ luoc tic	He who was proud will not return home
Ka ciɛ ruac Deaŋ	That will not be Deng's word
Nac bilual ci be ŋuna tiɛk	A red heifer was given by a lady
Cä pɛn piny ruacdä hän Mar	I, Mar, came down with my word
Rolä hän Deŋ healä kä rɔa	This is my world, I, Deng, which I alone own

That was the time I went with my mother. He then spat into my mouth. He told me, 'You will live long, you will be old. All these things we talked about, you will bring them after me.'[95]

[95] Tut Jiak Gai L21.1, also L21.2.

In the mid-1970s, when Tut Jiak Gai told this story, he was one of the few surviving members of the Dang-gonga age-set, the last age-set marked before Ngundeng's death. The story illustrates how the idea of DENG's strength spread through Lou society, and how Ngundeng took those opportunities offered him to foster the idea. Though the prospect of dying for refusing Ngundeng was certainly frightening, he was careful to emphasize that he offered something in return. The spiritual reward was manifest in a physical benefit, such as children, long life, good health, or wealth. What is also revealing here is the way that Ngundeng mixed Dinka with Nuer, employing both the Dinka and Nuer words for cow (*yang* and *weng*), and referring to Tut Jiak Gai's mother by the Dinka word *tiek*.

Ngundeng was later accused by the Anglo-Egyptian administration (who killed his son and destroyed his Mound) of having used his powers to get 'wives and cattle in untold numbers'.[96] This is clearly an exaggeration as far as his wives were concerned. His family maintain that DENG forbade him to marry very many wives, and that this is why his family section remains small today. Certainly compared to his contemporary Deng Laka (who had over fifty wives), or that most favoured of later Dinka government chiefs Deng Majok (who had nearly 200 wives),[97] Ngundeng does not appear to have increased the size and power of his immediate kin-group. Yet one grandson could count fourteen wives, eleven of whom were married after Ngundeng moved to Lou. Most came from Jikany sections, but there were some Gaadbal, Mor, and Rumjok wives as well.[98] It was not an extraordinary number of marriages, but it was more than most men could hope for. Still, Ngundeng appears to have used the cattle he requisitioned more to attract others to the Mound than to build up his family through marriage alliances. He provided milk and meat for those who came to visit, and cattle for those who came to settle.

Feeding visitors and attracting a following through food (the 1880s and 1890s were hungry decades) was a constant problem. Ngundeng maintained a large plantation of sorghum and maize around the Mound, a legacy of the period of the Mound's construction. There seems to have been no systematic conscription of labour to work the fields. The grain was weeded by members of his family, by his *dayiemni*, by those who lived in his village, and by those who came seeking his help. Usually supplicants would come in the dry season, bringing offerings of cattle, goats, or ivory, and if they happened to come during the sowing time, they would help to sow. Others would come and begin working in the fields until Ngundeng noticed them and asked them what they had come for. Sometimes Ngundeng himself would take to the fields to cultivate, and when this was noticed, others would join in. In this way enough grain was cultivated and stored for the hundreds of persons who came

96 Coriat (1939: 223).
97 Deng (1986: ch. 12).
98 Gatkek Bol Ngundeng L7.2.

to visit all the year round. The sorghum was usually eaten first, then the maize, and by the time both were exhausted the next harvest was ready. As this supply of food was also supplemented by gifts of animals and grain from supplicants, the area around the Mound became one of the few areas nearly always free from the hunger endemic to Nuer life.[99]

Such a cornucopia was a powerful attraction to Nuer and others in even less well-favoured lands. It was an incentive to those with problems to seek Ngundeng's aid. The system, however, was in practice for only the last dozen years of Ngundeng's life. Still, those who came because they would be provided for helped to provide for others through their labour or their own gifts. The giving of cattle strengthened the social bonds which reinforced the moral community Ngundeng was trying to create.

That community included the Dinka and other foreigners who came to the Mound, for Ngundeng advanced truly universal claims. 'Receive the Dinka', he admonished in one song, 'for DENG created people [*naath*], even if they speak nonsense.'[100] And, just as he urged the Nuer sections to cease fighting one another, so he urged them to stop raiding the Dinka. After the Battle of Pading he organized no raids against them, and he sanctioned no raids organized by others. Those songs of his that condemn Dinka are aimed specifically at those who attacked him at Pading, or who later guided the Anglo-Egyptian troops to the Mound in 1902.

It was difficult to get the Nuer to agree to his injunction. One who did not was the Dung-Rumjok prophet of DHOL, Thijok Dul. He lived near Pathai on the border with the Gaawar and maintained an autonomy of action not shared by the *dayiemni* resident at the Mound. Like his neighbour Deng Laka, he was an adopted Dinka refugee. 'DIU was a warrior', one of Thijok's sons explained. 'He and my father used to raid the Dinka.' The raids were usually instigated by Deng Laka, and Ngundeng acquiesced in them. Had he not done so, Thijok Dul might have joined Deng Laka entirely. As it was he behaved almost like a *dayiem* to both prophets.[101] There were other Lou who raided Dinka living along the mouth of the Khor Fulluth at the end of the century, and the Dinka there assumed that they did so with 'Dengkur behind'.[102] But the overwhelming testimony of Lou, Gaawar, Jikany, and Dinka today was that Ngundeng did not take the Lou raiding and tried to prevent them from doing so on their own.[103] Modern testimony is confirmed by a contemporary document. After a tour of the Gaawar and Dinka bordering the Lou in 1905, a British officer wrote,

[99] Garang Ngundeng L1.3, Nyakuil Tuel L8.

[100] Cuol Puyu L22.1.

[101] Cuol Thijoak L10.1, Marieu Thijoak L11.

[102] Dau Kur EHJP-3.

[103] Lou: Macar Ngundeng L2, Deng Bor Ngundeng L5.1, Bil Peat L12.1. Gaawar: Kulang Majok G6.2, Cuol Dual G13.2. Jikany: Gai Ruea Jk1.3. Dinka: Nyareweng elders D3, Lueth Ayong Yor EHJP-2.

Diu's Nuers, and the resident Dinkas themselves (*i.e.* not the 'fugitive' Dinkas of the Filus), all state that Deng Kur's Nuers were a most inoffensive lot, and that they did not go in for raiding now, and that if a Nuer went raiding he was kicked out of the 'merah' [cattle camp] by Deng Kur on his return.[104]

The Dinka who received the most favourable attention from Ngundeng were the Ngok and the Nyareweng. There had been some fighting between the Ngok and Lou during the Lou migration east. Ngundeng put an end to these raids by planting elephant tusks on the border between the two and cursing anyone of either tribe who might cross that boundary to raid. Ngundeng's peacemaking is commemorated in this Ngok song which recalls him by the Dinka pronunciation of his name, Wundeng:

What the chief of the Nuer once said
The chief Wun Deng spoke and said
We shall drink out of one gourd . . .[105]

The Ngok and Nyareweng had a number of social and economic ties with the Lou, with whom they intermarried, and intermarriage increased the risk that a raid against neighbouring Dinka would involve Nuer relatives. The Lou often relied on the Ngok for grain, just as the Ngok relied on the Lou for cattle. The Lou and the Nyareweng had similar bonds, their sons were often marked in the same age-sets together. Within ten years of Ngundeng's death their settlements were so mixed that bemused administrators were unable to separate them.[106] There is evidence that during Ngundeng's time the Lou and the Nyareweng (if not the Lou and the Ngok) did exchange bloodwealth payments in cases of homicide concerning the two tribes. Some twenty years after Ngundeng's death the local British administrator discovered this precedent and tried to reintroduce it.[107]

Ngundeng reinforced the symbolism of peace, not only through his references to Aiwel Longar and DENG, but in his own person. He was left-handed, and this has strong associations with peace. The right hand is the spear hand and is associated with men, strength, and war. The left hand is not the spear hand and is therefore associated with women and 'weakness'.[108] There are a number of female symbols also associated with Aiwel, and one, the woman's winnowing-tray, is used in Dinka peacemaking ceremonies.[109] The association between women and the left side, therefore, is not automatically one of weakness as a defect or a danger. It is, rather, not so

[104] Wilson (1905).
[105] Deng (1973: song no. 90, p. 208).
[106] Johnson (1982*a*: 191–8).
[107] Coriat (1926*b*).
[108] Evans-Pritchard (1956: 233–6), esp. 233 (bride's mother's family), 236 (femininity incompatible with fighting spears), against which must be set 235 ('right-handed peace').
[109] Lienhardt (1961: 288 n. 1).

much physical incapability, as the more positive quality of non-aggression. The association between female attributes and peace is expressed in both Nuer and Dinka society through the pacific relations required of men related through women, in the mother's brother and sister's son relationship. In Dinka society there is the further identification of the spear-masters as 'children of women'. When Ngundeng was addressed by the Lou it was more often as 'Gatnyayiel', the son of his mother (their sister), than as 'Gatbong', the son of his father (a stranger).

These associations between peace and the left hand are made explicit in certain contexts. DENG at Luang Deng is also known by the ox-name 'the left-handed one', and visitors to the shrine are not allowed to carry spears in their right hand—their spear hand—but must carry them in their left.[110] Though left-handed, Ngundeng held his baton in his right hand at Pading when he used it to kill those attacking him. That the left hand is associated with peace among the Nuer (perhaps now particularly because of Ngundeng), and that Ngundeng's peacemaking activities are evoked through his left-handedness is revealed in one of his prophecies recalled after the end of the first civil war in 1972. It was then remembered that Ngundeng had foretold the coming of the war, but that he had also foretold that peace would be brought by a left-handed stranger, and by a Nuer who was born of a left-handed woman. These were identified as two of the government's principal negotiators at the Addis Ababa Agreement, Abel Alier, a Bor Dinka, and Peter Gatkuoth, his Lou Nuer deputy.[111]

The peace and welfare the prophet brought came through his prayers for rain, cattle, and crops, through his sacrifices to combat infertility, epidemics, and illness, and through his prohibitions against fighting. It was, in fact, the overcoming of death, the gift of life. The Nuer desire for peace and for these gifts of life was revealed in the numbers of people who came first to build his Mound, and then to add to it. The Lou had been unenthusiastic about building a modest shrine at Juet in the early 1880s. By the early 1890s enough Nuer had suffered from drought, rinderpest, disease, and fighting to look to Ngundeng with hope and to join in the construction of a far larger Mound; refusal to participate then would have appeared to be courting death. But the Lou still fought among themselves, and Ngundeng still had to intervene to prevent feuds from spreading. The year the Dang-gonga age-set was marked (*c.*1895) he stopped a fight between Rumjok and Gaabal. He also intervened to prevent a much larger fight between the Gun and Mor.[112] At the time of his death in 1906 feuds were only contained, they were not eliminated. Mor Lou country was so riven by feuds that almost every village was at odds with its neighbour.[113] Shortly after Ngundeng's death the Gun–Mor conflict

[110] Howell (1961: 99); Wan Deng EHJP-9, Gony Yut G15. [111] Peter Gatkuoth Gual A3.1.
[112] Tut Jiak Gai L21.2. [113] O'Sullivan, 'Lau Nuers'.

which he had restrained broke out into a bloody war. The *kor luny yak* (War of the Hyena) is mentioned by Evans-Pritchard as an example of the ferocity that Nuer intersectional feuds can attain.[114] Ngundeng's gift of life and peace was remembered in its very absence.

Ngundeng and the north

It has been the consensus of ethnographers and administrators that Ngundeng arose as a Nuer response to foreign aggression. This conclusion was based as much on Old Testament models of prophets as on a lack of detailed knowledge of Nuer history. Before we can assess the crisis theory as it applies to Ngundeng, we must examine the historical facts of Nuer experiences of foreign aggression. We have already seen that Ngundeng's reputation was not based on regular raids against the Dinka. Chronologically he also began to flourish before the Mahdiyya in the Sudan (1881–98), and his influence was well established (if not at its height) before the appearance of the Anglo-Egyptian government. Neither the Mahdists nor the colonial government can take the credit for Ngundeng. It might still be possible to suggest, however, that Ngundeng responded to earlier pressures during the Turco-Egyptian presence in the Southern Sudan (1840–85).

Encounters with the 'Turuk' do not figure prominently in Lou accounts of the nineteenth century. It is difficult to see how they could. The Sobat was not a major route for the merchant companies who traded in the Southern Sudan from the 1850s to the 1870s. In the early period of trade exploration the Sobat appeared to offer a way to the gold-bearing hills of Ethiopia, and there were reports of merchants ascending the river. But the promise of this Eldorado was never fulfilled, and by the late 1870s there was no trading network from the Sudan which used the Sobat as a route to the southern Ethiopian kingdoms. Those merchants who did ply the river kept close to the banks and did not venture far inland.[115]

The lower Bahr el-Zeraf was first visited by ivory merchants in the late 1850s and between 1865 and 1874 was the main waterway south. It was during this time that armed camps were established in Dinka territory, and an overland route from the Zeraf to the Sobat, perhaps passing through Pul Turuk, linked the two rivers. The Lou, who lived closer to the Bahr el-Zeraf at this time, were affected by these camps. Marno found Lou slaves with the Zeraf companies in 1871, and the Lou mention Yuot Nyakong's dealings with the 'Turuk'. But contact was brief. The camps were closed in 1874, and Egyptian government posts were established at the Sobat mouth and Nasir up

[114] Evans-Pritchard (1940*a*: 144).

[115] Brun-Rollet (1852: 412; 1855: 107); Petherick (1861: 360–1); Heuglin (1941: 155); Baker (1875: i. 35); Chaillé-Long (1877: 27); Schuver (1883: 17, 20–1).

until 1883–4. They did have some impact on the surrounding populations (Dinka and Shilluk at the Sobat mouth, Anuak and Jikany at Nasir), and the Danaqla irregulars garrisoned at Nasir are said to have despoiled the area of Kuanylualthoan.[116]

Ngundeng left Jikany territory before the creation at the post at Nasir in 1874 and the subsequent devastation of Kuanylualthoan (through which he passed). There is no mention in his biographies of 'Turuk' active in the area. He may have settled in Lou before the Zeraf merchants made contact with Yuot Nyakong, and this would date his movements to the late 1860s or early 1870s. He was not entirely insulated from the world of the merchant camps, as his songs indicate. There are bits of camp Arabic: *aiwa* (yes), *lathkar* (*al-askari*: soldier), and even *thol* (*sol*: sergeant-major). *Kartum bari* is mentioned, which is either 'Khartoum on the river' (the Arabic *bahr* being adopted in Nuer), or the Arabic for Khartoum North, the dockyard from which so many flotillas set off for the south. The exterior of the armed camps is also described by their fences, the thorn barrier or *zariba* from which the whole encampment takes its name. There is a complete absence of any Islamic religious vocabulary. This suggests knowledge of the comings and goings of the people from the north, but not intimate contact. The Turco-Egyptian period was a disturbing time for other parts of the Sudan, but not for the plains south of the Sobat.

With the fall of Khartoum in 1885 and the withdrawal of Emin Pasha from Equatoria in 1888, the Mahdist army was able to enter the White Nile and Bahr el-Jebel, but it never maintained a strong presence along the length of the river, and certainly not on the major tributaries. Mahdist forces around Fadasi tried to penetrate Wallega Province of Ethiopia in 1889–90 but were expelled by Menilek's army; thus being denied access to the tributaries of the Sobat from that direction. A Mahdist raiding party did set off from the Blue Nile in about 1890 (following the famine of 1889) and raided the Anuak on the Baro and the Gaajok on the Pibor. It, too, retreated in the face of an Ethiopian army. Al-Zaki Tamal was sent to wage war against the Shilluk in 1891–2, but after that date there was only a fleeting Mahdist presence at Fashoda.[117] It is al-Zaki's army that figures in the oral history of the peoples of the Sobat mouth. The Dinka living around Khors Atar and Fulluth were brutally raided by the *ansar*, who are remembered for throwing the bodies of children down the wells and taking all the sorghum. Many Dinka fled for protection to the Gaawar and the Lou, but the *ansar* did not follow.[118] The Dinka suffered from this raid, not the Nuer.

[116] Marno (1874: 391, 394–5, 428–9); Gordon (1953: 155–8, 190, 203–4, 219–23, 317); *SIR* 163 (Feb. 1908), 2. See Ch. 4 below.

[117] Triulzi (1975: 68–9); Michel (1901: 186, 307–8); Evans-Pritchard (1940*a*: 145); Holt (1970: 209).

[118] Lueth Ayong Yor EHJP-2, Dau Kur EHJP-3, Philip Diu Deng A8.2.

The *ansar* are not mentioned in Ngundeng's songs; we hear only about the *marol* (a red ox which symbolizes the red foreigners), *rolmac* (gunmen), *lathkar* (soldiers). The only northern Sudanese people specifically named are the *Dunglaa*, Danaqla, the Mahdi's own people and the group from which many merchants came. Modern Lou do speak of a raid on Ngundeng's Mound by *ansar*, or *Turuk-ansar*. This attack took place between the initiation of the Dang-gonga and Luac age-sets. It is clear from a comparison of the account by an eyewitness to this raid, Garang Ngundeng, and the contemporary British record that it was *not* the Mahdists who raided Ngundeng, but the Anglo-Egyptian army, in 1902. No other confrontation between Ngundeng and the 'Turuk' has ever been mentioned by the Lou.[119]

Ngundeng was not, therefore, 'thrown up like some dictator' to confront the slavers, the Egyptians, or the Mahdists. His seizure by DENG pre-dated the Mahdi's announcement of his messianic mission by almost a decade. This does not mean that he was untouched by slave-raiding. It is reported that he married one daughter to an ex-slave, and another daughter was captured by slavers.[120] For all that Ngundeng and the Lou were relatively unscathed by the turbulence of armed raiders in the nineteenth century. They faced a far more potent and determined threat from the Anglo-Egyptian army, who conquered the Sudan ostensibly to rid it of slavery.

The new Anglo-Egyptian administration centred at Fashoda was at first confined to the rivers, just as previous occupying powers had been, and its knowledge of the interior was obtained mainly from those few persons who were willing to visit the new outposts or meet with officials on their steamers. Those 'sheikhs' who did come in very often represented no substantial political group, had no power base of their own, and hoped to enlist government aid in securing territory, cattle, or followers.

Some of the first 'sheikhs' to come to Fashoda were men representing those Dinka groups who had been defeated by Ngundeng at Pading and expelled from their country by Deng Laka. It was from them that the new government received an image of Ngundeng's implacable hostility to the government and the Dinka. Between 1899 and 1902 the government was told that Ngundeng (the 'Mek [king] of the Nuers') had threatened to kill all his cattle 'to prevent them from being taken, and will fight to the last'; that he had built a fort of ivory tusks 'taken from Dinkas, Shilluks, and Nuers in various raids'; that he 'declines to have anything to do with white men, and promises to kill all people other than his own tribe, and even them, if they are friendly with white people approaching his village'; that the Lou had been raiding the Twic and the friendly Dinka on the Khor Fulluth; that Dinka among the Lou lived as

[119] Johnson (1982*b*: 119–39).
[120] O'Sullivan, 'Lau Nuers'.

slaves; and that Ngundeng's popularity rested on successful raids against the Dinka.[121]

The reports, though constructing a false picture, contained some elements of truth. Ngundeng had a fence of tusks around his Mound, not a fortification but a display of offerings brought by many peoples. He had sacrificed great numbers of cattle, not as an act of war but as a rite creating a desolate tract of bush between himself and an advancing epidemic of rinderpest. His songs did denounce 'gunmen', but those of the *marol* of earlier regimes. The Twic Dinka had been raided, but by the Gaawar, not the Lou. By April 1902, when the administrator of Fashoda, Major Blewitt, led a punitive column of troops and Dinka auxiliaries against the Lou, none of these reports had been corroborated by a single Nuer.

The official report of 'the Dengkur patrol' is explicit that it met no organized resistance. Troops entered Ngundeng's village unopposed, looted the ivory around his Mound, burned his village, and seized cattle dedicated to divinities. For three more days they burned villages and seized cattle, firing on some Nuer only at Muot Dit. The patrol returned to Fashoda, reporting one minor affray between their Dinka auxiliaries and the Nuer on the way. The evidence presented of Ngundeng's hostility was entirely negative: he never answered Blewitt's summons. That he had not fought counted as much against him as if he had. It is solely on this report that Ngundeng's reputation for rallying oposition to the government rests.[122]

Other sources throw light on Ngundeng's response to the patrol. The messenger sent to Ngundeng with the administrator's declaration that he came 'as a friend' but would punish Ngundeng if he did not agree to meet him was a 'small Nuer Sheikh' called Bul Kan. Bul Kan, we know from Evans-Pritchard, was a renowned magician.[123] If he was already practising at this time it is highly unlikely, given the prophet's antipathy to magicians, that he would have gone to Ngundeng to deliver this ambiguously threatening message. When the column did reach the village the Dinka auxiliaries, led by the Luac chief Ayong Yor, were mainly responsible for desecrating the shrine.[124] In subsequent songs Ngundeng referred to the soldiers of the column as *Turuk Yuong*, 'Ayong's Turks'. The most revealing account of Ngundeng's response comes from Garang Ngundeng, who was between 12 and 15 years old when his father's village was raided.

As the patrol approached Muot Tot, Ngundeng was in front of it in the bush with three columns of warriors. Suddenly he shouted 'Stop!' and the

[121] Sparkes (1899: 10); Blewitt (1902); Hawker (1902: 5); *SIR* 72 (July–Aug. 1900), 2; 87 (Oct. 1901), 3.
[122] Blewitt (1902), repr. in Johnson (1982*b*: 122–7); Wilson (1903*c*: 6).
[123] Evans-Pritchard (1935: 72–3).
[124] Lueth Ayong Yor EHJP-2.

columns halted. Ngundeng raised his baton to the sky three times, then announced that Divinity was absent and called off the advance. The leader of one column, Kuony Gol, remonstrated with him, but Ngundeng refused to listen, and the force dispersed. The Lou then abandoned their villages and went deep into the bush. 'Divinity was walking with us, avoiding the war.' Ngundeng took the fishing-spear from the top of the Mound and some of his special cattle. Divinity seized him once they were all in the bush, and he stuck the fishing-spear in the ground to bring rain to relieve his people from thirst. He also sacrificed a number of black and white cattle to feed them. After the troops had burned the village around the Mound, Ngundeng announced that he would return to fight, but he never tried to catch them up. Instead he held back to supervise the planting and harvesting of that year's crops. He did not return to the Mound, but built a new byre near Waat, a few miles to the south.[125]

Both the government and Ngundeng suffered from the 'Dengkur patrol'. The gratuitous burning and looting by government troops did nothing to win over the Lou. Yet, they had clearly expected Ngundeng to repeat his performance at Pading, and destroy the invaders with his baton. Ngundeng saved the lives of his people by dispersing them, but he did not save all their cattle, nor did he free them from this new threat.

Blewitt's successor in Fashoda, Major G. E. Matthews, was convinced that the patrol had impeded the progress of administering the Nuer. He also reassessed the policy of protecting the apparently loyal and friendly Dinka of the Sobat and Khor Fulluth, on whose behalf Ngundeng had been attacked. The Dinka 'friendlies' reported Lou retaliation soon after the raid, but a new scepticism began to inform government dealings with its allies. Within a year of the patrol against Ngundeng the goverment no longer believed the 'false rumours' the Sobat Dinka spread against the Nuer, suspecting that they were motivated by the desire for legalized looting under government protection. Two years after the 'Dengkur patrol' the government realized that the Dinka were also raiding the Nuer and tried to halt this. In 1904, as retroactive punishment, the Dinka leaders who had urged the government to attack Ngundeng and had acted as guides in the patrol were briefly imprisoned for their part 'in the events leading up to the expedition against Deng Kur'.[126]

Ngundeng was not so utterly discredited as the government hoped, but his supporters became less fervent and his enemies more confident. Kuony Gol, who had earlier urged Ngundeng to fight, sent emissaries to Fashoda a year later to see what accommodation could be made. He then received a government official at his own village and agreed to try to persuade Ngundeng

[125] Garang Ngundeng L1.2, in Johnson (1982*b*: 128–9).

[126] *SIR* 95 (June 1902), 4; 96 (July 1902), 2; 105 (Apr. 1903), 2; Wilson (1904: 9); 'Return of Prominent Persons in Upper Nile—1909', SRO UNP (unnumbered).

to meet with the government, too. It was from Kuony that the government learned that some of Ngundeng's followers, 'having got tired of his continual flights . . . have settled under other Sheikhs'. Lam Tutthiang, the magician, openly aligned himself with the government.[127] Ngundeng's songs reflect the decline in visitors to his Mound. 'Ngundeng's Mound was built for nothing,' one laments, 'it is deserted except for Bong's son himself.' He then declares, 'I do not know the person who will defeat the foreigners [*rol*]'; but then invokes his own spear, 'My spear with which I killed the *marol* and the prophet [Deng Cier], let my spear kill all the destructive people [*ji juarjuari*].'[128]

Ngundeng did not abandon the Mound, but he no longer lived right next to it. He still visited it, but he also fled into the bush when he heard of any touring government inspectors near his territory. Coriat, later attributing the devastation of Lou villages to the 'Arabs' rather than to the government, wrote of Ngundeng during this period, 'alarms and escapes and a scattered people gave him little opportunity for the display of magic, but when he could he made encouraging prophecies and concocted plausible excuses for his impotence to stem the ravages of the foreigners'.[129] Most of his songs which mention *rol mayok*, *marol*, and *rolmac* come from this time. One which may date from after 1902, and which begins the verse quoted on p. 105, reaffirms his position as an earth-master from the Leak clan, as well as his inspiration from above.

Jin lap yɛnɛ canyɛ be dhil agurun	You do not believe me but I will be your father
Gatbuleak be nhialɛ	Buleak's son comes from above
Kuɛ dormi ŋundeaŋ	Let them talk about Ngundeng
Kartum Bari rɔl mayok	Khartoum Bahri belongs to *rol mayok*
Waŋda lony riɛm muoya wea	My eyes are filled with blood
Maida cuɔr maida cuɔr	My friend is a vulture, my friend is a vulture[130]

Other songs were less bloody. In the next one he mentions the carrion-eating birds Kueilit and Nyalaang, the divinities of two *dayiemni*, CUOL NYALJOK and GÖT, the Mor Lou section Nyabor, and his own village at the Mound, *wec Carlel*, or 'the cattle camp of the black ox'.

Ba tuŋ biɛ car piny	I will lay down the point of the Mound
A bi kuel rɔdɛ duany daar	The fig-tree will bend in the middle
Kueilit ɛn Nyalaaŋ pɛɛn cuɔrɛ 'wuu'!	Kueilit and Nyalaang, the vultures, drop—'wuu'!

127 *SIR* 105 (Apr. 1903), 3; 130 (May 1905), 6; 114 (Jan. 1904), 2; Nguth Kuny L14.
128 Nyang Kuac Agok L15.1.
129 Coriat (1939: 225).
130 Simon Mayan Tut, recorded at the Mound, 22 June 1975.

Cieŋ Nyabor palɛ gɔa	Pray well, Nyabor section,
Laaŋɛ gɔa riecdiɛn ni kɛlɔ	Supplicate well, their generation is the same
Riec ba kɛ nuar piny	The generation came down with the Nuer . . .
Tɔaŋa biɛ wec gaatkur	I built the Mound of Kur's children's camp
Tɔaŋa biɛ bi rɔɔl	I built the Mound which will heal up
Tɔaŋa yik	I built the shrine
Tɔaŋa biɛdɛ ŋundeaŋ	I built Ngundeng's Mound
Hän, DEŊ taadh	I, DENG, the one who moulds
Ca gɔny ca marɔl	Do not accuse me, I am not *marol*
Mut mi noŋ yiɛnɛ dhɔalä jɛ	I reject the fight you bring
Cia kuoth kɛnɛ guk coɔrɛ gak	Divinity and the prophet do not quarrel
Bie luoc mi yiɛn	You will be the one who returns it
Ram mi laat canɛ	Someone who says he is poor
bɛ wa mi buɔr ŋundeaŋ	he will come to Ngundeng's arms
Ba rɔ thacɛ tɛɛ mi luak	I will curl myself up in the byre
ba ruac thiec ka Lit	Lit will ask the word
CUOL NYALJOK yene GÖT	CUOL NYALJOK and GÖT
caŋ dhɔale ruac	even if you refuse the word
bi ruac jiac wec Carlel	the word will begin at Carlel's camp[131]

Here is a reaffirmation of peace, for 'divinity and the prophet do not quarrel'. Despite the aggressiveness of the foreign soldiers (*marol*), and despite the implied scepticism of some *dayiemni* (including Duop Thar, prophet of GÖT), he reminds people of the virtues of the Mound and the succour Ngundeng gives to those in distress.

With doubts about Ngundeng's ability to meet the threat of the gunmen both secretly and openly expressed, Ngundeng had need of new demonstrations of his spiritual strength. It was at about this time that he commissioned an Anuak blacksmith, War Nyigol, to make him a brass pipe. The pipe was in the shape of an ordinary Nuer *tony*, with a large brass bowl, a long stem decorated with brass rings, and a gourd mouthpiece (see Fig. 15). Ngundeng revealed it at a large gathering at the Mound. It was stored in its own hut near the Mound. Though unlit, it would smoke mysteriously. It became known as a death-dealing instrument; Ngundeng was supposed to be able to just shake it at an ox for the beast to fall dead. It is also said that he sometimes put a medicine (*wal*) called *nyangaat* in the bowl, and gave the pipe to people to smoke. It was something of a truth-testing ordeal, such as the use of the leopard-skin, testing the truth of what other persons said. If they were

[131] Nyang Kuac Agok L15.1.

lying to Ngundeng, *nyangaat* would kill them. In this way, some say, Ngundeng used the pipe to eliminate his enemies.[132]

Ngundeng's prestige may have suffered from the government presence, but administrators were soon in no doubt that Ngundeng was still an influence to be reckoned with. When there was crop failure and famine along the Bahr el-Zeraf in 1904 the Lou had a bountiful harvest in contrast, and such tangible proofs of Ngundeng's blessing continued to exert a powerful attraction to other Nuer. The Lou lay at the heart of Nuer country and appeared to be the 'root of the Nuer opposition to the Government'. Ngundeng, officials realized, had to be 'reconciled or removed' before the government could 'hope to do any real good among the Nuers'. But Ngundeng's 'antagonism to Government has apparently only deepened with time', wrote Governor Matthews in 1904. 'With the best possible intentions', he continued, apparently without irony, 'we may be unable to prevent the Nuers of the Sobat moving across to Den[g]kur rather than accept our pacific proposals.' He feared that Ngundeng could then 'undo our small efforts at progress with the Nuers in the Zeraf valley'. It seemed impossible to make any contact with the prophet through the intermediaries then available. Freed slaves had been used with some effect in other parts of the Southern Sudan, but they did not impress Ngundeng. One 'old Dinka refugee from Cairo' who had visited friends on the Khor Fulluth in the dry season of 1904 reported that 'Dengkur would hold no communication with him, and at the very sight of a man in clothes (indicative in these parts of his loyalty to the Government) he is said to cover his face and refuse to look on him.'[133]

It was because of the unfortunate consequences of the 1902 patrol that Matthews approached the other major prophet in the region, Deng Laka, more diplomatically. After the exchange of Nuer emissaries between Deng Laka and the government, the province's senior inspector, H. H. Wilson, finally met the prophet in his own home in March 1905. During this trip Wilson received a different impression of Ngundeng from the one the government had already formed. Ngundeng had a reputation as a peaceful man among his immediate neighbours, and both the Ngok and Nyareweng Dinka got on well with him. This was encouraging news, and the government redoubled its efforts to win over the Lou. Matthews appeared on the border of Lou country early in 1906 and personally returned Lou cattle and captives taken by the Khor Fulluth Dinka in raids since 1902. But in January 1906, just as another official was preparing to enter Lou country, Ngundeng died. 'The death of Deng Kur', Matthews reported with relief later that year, 'has apparently dispelled to a great extent the former objection on the part of the

[132] Coriat (1939: 225–6); Alban (1940: 200); Gatkek Bol Ngundeng L7.2, Tut Jiak Gai L21.1, David Koak A2.

[133] *SIR* 117 (Apr. 1904), 1–2; 118 (May 1904), 4; Wilson (1904: 9); Gordon (1903: 12); Matthews (1904: 7).

Nuer tribe in these parts to coming in touch with the government.' Administration could proceed without the prophet.[134]

Ngundeng's legacy

Many years later, when the province administration was at war with Ngundeng's son Guek and was determined to rid the Nuer of their prophets, it was claimed that Ngundeng perverted 'tribal custom' and lived merely to extort cattle from his credulous and fearful followers.[135] The impression obtained by the first administrator to visit the Lou in the month following Ngundeng's death was quite different. Captain O'Sullivan, in the report cited in Chapter 1, described Ngundeng as both beloved and feared, 'very just, always helped poor, never allowed killing'. There was even a sound stock-breeding explanation for his mass sacrifice of cattle: 'We have all laughed at the story of DUNG KUR [*sic*] telling the people to kill their cattle and he would get them others: he was quite right though, he saw that the time of the good cows was largely wasted in producing calves to these decrepit, mangy brutes and producing a very inferior breed'.[136]

This favourable assessment of Ngundeng, identifying those aspects of his career most valued by the Nuer, was buried in the files of the Intelligence Department in Khartoum and was lost to those later generations of administrators who came to govern the Lou. It entered neither the administrative nor the anthropological analysis of prophets in Nuer society. Its value as part of the historical record lies in the corroboration it gives to modern Nuer oral testimony. Ngundeng is still described in those terms first recorded immediately after his death.

The conflict between Ngundeng and the government, so forcefully documented in Ngundeng's own songs, is frequently glossed over by modern Lou. Instead, they stress Ngundeng's predictions about the coming of the 'Turuk' to rule them, and point to the similarities between Ngundeng's work and that of the government. Ngundeng's Mound (which buried all illness) and Ngundeng's blessings are equated with the government dispensaries and veterinary teams who looked after human and livestock health. His injunctions against fighting are compared with the government's subsequent prohibition. His *dayiemni* are likened to the government's native administration policemen. In fact, the modern description of Ngundeng's system of summonsing defendants by sending a *dayiem* with a metal ring is suspiciously similar to the government's own use of numbered metal discs to keep track of litigants and cases. The frequent assertion that disease, fighting, and magic have all spread

[134] *SIR* 128 (Mar. 1905), 6; 139 (Feb. 1906), 1; 145 (Aug. 1906), 4; Wilson (1905); Matthews (1906: 745).
[135] Willis (1928: 201).
[136] O'Sullivan, 'Lau Nuers'.

since Ngundeng's death is also paralleled by the notable decline in services and security which followed the departure of the British.

Times of relative peace always look more peaceful when viewed from the perspective of insecurity and war. We have already discussed the evidence contained in the oral record of feuds within Lou society during Ngundeng's time. There is further support in the documentary record for modern assertions of Ngundeng's efforts as a peacemaker.

O'Sullivan's 1906 report records widespread feuding among the Mor, and also one feud within the Gaadbal section among whom Ngundeng had lived. Thie Ruea, of the Ciec section, had been fighting Kuony Gol's son for harbouring Dinka refugees. Thie was also threatening Ngundeng's family. We know from modern testimony that there was no love lost between Ngundeng and the Ciec section, and we will see in Chapter 5 how this conflict continued in the succeeding generation. But this feud within the Gaadbal broke out at the very end of Ngundeng's life, during the period of his fatal illness. The impression given by O'Sullivan's report is of general security among those living closest to Ngundeng, with security declining as the distance from Ngundeng's Mound increased.[137]

A telling comparison can be made from reports in the 1920s written by Percy Coriat, the first administrator to gain an intimate knowledge of the Lou and their Gaawar neighbours. It is clear from his descriptions that feuding was much more severe among the Gaawar than among the Lou. The Gaawar were still struggling with the legacy of the nineteenth century, when their society was deeply divided between those who allied with the slavers and those who became the slavers' targets. The level of feuding, at least among the Gun Lou, was much lower. Coriat's main task there was to clear up feuds between the Lou and Dinka which had developed since Ngundeng's day. There is no recognition in any of Coriat's reports that the prophets were responsible for maintaining peace in the past, but his evidence of a lower level of violence among the Lou than among the Gaawar is suggestive of some influence on Ngundeng's part.[138]

It is clear that Ngundeng cannot be described as a 'crisis leader'. He defended the Nuer from attack once, but he did not gain strength by rallying the Nuer against the government. If anything, he lost followers by avoiding confrontation. Crisis cannot explain Ngundeng's appearance as a prophet, nor his continuing appeal to the Nuer and to others. Yet crises and disasters did influence his career, and for historians such disasters do 'expose, at a particular point in time, the inner workings of a society and illuminate the basic values and assumptions which inform its actions and govern its relations with outsiders'.[139] We can learn something by analysing how Ngundeng and the Lou responded to different crises.

137 Ibid. 138 Coriat (1926*a*, 1926*b*, 1929*b*). 139 Waller (1988: 74).

The formative period of Ngundeng's early life was spent among the Eastern Jikany in the aftermath of their crossing the Nile. It was a period when the leaders of the migration were increasingly ignored and disputes and feuds tended to be resolved by division as groups went off to settle new lands. This strategy could not be employed indefinitely. Migration brought the Nuer into contact and conflict with other groups; the Buongjak experience showed that there were also environmental limitations to Nuer movement. Ngundeng appears to have been deeply affected by these continuing difficulties the Nuer faced on their new frontier. The enduring examples of old Dinka shrines, divinities, and mythical figures offered a means to overcoming the divisive tendencies in Nuer society. Ngundeng combined the ideologies associated with DENG and Aiwel, the focus of a fixed central shrine, and the mediating role of the earth-master to persuade many Nuer to settle their own differences with greater regularity, and to enable them to live in security with those earlier inhabitants whom they had displaced.

Ngundeng's success may have been only partial, but it was cumulative. He began preaching (through his songs) before the Dinka threat of the late 1870s. He received only mildly favourable attention until he proved himself at Pading. His successful response to that challenge attracted more followers, but he maintained and expanded his following through the persuasiveness of his propaganda, the apparent efficacy of his blessings, and his manipulation of the networks of redistribution and generosity that he was able to create. By the time of the rinderpest epidemic of 1888–9 he had already articulated a philosophy of social harmony and had gained a considerable spiritual reputation. His actions in meeting the smallpox and rinderpest which swept in from Ethiopia may, or may not, have limited the effects of those two epidemics; but he gained the credit for having done so, and used that credit to mobilize labour on a large scale to build his Mound. The idea to build such a Mound pre-dated rinderpest; the willingness of the general population to build the Mound followed Ngundeng's response to the disease. People were persuaded to work on the Mound as a form of protection against future epidemics; once it was built it became a focus of religious and social attention which helped attract more persons to Ngundeng, thereby spreading his message further. Ngundeng did respond to a series of immediate crises. His perceived success in meeting these challenges enhanced his reputation; each success increased the popular willingness to accept his general message, thus improving his ability effectively to address challenges endemic to the Nuer community.

In so far as Ngundeng and the Anglo-Egyptian government wished to achieve the same goals, they were rivals and competitors for allegiance among the Nuer. Modern Nuer comparisons between the work of Ngundeng and the government implicitly acknowledge this. Because the government initiated violence, Ngundeng could not be reconciled, and the government could neither co-opt him nor restructure the religious and social network at whose centre he stood, as it was able to do with the king and the institution of kingship among the Shilluk. Neither Ngundeng nor the government could or would adapt to the other. The government was the final victor in its confrontation with the Nuer, and as such presented itself as the ultimate protector of Nuer values and Nuer society. It dismissed its earliest rival as an aberration of little lasting significance to the Nuer. Ngundeng has thus been consistently misrepresented in the official record of Nuer administration, and in the histories which are based on that record.[140]

Ngundeng's legacy is not without ambiguity. As a peacemaker he was not a pacifist: he fought at Pading, countenanced Thijok Dul's raids, and appeared willing to oppose Blewitt. The Lou clearly expected a prophet to fight in some circumstances, and this expectation resurfaced during Guek Ngundeng's confrontation with the government in 1927, and even later, during the Sudan's second civil war. But if periodic violence has interrupted the construction of peace, the prohibitions against fighting are constant, and to many Nuer today, as we shall see in the final chapter of this book, Ngundeng's life embodies the values they most prize, and his songs articulate both their ideals and their current hopes.

[140] Cudsi (1969); Collins (1971: 218); Digernes (1978); Sanderson and Sanderson (1981: 4–5); Daly (1986: 145–6).

4

Deng Laka: A Pragmatic Prophet

*Biographical contrasts—the Gaawar dispersal into their new territory—Nuaar Mer the slaver and Deng Laka the prophet—*DIU *and the social order—the prophet and the spiritual order—relations with the Dinka and foreign governments*

Biographical contrasts

Deng Laka's life among the Gaawar presents a sharp contrast to Ngundeng's prophetic career among the Lou. Both were foreigners to the communities in which they lived; but whereas Ngundeng's mother was a Lou 'aristocrat', Deng Laka's mother was a Dinka refugee. Ngundeng fixed his central shrine permanently in the middle of the Lou plain; Deng Laka was forced by floods to relocate himself to the south-eastern edge of Gaawar territory. Ngundeng built on the relatively stable settlements of the plains to establish the basis for a community at peace with most of its neighbours; Deng Laka lived in an unstable environment which placed the Gaawar in frequent competition for land and pastures; at best he could only contain the circle of hostility such competition fostered. Lou accounts of Ngundeng's seizure and early career emphasize the activities and intervention of Divinity; Gaawar tales of Deng Laka focus clearly on the man and his motives. Ngundeng made his Mound the geographical centre of converging spiritual and political networks; Deng Laka, through his many marriages, made himself the personal centre of a new social network. There is little information about Ngundeng in contemporary documents. He remained a phantom to the British administrators who tried to contact him at the end of his life, and an enigma to those who dealt with his successors. More is known about Deng Laka, who twice met and negotiated with government officials, and whose views on practical matters found expression in the official record during his lifetime.

Deng Laka's life can be contrasted not only with Ngundeng's, but with that of another Dinka refugee among the Gaawar: Nuaar Mer, the slavers' ally. Each man rose, through different routes, to a position of considerable power and wealth in Gaawar society. They established and maintained their positions at a time when the Gaawar had to deal with three major problems arising from their recent move into the Zeraf Valley: the progressive fragmentation of Gaawar society as it gradually occupied a territory constantly beset by floods;

the assimilation of Dinka living among them; and the intrusive influence of a new external force based in the Northern Sudan. Nuaar Mer, through his alliance with the early slavers, accelerated internal segmentation and increased the distance between Gaawar and Dinka communities. Deng Laka, in his role as a prophet, spent most of the rest of his life trying to overcome internal divisions while maintaining a selective hostility to a few external communities. To understand Deng Laka's later life, one must begin with those who preceded him.

The Gaawar dispersal into their new territory

The Gaawar occupation of the Zeraf Island (described in Chapter 2) was not a mass movement. Gaawar society grew through the incomers it attracted, not only from other Western Nuer groups, but from the Dinka whom it surrounded, engulfed, or displaced. The unity of the Gaawar and the authority of their leaders did not survive their victory over the Dinka at Pakuem, as Nuer settlements filtered into the newly available land and the leaders of these settlements sought a variety of means to increase their power. Buogh Kerpeil was blessed by his contemporaries and given leopard-skins by common consent, but others could also aspire to what he had attained. This was a time when strong leaders tried to bolster their positions with magic. The split between the Radh and Bar sections of Gaawar was hastened, in part, by the rivalry of two magicians.

It was Buogh's use of magic against his rivals which undermined the consensus on which his authority as earth-master rested and which led ultimately to his demise. Puol Bidiit, an influential man of the Bar primary section, went in search of magic for his own protection. He went to the Duk ridge, which was then still settled by the Dinka, but which in Gaawar legend was originally inhabited by animals in human shape (*let*). They bore the names of Yod, Kuei, Dor, Buk, Kuacdeng, and Paguir. According to the Gaawar these *let* were not Dinka (though the above are Dinka names), and they were not human; they were, however, dangerous strangers, like the 'lions' in Dinka 'lion' stories. Puol Bidiit is said to have befriended some of these *let* when they came hungry to Gaawar territory and ate one of his cows. They remembered his generosity and welcomed him when he came to their settlements on the Duk ridge and helped him when he explained the danger he was in from Buogh's magic. They gave him some magic of their own and taught him how to use it. He used it just once to kill Buogh. Released from Buogh's threat and influence Puol became the leader (*ruic*) of the Bar Gaawar. But there is more to the story. In one version the *let*, in addition to giving Puol the magic, made a circle around him and blessed him with their spittle. The significance of this is similar to the spittle given to Buogh by the Gaawar elders, but it goes further than that. As the *let* were supposed to be the original inhabitants of the country their blessing transferred the authority over their land to Puol and his descendants. The names of the *let* are all place-names in Bar Gaawar territory. The story legitimizes Gaawar ocupation of the new land.[1]

The problem of establishing a new legitimate authority over land which still contained its original inhabitants was a serious one for the Nuer east of the Nile. 'Original settlers' claiming new territory were original only in the Nuer sense. Any new settlements were bound to contain a good number of Dinka who really were 'original' settlers. The spiritual foundation of the power of the earth-master, too, was undermined by this new situation, for the question remained, whose earth was it? This is the significance of the Gaawar and Lou adoption of Dinka into earth-master lineages, and then making *them* earth-masters with the *post hoc* justification that they already came from Dinka 'earth-master' lineages. This claim was made of Yuot Nyakong, Nuaar Mer, and Deng Laka. The problem of establishing legitimate authority over the new land was ultimately solved by the prophets Ngundeng and Deng Laka, who, in addition to being earth-masters, were seized by sky divinities. Their authority over all inhabitants was superimposed from above.

Gaawar settlement of both banks of the Bahr el-Zeraf never fully displaced the Dinka there. Not only were Dinka and Gaawar villages found interspersed well into the twentieth century,[2] but the composition of Gaawar settlements was continually altered by a steady influx of Dinka, some coming as refugees, others coming on their own volition. The lives of Nuaar Mer and Deng Laka present instructive contrasts.

Nuaar Mer the slaver and Deng Laka the prophet

Nuaar Mer was a Thoi Dinka from the area west of Mogogh. When he was a child there was famine in Thoi country, as a result of either Nuer raiding, floods, or a combination of both. Mer Teny, Buogh Kerpeil's nephew, found Nuaar wandering alone in the bush, looking for food. Mer brought him home, adopted him as his own son, and gave him cattle. Upon the deaths of his father Teny Kerpeil and his uncle Buogh, Mer became the main leader of the Radh Gaawar. On Mer's death Nuaar succeeded to the leopard-skins, though not without dispute.

Mer chose Nuaar as his successor, but according to one Radh account Nuaar demurred when offered his father's skins, claiming that being a Dinka the Gaawar might kill him, and urging them to take 'the real sons of Mer'. Other accounts (from both Radh and Bar) recall that some among his own section objected to Nuaar receiving the skins because he was only an adopted

[1] Kulang Majok G6.4, Mar Kutien G5, Ruot Diu G10.2; Lewis (1951) for Buogh. See Lienhardt (1961: 69–70), and Deng (1974) for lions in Dinka myths and folk-tales.

[2] Coriat (1923).

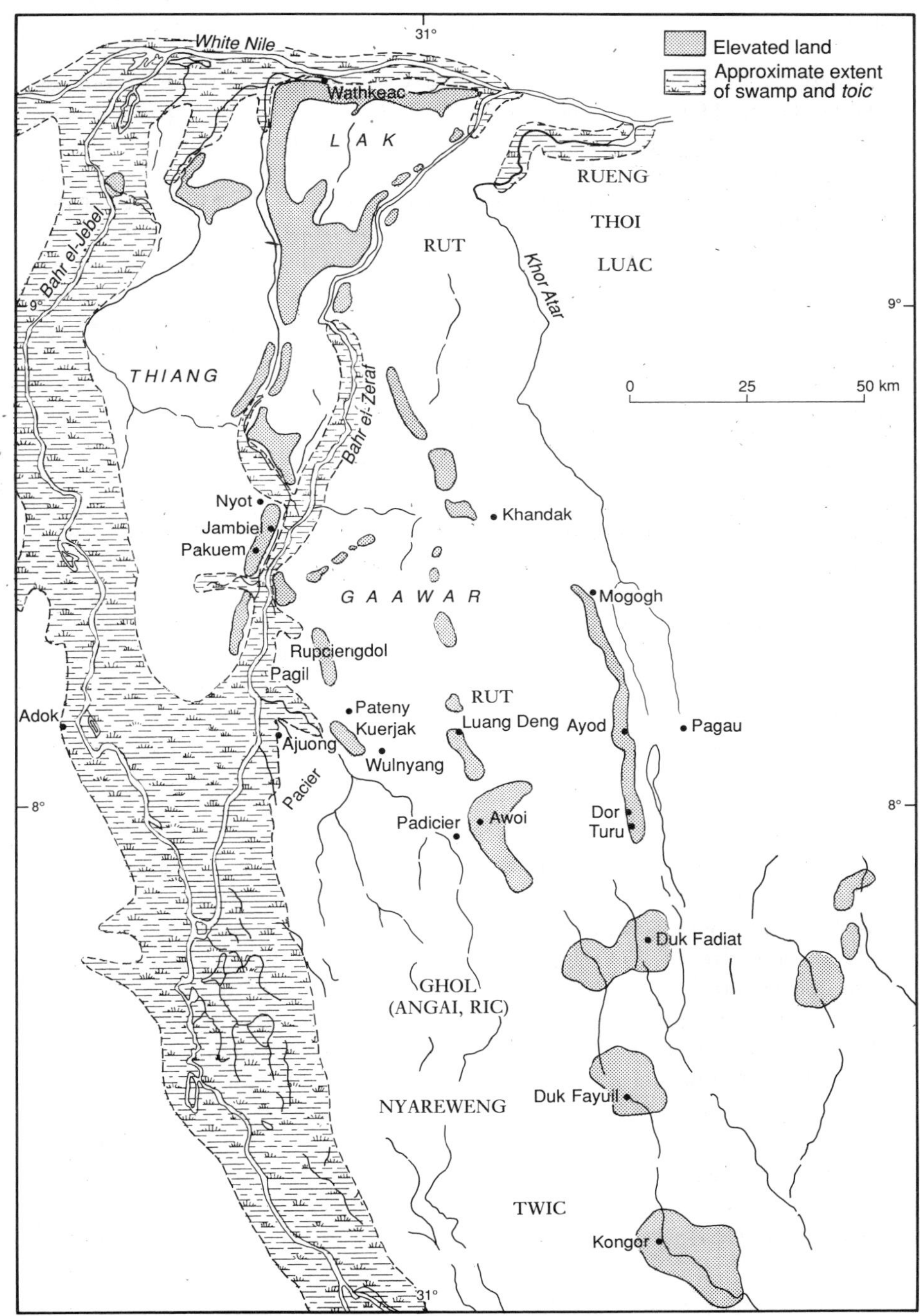

Map 4. Gaawar and southern Dinka territory

Source: JIT 1954.

son, but the 'Turuk', then at Jambiel, imposed him on the Gaawar,[3] and he is sometimes described today as merely a chief of the 'government' or the 'Turuk' (*kuaar ke kume or kuaar turuk*).[4] It was certainly from the 'Turuk' on the Bahr el-Zeraf that Nuaar derived his coercive power.

The Bahr el-Jebel was opened up to navigation by the Egyptians in 1840, after the Gaawar had already crossed to the Zeraf Island. The entire length of the Bahr el-Zeraf was traversed by shallow-draught boats by 1859, but it was not until the mid-1860s, when *sudd* completely blocked the Bahr el-Jebel, that the Bahr el-Zeraf briefly became the main river route south for commercial traffic. Ivory-hunting expeditions had made contact with a few Dinka and Nuer along the Zeraf in the 1850s, and in about 1865 Kuçuk Ali's trading company established a *zariba* near Jambiel. Later in the decade both the Kuçuk Ali and Ghattas companies established camps in the interior at Khandak and Ayod.[5]

Mer Teny first contacted the traders when other Gaawar were shy of approaching them.[6] Relations between Gaawar and merchants were friendly during his lifetime, but Mer's death coincided with the period when the traders strengthened their presence and expanded their operations along the Zeraf, becoming more actively involved in raiding. At first they raided mainly Dinka, but with Nuaar Mer's assistance they began raiding Nuer. Nuaar's insecurity as a Dinka adoptee led him to bring his powerful allies directly into lineage politics. A number of the Kerpeil section fought with Nuaar over cattle and defeated him. Nuaar then brought the troops of the local *zariba* at Jambiel into the fight and defeated the faction led by his paternal uncles. This split the Kerpeil, some staying with the 'Turuk' and Nuaar Mer at Jambiel, and others crossing the river for safety.[7]

After this Nuaar extended the range of his allies' activities, raiding Thiang, Lak, and Lou Nuer. The Gaawar were not immune, and some became special targets. It is now recalled that whenever Nuaar Mer quarrelled with anyone, whether from Bar or Radh, he would sell that person into slavery. He took so many people to the slavers that he often sold them for petty things, such as sugar or tobacco. When he wanted cattle he would enlist the aid of a few riflemen and go raiding. In a feud with the Nyadikuony section of the Radh Gaawar he used the slavers' soldiers to herd the Nyadikuony men into a small *zariba* which was then set alight, burning the people to death.[8]

3 Ruot Yuot G2.1, Ruot Rom G1, Diu Garadin G4.

4 Kulang Majok G6.2, Ruot Diu EHJP-5.

5 Johnson (1992*b*); Marno (1874: 394).

6 Ruot Rom G1. This is also claimed in Tangye (1910: 219), presumably on information provided by Matthews and Struvé, but he mixes events from Nuaar Mer's life with that of his father.

7 Ruot Rom EHJP-4, Ruot Diu EHJP-5.

8 Ruot Rom and Puok Banak G1, Ruot Diu G10.1, Ruot Yuot G2.1, Kulang Majok G6.4; Coriat (1923); Struvé (1908*b*: 656), for burning men in a *zariba*.

Nuaar Mer's chief ally was an Arab named Ali, and two men of this name seem to have been associated with the *zariba* at different times, Ali Nasir (or Nasir Muhammad) and Ali wad Rahma.[9] It was Ali Nasir whom Gordon found at the *zariba* when he closed down all the camps in July 1874. He enlisted Nasir into government service, sending him to the Sobat to found the post which now bears his name. The Zeraf camps were thus operational for only about nine years. Gordon's arrival by steamer was later described by Kulang Majok, the son of an eyewitness, Majok Juc, who as a boy worked voluntarily at the *zariba* for a soldier named Marjan:

> My father said that when they came the steamer arrived late in the day. It came and stopped. The Turuk came out, the Turuk who came from Khartoum, coming to take the Turuk who were living at Jambiel. My father said that the Turuk called Marjan who worked with him said, 'Majok, my son, we are being taken back. I would take these cows of ours; you take a heifer for yourself.' So he took one heifer with a white patch on its head. They spent the night. He said the following morning the Turuk all gathered together and went to the steamer.[10]

Gordon's own report largely confirms this. Arriving before dusk, he gave the slavers four days to evacuate, which they did, leaving their cows behind. 'One of the Nuehr chiefs, who was in alliance with Nasser', he noted, 'was in a bad way also. He said, "When you go away the tribes around will attack me." I said, "I cannot help that, but if you will assemble the neighbouring chiefs I will speak to them."'[11] Only one Nuer chief was at Jambiel with Nasir: Nuaar Mer. Kulang Majok reports that the advice Nuaar received was pessimistic. When leaving on their steamer the 'Turuk' said: '"You, Nuaar, you go to Mogogh. You go and be with the Luac and Thoi. If you stay on this side, you will be killed by Kerpeil section." Nuaar left. He came on his horse. He was a very big chief. He found the Thoi having many cattle.'[12]

Whether Gordon, or anyone else, had sufficient grasp of the complexities of local feuds to give Nuaar such precise advice, Nuaar did remove himself to Mogogh on the northern tip of the Duk ridge, where many Dinka still lived with their cattle. It was there that Nuaar was joined by many other Dinka and Gaawar, attracted by his own large herds and still in awe of his strength, despite the disappearance of his allies.

Nuaar Mer's activities had an unsettling effect on the Gaawar beyond the physical and social disruption of his raids. As the leading member of the Kerpeil section he was the head of the dominant section of original settlers which, unusually for the Nuer, was also the mediating section of earth-

[9] Ruot Diu EHJP-5; 'Memorandum by Lieutenant General Sir Reginald Wingate 1908', GRR 1908 195.

[10] Kulang Majok EHJP-8, also mentioned in G6.4.

[11] Gordon (1881: 20–2).

[12] Kulang Majok EHJP-8.

masters. The Gaawar experience demonstrates how difficult it is for earth-masters to be both dominant and neutral at the same time. It required a very delicate balance at the best of times. By victimizing other Gaawar, Nuaar Mer undermined the Kerpeil position as the dominant section; those raided by the Kerpeil could scarcely seek to associate themselves with it. As the creator of a number of feuds Nuaar could no longer mediate as an earth-master; there was no way to bring to an end the feuds which proliferated around him.

Deng Laka felt many of the same insecurities as a Dinka refugee that Nuaar felt, yet he was to overcome them in a most striking way. Deng was a Ngok Dinka of the Dut section, then living on the northern end of the Zeraf Island. His father's name was either Gil or Cuol.[13] During a famine (perhaps the same one which drove his contemporary Nuaar Mer from the Thoi) Deng Laka's father died. His mother Bol took Deng and her two daughters into Gaawar country, looking for her own sister who was married to a Gaawar man living at Ajuong. On the way they were picked up by a fishing party of Jamogh Gaawar, and Deng was adopted by a man named Lek Jiel, becoming known as Deng Laka (Deng, son of Lek). Lek wanted to marry Deng's mother, who had been taken with her daughters by yet another man, Jul Luak. Jul was unwilling to part with Bol until her sister in Ajuong learned of Bol's capture. The sister's Gaawar husband came to retrieve Bol, whereupon Jul hurriedly married her to Lek for eight cows, three of which went to Jul Luak, and the rest to Bol's Gaawar brother-in-law.[14]

Bol had a son by Lek, Kerjiok Laka. When this boy was still small, but when Deng Laka was fully grown, some of Nuaar Mer's slaver allies came raiding the Jamogh Gaawar. Deng Laka hid his brother in a pile of thatching grass and then ran to safety, but Bol and her two daughters were captured and taken away. Deng Laka went to Nuaar Mer to appeal for their release, but he was told by Nuaar that his mother would be released only if Deng either slept with her or ate human excrement. Deng refused and never saw his mother again. The two sisters, it is said, were sold to the slavers for sugar or tobacco. This was the beginning of Deng Laka's personal feud with Nuaar Mer.[15]

Deng Laka returned to Ajuong where many of Nuaar Mer's victims had retreated. There are some family stories which claim that he lived in poverty there, but during this time he married four wives. True, his first marriage was contested by some of his age-mates who objected to him, as a Dinka,

[13] Lueth Ayong Yor EHJP-2, Ruot Diu EHJP-5, Nyanyai Kal G8.

[14] Details provided by Deng Laka's children: Nyanyai Kal G8, Matit Kal G9.1, Ruot Diu G10.1 and EHJP-5. This agrees in general outline with Kulang Majok G6.1 and G6.2.

[15] Malual Mayom and Ruot Rom G1, Nyanyai Kal G8, Cuol Macar and Matit Kal G9.2 and G9.3, Ruot Diu G10.1, Mar Kutien G5. Untitled, undated (*c*.1943) note in New Fangak ZD 1.A.6. There is some disagreement among sources about Deng Laka's age at the time and whether he managed to ransom back his mother. Nuaar and Deng were members of the same age-set (Thut). It is clear from words attributed to Deng Laka after this event that he failed to obtain his mother's freedom.

marrying a Gaawar girl, and true, one of the wives was married in his half-brother Kerjiok's name, as the boy had died. But Deng Laka overcame the prejudice against his Dinka origin by his strength and bravery: he was (as his natural sons later were) exceptionally tall and strong. He paid bridewealth for all of his wives, so he could not have been entirely impoverished relative to the other Bar.[16]

This was not a time of great prosperity for the Bar, though. Not only did they suffer from Nuaar Mer's raids, but it was an unpropitious time to be confined to an area so close to the river. Ajuong is a small island of slightly elevated ground between the Bahr el-Zeraf and Khor Jurwel. It is well situated for dry season pastures but vulnerable to any substantial rise in the river level. The Bahr el-Zeraf was high throughout most of the 1860s until 1874, when the opening of a channel through the Bahr el-Jebel *sudd* cleared the main river again. The great flood of 1878 brought more troubles in its wake. Even before that a cattle disease called *puc* killed off many of the livestock along the upper Zeraf, leaving some Bar Gaawar families with only one animal each. Milk was so scarce it had to be measured out in clam shells, and people were reduced to eating water-lily (*yil*) with their fish soup.[17] Nuaar Mer's settlement on the northern end of the Duk ridge, however, seems to have been largely unaffected by either the cattle epidemic or the floods.

Nuaar Mer's oasis of relative plenty attracted many Nuer and Dinka. He projected an ostentatious life-style. He built his cattle byre between the large *kuel* (*Ficus platyphylla*) tree at Mogogh and a seasonal pool. In front of his byre, at the edge of the pool, he planted eight doleib palms in a row, where they could still be seen over a hundred years later. The palm trees were the tethering pegs for eight oxen of the black and white *kuaijok* pattern, from which Nuaar Mer took his own ox-name. He was also very fat, which only the very rich could be. Those who came to join him as individuals included Rut, Thoi, and Luac Dinka, some of his own Teny section of Kerpeil, and a few other Gaawar, Lak, and Thiang. Mogogh was a Gaawar village because of Nuaar Mer's central presence, but its inhabitants were as much Dinka as Nuer.[18]

Such a community became the focus of envy, anger, and fear. At the time when the Bar herds around Ajuong were decimated by disease a man named Biem Jiak announced that he had been seized by a divinity with the ox-name MAYAN YIETH TUT and would lead a raid against Nuaar Mer and seize his cattle. Deng Laka was among Biem's band of warriors who set out from Ajuong for Mogogh. But Nuaar still had a fearsome reputation, and Biem Jiak

16 Nyanyai Kal G8, Kulang Majok G6.2 and G6.6, Ruot Diu G10.1, Cuol Macar G12.1.

17 Kulang Majok G6.6.

18 Malual Mayom and Ruot Rom G1, Ruot Yuot G2.1, Kulang Majok G6.2 and G6.4, Ruot Diu G10.1.

was not up to the enterprise. He got no closer to Mogogh than Pateny when he suddenly panicked, claiming that his divinity had left him. He called off the raid, adding that they should quickly send some girls to Nuaar to atone for their audacity. Deng Laka was disgusted, exclaiming to his age-mates, as one of his sons later recalled, 'Boys, divinity has caught a coward!'[19]

Biem took his shrine-stick and started back, but Deng remained behind with a few of his companions, including Majok Juc, Wuor Yiec, and Both and Jok Diet. Deng stood on top of a termite mound, facing the direction of Mogogh, and said.

This fellow called MAYAN YIETH TUT wants to take us back to Gaawar where we will eat water-lily with our soup, while the cattle are over there with the Dinka called Nuaar Mer in Mogogh. If divinity had seized me—me, Deng Laka—I would add my spear [*tong*, Dinka]—my bravery—to it, and capture that Dinka and bring those cattle for us to eat![20]

It was then, according to one of his sons, that Deng raised his hands to the sky, saying, 'Grandfather, you keep all of yourself in the sky without giving me that little thing [*dung*] you can give me.'[21]

Biem stopped at Wuor Yiec's homestead, where there was one milk cow left which had survived the epidemic. Kulang Majok later recounted his father's reminiscence.

Biem knew there was a cow there, that is why he went to the byre. It was being milked into a gourd. My grandmother asked him if the battle was postponed. He said, 'Yes.' 'And what about the other people?' 'They are on the way.' The women began to cook porridge. Biem was given a mat to sit on, and he slept in the back of the byre. The milk of the cow was not shared out, it was put aside for the man with a divinity.[22]

His companions joined him, but when Biem was served with the little milk which was available Deng Laka intervened. 'The milk was brought in a gourd', Kulang Majok continued:

Deng Laka called one of the women named Nyathak Col. 'Who is that over there?' She replied, 'The man of divinity [*guan kuoth*].' 'Whose divinity?' 'MAYAN YIETH TUT', she replied. He said, 'If this divinity MAYAN YIETH TUT is a divinity, why did he fear Nuaar? If the cattle had been captured, would not people be satisfied with milk tomorrow? And what are you carrying?' he asked the woman. 'It is milk,' she said, 'He does not know milk!' He took the milk, the milk which was going to be eaten, and gave it to the other men. MAYAN YIETH TUT ate without milk. [Deng] threw the gourd down after pouring the milk on the food. He went and sat down. People called him to eat, but he refused.

[19] Ruot Diu G10.1.
[20] Kulang Majok G6.2 (similar to statement in EHJP-8).
[21] Ruot Diu G10.1.
[22] Kulang Majok EHJP-8. Throughout the interviews recorded in 1975–6 and 1981–2 the terms 'grandfather' and 'grandmother' were often used in the plural in the classificatory sense.

Deng Laka spurned all offers of food and departed suddenly, taking his age-mates with him. His abrupt actions were later understood by his companions to be signs that 'the divinity was already in him, but he did not know it', yet it was only after he returned to Ajuong that he began to exhibit peculiar and disturbing behaviour.[23]

According to his children Deng became ill after he returned home and got into a fight while fishing at Pacier. He was beaten, went to bathe his wounds, and cut his hand on some grass. The wound became infected, Deng became delirious, then mad, and went wandering in the bush where he was seen playing with snail shells, arranging them like cattle at the foot of termite mounds, a childish game.[24] Returning from the bush he would cry, 'Poo! Poo! Poo! I shake the ground with thunder [*märä piny*], and no one answers me! Yes, I subdue the world, I subdue the land [*kokä piny*], and there is no answer! I shake with thunder, and I stop!' As in the early stages of Ngundeng's seizure, it was the prophet's wife who was the most vocal sceptic, or so one member of Jithep-Radh, the section of Deng's senior wife, has perhaps mischievously claimed. Bol Roa, the mother of Macar Diu, scolded Deng, saying, 'Don't bring this "Poo!", you Dinka! You are just refusing to bring things for my children, pretending that you have a divinity!'[25] To Deng's age-mates, however, his illness was both mysterious and puzzling, something to be taken very seriously.

Deng remained indisposed throughout that rainy season. Wuor Yiec and the two Diet brothers learned of Deng's illness after the harvest and went to visit him. As far as they knew he had fallen ill as soon as he returned to his byre and had not left it. They found him lying in his byre, and Wuor questioned him about what was troubling him:

> He said, 'Deng, what is wrong with you?' He replied, 'I am ill.' 'How does it hurt you?' 'Yiec's son, at night I feel as if I am in the bush among all these termite mounds, up to that sausage tree [*luel*]. I gather up many snail shells, and there seem to be people [*nei*] gathering up a lot, but I do not know where. When I am in the bush I am insensible to the world. I do recognize when I am in the byre in the morning, it seems as if I am inside. Boys, this is how it looks. I do not hurt as if I will die, or hurt as if I will get better. I do not know the thing which takes me to the bush. I do not know what makes my legs move.[26]

This was Deng Laka's explanation, as later repeated by those who heard it. Some in Deng's family now say that he spent the entire late rains in the bush and was discovered by persons from his own village when the cattle were

23 Kulang Majok G6.2, EHJP-8.
24 Matit Kal G9.1, Cuol Macar and Matit Kal G9.2, Nyanyai Kal G8. For children playing with snail shells see Wilson (n.d.: 47).
25 Ruot Yuot G2.1. Deng Laka probably had not announced his seizure this early.
26 Kulang Majok G6.6.

moved out into the camps in the early dry season. They saw him sitting on a termite hill under a sausage tree with divinities dancing up and down the sides of the hill and in a circle around him. People who tried to approach him were knocked unconscious. It was only after many cattle were sacrificed that they were able to surround him and shepherd him back to his village, where he was watched closely and given cattle.[27] There is an element of exaggeration here, both in the number of divinities and cattle: *puc* had left few families with many cattle to spare. There is also perhaps the natural desire among those living closest to the prophet to assert their own early recognition of his true state. But no such explanation was given to Deng Laka's three friends. As they returned to their own village they agreed among themselves that Deng had a divinity and that others must be told about it.

They organized a dance and told the assembled dancers of Deng Laka's strange illness. They arranged to go to Ajuong to hold a prayer-meeting (*pal*) for him. The girls were each to bring a bundle of sorghum stalks, and Both Diet managed to find one big white ox which had survived *puc*. On the appointed day they processed to Ajuong singing, the women carrying their stalks, and came to a halt in front of Deng Laka's byre. Majok Juc was among the crowd. Kulang Majok gave his account of things:

> My father said they came and stood in front of his byre. The white ox was tethered in front of the byre. He [Deng Laka] was sleeping in the byre. Nobody yet knew that he had a divinity. After people had sung a lot he came running out of the byre, crying, 'I subdue the land, I subdue the land!' My father said that he cried, 'I subdue the land!' He turned this way. He went to the door of his wife's hut and said, 'Bring me my apron [*buong*], bring me my apron.'

Deng Laka was given a serval cat's skin (*thoan mibor*) which he put on. He began jabbing from side to side and people dodged him to get out of the way. He cried again, 'I shout and I stop. Pulwar [Gaawar], I have come.' Then he was asked, ' "What are you called?" He said, "I am called Diu." ' The people told him to take the white ox and kill it. 'My father said that we killed the white ox. They dug around it and piled up earth on top of it. Yes, that place became a shrine [*yik*]. Even now, when it has been eroded [by floods], it is still as high as an automobile, it is like an automobile, over there in Ajuong.' It was from that point that Deng Laka became known as Diu and 'spoke as a divinity'.[28]

The stories of Deng Laka's seizure by Diu offer us an insight not only into Deng's motives, but into the expectations of contemporary Gaawar society. The Gaawar already had examples of mantic persons who spoke with the voices of divinities. Not only was Ngundeng's fame spreading, but there was

[27] Ruot Diu G10.1, Nyanyai Kal G8.

[28] Kulang Majok EHJP-8 (also G6.2 and G6.6). He earlier identified the skin as *thoan mibor* but later called it a *tuac*, which could be either a serval cat or leopard-skin.

the nearby shrine-master of Luang Deng. Biem Jiak, who apparently began his career curing sick children with his blessing, was readily understood when he announced he had been seized by a divinity. The man of divinity, the *guan kuoth*, was afforded some special attention, as is illustrated in this story when food and milk is specially reserved for Biem. But while the Gaawar knew what to expect of a man of divinity, they could also be sceptics. A prophet who fails to deliver is treated without respect. Deng Laka spoke contemptuously of Biem's cowardice and deprived him of his milk, even before it was known that Deng, too, had been seized. Biem seems to have offered no resistance to this humiliating treatment.

Deng Laka's motives for seeking seizure are explictly stated. His is the one clear example we have of a prophet who 'set out systematically to acquire a spirit', and from examples in comparative religion we could conclude, as Evans-Pritchard did, that this seizure came about through 'fasting and solitude'.[29] This is not, however, the Nuer perception of the sequence of events. In their view Deng Laka was seized upon beseeching Divinity while perched on a termite hill. It was a divinity who then took him out into the bush and made him do peculiar things. But in order to get the divinity to speak, others had to recognize it. The opposition between the village and the bush are emphasized in this story as in no other account that I know of a prophet's seizure.

The plains between Ajuong, Pacier, and Rupciengdol—now under water since the 1960s floods—used to be littered with termite hills. In the dry season such expanses can present a deceptively populous and settled appearance. The low, rounded mounds produced by nature mingle with the low, rounded temporary grass huts and dung-ash hearths of the cattle camps fashioned by human beings. In the cattle plague year of 1981 I visited a camp in a termite hill-littered range not far from the site of Deng Laka's seizure. At even a short distance the mounds of the plain and huts of the camp resembled each other, so that one's sensations alternated between feeling alone on a vast unpopulated range, and feeling surrounded by settlements as far as the eye could see. It was difficult to distinguish when the termite hills infiltrated the cattle camp and when the camp intruded on to the landscape. Any distinction between the settlement and the bush was further blurred by the death of cattle. Cattle corpses lay just inside the camp as well as just beyond it. Carrion birds hovered in the air, swooping suddenly on the carcasses, or fluttering down to perch, hunched, on top of termite hills. At a distance these large birds even looked like sitting persons. These sights must be common during any year of widespread livestock death, such as the year *puc* carried off the Bar Gaawar cattle. I was forcibly reminded of Deng Laka on his own mound, not just because of the visual images around me, but because of the images

[29] Evans-Pritchard (1935: 61; 1940*a*: 186; 1956: 306).

evoked by the family's account of their father's appearance in the bush surrounded by divinities dancing up and down the mounds, playing with snail shells as if they were cattle at the foot of termite hills which were their byres. In a human settlement which was not quite settled I could imagine Deng Laka surrounded by people who were not people, playing with cattle which were not cattle, beneath cattle byres which were not cattle byres.

Deng Laka later claimed that he was seized by the divinity JOK as well as DIU, and that JOK came to him when he was sitting on the termite hill. This divinity, he stated, gave him cattle when he was playing in the bush with snail shells. As a prophet Deng Laka often poured milk over termite hills, in much the same way a man of cattle pours milk over the first cattle-peg of a new cattle camp, saying that his divinity was the termite hill, and that the hill was JOK's hill.[30] There are a number of associations between termite mounds and divinities and powers.[31] In the light of our earlier discussion about the division between divinity here below and divinity up above it is significant that Deng Laka, when he implored Divinity to take him, sat on a mound already associated with the activity of divinity on earth, while he raised his hands to divinity above, pleading for a portion of the strength associated with the transcendent Divinity.

After Deng Laka's appeal to Divinity to take him it needed the efforts and sacrifices of his age-mates and contemporaries to bring him out of the world of spirits, to provide the social recognition for his divinity so that it could be brought into society and become active there. When Wuor Yiec told the people of Dol section that Deng Laka was 'dying without a disease', he organized the prayer-meeting and sacrifice of oxen specifically so that Deng Laka's divinity could manifest itself and 'seize' him. Evans-Pritchard's assertion that a prophet need only announce his possession and the name of his divinity to begin to build up a personal following is, perhaps, too simple.[32] Social recognition of the seizure must come first. It is only then that a prophet is able to develop the connection between himself, his divinity, and his community.

The annunciation of DIU's name was followed by proofs of the divinity's strengths. Deng Laka predicted the appearance of a buffalo herd and blessed the spears used to hunt it. He did the same with an elephant herd and decorated his shrine at Ajuong with tusks taken from the slaughtered beasts.[33] In this way Deng Laka apparently provided food to replace lost cattle and built both his reputation and his following. He made no secret of his desire eventually to raid Nuaar Mer. For his part, Nuaar Mer kept himself informed of Deng Laka's activities.

[30] Matit Kal and Cuol Macar G9.3.

[31] Crazzolara (1953: 134); Lienhardt (1961: 109); Evans-Pritchard (1936*b*: 232).

[32] Evans-Pritchard (1956: 177).

[33] Ruot Yuot G2.1, Nyanyai Kal G8, Ruot Diu G10.1.

Kulang Majok's maternal grandmother was a father's brother's daughter to Nuaar Mer. She sometimes travelled from her village of Pagil, near Ajuong, to Mogogh. Nuaar Mer quizzed her about Deng Laka.

> My grandmother said he would ask, 'Nyawang.' 'Yes.' 'That flat-headed Dinka, is he there in Juong with a divinity?' She said, 'Yes. He says, "I will go to Mogogh. I will go capture Nuaar Mer."' 'Ah! Will that flat-headed Dinka really come to get me?' and he uttered the name of his ox. Then at night he would go to people [*naath*] and tell them, 'You Dinka, take these big oxen and kill and eat them, or that Dinka boy will come and take them all.' They disagreed, saying, 'Let us not waste cattle.'[34]

It may have been as many as three years before Deng Laka finally organized a raid against Nuaar Mer. By that time the flood of 1878 had overwhelmed the Zeraf Valley and a large portion of Nuaar Mer's followers had been killed with Deng Cier at the Battle of Pading. The flood did not begin to recede until well into the dry season. The ground was still wet when Deng Laka set off from Ajuong in March or April 1879. He announced, 'Now I will go to the man who took my people to the Turuk.' Deng had received encouragement from Nyang Macar (ox-name Cotrial), who defected from Mogogh bringing some of Nuaar's own cattle. 'Take these cattle, son of divinity [*gat kuoth*]', he is remembered as saying. 'If you have a divinity, there are many cattle with Nuaar in Mogogh. You can go and bring them if you really have strength.' But others were sceptical. Biem Jiak denounced Deng as a liar and predicted his defeat.[35]

The force Deng gathered was small. Many were still in awe of Nuaar Mer's reputation, and even some of those who set off with Deng deserted him before long. Those who remained were drawn from Nuer groups throughout the Zeraf Valley: Bar from Ajuong and Rupciengdol, Radh, Lak, Thiang, and relatives of persons captured by Nuaar Mer. Even some of the Bar were related to Nuaar; Majok Juc's father's sister was married to Nuaar's brother. Opposing them in Nuaar's camp were Nuaar's own section, individual Gaawar, Lak, and Thiang, and a number of Luac, Thoi, Rut, and Duor Dinka.[36] The forces Deng and Nuaar each rallied thus did not follow the structural lines of cleavage between segments of Gaawar society.

Deng Laka nearly repeated Biem Jiak's fiasco when on the way to Mogogh he danced in front of his group and announced, 'I have no divinity.' There were grumblings as the men asked themselves why they had been led out into the bush like that, but in the afternoon Deng began dancing again and said, 'We must reach the place. You will be up to your necks in butter tomorrow.'[37]

[34] Kulang Majok EHJP-8.

[35] Kulang Majok: G6.2, EHJP-7, EHJP-8, Ruot Yuot G2.1, Ruot Diu G10.1, Matit Kal G9.1. Coriat (1923) claimed this force was raised mainly through Nyang Macar.

[36] Ruot Yuot G2.1, Ruot Diu G10.1, Kulang Majok EHJP-8.

[37] Ruot Diu G10.1.

Thus reassured, the band spent the night in the bush and reached Mogogh in the evening of the next day. Their arrival seems to have been anticipated. They found the Dinka there dancing and singing, preparing for battle. Both forces spent the night camped near each other, but some of Nuaar Mer's followers persuaded him to decamp to Cieth, a few miles north-east of Mogogh.[38]

A dramatic account of the battle is given by Ruot Diu, Deng Laka's son. When the two sides advanced towards each other, Deng's force was led by his own white-headed black bull, whose right horn had been specially sharpened.

> The dogs of Nuaar's camp came out and fought the dogs who came along with DIU. Nuaar's dogs were defeated; my father stabbed the bull; they fought. Those people of Nuaar's camp, when they stabbed a man they only grazed him. But when one of Nuaar's men was stabbed, he was pierced right through. The people were killed—the people who sold his [DIU's] mother and two sisters. He conquered the man who took his mother and two sisters, the big chief of the Turuk.[39]

The dogs' combat is remembered by others, but Majok Juc's recollections, as retold by his son, give no prominence to supernatural intervention through Deng Laka's sacrifice. Quite simply, 'We went through the Dinka, we killed the Dinka. They were killed, they were killed.'[40]

Nuaar Mer was tracked down. His leopard-skins were removed from him before he was killed with a barbless fishing-spear at Deng Laka's order (another echo of Aiwel).[41] Then, according to some, Deng Laka's *dayiemni* cut open Nuaar's body and ate his liver, raw. Perhaps it was 'to acquire something of his remarkable personality and success', as one scholar has suggested, but it was an act repugnant to Nuer.[42] The eating of such unnatural food is regarded as dangerous. The *dayiemni* fell down as if dead. They were revived by Deng Laka who beat them with a sheepskin (*dual*). 'DIU used to call eating *cuit*. "This *cuit* will kill you. Why should you eat the flesh of a man?" DIU asked.'[43] Though the story was later told with some reservation, the remembered words have a ring of authenticity. 'Cuet' is Dinka for eating meat, for devouring food like a wild animal.[44] Deng Laka was born a Dinka, he grew up in a family which included his Dinka mother and older sisters; and Gaawar society contained many such Dinka. It is yet more evidence of how little distance then separated Nuer from Dinka.

Deng Laka's return to Ajuong was triumphal. He distributed cattle among

[38] Kulang Majok EHJP-8.
[39] Ruot Diu G10.1.
[40] Ruot Yuot G2.1, Kulang Majok EHJP-8.
[41] Ruot Diu G10.1, Kulang Majok EHJP-8.
[42] Ruot Yuot G2.1, Ruot Diu G10.1; P. P. Howell, 'The Defence of Duk Faweil', PPH MSS.
[43] Ruot Yuot G2.1.
[44] Nebel (1979: 21, 133).

his followers and brought more back to Ajuong. 'All the people became rich with cattle then.' They abandoned their fish soup for milk; young men now married wives; Deng Laka opened the initiation of a new age-set. Something of the sheer joy he felt at the reversal of his misfortunes can be seen in his actions when the new age-set emerged from seclusion. As they held their first dance Deng Laka joined in, waving his curved, copper-bound baton (*dang*) above their heads. From then on, he told them, they would be known as 'Dang'; and it is as 'Dang' that this age-set is still known among the Bar Gaawar.[45] But amid the joyous clamour of a triumph there is always a ruthless note of subjugation. All of Nuaar Mer's symbols of power were appropriated. Deng Laka destroyed Nuaar's homestead shrine at Mogogh. Nyang Macar, the same man who had brought Nuaar's cattle to Deng, placed Nuaar's leopard-skins in Deng's hands. Deng took them as his own, sacrificed cattle at Ajuong, and sprinkled their blood on the skins. Nuaar's special cattle were reserved for Deng's own divinities: some were dedicated to DIU, and the *kuaijok* cattle were renamed *kuaidiu*, though they remained dedicated to JOK. To announce his ascendancy Deng Laka even sent a cow to Biem Jiak with the message that he had killed the man Biem had feared. It was as complete a victory as the Gaawar could hope to see.[46]

DIU and the social order

The standard ethnographic description of the confrontation between Nuaar Mer and Deng Laka draws more on Evans-Pritchard's theory of structural opposition than on historical facts. Deng Laka, it is asserted, 'rallied the forces of Bar around him, inflicted a crushing defeat on the treacherous Nuer sections who had assisted [the Dervishes], and killed Nuar Mer'.[47] We have seen from the composition of the forces which fought at Mogogh that this is far too simplified an analysis. No sections rallied as groups to Nuaar Mer, and Deng Laka led a heterogeneous war-band. British administrators later interpreted Deng Laka's seizure of Nuaar's leopard-skins as an attempt to bolster his spurious claim to spiritual and political authority. They saw it as an instance of prophets undermining the legitimate authority of the chiefs, a misappropriation of 'the functions and insignia of more reputable experts'.[48] 'The Gawaar are emphatic', claimed one former district commissioner, 'that Deng Likea used his spiritual powers as a *guk* [prophet] to help him become *ruic* [leader] of the Gawaar.'[49] Deng Laka's action has been cited as a classic case of the opposition between the prophets and 'priests' among the Nuer.

45 Ruot Diu EHJP-5, Kulang Majok EHJP-8.

46 Malual Mayom G1, Matit Kal G9.1, Kulang Majok EHJP-8.

47 Howell (1954: 31). See Lewis (1951: 81).

48 Howell (1954: 216).

49 Lewis (1951: 82).

Gaawar society had been rent by feuds of Nuaar Mer's making. The Radh, in particular, were divided against themselves. In the end they rejected Nuaar and abandoned him to his fate. But if Deng's victory was to be anything more than a cattle raid, he had to try to re-establish peace among the Gaawar. The exchange of his own serval cat skin for Nuaar's leopard-skins was symbolic of more than just the victor's spoils. It was the first step in the reconstruction of internal peace.

The Gaawar had no earth-masters when they moved east and created their own. The principle of heredity subsequently transferred to others the possibility of acting as masters, but this was not by itself sufficient to establish legitimacy among the Gaawar. Nuaar Mer's eligibility to be a master came through his adoptive father, but he was chosen to be a master because, as a Dinka, it was assumed he would maintain neutrality better than his father's real sons. His failure meant that others had to assume a master's duties. None of Nuaar's own descendants functioned as masters among the Gaawar, though curiously enough one did among the Thoi Dinka.[50] Eventually younger members of the Teny section of the Kerpeil lineage emerged as masters, such as Mayom Kuài and Dag Mer, one of Mer Teny's natural sons,[51] but they were junior to Deng Laka. The Teny section still suffered from association with Nuaar's feuds, and no one from within that line could then restore equilibrium.

Deng Laka could. Having been adopted into the dominant lineage of the Bar, and claiming descent from a Dinka 'earth-master' lineage, he followed essentially the same route of acceptance by the Gaawar as had Nuaar Mer.[52] But his divinity transcended Gaawar social divisions, being a divinity not only for all Gaawar and all Nuer, but for Dinka, too. By combining leopard-skins and divinity he strengthened the earth-master's peacemaking role. Having taken Nuaar's skins as his own, Deng Laka performed the duties of a master in individual cases of homicide and presided over sacrifices after mediating the end to feuds between families.[53] This use of the leopard-skin was important to Deng throughout his career. Towards the end of his life he was worried when other Gaawar thought his favourite son Macar was an unsuitable potential earth-master, and he seems to have taken their advice to bequeath his skins to a more acceptable younger son.[54] The mediation of disputes, even when involving only a few persons, was, of course, essential in checking internal tensions before they developed into major feuds. For more serious threats to internal peace Deng Laka went beyond the leopard-skin to the divinity DIU. In order to allow the Radh and Bar to live in peace following the death of Nuaar Mer, without the endless negotiations individual homicide

[50] Struvé (1908*a*: 8); untitled, undated page on 'Nuar Mer', New Fangak ZVD 1.A.6.
[51] Coriat (1923); Lewis (1951: 81).
[52] Nyanyai Kal G8, Kulang Majok G6.2.
[53] Kulang Majok G6.2. [54] Matit Kal G9.1.

claims would entail, Deng held a peacemaking ceremony on the common boundary of the two sections. He cut down a large tree on the border and told the Radh and Bar each to go in peace;[55] an act reminiscent of the splitting of a sacrificial animal at incest-cleansing rites, and also echoing those myths in which the ancestors formally separate related sections. It explicitly recognized a social breach between the sections, but established a *modus vivendi* which allowed them to coexist.

Coexistence was difficult for the Gaawar sections, even without Nuaar Mer's legacy. The last two decades of the nineteenth century saw constant fluctuations in the river level. The Gaawar remember this as a time when their houses were demolished and their cattle killed by floods. Deng Laka was washed out of Ajuong and went to live at Kuerjak in Rupciengdol. Floods came to Kuerjak, and he moved to Wulnyang on the edge of Rupciengdol. He was flooded out of there and went east to Padicier, but found that place too muddy. It was not just floods which sped him on his way. When the banks of the Bahr el-Zeraf overflowed the relatively high land of Rupciengdol came under pressure as more people moved there. When Rupciengdol itself was flooded in the mid-1890s there was scarcely enough land even for the people of Dol section, not to mention the newcomers. There were fights between Jamogh and Dol and some men were killed. At Kuerjak, where Deng built a shrine, the Dol showed him little respect. One time, while his people were praying at the shrine and Deng was sitting, smoking his pipe, on top of a nearby termite hill, someone came up behind him and knocked him off the mound, breaking his pipe. The family recall this as the reason why Deng Laka left Kuerjak, but outside the family it is recalled that Dol outnumbered Jamogh and forced them to leave.[56]

During the rainy season the cattle, mired in the mud of Padicier, were afflicted by *tuok*, a disease attacking the hooves of cattle exposed to mud and water, making them rot off. It was then that Deng Laka learned of the availability of the Duk ridge.

A Dinka man named Deng Tap said to DIU, 'If you go to my grandfather's country, which is called Duk . . . if you go there, you could stay for the rest of your life. It has good soil.' Deng said, 'Do you know it?' and Deng Tap said, 'I know it.' 'Will you go if I give you people to go with you?' He said, 'I can take them.' He told [his son] Macar, 'Go with this Dinka to show you the place and see it with your own eyes.' The people left Padicier and spent the night on the way. The next day they reached Duk, they reached Dor, which is now called Dor Macar. They put soil in a gourd and left . . . They put the soil before DIU. [Deng Tap] said, 'This is the earth I was telling you about.'[57]

[55] Ruot Yuot G2.1.

[56] Kulang Majok G6.2, Mar Kutien G5, Malual Mayom G1, Ruot Diu G10.1, Matit Kal G9.1.

[57] Kulang Majok G6.2.

Deng Laka went with his family and a few followers and built seven byres at Dor. Others came after him. Deng had only recently established himself at Dor by the time the first British officers visited the Bahr el-Zeraf in 1898 and 1899. His dry season cattle camps were still at Ajuong and Pacier, but Pacier was subject to untimely flooding as late as 1903.[58]

The story of Deng's move to the Duk ridge illustrates the precariousness of the prophet's position. In the pattern of Nilotic migration familiar elsewhere, newcomers to an area were forced to settle on the most vulnerable land and were the first to move off when conditions became untenable. In time, after several moves, Deng established the first settlement on a part of the Duk ridge abandoned by the Dinka, and became himself the focus of a new settlement.

Deng Laka had a small family circle in those early days and, as a Dinka refugee, his kin-ties with the Gaawar were shallow. Nuaar Mer's experience showed how readily the Gaawar could abandon an adopted Dinka. Deng Laka overcame this vulnerability by marrying a large number of women, not to himself, but to all the divinities he co-opted and claimed as his own. He married wives to the divinities of the sleeping-mat (KAL), blood (RIEM), the mosquito, the vulture, 'fortune' (BANG), as well as to numerous other divinities, such as JOK. The full number of his wives may never be recalled. Certainly those outside the family do not know the exact number, and his children have difficulty remembering all of their mothers. Two of his descendants together could positively account for forty-eight wives, but there were at least fifty, and the final number may have been closer to sixty. Of those wives whose sections could be recalled, at least twenty-nine were Gaawar. Another twelve came from other Nuer sections (seven from the Western Nuer, two Lou, two Lak, and one Jikany), and only six or eight were Dinka, mainly southern Dinka, but including Ngok and Rut. Of the Gaawar wives over half were Radh, and of those the largest representation came from the Teny section, with nine wives in all.[59]

Deng acquired these wives in a variety of ways. The family of Nuaar Mer feared for their safety when he was killed and offered Deng one of Nuaar's sisters as a wife to protect themselves. Others, it is claimed by Deng's family, gave him wives out of gratitude for overthrowing Nuaar Mer. Still others wanted to derive some benefit from Deng's divinity. When people really knew that his divinity was like that of Ngundeng, one of his sons declared, they decided to give him wives.[60] But Deng did not wait for these offers. He manipulated his growing control over the age-set system to direct wives his way. Some time after Deng initiated the Dang age-set, before many of the young men were able to marry, he hung up one of his leopard-skins and

[58] Sparkes (1899: 9); Wilson (1903*b*: 8; 1903*c*: 3); Johnson (1992*b*).

[59] Matit Kal and Cuol Macar G9.2 and G9.3.

[60] Ruot Diu G10.1.

announced that no man should marry until his eldest son Gai was initiated and married. This prohibition applied to all Gaawar and it is said that it was observed for fear of Deng Laka's divinity. True, some girls got pregnant and gave birth, but no one married. How long the ban lasted is unclear, but it was not lifted until the initiation of the Lier age-set, in about 1896. Those who felt they had the most to lose by it were the young women of marriageable age. 'The girls were waiting. A mature girl, who is very big, if she felt ready, she would go to DIU's homestead and become his wife.'[61] It was in this way that, in the early days of his prophetic career, Deng Laka encouraged girls to become, not *his* wives, but the wives of his divinities.

It is unclear how much bridewealth Deng Laka paid for his wives after he became a prophet, or whether he paid any at all. His children were unanimous in declaring that he did pay bridewealth, even for his Dinka wives. The children could not be his if he did not. But another source was equally emphatic that, at least for the wives married during the prohibition on marriage, no cattle were paid. It is possible that Deng made only token payments. His daughter Nyanyai Kal remembered, 'he used to be given a wife freely—such as my mother—and later he pays only one cow to go and multiply itself. If someone from the girl's family wants to marry, then he comes and is given a cow.'[62]

To attempt to corner the market in marriageable girls is to court resentment, as Dr Francis Deng has described so well in the biography of his father Deng Majok, who in a later generation married some 200 wives.[63] Inevitably, Deng Laka found himself in competition with some of his followers. Kulang Majok's father, one of Deng Laka's own *dayiemni*, competed with Deng for one of his female singers.

> Father had a divinity, too . . . Mother was a singer. [DIU] said, 'That girl, who is going to marry Majok Juc, I will marry her myself. She will come and sing by the hearth, here.' My mother said, 'I don't want *you*, Deng Laka. I'm going to marry Majok Juc.' Mother was taken by Majok, and Deng relented.[64]

This does not mean that no girls were married to Deng against their will, but there were limits to Deng's coercive power. Some girls, at least, were not intimidated by the potential wrath of DIU, and Deng did have to defer to the prior claims of lesser men. His followers did not approach him in fear and trembling.

Deng avoided widespread resentment over his marriages by not keeping all his wives to himself. He announced that DIU forbade him to sleep with his

[61] Kulang Majok EHJP-8.

[62] Matit Kal and Cuol Macar G9.2, Ruot Diu G10.1, Kulang Majok EHJP-8 and G6.2 (he stated in the latter that Deng Laka did pay cattle for some wives), Nyanyai Kal G8.

[63] Deng (1986: chs. 12 and 13).

[64] Kulang Majok EHJP-8.

new wives. There are some recalled lapses to this rule, Dual Diu's mother among them, but most of his fifty or so wives were free to choose their own consorts. There is general agreement, even outside the family, that his wives made their own choices, but the range of choice seems to have been restricted largely to the immediate circle of Deng's own village. Deng is also said to have given wives to certain favoured men. Of the list of twenty-nine consorts which I was given by two of Deng Laka's descendants, most (sixteen in all) came from Deng's own Jamogh section, and a further five from other Bar sections. Very few Radh were included. Only three were recalled, but two of these were from Nuaar Mer's own Teny section, one being Dag Mer, Nuaar's younger brother. There were few other Nuer groups named, and none from the Dinka. The list is surely incomplete, and one son has claimed that a number of Dinka and other Nuer did settle in Deng Laka's village as consorts to his wives.[65] Unlike the case of Deng Majok, Deng Laka seems to have avoided quarrels with his sons over his many marriages. As an old man Deng Laka allowed his elder sons—such as Macar, Wol, Tung, and even one of Tung's friends—to take his younger wives as their consorts. Young men thus were not necessarily excluded by Deng's habit of marriage.

There were further rewards for the begetters of children on behalf of Deng's numerous divinities. One of his sons, so begotten, explained: 'A man who begot a child with one of DIU's wives, he took him and gave him cattle to marry a wife for himself. . . . All the people, our fathers, married women. Yes, our village became big. There were our fathers—but DIU was our real father—and our mothers' brothers were here, too.[66] Deng Laka's village grew with his family. By marrying so many wives from throughout Gaawar society, he placed a number of potentially hostile sections, such as Teny, in a mother's brother–sister's son relationship to his own children. It would have been difficult to raise a large enough force to attack a village so full of sisters' sons. Overlapping this were the ties created through his wives' consorts. Deng was the acknowledged *pater* of his children, but they had their own bonds of affection with their *genitors*, again, further entrenching DIU's family in Gaawar society. In turn, Deng Laka enabled these consorts to marry and have children in their own names; thus increasing the circle of families who, if not entirely dependent on him, were certainly obliged to him in some way. Deng's village at Dor, on the opposite end of the Duk ridge from Mogogh, was socially the opposite of Nuaar's old village as well. The people at Dor were not loosely bound by expediency to its central figure, whatever motives of self-interest originally brought them. The prophet may have been the spiritual and political focus of attention for his community, but in a social sense the women and their children were the real focus of the village. They were the ties which

[65] Matit Kal and Cuol Macar G9.2 and G9.3, Ruot Diu G10.1.
[66] Ruot Diu G10.1.

connected the rest of Gaawar society to Deng. Those who came to Dor because of the prophet, stayed because of the prophet's wives and children.

Perhaps the most important aspect of Gaawar social life that Deng Laka regulated was the marking of the age-sets. He marked and named three in his lifetime: Dang (1879), Lier (*c.*1896), and Yaal (*c.*1900). As initiations are not normally undertaken during periods of war, flood, famine, or epidemic, initiations at this time were not regular. Dang were marked after the battle of Mogogh, after which floods and the war known as Mut Roal (*c.*1896) intervened before Lier were marked. More floods and the disastrous Mut Mandong against the Twic followed Lier. The Yaal began to be marked before the final move to Dor was completed, but some seem to have been marked as late as 1905, the year the first British official visited Deng Laka.[67] Despite being marked so close to Lier, Yaal was the largest set Deng Laka initiated.

Those closest to him insist that Deng opened the initiation periods and named the age-sets for all Gaawar, Lak, and Thiang. He gave Dang their name from his own dance stick. Similarly, when Lier were marked he joined their first dance after initiation and sprinkled them with milk from a gourd ladle, *liera*, telling them that their name would be 'Lier'. The evidence from other age-set lists indicate that Deng Laka's influence over the naming of sets was not as great as is now asserted. While the names Dang and Lier were recorded by Coriat at Ayod in 1923 (and by me in the 1970s and 1980s), they do not appear in the age-set list for the Lak compiled by Evans-Pritchard in the 1930s, nor in the age-set names used by the Lak, Thiang, and Gaawar on the Zeraf Island published by Howell in the 1940s. The only age-set name which is common to all Gaawar is Yaal, a name not used by the Lak or Thiang. This indicates that Deng Laka's influence over the Gaawar had grown sufficiently by the end of the century for the Radh Gaawar living on the Zeraf Island to follow his lead. But the Lak and Thiang still went their own way in age-set initiations.[68]

The prophet and the spiritual order

When Deng Laka began establishing himself as a prophet among the Gaawar he had to compete with both the Dinka shrine at Luang Deng and the Lou prophet Ngundeng. Luang Deng was the oldest religious centre in the region and had set the idiom for spiritual manifestations. Deng Laka had to fit his own divinity and prophetic behaviour into the shrine's established range of spiritual activity. He was too close to compete with or co-opt the language of the shrine, as Ngundeng ultimately did with references to his own Mound as

[67] Ruot Rom, Cuol Macar, Gai Thung EHJP-4, Ruot Diu EHJP-5, Kulang Majok EHJP-8.
[68] Ruot Diu EHJP-5; Coriat (1923); Evans-Pritchard (1956: 251); Howell (1948*a*: 178).

the *luak* of DENG. Yet Ngundeng's earlier dealings with the shrine did create a precedent by which the shrine-master could recognize the autonomy of new Nuer divinities. Just as the major prophets later declared and imposed their seniority on those lesser prophets whom they recognized as *dayiemni*, so Deng Aguer, shrine-master of Luang Deng, asserted his seniority in granting the major prophets the recognition they sought. To this day, Deng Laka's family accept the spiritual primacy of Luang Deng. They may assert that DIU is DENG, but they also claim that all divinities first came from Luang Deng. Deng Laka sang hymns to DENG LUAK along with hymns to DIU and other divinities. To the DENG LUAK of Luang Deng is attributed the power of fertility regarding women and cultivation, and the control of rain and floods; powers also claimed by DIU, but clearly on licence, as it were, from Luang Deng.[69]

There was a practical alliance between the people of the shrine and Deng Laka. Deng married one or two wives from the Rut Dinka there. He also took cattle to the shrine to be sacrificed before going south to raid the Dinka and brought more as gifts if his raids were successful. This regular presentation of cattle in sacrifice and as gifts is remembered equally by the descendants of the prophet and the caretaker. The family of the caretaker attribute Deng Laka's success and survival to the sacrifices he made at their shrine. 'If he did not go to the byre', explained Wan Deng, son of Deng Aguer, 'he would not get cattle.'[70] The work of the Rut shrine-master and the Gaawar prophet may have been as one, he declared, but it was Deng Laka who was in most need of help:

> When the Gaawar came to this side they found Deng Aguer at Luang Deng. He gave them places to settle. DIU came and settled in Duk. DIU's work was one with Deng Aguer. Deng Aguer said to Deng Laka, 'If you want anything, you come to me and bring cattle. I will bless the cattle, kill them, and then you can go to fight the Nyareweng and Dinka of Duk.'[71]

The balance struck between Deng Laka and Deng Aguer was mutually beneficial. Deng Laka, as a Gaawar war leader, had a power which the small Rut community around the shrine lacked, but the shrine had the prestige Deng Laka craved. Deng Aguer secured his community's survival, as his father had done before him, by accepting, and even insisting on, Gaawar gifts and sacrifices. In return he legitimized the Gaawar appropriation of Dinka territory. In the shrine's view of things the new homes of the Gaawar were given by the divinity DENG, not taken by right of conquest. Yet the Rut did more than acquiesce in a new order imposed by the Gaawar; they actively

[69] Matit Kal and Cuol Macar G9.2 and G9.3, Pöc Nap Laka G11, Cuol Dual G13.1 and G13.2.
[70] Wan Deng D1.
[71] Wan Deng EHJP-9.

participated in its creation. Many Rut married into Gaawar families, and during the Gaawar occupation of the Duk ridge it was not unusual for Rut Dinka to join the Gaawar in their battles against the Ghol, Nyareweng, and Twic Dinka.[72]

In the early years of Deng Laka's prophetic career there was little regular contact between the Gaawar and Lou. There was no idiom of agnatic relationship (*buth*) between the two groups, much less intermarriage than now, and the Lou grazed and watered their cattle along the Sobat or at inland pools such as Paddoi and Muot Dit, while the Gaawar remained close to the Zeraf River. It was only later, when the Bar moved east to occupy the Duk ridge and some Lou settled close to the Nyareweng and Ghol that contact increased and tensions began to develop. The two prophets remained wary of each other; often critical or suspicious of the other's action, but never actively hostile.[73]

Deng Laka courted Ngundeng's recognition just as he had that of Luang Deng. It is now widely believed that not only did Ngundeng recognize Deng Laka as a prophet, but he foretold his coming. The stories told by the Lou about the Battle of Pading often contain this prediction. One of Ngundeng's songs is also interpreted by Gaawar as announcing DIU's appearance. Some Gaawar now claim that Deng Laka merely contributed to the work that Ngundeng began, adding his own hymns to Ngundeng's, and praising Ngundeng, too. One of DIU's hymns composed by Deng Laka's son Lel Nyang explicitly states, 'My father is Ngundeng.'[74]

It was when Deng Laka tried to present himself as Ngundeng's equal that the Lou prophet became scornful. After Ngundeng had built his Mound, but while Deng Laka was still in Kuerjak, Deng sent a deputation of eight of his own *dayiemni* to Ngundeng. Majok Juc was one of them. Deng gave them a cattle-rope and said, 'Take this to Deng Kur in Lou. Tell him that it was given to you by DIU.' According to Kulang Majok there was no other message.

My father said, 'We left, eight of us, the *dayiemni*. When we reached Ngundeng's Mound, Ngundeng himself was not there. He was tending cattle and in the evening he came back with the cattle. He found us sitting near the fence around the hut, we divinities.' He greeted the seven divinities but when he came to my father's divinity he shook his head. 'Are you the one who was given Dol Pajok?' Dol Pajok had been killed in Gaawar, and Ngundeng knew about it through his divinity. He asked, 'Are you the one?' 'I am', my father replied. 'I know', said Ngundeng.

Dol Pajok was a rogue red bull which had lurked in the woods between Lou and Gaawar country. It attacked a pregnant woman who went into labour and

72 Wan Deng D1, Cuol Dual G13.2.

73 Evans-Pritchard (1934: 31; 1940*a*: 62); Garang Ngundeng L1.2; *SIR* 99 (Oct. 1902), 1 exaggerates the rivalry between the two prophets.

74 Kulang Majok G6.6, Cuol Dual G13.1.

bore twins. Ngundeng is supposed to have foretold this in a song, saying, 'People of the earth, I send you this message that Dol Geng will bear twins | all the ghosts look from the bush to the fence' (*Jipinyɛ nopa yɛ dol gɛŋ be cuɛk | rɛk jɔɔk dial bi guic dɔr*). Majok Juc then killed it.

[My father continued] 'He shook his head. In the evening he killed an ox for us. When we were about to leave we told him, "Bong's son, this cattle-rope is given to you by Diu." He looked at it and said, "Diu is Diu!" He said, "He gave me this rope so that I would go raiding. I cannot go raiding. I am not a *dayiem*. Tell him Ngundeng said that he could not go capturing people. When I left our byre, Divinity did not tell me to capture people." He gave us an axe and a head-ring. "Take them to Diu", he said. We came and found Diu in his byre at Kuerjak. We put the axe and the head-ring before him. When Diu saw them he said, "Bong's son is Bong's son!" He said, "Pulwar will be finished. We will not remain in these places. We will be given a flood. The axe means that we will use it to cut these doleibs to have canoes with which to fish. The head-ring means that we will wander throughout our lives, carrying children [in baskets] on our heads."'[75]

Here Ngundeng expresses annoyance at Deng Laka's presumption in summoning him so ('I am not a *dayiem*'), and at the same time reiterates his own principle against raiding. He then demonstrates his superiority to Deng Laka by predicting—therefore helping to bring about—the floods which drove Deng from his home. It is such stories, originally told by persons who claimed to be eyewitnesses, which help to explain the strength of Ngundeng's reputation beyond the Lou. Deng Laka, though rebuffed, is not entirely humiliated. Only he understood the meaning of Ngundeng's reply; thus displaying his own insight.

This one-upmanship between the prophets is repeated in other stories. When Deng Laka's wife Nyawang Lul could have no children, Deng sent her to Ngundeng, who blessed her and told her she would give birth to a very talkative son. Nyawang returned home, chose a new consort, and gave birth to Matit Kal. But in return, Matit claimed when he told this story of his birth, Deng Laka foretold that Ngundeng's wife Nyaduong would have a child named Guek, thus taking the credit for Guek's birth.[76]

Deng Laka got the better of Ngundeng in a story widely told among the Lou. It is alleged that Deng Laka sent a man with witchcraft (*peth*—the evil eye) to kill Ngundeng. 'Of course, prophets in those days feuded with each other,' one of Ngundeng's grandsons explained.[77] Deng Laka is thought to have become envious of Ngundeng's numerous followers and brought over a man with witchcraft from Dor, in the Nyuong Nuer territory, west of the river. Ngundeng knew that the man had witchcraft but welcomed him anyway and killed an ox for him.

[75] Kulang Majok G6.2.
[76] Matit Kal and Cuol Macar G9.2 and G9.3.
[77] Gatkek Bol Ngundeng L7.2.

The man with witchcraft stayed two days and on the third day he returned to DIU. He told DIU that he could not do it because Ngundeng's body was filled by his divinity. DIU told him that his spinal cord was empty, so he told the man with witchcraft to bring out the spine. The man with witchcraft returned to Ngundeng and did it. People heard of Ngundeng's death but could not believe it. The following year DIU died.[78]

According to the Lou, Ngundeng foretold his own death resulting from this plot. This story was known in Evans-Pritchard's day, though apparently there were some Lou even then willing to defend Deng Laka from the accusation. The story was never told to me by Gaawar, though some must know it.[79] In his songs Ngundeng could be critical of Deng Laka and of the Gaawar for disputing his word. The Gaawar stories of relations between the two prophets suggests Deng Laka's need to measure himself against Ngundeng's reputation. Now the Gaawar insist that Ngundeng and Deng Laka did essentially the same thing, but this implies equality. The Lou story denies equal status to Deng Laka, because he has to rely on a man with witchcraft. It is uncharacteristic of all else we know of Deng Laka's career, but it is evidence of the rivalry which is implicit between prophets, especially prophets of nearly equal standing.

Ngundeng was able to build shrines at Juet and Keij. Deng Laka, we have seen, built a shrine at Ajuong and had to abandon it for one at Kuerjak, and had to leave that too. Unlike Ngundeng, he was unable to rely on a fixed centre and had mobility thrust upon him. He surrounded himself, instead, with the 'walking shrines' of cattle dedicated to divinities. When Deng looted Nuaar's herd at Mogogh he reserved all the hornless (*cot*), brown (*lieth*), white-headed (*kuei*), and brown-and-white-headed (*kueilieth*) coloured cattle for his divinities. An animal of one of these colours became known as a cow of JOK (*yang joak*).[80] Each time Deng Laka announced that he had acquired a new divinity he married a wife to it and dedicated cattle to it. Beasts so dedicated seem to have been cows as well as oxen, and they could not be sacrificed or given away. This was, perhaps, one way of maintaining the integrity of the herd, but it also meant that Deng Laka's 'shrines' travelled with him. The cattle-pegs of the dedicated cattle became the focus of worship for the individual divinity. Certain divinities had their own cattle-pegs placed in Deng Laka's homesteads.

Deng Laka did not fall ill each time he was 'seized' by a new divinity. Rather, it seems truer to say that he 'seized' them by announcing their existence and adding them to his collection. In addition to the invented

78 Nyang Kuac Agok L15.3.

79 Evans-Pritchard (1935: 60), where Deng Laka himself is accused of having *peth*. Other Lou versions are essentially the same as cited above: Gatkek Bol Ngundeng L7.2, Cuol Thijoak L10.1, Bil Peat L12.1.

80 Matit Kal G9.1.

divinities already mentioned a number of better-known divinities appeared among his cattle. There was CAK ('creator'), TENY (known in the west), and JOK. There were variations on DENG, referred to by praise-names or attributes different from those employed at Luang Deng and Ngundeng's Mound. Deng Laka included a NYADENG (daughter of DENG); cattle colours such as KUAIJOK DENG, YIAN DENG, MAYAN DENG, and DENG MAROAL; names of places or persons such as DENG PALOI, and DENG GIL.[81] If Deng Laka's Dinka father was named Gil, as stated by one of his sons, then this last divinity was Deng Laka's original name.

The divinities' attributes were explained in a number of ways. CAK was prayed to for the birth of children; NYANWIR paralysed people's legs and killed them; PAJOK returned stolen property and killed thieves.[82] But while these divinities can be described as very minor in relation to DIU, some had an independent existence before Deng Laka claimed them. CAK is known as creator of the universe or creator of people[83] and is sufficiently important to merit its own permanent cattle-peg at the graves of both Deng Laka and his son Dual Diu. PAJOK is one of the divinities represented at Luang Deng, but it is also the name of a type of magic associated with the red cobra. Gaawar seem to be genuinely uncertain whether it is a divinity or a Power. Deng Laka claimed to have found it in the bush near his homestead on the Duk ridge and took it as a personal divinity for the protection of his family. It is from his family that we learn that when Deng adopted it he claimed that he had been born after his mother had passed menopause, but that his PAJOK would protect his descendants from being born in similar circumstances.[84] There are two points to note about Deng Laka and PAJOK. First, he seems to have adopted PAJOK's association with Luang Deng as a divinity rather than an earthly Power. Second, with the belated (and somewhat unconvincing) story of his birth he seems to have attributed to himself one of the more striking features of the biographies of Aiwel and Ngundeng. The Aiwel imagery has not stuck; most Gaawar are unaware of any peculiar manner of his birth.

Deng Laka was known for his war songs and may have been content to borrow hymns from Luang Deng and Ngundeng. One of his few religious songs is a catalogue of lesser divinities. The imagery of sky-divinities is maintained throughout, and one verse declares, 'Big divinities, small divinities, fell to earth with all their children.' It extols Divinity and individual divinities for their 'good character' (*ciaŋ mi gɔa*) and their 'rich breath' or life (*bany yiɛ*). It urges all the 'the children of the ants' to walk together, and tells them to pray for a good world. It is also critical of some divinities (BANG, KAL, and YUOL are named) for disputing with DIU out of jealousy (perhaps a reference to insubordination among the *dayiemni*). It also celebrates victory over the 'red

[81] Ruot Yuot G2.1, Matit Kal G9.1.
[82] Cuol Dual G13.2.
[83] Evans-Pritchard (1956: 4–5).
[84] Matit Kal G9.1.

oxen', the 'Turuk'. But most of all it exhorts people to believe in Diu, the lesser divinities, and the prophet of Diu. Some of the central verses state:[85]

Wee cuk ee palɛ hɔu gɔa	Go ants, pray for a good world
Jitikni palɛ hɔu gɔa	People of the beads [*dayiemni*], pray for a good world
Palɛ hɔudan no	Pray for our world
Palɛ yɔŋ	Pray for the mad man [the prophet]
Cuarɛ kuuth yap	Do not deny divinities
Cuarɛ kuuth yap te ki mi latkɛ ka thuok	Do not deny divinities who tell the truth
ɛni mi walɛ mi nin ŋu ca ku nɛn hal	I have seen where someone thrashes about
Wut mi lat guai ca ku nɛn hal	I have seen where someone speaks nonsense
Wut mi kuin piy ca ku nɛn hal	I have seen where someone eats the porridge stick
Ci Jok ben cɛ rɔdɛ mat gan	Jok came down himself to collect children
Palɛ gɔa ci tuolɛ ben piny	Pray well, his smoke came to earth
Ci Doaŋ ben cɛ rɔdɛ mat dɛni	Doang came herself to collect hers,
Palɛ gɔa ci tuolɛ ben piny	Pray well, her smoke came to earth
Nɛna Nyadeŋ ci lɛ nyur luak	I see Nyadeng who sits in the byre
Ram mi gor yaŋ a wa ka Nyadeŋ	Someone who wants a cow, let him go to Nyadeng
Ditdial wea ka Mayian Deŋ	All you old men, go to Mayan Deng
Garri Jok Kuoth ci du gɔa	Your father, Jok divinity, is good
Ditdial wea ka Mayian Deŋ	All you old men, go to Mayan Deng

The final verses say:

Tut cuea mi cokɛ ŋuan	Big four-legged one
luɛk kɛ wɛŋ wɛŋni kɛ yɔŋ yɔŋni	shake the cattle, shake the madmen
Kɛ yie lo guari	It is a soul father,
ci cuk kɛ liŋ yiee	may the ants hear the souls
Kɛ yie Nyabit	It is a soul, Nyabit,
ci cuk kɛ liŋ yiee	may the ants hear the souls
Kɛ yie Yian Deŋ	It is a soul, Yian Deng,
ci cuk kɛ liŋ yiee	may the ants hear the souls
Gati cuk guandan a bee na	Children of the ant, our father is coming
Magurgur bani ben lar mɛ	Come, Magurgur and say:
Ram cii kɔn gai ci gai bi nyok nen	Someone who was poor, will not see poverty again
Ram cii kɔn tek ci tek bi nyok nen	Someone who was rich, will not see wealth again
Mi cii gai du dit bɛi ci can bi nyok nen	And he who was the poorest will not see poverty again

[85] Nyanyai Kal G8.

Dor mi wa kuom ba kuom ni dei laŋda kɛ nuani	Any village where I am, the growling of my copper hammer will be heard afar
Cieŋ mi wɛa jal ba jali dei laŋ kɛ nuani	Any territory where I walk, the copper hammer will walk far
Wei maroal coala kɛ mari ci waŋ	The camp of the red oxen will be struck and burned
Ca ku thui larɛ KERJOK ci gieree	I told you that KERJOK shouted and shook
ku marpiny, mar kendial hɔaa	the land, struck the whole world
DEŊ MAROAL ber mar kendial	Come, DENG MAROAL, and strike them all
Mar thil DIU	Strike all but DIU
Wei wa tuol bi we tom	The camp is burning
Ci we riɛk yith jiath	I heard the throbbing
Ca we hɔɔ	and I said yes
Ca we gir ci Kuoth gir	There was shouting, Divinity shouted
Ci we jiath ca we hɔɔ	I heard the sound and I said yes

The images and assertions are similar to other religious songs of other prophets. Deng Laka's baton (referred to here as a 'copper hammer') is introduced as a symbol of his strength. The power of the divinities to confer wealth or poverty, to reverse good fortune, is explicitly stated, perhaps with the fate of Nuaar Mer in mind. The incident of Deng Laka's seizure is recalled with divinity sounding and shaking the world, and Deng answering 'Yes!' Finally there is the assertion of DIU's primacy over all other divinities. But for all this, with the enumeration of so many divinities the effect is diffuse. There is nothing comparable to those verses in Ngundeng's songs such as 'I, DENG, am the prophet of the universe', or 'It is Ngundeng Bong who will gather together the earth and clouds.' Where Ngundeng and his Mound presented a spiritual monopoly, Deng Laka and his cattle appear more as a spiritual collective.

Deng Laka exerted some control on the appearance of divinities in others, in the *dayiemni* he collected around him. As Kulang Majok, whose father was a *dayiem*, explained, the *dayiemni* were not always seized by illness. Rather, they would think they had a divinity because they found they suddenly could do strange things. They would go to Deng Laka to find out the name of their divinity, and he would tell them. Sometimes he would tell them they had no divinity. He could even, apparently, reassign divinities. Biem Jiak's MAYAN YIETH TUT was assigned to a *dayiem*. The *dayiemni* had very little power of their own, having only 'small divinities'. They would help Deng Laka perform some of his rites (Majok Juc carried the firesticks Deng Laka always used when having a fire lit). Occasionally they would help persons when the prophet was not available. Since the *dayiemni* were among Deng Laka's most constant companions, they were among those who became consorts to his wives.[86]

Deng Laka's most important and influential *dayiem* was a woman, Nyacan Ruea. Nyacan was an unmarried girl at the time Deng Laka was seized by DIU. After DIU's annunciation, but before the attack on Nuaar Mer, Nyacan was suddenly seized by a divinity and ran, shouting, from her parents' home to Deng Laka's. Deng took her in and subsequently announced that she was seized by the 'mother of DIU', or MANDIU. Nyacan became known as MANDIU, or sometimes as MANDONG (grandmother), or simply DOANG. She became DIU's mother rather than Deng Laka's wife. She helped in raids on the Dinka, performing ceremonies which 'tied up' the Dinka when the Nuer went cattle rustling at night. She was finally killed by the Twic in the war which bears her name, Mut Mandong.[87]

Deng Laka's spiritual strength was demonstrated in hunting and in war but it was also manifest in a number of beneficent acts. He prayed for (and provided) rain, blessed crops, gave forewarning of plagues and raids, and sacrificed cattle against epidemics. He blessed the sick and barren women. He also tried to suppress harmful spiritual activity. According to one member of his family DIU completely suppressed witchcraft (*peth*) during Deng Laka's lifetime, the Lou story of Ngundeng's death to the contrary. Deng also took active steps against the use of magic, both *wal* and *kulangni*. Through his divinity he revealed the names of magicians, cured those afflicted by magic, and is even said to have beaten persons owning fetishes until the Power in the fetish left them. In one large ceremony he gathered people together along with a number of fetish gourds. With the aid of his young uninitiated son Dual Diu, he broke the gourds and threw them in the river, washing them all away. It is mainly his family who assure us of the overall efficacy of Deng Laka's suppression of magic. We know from the experiences of the Lou under Ngundeng and the Western Nuer under their prophets (to be described in Chapter 7) that the suppression of magic is never complete, but whenever a prophet is active public anxiety about the threat of magic is reduced. Among the Gaawar, as among other Nuer, there is the general impression that people were safer from the individual use of magic in the prophet's day than they are now.[88]

Relations with the Dinka and foreign governments

We already have examples of the important influence of Dinka living among the Gaawar, and the ambivalent attitude of Gaawar to them. Both Nuaar Mer

[86] Kulang Majok G6.2 and G6.6.

[87] Ruot Yuot G2.1 and G2.2, Kulang Majok G6.2. *Mandong* was killed before 1905; therefore she cannot be 'the woman behind the throne' mentioned in government reports.

[88] Ruot Yuot G2.1, Kulang Majok G6.2, Cuol Dual G13.2, Matit Kal and Cuol Macar G9.3, Ruot Diu G10.2.

and Deng Laka were Dinka. In their mutual abuse each would insult the other by calling him a 'Dinka' (*jaang*). Yet, it was a Dinka who led Deng Laka and the Jamogh to safer homes on the Duk ridge, and the Dinka shrine at Luang Deng actively aided Deng Laka in many of his raids. In fact, Deng Laka had a complicated set of relations with the Dinka living in and around the Gaawar which subsequently affected his initial contact with incoming foreign governments.

There was a history of conflict between the Gaawar and Dinka, dating from the Nuer intrusion into the Zeraf Valley, but Deng Laka's hostility to his Dinka neighbours was selective. He tended to ignore the Dinka living along the Khors Fulluth and Atar, in so far as he could, and directed his raids against those living to the south: the Nyareweng, the Ghol, and the Twic. Despite this, all Dinka were affected by the aftermath of the battles of Pading and Mogogh. Those Luac, Thoi, and Rut living with Nuaar Mer fled north from Mogogh after Deng Laka's victory. A number of other groups of Rut, Ric, and Thoi went to the Khor Fulluth. The Luac and Angai split, some to go north to the Fulluth, others going south to the Twic.[89] A few may have been particular targets because of having been allied with the slavers on the Zeraf, but on the whole Deng Laka does not seem to have pursued any systematic feud with them. Kulang Majok claims that Deng Laka fought the Luac merely because he found them together with Nuaar Mer in Mogogh. When they fled to the Fulluth Deng declared that he would not raid them, since he came from that area. There was no sustained fighting after that.[90] This claim is supported by other sources.

In a meeting in 1905 between Deng Laka, H. H. Wilson, and Dinka chiefs, Deng Laka asserted that he had offered the Dinka the option to continue living in their old homes after their defeat, but that they had refused and moved off.[91] This is partially confirmed by Lueth Ayong, son of the Duor chief Ayong Yor. According to the Gaawar Ayong was associated with the slavers on the Zeraf, but he was not an ally of Nuaar Mer's.[92] After the Battle of Mogogh Ayong searched for a suitable site along the Khor Fulluth and, finding one, returned to bring the Duor and Luac there. They were not harried by the Nuer as they moved; their greatest tribulation on the way seems to have been floods.[93] The Duor and Luac thus left because of Deng Laka, but they were not driven out by him. They had lost their cattle in his attack on Nuaar Mer, and this was a source of friction for many years to come, but there is little evidence of systematic harassment.

The steady Gaawar encroachment during the 1880s and 1890s on lands

[89] 'Return of Prominent Persons in Upper Nile—1909', SRO UNP unnumbered; 'Dinka-Shen Rut', W.M., 15 May 1931, SRO BD 66.B.1/3; 'Notes on the Luac Court held at Wungnab 26th to 30 Dec '39', New Fangak ZD 1.A.6; Struvé (1909).

[90] Kulang Majok EHJP-7.

[91] Wilson (1905).

[92] Ruot Rom, Cuol Macar, Gai Thung EHJP-4, Kulang Majok EHJP-7.

[93] Lueth Ayong Yor EHJP-2.

formerly occupied by the Dinka may have been one factor in the northward migration of some groups. Yet, by the beginning of the twentieth century it was clear that many Dinka had not chosen to leave when the Gaawar came, and many original inhabitants were still to be found in Gaawar territory.[94] The Gaawar and Dinka also claim that most of the territory the Gaawar occupied had already been abandoned by the Dinka. Some time before the Battle of Mogogh the Luac living south of Luang Deng initiated a war with the Rut. The Rut allied with the Cuor Dinka living around Duk Fadiat and chased the Luac away after great slaughter of men, women, and children. The Luac, Duor, and Nyareweng living along the Duk ridge were also harried by the slavers from their *zaribà* at Ayod, and left to seek refuge with other Dinka.[95] This helps to explain why the Dinka living along the northern watercourses felt dispossessed of their land by the Gaawar, but while there was resentment, there was no feud.

The Gaawar need for cattle and dry season pastures, and their move to the Duk ridge, brought them into direct conflict with the Dinka living further south. It was this competition which fuelled their feud with the Ghol, Nyareweng, and Twic. The floods of the 1880s and 1890s meant that the preferred riverain pastures along the Zeraf and at Ajuong and Pacier remained under water late into the dry season, or even for the entire dry season. Alternate pastures could be found only by moving south along the network of watercourses into Nyareweng territory. The Gaawar need for this territory increased after they occupied the southern part of the Duk ridge, since even in good years they had to cross this region to bring their cattle to the river.

In addition to the need for pastures there was the desire for cattle. The southern Dinka had not suffered from Nuer and slave-raids to the same degree as those further north, and they still had large herds. Certainly it is the desire for cattle which the Gaawar remember as being the main reason for their wars against the Nyareweng. Whatever his spiritual attraction, Deng Laka could maintain a following only by providing cattle. Gifts from followers and supplicants increased his herd, but it was increased far more by capturing Dinka cattle. Deng Laka's herd grew so large that it frequently produced more milk than his large family and followers together could consume, and it had to be poured away. Many a poor family is said to have grown rich through Deng's generosity in cattle. Many a young man, both Nuer and Dinka, came to Deng for marriage cattle. A reputation for success in raids helped to raise large forces when going into battle. Not only would other Nuer, such as the Lak, join him, but so would Dinka, such as the Rut.[96]

94 Wilson (1905); G. B. Wauhope to governor UNP, 22 Apr. 1913, NRO UNP 1/12/101.

95 Ruot Diu EHJP-5, Makor Guot D3.

96 Nyanyai Kal G8, Ruot Diu EHJP-5, Kulang Majok G6.2, Wan Deng D1, Mar Kutien G5; 'Return of Prominent Persons in Upper Nile—1909', SRO UNP unnumbered; J. L. F. Tweedie to governor UNP, 8 Jan. 1914, SRO UNP SCR 14.1.

The first Dinka groups to suffer from these raids were those living on the frontier with the Gaawar. The Ghol, Angai, and Cuor were broken up and fled to the Nyareweng. The Nyareweng, too, were attacked and retreated further south, many seeking refuge with the Twic. The Twic prospered from this influx. Not only did their own numbers swell, but they extracted cattle from the refugees as the price for the protection they were able to provide. Five clans of the Twic united to defend themselves against all aggressors—the Murle, the Nuer, and the Mahdists. When Deng Laka raised a force of Gaawar and Lak to raid the Ghol, Nyareweng, and Twic at a place called Juac sometime in the 1890s, he was decisively repulsed.[97]

Deng Laka's raids south increased towards the turn of the century, especially after he settled at Dor.[98] His three largest battles against the southern Dinka were the Battle of the Foreigners (Mut Roal), the Battle at Juac (Mut Juaca), and the Battle of the Grandmother (Mut Mandong). We are not yet certain of the dates, but they all appear to have taken place during the 1890s, and the last, and largest, battle probably around 1900. The Battle of the Foreigners was the first time that the Dinka enlisted outside help to meet Deng Laka's threat. Deng Laka had moved to Kuerjak and, having lost cattle in a recent epidemic, raided the Dinka to the south of him. The Twic went to Bor seeking the aid of the local Mahdist garrison. The man who was the main intermediary with the *ansar* was Mabur Ajuot, an Angai Dinka who had been a slave in Omdurman but had managed to return to his home territory. Once back among his own people he learned that the Nuer had come and occupied their land. It was this land he wanted back. The Mahdist commander at Bor was Arabi Dafaʿallah. He had his own difficulties at this time, cut off as he was from Omdurman by *sudd* blocks on the Bahr el-Jebel. Early in 1896 he sent a large force of riflemen north with Mabur as his guide, hoping to reopen the old road that led from the Duk ridge to the Sobat. The force that Deng Laka raised to meet the 'Turuk' coming from Bor consisted of Radh and Bar Gaawar as well as Rut Dinka. According to the Gaawar the Dinka and 'Turuk' failed to co-ordinate their advance and were defeated individually, the 'Turuk' first and then the Dinka. When attacking the 'Turuk' Deng Laka sacrificed an ox and then pointed his baton. There was thunder in the sky, and when the 'Turuk' tried to shoot their guns, the guns broke. The Nuer rushed on the 'Turuk' and killed them; Deng Laka himself speared their leader. The Gaawar gathered up the rifles and ammunition of the enemy, taking some to Luang Deng as an offering to DENG, and using the metal bits of others to dig post holes for huts. This battle ended Arabi Dafaʿallah's hope of re-establishing contact overland with the main Mahdist forces

[97] J. W. G. Wyld, 'Report and Notes on Bor-Duk District', Nov. 1930, NRO Civsec 57/2/8; Stevenson-Hamilton (1920: 390–1); Ruot Diu EHJP-5.

[98] Stevenson-Hamilton (1920: 390); Kulang Majok G6.2.

in Fashoda and Omdurman. It also ended any possible alliance between the Mahdists and the Dinka. After that the Mahdist force concentrated at Rajaf, but was expelled from there by the Belgians in 1897. Retreating to Bor they were increasingly isolated and beleaguered, raiding the Dinka for food, and frequently meeting defeat at their hands.[99]

The battle, though decisive, was not as great a blow to the Dinka as to the Mahdists. Though it was fought in Twic country, the main Dinka ally was Mabur Ajuot, who was a refugee Angai. The victory may have encouraged Deng Laka to overstretch himself. Many of his war songs, which may date from this period, celebrate his defeat of the *marol* and the Dinka, sometimes invoking other divinities in the fight, as in 'I am DENG LUAK, my strength increases and will remain here | I beat the Dinka in a fight | I, TENY, am good | I strike the Dinka [*mar jaang*] and they flee.' He threatened the Dinka with further violence, declaring, 'You Dinka . . . you of Malual's camp, you have exceeded your strength | We will fight the Dinka in a fierce fight.' But his next invasion of the Dinka was met and repulsed by a combined force of Twic, Nyareweng, Ghol, and even Cic and Bor.[100]

The last battle in Deng Laka's career occurred just as the Mahdist state came to an end and the British were entering the White Nile and Sobat valleys. Deng Laka had recently come to Dor when Nyacan Ruea (MANDONG) proposed and helped organize a raid to the south, directed against the Twic and the Cuor from Duk Fadiat living among the Twic. It was a hard-fought battle, with many Twic, Cuor, and Gaawar dying. The Twic caught Nyacan. It is said that spears could not pierce her, so they killed her by hammering a cattle-peg up her vagina. The Gaawar broke and began to flee, but they were rallied by Deng Laka himself, and the Twic were driven back with heavy losses. One of those to suffer was Mabur Ajuot, who was driven from his home at Awoi in 1900, which may be taken as the latest probable date for this battle.[101]

This was the last big battle the Gaawar fought with the Dinka in the nineteenth century. If it was a victory for Deng Laka, as the Gaawar claim, it was a Pyrrhic victory. It marked the extent of Gaawar military strength; for the Twic contained the Gaawar advance on their own, without any aid from external armies. By 1903, when Deng Laka was reported to be threatening another raid on the Twic, the new Anglo-Egyptian government had enough knowledge of the relative strengths of the two peoples to assume that Deng would 'get a salutary lesson' if he did attack. The Ghol and Nyareweng living between the Gaawar and the Twic were fragmented and dispersed by the

[99] Johnson (1993*b*). Also Collins (1962: 133–4, 158, 165–8); Stevenson-Hamilton (1920: 391).

[100] Song: Cuol Dual G13.1. Ruot Diu EHJP-5.

[101] Cuol Macar EHJP-4, Ruot Diu EHJP-5, Cuol Cany Bul, Pok Tuot, Jal Wang EHJP-6, Kulang Majok EHJP-7 and EHJP-8; Liddell (1904: 6).

Gaawar battles, and continued to be harassed by smaller raiding parties, but the Gaawar could push no further.[102]

Given Deng Laka's history of war with the southern Dinka it is not surprising that they refused to accept his divinity. There is a story of the founding of the Twic chiefly lineage of Pan Bior in Kongor which has now been expanded to accommodate Deng Laka. The ancestor of Pan Bior is said to have been a 'lion', or 'man-eater' (the equivalent to the Nuer *let*), living among the Ngok Dinka. The Ngok finally despaired of his predatory ways and rose up and killed him, but he was able to send his wives and children away before he died. One came to Kongor with her son Aguer Ayuel, who became the founder of Pan Bior. It is now said that another of the wives of the 'lion' was the mother of Deng Laka, and she brought Deng to Gaawar. Therefore, Deng Laka, though exceptional like the Twic chiefs, is the son of a 'lion'.[103]

When the Anglo-Egyptian government occupied Fashoda and set up posts along the Sobat and the upper Bahr el-Jebel, eventually reoccupying Bor, its first information about Deng Laka came from Ayong Yor, Aguer Wiu, and Mabur Ajuot. They were no more flattering of Deng Laka than they were of Ngundeng. The government learned little to the prophet's credit, and was further disturbed by his religious, as opposed to hereditary, position, likening him to a 'fakir' or a 'Mahdi', usurping the legitimate position of the Teny family. The only thing which told in his favour was that he was supposed to be at enmity with Ngundeng.[104]

The new government's presence immediately affected Nuer–Dinka relations. Ayong Yor, Aguer Wiu, and Mabur Ajuot saw an alliance with the government as a way by which the land now occupied by the Gaawar could be returned to them. They were all involved in the 1902 expedition against Ngundeng, and they continued to agitate against the Gaawar. Ayong even halted the slow process of intermarriage between his Luac and the Gaawar. He forbade the Luac to marry their daughters to the Gaawar and forced those who had to return the marriage cattle. The Dinka living along the Khor Fulluth began visiting their relatives living among the Gaawar for the purpose of rustling Gaawar cattle, and the Gaawar assumed that this was done under the new government's protection.[105]

With the government's realization of the folly of Blewitt's attack on Ngundeng came a reassessment of its policy towards the Khor Fulluth Dinka and the Nuer. By 1902 friends of Deng Laka, and even putative emissaries from him, began arriving in Fashoda bearing a friendlier portrait of Deng

[102] Wilson (1903*c*: 7). For devastation of country see Liddell (1904) and Wilson (1905). The desolation was due in part to floods, but the appearance was accentuated by the fact that the villages were deserted for the dry season. For raiding, Marol Ater EHJP-10.

[103] Makor Guot D3, Bior Aguer Bior EHJP-12.

[104] Sparkes (1899: 10); Blewitt (1902); Wilson (1902: 3; 1903*b*: 9; 1903*c*: 6–7).

[105] Lueth Ayong Yor EHJP-2; Wilson (1905).

Laka than that presented by the Dinka. One, Thoi Thiep, a Thiang Nuer chief, was so friendly to the government that his word was generally accepted. Another, Cany Reth, a former warrant officer (*buluk amin*) in the old Egyptian army and a nephew of Nuaar Mer, was less reliable an informant. He exaggerated Deng Laka's hostility towards the Dinka and Ngundeng, but even he reassured officials somewhat before he began to manœuvre for government support for himself against Deng Laka. But by this time other intermediaries began to appear. The Gaawar had suffered more than the Lou from slave-raids, and during the first decade of this century a number of Gaawar ex-slaves returned home. Many were old soliders and continued to act as official or unofficial interpreters. One such man, Nuang Lol ('Farag Osman'), helped the government construct its telegraph line to Bor. His sister was married to Deng Laka. The government soon came to know more about the Gaawar from Nuer sources than it had known about the Lou. Deng Laka learned that he could present his case through known and trusted intermediaries.[106]

Deng Laka was still reluctant to meet directly with government officials, but a meeting finally was arranged with H. H. Wilson, the senior inspector of the province, in March 1905. It got off to a bad start. Wilson stood on his precarious dignity, sending a message to Deng Laka that he was a *bint* (Ar.—girl) if he did not come in person. It is unlikely that his insults and threats were even conveyed in full. When the meeting did come off, it went entirely in Deng Laka's favour. He explained his version of the events of the last quarter of a century, 'which the Dinka Sheikhs, confronted by him, were unable to deny'. In telling his story Deng Laka presented himself as the moral ally of the government against those Dinka who were currently collaborating with it, claiming to have avenged the death of the previous government's agent Yuot Nyakong. Having gained the government's sympathy on this point, he then explained that the Dinka were keeping up 'a kind of guerrilla warfare' against him, which he assumed was done with the government's approval.[107] The government not only had to deny this, it had to prove the opposite.

In return for his assurances that he would not take matters into his own hands and raid the Dinka, the government for its part promised Deng Laka to keep them under control. It reiterated this promise in a second meeting in 1907 when Governor Matthews himself and Inspector K. C. P. Struvé travelled to meet the prophet. Deng Laka cemented this friendship by promising to give the government the left tusk of every elephant killed.[108] The outcome of these visits was that the government ceased to believe Dinka

[106] *SIR* 99 (Oct. 1902), 1, 3; 106 (May 1903), 3; 159 (Oct. 1907), 2; Liddell (1904: 5); Wilson (1903*c*: 6; 1905); Matit Kal G9.1, on Nuang Lol.

[107] Wilson (1905).

[108] Matthews (1907); Ruot Diu EHJP-5. The tribute agreement is confirmed in *SIR* 143 (June 1906), 2.

FIG. 5. Matit Kal at Deng Laka's grave, Dor, 1976 (the ship's bell was given to Dual Diu by an official of the Sudan Railways and Steamers)

stories of Deng Laka's hostility and were favourably disposed towards the Gaawar in future Gaawar–Dinka disputes.

Deng Laka died during the rains of 1907, in about August, only a few months after meeting the governor (Fig. 5). He outlived Ngundeng by one year and was looking forward to a period of unrivalled influence among the Nuer, hoping, even, that the government would recognize him as 'paramount' of all the Nuer.[109] What he envisaged by this we do not know, for this ambition is not mentioned by any of his living relatives. He had proved his reasonableness in his dealings with the government, despite affecting the mannerisms of a 'kujur'. He accepted the government's presence and strength as a fact of life but put his own case before it with great persuasiveness. At the time of his death the government was convinced of his personal goodwill.

Deng Laka's life at first sight appears to confirm the ethnographic stereotype of the Nuer prophet. He has been presented as the focus of Gaawar unity against the Dinka, the slavers, and the government; yet this is only partially true. He did raid the southern Dinka until they blunted his advance, but he did not raid the northern Dinka. He did defeat the Mahdists, but only when they intervened in a war between the Dinka and the Gaawar. He did not extend this hostility to the Anglo-Egyptian government, despite

[109] *SIR* 143 (June 1906), 2; 159 (Oct. 1907), 2; Matthews (1907).

their alliance with the Dinka. Rather, as his son and successor Dual Diu was to do more than a dozen years later, he adopted a pragmatic approach in dealing with this new force and tried to reach an accommodation with its representatives.

Deng Laka's career cannot be explained by reference to a succession of external threats. We have to examine his response to the internal conditions of Gaawar society. From the first we can see that he was concerned with the Gaawar moral community. He had a personal reason to hate Nuaar Mer, but in overthrowing Nuaar he was overthrowing someone widely perceived as a violent and unjust leader. The prophet thus made his stand by confronting tyranny and the misuse of power. His actions subsequent to the Battle of Mogogh demonstrate that he attempted—perhaps with less success than his partisans allow—to re-establish a moral equilibrium within Gaawar society. His attempt to bring peace to the Radh and Bar, to mediate disputes, to suppress witchcraft and magic, were all part of the effort to reconstruct the moral community of the Gaawar. We have seen some of the reasons why he may have been less successful in this than Ngundeng: Nuaar Mer's feuds ran too deep, the environment fostered competition both internally and externally. It was only later in this century that his sons—including Dual Diu—were able to build on the kinship ties he initiated to reduce tension between the Gaawar and the Dinka (see Chapter 6). The broader vision of Ngundeng's hymns seems to be missing with Deng Laka. Yet, that peace was important to him—peace for the Gaawar community—we cannot doubt.

5

Guek Ngundeng and the Minor Prophets: Divinity Dispersed

Ngundeng's family—the reappearance of Lou prophets—prophets and the contest for leadership—Guek and the 'Nuer Settlement'—aftermath

Ngundeng's family

Nuer country at the time of the death of Ngundeng and Deng Laka was still largely free from government interference. Large parts of the Nuer frontier were subjected to exploratory probing from outposts along the main rivers, but there was no sustained contact. The whole of the Western Nuer had been bypassed. The prophets there, as we shall see in Chapter 7, were locked in closer competition with each other than was the case in the east, and had not yet impinged on administrative consciousness. Among the Nuer of the frontier there was a hiatus between the death of the great prophets and the establishment of their successors. In the interval government influence became more pervasive and changed the political geography in which the prophets could operate. Dual Diu (Chapter 6) ultimately continued his father's diplomatic chess game with administrators in the 1920s. Among the Lou there was the inclination to follow Ngundeng's model of aloof detachment, but less chance of success.

Ngundeng left no direct successor when he died. By definition all of his *dayiemni* were motivated by lesser divinities, and these were in any case widely scattered throughout Lou and Jikany territories. At the time of Ngundeng's death his family's position as earth-masters was even being challenged by a second generation rival. Thie Ruea, son of the Dinka stranger Ruea Kerjiok whom the Ciec section had preferred to Ngundeng, was already feuding with the family of Ngundeng's ally Kuony Gol.[1] The feud revolved largely around Kuony's son's refusal to hand over Dinka refugees, as if they were slaves. By the time Ngundeng died this feud threatened to engulf his own family as well.[2] The threat came to nothing, partly because of O'Sullivan's timely arrival, but it illustrates how little of Ngundeng's sanctity lingered after his

[1] H. D. E. O'Sullivan, 'Lau Nuers', 14 Mar. 1906, NRO Dakhlia I 112/13/87. For Thie Ruea ('Thie Rue') see Evans-Pritchard (1935: 48).

[2] O'Sullivan, 'Lau Nuers'.

death. Thie Ruea's own meeting with O'Sullivan also marked the beginning of friendly contacts with the government which his son Guet Thie would later build on to his personal advantage.[3] The threats to Ngundeng's family and the divisions which were becoming all too evident among the Lou clearly could be overcome only by a strong reassertion of Divinity.

The major division between the Gun and Mor Lou was a product of their separate history as two groups and was maintained by their patterns of settlement and intermarriage with their neighbours. The Mor were close to the Jikany, and their settlement in the eastern half of Lou territory meant that they looked to the Sobat and Pibor rivers in their seasonal movements. They intermarried with the Anuak and Jikany, and their orientation remained an eastern one. The Gun, on the other hand, settled on the plain formerly occupied by the Dinka and looked to the western watercourses and even the Bahr el-Jebel in the dry season. When they married out of Lou society they usually married Dinka and Gaawar. A continuous southern movement along the watercourses and intermarriage with the Dinka encouraged the division of the Gun into two largely autonomous segments, the Gaadbal and the Rumjok. The Rumjok settled along the southern reaches of the Khor Fulluth and mingled inextricably with the Nyareweng and Padang Dinka. They became virtually a third primary section of the Lou.

These divisions were sometimes the result of amicable settlement, but a section's autonomy was just as often increased and maintained by feuds. Ngundeng's attempts to contain the hostility between Gun and Mor and Rumjok and Gaadbal have already been mentioned. After his death Gaadbal and Rumjok drifted further apart from each other, uniting only in common opposition to Mor during *kor luny yak* which occurred sometime between Ngundeng's death (1906) and the Anuak raids (1911). This war was described by Evans-Pritchard as 'one of the worst wars in Nuer history', in which 'men displayed unusual ferocity' and 'so many people were killed that the dead were left for the hyenas to eat'. The government was so remote from Nuer affairs that no hint of the war appears in any surviving contemporary document. It was not the only conflict to overwhelm the Lou. Late in 1911 several groups of Anuak, armed with rifles from Ethiopia, traversed and devastated Lou country. Lou disunity may have contributed to the success of these raids, and Lou unity, rent by *kor luny yak*, was loosely reassembled only in the face of this new threat.[4]

Ngundeng's Lou *dayiemni* played no sustained part in any of these events. Only one, Thijok Dul, seems to have attempted to maintain internal peace, with little success. Sometime in about 1912 he tried to stop a fight between

[3] Ibid. For continuing contacts: Matthews (1907); Woodward (1912: 253).

[4] Evans-Pritchard (1940*a*: 144). G. S. Symes, 'Note on the Arms Traffic', 28 Nov. 1911, SRO UNP SCR 5.5; Intelligence Dep., 'Summary of Information on the Anuak Country', 1 Feb. 1912, NRO Civsec 112/3/10.

his own and another Lou section and was himself wounded in the fray. The injury was not fatal, but it troubled him for the rest of his life, and his family tried to claim compensation for a delayed death (*thung nyindiet*) when he finally died in the mid-1920s.[5] The Lou prophets who subsequently became active between 1914 and 1920 each ultimately justified his position by reference to Ngundeng, but for several years the Lou lacked any clear prophetic direction. During that time prophets did flourish further afield, among the Jikany, but their influence was largely restricted to small groups along the Ethiopian border, and they did not add significantly to the prophetic idiom created by Ngundeng.[6] His prophecy was to be further developed mainly among the Lou.

The reappearance of Lou prophets

The Lou tend to see much of their recent history as a fulfilment of Ngundeng's prophecies. Thus the Anuak raids of 1911 were said to be compensation to War Nyigol, the Anuak blacksmith who fashioned Ngundeng's brass pipe. When War asked for payment, Ngundeng rubbed his mouth with butter, saying his reward was yet to come.[7] It came with a vengeance in 1911. Thus, too, the appearance and disappearance of new prophets are all linked to Ngundeng in various ways. Car Koryom, Pok Kerjiok, and Guek Ngundeng each asserted a link to Ngundeng or the divinity DENG. Opposition to these prophets also sometimes stemmed from earlier opposition to Ngundeng: Guek's main opponent was Thie Ruea's son Guet Thie.

Prophets first reappeared in the Rumjok area bordering the Gaawar Nuer and the Ghol and Nyareweng Dinka. This area was very mixed, with some Lou living close to the Gaawar, and others living in the same villages with Dinka. It was unadministered until 1909–11, when an attempt was made to define the boundary between the Gaawar, Lou, and Dinka, and to fix it with an administrative border between Upper Nile and Mongalla Provinces. This affected Lam Tutthiang, who had moved from the Sobat to live in Ghol Dinka country. Lam's move to the Dinka frontier inevitably brought him into contact with the Gaawar, his people sometimes quarrelling with the Gaawar and at other times collaborating with them in raiding the Dinka. Lam, an old enemy of Ngundeng's, had visited the province headquarters at Kodok as early as 1904 and had maintained friendly relations with the government ever since. He therefore accepted the government's order in 1909 to leave Ghol territory, but the move was difficult to enforce. Some of his people came into conflict with the police and attacked the outpost at Duk Fadiat in 1910. Others

[5] Johnson (1985*a*: 142).
[6] Johnson (1992*a*).
[7] Tut Jiak Gai L21.1.

resisted the eviction order and had to be prodded out of Mongalla Province by troops in 1911. Lam was himself arrested and transported to Kodok to encourage his people to move.[8]

The provincial border proved difficult to police and the tribal boundaries impossible to enforce. The Gaawar continued to encroach on Dinka territory to the south; the Lou and Dinka used the same and adjacent pastures; individuals from either side of the border settled wherever they liked, unmindful of how this upset tribute assessment and collection in the two provinces; provincial interference in cattle cases and cattle rustling only aggravated antagonisms as the Nuer came to identify Mongalla Province as the ally of the Dinka. After the 1911 Anuak raids, and partly in response to increased government tribute demands, some Lou sections began raiding the Nyareweng, Twic, and Bor Dinka, often raiding in parallel with the Gaawar or being joined by Dinka allies.[9] The border presented great potential for conflict: government against Nuer, Gaawar against Dinka, Gaawar against Lou, Lou against Dinka, and even Dinka against Dinka. There would appear to be much demand and great scope for a warrior-prophet, but the prophets who did emerge had to mediate a complex set of relations among and between the Lou, Gaawar, and Dinka. The two Rumjok prophets, though referring directly back to Ngundeng, offered different approaches to the situations which confronted them.

Car Koryom was a Maiker-Rumjok man of cattle and a nephew of Lam Tutthiang. He was a Dang-gonga and once visited Ngundeng to give him a white ox—the same colour as that which Ngundeng had earlier sacrificed for the birth of that age-set. When Car fell ill in about 1914 he announced that he was seized by the divinity DENG. He does not seem to have claimed that it was the DENG of Ngundeng; in fact his seizure is sometimes attributed to Deng Laka. Car's father Koryom Bidiet was a western Rengyan Nuer immigrant. Though settled among the Lou, he visited Deng Laka to ask for a gift for his children. Deng Laka gave him a spear for any one of his sons. Koryom gave the spear to Car because, though Car had sisters, he was the only son of his mother (a parallel with Aiwel, Ngundeng, and Deng Laka). After Car was later seized it was said that his divinity was a gift from DIU. Car was thus linked to the two most powerful prophets of the preceding generation, whose influence overlapped along this frontier area.[10]

Car had suffered as much as any Lou from the Anuak raids, losing seven of his half-brothers. He took part in fighting just like any other Nuer man, but

[8] Johnson (1982*a*: 194–2). *SIR* 114 (Jan. 1904), 2; 157 (Aug. 1907), 3; 165 (Apr. 1908), 3; 174 (Jan. 1909), 4: 202 (May 1911), 4; Struvé (1909); G. B. Wahab to governor UNP, 29 June 1910, SRO UNP GOV CORR 34 1910; O'Sullivan (1910: 407); Woodward (1911: 245–6).

[9] Johnson (1982*a*: 193–7).

[10] Gany Car L26, Gabrief Yoal Dok A4; Bacon (1917). This perhaps explains the story that Car's father was a Dinka who had first been seized by DENG (J. W. G. Wyld to governor UNP, 26 Apr. 1928, SRO UNP 66.E.4).

his seizure began to mark a change in his behaviour and also marked a change in relations between the Maiker and the Dinka. Ngundeng had already established the character of DENG as a divinity who disliked fighting. The event that appeared to prove Car's seizure by DENG occurred during the 1914 Lou invasion of Bor District, which Car joined as an ordinary warrior. On their way back from Bor the Lou were surrounded by the Twic and faced annihilation. Car plunged his spear in the ground, and by that gesture opened up a path of escape. After this people began to believe he had a divinity. After this, too, Car began to develop a reputation as a peacemaker, especially in relation to the neighbouring Dinka.[11]

Car had many contacts with the Dinka. He married a Nyareweng captive, paying ten head of cattle in bridewealth to her Dinka father. His sister married a Nyareweng man who sought refuge with Car from Gaawar raids. After being seized by DENG Car visited Luang Deng with offerings of cattle. A large number of Nyareweng lived at his village of Padiak; in 1918 it was estimated that almost all of his followers were Dinka. Unlike many other Lou chiefs of his day, he openly trusted the Nyareweng and did not allow small incidents of theft to disturb the general peace. He even intervened to prevent a fight between the Ghol and Nyareweng Dinka.[12]

Car was not alone in trying to maintain settled relations with the border Dinka. Two neighbouring Maiker chiefs, Bayak Bior and Nyok Biciuk, were also reported to have a majority of Dinka among their followers, and in 1919 Bayak was attacked by the Mor Lou after he refused to allow them to pass through his territory to raid the Dinka.[13] The Lou who lived intermingled and intermarried with the Nyareweng had few reasons to start a quarrel with the Dinka and many reasons to contain such quarrels if they did start. Car's introduction of the divinity DENG directly into this frontier area reinforced other efforts to maintain and extend peace.

The reappearance of DENG came at a time when Lou–Dinka relations were under strain. The Lou had lost large numbers of cattle, women, and children to the Anuak in 1911, and though there is no direct evidence that this stimulated raids against the Dinka to the south-west, it is known that for years (even decades) after the raids many Lou sections did rebuild their numbers through the absorption of Dinka incomers. The Gaaliek-Mor deliberately welcomed refugees from Bor district, but more forceful methods of assimilation were also tried. The large numbers of women and children that

[11] Gabriel Yoal Dok A4 and A5.

[12] Gany Car L26, Mier Deng Reng D2, Wan Deng D1; J. Stevenson-Hamilton to Godwin, 14 Apr. 1918, Malakal UNP SCR 14.A; Stevenson-Hamilton, Supplementary MPMIR, Mar. 1919, NRO Intel 2/48/408.

[13] J. Stevenson-Hamilton to Godwin, 14 Apr. 1918, Malakal UNP SCR 14.A; MPMIR May and July 1919, NRO Intel 2/48/408.

the Lou abducted from the Bor Dinka in 1914 indicate that wives and children were in demand.[14] But there were other strains. The Nuer who settled west of the Khor Fulluth before 1909 sometimes took their cattle to the Bahr el-Jebel during the dry season, but access to the riverain pastures was made difficult by the 1909–11 border settlement. The Lang region east and south-east of Khor Fulluth was a usually well-watered source of dry season pasture, but it was close to those pastures between Khors Kwanyor and Fulluth which the Dinka also used. Dry years and years of badly spaced rainfall could result in competition and confrontation. This seems to have happened in 1913, a year of low rainfall and near universal drought throughout the Sudan. More Lou than normal moved to the southern reaches of the Khor Fulluth as many avoided government tribute collection patrols along the Sobat. They grazed close to the Twic Dinka, who looted their cattle. When the Lou protested to the government the Twic were forced to return some cattle but were allowed to keep others in payment of outstanding bridewealth debts. This provoked the 1914 raids which went beyond the Twic to include the Bor Dinka, who were not party to the original dispute.[15]

If Car's seizure by DENG produced at least a partial conversion to non-violence, he did not influence all Rumjok. Those who lived away from the frontier stood to gain more than they lost by raiding the Dinka, and they found their champion in another prophet, Pok Kerjiok. Pok also traced his spiritual pedigree to Ngundeng, but his personal genealogy connected him with Deng Laka. He was closely involved with the Gaawar at different times of his career, and this influenced his attitude towards the Dinka.

Pok's grandfather, a Ngok Dinka named Dieu, shared a common ancestor with Deng Laka. Pok's father Kerjiok Dieu settled among the Nyajikany-Rumjok, and Pok lived in Muot Tot, some twenty-five miles east of the Gaawar and about forty miles north-east of Car Koryom's village of Padiak. He was thus close to the Gaawar but separated from the Dinka by the Maiker-Rumjok. Kerjiok Dieu had been one of Ngundeng's bards at the Mound. It is now said that Ngundeng bequeathed the divinity GÄR to Kerjiok's family, and there is a Ngundeng song announcing the appearance of GÄR, following the form used in songs announcing the divinities DIU and GÖT. Pok was seized by GÄR shortly after Car was seized by DENG. His seizure by a divinity was said to be proven when he located lost cattle and resurrected his son who had been burned to death in a brush fire. He shared with Ngundeng, then, the gift of life, and he demonstrated this in other ways,

[14] A figure of 421 women, 655 girls, and 352 boys was given (J. Stevenson-Hamilton, 'Notes on Patrol 33', 6 May 1917, NRO UNP 1/13/118). Just as bridewealth cattle were often included in numbers of those stolen, so women earlier married to Nuer might have been included in the total of those abducted.

[15] 'Report on Lau Patrol 1917', SRO UNP GO 15/10.

such as curing barren women and providing abundant harvests through his prayers. His reputation extended to the Gaawar.[16]

One of Pok's close companions was his father's brother's son Lam Liew Dieu. Liew Dieu had also been a singer for Ngundeng and a composer in his own right. Lam was still a boy when the Anuak raided and narrowly escaped capture. As a young man he earned a reputation both for singing and for bravery. He helped Pok organize all his raids and also led the singing at prayer-meetings. Because of his ancestral link with Deng Laka he also became a close friend of Dual Diu, who shared with him the Ngok Dinka clan-divinity WIU. Lam reinforced Pok's link with the Gaawar and was probably an intermediary between Pok and Dual. Lam also sang Ngundeng songs at Dual's prayer-meetings.[17]

In the late dry season of 1916 some Lou cattle were stolen by Bor Dinka. When the Lou went to retrieve their cattle they were arrested in Mongalla Province and their complaints were ignored. This was a period of extensive cattle rustling between the Gaawar and Dinka, and Dual Diu had come into conflict with the government (especially Mongalla Province) after raiding the Ghol and Nyareweng in 1914–15 (see Chapter 6). The Nuer thus already perceived the government as a Dinka ally. The Lou turned to Pok (the Nyajikany, too, had lost cattle to the rustlers), and he gave them inspiration for a retaliatory raid against the Bor late in May. Many other Nuer joined just to get cattle for themselves.[18]

The Lou were intercepted by a patrol of some sixteen soldiers of the IXth Sudanese battalion under a Sudanese captain, Saʿid Nur. Pok had some 3,000 men in his force, but the detachment probably encountered less than the full number. The Lou held back when confronted by the soldiers near Ajak, but Pok ordered the attack. The troops fired until their ammunition ran out and then fought with bayonets until they were all killed. As the Lou returned home they were harassed by the Twic Dinka, who recovered 1,000 head of cattle, but the Lou raiders still managed to retreat with between 2,000 and 3,000 cattle. This battle is known to the Lou as *kor rialbeagh*, the War of the Saddle-bill stork, after Saʿid Nur's ox-name. Rialbeagh was killed, they say, only because he sided with the Bor.[19]

The battle was unfortunate for the Lou in that the government was shocked out of its complacent assumption that its troops would prevail in any

[16] Stephen Ciec Lam, personal communication; C. R. K. Bacon, 'Patrol No. 71—Political Report', 19 June 1920, NRO UNP 1/13/117; 'Précis of Information Concerning Gwep [*sic*] of Dengkur, January 1921', NRO Dakhlia I 112/13/87.

[17] Stephen Ciec Lam L24.3 and L24.4.

[18] Garang Ngundeng L1.2, Tut Jiak Gai L21.1 and L21.2, Stephen Ciec Lam A5.

[19] OC Troops Bor to governor Mongalla, 2 June 1916, Mamur Kongor to governor Mongalla, 4 June 1916, 'Statement of Sheikh Ajak 6 June 1916', and 'List of Persons Killed', all in SRO UNP SCR 14; *SIR* 262 (May 1916), 4; 263 (June 1916), 3; 265 (Aug. 1916), 4; Bacon (1917); J. Stevenson-Hamilton, 'Notes on Patrol 33' for highest estimate of Bor losses; Tut Jiak Gai L21.2.

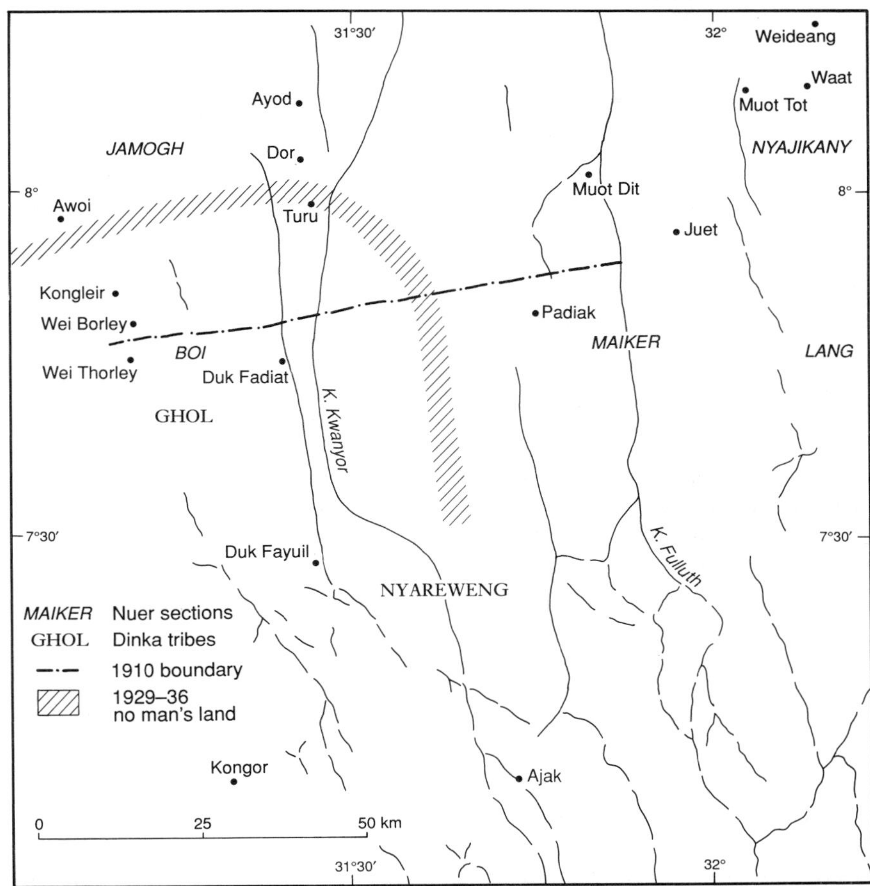

Map 5. The Nuer–Dinka border, 1910–1936

confrontation with the Nuer.[20] The government was obliged to retaliate with its own punitive campaign, aimed at all Lou and taking a perfunctory swipe at the Gaawar. The campaign was carefully planned, with two columns of troops converging in Lou territory, while a third patrolled the Gaawar border. The main body met 500 Nuer near Muot Tot on 18 March 1917. Pok advanced behind a black bull, but the bull was machine-gunned before Pok could sacrifice it, and many Lou, too, were killed before they scattered and fled. The rest of that dry season troops roamed the countryside seizing civilian

[20] R. C. R. Owen to the adjutant general and chief staff officer, 6 June 1916, SRO UNP SCR 14.

hostages and capturing some 4,000 head of cattle and 3,000 sheep and goats. In order to redeem their kinsfolk and retrieve part of their livestock the Lou had to hand in their rifles at either the old Sobat outpost of Abwong or the new administrative headquarters at Nyerol. Some who did come in early, such as Lam Tutthiang and Guet Thie (Thie Ruea's son), were appointed chiefs in the new administrative hierarchy which was set up after the campaign.[21]

Pok's role in the hostilities illustrates the range of spiritual activities a prophet could employ in war. Both Nuer and government sources agree that Pok was not the instigator of the 1916 raid against the Bor but became involved after being approached by the Lou. According to a contemporary report Pok was consulted and 'prophecied [*sic*] victory and success saying he could see blood, and it was the blood of enemies'. From then on he took a leading role in organizing the Lou for war, commanding the attack on the IXth Sudanese patrol, and advising against a second raid on the Dinka during the rains. When the governor of Upper Nile Province made a reconnaissance up Khor Nyanding on an armed steamer in October 1916, Pok perfomed a *muot* sacrifice against him, killing and partially burying a dog, a chicken, and a sheep. It was after this that Pok held a meeting of Gun and Mor leaders to decide their strategy in the imminent war.[22] Finally, at the battle of Muot Tot, Pok attempted to sacrifice a bull in the face of the enemy, as Ngundeng had done at Pading.

None of these were exceptional actions. The *muot* rite is frequently performed by an earth-master or other mantic person to defeat an enemy prior to battle. The Nuer, like all Nilotes, seek spiritual reinforcement before going to war. The Lou had two prophets whom they could approach, both of whom had established reputations for beneficent works. If Pok was not the initiator of hostilities, we must ask why his services, and not Car's, were sought in 1916.

Car was well known for praying for rain, and he was also known as the prophet of a divinity which disliked fighting. It is clear from contemporary sources that Car had no reputation as a raider. He had only a moderate herd of cattle, built up entirely from bridewealth payments and gifts from supplicants. Whether he was approached and refused or was never asked, Car and the Maiker kept out of the 1916 raid and avoided confrontation with the army in 1917. Pok's appeal before 1916 was limited to the Gun Lou; certainly the Mor did not come to him with their problems. But the story of Pok's resurrection of his son may be evidence of a flamboyant style of self-publicity which could have encouraged the Lou to seek his services. This is indicated in the contemporary report, but surely the most telling factor in his favour was

[21] 'Report Lau Patrol 1917', and C. C. Godwin, Nyerol, 23 Apr. 1917 and 25 Apr. 1917, all in SRO UNP 15.10; 'Monthly Report—Nyerol—May 1917', and 'Notes for Inspector Lau Nuers' (1918), both in Malakal UNP SCR 14.A; *SIR* 273 (Apr. 1917), 3; Tut Jiak Gai L21.2.

[22] Bacon (1917).

his willingness to raid the Dinka. He increased both his prestige and his herd as a result.[23]

The government did not withdraw from Lou territory as it had done after previous patrols. About a month after the battle at Muot Tot Pok's cousin Lam Liew visited the newly installed inspector at Nyerol and told him that Pok 'was absolutely finished and no longer of any account'. He spoke in detail of how Pok had 'lost his head and his influence', had wandered aimlessly in the bush bereft of shelter, cattle, or followers, and was now living under the trees eating nuts. There was no point in trying to capture him, as he would only run away. The inspector took this advice. 'When first questioned about the Kajur', the inspector reported, 'Lam Lau laughed heartily and seemed very tickled at the idea of enquiries being made about him.'[24] (So, might I add, did Lam's son laugh over seventy years later when I quoted this report.) The effect of Lam's account of Pok's destitution—whether accurate or not—was that Pok was downgraded as an immediate threat and almost completely disappeared from official view. Ten years later he was scarcely known to administrators, and his role in the events of 1916–17 was all but forgotten.[25]

The Lou had suffered a series of misfortunes since Ngundeng's death: *kor luny yak* between Gun and Mor, the Anuak raids of 1911, the 1917 war, followed by floods which reached Lou territory in the rainy season of 1917–18, producing starvation in the land and sending many Lou fleeing to Jikany.[26] The contemporary prophets had provided little protection from these events. Pok was now in hiding, Car was back in his village on the frontier. Neither had been destroyed by the war, but their reputations had suffered. Despite their retroactive links with Ngundeng, they were not entirely adequate successors. It was only after this was clearly demonstrated that DENG reappeared in Ngundeng's family.

When Ngundeng died his elder son Reath took possession of his pipe, spear, baton, drums, and leopard-skin, because they were the property of Divinity and it was not considered right that they should be discarded. Reath sometimes carried them when the Lou fought their enemies, but at no time did he claim to be seized by DENG, and no one thought of him as the prophet of DENG. He was a man of no special importance, appearing once on a list of

[23] For Car and rain see Evans-Pritchard (1935: 43–4). For Car's herd: Gany Car L26. For Car's reputation (attributed to his failure in 1914 rather than to saving the Lou): Bacon (1917). For Car's movements in 1916–17 (where it is always rumoured that he is about to fight but never does): Fanar Duk Fadiat, Kongor, to Sanduk Mongalla, 10 June 1916, SRO UNP SCR 14; J. Stevenson-Hamilton, 'Notes on Patrol 33'. For sections in 1916 raid see *SIR* 265 (Aug. 1916), 3–4. For limits of Pok's reputation: Tut Jiak Gai L21.2.

[24] Godwin, Nyerol, 23 Apr. 1917, SRO UNP SCR 15.10.

[25] J. W. G. Wyld to governor UNP, 18 Sept. 1927, NRO UNP 1/5/27 and Civsec 5/2/10; Coriat (1928).

[26] *SIR* 283 (Feb. 1918), 3.

Lou sectional chiefs before the campaign of 1917 but absent from all subsequent lists of chiefs and prominent persons.[27]

It was on one of Ngundeng's youngest sons that DENG fell. There were special circumstances in Guek's birth which were later used to justify or explain his seizure. It is said that Guek's mother Nyaduong, who came from Jikany, was the only one of Ngundeng's wives who looked after him during his madness. Nyaduong had difficulty conceiving or bearing live children, and Ngundeng seemed unable to cure her. He finally asked some Ghol Dinka to bring a frog, hoping that the divinity of the Dinka would succeed where he failed. Ngundeng cooked the frog and gave it to Nyaduong to eat. Shortly after that she conceived and gave birth to a son who was then named Guek, 'frog'. At about this time Ngundeng's divinity spoke through him, saying, 'My speech will be ended with Nyaduong.' Thus, it is said, Ngundeng foretold his son's seizure and death.[28]

Guek was still a boy when his father died. He was initiated into the Luac age-set (*c.*1908) and was married to one wife when the government invaded Lou in 1917. He fled to his maternal uncles in Jikany, and it was while he was with his mother's people that he fell ill and became mad. The madness resolved itself into seizure when the divinity DENG spoke through Guek's mouth announcing who it was. Guek then returned to his home in Lou and recovered his father's relics from Reath.[29]

Guek's seizure resembled his father's in three ways: his birth was supposed to have been brought about by divinity's intervention; he was the only child born of his mother to live, making him the only child of his mother; and his seizure by DENG was announced while he was residing among his maternal kin. The combination of these factors may have predisposed Guek to seizure by a divinity more than his brothers. The similarities may certainly have predisposed Guek's contemporaries to accept that his seizure was a replication of his father's.

Evans-Pritchard later stated that Guek 'appears to have realised that if you wish the spirit which possessed your father to enter your body you must go half way to meet him'.[30] This may only refer to Guek's attempts once back home to prove his seizure to others, and to take full possession of his father's place. Percy Coriat, the first district commissioner capable of conversing with

[27] Macar Ngundeng L2, Deng Bor Ngundeng L5.2, Garang Ngundeng L1.2. Evans-Pritchard's claim (1935: 60) that Reath was possessed before Guek was repeated by Seligman and Seligman (1932: 232) and Coriat (1939: 226). Bacon (1917); Bramble, 'Intelligence Notes on Lau Nuer' (1918), 'Diary—Nyerol—April 1917', and 'Notes for Inspector Lau Nuers' (1918), all in Malakal UNP SCR 14.A.

[28] Bil Peat L12.1 and L12.2, Deng Bor Ngundeng L5.2; Evans-Pritchard (1935: 60). Both Jackson (1954: 164) and Coriat (1939: 226) assumed Guek was so named because of his short and stumpy build.

[29] Deng Bor Ngundeng L5.2, Bil Peat L12.2, Garang Ngundeng L1.2.

[30] Evans-Pritchard (1935: 60).

Guek in Nuer, reported that most of Guek's demonstrations centred—quite literally—on the Mound. Guek was seen standing on his head on the apex of the Mound, chattering all night in an unknown tongue, and finally gained acceptance by appearing on top of the Mound holding his father's brass pipe.[31]

Any true successor of Ngundeng's would have to establish his control over the Mound if he were to assume anything like the old prophet's influence. The Mound had been slightly damaged in 1917 when the army removed the fishing-spear from the apex and unsuccessfully tried to blow off the top. In 1920 a smallpox epidemic passed through the Lou, and Guek took this opportunity to organize the repair and reconstruction of the Mound in order to rid the land of the disease. He called people from all over Lou and Jikany to help. It is even reported that he invited Dual Diu, who refused to come. Guek enlarged the Mound and replaced some ivory tusks. While work was under way eight to ten oxen were killed daily to feed the assembly. Guek expanded the cultivation of maize and sorghum near the Mound, but his plantation never reached the extent of his father's.[32]

The scale of the labour Guek could command at this earliest stage of his career can be judged by his enlargement of the Mound. The Mound's size was estimated in 1917 at 50′ (high) × 100′ (base). Precise measurements made by the Royal Engineers in 1928 before they blew up the Mound showed it to be 62′ × 150′.[33] These measurements suggest an increase from 131,250 to 366,187 cubic feet. Even allowing for an underestimation in 1917, or a broadening of the base due to rain erosion, Guek may have at least doubled the volume of his father's Mound. A comparison of photos taken in 1902 and *c.*1924 (see Fig. 1 and frontispiece) does reveal an alteration in the height and the shape of the Mound. This was a considerable achievement for a man less than 30 years old.

Both Guek and Pok were members of the second youngest age-set, the Luac, which was beginning to assert itself in public affairs. This was not entirely welcomed by older Lou, who resented the independence of the younger generation. The older leaders who came to Nyerol in 1917, including Lam Tutthiang (Boiloc age-set) and Guet Thie (Dang-gonga age-set), all urged the capture of Pok and claimed that a post at Nyerol would help to keep the young men in check. 'This they look upon as most important. Their common cry is that they cannot control their young men.' This seemed especially so of Lam Tutthiang who, though an enthusiastic supporter of

[31] Coriat (1939: 226).

[32] Bil Peat L12.2; H. C. Jackson, 'Safaria Notes January–February 1921: Lau Country', SAD 465/4; C. R. Bacon to governor UNP, 30 Sept. 1920, NRO UNP 1/13/117; 'Précis of Information Concerning Gwep'.

[33] Stigand (1918*b*: 210); 'Patrol S.8 Report on the Destruction of Dengkurs Pyramid', NRO Civsec 5/2/11.

government and thought to be 'useful & loyal', had 'little influence'. By 1918 he had left his old home among the Maiker, where he no longer had much authority, and moved first to Nyerol and then to Kurmayom near Abwong just to be close to the government. Guet Thie, on the other hand, was judged 'the most useful' of the Lou chiefs and visited Nyerol frequently.[34]

Nyerol was an unpopular location, being uncomfortable and unhealthy in the rains. It was closed down after the inspector was invalided out during 1918, and no British administrator was assigned the duty of regularly supervising the Lou until 1924. Those who hoped the government might help them assert their own control were bereft of an ally. Those who hoped the government might assert a neutral control over internal disputes were also disappointed. In the absence of any other active judicial authority Guek began to mediate disputes among the Lou, hearing cases at the same time that he began repairing the Mound. He reintroduced his father's system of sending metal rings to those against whom complaints were brought, obliging them either to admit guilt or prove their innocence.[35] By establishing himself at the centre of his father's old network of mediation, Guek activated a rival judicial system to the government's. By doing so he came to official attention as a potentially serious challenge. Even though Guek was an earth-master (and therefore a 'traditional' leader), the greater sanctions he could bring to bear as a prophet (one who could know the truth) set him outside the supervised legal system the government was trying to create, and through which it hoped to govern.[36]

The government first learned of Guek's alternative court when the Jikany (including some from Ethiopia) began taking their cases to him rather than to the inspector at Nasir. The reason, when discovered, was sound enough. The inspector at that time was a man who spoke neither Nuer nor Arabic. He relied on a corrupt Anuak interpreter who took bribes before he would even present a case. The inspector knew no customary law and judged all cases according to the Sudan Penal Code. The Jikany felt they could get no justice in Nasir, while Guek's justice was comprehensible and more to their liking. This development annoyed the inspector, who declared Guek was 'swollen headed' and 'unfriendly'. It also alarmed the interpreter, and perhaps even Dual Diu, who was now at peace with the government. By August 1920 garbled reports began to reach the province headquarters at Malakal that Guek was working on his father's 'mausoleum' and bringing in Gaajak (who had recently been in revolt) to do the work; that he had 'instructions from Nyallitch (their tribal god) to raid the Dinka and then attack the government'.

[34] Godwin, Nyerol, 23 and 25 Apr. 1917, SRO UNP 15.10; C. C. Godwin to governor Malakal, 28 Apr. 1918, and 'Notes for Inspector Lau Nuers' (1918), both in Malakal UNP SCR 14.A.

[35] Bil Peat L12.1.

[36] Johnson (1986*b*: 69–70).

But some loyal Lou chiefs, including two old magicians, Lam Tutthiang and Bul Kan, surprisingly came to Guek's defence. Early in January 1921 the senior inspector (deputy governor), H. C. Jackson, was sent out with a small escort of police and a medical officer armed with smallpox vaccine to try to contact Guek and determine if he was 'of the right stamp'.[37]

Jackson arrived at Weideang on 30 January 1921. Observing the enlarged Mound he noted with misplaced optimism, 'a conspicuous mark . . . Could be easily bombed from the air'. Guek did not appear but sent a present of tobacco and a message that he was much disturbed by the false rumours the government had heard about him. Later he arrived escorted in a state of near seizure. His chattering teeth and trembling Jackson attributed to fear. In their discussion Guek confirmed the reports of the Nasir interpreter's extortionate practices. He also informed Jackson that some of the hostile rumours came from the Khor Fulluth Dinka, who had also warned Guek that Jackson intended to attack Weideang with his small escort of police. Each tried to convince the other of their good intentions. Guek requested that Nyerol be reopened in order to keep his northern Dinka neighbours under control, and also suggested that the current Upper Nile–Mongalla border be incorporated within Upper Nile, a proposition which coincided with the province government's own thinking.[38]

Many years later, after Guek had been killed, Jackson described him as 'an epileptic with a lust for power', but his first impressions were more favourable. 'Guek', he wrote almost immediately after their meeting 'seems a good fellow though still anxious about the intentions of Government.'[39] Once reassured of those intentions Guek seemed prepared to co-operate in various ways. He even sent people to Jackson to be vaccinated for smallpox, despite his earlier assurance that vaccination was unnecessary now that the Mound was repaired.[40]

The most important question to be resolved in this meeting was the question of Guek's mediation of disputes. Before setting off Jackson had been instructed by Governor Struvé to 'Inform Gwep [*sic*] also that the Government not only has no objection to but actually favours the hearing and settling of disputes by himself and other chiefs; the Government however reserves the right to act as a court of appeal in any case of injustice by the chiefs.'[41] This is a significant statement given a later governor's charge that Guek 'ran a ritual

[37] Jackson to Butts, 15 Nov. 1927, NRO Civsec 5/2/10; id., 'Lau Nuer Country', SAD 465/4; id. (1954: 153); C. R. Bacon to governor UNP, 20 Sept. 1920, NRO UNP 1/13/117; 'Précis of Information Concerning Gwep'; senior inspector to governor, 13 Jan. 1921, SRO UNP SCR 14.

[38] Jackson to Butts; 'Lau Nuer Country'; id. (1954: 160–5).

[39] Jackson (1954: 153); id., 'Lau Nuer Country'.

[40] Bil Peat L12.2; Jackson, 'Lau Nuer Country'.

[41] Governor UNP to senior inspector, 17 Jan. 1921, SRO UNP SCR 14.

and law of his own'. Lou claim that the government and Guek initially agreed on a division of court work. Jackson tends to confirm this, writing later that Guek's judgments 'gave general satisfaction'.[42]

Guek nevertheless was reluctant to be fully incorporated into the government's hierarchy of chiefs and preferred to be represented by his brother Bol Ngundeng. Jackson duly appointed Bol 'head of the Lau Nuers', but this arrangement did not last long. By 1923 Bol had fallen out of favour and was detained in Abwong. The government decided that it must bring Guek into the administrative structure, whether he liked it or not, because he clearly had more influence among the Lou than any other leader. Percy Coriat, the Nuer-speaking district commissioner from Ayod, was sent to inform Guek of the changes. Coriat was a warm friend of Dual Diu's, so he did not come with a fixed prejudice against prophets. But Guek was different from Dual in both appearance and manner. Where Dual was tall and powerfully built, Guek was short, stumpy, had 'an unpleasant tendency to slaver at the mouth', and appeared to Coriat to have 'a stupid and sheepish air about him'. Where Dual and Coriat frequently exchanged visits, Guek avoided Coriat, spending much of his time on top of the Mound, occasionally shouting at the top of his lungs. Guek demurred at Coriat's insistence on dealing with him directly, stating that his divinity would not allow him to leave home. Coriat none the less appointed him a subchief of his own section (not 'head of the Lau Nuers') and advised him to get a special dispensation from his divinity to engage in government work. Guek appeared to accept this new situation. He visited Coriat at Abwong twice in the next three years and complied with government orders, while seeking at the same time to minimize his official responsibilities.[43]

Guek's obvious reluctance to deal with the government was in keeping with his father's earlier aloofness, but it was in contrast to Dual's pragmatic acceptance of government presence and power. Lou Nuer administration was thus built up despite Guek, making no clear place for him because he seemed to prefer no fixed role. Because he was hesitant about all government proposals, administrators ceased to treat his hesitations seriously and were suspicious of his motives when later he voiced a major objection to government policy.

Prophets and the contest for leadership

Guek emerged as a prophet at a time when there was no effective authority over all Lou. The Rumjok prophets, Car Koryom and Pok Kerjiok, each restricted the other's influence. They represented different sections, so

[42] Willis (1928: 201); Bil Peat L12.2; Jackson (1923: 107).

[43] Jackson, 'Lau Nuer Country'; Coriat (1939: 226–7; 1928); A. H. Alban, 'Abwong District', 17 Dec. 1930, NRO Civsec 57/2/8 and SAD 212/14/214.

neither could gain the support of all the Rumjok; they had opposite approaches to the Dinka, which further divided Lou society on the frontier; and after 1917 they followed different paths in their relations with the government, Car dealing directly with Mongalla Province administrators and Pok remaining a fugitive. The 1917 campaign further curbed the expansion of any networks of influence beyond their own sections. But the government, too, exercised only limited authority with restricted territorial jurisdiction. It had no sustained presence after the closing of Nyerol post. From 1919 to 1924 administration functioned around the fringes of the Lou from centres situated outside their territory at Akobo, Abwong, Ayod, and Duk Fadiat. Promises of alliance made to leaders who presented themselves at Nyerol went unfulfilled. Guek, by reviving his father's divinity, central shrine, songs, and teachings, reanimated an old network of influence, authority, and relationships just when attempts to create new ones had faltered. Nuer expectations of the benefits to follow the divinity DENG's return to Weideang can be partially gauged by the distances they travelled—some walking as much as 300 miles—to take part in the labour of enlarging the Mound or to have their disputes arbitrated by Guek.

Guek was widely welcomed on the strength of his father's reputation, but Ngundeng's networks had already begun to wither at the end of his life and atrophied further after his death. They could not be reactivated without resistance. Just as there were Lou who felt they had cause to be suspicious of this revival, there were others outside who felt threatened by any new efflorescence of prophecy among the Lou. The confrontation between Guek and the government, which has been explained in basic personal or political terms by administrators and anthropologists, was produced by a convergence of opposing fears, ambitions, and expectations among the Lou and those who dealt with them. To understand Guek's fall, and how he came to be pushed, we must examine the rivalries for leadership and the tensions produced by conflicting expectations within the structures of both Lou society and local administration.

Two Lou leaders who made an immediate impression on officials in 1917 were Lam Tutthiang and Guet Thie. Both had reasons to be unfriendly to Ngundeng's family, and both were magicians. Lam, according to one son, was opposed to most prophets. He had urged the capture of Pok Kerjiok, but being an uncle of Car Koryom's he could scarcely have done otherwise. By 1918 he was no longer directly involved in any competition for leadership, having left his people to settle near Abwong. It is now said by his family and others that Lam accepted Guek's divinity and did not actively campaign against him. This is borne out by the few surviving records in which he is named. Any propaganda against a prophet of DENG for which he was responsible seems to have been retroactively aimed at Ngundeng. But if Lam was no longer personally involved in the administration of the Lou, his son

Mayan was. Mayan Lam was one of the first Lou to go to the mission school at Nasir and became the official interpreter at Abwong. Though Lam's family are now cautious in saying anything against Guek and about their own role in the events which led to his death, they were unambiguously on the government's side in the conflict.[44]

Guet Thie had a number of reasons to resent Guek's rise. Guet's grandfather and father, as we have already seen, were established earth-masters and competitors with Ngundeng. Guet Thie had only just succeeded his father when the government invaded Lou in 1917. During the occupation he proclaimed himself an opponent of Pok Kerjiok and was recognized as the government's most useful ally, but then the post at Nyerol was closed and government influence receded to Abwong. As well as being an earth-master, Guet Thie possessed magic which had the reputation of killing people.[45] Thus at the time of Guek's annunciation Guet Thie was an anti-prophet magician recently deserted by the government. The rival he now faced not only came from a family opposed to his, but was a member of the age-set immediately junior to his own.

The prophets established a style of behaviour and dress which magicians frequently imitated, and Guet Thie seems to have decided to accommodate himself as best he could to the new spiritual power in the land. It was thus that Jackson found him at the Mound on his visit in 1921 and dismissed him as 'Gwaat Thieh, a Kujur touched in the head'. Having been left in the lurch once before, Guet Thie did not rush to declare allegiance on the government's reappearance. Following Guek's lead, he appeared to have seizures and told officials twice that his 'kujur' would not let him do government work. But administrators visited the Lou annually between 1921 and 1924, and the arrival of a Nuer-speaking district commissioner in the person of Coriat made regular communication much easier. By 1924 Guet Thie was being described as 'the most powerful Chief of the Lau' and personally assisted in the collection of cattle tribute. He began to shed the mannerisms of a magician as he learned those of a model chief.[46]

The Mor Lou responded to Guek in a number of ways. Groups of Mor had united with the Gun at different times since *kor luny yak*: in 1914 against the Anuak, in 1916 when Pok raided Bor, and in 1917 when the government invaded their territory. But there had been no universal reconciliation, and during 1917–24 many Mor continued to move east, away from the Gun, seeking to establish rights to the water holes along Khor Geni in Anuak

[44] Madhir Lam L20, Bil Peat L12.2; 'Précis of Information Concerning Gwep'; Coriat (1929*a*); Alban, 'Abwong District', NRO Civsec 57/2/8 and SAD 212/14/214.

[45] Moses Cot Dak A9.

[46] Jackson, 'Lau Nuer Country'; Coriat (1929*b*); 'Upper Nile Province Personality Sheets no. 5', NRO UNP 1/34/276; *SMIR* 355 (Feb. 1924), 4.

country.[47] There was thus considerable social and political distance between Gun and Mor early in 1921, when Guek assured Jackson that he had 'complete control over the Gun section' and soon hoped 'to manage the Mor'. His management included retroactive intimidation. Guek received the credit for the destruction of Mor crops during heavy rains later that year, and he followed up that misfortune by ordering the Mor to obey the government, stop stealing, and cease fighting.[48]

There were individual Mor who were sympathetic to Guek. Tut Jiak Gai, who had recently been appointed a subchief for his section of Bul-Mor, had been blessed by Guek's father as a boy; and Kong Pan, a Buth-Mor earth-master whose father had been killed by the Anuak, supported Guek and imitated him by developing 'signs of being also in communication with above'. Guek had marriage ties with the Jimac-Mor, which later secured that section's support in his confrontation with the government. His spiritual activities were also sometimes more benign than destructive, and the Mor credited him with containing an outbreak of smallpox in 1923. But on the whole there were greater inducements for autonomy among the Mor than there were ties encouraging co-operation.[49]

Autonomy of all sections of Lou was encouraged after 1924 when the policy of local administration began to support the individual and collective authority of recognized chiefs, arranged in a system of courts, assisted by locally recruited chiefs' police. The change in administrative theory in the early 1920s (described in Chapter 1) meant that the government was committed in principle to creating hierarchies of chiefs with specific judicial and administrative powers. The district commissioners began to organize recognized sectional leaders into courts empowered to settle disputes according to customary law, and supervised the recruitment of a body of police from among the chiefs' own followers with which to enforce judgments. Coriat had begun recruiting such police among the Gaawar as early as 1922, but it was not until 1926 that chiefs' courts began to function effectively among the Lou. Chiefs meeting with the district commissioner began to standardize procedure, settle feuds through the enforcement of compensation payments, and participate in intertribal meetings with the courts of other tribes from neighbouring districts.[50]

[47] 'Upper Nile & Pibor District Monthly Diary', Jan. 1922 and Mar. 1923, NRO Civsec 57/3/12; E. C. Tunnicliffe, 'Akobo', NRO Civsec 57/2/8 and SAD 212/14/89.

[48] Jackson, 'Lau Nuer Country'; *SMIR* 326 (Sept. 1921), 4.

[49] Tut Jiak Gai L21.1 and L21.2. For Kong Pan see: Lee to governor, Malakal, 16 Oct. 1927, NRO UNP 1/5/27 and Civsec 5/2/10; A. H. Alban, 'Note on the Indigenous Basis of the Present Administrative System', 26 June 1935, SRO UNP 32.B.1. For the Jimac Mor see: governor UNP to civil secretary, 19 Feb. 1929, Nasir ENRC 66.A.1; Coriat (1929*a*). For smallpox see 'Upper Nile & Pibor District Monthly Diary', Oct. 1923, NRO Civsec 57/3/12.

[50] Johnson (1986*a*: 67–70; 1991*b*); Coriat (1926*b*); *SMIR* 381 (Apr. 1926), 8; 382 (June 1926), 5; 394 (May 1927), 9.

The courts were organized on a territorial basis, and chiefs were appointed by sections, ostensibly representing descent groups. The system defined and regulated the powers a sectional leader could wield. Through the promise of government support and the deployment of chiefs' police (often recruited from a chief's family), it gave many potential leaders a real chance to attract, strengthen, and retain a personal following. Even though the chiefs were required to work collectively in the courts, the support the new system gave offered them the prospect of some measure of sustainable individual autonomy.

This applied to the Dinka as well as to the Nuer. The reconstruction of Dinka communities along the southern border of the Nuer through the repatriation of refugees was proposed as early as 1904.[51] The resolution of conflicts along that frontier after 1918 did encourage a number of Dinka living among the Twic to resettle around Duk Fadiat and Duk Fayuil. The government committed itself to constructing new tribes—new administrative units—out of remnants of other groups, under loyal and acceptable leaders such as Deng Malual of the Nyareweng and Monykuer Mabur of the Ghol. It was also committed to providing these new leaders with a credible authority *vis-à-vis* their Nuer neighbours. Since the authority of a Nilotic leader is determined to a great extent by the size of his following, the government inevitably involved itself in helping its appointees and allies secure such a following. The Dinka chiefs—Deng Malual of the Nyareweng especially—came to expect government support in their competition with Nuer frontier leaders for those Dinka living with the Gaawar and Lou. Thus in its early stages the policy of devolution intensified, rather than moderated, tribal confrontations in this region, because it required a clear definition between tribes. There were some peculiar results. When Dinka sections were 'extracted' from the border Lou communities after 1930, many groups who had previously sided with the Lou against the Nyareweng were redefined as Dinka, and a few Nuer chiefs became Dinka chiefs.[52] The competition along the border was a significant factor in the developing confrontation between the government and Guek.

The direction a policy takes depends on those who implement it. One attractive feature of devolutionary policy as applied in the Sudan was that it was so flexible it could be used to justify virtually any action, from direct intervention to *laissez-faire*. This was the case in Upper Nile Province in the mid-1920s, and the internal tensions this created within the provincial administration were another contributory cause of Guek's ultimate demise. Some account of administrative thinking at this time has already been given. Contact with Guek had been initiated under K. C. P. Struvé, who had

[51] *SIR* 117 (Apr. 1904), 10; 128 (Mar. 1905), 7–8.

[52] See 'Nyareweng Dinka–Lau Nuer Relations: Panyok Meeting February 8th 1944', SRO BD 66.B.3.

been an inspector in the province before the war and had returned after it as governor. He favoured the gradual, evolutionary approach to native administration. Constrained by the central government, which was reluctant to spend any money on the province, Struvé had to make a virtue of necessity and gave his district commissioners considerable latitude in developing the powers of the chiefs in their districts.[53] His successor C. A. Willis, who took over at the end of 1926, was by temperament a more interfering administrator. The humiliation of his transfer from the Intelligence Department to Upper Nile Province, and the effect this had on his approach to administration, has already been described. He claimed to be one of the initiators (if not the founder) of devolutionary policy in the Sudan, but his commitment to tribal custom was ambiguous. 'I am . . . quite convinced that the building up of a native administration on the foundations of tribal custom is the only sound method of tackling these tribes,' he informed his rival and superior Harold MacMichael, 'even to the point of inventing an organization where, as with the Dinka, they have lost their own.'[54] Yet he judged the prophets guilty of precisely this sin of invention.

It was in Struvé's nature to advise caution and in Willis's to ignore such advice. Struvé's handing-over notes are instructive, as they contain warnings about matters which did arise within Willis's first year; therefore it can be said that some of the consequences of ignoring this advice could have been anticipated. Struvé advised against building a road—its construction was impractical on local soils (he did not say it would disrupt administration). He suggested that province mounted police be concentrated annually and used to deal with any sections reluctant to carry out orders, as this was an easy way of imposing security which did not require approval from Khartoum and did not disturb other districts. He also warned Willis that on his own departure from the province there would be 'a lot of stirring of old antagonisms' along the Nuer–Dinka frontier, with the Dinka chiefs full of rumours of impending Nuer raids. Struvé had negotiated the border settlement in 1909–10 and refused to listen to 'old intrigues' against the Nuer from the Dinka chiefs. It was not that Struvé had a romantic view of the Nuer; he found them 'very low in the scale of humanity' and the Lou and Gaawar 'as hopelessly backward and uncontrollable as they were when I first went among them'. But he knew the history and pattern of the border disputes; suspected the interpreters and *ma'murs* of Duk District as biased sources of information; and was convinced that the new district commissioner, Major Wyld, was too precipitate, too committed to his charges, and therefore susceptible to their intrigues, for his judgement on the border area to be entirely sound.[55] This advice was not

[53] Struvé (1926: 414–15).

[54] Governor UNP to civil secretary, 18 Feb. 1929, NRO UNP 1/44/329.

[55] K. C. P. Struvé, 'Handing Over Notes July–Aug, 1926', SAD 212/9. For Struvé on the Nuer see *Blue Book, Egypt No. 2 (1921)*, 132.

taken: the road was built, the rumours of raids were believed, the police were not used at an early stage in lieu of the army. But this is to anticipate events.

Willis stamped his mark on the province early in his first year by expanding the organization of Nuer and Dinka chiefs' courts and the recruitment of chiefs' police. This was coupled with other development projects, the key of which was the building of a road from the Sobat across Lou country, eventually connecting up with Akobo and Duk Fayuil.[56] Coriat and Wyld particularly welcomed the accelerated pace of administration and promise of even greater things to come which Willis proposed; for their districts now seemed guaranteed more attention and resources. Both men were in favour of building up the authority of select chiefs in their districts; Coriat especially liked strong men who were capable of enforcing orders and taking decisions on their own.[57] He was less protective of his charges than Wyld, who saw Coriat's Nuer as a persistent threat that had to be curbed. But both men agreed on the need for fostering strong authority within their districts and supporting those who were the main recipients of their favour. When, for different reasons, their principal allies among the Lou and Nyareweng expressed hostility to the prophets, Guek in particular, they were agreed that Guek should be removed. Where they disagreed was on how far the operations against Guek should extend to the rest of the Nuer. Coriat hoped to confine the disturbance in his district to a small radius around Guek, while Wyld had long advocated the final and complete subjugation of the Nuer as a prerequisite to progressive administration in his own district. The degree of force in the administrative response to Guek's challenge thus depended on what other aims might be advanced by his removal.

Coriat originally intended to make Guek chief of the Ciec section, and possibly of all Gun, but soon concluded that he was not 'fitted as a Chieftain', though essentially harmless and friendly. As he was unable 'to combine with other Chiefs in administrative matters', Guek was retained only as a minor chief.[58] Coriat was attempting to organize territorial chieftaincies representing specific descent groups, and while this was difficult enough to achieve among the Lou, it was even more difficult to incorporate Guek into such a hierarchy. He was attached to the Gaadbal through a grand-maternal kin link. The Puol section with whom his father Ngundeng had settled was territorially close to Ciec but genealogically distant. But more than that Guek's position as a prophet was enhanced, just as his father's had been, by his standing outside sectional politics, by his being able to call all Lou his mother's brother's sons. Coriat had been able to recognize the prophet Dual Diu as 'paramount chief' of the Bar Gaawar, but Dual had a different kinship attachment to the Gaawar

[56] Willis, 'Duk Faiwel District', 27 Nov. 1926, SAD 212/9.
[57] Coriat (1929*b*); Johnson (1993*a*).
[58] Coriat (1928).

from that of Guek to the Lou. It is no wonder, then, that Coriat found Guek difficult to place and reluctant to be placed.

Coriat and Guek were creating two different networks. By his recognition, appointment, and dismissal of chiefs, by his recruitment of chiefs' police, and by his hearing cases on appeal from the chiefs, Coriat stood at the centre of a new network of authority. But Guek, through his prayers and sacrifices, his blessings, and his mediation of disputes, stood at the centre of another network of influence, founded by his father and asserting primacy in spiritual matters. As this encompassed questions of right and wrong, which inevitably arose in disputes brought to court, these two networks clashed. The Lou were thus presented with a dilemma which was not entirely their own making, but forced on them by government innovation. When the issue came to a head over labour demanded for road construction, the Lou had to choose between the prophet and the district commissioner: to put mud on the Mound and bring their problems to Guek, or put mud on the road and take their cases to Coriat and his chiefs.

Coriat's apparent innovations were an outcome of government policy, but the Lou saw the confrontation between Guek and Coriat in their own terms of personal ambition and competition. It was a competition for authority (*ruec*) and leadership (*ruic*); not only who was to lead the Lou, but who was to represent them, to speak on their behalf within the broader government framework. It is thus that Guek is remembered today to have told people 'that he was the only one in the land to whom people should listen'. In the early stages of the confrontation Coriat found that the Lou chiefs tried to avoid involvement, telling him that 'the trouble was a personal matter between Gwek and myself'. Years later Coriat's successor B. A. Lewis understood the Lou to be saying that 'when Gwek tried to make himself Ruiic Curiath [Coriat] fought with him'.[59]

Leadership among the Nuer implies listening to people as well as persuading them, articulating their views as well as producing a consensus. The question of who was speaking, who was listening, and what was being said is crucial in discovering why the confrontation between Coriat and Guek developed to its final, violent conclusion, affecting so many Nuer not involved in the original dispute. If we are to understand the pressures each of the main participants faced we must recognize that there were a number of conflicting expectations: what the Lou expected of a leader, what the government expected of a chief, what the government expected of a 'witch-doctor'. We must examine how rumour was an indication of these expectations and both influenced and restricted the responses which were made. We must identify the loyalties which were called into play.

[59] Bil Peat L12.2; Coriat (1928); Bazett Lewis to Paul [Howell], 6 Apr. 1943, PPH (Private), PPH MSS.

Guek and the 'Nuer Settlement'

Modern Lou testimony reports the pressure Guek was under to represent Lou objections to government policy; contemporary documents do not. The documents instead record speculation on Guek's personal motives. They also repeat second- and third-hand accounts of Guek's activities. There is some convergence of agreement when the oral testimony and the contemporary documents record the same events, and it is only then that we are given a glimpse of how the Nuer and the government misapprehended each other, and how they interpreted the situation differently. The Lou acknowledge that Guek objected to the building of the road and the recruitment of chiefs' police, and they do not deny his attempts at obstructing both. To this extent modern testimony and contemporary documents agree. Where they are in fundamental disagreement is over the intended scope of Guek's opposition and the motives for it. The government ascribed purely personal motives to Guek, claiming that he was trying to stop the erosion of his power which began to decline with his defeat in 1917 and the end this brought to his raids against the Dinka (Guek's role being confused with Pok's). The consensus among the Lou is that Guek never intended a full-scale rebellion, and certainly had no designs on the Dinka, but that he was manœuvred into a fight which, listening to his age-mates rather than to his divinity, he lacked the strength of character to avoid. It is when we compare the evidence contained in the two sets of sources that we find that there is much to support the Lou interpretation of events.

In the dry season of 1927 Coriat and Governor Willis toured the Lou to explain the proposals for expanding the courts and recruiting police. The Lou chiefs were also told about the road project and their expected role in providing labour for road construction. In other parts of the Southern Sudan, government introduction of corvée (such as porterage and road-clearing) had often been met with strong resistance; it was therefore necessary to prepare the way carefully before work could begin. A general meeting to allocate road work was called for May.[60]

None of the chiefs was enthusiastic about the road, and nor were their people. But the chiefs owed their present position as much to government recognition as to popular support. They benefited from the organization of courts and recruitment of police, and as these projects were linked to the new road, the chiefs were inhibited from objecting. Whatever complaints their people relayed to them, it was Guek who focused popular discontent. When the government announced its plan to build a road, a number of persons approached him saying,

[60] *SMIR* 392 (Mar. 1927), 7; Coriat (1928). For Dinka resistance to corvée, see Mawut (1983: 15–17, 24–5).

'If you accept this, we will consider you a coward.' These people said, 'Why should we construct something for these people [*nei*]? Why should these white men not use the path which ordinary people [*naath*] use? These followers said, 'If it were Ngundeng, who killed the Dinka with the baton, he would not agree to hoe.' Guek told his followers, 'These men are different and we should not clash with them.' The people refused to work.[61]

A spokesman must listen if he is to speak, or he loses his credibility. Guek was being forced to listen and urged to speak on behalf of his people. He is the only Lou leader on record as having done so.

Coriat has left two accounts of his meeting with the Lou chiefs in May 1927. The first, written less than a year after the event, underplays Guek's objections and explains why Coriat did not identify Guek as a significant threat.

Gwek arrived at the meeting after all the other Chiefs had assembled, whether by accident or design I am uncertain. He was accompanied by some twenty followers and minor Kujurs. . . . I was surprised at the manner of his arrival as I was later by his demeanour.

Chiefs and followers were seated round me in a semi-circle and room was made for Gwek in the centre of this by the Chiefs and on their own initiative. I discussed other matters with the Chiefs before addressing Gwek and then informed him that I had sent for him in order to let him know that a road was to be cleared through the Gun Lau country and that I should expect his section to give any assistance required by Chief Gwet Thi of the other Subsection of Shish. He replied that the Lau were unable to make roads and such work should be confined to the Dinkas. I explained that the question of whether a road could or could not be made did not rest with him but with the Government, also that I had already discussed the matter with the leading Chiefs on whom the work devolved. The conversation continued in this strain for some time, until, after informing Gwek that as a lesser Chief I expected him to carry out the orders of the Shieng [*cieng*] Leaders, he asked whether there was any further matter I wished to discuss with him and whether he could take his leave, to which I replied that there was not and that he was at liberty to return to his village. He then rose and with his twenty followers made off singing lustily.

I considered it correct to show my disregard of Gwek and to diminish any prestige this local show of truculence may have given him in the eyes of the Nuer by affecting to ignore the result of my discussion with him and the manner of his departure. . . . The Chiefs made no sign of their having been influenced by Gwek and no reference was made to the interlude; the meeting being terminated after each section had been allotted its sector of road and it being understood that the road would be cleared and ready for use by the beginning of the 1928 dry season.[62]

His second version, written many years after Guek's death, when Guek could no longer speak for himself, depicts a more dramatic confontation, at odds with the report of a more rational, if obstinate, debate.

[61] Dhieyier Bol Ngundeng L6.2, confirmed by Bil Peat L12.2 and Madhir Lam L20.
[62] Coriat (1928).

There was a sullen and apathetic air about the meeting quite unlike the hearty gatherings common to the Nuer. It was while I was labouring heavily on the benefits conferred by easy communications that the sound of singing was heard. From the trees at the fringe of the camp emerged a group of Nuer 40 to 50 strong all singing heartily and led by an individual whom I soon recognized as Gwek. Advancing to the group of Chiefs who were seated in a semi-circle facing me, Gwek held up his hand for the chorus to cease and stepping past the men in front of him squatted down beside the senior Chiefs present. There was no surprise evinced at his arrival and as there was much ostentatious movement to the side to make way for him it was obvious that he had been expected. Gwek spoke no word and made no signal of any kind but sat staring at the ground in front of him. I retorted by ignoring the interruption and continuing my discourse on roads but I had not spoken for more than ten minutes before Gwek rose to his feet. 'The Lau know not how to make roads. Drive your Dinkas. Let the road be for such as the Dinkas' and with that he stalked off accompanied by his chorus who again broke into song as they vanished from sight into the trees. I felt prompted to do several things but chose the alternative I liked least by assuming an air of indifference to the episode. A desultory and uncomfortable quarter-hour followed after which, expressing the hope that the coming dry season would see the road well on its way to the south, I left the meeting.[63]

The testimony of some of Guek's companions (including one of his wives) tends to support Coriat's first version rather than his second. They give no detailed account but say that Guek expressed his opposition to the road because of the labour involved and the timing of the work, which he thought would interfere with the harvest.[64] The objections might have been specious, but they could equally have been genuine. The first and second sorghum crops are harvested between September and December, and Coriat seemed to be suggesting that the work should be well under way by the time he returned from leave in November.

There was no contact between Guek and Coriat after that. Guek was instructed to come to Abwong with other chiefs in June to meet the governor-general, but he failed to show. One man who may have influenced Guek was chief Dhiew Dieng of the Manthiep section, living between Guek and Guet Thie. He was well liked by Coriat and on good terms with Guek. He arrived at Abwong and asked Coriat to talk to Guek again before road work began. 'I informed him,' reported Coriat, 'that I should expect the road to be cleared as arranged and that on my return from leave I should take steps to see that the young men had obeyed their Chiefs['] orders, also that I did not see how a minor Chief such as Gwek could influence the sections or run contrary to the orders of Government.'[65] Dhiew Dieng is remembered as one of the first who warned Guek that the government meant him harm. He, too, failed to show at Abwong that June.

By June 1927, then, Guek was under pressure from those nearest him to

[63] Coriat (1939: 231–2). [64] Nguth Kuny L14, Nyakuil Tuel L8. [65] Coriat (1928).

oppose the road and had, alone of all chiefs, publicly stated an objection many held. His protest was rejected, as was Dhiew Dieng's tentative mediation. In dismissing Guek's protest Coriat twice stressed Guek's junior position in the hierarchy of chiefs and specifically subordinated him to Guet Thie, a long-standing rival. If Guek appeared truculent, Coriat was intransigent, offering Guek no inducement other than compulsion to accept government policy.

From this point until December 1927 rumour and speculation took over. Coriat was out of his district from June to November, and out of the province from July. The rumours that circulated in his and neighbouring districts were uncorroborated for five months, feeding off each other until they finally took on a life of their own. They expressed the expectations of the peoples in the rural areas and were the basis of the government's response. It is difficult at this distance to identify the origin of each rumour. While it has been possible to identify some of the false stories, it has not been possible positively to identify those which were true. One can only analyse the sources of the rumours to judge what may have lain behind them.

For the first several months none of the informants was Gun, and very few were Lou at all. They were Dinka from Wyld's district, his *ma'mur* at Kongor (about whom Struvé had been especially suspicious), a Dinka interpreter, an ex-policeman, a 'Morised' Dinka, two Mor chiefs' police, and some Jikany who were in touch with the Mor. They reported that Guek was trying to raise a revolt and was holding back the rains to prevent people from working on the road. He was planning to lure Coriat to the Mound to be killed by Guek's 'kujur'. He was collecting government taxes for himself; he was holding daily sacrifices at the Mound; he was planning to raid the Dinka and offered 'raiding rights' to various tribes; he was gaining support among both the Gun and Mor Lou. It was also said that he had publicized one of his father's predictions which foretold the coming of the 'Turuk', the recruitment of chiefs' police, the building of the road, but also the 'Turuk's' ultimate destruction by the Nuer. No police rifles would fire in the vicinity of the Mound; any government man who laid hands on Guek would die.[66]

Struvé would have accepted none of this as reliable evidence of an incipient rebellion. Both Wyld and Willis did, but the evidence they supplied to Khartoum also supported their proposals for future administrative action which Struvé, in relation to Wyld, and Khartoum, in relation to Willis, had earlier been reluctant to consider (see Chapter 1). Wyld, citing the support of Deng Malual, pressed for a campaign against Guek 'and other kujurial power' to advance local administration, and further urged the purging of Dinka living with Nuer sections and their return to his jurisdiction. Willis supported this

[66] 'Extract from UNP Monthly Diary', July 1927, NRO Civsec 5/2/10; Mamur Kongor to Discom Duk Faywil, NRO UNP 1/5/27; Wyld to governor, 18 Sept. 1927, NRO Civsec 5/2/10 and UNP 1/5/27; Wyld to governor, 2 Oct. 1927, Alban to governor, 14 Nov. 1927, acting governor UNP to civil secretary, 22 Oct. 1927, all in NRO UNP 1/5/27; Coriat (1928).

and insisted to Khartoum that administration could proceed only after Guek's influence had been eradicated and the Nuer disarmed, section by section. The proposal for a punitive campaign was presented as early as August and was approved on the basis of the evidence accumulated up to then.[67]

The rumours do suggest a widespread anticipation that the confrontation between Guek and Coriat would have to be resolved in some way after the rains. Though they are repeated mostly by persons who were not Lou, they are expressive of the expectations of those who either hoped, or feared, that Guek had the power to stop the road. The reports suggest an unusual level of activity around the Mound during the rains, but this need not have been so. Visits to the Mound were most often made during the rains, when water could be found on the way and food was available for visitors. The rainy season of 1927 was particularly dry, and more persons may have come with individual needs. Cattle would have been slaughtered as sacrifices on their behalf, and to feed them. But visitors did try to persuade Guek to resist the government, and members of Guek's age-set particularly pressed him hard, saying about Coriat, the 'Englishman' (*linglith*): '"Why don't we fight him? Ngundeng was able to kill people with his baton. We will kill them as we killed the Dinka." Guek told them, "Divinity has not shown me this." They said to Guek, "You are afraid."'[68]

Ngundeng's victorious use of his baton when attacked by the Dinka at Pading in 1878 was one obvious precedent guiding expectations of what the prophet could do when faced with a threat. But Ngundeng more often avoided fighting. He used to restrain his followers from coming to his defence. 'Do not defend me', DENG said repeatedly through Ngundeng and Guek, implying that DENG's retribution would come to those who harmed his prophets. At one point Guek is said to have finally conceded that he would fight if attacked.[69] Thus Coriat's death by spiritual means was being discussed; fighting the Dinka in the past was mentioned; DENG's ability to prevent enemies from harming his prophet was invoked. We have evidence that some persons hoped that DENG would inspire Guek to fight, but we have no evidence that at this stage Guek was committed to fighting.

Some of the rumours which reached the government were based on what was being discussed among the Lou at the time. Others were completely false, but were proved to be false only in time. In September Wyld reported that a number of chiefs, including Guet Thie of the Gaadbal and Rial Mai of the Nyajikany, had recently thrown in their lot with Guek under pressure from Guek's age-set. Of all the chiefs listed only one did join Guek, and neither

[67] Wyld to Willis, 5 Aug. 1927 and 6 Aug. 1927, NRO UNP 1/44/329; governor UNP to civil secretary, 6 Aug. 1927, NRO Civsec 57/2/8; 'Note of Discussion at Khartoum on August 13th, 1927', NRO Civsec 5/2/10 and UNP 1/5/27.

[68] Dhieyier Bol Ngundeng L6.1.

[69] Deng Bor Ngundeng L5.1.

Guet Thie nor Rial Mai ever wavered in their loyalty to the government. The next month it was rumoured that the prominent Mor chief Weituor Begh had suddenly, and suspiciously, died after criticizing Guek for opposing the government. Weituor, in fact, supported Guek and three years later was punished with imprisonment in Malakal for having done so.[70]

Throughout this there were occasional witnesses supporting Guek. In September a Maiker-Rumjok man of cattle denied to the *ma'mur* at Duk Fayuil all rumours of Guek's disloyalty (but then sent cattle to Guek's Mound to be sacrificed). In October a Jikany chief confirmed that Guek objected to the road work (which everyone knew) but stated categorically that Guek was not against the government or Coriat personally.[71] But these were isolated denials of what was accepted as overwhelming evidence of disloyalty. By the end of November the rumours circulating amongst government officials had been distilled to such an extent as to be purified of qualification. As far away as Shendi, north of Khartoum, the officer commanding the mounted infantry detachment chosen to fight Guek noted:

> The trouble has arisen through a bloke called Aguek Wonding [the Dinka version of his name] who lives at a place called Deng Kurs in the Lau Nuer district... He has got rather an exaggerated opinion of himself & has threatened to kill the district Commissioner when he makes his tour to collect taxes... There was a patrol in the district in 1917 when there was trouble then. They then raised a pyramid to shew their allegiance to their chief by throwing mud in a heap resulting in a mound as big as a tree (20 or 30 feet I suppose)—They have apparently now started throwing mud at this pyramid again to shew allegiance to Agwek & the whole area is in a state of unrest.[72]

Military operations would not begin until Coriat's return, and he had only a short time to verify reports. Because of the rumours of plots against his life, he was ordered not to attempt to arrest Guek himself. He found Abwong in a state of turmoil when he arrived on 26 November. Dinka chiefs came in with alarming tales; the old magician Bul Kan (whom Blewitt had sent as a messenger to Ngundeng in 1902) gave less alarmist information about the extent of Guek's support; a Mor chief came in with his police and followers, urging Coriat to intervene with a large force before Guek's support among the Mor could grow.[73] Apparently Lou chiefs had avoided Mayan Lam, the interpreter, and had told him nothing. Coriat was convinced that Mayan was hiding information and beat him with a stick—an incident commemorated in

[70] Wyld to governor UNP, 18 Sept. 27, NRO Civsec 5/2/10 and UNP 1/5/27; Coriat (1929*b*); Lee to governor Malakal, 16 Oct. 1927, NRO Civsec 5/2/10 and UNP 1/5/27; Gabriel Gai Riam, personal communication about this grandfather Weituor Begh.

[71] 'Extract from a Report Received from mamur D/Faywil' (*c.*Sept. 1927), and Alban to governor UNP, 14 Nov. 1927, both in NRO UNP 1/5/27; Lee to governor Malakal, 16 Oct. 1927, NRO Civsec 5/2/10 and UNP 1/5/27.

[72] Eastwood to his mother, letter dated Cavalry Mess, Shendi, 26 Nov. 1927, Eastwood MSS.

[73] Coriat (1928).

the name Mayan gave to his son born during that time, Wat (stick). But it was Guet Thie, according to Mayan's brother, who came to Coriat with the most convincing stories of Guek's hostile intentions.[74] Preparations for fighting were well under way on both sides, with a landing strip for the RAF being cleared at Abwong with Dinka and Lou labour.

One person who observed these preparations and reported back to Guek was Dhiew Dieng, the chief who had suggested a second meeting between Coriat and Guek in June. He came to Abwong with a tusk of ivory from Guek early in November, offering it to Captain Alban, who was supervising the clearing of the landing ground, and excusing Guek's failure to clear the road. The tusk and the excuse were both refused. Dhiew then reported that the Lou were willing to clear the road but Guek had said they would die if they did. After Coriat's return Dhiew, accompanied by Bol Ngundeng (Guek's half-brother) and other Lou chiefs, came with another tusk, saying 'that they had heard that for some reason the Government was angry and they had only been awaiting my return before starting on the roads'. Coriat rejected so lame an excuse, instructed the chiefs to await him at Nyerol where he would discuss 'the matter of certain ill reports' he had heard, and informed them that 'I was not satisfied with the conduct of Gwek and some of his followers during the rains and that consequently Bul Wundeng would be detained.'[75]

Bol's arrest ended any chance of reconciliation. 'Guek attempted to settle his differences with the government,' explained Bil Peat, whose brother Kueth Peat was one of Guek's emissaries to Coriat. 'As a sign he sent two men, Bol Ngundeng and Kueth Peat, to take an elephant's tusk to the government as his gift. But unfortunately the government refused to take the gift and arrested Bol Ngundeng instead.'[76] Dhiew Dieng and Kueth Peat warned Guek not to go to Nyerol, where Coriat was assembling his friendly chiefs. They told him:

> 'The Turuk is calling you, and he will arrest you. That is why he is calling for you. He is not calling for you so that you will discuss your relationship [*mar*], he wants you because he will arrest you. He will arrest you, he will take you. That is why he called for you.' That was the point that frightened Guek, that one. He was afraid. Guek was thus frightened, he was afraid himself. He did not intend a battle. It was because Guek was frightened about this point that he said, 'Yes, if he will arrest me, I will not go.'[77]

But Dhiew, Kueth, and others urged more than this. 'I knew those men who made Guek fight with the Turuk,' Guek's nephew Deng Bor Ngundeng later testified. 'They are: Kueth Peat, Dhiew Dieng, Wuol Kor and Nyak Kuic. Guek refused to fight the Turuk, but these men accused Guek of being a coward.'[78]

[74] Madhir Lam L20.
[75] Alban to governor UNP, 15 Nov. 1927, NRO UNP 1/5/27; Coriat (1929*b*).
[76] Bil Peat L12.2.
[77] Tut Jiak Gai L21.2.
[78] Deng Bor Ngundeng L5.2. Wuol Kur may have been one of Guek's *dayiemni*; Nyak Kuic was a Nyajikany-Rumjok.

By the time that Coriat reached Nyerol there appeared to be signs of 'definite resistance' among the Rumjok sections Nyajikany and Palker, as well as in those sections immediately surrounding the Mound. Madhir Lam, the interpreter's brother, who was among those sent to the Mound to investigate, found that the people there were preparing for war. Even then, Coriat judged that the situation could be handled by a full squad of mounted police, but Willis vetoed this when Coriat reported back, and the army and air force were brought in for a full-scale punitive campaign.[79]

Twice in seven years the government had been disturbed by rumours surrounding Guek. In both cases the rumours originated from persons at some distance from him, including those who felt their own position was either threatened by Guek's activities, or would be advanced by his demise. In the early 1920s the provincial government was deterred from taking immediate offensive action by the cost and example of the Gaajak campaign, and by a suspicion of the sources of the rumours. By 1927 the balance of opinion had shifted within the province, and the two men most affected by the rumours, Wyld and Willis, were also the least suspicious of 'Dinka intrigue' or aware of internal Nuer politics. Instead the rumours confirmed their expectations of 'kujurs'. As early as July Willis reported to Khartoum that 'Gwek Wonding has taken a hostile attitude to Government from the very beginning, and for many years prevented the Lau Nuer from coming into Government',[80] though the files then in Malakal, and even back issues of the official intelligence reports (which Willis, as director of intelligence, had edited), disproved this claim. Had provincial authorities been guided by all the facts at their disposal, it is unlikely that they would have been so easily agitated by the reports they received, or embellished the rumours which they passed on.

Rumours during times of impending crisis have been identified elsewhere in Africa as inducing religious leaders to accept the prophetic role thrust upon them by popular expectation.[81] Rumour certainly influenced both Guek and the government into making preparations which, in the end, confirmed the worst fears each had about the other's intentions. The rumours circulated within two communities: that of the Lou and their neighbours, and that of the government. In both communities the rumours represented what Peter Lienhardt has described as 'complexities of public feeling that cannot readily be made articulate on a more thoughtful level', being 'the voice of the mob before the mob itself has gathered'.[82] In Upper Nile Province in 1927 two mobs were gathering, that of the government and that of the Lou. Guek was caught between the two.

[79] Coriat (1929*b*); Madhir Lam L20; Coriat to wife, undated (*c*.Mar. 1928), quoted in Johnson (1993*a*).

[80] 'Extract, UNP Monthly Diary, July 1927', NRO Civsec 5/2/10.

[81] Schoffeleers (1974: 78–80).

[82] P. Lienhardt (1975: 130–1).

The military operations against the 'witch-doctor' favoured by higher authority were far more elaborate than Coriat's preferred police strike, and as aeroplanes had been used with some effect in the Gaajak campaign of 1920, it was decided to use them again to prove that the government had the stronger 'kujur'. Coriat was instructed to announce in advance that on 18 December four (obsolescent) DH9a bombers, loaded with 20lb. bombs and incendiaries, would attack and destroy Guek's Mound. Officials first began to doubt whether this was enough to demolish an earthen structure sixty feet high with a 150-foot base when it was learned that Guek had countered Coriat's announcement with his own prediction that the planes would come and go, doing little damage. Logistical problems then delayed the arrival of the planes, and the expected day came and went with no bombing raid. Those Nuer working on the road immediately deserted. As government prestige sank a more ruthless demonstration was planned (perhaps influenced also by reaction to the unrelated murder of Captain V. H. Fergusson among the Nyuong on 14 December), now extending to include 'hostile concentrations' of persons and cattle.[83]

In the bombing raid over the Mound on 19 December the incendiary bombs set fire to the surrounding grass but not the village, and the other bombs either missed the Mound, or were muffled by its soft earth, or failed to go off. Another raid the next day interrupted a sacrifice of a white ox, and the Nuer hid in their sorghum fields as the planes machine-gunned the area. Over several days there were more raids as the planes tried to track down groups of scattered and fleeing Nuer. While the 'morale effect' of these raids was considered excellent the total casualties were finally tallied at two old men and 200 cattle killed, while a single Nuer rifleman wounded one pilot in the thigh, effectively grounding his plane for the duration of the patrol. The effect on the Lou was perhaps opposite of that intended. After the first bombing raid the Lou noticed that only those bombs falling outside the village of the Mound exploded, and this confirmed their belief that government weapons would not work in the vicinity of the Mound. One veteran later recalled that Guek ordered the people to lie down in the grass to avoid being spotted by the planes; thus reducing their casualties.[84]

The government had yet to demonstrate its strength over Guek's 'kujur' so it ordered the Royal Engineers to level the Mound with explosives in front of

[83] Willis, 'Lau Nuer & Gwek Wonding', 10 Dec. 1927, NRO Civsec 5/2/10 and UNP 1/5/27; Kaid el 'Amm, 11 Dec. 1927, NRO Civsec 5/2/10; Discom Bor to governor Malakal, 11 Dec. 1927, NRO UNP 1/5/27; governor Malakal to civil secretary, 12 Dec. 1927, 'Note on the Conference Held at Road-Head on the Nyerol-AFIO Road on December 18, 1927', and governor UNP to civil secretary, 18 Dec. 1927, all in NRO Civsec 5/2/10.

[84] Telegrams: Mosely Bey to HQ SDF, 19–21, 23, 28, and 29 Dec. 1927, 'Details of Objectives Actually Attacked', 'Note on a Meeting Held at Nyerol on Christmas Day, 1927', all in NRO Civsec 5/2/10. For the Lou reaction: Peter Gatkuoth Gual A3.2, Deng Bor Ngundeng L5.2.

an audience of thirty-four Lou chiefs. There was the atmosphere of a conjuring show on 8 February 1928 as Coriat announced that he would make the Mound disappear in a puff of smoke at the drop of a handkerchief. The handkerchief was dropped, the charge set off, and 'the result was something of an anti-climax', Coriat later wrote. The wind blew the sound away, and all that was seen was 'a puff of white smoke and a few lumps of earth tumbling down the side'. Symbolic of the government's entire effort only the top forty feet of the Mound had been removed, leaving the base intact (Fig. 6). Nevertheless the information office in Khartoum announced to the papers back home and to the world at large that the 'pyramid' had been 'completely destroyed' and that 'the destruction of this stronghold of wizardry symbolises the downfall of the kujurs'.[85]

The first rule in colonial warfare was to concentrate the enemy's main force in one place where it could be annihilated by modern weapons, as had been done so effectively at Omdurman in 1898. This rule was broken in the Lou patrol. The Nuer were scarcely damaged and certainly were not overawed by the wizardry of the planes. Rather they scattered in all directions and troops had to be sent into the swamp and plains to round them up. 'At first we expected resistance & possible attack', wrote the commander of the mounted infantry, after traversing some 600 miles of Nuer country, 'but there has never been any sign of it'. Instead he found many sections of Nuer 'sitting peacefully with their cattle waiting for us. Others have fled at our approach & we have been unable to attack them.'[86]

Military operations were now extended to other sections of the Lou and to the Gaawar where many Lou had fled, to capture fugitives and give the Nuer an unambiguous demonstration of government strength. The campaign against Guek was thus expanded to include the prophets Dual Diu, Car Koryom, and Pok Kerjiok, each of whom had earlier been reported as sympathetic to Guek.[87] The alienation of Dual Diu through the behaviour of troops and Dinka auxiliaries will be described in the next chapter. Of the two Lou prophets, Car tried to avoid involvement while Pok was a central figure in subsequent events.

Car was considered harmless by the government before 1928. During the operations following the bombing of the Mound it was reported that Car had persuaded Guek to flee to the Lang area, where Car's section had their dry season pastures. An aeroplane was sent to circle Car's cattle camp, and he surrendered without resistance when Coriat arrived with mounted troops. He presented himself to Coriat dressed in a beaded skin and carrying an ostrich plume fan (see Fig. 7), and explained that he had tried to dissuade Guek from

[85] Coriat (1939: 234); 'Patrol S.8 Report on the Destruction of the Dengkurs Pyramid', NRO Civsec 5/2/11; McMeekan (1929); press communiqué, 14 Feb. 1928, NRO Civsec 5/2/11.

[86] Eastwood to his mother, letter dated Fadding, 5 Feb. 1928, Eastwood MSS.

[87] Lee to governor Malakal, 16 Oct. 1927, NRO Civsec 5/2/10 and UNP 1/5/27.

FIG. 6. Ngundeng's Mound after demolition, 1928 (Coriat)

FIG. 7. Car Koryom under arrest, 1928 (Eastwood)

fighting. He was taken into custody but not placed under guard. That night he jumped the camp wire and escaped. Though there were many reports about his movements after this, he was not present at any of the subsequent battles of the next two years.[88]

Pok was more consistently associated with anti-government activities. When rumours began circulating in 1921 it was reported that Pok had visited Guek to urge him to fight the government. It was now alleged that he had constantly been with Guek since the rains of 1927, and it may have been his influence which brought the Nyajikany to Guek's side as early as November. When the Lou scattered from the Mound Pok fled to the Gaawar, staying briefly in the camp of a Gaawar chief, Dag Mer (the brother of Nuaar Mer), before absconding with Guek to Jikany territory in May, and back to the Mound in July 1928.[89]

When Dual Diu decided to break with the government and raid the Dinka at Duk Fadiat and Duk Fayuil, it was Pok, his distant relative, who assisted him and brought in Lou reinforcements. Pok was reported to have visited Dual before the Duk Fayuil raid in August 1928. It was another of Dual's clansmen, Lam Liew, who helped Pok organize the Lou raiders, but their numbers were few. Only about sixty men, mainly from the Nyajikany- and Palker-Rumjok, but including individuals from such Gaadbal sections as Dhiew Dieng's Manthiep, raided parallel to Dual.[90]

The Duk Fayuil raid was seen as proof of a co-ordinated rising of 'kujurs' whose main goal had always been the looting of Dinka cattle. But the Gaawar-initiated raid disturbed internal relations among the Lou. Aside from Pok, who was related to Dual, the Lou prophets were hardly involved. Guek and Dhiew Dieng, who had both lost cattle to government troops, tried to organize a contingent to join Pok, but they were stopped by Ding Tuil, a young Palker-Rumjok chief who objected to his Dinka relatives being raided. Some Maiker-Rumjok joined Pok's raid but Car did not. It was reported that Car tried to seize Nyareweng cattle then in the safe-keeping of some Maiker chiefs. Fighting was avoided when two other Rumjok chiefs (from Nyajikany and Palker) intervened, arguing against an inter-Lou sectional fight over Dinka cattle. These are the only two instances reported of either Guek or Car

88 Political, Patrol S8 to governor Malakal, 1 Jan. 1927 [*sic*], NRO UNP 1/5/27; governor UNP to civil secretary, 22 Feb. 1928, NRO Civsec 5/2/11; Coriat (1928). Car's fan is now in the Pitt-Rivers Museum, Oxford.

89 'Précis of Information Concerning Gwep'; 'Intelligence Report on Situation of S8', 25 Dec. 1927, NRO UNP 1/5/27; governor Malakal to civil secretary, 11 Jan. 1928, NRO Civsec 5/2/11; 'March through Gaweir Country', and 'Extract from Upper Nile Province Monthly Diary July 1928', both in NRO Civsec 5/3/12; Coriat, 5 May 1928, Coriat MSS.

90 H. G. W. Maxwell, ADC Fangak, to governor UNP, 1 Nov. 1928, NRO Civsec 5/3/12 and 'Duk Faweil', PPH MSS; 'Note of a Meeting Held in the Office of the Kaid el 'Amm on 8.9.1928', NRO Civsec 5/3/12; Stephen Ciec Lam, personal communication; ADC Abwong to governor UNP, 30 Aug. 1928, and ADC Southern District to governor UNP, 20 Dec. 1928, both in NRO UNP 1/7/46; 'Guncol Narrative Nuer Settlement', NRO Civsec 1/3/8.

having designs on Dinka herds. They are considered atypical of the two prophets by modern Lou, and the motivation can be traced to their having lost cattle to government troops. Car had a number of Dinka living with him, and this is the reason now given by both Lou and Dinka relatives why he took no part in the raids. Coriat was certainly convinced, shortly after the Duk Fayuil raid, that the Dinka were in no great danger from the Lou, declaring, 'unless we make a mess of it I swear the Lau will keep quiet'.[91]

Willis had confidently predicted a general rising of prophets, and he now had one. Radical action was required to put it down, and in January 1929 Khartoum agreed to combine large-scale military action ('the Nuer Settlement') with administrative reorganization to isolate the prophets from their potential followers, separate the Nuer from the Dinka, rebuild a strong Dinka district facing the Nuer by repatriating all Dinka to Duk Fayuil, and then impose 'tribal discipline' through the chiefs' courts and their police, the building of roads, and various other schemes. The administrative plan was very much what Willis had proposed two years earlier. It was now granted funding as a necessary security measure, to be imposed by force rather than persuasion.[92]

The 'armed assistance' of the Nuer Settlement involved herding the Gun, Mor, and Gaawar into concentration areas by early February. Those found outside the areas after the deadline would be declared rebels and would be attacked by police and troops. The Mound was outside the Gun concentration area, and Guek's return there made catching him easier.

It was said by the government that Guek returned to the Mound to revive his shattered reputation by a successful contest of arms with government troops.[93] Lou sources present a different picture, but modern Lou testimony is struggling to reconcile the result of the battle with Ngundeng's teachings as they are now understood. Guek was joined for the first time by both Lou prophets, Pok and Car. Car was elder to Guek as a member of the Dang-gonga age-set, was also a prophet of DENG, and had declared his prophecy before Guek. There was thus an inherent competition between these two prophets which had prevented them meeting face to face before. According to the story now told by Car's family, on the night before the battle with the government Guek brought out his spear and invited the leaders of the various sections to try to stab an ox. He spat on the spear as he handed it to each leader, and found they could not pierce the ox. Car, however, prevented Guek from spitting on the spear, stabbed the ox, and killed it. He cut off a foreleg and gave it to the members of the Dang-gonga age-set, whom he then

[91] ADC Southern District to governor UNP, 20 Dec. 1928, NRO UNP 1/7/46 and Civsec 1/3/8; Deng Bor Ngundeng L5.2; J. W. G. Wyld, 'Report on the Duk Raid', 10 Dec. 1928, NRO Civsec 5/3/12; Gany Car L26, Mier Deng Reng D2; 'Extracts from Private Letter from Coriat to Alban', 22 Aug. 1928, 'Duk Faweil', PPH MSS.

[92] Willis, 'Nuer Settlement 1929', 28 June 1929, NRO Civsec 1/3/8; governor-general to high commissioner for Egypt, 9 Jan. 1929, NRO Civsec 1/3/7.

[93] Coriat (1929*a*).

addressed, telling them they had no fight with the 'Turuk', reminding them that Ngundeng had not fought the 'Turuk', and ordering them to leave and roast the foreleg on their way home. Half the assembled Rumjok left with Car that night; the other half stayed with Pok.[94] In this story Car proved that he, not Guek, was the real prophet of DENG, the real prophet of peace.

Guek's nephew Deng Bor Ngundeng made no mention of Car's challenge, but gave a vivid account of Guek's uncertainty before his death:

> Guek did not prepare or plan to fight the Turuk. It was the Turuk who came to fight him. I was present at that fight. . . . When the Turuk came Guek told people to leave the place, but they refused. The following morning Guek's divinity left him.
>
> When the Turuk came, Guek took an ox and walked towards the Turuk. The Turuk said Guek was going to reconcile with them. But the black people [soldiers] who were together with the Turuk said that Guek was going to kill them with the ox as he usually does. Guek tried to spear the ox, but the ox turned away. He did this again and the ox did the same, he did this again and the ox did the same until he wept and the Turuk shot him and also shot the ox. When we saw that Guek had been killed we fled. The Turuk killed thirty persons from the family of Ngundeng, of which I am a member. The Turuk took all our cattle and children which remained behind, and took them to a place called Muot Dit.[95]

Guek was clearly trying to recreate his father's success at Pading, as he had been urged to do from the very start. According to government accounts, when the troops arrived and formed a square facing the Mound the Nuer made no motion to attack. Shots were fired in the air, and Guek then advanced, carrying his father's brass pipe and barbless iron fishing-spear, driving a white ox in front of him, before he was shot.[96] The barbless spear (*rip*) is associated with Aiwel Longar, featuring in some Nuer stories as the weapon used to kill him. Guek's failure has become the final proof to the Lou that DENG did not sanction Guek's fight. DENG did not fail as a divinity; rather it was Guek who failed as DENG's prophet, and the Lou are still trying to answer the question of why he failed. Some say that it was merely because he chose to listen to the members of his age-set rather than to his divinity. Others say that DENG abandoned Guek out of displeasure with his having sex with women who came to be cured of barrenness. Yet others claim that Pok had advised Guek to meet the troops by going around the eastern side of the Mound (the side of good things), but Guek went out by the western side (the side of bad things) instead. There are still others who insist—improbably—that Guek's attempted sacrifice before the battle was intended as a peace offering, an appeasement to his divinity which was misunderstood.[97]

Guek's body was taken from the field and hung from the branches of the

[94] Gabriel Yoal Dok A4, Gabriel Yoal Dok and Stephen Ciec Lam A5.

[95] Deng Bor Ngundeng L5.2.

[96] Coriat (1929*a*; 1939: 237); Jackson (1954: 170).

[97] Macar Ngundeng L2, Dhieyier Bol Ngundeng L6.2, Gabriel Yoal Dok and Stephen Ciec Lam A5, David Koak A2, Peter Gatkuoth Gual and Biel Lel Ngundeng A3.2.

FIG. 8. 'I will lay down the point of the Mound, the fig-tree will bend in the middle.' Guek's body, hanging from the Tree of Bad Things, 1929 (Coriat)

Tree of Bad Things near the Mound (see Fig. 8). A souvenir hunter among the soldiers cut off his testicles. After the troops had left some of Guek's wives returned and found him hanging there. He was taken down and buried, but not in his cattle byre, as was customary, as all the huts of the village had been burned.[98] The site of his grave, unlike Ngundeng's, is still kept secret from any enquiring latter-day 'Turuk'.

Aftermath

Guek's death intimidated the other Lou prophets. His *dayiemni* stripped themselves of their beads and feathers, shaved their beards and hair, and denied all association with Guek.[99] Magicians, too, stopped their outward imitation of prophets, and chiefs in the government hierarchy who had previously claimed some magic or divinity quickly abandoned the outward signs of their claims.[100]

[98] Bil Peat L12.2.

[99] Nyang Kuac Agok L15.5.

[100] A. H. Alban, 'Note on the Indigenous Basis of the Present Administrative System', 26 June 1935, SRO UNP 32.B.1.

Pok survived the battle of the Mound, receiving three grazes which he later claimed were from bullets which bounced off him. Car, who was on his way home at the time of the battle, was reported to be on his way to the Mound with reinforcements. Both men remained at large for the better part of two years. In 1930 troops surrounded Muot Dit and took hostages to try to force the Lou to give up Pok and Car. The soldiers however merely succeeded in flushing Evans-Pritchard out of the camp and brought an end to his first season's field-work among the Nuer. Since the hostages taken were not from the same lineages as the prophets, the Nuer felt aggrieved. Neither Pok nor Car were captured, but because of the activities of troops in the area their relatives put pressure on them to give themselves up, which they eventually did towards the middle of 1930.[101]

Both prophets were imprisoned in Malakal under a governor's warrant and were never tried. Dual Diu, who had been captured in January 1930, attempted to shield Pok by falsely claiming that it was Car, not Pok, who had brought the Lou to Duk Fayuil. It did not work. Pok was considered 'crafty, ill disposed to Government and thoroughly untrustworthy' and 'probably partly insane'. Both he and Lam Liew were exiled, though Pok subsequently persuaded the authorities to release Lam and let him return home on the grounds that Lam was only a singer of songs and had no divinity himself. He gave Lam a spear before leaving and told him to use it for sacrifices on behalf of the family.[102] Pok died in exile.

Car was treated more leniently. Major Wyld mistrusted him, and wrote, with his usual idiosyncratic spelling, 'a master of plausibility but a deffenite ante Government Influence'. Car was briefly imprisoned in Malakal with Dual Diu. One night Dual said to him, 'All of us will not die here. Tomorrow you will go free and I will remain.' The next day Car was released. He returned to his home and lived until 1948, maintaining his reputation as a prophet and a man of peace who would not let people fight. He used to speak to Divinity in the cattle camps, waving his spear towards the sky to emphasize his words. These invocations would not always be followed by a sacrifice, but the whole cattle camp would go silent, listening to him. One of his nephews remembers being frightened as a child watching him, but also being impressed that Car really seemed to be conversing with Divinity. The last time Car spoke in this way was shortly before he died. Dual Diu was still in exile. He had sent a messenger to Car asking for a goat with a white head and a brown body. Car refused, so the messenger took the goat anyway and, as previously instructed by Dual, killed it in front of Car's homestead, taking only a foreleg. Within the

[101] Coriat (1929*a*, 1929*b*); Evans-Pritchard (1940*a*: 11, 160); 'Nuer Settlement Report 1930', NRO Civsec 1/4/9; *SMR* 19 (July–Aug. 1930), 3; A. H. Alban, 'Abwong District', 20 Dec. 1930, NRO Civsec 57/2/8 and SAD 212/14/203.

[102] 'Statement by Dwal Diu taken on February 3rd. 1930', SRO UNP 5.A.3/43; Coriat (1931*c*); Stephen Ciec Lam A5.

year Car fell ill. He gathered all his cattle together and summoned his village. He stood in the centre and danced and sang, announcing that he was going to die soon, interrupting his song to give individuals advice. Soon after, he died. Thus the divinity given to the Lou by Deng Laka was taken away by Dual Diu.[103]

Guek foretold Lam Tutthiang's death before his own, but Lam lived until 1931. His mortuary ceremony is described by Evans-Pritchard, and it is significant, given the old conflict between Lam and Ngundeng, that the hymn to DENGKUR, which Evans-Pritchard said was sung at most Nuer mortuary rites, was not sung at Lam's. There are now two versions told of Ngundeng's curse when Lam slapped him so many years ago. According to Ngundeng's family Ngundeng said, 'I will add Lam Tutthiang to the foreigners (*rol*), whom I am holding in my right hand. All the descendants of Lam will vanish in the foreigners. If something comes later, it will find the descendants of Lam with the foreigners.' According to Lam's son, Ngundeng saved Lam from being killed, saying, 'Lam Tutthiang has a very difficult task. When the foreigners come, he will serve them.' Lam's family have transformed Ngundeng's curse into a prediction and a blessing, and are thus able to accept the divinity their father denied.[104]

Guet Thie abandoned all outward signs of being a magician. Guek's section was added to his, and he was president of the Gaadbal court until 1937, when it was divided into two. He was known to succeeding district commissioners as 'an old pal of Coriat's'. Despite the secularizing trend of Nuer administration during those years, he was much in demand as an earth-master, finally handing his leopard-skins over to his son Wang Guet in 1949. He was still alive when the last British administrator left the district in 1954.[105]

The Nuer still speculate on the reasons for the betrayal of Guek in 1927. There are some who say that 'rich people' turned the government against Guek out of jealousy and greed.[106] Guet Thie's actions are comprehensible, because Guet's competition with Guek is well known. Kueth Peat, who died with Guek at the Mound, is said to have misled the British about Guek at the same time that he was urging Guek to fight, but there is no documentary evidence of this. Dhiew Dieng, too, is charged with double dealing, for which there is some evidence in the contemporary record. He served some time as a political prisoner in Malakal after the Nuer Settlement (along with Reath Ngundeng and Weituor Begh). Coriat was puzzled by his behaviour too,

[103] Wyld, 'Handing Over Note Three Southern Shens Gun Lau: Personality Reports', n.d. (*c.*1930), SRO BD 66.B.1/3; Gabriel Yoal Dok A4, Gabriel Yoal Dok and Stephen Ciec Lam A5.

[104] Coriat (1929*a*); Evans-Pritchard (1949: 62); Deng Bor Ngundeng L5.1, Madhir Lam L20.

[105] 'Upper Nile Province Personality Sheets no. 5', NRO UNP 1/34/276; P. L. Roussel, 'List of Notables, and of Chiefs Now Retired or Dismissed', 2 Nov. 1954, SRO LND 10.A.

[106] Jok Jang Jk1.2.

writing that he was 'the only native I have known who can be effectively ironic. Had a dog he called "Kai Lora" (All Lies); the other Chiefs now say that the dog was the only person who knew Dtho's [Dhiew] mind and that it was "All Lies" anyway.'[107]

In the two decades which passed between Ngundeng's death and his son's war the government progressively restricted the scope of prophetic action. During that period prophets appeared where government presence was at its weakest, rather than where it was most entrenched. Most prophets among the Lou tried to recreate Ngundeng's ideal community to overcome the internal tensions of Lou society. The divinity DENG reappeared along the Dinka border where there was the greatest tension—in part aggravated by the government definition of that border. It reappeared centrally among the Lou after the earlier prophets had failed, but before the government could assert its authority. Government response to the prophets was, over the long term, hostile and suspicious. It was the government which was inevitably opposed to the prophets, not the other way around.

Guek's prophetic career lasted less than ten years, too short a time to establish a distinct difference between himself and his father. Guek, the Lou say, did nothing different from his father, and this, perhaps, allows them to assimilate his defeat and death so that it does not disturb the continuity of the combined careers of all prophets of DENG. No prophet attained Ngundeng's stature; for the government effectively curbed any prophet who had such ambitions. The prophets either operated in restricted territorial and political settings, or they worked in association with each other. There was, however, a potential for rivalry, and the rivalries were never entirely submerged. Divinity during this time looked, and was, more fragmented than during the preceding generation.

[107] Coriat (1929*a*).

6

Dual Diu and the Continuity of a Prophetic Tradition

The descent of DIU*—Dual, the government, and the border—Dual, divinity, and the regulation of Gaawar society—from the 'Gaweir March' to the 'Nuer Settlement'—exile, peace, and war*

The descent of DIU

Dual Diu, son of Deng Laka, was born at the end of the nineteenth century. He first came into conflict with the Anglo-Egyptian government in 1914. After a period of co-operation with local administrative officials he again clashed with the government in 1928, was captured in 1930, and spent the rest of the Condominium period in exile. Thus for most of his adult life, and throughout his career as a prophet, he had to come to terms with a government presence and the restrictions that presence placed on his range of action. Despite his willingness to work with the government, and despite his central position in the native administration of the Gaawar in the 1920s, he suffered a fate similar to those Lou prophets who had earlier held aloof from any contact with government officials. Yet Dual outlived the Anglo-Egyptian government, returning to his home just before the Sudan's independence, and dying there in 1968 during the Sudan's first civil war. He is thus a link between the earliest and the most recent periods of prophecy among the Nuer, and his life demonstrates a continuity within the broader prophetic tradition.

The story of Dual Diu's birth told by his family asserts an early link with divinity. Dual was the only child of his mother, just as Aiwel, Ngundeng, and his own father were said to have been. Dual's early life follows the archetypical pattern of a man of divinity more closely than his father's, whose claim to special circumstances in his birth came rather late in life (see above, p. 152). Because the story of his birth also identifies Deng Laka as Dual's true father, it reinforces by association Deng's own claim to an early special relationship with divinity.

Deng Laka married many wives, but he announced that his divinity forbade him to sleep with them, so they were all allowed to take consorts and beget children by them. Dual's mother Nyakera Maluoth was from Western Nuer.

Before she could choose a consort, it is said, Deng Laka came to her secretly one night and lay with her. Nyakera became pregnant, but Deng Laka warned her not to tell anyone how the child had been conceived. After Dual was born he looked so much like Deng Laka that Nyakera's co-wives became curious. According to one of Dual's half-brothers:

> When the lady gave birth she was asked by the other wives, 'Why does this child resemble his father? Who begot this child, Nyakera?' 'He was begotten by such and such a man', but he did not resemble him, 'he was begotten by so and so', but he did not resemble him. Once when she was conversing with her girlfriends she said, 'My sisters, if I tell you, you will tell others and I will be found out.' She told it. When she told it Divinity heard that this lady had told what had happened. A storm cloud formed at the village of Thil. [Lightning struck.] The mother of Dual was burnt in the hut with a younger wife . . . There remained a very small portion where Dual was covered with a sheepskin [*dual*], the sheepskin which a woman uses to cover her child when it rains. Dual survived. His mother died on the spot. People came to collect the dead bodies to be buried and Dual was found alive. His father sacrificed cattle, he killed an ox. He took his son and gave him to his grandmother, the mother of the mother, the mother of his wife. She was given her daughter's son.[1]

Dual grew up to be as tall and as powerfully built as his father and his father's other natural sons, Macar and Wol, 'but he was only one from his mother, he had no brother and he had no sister, only himself alone'. As a child he was reserved, and for this reason his father took a liking to him, including Dual in some of his rituals, such as the washing of the *kulangni* (mentioned in Chapter 4), when gourds used in invoking lower Powers were thrown into the river. Dual grew up to be a quiet and calm man, which is one reason why many persons accepted his later claim to seizure. His infant association with Divinity may have induced him to seek seizure later in life, just as it seems to have done with Ngundeng. At the time Dual was initiated into the Yaal age-set at Kuerjak in *c.*1900 the divinity DIU is supposed to have come to him at night and said, 'You have no brothers and no sisters. Now, I will come back and stay with you. Now, if I do not stay with you, you will be mistreated for you have no sisters' people and no brothers' people.' This revelation, later repeated by one of his half-brothers, can only be Dual's own explanation for his later seizure. It is, perhaps, an admission that the idea occurred to him some time before his father's death, and may be the origin of one administrator's later assertion that Dual inherited DIU at birth.[2]

The contemplative Dual was easily overlooked during the activity surrounding the visits of Anglo-Egyptian officials in 1905 and 1907. Deng Laka nominated an elder son, Wol, as his ambassador to the government, travelling to Kodok and Khartoum to be received by the governor and

[1] Ruot Diu G10.1.

[2] Ibid. (all quotations), Kulang Majok G6.3, Ruot Yuot G2.2; Coriat (1923).

governor-general, but it was Macar Diu whom he favoured as political heir. Macar was an elder—though not eldest—son, and impressed himself on Gaawar and British contemporaries alike as intelligent, headstrong, and aggressive. Deng Laka's preference for him was manifest shortly before the government came, when Macar quarrelled with another youth over Dinka cattle taken in a raid, and was badly beaten. On seeing his son bloodied, with his spears broken, Deng Laka became angry and shut himself up in his hut for several days. It was only when a crowd gathered singing DIU's praises that Deng Laka emerged, and speaking in DIU's voice warned the people not to harm Macar, but to listen to him.[3]

Deng Laka's confidence in his son was not shared by others. As Deng lay dying during the rains of 1907 a number of his in-laws came to him to urge him not to hand over his leopard-skins to Macar, who, they claimed, did not have the character suited for an earth-master. Deng Laka acquiesced in their objections, giving some leopard-skins to a younger son, Matit Kal. While none of Macar's brothers disputed his position as war leader, the spiritual succession remained unresolved. Macar assumed that if DIU were to go to anyone, it would be to him, but he never claimed to be seized.[4]

It was not until some five rainy seasons had passed, in about 1912–13, that Dual was seized. He suddenly became mad the day after an elephant hunt and, as his father had done, went wandering in the bush. It is said that DIU would take him to the forest and place him up to his neck in a hole full of blood. This aberrant behaviour resolved itself into something more than madness when Dual predicted the arrival of an elephant herd.[5]

Up until that time there had been no overt friction between the reserved Dual and his boisterous brother Macar. But as the word of the descent of DIU spread, people began to come to Dual to give him cattle. Even members of the family gave him cattle; his half-sister Nyanyai Kal brought him a black bull and put it in his hand herself. Macar was furious at such attention and ridiculed Dual's claims. Whereas many persons accepted that DIU had seized Dual because he was the only child of his mother, Macar argued that it was precisely because Dual was an only child that divinity could never seize him. Few seemed impressed by this argument, and Macar alone among the family openly opposed Dual. Yet this isolation did not inhibit his threats. Once 'when Dual was smoking his pipe, Macar came and fired a gun over his head, blowing off a feather stuck in his hair. He said, "Your divinity is gone!" and Dual laughed.'[6]

[3] Kulang Majok G6.3.

[4] Matit Kal G9.1, Kulang Majok G6.3; Coriat (1923), which is contradicted by Coriat (1931*c*).

[5] Ruot Yuot G2.2, Nyanyai Kal G8, Kulang Majok G6.3; *SMIR* 331 (Feb. 1922), 4. He was known as 'Machar's Kujur brother' by the end of 1913 (J. L. F. Tweedie to governor UNP, 30 Dec. 1913, SRO UNP SCR 14).

[6] Nyanyai Kal G8, Ruot Yuot G2.2, Kulang Majok G6.3, Ruot Diu G10.1, all quotations Matit Kal G9.1.

The dispute went deeper than cattle, as Deng Laka's herd had been distributed among his sons' and wives' households before his death.[7] It was an almost stereotypic confrontation between the hidden strength of a prophet and the unpredictable, violent, and therefore dangerous activities of an unpopular leader, reminiscent of the confrontation between Deng Laka and Nuaar Mer nearly forty years earlier. By this time Macar's behaviour, so admirable for leading raids against the Dinka, was alienating many Gaawar. Doubts about his character seemed justified. He made some attempt to settle murder cases and stop feuds, but with little success. He had neither the diplomatic skills nor the spiritual authority of his father, and Gaawar society became increasingly divided by fighting.

Macar's main problem was his own involvement in creating feuds. Before his death, Deng Laka had advised his son, saying, 'Macar, these eight sections of Gaawar you must be good with them. Endure what evil they say to you. All these cattle I gave them they will not give to you. If they will be the ones to attack you first, you will kill them . . . And if you will be the one to attack them, you will see the consequences.' But Macar is said to have forgotten this advice. He killed his father's brother-in-law Wol Kan, whom he suspected of adultery. Wol's father Kan Boi had to flee with his family to the Ghol Dinka, where he was welcomed by Deng Laka's old enemy Mabur Ajuot. Macar's quarrelling thus intruded directly into family affairs, threatening not only to upset the alliances Deng Laka had made through his many marriages, but to dissolve the family itself. There were good reasons, then, why Macar's brothers and sisters would want someone else to take the lead in family matters, and why Dual, as one of his half-sisters later explained, 'became our father when DIU came to him'.[8]

Macar was under increased pressure from the government at this same time. In his early contacts he had made a favourable impression on administrators, for though he had taken the initiative (at his father's request) in raiding the Twic Dinka, and forcefully put the Gaawar case for annexation of Dinka land, he had also shown willingness to accept government arbitration in outstanding disputes between the Gaawar, Ghol, and Twic. He even paid his fines and taxes on time. He was tractable as long as the government appeared reasonable, but after 1910 the government increased its tax demands and multiplied its armed tribute-collecting patrols. By 1913 the Gaawar were in a mood to resist.[9]

The army collected tribute in April, June, and December 1913, and in each month faced opposition. When troops halted outside Macar's cattle camp on

[7] Ruot Yuot G2.2.

[8] Nyanyai Kal G8 (all quotations). Feuds: Ruot Yuot G2.2 and Coriat (1923). Kan Boi: Nyanyai Kal G8, Kulang Majok EHJP-8, Coriat (1923, 1925). Compare with the break-up of Deng Majok's family after his death (Deng 1986: chs. 15 and 16).

[9] Johnson (1982*a*: 193–6).

22 December 1913 they were met by Macar and nearly 1,000 Gaawar, many armed with rifles. Two of Macar's men, one of them an ex-policeman, opened fire, followed by the rest of the Gaawar riflemen, before the troops returned fire and drove them away.[10] For the next month the army and Macar raided each other for cattle. Early in the campaign the British inspector tried a parley with Macar and arranged a meeting where he spoke to Macar through a police interpreter. The inspector held Macar solely responsible for the rising and warned him, 'You had better surrender. Eventually you will be caught, probably shot and your country ruined.' But Macar refused and stalked off, demanding his cattle.[11]

This prediction of the ruination of Gaawar country was fulfilled. The Gaawar were harried from place to place, littering their route of retreat 'with dura, hides, raikas [baskets] and dead and dying calves'. Dinka friendlies sacked Macar's village. 'Several Nuers were run to a standstill by the Mounted Infantry and died of exhaustion.' Few were killed or taken prisoner, but over 1,000 head of cattle, in addition to numerous calves, sheep, and goats, were captured. Only lack of water during the height of the dry season prevented the troops from pursuing Macar any further.[12]

Very early on government officers identified Macar's 'Kujur brother' Dual as a sinister influence behind Macar's rebellion. It was Dual who was supposed to have fired the first shot, Dual who was the leader of 'the militants', and Dual whom the troops tried to capture. Dual did fight, but he took no leading role. In fact Macar refused to co-operate with him and continued to threaten Dual, shouting at him, 'You are pretending to have a divinity. Why should my father's divinity leave and go to you? You are a liar!'[13]

The Gaawar were now in dire straits, having lost much of their stored grain, herds, and flocks to the soldiers. At the beginning of the rains Macar left Dual, gathered a few of the eldest brothers around him, and set off for the Duk ridge as if to cultivate. In fact he went south, raiding the Ghol of Monykuer Mabur near Duk Fadiat. After an initial success Macar's band was counter-attacked and first Thoi, then Wol, and finally Macar Diu himself were killed. It was Dual, deliberately excluded from this raid by his brother, who organized retaliation. In June 1914 both Radh and Bar Gaawar gathered for vengeance, swept down on the Dinka, seizing women and children and

[10] G. B. Wauhope to governor UNP, 22 Apr. 1913, NRO UNP 1/12/101; Kulang Majok G6.2 and EHJP-7; Bimbashi Fairbairn to governor UNP, 30 Dec. 1913, SRO UNP 14.

[11] Tweedie to governor UNP, 8 May 1914, SRO UNP 14.

[12] J. L. F. Tweedie to governor UNP, 23 Jan. 1914; Bimbashi Fairbairn to governor UNP, 30 Dec. 1913, both in SRO UNP 14; 'IX Sudanese Regimental Historical Records', SAD 110/11/82.

[13] Bimbashi Fairbairn to governor UNP, 30 Dec. 1913, J. L. F. Tweedie to governor UNP, 30 Dec. 1913, 3 Jan. 1914, and 28 Jan. 1914, and Kaimakam Fairbairn, commandant of Zeraf patrol, to governor UNP, 10 Feb. 1914, all in SRO UNP 14; Ruot Yuot G2.2, quotation from Kulang Majok G6.2.

sometimes killing them (unusual in such raids), looting cattle, and even burning down the police post at Duk Fadiat. The fact that Dual organized such a spectacularly successful and devastating raid, and came out of it unscathed, was the final proof to many that he was seized by DIU. It was an irony that Macar would not have enjoyed.[14]

Dual, the government, and the border

The creation of tribal and province boundaries in 1909 made the Bar Gaawar on the Duk ridge into a border people. This had a profound impact on their relations with the government. Any Gaawar movements in search of new pastures or settlement sites automatically threatened the maintenance of the border; thus bringing the Gaawar into direct conflict with the government. The division of authority between Upper Nile and Mongalla Provinces, moreover, produced opposing definitions of border threats and responsibilities. Mongalla Province saw the Nuer as a constant threat to the peaceful administration of the Dinka, and the administrative practices of Upper Nile Province as regularly provoking the Nuer into invading its territory. Upper Nile Province viewed the Dinka as liars and schemers who consistently upset the fitful progress of Nuer administration. These antagonistic attitudes prevented any agreement on joint administration. The inability of the two provinces to adopt an effective border policy was most marked during the years coinciding with World War I.

The governor of Mongalla Province felt very strongly that Dual must be punished for his 1914 raid and for continued atrocities against the Dinka. The governor of Upper Nile Province, on the other hand, believed that the defence of the Dinka was solely Mongalla Province's responsibility and was unwilling to disturb the Gaawar by another punitive campaign. The two provinces co-operated in a tribute-collecting patrol in force around Woi at the beginning of 1915, but Dual and his brothers split up into three groups, and the governor of Upper Nile sent the Mongalla troops back home without making a determined effort to chase Dual. During the Lou campaign of 1917 the Upper Nile Province administration objected to any plans to send troops to 'punish' the Gaawar for previous raids against the Dinka. A column was sent to secure the Duk ridge against Lou retreat and clashed briefly with bands of Gaawar, but did little damage, much to the regret of the governor in Mongalla. For all the government could do between 1914 and 1918, the Gaawar existed in an administrative limbo.[15]

The level of hostility between the Gaawar and Dinka at this time is difficult

[14] Kulang Majok EHJP-7, Ghol Dinka EHJP-10, Ruot Yuot G2.2; governor MP to governor Malakal, 23 June 1914, SRO UNP 14; P. P. Howell, 'The Defence of Duk Faweil', PPH MSS.

[15] Johnson (1982*a*: 197–8); C. H. Stigand, governor UNP to inspector Zeraf, n.d. [*c*.July 1917], NRO UNP 1/13/118.

to assess. There were no reports during 1915 and 1916 of any Gaawar raids, but such claims did surface in 1917 when the Dinka hoped that cattle seized by troops from the Lou and Gaawar might be distributed to them. Mongalla Province accepted a total claim of several thousand head of cattle. As border Dinka chiefs were known to claim back cattle paid to the Nuer in bridewealth, and as previous attempts to verify Dinka claims had produced much reduced figures, the Upper Nile Province authorities refused to consider such a figure seriously. The most that could be said was that there had been regular seizures of disputed cattle on both sides of the provincial boundary.[16]

Two points emerge from oral testimony concerning this period. First, there was little opportunity for any large-scale raiding. The floods of 1916–18 prevented the Gaawar from doing anything except protect their cattle from the sudden disappearance of many of their pastures and settlements. Age-set initiation was postponed; cattle were herded close to the homesteads along the Duk ridge or sent to the Lou; young men went out in small groups to secure endangered camps from flooding or to fish and hunt hippos for food. Second, after Dual's raid in 1914 the Ghol Dinka organized their own retaliation. They sent groups of fifty men into Gaawar country on a campaign of arson, burning down Gaawar houses and killing many persons until Dual himself declared there must be peace.[17]

The real dispute between the Gaawar and the Ghol was over land, and land became increasingly important after the 1916–18 floods when the Duk ridge became excessively dry, nearby pastures had been spoiled, and the Gaawar had to move south looking for new places to live. After the floods subsided Dual's Gaawar and the Ghol Dinka began to use the same *toic*. Between 1918 and 1925 the government received repeated warnings from the Dinka in Mongalla Province that the Nuer were going to invade. Alarms were raised nearly every year, and sometimes several times a year, but the invasions never materialized. These scares may have been 'the usual annual crop of Dinka lies', but they were indicative of a very real anxiety about persistent Nuer encroachment. The invasion was insidious rather than violent. The real threat to the security of the border came from the presence of Gaawar on either side of it.[18]

Kan Boi's Cam section who fled from Macar Diu settled with Mabur Ajuot north of Duk Fadiat. Kan married one of his daughters to Mabur's son Monykuer, a contemporary of Dual's. There was still a blood feud between Kan Boi and the family of Diu. In April 1918 Dual attacked Kan's village and another Gaawar group who had moved south because of the floods and were then friendly with the Dinka. Dual then raided their Dinka neighbours

[16] Stigand to inspector Zeraf.

[17] Kulang Majok EHJP-8, Ghol Dinka EHJP-10.

[18] Johnson (1989*c*); Kulang Majok EHJP-8; Coriat (1925); MPMIR, Oct. 1924, NRO Intel 2/48/408 and SRO TD SCR 36.H.2.

because they were occupying land Macar Diu had once taken. Later the same year Kan's people stole some of Dual's cattle and ran off to Lou.[19] In 1925 a similar clash took place when Dual's people began building huts very close to Dinka territory and were attacked by Kan Boi's people (Kan having died in 1922).[20] It was partly the prolonged nature of this feud which forced the two provincial governments to adopt a united policy and establish direct contact with Dual.

Dual's incursion against Kan Boi and Monykuer Mabur in April 1918 renewed anticipation of extensive Gaawar raiding. No raids followed, but the government began to plan a pre-emptive patrol. By this time, however, Mongalla Province's inspector at Bor had realized that enforcement of the tribal boundary was a major contribution to Nuer–Dinka friction. He held a series of meetings between the Lou and Nyareweng to reduce border tension. It was to him that Dual sent his two brothers Gai and Biel in August 1918. They explained that Malakal, the capital of Upper Nile Province, had always been too distant for them to know its intentions, and that Mongalla appeared to be a Dinka ally. Their version of the Gaawar–Ghol fighting was that 'We are Nuers and do not steal cattle, and so when the Dinkas stole our cattle the only way we knew of getting them back was by force and by punishing the thieves so that they would be afraid to do it again.' Now, however, Dual was willing to submit to the government.[21]

On receiving this good news Upper Nile Province dispatched one of its own inspectors to visit Dual at his home in Buk, south of Ayod. 'Dwal', he reported, 'is a very tall man of about 25 (6 ft. 6 I should say) well built and well fed. He has a pleasant face, short hair and wears no clothes at all, he also has a rather cunning eye' (Fig. 9). Dual received the inspector graciously, announced his pleasure that the government had come to stay, explained that he never left his own territory, but offered his brothers as intermediaries. Gai returned with the inspector to Malakal, and shortly after that work began on building a government station at Ayod.[22]

Direct contact helped overcome lingering suspicions on both sides, but they were not immediately dispelled. Prior to the Upper Nile Province inspector's meeting with Dual a rumour had been started by Dag Mer—Nuaar Mer's brother and a former government interpreter—that the inspector intended to behave treacherously. Dual ignored the warning, but when the inspector sent ahead asking for porters the men Dual selected for the job absconded to the

[19] Inspector BD to governor MP, 25 Apr. 1918, SRO UNP SCR 14; MPMIR, Apr. and Oct. 1918, NRO Intel 2/48/408 and SRO TD SCR 36.H.2; Coriat (1923), where he mistakenly gives the date as 1916.

[20] Coriat (1925).

[21] Ibid.; J. Stevenson-Hamilton, inspector BD, to governor MP, Sept. 1918, Malakal UNP SCR 14.A.

[22] W. Pollen, inspector Lau and Gaweir, 'Report on Visit to Buk on the Duk (Dwal Diu's Ballad)', n.d. [*c.*Oct. 1918], Malakal UNP SCR 14.A.

FIG. 9. Dual Diu, *c.*1924 (Coriat)

Lou border in Mongalla Province, where they fought with the police, killing one corporal before fleeing back to Upper Nile Province. Dual replaced the porters with members of his own family and immediate followers, and promised to extract cattle compensation for the dead policeman. But even after his assurances that he 'wanted to be at peace with everyone and to obey the Government in all things', the government was warned by one of its soldiers that Dual was under pressure from some Gaawar to attack the new station at Ayod. The Bor inspector was convinced that Dual was 'a good chief with considerable influence among his people', but clearly expressions of good faith could be accepted only as an act of faith by both sides for some time.[23]

Dual seemed determined to be on good terms with officials south of the border. He authorized Biel, his main intermediary, to tell the Bor inspector that it was entirely due to that inspector's efforts that Dual had submitted to the government. If there was any policy in Dual's compliments, the reason may have lain in the deterioration of the environment around the southern end of the Duk ridge after the floods. In the dry season of 1920 Dual came with his cattle to Duk Fadiat and proposed to the local *maʿmur* that he be

[23] MPMIR, Dec. 1918, NRO Intel 2/48/408 and SRO TD SCR 36.H.2.

allowed to settle west of Duk Fadiat and transfer all his people to the jurisdiction of the headquarters there. He explained that the Duk ridge was too dry and his pastures in Upper Nile were now bad, and further suggested that by transferring to Duk Fadiat all his disputes with the Dinka would end.[24]

Dual's request was refused by Upper Nile Province, but the problem persisted. Throughout the first half of the 1920s Gaawar shifted away from the Duk ridge, either to the western settlements formerly abandoned to the great flood, or south to areas once claimed by Macar Diu. A number of small groups settled next to Kan Boi inside Dinka territory. It was partly to regulate Nuer–Dinka disputes more effectively that Duk Fadiat and Duk Fayuil were transferred to Upper Nile Province in 1926. At the end of 1925, before the transfer was made, Dual moved into the area south-west of the ridge which Macar had once occupied and began building new cattle byres there. The Boi section feared that he intended to reopen the blood feud with them, and the Ghol feared that he planned to annex their land. There was a skirmish between the Boi section and some of Dual's men. It was at this point that the inspectors from Upper Nile and Mongalla Provinces met to redefine the boundary. In December 1925 it was decided that parts of the disputed area could be occupied by the Gaawar, and part by the Dinka, with the intervening territory remaining temporarily unoccupied. All Gaawar living with the Dinka were to return to their old homes. Both Dual and Monykuer accepted this arbitration. However, the following year Dual once again grazed his cattle in the disputed *toic* and was personally warned by the province governor to stay out of Dinka territory completely.[25]

The territorial expansion of the Gaawar to the south and south-west of the Duk ridge was thus halted by government intervention. Dual co-operated in government arbitration but continued to press for increased freedom of movement. He never fully abandoned his claim to territory west of Duk Fadiat and was to raise the issue again on his return from exile in 1954. The government balanced Gaawar needs against their own policy of resettling and reorganizing the southern Dinka communities and expanding the powers of selected leaders. Dual was the only Gaawar leader with the potential to threaten this process. Not only could he rally support among the Gaawar to lead them into the land they wanted, but he could undermine the emergent Dinka leaders who confronted him across the artificial boundary by attracting their followers. It was his strength which led to his fall. The rehabilitated Dinka communities could be nurtured only if Dual was restrained. When the government finally came down unequivocally on the side of Dual's Dinka

[24] Ibid.; Ibrahim Abd el Rahman, Mamur Kongor, to governor Mongalla, 9 June 1920, SRO UNP 66.B.11.

[25] Pollen to governor UNP, 20 July 1920, SRO UNP 66.B.11; Coriat (1925); J. W. G. Wyld, 'Report on the Duk Raid', 10 Dec. 1928, NRO Civsec 5/3/12.

neighbours, it did so in a way which undermined Dual's own position among the Gaawar.

It was some time before matters came to that point. Prior to the amalgamation of the Nuer and Dinka districts, Upper Nile Province administration was less interested in conciliating the Dinka and more concerned with obtaining the loyalty, or at least the acquiescence, of major Nuer leaders. Progress was halting after 1918. Dual tried to insulate himself from the occasional official who visited him, preferring to use his brother Gai as intermediary and spokesman. But in 1922 Gai died and Percy Coriat arrived as district commissioner in Ayod and stayed through the rains. He was the first British administrator the Gaawar met who learned to speak Nuer. Given the ox-name Girkuai, he became well known to the Gaawar and Lou, whom he administered between 1922 and 1929, as a frequently harsh but also approachable figure. He made some genuine friendships among the Nuer (even taking a wife from among the Gaawar), and he was the first British official who liked Dual and regarded him as a 'great friend'. The personal friendship which developed between the two men encouraged Dual to deal more directly with the government. In the next two years Dual began to wear the chief's clothes government sent him, visited Malakal twice, and was even awarded a Sword of Honour. Government confidence in him grew, and he was no longer referred to in the derogatory terms reserved for other 'kujurs'. 'Apart from our fears regarding his designs on the Dinka', Coriat later wrote of this period, 'he proved himself a capable and trusty chief. Dwal was young and hot headed as are most Nuer young men but his frankness, energy and sense of humour ensured him a friendly reception at the hands of District Commissioners who knew the Gaweir.'[26]

If the government were now convinced that Dual was a real 'chief' and a reasonable person with whom to deal, they still treated him with some reserve. It was his independence which inspired such reservations, for Dual, more than any other Gaawar at the time, could still deal with the government very much on his own terms. There were others with less independent power who showed more whole-hearted loyalty. The 'most efficient and loyal' chief of the Gaawar was Guer Wiu of the Long section of the Gaakuar-Bar. He helped the government as early as 1914 and was Coriat's constant companion on his early tours of the district. Through his energetic willingness to work with government he gained a reputation for being 'the most enlightened and useful Chief in Gaweir'. Like Dual, his father had been a Dinka and his section lived near Dual's on the Duk ridge. Yet Guer had a quarrel with Dual and lived further off, in Rupciengdol.[27] In seeking Gaawar loyalty, government found itself involved in inter-lineage politics.

[26] Johnson (1993*a*); *SMIR* 338 (Sept. 1922), 3; 348 (July 1923), 5; 363 (Oct. 1924), 4; Coriat (1926*a*, 1931*c*).

[27] Coriat (1926*a*); governor UNP to civil secretary, 26 Nov. 1928, NRO Civsec 5/3/12.

Later, official suspicion of Dual was retroactively justified by reference to his breach with the government in 1928, proof that 'kujurs' were anti-social, unreliable, and incapable of being absorbed into native administration. But the administration's inability to absorb the prophets was a problem as much of its own digestion as of prophetic obduracy. While government claimed to be administering the people through their own customs, institutions, and leaders, it also claimed to be the ultimate source of administrative authority. Political power was derived through established institutions, not inspiration, and government was then in the process of defining native institutions and choosing those most adaptable to administration.

Dual, divinity, and the regulation of Gaawar society

Dual came to government notice as a warrior, but it was as a prophet that he achieved influence and fame among the Gaawar. It was as a prophet that he tried to regulate spiritual activity within Gaawar society. It was also as a prophet that he continued his father's activities in regulating social relations, organizing age-sets, and composing feuds. The social and spiritual spheres merged into one another, so that in maintaining his social authority he reinforced his spiritual authority.

Dual usually impressed British observers with his reasonableness. The 1918 description of him having short hair and wearing no clothes at all is striking in the absence of any mention of those identifying marks of a prophet: long unruly hair, beard, beads, feathers, leopard-skins, and other ornaments. Coriat, who knew Dual long and well, gives no hint that he ever behaved in an outlandish manner (in distinct contrast to Guek), and there is no mention of 'kujurial frenzy' during his long exile. However many times he was seized by a divinity in front of the Gaawar, there appears to be only one occasion when such a seizure was witnessed by a government official. In February 1922 a district commissioner visited him, unannounced, at his cattle camp, where some 150 persons were gathered:

> Upon the face of each, as I stood scanning this array of martial zeal, there was a strong expression of expectant interest, and an air of gravity that is not usually associated with these folk hung in the air and charged it with uncertainty about the things to come. Within a very little space of time, however, matters were free from doubt, for an extraordinary apparition burst through the attendant ranks of Nuers in the persons of two savages supporting in their arms the seemingly half drunken figure of the 'kujur' Dwal. Staggering forward thus, the latter now approached by intermittent lurches to within five yards of where I stood, remaining there a short while in a state of well-feigned helplessness, his body limp and he pretending to be dazed, and foaming at the mouth. . . . As he stood there, foaming and muttering, the two supporting henchmen seemed to be reasoning with him, urging him forward, and taking a firmer grip upon his body. . . . A frenzy of excitement and exuberance dominated all the watching host, and they commenced in raucous unison to sing a war-song of their own.

This primitive cantata was continued for about a minute, during which the 'kujur' seemed to be regaining something of his former strength, and at its termination he showed every sign of having once again become a normal man.[28]

Neither the meeting nor the performance was fortuitous. The government had heard rumours that Dual 'had recently become invested with the specious signs of a "kujur"', that he was opposed to government, and had gone mad. Since religious frenzy was virtually tantamount to subversion in the Anglo-Egyptian Sudan, the district commissioner was sent on a surprise visit to catch Dual unawares and discover his true inclinations. No British official was ever impressed by a 'kujur' in a trance, but the censure passed on Dual was light. Dual was not really anti-government, 'but is afraid of losing caste with his people by giving in, and he is quite simply and naturally conceited and ambitious'.[29]

Something far more serious than the very English fear of 'losing caste' was involved, and the government were not as central in Dual's calculations as they assumed. In May 1921 Dual had announced that he was seized by a new divinity called GOG. He did not fall ill, as with DIU, but announced the divinity's name and gave it (as a nickname) to the Pilual age-set marked that year.[30] The assumption of a new divinity marked a renewal of spiritual authority. It was as much a reassertion as a revival. Not only had Dual's family ceased to provide effective earth-masters after the death of Deng Laka, but Dual was also being challenged by a rival from the Kerpeil section who not only had government support, but was a magician.

Cany Reth was a Kerpeil who had been captured by slavers while still a boy and had grown up to serve in the army. He learned to speak, read, and write Arabic, became a company quartermaster sergeant (*buluk amin*) in the army, and eventually returned to the Gaawar. When the Anglo-Egyptian government re-established itself at Fashoda he was sent by Deng Laka as an emissary as early as 1902. He seems to have been a rather unreliable messenger, sometimes alleging Deng Laka's hostility towards government while asserting his own loyalty. He appears to have been manœuvring for government support as early as 1904. Under his Arabic name and rank, Faragalla Buluk Amin, he was employed on and off as a guide and interpreter, but it was not until after 1918 that he was recognized as chief of a group of Radh Gaawar living around Khandak (an old *zariba* site) while still acting as interpreter at Woi (replacing Deng Laka's in-law Nuang Lol). He was older than Dual, had lost an eye in battle, and 'scorned his fellows' nakedness, appearing always clad in flowing robes; his wives likewise were adorned in finery associated more with the peoples of the north than with the unclad south'.[31]

[28] Ben Assher (1928: 260–1). [29] Ibid. 257; *SMIR* 331 (Feb. 1922), 4.

[30] *SMIR* 331 (Feb. 1922), 4; Coriat (1923); Kulang Majok G6.3.

[31] *SIR* 99 (Oct. 1902), 1, 3; 119 (June 1904), 5; 'Return of Prominent Persons—Upper Nile 1909', SRO UNP (unnumbered); Coriat (1923); Ben Assher (1928: 183).

Being a member of the Kerpeil section Cany was a potential earth-master, but he does not seem to have been as renowned an earth-master as Mayom Kuai and Dag Mer, two other members of his lineage who were his contemporaries. In fact, Cany Reth was best known as a magician (*guan wal*), practising magic openly after Deng Laka's death. He gained a reputation for controlling rain, amassed a large herd of cattle, and was feared within the Radh section, for his magic was known to kill.[32] Such a powerful magician among the Radh was a direct challenge to the authority of a prophet among the Bar. But added to Cany's challenge to Dual was his seniority, his membership of the earth-master family Dual's father had displaced, and his close alliance with the government as a literate (and therefore administratively useful) ex-soldier.

Dual had inherited a number of blood feuds from his brother, including feuds within the Bar Gaawar. He began to act as an earth-master after his brother died, but the period 1914–18 was overwhelmed by warfare and flood and he had little chance to assert his authority among the Gaawar in any substantial way. He initiated the second half of the Karam age-set following Macar's death in 1914, but the floods of 1916–18 delayed the initiation of the next age-set until 1921. It is understandable, then, why he may have felt the need to reinforce his spiritual authority in publicly proclaiming seizure by an additional divinity at the same time that he opened the new age-set.

The first test of strength between Dual and Cany after the annunciation of the new divinity came in October 1922 when Dual gathered together a number of section heads and proposed to end all outstanding feuds on the general payment of only six head of cattle per death. Some Radh Gaawar objected, specifically mentioning the unpaid blood-money owed by the people of Kan Boi, then residing among the Dinka. They appealed to Cany Reth, as a lineal descendant of Teny Kerpeil and 'a wise kujur'. Cany insisted that the full blood-money of fifty to sixty head of cattle be paid for each case. Dual refused, tried to rally the Jamogh around him, but no agreement could be reached. At the time it was said that Cany had opposed Dual out of 'jealous motives and a fear of losing cattle', but the dispute is now remembered as being for leadership and domination, Cany wanting to gain control of the Bar, as well as Radh, Gaawar.[33]

Shortly after this the government appointed Cany paramount chief of the Radh Gaawar and confirmed Dual as paramount of the Bar. The motives for Cany's elevation seemed mixed. He was required to spend most of his time among the Radh on the Zaraf Island, leaving Dual to get on with his efforts in

[32] Coriat, 'Barr of Southern Gaweir—Précis of Note by Coriat', 19 Jan. 1923, NRO Dakhlia I 112/13/87; Coriat (1923); Kulang Majok EHJP-7.

[33] Coriat, 'Barr of Southern Gaweir—Précis of Note by Coriat', 19 Jan. 1923, NRO Dakhlia I 112/13/87; Coriat (1923); Kulang Majok EHJP-7.

settling blood feuds.[34] But Cany returned to the Duk ridge for another confrontation. When the 1924 rains were ending the young men of the Pilual age-set held a dance at Dual's village, Turu. Kulang Majok, the son of Deng Laka's companion Majok Juc, and an initiate of Pilual, recalled:

> Pilual were dancing. Cany Reth came and threw his spear down on the ground and said, 'You, Pilual! Which one of you will pick up my spear?' We all just stopped and looked at him. Dual heard that the drums had stopped and came to see what had happened. He was told of Cany's challenge, so he picked up the spear and threw it away. The dance resumed. Later a man of Pilual named Lel composed a song mocking Cany. Cany threatened Lel, so Lel decided to kill him.[35]

By so threatening the young men Cany effectively challenged Dual in his own village in front of the age-set he had opened and named. Dual humiliated Cany before those he had tried to intimidate. Cany's humiliation was commemorated by one of Dual's own singers; for Lel Lublub had been a poor man whom Dual brought into his own circle. He had been given cattle by the prophet and had become the consort of one of Deng Laka's many young widows. In return he placed his talent as a composer and singer at the prophet's disposal.[36] The mocking song had official sanction. Cany was still a known magician with many deaths to his credit, but his danger was being neutralized through laughter. There is a note of desperation in his threat to kill Lel. Lel took this threat seriously, but he met it in the old way, killing Cany in cold blood on 22 October 1924. When retribution for Cany's death came it came not through his magic, but through the government. After fleeing to Lou and Nyuong, Lel was apprehended in 1925 (through the assistance of another of Dual's rivals, Guer Wiu), tried, and executed.[37]

The government was insufficiently entrenched either effectively to support Dual's peacemaking efforts or to prevent a confrontation between Dual and Cany. In fact, the government decided only after 1922 that Dual was worth supporting. But Coriat was impressed enough by Dual's approach to reducing compensation for old feuds that he introduced the same reform to the Lou after he took over the administration of that district.[38]

The rivalry between Dual and Cany was more than just a continuation of the original enmity between Deng Laka and Nuaar Mer. Cany's use of magic made it a spiritual contest too. Dual, like all major prophets, was ardently and publicly hostile to magic and the secret manipulation of Powers for individual gain that the use of magic entailed. He particularly disliked the talking Powers (*kulangni*) which had become increasingly prevalent at the end of the previous

34 *SMIR* 343 (Feb. 1923), 4; Coriat (1923).
35 Kulang Majok EHJP-7.
36 Cuol Dual G13.2.
37 *SMIR* 364 (Nov. 1924), 7; 365 (Dec. 1924), 4; 373 (Aug. 1925), 6; Coriat (1926*a*).
38 Coriat (1926*b*).

century. Even involuntary witches, those with the 'evil eye' (*peth*), came under Dual's ban.[39] For these reasons modern Gaawar tend to remember Dual's heyday as a time when the private use of spiritual power for personal ends was less than today.

The suppression of the lower Powers was only one way in which Dual reasserted the primacy of his divinity. He continued his father's accumulation of divinities, dedicating cattle to all the divinities whom his father had honoured. He even seems to have tried to co-opt the more famous divinities to the east and west, dedicating cattle to DENGKUR and MAANI. But he did not suppress other *guan kuoth*, those mantic persons with inherited tutelary divinities. Rather, he used them, inviting them to perform their rites, especially before battle during those years when he was raiding the Dinka. But he could not and did not even try to co-opt the shrine at Luang Deng. As his father had done, and as other Gaawar prophets would later do, he sent offerings of his own cattle to the shrine. The alliance between the shrine-master of Luang Deng and the prophet of DIU founded by Deng Laka continued under Dual, and Dual sent cattle to Luang Deng both before and after attacking the Dinka to the south.[40]

Dual built on other aspects of his father's legacy to ease some old tensions in Gaawar society and assert control over his own family. Deng Laka had married one of Nuaar Mer's sisters. Dag Mer, a younger son of Mer Teny and a renowned Kerpeil earth-master, thus became an in-law. Dag Mer was a frequent supporter of Dual's,[41] and perhaps they were also drawn together by mutual rivalry with Cany Reth. Dual also co-opted his father's authority to advise and guide his numerous brothers, sometimes claiming that his father spoke to him in dreams. Thus he relayed posthumous advice to his younger brother Matit Kal, to whom Deng Laka had bequeathed his leopard-skins. Matit, Deng Laka instructed Dual to say, must not quarrel with anyone, especially members of his own age-set. He should be generous and give to persons in need, even his enemies. Dual and Matit were 'to speak as one'.[42] It was, perhaps, unexceptional advice, and no more than any Nilotic elder would give to a junior. But it gave the elder brother added parental, rather than prophetic, authority, which may have been more effective within the context of family politics. The favour Deng Laka had explicitly shown Matit by giving him the leopard-skins before his death was now co-opted by Dual.

This is not to say that Dual was treated with reverence and awe by his family. The story is told how a renowned Lak Nuer warrior despaired of the behaviour of his wives and went to Dual for advice. He explained that his wives never obeyed him and were always quarrelling with him. Was this

[39] Cuol Dual G13.2.
[40] Nyanyai Kal G8, Cuol Dual G13.2.
[41] Lewis (1951: 81).
[42] Matit Kal G9.1.

because he did not know how to handle his wives, or was it the way of women? When he had finished, Dual called to one of his own wives and demanded the ostrich egg-shell necklace she was wearing. She emphatically refused, and left the two men with some well-chosen words. Dual said nothing more, but his visitor departed satisfied, saying that if even the wives of a prophet did not fear him, then there was nothing he could do about his own womenfolk.[43]

Dual's wives were not as numerous as his father's, but he married them for himself rather than for other divinities, and all his children were known to be his own. His wives included at least one Lou, two Western Nuer, a Ngok and a southern Dinka, but most were Bar Gaawar, many from the Bang section (closely related to the Jamogh), and at least one from Guer Wiu's Long section.[44] The pattern of Dual's marriages indicates that he did not feel the need to make the extensive marriage alliances his father had, but rather strengthened his relations with sections close to the Jamogh. The family of DIU had become, in the space of one generation, a large but compact unit tied to many of the most important groups of the Zeraf Valley, Dinka as well as Nuer. Even the younger widows of Deng Laka continued to attract new members during Dual's lifetime, as they were still allowed to choose their own consorts, some coming from Dual's personal *dayiemni*.[45] Deng Laka's descendants were becoming a section of their own, with a security and confidence quite in contrast to their father's origin as a refugee waif.

Macar Diu's death along with many of his brothers who were also his age-mates removed his generation from effective control within Deng Laka's family. Dual's accession to power elevated his age-set as well, and even after Dual's exile in 1930 other members of his Yaal age-set, such as his brother Gau Bang, exercised considerable influence in Bar Gaawar affairs. Dual himself assumed the duties for opening, closing, naming, and dividing age-sets, duties he exercised even in exile. He did not do the actual marking of initiates, as a man of cattle would do, but in all other ways he regulated the age-set system, at least for the Bar. In the 1920s he initiated three groups—Pilual, Cayat, and Paduom—pairing Pilual and Cayat together as one age-set (Pilual), and cutting an ox between them and Paduom to separate Paduom from the rest.[46]

Dual's divinity had first revealed itself in hunting elephants. It became active during a period when the Gaawar were becoming increasingly involved in the ivory–gun trade conducted by Ethiopia through the Gaajak Nuer. The Gaajak used to come in small groups to Gaawar country, exchanging Ethiopian

[43] John Kaan Wuawu A17.

[44] Matit Kal and Cuol Macar G9.2, Cuol Dual G13.2; 'Statement by Dwal Diu taken on February 3rd. 1930', SRO UNP 5.A.3/43.

[45] Cuol Dual G13.2.

[46] Ruot Diu EHJP-5, Kulang Majok EHJP-7. The names of the age-sets used on the Duk ridge do not appear to be the same as those used on the Zeraf Island, which may indicate that Dual's influence did not extend to the Radh. See Howell (1948*a*: 179).

rifles for ivory, and sometimes the Gaawar would go, individually or in groups, to the Gaajak near the Ethiopian border to exchange ivory for guns. The demand for rifles among the Nuer increased in 1911 when the Anuak, having armed themselves, rampaged through Lou country almost as far as the Gaawar. Macar Diu is known to have organized a sizeable trading party to get guns from the Gaajak just before he broke with the government in 1913, but the height of Gaawar involvement in the trade occurred when Dual was active as a prophet. There are diviners who perform minor rites with bundles of grass to 'call' elephants prior to a hunt, but during this period (1914–27) Dual called on his divinity to bring elephants for the benefit of his own section. One of his warriors, Kulang Majok, gave this description:

> Dual was caught by his divinity. He told the people, 'Tomorrow elephants will come very early in the morning and you will kill them.'... When people were singing, Dual himself took the rope of an ox and turned it around, and untied [the ox], and speared it, speared it, speared it. In the evening he again tied it down and the elephants would come from their place. They would go and in the morning they would be killed around the village.[47]

One tusk of each elephant killed by Dual's section went to Dual. The rest were disposed of by the families of the hunters, and the guns obtained were owned and distributed without reference to Dual. Dual does not seem to have made use of the ivory given to him to trade on a large scale. Any ivory taken specifically to the grave of his father became the ivory of the divinity Diu and could never be traded. In the 1920s Dual also revived his father's arrangement of giving tusks to the government, a direct result of his friendship with Coriat. Thus half of his section's ivory was traded to the Gaajak, and much of the other half went to the government. The reputation Dual gained for 'calling' elephants during the height of the Nuer ivory-trading period was thus a considerable asset. While Dual exerted no direct control over the trade itself, he manipulated the distribution of tusks in such a way that he increased his section's stock of rifles at the same time that he improved his relations with government. Through Dual's action the provincial government benefited from the increase in Gaawar hunting in a way it had never benefited from Gaajak trading. Thus, while the government was worried about the level of Nuer ivory exports and firearm imports, as late as 1926 the governor was convinced that Gaawar participation in this trade presented no serious threat to public security. Much of the credit for that belief must go to Dual.[48]

By 1927 Dual and the Gaawar had enjoyed some ten years of relative peace, both internally and externally. Dual still had not attained the widespread reputation enjoyed by his father, but he had engaged in activities

[47] Kulang Majok EHJP-8. For other methods of 'calling' elephants see Howell (1945*a*: 98–9).
[48] Johnson (1986*b*: 235–6).

which demonstrated that his divinity had become 'very big'.[49] He had asserted his control over the age-set system of the Bar, become more active than his brother in composing feuds, begun to co-opt other divinities in the area, successfully fended off the challenge of a magician, and extended his expertise to elephant hunting. In all this he had also maintained satisfactory relations with representatives of the government and had shown willingness to allow them to mediate his disputes with his Dinka neighbours. He had, in other words, used his influence and his divinity in maintaining peace and social order and appeared to be all the government could hope for in a paramount chief. The contrast with Guek and most of the Western Nuer prophets could not have beem more complete. Yet Dual, too, was to fall from grace in 1928.

From the 'Gaweir March' to the 'Nuer Settlement'

The changes in province personnel which led to a change in Nuer policy affected Dual and the Gaawar. In 1926 Coriat, now based in Abwong, handed over responsibility for all the Gaawar to the district commissioner at Fangak. Also in 1926 the northern half of Bor District was transferred from Mongalla to Upper Nile Province, along with its district commissioner, Major Wyld. This meant that while Dual would continue to have Wyld as his neighbour, he no longer had Coriat in his own district as an ally. Dual could hold his own in the meetings along the border, but he had no real spokesman to put his case for him in Malakal.

Dual's troubles began in neighbouring districts. The campaign against Guek and the Lou and the murder of Captain V. H. Fergusson among the Nyuong in Western Nuer country both occurred in December 1927. Refugees from both areas came not just to the Gaawar but to Dual, and government troops came after them. Dual was caught trying to balance his obligations to other Nuer with his loyalty to government, and this the government would not allow. Being an exemplary government chief precluded being an exemplary Nuer prophet. This had always been implicit in government policy towards 'kujurs', but it became explicit in 1927–8.

The Gaawar had strong kin-ties with the Nyuong. Many Nyuong had settled among the Gaawar, there was frequent intermarriage (Dual's mother came from the west), and the Gaawar often lent the Nyuong their rifles. The Bar Gaawar had also developed more recent ties with many Lou sections. Some Lou had settled and intermarried with the Bar in Macar Diu's time. There were also older kin links between some Lou and Gaawar, based on their mutual Dinka ancestry. Thus, Dual himself shared a Ngok ancestor with the Rumjok prophet of GÄR, Pok Kerjiok, and was a close companion of Pok's relative Lam Liew. All three claimed the same clan-divinity, WIU, through

[49] Cuol Dual G13.2, Kulang Majok EHJP-7.

their Ngok origin. Dual had a Lou wife as well as at least one Lou *dayiem*. These were personal loyalties far older and far deeper than the supreme loyalty government insisted was owed them.[50]

Thus, when Gatkek Jiek, one of Fergusson's murderers, came and stayed with Dual for a month, Dual did not arrest him, as the government expected him to, but advised him to leave as the government always visited Dual's camp. Similarly, when the Lou refugees began to come to Gaawar neither Dual nor his brothers were prepared to surrender those in-laws among them to government troops.[51] Yet in giving refuge to his own relations Dual did not see himself as acting against government. He had consistently remained aloof from Guek even when, according to some reports, Dual was urged by his own people to join him.[52] The government certainly feared a combination between the prophets and assumed one was likely merely because they were prophets. Yet, when it came to it, Dual was scarcely rewarded for his greater loyalty in spurning Guek, but punished severely for the lesser disloyalty of harbouring his own relatives.

After the bungling of the military operations against Guek the province government decided to send troops into Gaawar country to 'eliminate hostile elements' of Lou and Nyuong and bring the Gaawar 'under discipline'.[53] The new district commissioner at Fangak, Wedderburn-Maxwell, was to accompany troops along the Zeraf and then meet Coriat, coming from Lou, and Wyld, coming from Duk Fayuil, at Dual Diu's cattle camp. A month before the 'Gaweir March' began rumours surfaced in Duk Fayuil that a new 'kujur', who proposed to settle all inter-Nuer feuds by raiding the Ghol and Nyareweng, was active in Rupciengdol.[54] This 'kujur' was the first target of Wedderburn-Maxwell and the Equatorial Corps under Captain Romilly.

The new prophet was Gatbuogh Yoal, seized by a divinity with the ox-name KERBIEL, and it was as KERBIEL ('Kurbiel' in official reports) that he became known. He was every administrator's nightmare of a 'kujur'. Not only was he dangerous, he was obnoxious. In conversation 'he made extraordinary noises and went into convulsions', and it was reported that he was 'constantly having fits', drinking his own urine, and 'such like tricks'. He was later diagnosed as an epileptic 'and generally not responsible for his actions',[55] but while he was at large there was no telling what harm he might do.

[50] Coriat (1923, 1926*b*); Cuol Dual G13.2.

[51] 'Statement by Dwal Diu'; Matit Kal G9.1.

[52] 'Précis of Information Concerning Gwep [*sic*] of Dengkur, Jan. 1921', NRO Dakhlia I 112/13/87; J. W. G. Wyld to governor UNP, 18 Sept. 1927, NRO Civsec 5/2/10; 'News of Gaweir Brought to Malakal by one Yirok Ker, Lak Nuer 17/11/27', NRO UNP 1/5/27.

[53] Governor Malakal to civil secretary, 30 Jan. 1928, NRO Civsec 5/2/11.

[54] 'Extracts from Report of District Commissioner Bor and Duk', 29 Dec. 1927, NRO UNP 1/5/27.

[55] [Wedderburn-Maxwell], 'Encounter with Kurbiel 21.2.28', 'Duk Faweil', PPH MSS; 'Nuer Settlement Report 1930', NRO Civsec 1/4/9; Coriat (1931*c*).

Administrators assumed that Gatbuogh was a direct challenge to Dual, who was both prophet and paramount chief of the Bar Gaawar. They feared that Gatbuogh appealed to the latent dissatisfaction of younger Gaawar with Dual's willingness to end raids against the Dinka. Modern testimony suggests, rather, that the two prophets were complementary, and one of Dual's young men, Kulang Majok, recalled that 'KERBIEL seized Gatbuogh Yoal of Long section. He was having his divinity in his section, and Dual was having his divinity in his own section.'[56] Gatbuogh came from the same section as the government's most loyal chief, Guer Wiu. Had Gatbuogh become a successful prophet he might ultimately have challenged Dual, but he was a more immediate trial to Guer Wiu, and his anti-Dinka utterances may have been made with Guer's Dinka parentage and relatives in mind. It was Guer who was the first to inform on Gatbuogh to the government.[57]

On being informed by Guer of Gatbuogh's whereabouts, Wedderburn-Maxwell, Romilly, and ten soldiers went to his camp on 21 February but were there surrounded by 200 Nuer warriors. Gatbuogh agreed to give the officials three bulls in tribute but refused to accompany them. The troops withdrew and Gatbuogh absconded. 'An unpleasant show altogether', Romilly confided to his diary. The next two weeks were spent unsuccessfully trying to surprise Gatbuogh and burning the huts where he had stayed.[58] In the middle of these efforts to capture Gatbuogh the troops joined Coriat and Wyld at Dual Diu's camp at Pajilil.

Despite the civil secretary's clear instructions that no military operations, other than those forced on the troops *en route*, would be sanctioned during the march,[59] the military imperative, so reminiscent of earlier encounters with the Nuer, was beginning to dominate the conduct of the patrol. Wyld preceded Coriat and Wedderburn-Maxwell with 300 Dinka warriors who had joined him voluntarily when they learned he was going to Gaawar country. Dual was now confronted by a large combined force of regular soldiers and Dinka auxiliaries, accompanied by one district commissioner who was actively hostile to him (Wyld), one district commissioner whom he had never met (Wedderburn-Maxwell), and only one friend (Coriat). All other known prophets among the Lou and Gaawar had avoided the troops as best they could, but Dual, relying on his friendship with Coriat and past dealings with the government, chose to meet them. At first the day was, as Romilly noted, 'very pleasant'. Dual and Coriat each assured the other of their friendly intentions,

[56] Kulang Majok EHJP-8.

[57] [Wedderburn-Maxwell], 'Encounter with Kurbiel'.

[58] Ibid.; Romilly Diary 1928, SAD; Wedderburn-Maxwell to governor UNP, 23 Mar. 1928, NRO UNP 1/6/23; 'March through Gaweir Country', NRO Civsec 5/3/12; 'Note by Mr. Wedderburn-Maxwell on the Duk Faiyuil Affair: August, 1928', 16 Sept. 1928, NRO Civsec 5/3/12.

[59] Civil secretary to governor Malakal, 31 Jan. 1928, NRO Civsec 5/2/11.

and Dual denied he was hiding rifles. Wyld remained unsatisfied, and after Dual left he had a fierce argument with Coriat. Against his better judgement Coriat agreed that Dual's camp should be surrounded by troops that night and searched in the morning. Romilly, who was in charge of the troops, was later to recall how his soldiers went in with fixed bayonets at dawn on 29 February and 'generally beat the place up'. Some Lou refugees were surprised and captured in the round-up, and a few rifles were found in the grass outside the camp. Dual was accused of lying and punished with the confiscation of thirty-three rifles, representing a considerable investment in ivory and cattle by his people.[60]

Dual felt betrayed and was further aggrieved by the behaviour of the Dinka auxiliaries. Deng Malual, Monykuer Mabur, and their followers accompanied Wyld to Dual's camp. After the troops' action Dual presented the three officials with one of his special oxen which he claimed had been mutilated by the Dinka auxiliaries. He also complained of another ox whose hump had been cut off by Dinka in the *toic*. He expected Coriat to hear both complaints, but 'Girkuai ignored it. He did not consider it.' Coriat, Wyld, and Deng Malual examined the wounded beast but declared it had been gored by a bull. The case of the ox in the *toic* was not investigated.[61]

It was Coriat whom the Gaawar blamed for this miscarriage of justice, but it was Wyld who refused to consider the possibility that his Dinka might have mutilated Dual's cattle, claiming that if they had any designs on Nuer animals, they would have stolen or slaughtered them. But intimidation, not acquisition of cattle, was the object of the exercise. Throughout the early 1920s the government had been trying to build up the Dinka settlements along the border, encouraging new settlers and defining the limits of the Gaawar use of seasonal pastures. The Gaawar claim that when they came that dry season to pasture on Khor Nyang, close to the boundary, the Dinka cut off the humps or horns of any Gaawar cattle they found in the *toic*. Mutilation of special oxen in this way is an insult to the owner of the cattle, inflicting greater damage on his prestige than would the loss of the animals. The stealthy attack on Nuer cattle grazing along the boundary was one tactic in the border skirmishes of the time, similar in character to the Ghol arson campaign after 1914. The intention seems to have been the same, to frighten the Gaawar away from the border, making room for the Dinka to expand their use of the territory.[62]

[60] Romilly Diary 1928, SAD; governor UNP to civil secretary, 27 Mar. 1928, NRO UNP 1/6/31; 'Note by Mr. Wedderburn-Maxwell on the Duk Faiyuil Affair'; B. A. Lewis to Marwood, 10 June 1936, SRO UNP 66.B.11 and BD 66.E.3. At this time one rifle was traded for about two bulls and a cow (Johnson 1986*b*: table 5). Dual was fined the equivalent of sixty-six bulls and thirty-three cows.

[61] 'Statement by Dwal Diu'; quotation from Ruot Diu G10.1; Ghol Dinka EHJP-10; P. Coriat, ADC Western Nuer, to governor UNP, 10 Feb. 1930, and J. W. G. Wyld, ADC Bor and Duk District, to governor UNP, SRO UP 5.A.3/43; Coriat (1931*c*).

[62] Kulang Majok EHJP-7; P. P. Howell, 'The Defence of Duk Faweil'.

The official assessment of the 'Gaweir March' was curiously self-deluding. Dual was described as 'loyal', the confiscation of his rifles as 'a precautionary measure', and the presence of the troops as a necessary support to Dual's authority over the young men. Governor Willis concluded with satisfaction that the result of the march 'has been to bring the Barr section of Gaweir completely into submission. The Kujur have been discredited and it has been brought home to the tribesmen that if they harbour rebels or refugees they get into trouble.'[63] No mention was made in the final reports of the methods of the troops, the behaviour of the Dinka, or Dual's complaints. It was only later, after Dual's attack on Duk Fayuil, that a more critical description of the conduct of the patrol entered the official record. Wedderburn-Maxwell admitted some months after the march that Dual considered the reason for the confiscation of his section's rifles as an excuse to disarm him, 'and his idea is not unreasonable; had he been a weak man with an unarmed following, the number of cattle he would have been fined for this offence would not have approached the equivalent of 30 rifles'. After Dual's capture in 1930 Coriat commented that 'in my opinion Dwal had material cause for grievance at the action taken on the Gaweir march.' Later, when both Wyld and Willis, the men responsible for Dual's treatment, had left the province, Coriat was more emphatic when describing to the new governor the mutilation of Dual's cattle and the sequel of his attack on Duk Fayuil, concluding, 'I do not consider his behaviour was surprising.' Romilly, after leaving the army and becoming a Nuer district commissioner, later insisted that 'Dwal got a very dirty deal from Government'.[64]

None of this surfaced officially at the time, and there is no reason to suspect that Dual was given any hope for future redress. Even today, the Gaawar sense of betrayal remains strong. It no longer made sense to put any faith in a government which had so unaccountably broken faith on its own and now seemed unequivocally on the side of the Dinka. The injustice could be righted only by the Gaawar themselves, and they felt capable of doing so. Dual had initiated three age-groups between 1921 and 1927, and they had amassed many rifles in their trade with the Gaajak.[65] Before the troops and their followers left, Dual is reported to have asked Deng Malual, 'Is it only guns they are after?' Deng Malual replied yes. Dual then asked whether the Gaawar had any guns when they last raided Bor? 'You look out', he warned, 'there is war this year.'[66]

[63] 'Note by P. Coriat Esq.', 2 Aug. 1928, NRO Civsec 5/3/12; governor UNP to civil secretary, 27 Mar. 1928, NRO UNP 1/6/31.

[64] 'Note by Mr. Wedderburn-Maxwell on the Duk Faiyuil Affair'; P. Coriat, ADC Western Nuer, to governor UNP, 10 Feb. 1930, SRO UNP 5.A.3/43; Coriat (1931*c*); B. A. Lewis to Marwood, 10 June 1936, SRO UNP 66.B.11 and BD 66.E.3.

[65] Kulang Majok EHJP-8.

[66] B. V. Marwood, DC Bor, to B. A. Lewis, 2 June 1936, SRO UNP 66.B.11 and BD 66.E.3. See also 'Statement by Dwal Diu'.

Dual's tribute cattle arrived in Fangak late that year, just before Wedderburn-Maxwell closed the station down for the rains. Dual then began to prepare for war. He gathered large contingents from the Bang, Jamogh, Cam, and Dol sections of Bar, a few members of the Kerpeil section from Radh, and individuals from most other Bar sections and even some from the Lak and Thiang. Dag Mer, who used to assist Dual in raiding the Dinka, now held aloof, but the attitude of Mayom Kuai was ambivalent, it being warriors from his section of Kerpeil who joined the raiders. Gatbuogh joined with men from his own Gaakuar section, and Dual also enlisted some fifty-one Angai Dinka.[67]

Dual also sought the help of the Lou. It is said that he mysteriously sent bullets to Guek. 'The bullets went alone and fell before Guek. Then Guek immediately knew that these things were from Dual. Guek called all the Lou and told them that "I received a message from Dual that he wanted us to go and help him in raiding the Dinka." '[68] But Dual got very little help from either the Lou or the Lou prophets. Guek, as we have already seen, was unable to arouse enthusiasm for such a raid. Car Koryom also took no part, and even some of the Lou who had earlier taken refuge with Dual wanted nothing to do with raiding the Dinka. Only Pok Kerjiok, Dual's distant clansman traced through their mutual Ngok ancestor, joined. He is reported to have visited Dual before the raid, but the organization of the small Lou contingent was left to Lam Liew, who was a close friend of both Dual and Pok. Only about sixty warriors came, mainly from the Palker and Nyajikany sections of Rumjok. This was not, then, 'a revolt of the Kujur as a body', as Willis proclaimed, but the recruitment of a large raiding party following extended, and in some cases very old, kinship lines.[69]

The total raiding force numbered between 2,000 and 3,000. It invaded Dinka territory on 2 August 1928, divided to carry out a series of raids throughout Ghol and Nyareweng territory (including an attack on Duk Fadiat), and then recombined to assault the police post at Duk Fayuil on 6 August. There were some 1,500 Nuer with 100 rifles in the final attack. They had passed through Deng Malual's village and, finding no cattle, burned the houses there. According to one Dinka, who accompanied the raiders in order to recover some of his own cattle from the Ghol, 'they also cast a spell on

[67] 'Note by Mr. Wedderburn-Maxwell on the Duk Faiyuil Affair'; Percy Coriat to governor UNP, 30 Aug. 1928, and ADC Fangak to governor UNP, 6 Sept. 1929, both in NRO UNP 1/7/46; H. G. Wedderburn-Maxwell, ADC Fangak, to governor UNP, 1 Nov. 1928, NRO Civsec 5/3/12; 'Decisions Arrived at by Meeting of D.C.s Duk Faiyuil and Zeraf Valley Districts held at Fagillil from May 4th to May 7th 1931', SRO UNP 66.B.11.

[68] Ruot Yuot G2.2.

[69] H. G. Wedderburn-Maxwell to governor UNP, 1 Nov. 1928, NRO Civsec 5/3/12; ADC Southern District to governor UNP, 20 Dec. 1928, NRO UNP 1/7/46; Coriat (1929*a*); 'Extracts from Private Letter from Coriat to Alban', 22 Aug. 1928, PPH MSS; Stephen Ciec Lam, personal communication.

Deng's luak [byre], slaughtering three goats, burying a dog alive and making flags of Marabou feathers'. Dual was assisted in laying this spell by another man. The night 'was spent in orgies of slaughtering sheep, goats and cattle, raping women and feasting'. The next day Dual, accompanied by his brothers Gau and Diop (who carried his drum), Gatbuogh, but none of the Lou prophets, attacked the police at Duk Fayuil. Fighting lasted several hours, but the police repulsed the Nuer, killing some thirty and wounding eighty while suffering no losses of their own.[70]

Despite their heavy losses in this last battle, the Nuer retreated with so much looted livestock that some remember the expedition as a victory.[71] Deng Malual was the main target, as he was then chief of all the border Dinka, but the Ghol (who were most active in the border skirmishes) were hardest hit. Some 668 cattle were lost (of which 425 were Ghol), 120 women and children captured, and ninety persons killed. In addition to this cattle byres were burnt so that many cattle sickened and died during the remainder of the rainy season, and the first crop of sorghum was destroyed just before harvest. The three main Dinka border groups, Nyareweng, Ghol, and Duor, were made homeless during the height of the rains, and many had to seek refuge among the Twic Dinka and the Lou Nuer. The officials who visited the abandoned Dinka settlements reported a scene of utter devastation.[72]

It was not just the scale of destruction which now placed Dual beyond the pale, it was the deliberate attack on a government outpost. In 1914, the Gaawar remember, they fought the police at Duk Fadiat only when they became mixed up in the Dinka defence. This time the raid on Duk Fayuil was premeditated. That is what grieved Coriat when he learned of the raid, as Dual had now gone beyond 'the reach of government forgiveness'. Dual's retaliation also allowed administrators to absolve themselves of any blame in their handling of him in February. It did not matter that by the end of 1928 they learned from Nuer that Dual had claimed that, as the government refused to hear his two cases against the Dinka, 'and had confiscated his rifles on Dinka complaints and seized his country, he refused further to believe in the integrity of Government'.[73] The official version of the raid on Duk Fayuil was that it was a result of the Nuers' 'inborn conviction that Dinkas existed merely to be raided'.[74]

To retaliate during the rains was no easy matter. Regular soldiers could

[70] Quotations from 'Statement Jok Achinpiu', SRO UNP 5.A.3/43 and PPH MSS; 'Note by Mr. Wedderburn-Maxwell on the Duk Faiyuil Affair'.

[71] Kulang Majok G6.1.

[72] J. W. G. Wyld, ADC Bor and Duk, to governor UNP, 30 Oct. 1928, and H. G. W. Maxwell, ADC Zeraf River, 30 Oct. 1928, both in NRO Civsec 5/3/12; J. W. G. Wyld to governor UNP, 10 Mar. 1930, SRO UNP 5.A.3/43; J. W. G. Wyld, 'Report on the Duk Raid', 10 Dec. 1928, NRO Civsec 5/3/12.

[73] ADC Southern District to governor UNP, 20 Dec. 1928, NRO UNP 1/7/46.

[74] 'Police Operations Subsequent to Patrol S.8', NRO Civsec 5/3/12.

not be used and Wedderburn-Maxwell was sent with police to patrol as best he could in early October. The countryside was still flooded, but he managed to wade to the Duk ridge and surprise Dual and Gatbuogh at Turu. The two-hour fight in the high grass and through the long, straggling village was a drawn-out, desultory affair. The police 'fired a few rounds, but there was nothing to shoot at except smoke'. The Nuer were too busy untethering their cattle and driving them away to counter-attack. Five Nuer—one Lou and four Bar—were killed, including Ruop Jiak, the ex-policeman who had fired the first shot against government troops back in 1913.[75] The Gaawar were disconcerted at being attacked in their homes during the rains, but Wedderburn-Maxwell was unable to follow up his surprise.

Despite the fact that some Lou (including a few Dinka living among them) joined Dual, the raid and its aftermath considerably upset relations between the Gaawar and those Lou bordering the Dinka. Dual's Lou mother-in-law Nyanhial exchanged angry words with him 'because of my relations that had been killed in the Gaweir raid' in August. She protested again in November after a band of Jamogh massacred a small group of Nyareweng at Famenkwai and abducted their wives and daughters. One of the men killed and one of the girls stolen were Dung-Rumjok Lou, not Dinka, and some of the other women were related to the Lou chief Kuny Nyang. But feeling was running high in Dual's camp, and Dual refused to speak to either his mother-in-law or a party of Kuny Nyang's people who came to reclaim their women. While Dual lay on his back under a tree, taking no active part in events, his young men beat Nyanhial and the Lou envoys, killing one who was a Dinka raised among the Nuer. Nyanhial managed to escape with the help of some of the Gaawar women in the camp and further deaths were avoided by the intercession of one of Deng Laka's elderly widows. When Dual finally did speak to his one remaining Lou prisoner, he complained of the way Kuny Nyang and other Lou chiefs had befriended the Dinka during his raid, adding 'that if it was not for the Government he would go and fight them too'.[76] The killings at Famenkwai and the response of the Lou again demonstrate the complexity of Nuer–Dinka relations in this region.

Dual was a fugitive from the end of 1928 until January 1930, when he was captured. After the attack at Turu he split with Gatbuogh. He made at least two overtures to the government, using his brother Gau Bang as intermediary asking for terms of surrender, but on being told to surrender unconditionally and to make complete reparation and compensation to the Dinka and the government he did not come in. From February to May 1929 the troops known as the 'Bar Column' of the Nuer Settlement traversed Gaawar country,

[75] H. G. W. Maxwell, ADC Fangak, to governor UNP, 27 Oct. 1928, NRO Civsec 5/3/12 and PPH MSS; Kulang Majok EHJP-7.

[76] 'Killing of Chan Deng', SRO UNP 5.A.3/43 and PPH MSS. See also governor Malakal to civil secretary, 1 Dec. 1928, NRO Civsec 5/3/12; Wyld, 'Report on the Duk Raid'.

enforcing the concentration order, and chasing Dual and his young men from one hideout to another. On 3 May 1929 Wedderburn-Maxwell again ambushed Dual at his camp in the *toic*, and this time Dual was wounded. Because of the concentration of the Gaawar and the movements of the troops during the Nuer Settlement, Dual became progressively isolated from his people, and finally decided to leave Gaawar country altogether.[77]

Dual, now accompanied only by his brother Diop, was given refuge by Giet Majok of the Guandong section in Gaajok country along the Sobat. Giet Majok was related by marriage to Guek and had earlier harboured him. A Nuer ex-soldier learned of his hiding place and alerted the district commissioner at Nasir, C. H. Armstrong ('Latjor Dingyan'). Armstrong arrived at the village on 24 January 1930, there was a brief struggle with Diop, but both Dual and he then surrendered. Armstrong handcuffed himself to Dual for the entire steamer journey to Malakal, and only on arrival learned that Dual was now suffering from smallpox.[78] Dual's life as a fugitive was over, and his long exile had begun.

Exile, peace, and war

Dual's arrest followed Guek's death and preceded the surrender of Pok and Car in 1930, and Gatbuogh in 1931. Dual, Gatbuogh, and Pok were all imprisoned in Malakal under a governor's warrant, and in the end none of the prophets was tried on any charge. The circumstances which led to Dual's breach with the government, and the campaign which followed that breach, reveal the psychological need within the government (explicitly voiced by Willis and Wyld) to demonstrate its control over the Nuer by removing the prophets. The collective fate of the prophets, which included death in battle or in prison, exile, and release, showed that the power to manipulate life and death had passed from the prophets to the government.

Wyld preferred Dual either dead or imprisoned for life, and Willis was inclined to agree with him. It was only after both men had left the province early in 1931 that Coriat persuaded the new governor, A. G. Pawson, to reconsider Dual's case, by suggesting that Dual be allowed to settle in Coriat's new Western Nuer District near the Catholic mission station of Yoinyang. Dual had promised Coriat he would settle quietly. Pawson, impressed by Coriat's description of Dual's treatment in 1928, agreed and obtained

[77] Governor UNP to civil secretary, 26 Nov. 1928 and 21 Dec. 1928, both in NRO Civsec 5/3/12; 'Barcol Diary', and Willis, 'Nuer Settlement 1929', 28 June 1929, both in NRO Civsec 1/3/8; governor UNP to civil secretary, 27 May 1929, SRO UNP 5.A.3/42; 'Statement by Dwal Diu'; Kulang Majok EHJP-7.

[78] C. H. Armstrong, DC ED, to governor UNP, 25 Jan. 1930, and 'Dwal Diu & Diop Diu—Capture of', both in SRO UNP 5.A.3/43; 'Statement by Dwal Diu'; *SMR* 13 (8 Mar. 1930), 2.

permission from Khartoum early in 1932. Gatbuogh and Pok, on the other hand, were deemed incorrigible and were exiled to Wau, the capital of Bahr el-Ghazal Province, and ended their days there.[79]

It is not clear from the surviving record whether Dual did go to Western Nuer in 1932. By 1935 he was still detained in Malakal, this time unanimously recommended by all Nuer district commissioners to be the 'chief' of a 'tribal village' set up on the outskirts of town for Nuer and Dinka migrant workers. There he registered immigrants, collected rents, kept the huts in repair, and advised the district commissioner of Malakal on magistrate's cases arising in his village. The duties were light, but the position gave him a slight income and a place where he could entertain visitors. With the outbreak of World War II and the increased influx of migrant workers to Malakal, the tribal village was abandoned, but by that time Dual had been transferred to Adok.[80]

Meanwhile, the Gaawar and their Dinka neighbours were undergoing a reorganization which not only excluded Dual, but was predicated on his absence. The amalgamated Dinka groups of Nyareweng and Ghol were separated from each other, and their two paramount chiefs, Deng Malual and Monykuer Mabur, were given increased responsibilities. The elevation of the Dinka border chiefs was achieved in part by levelling the Gaawar. Administrators set their faces against allowing anyone among the Gaawar to achieve the same influence and power Dual had had. While Guer Wiu became the 'leading chief' of the Bar, no one was appointed 'paramount' of the Bar Gaawar in Dual's place. Smaller lineage heads were recognized and proliferated under the court system. When at last the need for a more powerful administrative chief was recognized in the early 1940s, authority was not vested in one paramount, but was divided between a court president and an executive chief. There were to be no more Dual Dius.[81]

In the aftermath of the Nuer Settlement those Gaawar leaders who had the closest ties with the Dinka, and who had shown the greatest loyalty to the government, assumed the most influential positions in the new structure of native administration. Guer Wiu was relied on and praised by all district commissioners until his death in 1937. Getting on with the Dinka almost became the test of a 'good' chief. Even Dual's brother Gau Bang as chief of the Jamogh gained a good reputation for settling disputes of all kinds and for maintaining good relations with the Dinka. He even married a Ghol wife in

[79] Coriat (1931*c*); A. G. Pawson, governor UNP, to civil secretary, 30 Nov. 1931, NRO Dakhlia I 1/2/6; E. G. Coryton, acting governor UNP, to DC Fangak, 12 Feb. 1932, PPH MSS.

[80] Governor UNP to civil secretary, 28 Jan. 1935, 'Tribal Re-organization in Malakal Town', 18 Nov. 1935, and DC Northern District to governor UNP, 7 Aug. 1943, all in SRO UNP 66.B.12; Coryton, 'Handing-Over Notes', 1939, NRO UNP 1/45/332.

[81] W. L. Sherratt, ADC ZVD, to governor Malakal, 2 Nov. 1935, SRO UNP 32.B.1; J. Winder, 'Note on the Evolution of Policy in Regard to Chiefs Sub-chiefs & Headmen', 17 June 1942, Nasir END 1.F.1 and 2 vol. i; Johnson (1986*b*).

1938. There grew up a myth among administrators, deliberately fostered by Deng Malual, that past bad relations between the Gaawar and Dinka had been due to Dual, and to Dual alone.[82]

Dual maintained a keen interest in home affairs during the first ten years of his exile. He kept in touch through numerous visitors who came to stay with him in exile and sent word to Gau Bang whenever he thought the time was right to initiate a new age-set.[83] He was concerned about his own position and did not seem, at first, to understand the finality of his exclusion. In 1936 he sent a note to the district commissioner of Malakal complaining about the activities of Guer Wiu and Dag Mer in trying to usurp his position as 'Head Chief' and in oppressing his people. He was severely reprimanded for this attempted interference and warned that if he continued he might lose his 'present easy job' as chief of the tribal village and be deported from the province. Apparently visitors continued to complain to him about court cases that went against them. The Zeraf district commissioner finally asked for Dual's removal, and he was transported to Adok in Western Nuer District to live on a government allotment.[84]

Dual had been physically powerful and intellectually active and clearly had difficulty adjusting to this prolonged period of trivial activity. In the presence of visiting district commissioners in Malakal and Adok he was either excitable or withdrawn. He appeared to them as a burned-out case who had gone to fat and turned to drink. By the end of the 1940s he was reduced to begging for money with which to sustain himself. All of this contributed to the impression that he was temperamentally incapable of returning to the Gaawar and settling down in peace. From time to time either Dual or the Gaawar would ask for his return. By the early 1940s it was thought possible that Gaawar–Dinka relations were sufficiently stable to make the experiment, were it not for the World War and the need to keep the country completely secure. Dual's strongest supporter within the administration was Wedderburn-Maxwell, now district commissioner Western Nuer and responsible for Dual's upkeep. Though Monykuer Mabur and even Deng Malual expressed no overt objections, two arguments were advanced against Dual's return: (1) that his presence might undermine Gau Bang's position, not only in his court work, but in his relations with the Dinka, and (2) that as Dual still had a divinity he could never be trusted to hold a position within the administrative

[82] Sherratt to governor Malakal, 2 Nov. 1935, SRO UNP 32.B.1; 'Duk Fadiat Meeting 1938', SRO BD 66.E.3; A. Forbes, ADC Bor, to governor UNP, 30 May 1941, SRO BD 66.B.3; ADC ZVD to governor Malakal, 23 Oct. 1936, SRO UNP 66.B.11; B. V. Marwood, DC Bor, to governor UNP, 28 Feb. 1936, SRO UNP 66.B.11 and BD 66.E.3.

[83] Ruot Diu EHJP-5.

[84] Dual Diu to DC Malakal Town, 16 Jan. 1936, W. Sherratt, ADC ZVD, to governor Malakal, 28 Jan. 1936, governor UNP to DC Malakal, 1 Feb. 1936, and DC Malakal to governor UNP, 6 Feb. 1936, all in SRO UNP 66.B.12; B. A. Lewis, DC Pibor, to governor UNP, 16 Feb. 1944, SRO BD 66.B.3.

organization. It was felt that even if he tried not to settle court cases on his own, the Gaawar would insist that he did. There were some grounds for this latter fear. Gau Bang had indicated several times that he considered that he was only temporarily standing in for Dual, and even today the men who followed Dual as warriors recall that they could not respect Gau as much as they did Dual.[85]

Dual continued his spiritual work, but even that was probably less in Adok than in Malakal. In Malakal he had cured barren women by anointing their stomachs with butter or his own spittle (Lam Liew, Dual's Lou friend, sent his wife to Dual to be cured in this way). He extended his services to the *gatkume*, 'children of the government' (i.e. townspeople), and cured sick children by sacrificing goats. 'He became the divinity of all the people, even the Turuk.' But Adok was smaller than Malakal, with fewer residents and visitors. In 1942 the Gaawar, Lak, and Thiang all petitioned the governor-general, then visiting Fangak, to release Dual so that he could bless their crops, but this was turned down. Dual's application to return to Gaawar was finally rejected in 1944, but he still longed for home. He was involved, even at a distance, in the negotiations which led to the marriage of his son Gatkuoth Dual to Deng Malual's daughter in 1944, hoping it would help to overcome that old adversary's residual mistrust. He made an unauthorized crossing from Adok to the Zeraf Island in 1948, but still the government would not sanction his return.[86]

It was when the government was distracted by the preparations for Sudanese independence that Dual made his escape. In April 1953, at the urging of his divinity, he left Adok and returned to Gaawar. The district commissioners failed to apprehend him before the onset of the rains. Throughout the rains Dual blessed crops and cured the sick, and providentially the Gaawar alone along the Zeraf had a good harvest that year. By the time the roads had opened at the beginning of 1954, the Gaawar would not give Dual up without a fight, and that could not be countenanced with elections to the National Assembly about to take place. But what surprised the government the most was that Dual's Dinka neighbours raised no objections to his return (Deng Malual having died in 1946). The governor, John Winder (a former Zeraf Valley district commissioner), interviewed him, was convinced he meant no harm, warned him to behave, and let him go.[87]

85 'Upper Nile Province "Who's Who"', Malakal UNP SCR 66.D.4; C. G. Davies, governor UNP, to DC Bor, 13 May 1941, A. Forbes, ADC Bor, to governor UNP, 30 May 1941, H. G. Maxwell, DC Western Nuer, to DC Zeraf, 22 Nov. 1943, P. P. Howell, ADC Zeraf District, 2 Jan. 1944, J. F. C., DC Bor, to DC Zeraf, 14 Feb. 1944, and B. A. Lewis, DC Pibor, to governor UNP, 16 Feb. 1944, all in SRO BD 66.B.3; Kulang Majok G6.1 and EHJP-7.

86 Stephen Ciec Lam L24.3, Kulang Majok EHJP-7; John Winder to Davies, 1 July 1942, SAD 541/1/157; Lazarus Leek Mawut, personal communication; F. D. MacJannet, DC Western Nuer, to DC Central Nuer, 24 Apr. 1948, SRO BD 66.B.3, vol. ii.

87 John Winder, governor UNP, to permanent under-secretary, Ministry of Interior, 29 Apr. 1954, NRO UNP 1/34/276.

At home Dual seemed a different person from the pathetic exile, now impressing visitors with his 'commanding presence and personality'.[88] He also impressed the first Northern Sudanese district commissioner of the Gaawar, Hassan Dafa'allah, who arrived towards the end of 1954 and found Dual 'old but still strong. He received me cordially and he was pleased to see the British go for ever,' a statement we need not doubt was genuinely expressed. Early in 1955 Dual met the new Sudanese governor, gave him one of his own ox-names (Carkur), and sacrificed an ox to signal the end to the feud between himself and government. The Northern Sudanese officials were highly pleased with his attentions, but they, too, reiterated the instructions of their British predecessors: Dual was to stay out of court business, confine himself to spiritual work, and advise his people not to make trouble with the Dinka.[89]

The latter injunction was to prove the most difficult to follow. The problem was the old one of border grazing areas. An agreement had been reached at a Nuer–Dinka chiefs' meeting in 1947 that the Gaawar should graze north of Khor Nyang, even though Khor Nyang itself was just north of the province boundary. In 1954 Dual twice asked Winder, before a number of Nuer and Dinka witnesses, if he could graze along the watercourse and was told he could. On going to the *toic* in 1955 he brought a mounted police escort to ensure that there would be no trouble between himself and the Dinka. He crossed Khor Nyang with his cattle and camped to the south of it, between two Angai Dinka cattle camps.[90]

This was clearly a provocative act, even if it did not presage hostilities. Word got back to Malakal from various Dinka sources that 'Dual is being told by his Kujur to kill the bulls and fight the Dinka this year.'[91] The new Northern Sudanese district commissioner at Bor became extremely alarmed, wiring the governor that 'it is reported that Dual Diu started his 1928 wars with the Dinka in similar manner', which was, in fact, false.[92] But there was something disturbing happening on the border, and the Dinka from Kongor and Duk Fayuil were rushing to the aid of the Dinka in the *toic*. Hassan Dafa'allah sent Dual a note asking him to withdraw to the north of Khor Nyang. A force of two companies of the Sudan Defence Force (one Camel Corps and one Equatorial Corps), accompanied by the deputy governor, district commissioners Fangak and Bor, and the chief inspector of police, assembled at Duk Fadiat to bring Dual in. The Sudanese administrators, having no previous experience in the province, felt that their authority was

88 "Upper Nile Province 'Who's Who"', Malakal UNP SCR 66.D.4.

89 'Dual Diu', New Fangak ZVR/SCR/1.B.9; Hassan Dafa'allah (Dingnyang), DC ZVD, to Matet Kan, 20 Jan. 1955, and Hassan Dafa'allah to Dual Diu, 20 Jan. 1955, both in NRO UNP 1/28/217 and New Fangak ZVR 66.A.1.

90 The following is based mainly on papers in NRO UNP 1/28/217–18. Specific references are given for cited passages.

91 'Cpl Barang Abit and Ch. Thon Malek & Majok Kuacuol', NRO UNP 1/28/218.

92 DC Bor to governor UNP, Mar. 1955, NRO UNP 1/28/217.

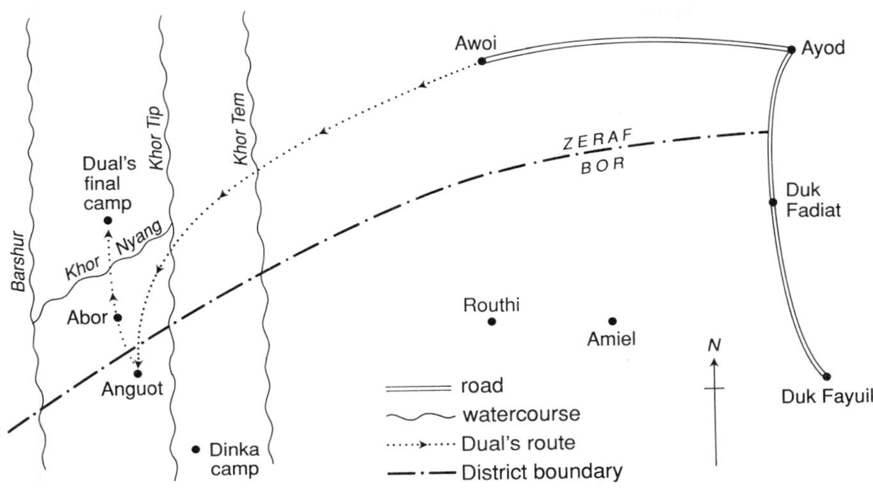

FIG. 10. Dual Diu's return, 1955 (from a sketch in NRO UNP 1/28/218)

being tested. They were nervous about Dual's intentions, having only a general impression of Dual's history of conflict with the government. Dual retired north of Khor Nyang but pleaded age when ordered to come to Duk Fadiat and requested a delay. Hassan Dafaʿallah was sent to Dual's camp with a platoon of Camel Corps. When Dual heard they were coming he commented casually to the young men present that he had longed to eat the fish of Khor Nyang when he was in exile and would like some fish now. The young men immediately left to fish in the watercourse; thus they were absent when the district commissioner arrived.[93] Hassan Dafaʿallah summoned Dual to appear, and 'he complied without hesitation. I explained the accusation to him and declared his immediate arrest. He obeyed the order in very good spirit.'[94]

The tension within the administration was clearly communicated to the Gaawar. Kulang Majok, one of the chiefs' policemen present, remembers Hassan Dafaʿallah as the man who prevented any rash act of bloodshed:

> the Turuk were coming. They met and they said 'We will go and shoot at Dual's camp.' There was a certain man who was the district commissioner, an Arab named Hassan Dafaʿallah—after the English had gone, he came when there was Arab rule—he was brave. At once he said, 'All you Turuk, I see you. No one will go to Dual's camp. I will go, I myself alone.' They said to him, 'If you do you will be killed.'

[93] Bullen Alier Buttic, personal communication.
[94] DC Zeraf District to governor UNP, 17 Mar. 1955, NRO UNP 1/28/217.

He said, 'I am the man who was given to them.' He then went. He came to us in Nyang. 'Right', he said. 'Now you policemen—Kulang, Thoncar, Kaydol, Matet, and Cuol—you five who are here in this place, stand guard between the Dinka and the Gaawar. Right. Let me go. I will take Dual,' and he took Dual to Malakal.[95]

The arrest of Dual caused quite a stir. Hassan Dafa'allah insisted that Dual's history under the British should not influence the investigation into the charges that he had invaded the Dinka *toic*, threatened to fight them, and threatened to fight the government. The district commissioner in Bor resembled Major Wyld in prejudging Dual's guilt. Buth Diu, member of parliament for the Zeraf District, wrote to find out what was happening. The case had to be handled very circumspectly. The most senior administrators of the province also felt that a new Sudanese administration should act with greater respect for the rights of citizens than they believed the British had done. The chief inspector of police was assigned the task of investigation. As Dual had entered an ill-defined border area where district jurisdiction was uncertain, it was decided that Dual should be tried by a neutral court of two Nuer, two Dinka, and one Murle chief.

The chief inspector investigated the three allegations of criminal trespass, inciting disturbance of the public peace, and being a member of an unlawful assembly, and found Dual innocent of all charges. Witnesses had recalled that John Winder had given Dual permission to graze in the area. Dual had obeyed the district commissioner Fangak's order to return to the north of Khor Nyang. Not only had Dual not made the bellicose threats attributed to him, he had tried to calm some of his followers when confronted by the Dinka. Some of the other Nuer and Dinka participants, however, were found subject to prosecution.[96]

Dual's statement at his trial is worth quoting, even if it is in the language of the official recorder, as it does indicate how he judged his circumstances in the new Sudan:

I never intended to fight the Dinka. I myself have married to 5 Dinka wives & my son is married to a Dinka girl.

I was very pleased when the Birtish left the country and the country was ruled by the Sudanese themselves. I was also very pleased when the present Governor told me that good relations should be maintained between the Dinka & Nuer. After this I believed that the whole country was one & that every Sudanese has the right to move anywhere. Last year after I was released from my exile I went to the toich. I killed 3 elephants & distributed the meat both to the Nuer & Dinka alike.

This year when I intended to move to the Toich I asked the present Governor in order to allow 10 Mounted Policemen to accompany me to the Toich as I expected that the Dinka would make many rumours about fighting them and bad intentions

[95] Kulang Majok EHJP-7.

[96] I. M. Korshid, investigator, chief inspector of police, 'Case against Accused Dual Diu & Others', 31 Mar. 1955, NRO UNP 1/28/217.

towards them. I moved to the Toich and I did not at all try to instigate anybody to fight and was all the time living there very peacefully.

Early this year Sayed Buth Diu visited me in my Luak in Toro [Turu]. I asked him about the state of affairs in the Country & whether the people supported the present Government. He told me that the British have gone for ever & we must all support our new Government. Up to this moment I don't see any reason for all these troubles & I know of no fault which I committed. . . . I knew the place to where I moved in the first place was a Dinka area. I moved to there in the belief that the old conditions have changed and that I will not be objected if I move there especially this place which was mine before my exile in this particular place I killed 10 elephants.

Last year when the Dinka visited me at Ador where my father is buried I killed a bull in courtesy for them.

The only thing the Dinka wants is to see me dead. I wrote a letter to the Governor . . . I told the Governor that I came in the Toich only for food as my people were starving.

. . . I welcome[d] the new Sudanese Government when [it] came into power & I was really very pleased. As a sign of my good intentions towards our Government I killed a bull as a sign of peace between the Govt. & Nuer & I gave my own bull name Char-Koor to the present government since then I believed all the lies of the past had gone into the oblivion. . . . All the British Governors since my exile were trying hard & asked me repeatedly to kill a bull to end the hostilities between the Nuer & the Government. I refused.[97]

It was not so much Dual's personal behaviour which was found at fault, as the excitement he aroused among his own young men and the Dinka opposite following his reoccupation of this area of the *toic*. Despite the report of the chief inspector of police, the five chiefs sitting in judgment fined Dual thirty head of cattle for trespassing on Dinka grazing. In order to preserve public order along the boundary the Governor ordered that Dual reside in Malakal for a further two years.[98]

Dual was thus in Malakal on 22 August 1955 when news arrived of the mutiny of the Equatorial Corps in Torit. This was the prelude to the first civil war in the Southern Sudan which was brought to an end only in 1972 by the Addis Ababa Agreement. The news of the Torit mutiny sparked off a shoot-out between the (northern) army and the (southern) police in Malakal. Many police and prison warders fled the town, and many prisoners escaped at the same time. Dual was among those who fled to the bush. When he arrived at his old home he sent a letter to Monykuer Mabur to reassure him that he had left Malakal only to get away from the fighting, and that he would soon proceed to Fangak. Meanwhile the governor and the district commissioner

[97] Statements of Dwal Diu, 20 Mar. 1955, 11. 30 a.m., and 24 Mar. 1955, 11. 30 a.m., NRO UNP 1/28/218.

[98] Governor UNP to permanent under-secretary, Ministry of Interior, 27 Apr. 1955, and Residence Order, M. O. Yassin, governor UNP, 25 May 1955, both in NRO UNP 1/28/217; 'Dual Diu', New Fangak ZVR/SCR/1.B.9.

Fangak were sending letters to Dual ordering him to return. The mounted police who were sent to arrest him found him at Ayod, on his way to Fangak, and he was brought in, exhausted and foot sore.[99]

Despite the fact that the police had cleared Dual of any criminal activity, and that he had been found on his way back to Fangak after the Malakal incident, his reputation as a 'kujur' ensured that his past history and present motives would be misrepresented in the final report of the Commission of Inquiry into the 1955 disturbances:

> One of the famous prisoners who had escaped from Malakal during the shooting was a Kujur, called Dual Diu, an old Nuer warrior who had troubled the authorities for a long time. This gentleman had been a trouble maker since the 1930's. He commands great authority and respect from his people and he often raided the land of the Dinka and stole their cattle. He was therefore, during the old regime, confined to the town of Malakal, but before the British left, and as an act of grace, the then Governor allowed him to go back to his land and die in peace. He was duly released in September 1954. But early in March 1955 Dual Diu thought of testing the strength of the new Government and attempted to raid the Dinka again. A Camel Corps Company with support, and a Company from the Southern Corps . . . were at him in a short while and Dual surrendered without any bloodshed and was brought to Malakal, given a house and was told to stay there. So when he ran away after the shooting, the authorities were faced with the additional problem of dangerous rumours spreading to the effect that there was 'no Hukuma' [government] and the old tribal raids would start. . . . However, Northern troops and police were quickly on the spot and Dual was arrested shortly afterwards.[100]

It was a mercifully short exile in Malakal this time. Dual was allowed to return to home in 1957. A peacemaking ceremony was held at Duk Fadiat between Dual, representing the Gaawar, and Monykuer Mabur, representing the Ghol. Dual was told by the government that he could go home, but he could not go to the *toic*; he could 'practice his Spiritual influence', but he was to take no part in administration. Then Dual and Monykuer shook hands and each sacrificed an ox. Both fell facing the *toic*, which was interpreted as a good sign.[101] But Dual and Monykuer went beyond the official ceremony. Dual married one of Monykuer's daughters, and both men regularly visited each other. To the Ghol Dual's wife was their 'bridge', and Dual last visited Duk Fadiat shortly before his death in 1968.

The eleven years between Dual's formal peace with the Ghol and his death were years of new difficulties. Dual was now an old man and seemed to want

[99] Hassan Dafa'allah, DC Zeraf District, to governor UNP, 6 Oct. 1955, SRO BD 66.B.3, vol. ii; UNPMD, Oct. 1955, p. 2.

[100] *Report of the Commission of Inquiry into the Disturbances in the Southern Sudan during August 1955* (Khartoum, 1956), 69–70.

[101] 'Minutes of the Inter-Districts Meeting . . . Duk Fadiet . . . 6th–10th March 1957', SRO UNP 66.B.5/3.

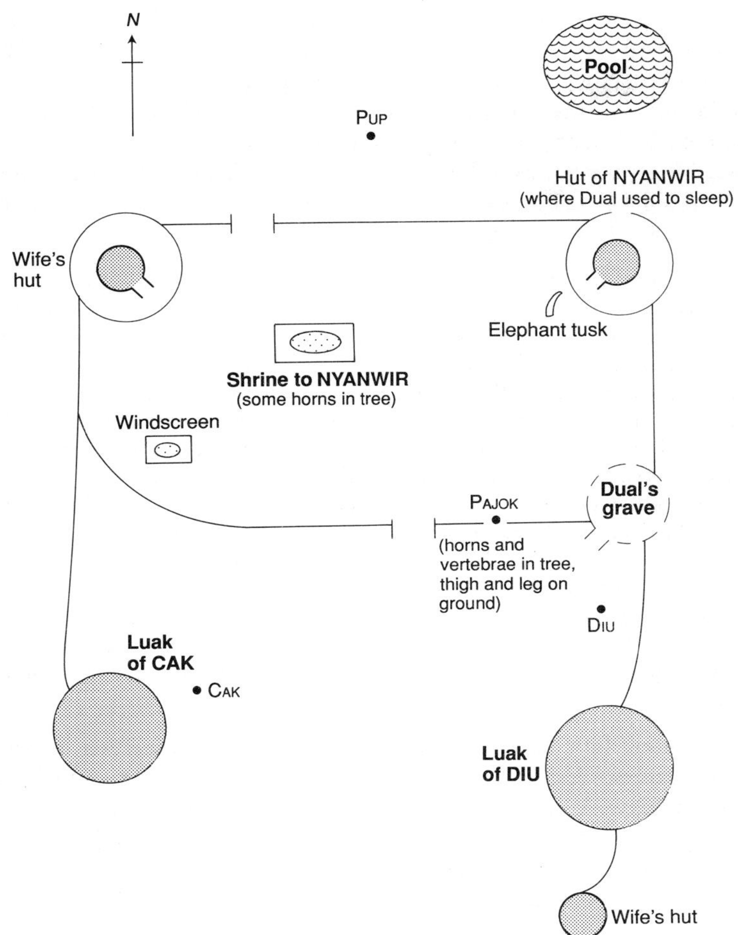

FIG. 11. Diagram of Dual Diu's homestead and grave, 1976 (not to scale)

to live a quiet life. At his homestead, which has since become a shrine associated with his grave, he accumulated a number of divinities, sometimes dedicating cattle to them, with special shrines and cattle-pegs. His two main byres were dedicated to his own divinity, DIU, and to CAK (creator), each with large cattle-pegs where sacrifices to those divinities were made. He also had a hut and a shrine dedicated to the divinity NYANWIR (daughter of the river, a clear reference to the Aiwel myth), and to PAJOK, the maternal uncle of DENG (Figs. 11, 12). He was not as energetic an opponent of magic on his return from exile, though magic was spreading more widely at this time than at any

FIG. 12. Nyup Dak (widow of Lam Liew) (l.) and Riei Pok, the prophet of GÄR, clear the ground around the shrine to NYANWIR at Dual Diu's grave, 1976

time in his life. Instead he dedicated a shrine to one new divinity, PUP, and cattle to another, KUOTH PINY, both being divinities he claimed to have found during his exile in Western Nuer. PUP is known as a talking fetish in the west. Perhaps in this way he hoped to co-opt the *kuuth piny* of the magicians without having to confront the magicians themselves.

But the main threat came, not from the Dinka, nor from the magicians, but from the civil war, which began in earnest in the south in the early 1960s with the founding of the Anyanya guerrilla army. The 'people of the bush' (*jidoar*) were not active in the Gaawar area until about 1965. Dual, who did not want to take part in the fight, tried to remain neutral and managed to persuade both the government and the Anyanya that he was on their side. Kulang Majok remembered:

> If the Arabs came, they would say, 'Grandfather, let us be in peace', and he would give them something to eat, and they would go on their way. If the people of the bush came they would say, 'Grandfather, let us be in peace', and he would give them something to eat and they would go on. He sided with no one and he rejected no one.[102]

Thus the government reported that, after the guerrillas had stolen his cattle in 1965–6, Dual ordered his people to defend themselves against the

[102] Kulang Majok EHJP-7.

'outlaws',[103] while those with the Anyanya reported that he placed his healing powers at their disposal to help their wounded.

Dual died on 23 March 1968 and was buried at his homestead in Turu. Perhaps the most ironic fact about his life was the epitaph written by the district commissioner Fangak on his death. 'Many telegrams of condolences for the death of this great man who served his Country faithfully were received from various parts of the country. We offered our sympathy to his relatives too. May almighty God let his soul rest in peace.'[104] He was a prophet at peace at last.

In Dual Diu's life there is a stark contradiction between his actions and the official interpretations of those actions. Superficially, the official record confirms him in the stereotype of the prophet as resistance leader, representing Nuer hostility to both the Dinka and foreign invaders. He first comes to notice in 1913 as the man really behind the Gaawar rising. After his capture in 1930 he is consistently represented as implacably hostile to the Dinka, and his raids were remembered while his attempts at reconciliation were forgotten. Even the new Sudanese government was willing to punish him for his reputation rather than his actions.

Yet the reality of Dual's life demonstrates the consistency of the prophetic idiom and the continuity of the prophetic tradition of DIU. Dual's emergence as a prophet was greeted with relief by his family as counteracting the wilder behaviour of his brother Macar. He took no leading role in the 1913 rising. His first raid against the Dinka was undertaken to avenge his brothers' deaths, and his subsequent confrontations responded to similar threats. The ecology of the Zaraf Valley is such that competition for land was a more marked feature in his relations with the Dinka than was the case between the Lou and Dinka during Ngundeng's life. But peacemaking was a significant feature in Dual's prophetic career, even if contained within a more restricted circle than that of the Lou prophet. He first attempted to reconcile feuding factions within the Gaawar; he worked with the province administration in the 1920s to effect a reconciliation with the Dinka; he maintained and strengthened that reconciliation throughout the 1950s until his death. His prophetic powers did not disappear with his removal from the political scene, nor was his importance to his people diminished. Healing, the giving of life, and mediating personal relations with divinity through sacrifice and prayer marked both his life in exile and his return. His prayers and his blessings were extended to all who wanted them—Nuer, Dinka, the townspeople of Malakal, and finally both government and their opponents in the troubled years after Sudanese independence. So Dual Diu—the warrior 'kujur', the predator of the Dinka, the inveterate rebel—even Dual Diu tried to be, and is remembered by some as having been, a prophet of peace.

[103] 'Dual Diu', New Fangak ZVR/SCR/1.B.9. [104] Ibid.

7

Prophetic Rivalries in the Western Homeland

The Western Nuer in the ethnographic imagination—the nineteenth-century background—prophetic rivalries, 1883–1921—the arrival of government, 1921–1923—the suppression of the prophets and the assassination of Fergie Bey, 1924–1927—reinstatement, surveillance, and survival, 1930–1973—contrasts

The Western Nuer in the ethnographic imagination

The most dramatic and best-known murder of a British officer in the Sudan, after that of Gordon in Khartoum, is the assassination of Captain V. H. Fergusson by two Nyuong Nuer on 14 December 1927. The events surrounding Fergusson's death were immortalized in a memorial volume about his life, commissioned by his mother and introduced by no less a personage than the former governor-general Sir Reginald Wingate.[1] This book has had some influence on both popular and academic perceptions of the Nuer. In so far as it also falsely accuses one prophet, Gaaluak Nyagh, of instigating the murder it further reinforces the old image of the prophet as resistance leader. The murder and official retaliation overlapped with the larger and more elaborate military campaign against Guek begun in the same year, and it is not surprising that the two episodes—separated as they were by over 100 miles—are sometimes conflated. One recent book has even identified Guek as the leader of 'a rising of Nuer in which a British district commissioner, V. H. Fergusson, and his retinue were killed'.[2]

Fergusson's murder has also been attributed to the structural hostility between Nuer and Dinka. The final report of the Jonglei Investigation Team noted that the Dinka pastures on the Lau river system present the Nuer with an alternative to Bahr el-Jebel pastures in years of high Nile rivers when the latter remain under water during the crucial period of the dry season. Because of this, it postulated, the Nyuong would probably have seized this area, had government not intervened.

> Indeed the prevention of raids and incursions into Dinka country was one of the main causes of discontent which ultimately led to revolt and the assassination of Captain V.

[1] Fergusson (1930). [2] Deng and Daly (1989: 173 n.).

Fergus[s]on, then District Commissioner of the area, in 1928 [*sic*]. It is significant that the year preceding this event was one of comparatively high Nile and a high minimum during the dry season (66.6 at Mongalla) after six previous years of low minimum. Large areas of grazing on the Bahr el Jebel *toiches*, previously accessible, were that year reduced by permanent flooding throughout the dry season. It is therefore reasonable to suppose that feelings of frustration at not being able to penetrate into Dinka country, where alternatives could be found, were one of the basic causes of this revolt, though it would be a mistake to consider this the only cause.[3]

Fergusson's murder thus has been used to illustrate some of the dominant themes of Nuer ethnography: the opposition of Nuer to both Dinka and government, and the prophet's involvement in focusing that hostility. The story as told contradicts the portrait of Nuer prophets presented in the preceding chapters. Yet, two points emerge from examining the events surrounding Fergusson's death. First, the established interpretation finds little support in the known evidence. The plausibility of the ecological hypothesis cited above, for instance, depends on misdating the murder by a year. Second, the prophetic idiom in the western homeland developed differently from that on the eastern frontier. The Western Nuer prophets were more regularly involved in warfare and constrained by rivalries than those of the east; they were less influenced by the symbols and imagery of the Dinka divinities and spear-masters; while clearly inspired by the appearance of prophets on the frontier, they fashioned their own idiom from a more local range of spiritual activities.

Despite this historically later development of the Western Nuer prophetic idiom, there has been a tendency in the ethnography to cloak all Nuer prophets in images taken from the west. This is because both Evans-Pritchard's and Crazzolara's most detailed descriptions of Nuer religious practice are drawn from observations there. Evans-Pritchard began and ended his field-work in Western Nuer District, while Crazzolara was confined almost exclusively to the Leek who surrounded the mission at Yoinyang. Prophets having recently been suppressed in the east, it was only in the west that Evans-Pritchard observed active prophets or cases of spirit seizure. Both he and Crazzolara drew their evidence of prophetic involvement in raiding almost exclusively from Leẹk Nuer testimony, where Kolang Ket, the prophet of MAANI, was best known. Crazzolara in particular relied on an anti-prophet government chief, Twil Ran, as an informant. The evidence he cites refers to the activities of Twil's twentieth-century opponents, but he extrapolated from this the hypothesis of a centuries-old pattern embracing the Nuer beyond the horizon of his mission station.[4]

The reconstruction which follows is frankly more speculative than the

[3] JIT 1954: i. 237.

[4] Evans-Pritchard (1940*a*: 127–9); Crazzolara (1953: 35, 165–6). Twil Ran was a Jikany chief in charge of the Leek. See AMC A/112/8 and Coriat (1931*a*).

preceding chapters. The data available to me concerning the lives of the Western Nuer prophets are more fragmentary and less detailed than the data I gathered for the Lou and Gaawar prophets. This chapter attempts to make sense of some contradictory evidence, and I stress that much more must be known about Western Nuer history generally before an interpretation of their prophets can be offered with confidence.

The rivalries which dominated the careers of many western prophets and limited the spiritual influence they could achieve were fuelled in part by the topography of Western Nuer district. Here, unlike the territory east of the Bahr el-Zeraf and Bahr el-Jebel, there are no broad dry plains intervening between settlements and pastures. The sandy ridges where settlement is possible are clustered close together, making communication easier. Nowhere in the dry season is water too distant. During the rains seasonal swamps in the south and west sometimes merge to form a temporary continuous barrier. Changes in the environment are felt more uniformly south of the Bahr el-Ghazal than is the case east of the Bahr el-Jebel. Social groups have tended, therefore, to be territorially more compact than in the east; there has been less seasonal movement; and, given the environmental constraints on both movement and settlement, there has been more interdependence between large groups than is found in the east, with more frequent intermarriage.[5] This propinquity meant that, in contrast to the Lou and Gaawar prophets who were able to remain aloof from one another, the Western Nuer prophets were forced both to compete and co-operate with each other to a far greater degree. In any wider sphere of activity they had to seek the same following. One prophet's rise in fortunes usually paralleled another's decline.

Relations with the Dinka have also been complex. The ethnographic image of constant Western Nuer military superiority over their Dinka neighbours is derived primarily from Evans-Pritchard's and Crazzolara's Leek Nuer informants, who were distant from any scene of conflict.[6] Other sources give a more varied picture. We have already seen in Chapter 2 how a powerful Dinka presence prevented the Jikany from moving west at the beginning of the last century, and how strong contacts were forged between the Jikany and Rueng Dinka. Further south the Nyuong Nuer both traded and married with the Agar, Cic, and Angai Dinka, despite the persistence of their conflicts over grazing and cattle. But the periodic isolation of the Western Nuer territory, imposed by the recurring seasonal swamps to the south and west, inhibited the growth of contiguous Nuer and Dinka settlements, as developed among the Gaawar and Lou. Marriage ties therefore do not seem to have expanded and stabilized relations between the Western Nuer and their Dinka

[5] JIT 1954: i. 145–6, 212–13; Evans-Pritchard (1940*a*: 55, 62–3, 111; 1947: 118).
[6] Evans-Pritchard (1940*a*: 127–9); Crazzolara (1953: 35).

neighbours to the same extent as they did in the east. Conflicts between the same groups of Nuer and Dinka recur frequently. Nor did the Western Nuer achieve an obvious military advantage. By 1913 the Sudan government were approached by the Jikany for protection from the Kuil Dinka,[7] and for nearly forty years, from 1883 to 1923, the Agar under Wol Athiang were a regular threat to the Nyuong, Dok, and Jagei.

The conflict between the Agar and the Nuer stemmed from the aftermath of the fall of the Egyptian garrison of Rumbek in 1883, when Wol Athiang turned on his Nuer allies. Over many years a succession of Nuer prophets confronted Wol, and the persistence of this hostility finally forced the Anglo-Egyptian government to extend its administrative authority to the Western Nuer when it sent Captain Fergusson to their country in 1921. Because the Nuer–Dinka conflict was the spur to government action and so dominated the early approaches to the prophets, we must first examine the nineteenth-century background to twentieth-century events.

The nineteenth-century background

The Jagei, Dok, and Nyuong Nuer have their main dry season pastures along the banks and watercourses of the Bahr el-Jebel. The Jagei and Dok also make use of pastures on Khor Bilnyang to the west and south-west of their main settlements, as do the northern Nyuong, but the southern Nyuong must use pastures to the south-west, in the Lake Nyubor region. The Jagei and Dok, therefore, often have dry season camps in the swamp bordering the Rek Dinka of Meshra el-Rek and the Gok Dinka, while the Dok might also find Agar pasturing near their southernmost camps. The Nyuong similarly sometimes find themselves grazing close to the Agar and Luac Dinka of Rumbek and the Cic Dinka between Shambe and the River Lau. Lake Nyubor has been a frequent meeting-point for the Nyuong Nuer, the Atuot, the Agar, and even the Cic Dinka.

In the early to mid-nineteenth century the Dok and Nyuong moved south and occupied Dinka territory bordering the Bahr el-Jebel, but in the last half of the century access to the western lands was by no means assured. Schweinfurth described the Western Nuer in 1869 as 'evidently hemmed in by hostile neighbours'. There were a number of observed incidents of Nuer–Dinka hostility along the Bahr el-Ghazal, yet during the slaving wars of the late 1870s, culminating in the revolt of Sulaiman Zubair in 1878, numerous groups of Dinka from around Meshra el-Rek fled with their herds to the Nuer for refuge. When they returned in 1880 as many as 359 Nuer families, encouraged by Gessi Pasha, settled near the Meshra. This was a period of very high and sustained flooding along the Bahr el-Jebel, and it is just possible

[7] Bimbashi Marshall, Talodi, 1 Apr. 1913, NRO Civsec 1/2/5.

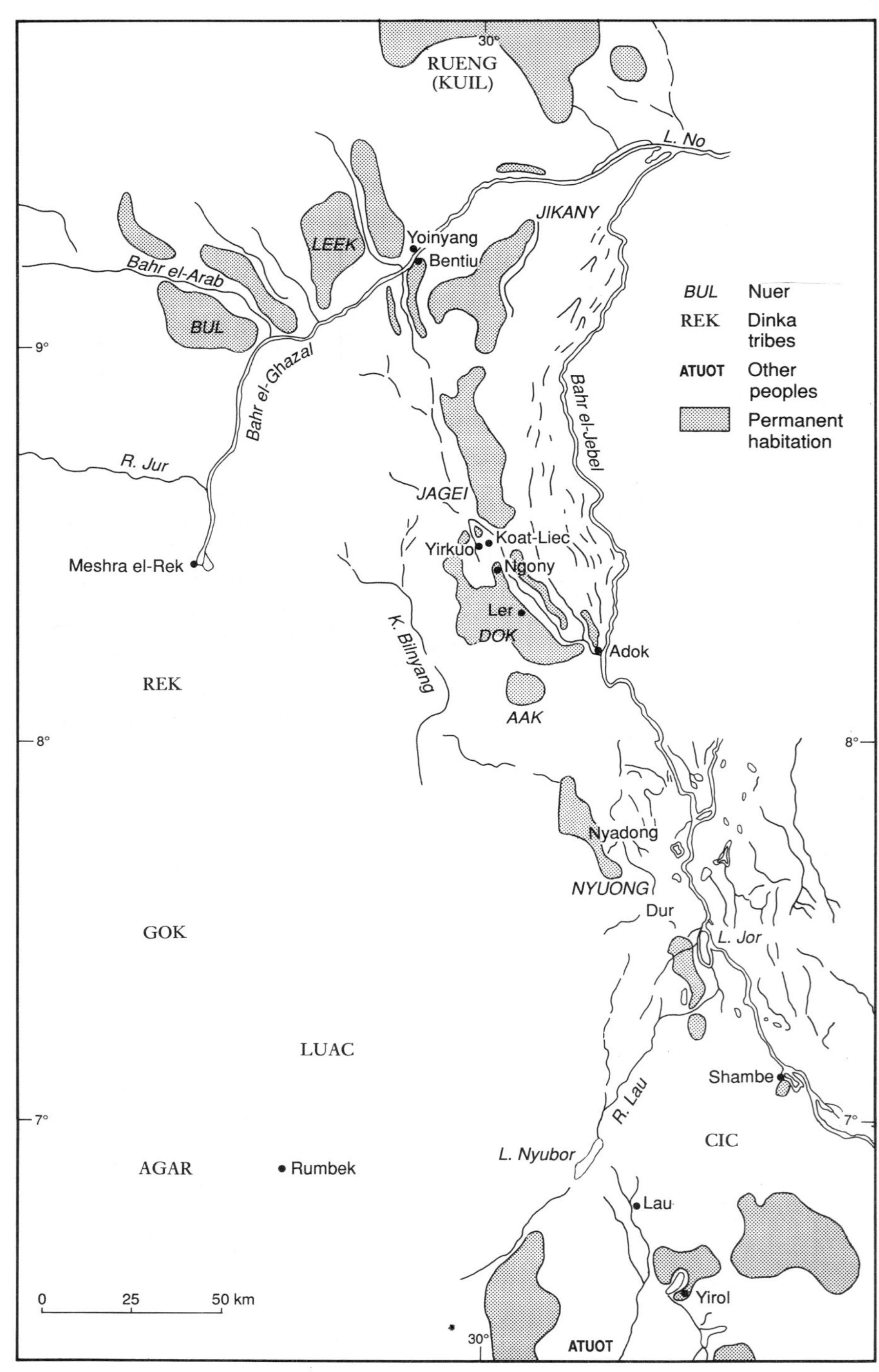

MAP 6. Western Nuer territory. *Source*: JIT 1954.

that this temporary settlement in Dinka territory was offered as reciprocation for Nuer shelter against the slavers.[8]

Dok and Nyuong relations with the Dinka further south after the fall of Rumbek in 1883 may have been influenced by environmental problems, but for this we have no firm evidence. The 1880s and 1890s were decades of variable Niles and recurring *sudd* blocks, with generally low rivers throughout the 1880s, and a period of sustained floods between 1893 and 1896. The Dok and Jagei explanation for their intermittent war with the Agar stresses vengeance for Wol Athiang's treachery after Rumbek and the desire to get more cattle, not the need to acquire alternative pastures. Kolang Ket successfully raided the Agar at the turn of the century during a long drought remembered for the death of cattle rather than the loss of *toic*.

Contemporary documentation of Western Nuer raiding begins only in 1914. In December 1914 a large force of 'Adul' Nuer (Dur Nyuong), led by a 'medicine man' named 'Kwoin', penetrated the Cic country as far as the CMS mission station at Lau where, thanks partly to the military intervention of Archdeacon Shaw, the Nuer were repulsed. The motive for the raid reported at the time was recent Nuer loss of cattle to an unnamed disease.[9] We will speculate on the identity of the 'medicine man' later, but an account of these raids gathered from the Nuer in 1921 gives a slightly different motive. The Nuer alleged that Wol Athiang made peace with the Nyuong and Jagei in 1913 but broke the peace by raiding the Nyuong in 1914. Kolang Ket, though not himself the target of Wol's raid, organized Nuer retaliation. They recovered some cattle, but Wol escaped their total vengeance, so they turned on the Gok and Rek Dinka as well.[10] The contemporary record of Nuer raids into the Meshra el-Rek area in May–June 1915, however, speaks only of Nuer retaliation for combined Dinka–Bongo forays into their country.[11] It also gives details only of the damage the Nuer did to the Dinka, saying nothing about the losses the Dinka inflicted on the Nuer. It was during this time that, according to Jagei testimony, MAANI was 'driven back' by Wol Athiang.

The Jagei imply that it was this check by Wol that brought their own raids against the Agar to a halt, and certainly even that devastation hinted at in contemporary reports suggests that all participants needed to call a halt to the war. The great floods of 1916–18 would be another reason why the official record ceases to mention any further raids along the Bahr el-Jebel. As with

[8] Fergusson (1921*b*: 154–5); [Wedderburn-Maxwell], 'The Nyuong', n.d. [1945], PPH MSS; Fergusson, 'Report on Eastern District (Nuers) Bahr el Ghazal Province', NRO Civsec 57/1/5; Selim Bimbachi (1842: 86–7, 90); Thibaut (1856: 84); Brun-Rollet (1855: 147); Petherick (1861: 367, 370); Gordon to Khairi Pasha, 16 Aug. 1874, in Gordon (1953: 164); Gessi (1892: 191, 381–2, 430).

[9] *SIR* 245 (Dec. 1914), 4; [Wedderburn-Maxwell], 'Dok and Aak Nuer', PPH MSS.

[10] Fergusson (1921*b*: 152–3).

[11] *SIR* 250 (May 1915), 6; 251 (June 1915), 5; 253 (Aug. 1915), 3.

the Gaawar and Lou to the east the flood 'Pilual' put an end to any activities except those ensuring basic survival. It was only after 'Pilual' had fully subsided, during the 1918–19 dry season, that aggression could resume. Sometime in 1918 a band of Nyuong attacked but were defeated by the Agar. In June 1919 a group of Nuer, probably Jagei but possibly Dok, raided the Loic-Rek Dinka south-east of Meshra el-Rek, and in January 1921 another group of Dok and Nyuong Nuer raided Wol Athiang's Agar and were defeated.[12] The government, which had been unable to take any effective action during the height of the 1915–16 raids, now felt both able and compelled to extend its administrative network to include the Western Nuer. On entering the country in 1921 Captain Fergusson found that not only were Nuer leaders in conflict with Wol Athiang, but many were in conflict with each other. It is to these rivalries we now turn.

Prophetic rivalries, 1883–1921

By 1921 four major prophets were established among the Western Nuer. Kolang Ket of Jagei had considerable influence and prestige throughout the area as the prophet of MAANI, and other prophets were careful to appear to work parallel with him. Buom Diu had revived the Dok divinity TENY in the shadow of Kolang. Gaaluak Nyagh worked from an older spiritual base in Nyuong but translated it into the modern idiom of prophecy. Wuon Kuoth set himself up as a rival to Gaaluak among the Nyuong, reintroducing the divinity DIU, which enjoyed considerable prestige among the Nyuong through its association with the highly successful Gaawar prophets. All four prophets had organized raids against the Dinka, but at least three of them—Kolang Ket, Buom Diu, and Wuon Kuoth—as well as one magician, Tiep Kolang, had experienced setbacks in their raids. Despite this, all four prophets were the focus of considerable attention within their own areas, attracting various satellite divinities as well as ordinary Nuer anxious to gain benefits from association with successful prophets.

During the nineteenth century the new prophetic idiom which arose in the east was incorporated in the homeland with other older forms of mantic activity and spiritual inspiration. The prophets became one more among a number of categories of *guan kuoth* (owner of a divinity), and that idiomatic term is still more commonly used to refer to prophets in the west than the descriptive *guk kuoth* (vessel of a divinity). The introduction of divinities appears to have been more individual and haphazard in the homeland than on the frontier, and new divinities often came from sources closer to earth. They were found in the grass; they came out of dogs; there seems to have been a

[12] Fergusson to governor Wau, 29 May 1923, SRO UNP 66.D.1; *SIR* 299 (June 1919), 4; Fergusson (1921*b*: 153).

less clear distinction between divinities of the 'above' and the 'below'; and while the opposition between prophet and magician was usually asserted, it was not always observed. This all had a bearing on prophetic rivalries and the direction the prophetic tradition was to take among the Western Nuer.

Western Nuer prophets came to prominence in the early 1880s. One of the first was a Jagei woman, Nyapuka Dan, who was seized by DENG. About the same time a Dok man, Macot Nyuon, was seized by a divinity called TENY, and the two joined forces when invited by Wol Athiang to help the Dinka attack the Egyptians at Rumbek in 1883. During the assault Macot Nyuon was shot dead and TENY immediately passed to his brother Puot Nyuon. When Wol Athiang turned on the Nuer, attacking them and capturing the cattle they had taken at Rumbek, both Nyapuka and Puot organized Nuer retaliation. They were not always successful, and Nyapuka herself was killed during a raid on the Dinka sometime in the 1890s. Before this the prophet and the prophetess continued their earlier collaboration, and Puot, at least, prevented any other prophets from rising to prominence. He threatened an early prophet of DIU until the latter fled the country. When Kolang Ket, a Jagei man living among the Leek, was seized by the divinity MAANI he, too, had to leave home to escape Puot's threats. This was during the latter years of the Mahdiyya and Kolang is said to have gone to the Mahdist capital of Omdurman for three years, returning shortly after its fall to Kitchener's army.[13]

The period 1899–1901 when Kolang returned to Jagei was a time of successive low rivers and failed rains, bringing scarcity and near famine throughout much of the White Nile Valley.[14] Jagei now offered more favourable prospects to Kolang than when he had left. Nyapuka was dead. Puot was still alive, but cattle were dying throughout the country. Kolang renewed his contest with Puot, cursing his herd, which soon after perished. An impoverished prophet has little appeal. TENY left Puot, it is said, because he had no cattle and only one surviving brother and sister. People began to turn to MAANI. Kolang then successfully predicted an end to the cattle deaths, delaying the marking of the next age-set until after he had organized a raid on the Dinka. He was now on his way to becoming the most renowned prophet of the Western Nuer.[15]

Kolang Ket had no claim to any special association with divinity before MAANI seized him. He was neither an earth-master nor a man of cattle. His father was quite ordinary (*duek*); only his maternal uncles were 'aristocrats' (*diel*). The available evidence gives no clear idea of his motive for seizure. That he achieved considerable spiritual authority in his lifetime is evident from both contemporary records and modern testimony. Yet he did not gain

[13] Johnson (1993*c*).
[14] Johnson (1992*b*).
[15] Biel Tip Gai Dk1, Kuol Kolang Ket, Jg3.

the material abundance which is associated with both Ngundeng and Deng Laka. He accumulated a large herd, but it is not remembered as very large; he had some wives, but not very many. He does not even seem to have achieved a considerable reputation for organizing raids. True, he is remembered to have taken people raiding and to have captured Dinka cattle, especially immediately after his return to Jagei. When he tried to repeat his success later Wol Athiang defeated him. As one of his younger generation of warriors recalled, 'MAANI went once and he never repeated it. This was when he was driven back.' The source of Kolang's influence and authority lay elsewhere.[16]

Kolang was fortunate in that his rivals had disappeared or suffered in his absence. No independent prophets seriously challenged his influence until his old age. After leaving Puot Nyuon, TENY made the unfortunate choice of seizing Tek Macot, Macot Nyuon's son. Tek used to have sex with women seeking cures from his divinity, until their enraged menfolk seized him and cut off his penis.[17] That ended TENY's career for some years to come. Both DENG and DIU were prudent enough to remain quiet until the 1920s. This does not mean that no one was seized by a divinity during Kolang's career. MAANI accumulated a number of satellite divinities in Kolang's *dayiemni*. As with Ngundeng and Deng Laka, seizure was defined through Kolang's presence, persons seized by minor divinities became minor prophets in his service. They composed or sang songs in praise of MAANI, ridiculing the pretensions of other divinities and threatening sceptics. The songs of Kolang's most able *dayiem*, Dak Dhon, are still sung, and Dak attempted, but failed, to succeed Kolang after the latter's death in 1925.

Kolang offered a full range of prophetic services. He cured the ill; he sacrificed against smallpox, chicken pox, and cattle diseases; he advised people to stop fighting among themselves; he denounced the use of magic and told people not to sacrifice to useless Powers. Like other prophets he tried to destroy magic (*wal*), and it is said that when he learned of anyone using it that person usually died.[18] In this way Kolang dominated the spiritual life of the Western Nuer for some two decades. His influence extended not only to the Jagei, Leek (where the divinity first seized him), and Bul, but to a lesser extent the Jikany, Dok, and Nyuong. Persons from the east, as well as some Dinka and Mandari, are said to have visited him.[19] It was only around 1919 that independent prophets began to establish themselves successfully in other parts of Western Nuer. This was a period when people had to contend with the consequences of another series of high floods as well as the intrusion of the

[16] Anon., 'Jagei Nuer', PPH MSS; Lili Goak Ruot Jg1 (on herds and raiding), Kuol Kolang Ket Jg3 (naming only four wives).

[17] Biel Tip Gai Dk1. Many persons do not remember TENY seizing Tek before Buom Diu.

[18] Kuol Kolang Ket Jg3. See also Ruay (1981: 3), on MAANI ('Mathy') suppressing fighting among the Western Nuer.

[19] [Wedderburn-Maxwell], 'The Jagei Nuer', 16 July 1945, and Anon., 'The Jagei Nuer', both in PPH MSS; Kuol Kolang Ket Jg3.

Anglo-Egyptian government. By this time Kolang Ket was visibly declining, displaying all the stubbornness and inflexibility born of an old man's failing memory.

The divinity TENY was quiet after Kolang Ket's successful confrontation with Puot Nyuon. Puot had belonged to the Tigjiek section of Dok, and in about 1919–20 TENY reappeared in Buom Diu, a man from the Dogwar section, unrelated to Puot. Buom came from an 'aristocrat' family but, being neither an earth-master nor a man of cattle, he had no hereditary association with divinity. His mother had been captured by slavers in the nineteenth century but had managed to escape and return to her people, where she married and subsequently had two daughters and Buom, her only son. As a young man Buom was relatively prosperous, since his sisters were married before him and there were no full brothers to contend for shares in the bridewealth. Buom is remembered as having a sizeable herd prior to his seizure. As an adult he was renowned as a warrior against the Dinka and as a quarrelsome man among his own people around Ler, where he also gained a reputation for seducing other men's wives. In distinct contrast to the characters of some eastern prophets, such as Ngundeng and Dual Diu, he seemed an unlikely candidate for seizure by a divinity.

Buom was seized quite suddenly one night while sleeping inside a cattle byre. He woke to find the byre filled with light, 'like many stars', he later explained. He felt his head spinning and, without knowing what he was doing, ran outside into the night, returning later in the day. He never fell ill; he was normal in the daytime, but at night he would see lights in the byre and would run outside. Buom did not announce that he was seized by TENY. This was deduced by those around him. After Buom began acting strangely different persons sacrificed cattle in front of him because of this mysterious happening. Eventually Buom himself sacrificed the cattle brought to him and then sacrificed his own. People said he had a divinity. One old man, Tip Gai of Puot Nyuon's section, who had been present with Macot Nyuon at the fall of Rumbek nearly forty years earlier, gave Buom a red and white ox. There were, however, sceptics. One man criticized Tip for giving away his ox to 'a mad man', but later, when the same man went fishing and found that his fishing-spear got stuck in the riverbed and could not be pulled out, he, too, gave Buom a white ox admitting that 'TENY has really come'. It is also said that people began to claim that Buom had been seized by TENY when he stabbed two men dead, left them lying in the sun all day with flies and insects gathering in their mouths and eyes, and then resurrected them, completely healed, with a touch of his baton (*dang*). In any case it was those around him, not Buom, who first claimed that TENY had come, and Buom accepted the claim.[20]

[20] John Wicjaal Buom A1.1, Biel Tip Gai Dk1, Nyakieneu Teny Dk3, Biel Teny Dk4. One of the men so killed and resurrected was Ngundeng Kuong Puoc, father of the headmaster at Ler, Clement Gatut Ngundeng; he finally died some time between 1976 and 1981.

Buom's personality is said to have changed after he was seized by TENY. He appeared to calm down, not getting personally involved in fights with other Nuer, even telling people generally that they should not fight. Some now claim that had TENY not seized Buom he would have ended up either killing someone or being killed. 'People were at peace when he was caught by TENY.' A toughness of character never left him, and Europeans who later knew him in the 1930s judged him to be difficult, tactless, ambitious, and despotic.[21] That was a period, however, when Buom was more active as a government chief than as a prophet and, as Nuer tend to explain it now, his divinity was further from him.

These stories suggest that TENY was as much imposed on Buom as sought. The question which this raises is not so much why Buom would court seizure, as why the Dok would seek a prophet? At this time Dok country was suffering from starvation. Dramatically high floods began at the end of 1916 and from 1917–1919 there were high river levels during the dry season. Dok settlements begin at Adok, near the river's edge, and this area is more susceptible to flooding than many other parts of Western Nuer District. A moderate rise in the flood level will swamp cultivations, flood dry season pastures, and leave water too deep for fishing. Not only were the Dok suffering from the consequences of the floods, their cattle were dying from an epidemic known as 'Nyai Car' which followed 'Pilual'. After it was decided that Buom had been seized by TENY he began sacrificing to protect cattle and crops. In the year following Buom's seizure the cattle disease disappeared and the harvest was abundant. This would be consistent with the much lower river level of 1920.[22]

This partially explains why the Dok sought a prophet within their own territory, rather than rely on Kolang Ket, who lived further away in better-protected country, but it does not fully explain their choice of Buom. Buom, as an 'aristocrat', came from a reasonably prosperous family. He had some means at his disposal for generosity, and he was a proven warrior. Once prophethood was thrust upon him he took a leading role in raids against the Dinka. Kolang Ket's prestige was such that Buom still approached him for joint expeditions, or at least kept Kolang informed of proposed raids. It is still uncertain how many raids there were. Buom may have been responsible for the attack on the Rek in 1919, but he is best remembered for raiding the Dinka of Rumbek District. He was not always successful, and a raid he

[21] Biel Tip Gai Dk1; Evans-Pritchard (1940*a*: 186); Crazzolara (1953: 162); John Winder, 'John Wicjaal Buom', 1976, SAD.

[22] Thesiger (1986: 299); JIT 1954: i. 239 for flood levels; Biel Tip Gai Dk1, Biel Teny Dk4, Nyakieneu Teny Dk3; John Winder, 'Notes and Queries', SAD 541/9. Winder dates 'Nyai Car' to 1921, but as there is reference to annual outbreaks of Bovine Pleuropneumonia in Fergusson's 1921 reports, we can assume that it was earlier.

organized early in 1921 with the Nyuong prophet Wuon Kuoth ended in defeat.[23]

The Nyuong Nuer at this time were split by rivalries within the new generation of leaders. The migration of Nyuong from Jagei into Adok began in the first half of the nineteenth century as a fairly uniform movement of people, but colonization of the southernmost Nyuong territory during the end of the nineteenth and beginning of the twentieth centuries took place in a series of short movements by small fragments, each under its own leaders. Some of these men were mantics, others had more ordinary backgrounds. The strongest rivalries were found in the recently colonized territory of the south. At about the same time that Buom was seized by TENY two prophets and one magician were competing for power in Nyuong. Gaaluak Nyagh redefined an old tutelary divinity, DAPIR; Wuon Kuoth revived the known divinity DIU; and Tiep Kolang profited by importing Dinka magic.

The leader of the earliest migrations was Bilieu Wayu, a man of cattle. He led the Nyuong into the Dinka country around Nyadong, and then brought them south-east into Dur country, a larger and more fertile region which ultimately became the main area of Nyuong settlement. The two primary Nyuong groups were Nyawar and Nyal, with Nyawar subdivided into the Gamuk and Galieth, and Nyal into the Luac, Thak, and Leik sections. Though the area of Nyadong is identified with Galieth, and the area of Dur is identified with Luac and Thak, the uneven distribution of dry land, water, and pastures is such that there is no territorial exclusivity. Groups of Nyawar and Nyal are to be found settled all over Nyuong. This was a point not fully understood in the early years of British administration when territorial chieftaincies were created.[24]

Bilieu Wayu seems to have derived extra authority from a tutelary divinity, DAPIR, which he found in the grass by the river in the Adok area. The character attributed to this divinity at the time is unclear. Usually only earthly Powers are described as being found in the grass. Given the association of Western Nuer men of cattle with such lower Powers as BIEL, which often become tutelary divinities, and the tendency of spiritual experts to strengthen themselves by the use of magic, it is possible that DAPIR at this time was such a Power. It figured in a spiritual duel between Bilieu and one of his brothers, a duel in which DAPIR proved Bilieu's greater power over cattle. DAPIR became inactive after Bilieu's death, and was revived three generations later

[23] 'Nuer Chiefs and Persons of Note: Bahr el Ghazal Province (1927)', NRO Dakhlia I 112/13/87, mentions his success. [Wedderburn-Maxwell], 'The Nyuong', PPH MSS, mentions his defeat in *c.*1921. Fergusson (1921*b*: 153) attributes the defeat in Jan. 1921 to 'Chief Teng of Therk [Thak] clan', (southern Nyuong) rather than to 'Chief Teng of Adok'.

[24] [Wedderburn-Maxwell], 'The Nyuong', PPH MSS.

by his great-grandson Gaaluak Nyagh. This, too, is more consistent with the random activity of Powers than with free-divinities.[25]

Gaaluak Nyagh (Fig. 13) was descended from Bilieu Wayu though Bilieu's granddaughter Nyagok. Nyagh, Gaaluak's father, was a poor man with no cattle who lived by fishing. He was befriended by a wealthy patron who gave him a wife (a thrice-divorced woman) and cattle and brought him out of the *toic* into the village. Gaaluak was born in Nyuong but later attached himself to a Gaawar patron in Adok. Gaaluak lived among the Dok for a while until he committed adultery with his patron's wife, and then was seized by DAPIR, though in which order is unclear. He had to return to Nyuong.[26]

Nyuong country is set in low-lying land, highly susceptible to floods, the Nyadong area particularly. The Nyuong suffered from the 1916–19 floods. Gaaluak is said to have organized a successful raid against the Agar as early as 1919.[27] He is remembered as having proven his seizure by DAPIR by capturing Dinka cattle, but he offered other proofs through curing barren women, not by anointing their bellies with butter or spittle as is common with other prophets, but by spitting in milk which he gave them to drink.[28] This has clear symbolic associations with the office of man of cattle. He thus seems consciously to have combined older forms of mantic activity and spiritual power with the new idiom of free-divinities.

Gaaluak, a Galieth Nyuong, lived at Nyadong, which is frequently cut off from Dur in the south by seasonal swamps. Shortly after Gaaluak's return to Nyuong a prophet from the Luac section appeared in Dur country. Wuon Kuoth, an earth-master, was struck by lightning while standing by the river during a daytime rainstorm. He survived and announced that he was seized by DIU. A middle-aged woman struck by the same bolt claimed to be seized by MANDIU, 'mother of DIU'.[29] The parallels with Deng Laka and Nyacan Ruea in the previous century are obvious. Given the very close kin-ties between the Nyuong and Gaawar, this conscious imitation is not surprising. Gaaluak had the edge over Wuon, and Wuon attempted to strengthen his position by allying with Buom Diu in Dok. The two of them combined in a raid on the Dinka early in 1921, but Gaaluak withheld both his consent and most of the Nyuong, and Buom and Wuon were defeated.[30]

Tiep Kolang was the son of one of the early leaders of Luac-Nyuong

[25] Riel Gaaluak Nyagh Ny1, on DAPIR in the family. Fergusson (1921*b*: 151) for the duel between 'Dafeer' and 'Leeay'.

[26] Riel Gaaluak Nyagh Ny1.

[27] 'Nuer Chiefs and Persons of Note: Bahr el Ghazal Province (1927)', NRO Ɗakhlia I 112/13/87.

[28] Riel Gaaluak Nyagh Ny1.

[29] Coriat (1931*a*); Crazzolara (1953: 162). Crazzolara states that Wuon Kuoth and Buom Diu were both seized in the same year as the death of Majok Kolang (1922). Fergusson mentions 'kujurs' Due (Wuon Kuoth) and Teng (Buom Diu) as early as 1921.

[30] [Wedderburn-Maxwell], 'The Nyuong', PPH MSS.

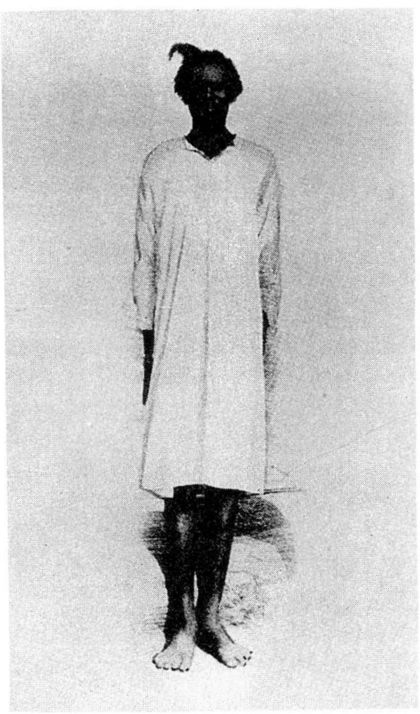

FIG. 13. Gaaluak Nyagh, *c.*1925 (from Fergusson, *The Story of Fergie Bey*)

settlement in the Dur region, but sometime in the late 1870s Tiep's father crossed the river to live with the Gaawar, where he married a number of wives and raised a large family of many sons. In Gaawar Tiep befriended a Nyareweng Dinka fleeing famine in his own country at the end of the last century. From this Dinka Tiep obtained the magic root NAI, to which goats were sacrificed in order to cure barren women or kill enemies. With a judicious use of NAI Tiep amassed a sizeable herd, but also spread fear within the Gaawar community where he lived. Sometime around 1914 the Gaawar attacked Tiep's family and killed two of his brothers. Tiep and the rest fled back to Western Nuer, some seeking refuge with Kolang Ket, some settling in Adok, and Tiep and the others settling in Dur. The elder generation of leaders in Dur were now gone: Dak, who had brought the Thak-Nyuong to Dur at the turn of the century, was dead, and Riak, the main leader of the Luac-Nyuong, had just been killed by the Cic Dinka. Tiep had managed to bring most of his cattle with him and with these, his circle of brothers, and the magic NAI he made a reputation for himself. He was strong enough to frighten off Dak's son Dor Dak, when the latter tried to assume his father's leadership position among the Thak-Nyuong. Tiep also organized raids against the Dinka, though without great success. He seems to have been the 'medicine man' who attacked Lau mission station in 1914, and in about 1918 he was again defeated in a raid against the Agar.[31]

Rumbek District in Bahr el-Ghazal Province had been at the sharp end of most of the Nuer raids which followed the 'Pilual' flood, and it was from Rumbek that the inspector, Captain Fergusson, set out in February 1921 to try to bring them to an end. Fergusson was to adopt a different approach to the prophets from that employed by Upper Nile Province before the war.

The arrival of government, 1921–1923

Fergusson's arrival among the Western Nuer in March 1921 was one step in the progressive incorporation of the Nuer during the steady expansion of administrative networks throughout the Southern Sudan after World War I. Though the Nuer were seen as troublesome aggressors, the administration was not predisposed to favour the Dinka over the Nuer at this time. The Agar chief Wol Athiang, especially, was considered difficult, having refused to pay taxes for two years and displaying a 'contumacious attitude'.[32] Throughout 1921 and 1922 there were other disturbances among administered Dinka. From April 1921 to March 1922 the Dinka prophet in the north-west, Arianhdit, caused considerable excitement among Dinka and administrators alike. Throughout much of 1921 the Zande *biri* secret society appeared in Rumbek District. Coinciding with this there was activity around a new 'holy lake' in Atuot country, which necessitated Fergusson's intervention. And finally from late 1922 through early 1924 administrators were chasing down *matthiang goh* magic as it bubbled up throughout Eastern and Central districts.[33]

The Nuer, if brought in on the government's side, could be used to counterbalance and control the Dinka. Fergusson declared at the beginning of his tour, 'I hope to prove that the old theory of Nuers' hostility is false.' In the Nyuong country he found the Nuer 'an inhospitable lot' but the general response to his announcement of the government's intention to bring the Nuer under administration was favourable, the Nyuong especially realizing 'that it is the only way grievances against the Sheesh [Cic] Dinka can be settled'. Fergusson's announcement that he planned to extend administration

[31] Fergusson (1921*b*: 154–5). This account was later corrected in Fergusson to governor Wau, 29 May 1923, SRO UNP 66.D.1.

[32] Fergusson, 'Visit to the Nuong Nuers', 6 Mar. 1921, NRO Civsec 1/2/5; *SMIR* 323 (June 1921), 7.

[33] For *mathiang goh* see Lienhardt (1961: 64–8), and above, Ch.1, p. 27. For *biri* see Johnson (1991*a*).

to all the Nuer up to the Nuba Mountains Province met with more voiced opposition from the Dinka than from the Nuer.[34]

The Nuer had good reason to be hopeful. Fergusson spoke to only a few Nyuong leaders but sent messages to both Kolang Ket and Buom Diu. From intermediaries he learned that they accepted his proposals 'but reserved to themselves the right to make one more attempt before the establishment of Government control to pay off old scores on Wal Atiang of the Agar Dinka'. He found further grievances against other chiefs of the Rek and Cic. 'I saw from the start that they would not entertain the idea of leaving them alone until they had one more attempt to pay off old scores,' Fergusson wrote in the unpublished section of his report. He told the Nuer that he realized they would want to have 'one more good fight and get it over for good and all. Any doubts that the chiefs had about the friendliness or otherwise of the mission were absolutely dispelled.' Commenting that, if Nuer charges were true, the Dinka chiefs would only get what was coming to them if raided, he added that peaceful behaviour by the Nuer 'would be absolutely necessary once an Inspector had taken over'.[35] Thus there seemed scope for independent action before Fergusson's promised return later that year.

Fergusson's reports clearly indicate that the Nuer were aware the Dinka had recently scored against them but were only waiting for the chance to score back. One of MAANI's songs from this period threatens the Dinka thus, 'Wuol, I will follow you, I shall find you in all circumstances . . . You children of the Dinka, do not curse me, curse Wuol Thian . . . I shall kill him and start such a massacre that his land goes to ruin.'[36] But Wol had to be caught first. Fergusson judged that the Nuer and Dinka were evenly matched and thought that 'the fighting qualities of the tribe have been greatly exaggerated and I do not see why they should be superior in this respect to the Agar or Sheesh of the Eastern District'.[37]

The government insisted on its right to settle all grievances, and shortly after Fergusson's visit some Nuer and Cic brought cases to Rumbek to be heard.[38] But Fergusson's return to the Western Nuer was delayed by the need to deal with Arianhdit's propagandists, the *biri* society, and the Atuot 'holy lake'. Wol Athiang and a Cic chief told the Nuer that Fergusson would not be returning. The government responded by exiling Wol to Wau. Kolang Ket, Buom Diu, and Tiep Kolang sent messages to Rumbek urging Fergusson to come and deal with Agar and Cic rumours. Then, in February 1922, Gaaluak Nyagh raided the Agar. The next month, with Wuon Kuoth's assistance, he

[34] Fergusson (1921*a*; 1930: 117, 134).

[35] Fergusson, 'Visit to Nuong Nuers', NRO Civsec 1/2/5.

[36] Crazzolara (1953: 169).

[37] Fergusson (1921*a*).

[38] Governor BGP to civil secretary, 30 Apr. 1921, NRO Civsec 1/2/5; *SMIR* 321 (Apr. 1921), 6.

raided the Cic, capturing over 800 head of cattle and killing a Cic chief. The government did not punish the Nuer. Rather, the Cic were forbidden to retaliate, as the Nyuong raid was deemed a response to Cic provocation.[39]

Gaaluak had taken advantage of the removal of Wol Athiang to pay off one of the old scores. Kolang Ket, however, took an opposite line. Kolang was an old man (reports estimated his age at between 80 and 90). He knew something of the government's power from witnessing its victory at Omdurman in 1898, and he was inclined to acquiesce in its demand for peace. He gave out a prophecy concerning Fergusson's riverboat, saying 'Now it is very bad. This animal that walks on the back of the river, it comes, it comes to us. There is no more war.' He was even reported to have ordered Gaaluak to return the Agar cattle he had taken at the beginning of 1922. During the dry season of 1922 Kolang took his cattle west to the pastures shared by the Rek to show that he was keeping his promise not to raid the Dinka.[40]

Kolang Ket's actions were resented by some of his young men, and they began to rally around his elder son Majok. Majok Kolang seems to have tried to rival his father, not as a prophet of MAANI, but as a prophet of TENY. It was an indirect challenge to his father, apparently aimed at one of his principal supporters outside of Jagei, but also harking back to TENY's original precedence over MAANI. The old MAANI–TENY confrontation was revived and redrawn along generational lines within Kolang's own family. Majok used a dispute over fishing rights between the Rek and Jagei in the *toic* as the *casus belli* for renewing raids against the Dinka. As Majok led out his raiding party at the end of May 1922, Kolang Ket is remembered to have called out to his wife, 'Mother of Majok, come and look at your son, you will not see him again.'[41]

Majok's first surprise raid was a success. In a second raid on 1 June Majok distinguished himself by killing a Rek chief, but was himself killed by the chief's people. By this time police had arrived from Meshra el-Rek and counter-attacked, forcing the Nuer to retreat. The Nuer ambushed a pursuing group of Dinka and escaped. The death of his son brought Kolang into the war. He called on Buom Diu for aid, and on 7 June a combined force of Jagei and Dok attacked a third time. The two groups were not well co-ordinated, and the police, now reinforced from Tonj, fought a running battle with the Nuer, repelling this final invasion. Reports later put Nuer losses at between

[39] *SMIR* 331 (Feb. 1922), 4; 333 (Apr. 1922), 8; 334 (May 1922), 5; governor BGP to civil secretary, 4 June 1922, and 'Extracts from Bahr El Ghazal Province Intelligence Reports', both in NRO Civsec 1/2/5; V. Fergusson to governor Waw [*sic*], 9 June 1922, NRO Civsec 1/8/5; [Wedderburn-Maxwell], 'The Nyuong', PPH MSS.

[40] Crazzolara (1953: 168), my translation of his Nuer text. Lili Goak Ruot Jg1 told a similar story. *SMIR* 331 (Feb. 1922), 4; 336 (July 1922), 6.

[41] Crazzolara (1953: 168–9); Fergusson (1923*b*).

130 and 177 men, an exceedingly high figure for the battles the Nuer were accustomed to fighting.[42]

This pattern of raiding could be stopped only by making direct contact with the prophets. After his first tour Fergusson had written, 'Unfortunately the status of the chiefs has been destroyed by the "kujur" men', but he saw 'no way out of working with these "kujur" people until such times as a satisfactory solution of the problem can be found'.[43] Early in 1922, before Majok Kolang initiated his disastrous series of raids, Fergusson began building an outpost at Adok and visited Buom Diu.

Buom is also now remembered to have predicted the arrival of the government. At a dance he prophesied, 'Children, I will bring you a man whom you will deny, I will bring you a man to whom you will have to listen. He will beat you with a stick . . . If he calls you even when you are eating, you will have to go.'[44] Fergusson reported that Buom was reluctant to meet him but was well informed about government activities elsewhere. When Fergusson began constructing a post at Adok early in 1922 Buom held aloof until Fergusson sought him out in Ler, his own village. There, in a long interview, Buom's main concerns emerged as maintaining internal peace among the Dok (he was 'much troubled' by fights among his people) and meeting the Agar threat. He outlined for Fergusson the recent history of the country: how during the brief reign of the Turkish government the country had been denuded of cattle, forcing the Nuer to go north and south to obtain replacements; how the first *guan* TENY (which Fergusson misunderstood as referring to Buom's own father) brought some prosperity and order back to the people; and how the Dok remained suspicious of government, especially as the Gaawar had warned them 'that it was the Government trickery to take over a country peacefully at first and then gradually force the people into a state of submission distasteful to them'. Buom, however, was willing to listen to Fergusson's proposals because of the way in which the government had punished 'their common enemy' Wol Athiang. He asked Fergusson his true intentions, and whether he really meant to rule the country without police or soldiers.

Fergusson tried to reassure Buom that the Dok had nothing to fear from government, as long as they refrained from raiding their neighbours. His main object was to stop raiding and settle intertribal grievances. He did not expect

[42] Fergusson to governor Waw [*sic*], 9 June 1922, NRO Civsec 1/8/5; 'Extract from the Bahr El Ghazal Intelligence Report for June 1922', NRO Civsec 1/2/5; *SMIR* 334 (May 1922), 5; 336 (June 1922), 6; 350 (Sept. 1923), 5; Titherington (1927: 198); [Wedderburn-Maxwell]: 'Dok and Aak Nuer' and 'The Jagei Nuer', PPH MSS. One contemporary report announced the death of both 'Teng and Madi'. Wedderburn-Maxwell implies that Buom's involvement was at his own initiative, but Nyadak Cilieny (Dk3), Buom's wife, who was present, stated that MAANI requested TENY's aid.

[43] Fergusson (1921*a*).

[44] Biel Tip Gai Dk1.

to be obeyed immediately, but he only wished free access to the country and the people, to deal with the people through the chiefs, and so gain their confidence. Buom, Fergusson says, replied:

> 'The country is yours. Go where you like and do what you like and you and I like brothers will govern these people. The young men are wild and pig headed, you don't know them yet but you will understand later. If they don't obey us then you and I will leave the country together.'
>
> Teng didn't even offer a parting greeting but got up without another word and left. I saddled up my horse and started on my homeward journey . . . On the road everyone we met questioned the guide as to Teng's decision, some seemed pleased and others the reverse but it was obvious that the atmosphere of suspense had been removed. . . . I knew that Teng was a man with a certain amount of power over the country but I never thought that he had such control as he has. His word is absolute law and it is indeed fortunate that we have been lucky enough to make a favourable impression on him.[45]

Next Fergusson tried to reach the Nyuong prophets, Wuon Kuoth and Gaaluak. In Nyuong Fergusson found a vocal opposition to 'kujur men' among those claiming, or aspiring, to be 'chiefs'. Dor Dak, son of the nineteenth-century Thak-Nyuong leader, urged government intervention against the magician (and outwardly friendly) Tiep Kolang; a man of cattle, Bakkam, insisted that he was the rightful chief of the Nyuong, but that his position had been usurped by his nephew Gaaluak Nyagh; Wuon Kuoth's 'wakil' (deputy), Cak Riang, became an early supporter of the government; while Rundial, a Gamuk-Nyuong 'chief', warned Fergusson as early as 1921 against all 'kujurs'. Both Cak Riang and Rundial were to play a further part in Gaaluak's downfall after Fergusson's murder in 1927.[46]

Wuon Kuoth repented his collaboration with Gaaluak and sought peace with the government through the Dok intermediary Caath Obang, an early friend of Fergusson's who had neither hereditary nor spiritual claims to leadership. Wuon soon learned the benefit of government friendship when he persuaded Fergusson to exile the magician Tiep Kolang from his territory. Gaaluak, too, seemed to want peace, but his position was complicated by his uncle Bakkam pressing a doubtful claim of chieftainship over all the Nyuong. Early in 1923 Fergusson entered Nyuong country with troops and recaptured some of the Cic Dinka cattle Gaaluak had taken the previous year. Gaaluak came in to Fergusson's camp with an offering of ivory, declared that he wanted no hostility with the government, and agreed to return all captured Cic cattle. Then, as he was leaving Fergusson's tent, he saw his uncle Bakkam sitting outside, clubbed him, and fled. Fergusson followed with troops until he was attacked at Gaaluak's village. Fergusson repulsed the attack and burned

[45] Fergusson, quoted in [Wedderburn-Maxwell], 'Dok and Aak Nuer', PPH MSS.

[46] 'Nuer Chiefs and Persons of Note: Bahr el Ghazal Province (1927)'; Fergusson, 'History of Nuong Nuers' (1921), NRO Civsec 1/2/5; 'Bahr El Ghazel Province Intelligence Report, March 1923', NRO Intel 2/27/217.

the village, Gaaluak fleeing to the swamps, from where it was reported he was seeking asylum with Kolang Ket. Gaaluak's behaviour served only to reinforce Bakkam's standing with the government.[47]

With these developments in Nyuong and Kolang Ket's reported wavering after the death of his son, it was imperative that Fergusson meet Kolang in person. Fergusson set out from Ler, accompanied by a number of Dok Nuer, and met the Jagei prophet at his home in Ngony on 25 July 1923. Kolang appeared surrounded by a group of women, girls, and young men, all singing his songs. 'He seemed very nervous and at a loss to know what to say or do. His kind old face and rather pleasant smile could not but impart a good impression, and in his day he must have been a very fine looking man, for he now stands well over 6 feet and holds himself perfectly.' He astounded Fergusson by distinguishing between the Turks and Arab merchants of the old government and the 'Englizi' of the new:

> He stated that his 'kujur' had taken him one night to England, where he had seen all the English and learned that their word was always to be trusted. On his arrival there the English asked where he had come from, and he told them from God. He was then asked where God lived, and Madi [MAANI] replied that he lived in a small pot which he pointed out to them in England. The English then stated that they wished to fight with the clouds, but he replied that, although the clouds appear near, they were in reality far off and impossible to reach. He saw people reading and writing from sunrise to sunset, and was told by God to respect them always. The time had now come to obey God's commands, and he therefore placed himself in the hands of the Government knowing that all his people, which constituted the Nuong and Gair [Jagei] Nuers, would be well treated. The speech rather taxed his strength, and the meeting broke up.[48]

This promising beginning was not sustained the following day. Kolang announced that Divinity had told him that the government would help avenge Majok's death and defeat the Dinka.

> He then burst into tears and it was quite 15 minutes before he regained his composure and was able to appreciate any reply. The situation was awkward in the extreme for there is no doubt that the poor old man fully believed all that he had said. My reply that no fighting could take place under any circumstances finished him, and he collapsed and had to be helped back to his house.[49]

[47] 'Extract from Bahr El Ghazal Province Intelligence Report for December 1922' and '. . . March 1923', both in NRO Civsec 1/2/5; *SMIR* 342 (Jan. 1923), 4; 334 (Mar. 1923), 4; 346 (May 1923), 5. In fact, as early as 1913 it had been recognized that the Nyuong had no paramount chief and that Bakkam commanded only 'a certain amount' of local respect: *SIR* 224 (Mar. 1913), 5.

[48] Fergusson (1923*b*). If Kolang was at Omdurman when Kitchener arrived, the *cieng* or *wec inglizi* of the Anglo-Egyptian army camp would have appeared very much as he describes here. During the battle howitzers, shooting with a high trajectory, were used to bombard the city and the Mahdi's tomb, perhaps giving the appearance of shooting at the clouds.

[49] Ibid.

It took some time before Fergusson, using Kolang's close friends and advisers as intermediaries, could get the prophet to agree to put aside thoughts of revenge and leave the matter of ultimate justice to the government. Negotiations were often at cross-purposes as 'talking with him is difficult, as he is so old, and they tell me that his memory is very bad, and at times it is almost impossible to make him understand anything'. But in the end Kolang even offered to persuade Gaaluak Nyagh to surrender, and Fergusson left, hopeful that his approaches would bring about a lasting peace with the prophets.

Fergusson's meetings had revealed two things. First, that the prophets were anxious to establish peace; and second, that rivalries and feuds undermined peace. All prophets had been cautious in dealing with Fergusson, and given the experience of the Gaawar between 1913 and 1918 they had reason to be suspicious of stated government intentions. Both Buom Diu and Kolang Ket saw in the government's presence a power which could potentially be harnessed to their own efforts to consolidate their control over and maintain peace within their own communities. Buom from the first announced his concern about his own people fighting among themselves; Kolang Ket declared his willingness to place the Nyuong and Jagei in government hands. Peace with the Dinka, which the government also insisted on, meant something different; to the Nuer it meant an end to Dinka raids more than an end to raiding Dinka. Still, Kolang, and possibly Buom Diu, appreciated sufficiently the prudence of deferring to the government for the time being, and they may have also appreciated that more settled relations with the Dinka on their borders could contribute to more peaceful conditions among the Nuer.

It is clear from Fergusson's description that Kolang Ket was well past his prime. His stubbornness was becoming irksome to those around him, his pronouncements were no longer lucid. The younger generation wanted to escape Kolang's strictures, and his ultimate rival was his son. Whatever Kolang thought of his son's initial challenge, Majok's death brought him personally into a feud with the Rek, and his standing with the Jagei ultimately rested on his pursuit of that feud. Rivalry between Nyuong prophets was also expressed in the competitive organization of raids against the Dinka. Gaaluak Nyagh, Wuon Kuoth, Tiep Kolang, even the Dok prophet Buom Diu, vied with each other in this respect, and temporary alliances between two leaders (as between Buom and Wuon) could be indirectly aimed against the position of a third.

Conflicts between leading personalities were most sharply drawn in the Nyuong area, the region most recently colonized through fragmenting migrations. Rivalries between leaders were often expressed in spiritual terms, not only in the activities of prophets but in the ambitions of magicians. Fergusson described these rivalries in terms of legitimate authority and usurpation, and he dismissed all spiritual claims as undifferentiated 'witchcraft'. Given the recentness of Nyuong settlement there had not been sufficient time for any 'authority' to become so well entrenched as to claim 'legitimacy'. No leader could count on a firm following. Fergusson's early reports give a clear picture of the internal political instability of the Nyuong and the intrigues of lineage politics, in contrast with the Dok and the Jagei. The fighting that broke out between the government and the Western Nuer in 1924–5 occurred more as a consequence of these intrigues than of the machinations of 'kujurs'.

The suppression of the prophets and the assassination of Fergie Bey, 1924–1927

While Gaaluak Nyagh remained at liberty the government's position with the other prophets remained in doubt. He was related to Buom Diu by marriage, and his hiding among the Jagei could influence Kolang Ket. When Gaaluak emerged from Jagei country early in January 1924 Fergusson went after him, defeated his force, and Gaaluak retreated to Jagei. By the end of 1924 it was reported that under Gaaluak's influence Kolang Ket was turning hostile towards government. Buom Diu was wavering. Fergusson visited Kolang late in November 1924 to try to arrange Gaaluak's surrender but found the village full of Kolang's warriors, with more expected. Kolang tried to disperse the young men but could not, and advised Fergusson to leave immediately, which he did. Kolang's apparent deference to Fergusson alienated many of his followers, who began to rally to Gaaluak. Riak Cany persuaded his uncle Kolang to join with Gaaluak, and while they were unable to muster all the Jagei the three leaders between them gathered together a large number of Jagei, Nyuong, and Dok.[50]

The government was alarmed by persistent reports of Kolang Ket's increasing hostility, rumours of impending raids on the Dinka, and the growing reputation of Jagei country as a magnet for 'evil-doers' throughout the Western Nuer. The first major military patrol into Western Nuer country was now planned. Buom appeared uncertain in his loyalties (he had responded to Kolang's invitation in 1922 to avenge Majok's death) and was removed from the district. Late in December the patrol, armed with machine-guns, set out with Fergusson as political officer. The main Nuer force of some 2,000 warriors under Gaaluak and Riak Cany attacked the column at Khor Yirkuo on 6 January 1925 and was decimated by concentrated rifle and machine-gun fire. The patrol advanced and burned Kolang's byre. In all 323 Nuer were

[50] 'Summary of Events leading to the Trouble in the Nuer Country Bahr El Ghazal Province in December 1924', NRO Intel 2/27/217 and Civsec 1/2/5; governor BGP to civil secretary, 13 Mar. 1924 and 12 Nov. 1924, both in NRO Intel 2/2/217; *SMIR* 364 (Nov. 1924), 9; 365 (Dec. 1924), 5–6.

killed, 71 prisoners taken, and 1,500 cattle captured. The Jagei alone lost 150 men, Riak Cany among them. Some Jagei had already deserted to the government before the battle; now more started coming in and paying cattle fines. Both Kolang and Gaaluak surrendered at the beginning of March. A decisive defeat in the heart of the Nuer homeland, Yirkuo capped the series of reverses which the Nuer and Kolang had, up to now, met only beyond their borders.[51]

The defeat of the prophets incidentally assisted the introduction of another religious order to the Western Nuer. The Catholic Verona Fathers, operating from the Shilluk village of Tonga on the White Nile, were setting up a new station among the Nuer on the Bahr el-Ghazal. Their compound at Yoinyang was built by Nuer prisoners of war provided by Captain Fergusson in 1925. Fr. Crazzolara recruited some of these prisoners as Nuer language informants. But progress in language study and the propagation of the faith was slow. The labourers-cum-language teachers kept escaping. With a staff of never more than five, the missionaries could not keep all the boys brought by local chiefs on the station either, especially after Fergusson's murder in 1927. By 1930, the year Evans-Pritchard began his field-work around Yoinyang, the mission could record few Nuer converts. Out of a total of thirty-four 'indigenous' Catholics, two 'mulatti' were Captain Fergusson's children by a Dinka woman, and a number of others were Dinka and even Anuak enrolled by the government for clerical and medical training. The census of the remaining denominations in the district told the true story of the state of religious competition at that time: 'Dissidenti di rito orientale' (Greek Orthodox): none; 'Protestanti' (Protestants): none; 'Ebrai' (Jews): none; 'Musulmani' (Muslims): three; and 'Pagani' (Pagans): *c.*10,000.[52] At Yoinyang, as at other missions, attendance at schools, and therefore conversion to Christianity, did not increase until the 1940s, when British administrative policy changed and actively encouraged education in the Southern Sudan in order to meet the challenge of the Sudan's coming independence.[53]

If the prophets had been the main obstacle to administration, now was the time to remove them. With Kolang and Gaaluak in captivity and Buom in exile there were plenty of men willing to replace them. Caath Obang of the Dok was one. He was an early friend of Fergusson's, had visited Khartoum in 1923 (clad in Fergusson's kilt), had acted as chief of the Dok during Buom's

[51] SMIR 367 (Feb. 1925), 4; governor BGP to civil secretary, 12 Nov. 1924, 'Patrol S.1, Intelligence Reports' Nos. 2–4, Fergusson to CSO and AG Khartoum, 26 Jan. 1925, and Fergusson to civil secretary, 7 Mar. 1925, all in NRO Intel 2/27/217; [Wedderburn-Maxwell], 'Dok and Aak Nuer' and 'The Jagei Nuer', PPH MSS; Fergusson (1930: 184–6).

[52] 'Diario Stazione Yoynyang dal Nov. 1923 al Nov. 1935', AMC A/145/15; Father Stephen Mlakic to Mr Kidd . . . 11 Oct. 1928, and 'Rosoconto Spirituale 30/6/1929–30/6/1930', both in AMC A/169/3; Coriat (1931*a*).

[53] Sanderson and Sanderson (1981: esp. 187, 449–50).

exile, and had provided scouts and 'friendlies' for the 1925 patrol against Kolang and Gaaluak. Kolang Ket was placed in Caath's care in Adok, and it was there that Kolang died on 24 June 1925. The story now widely told is that Caath buried Kolang alive. Another man of obvious ambition was Cak Riang of the Luac-Nyuong. He had been a subordinate of Wuon Kuoth's but gravitated to the government as soon as Fergusson entered the country. Then there were Gaaluak's uncle Bakkam and Dor Dak, the victim of Tiep Kolang's persecution.[54]

Justification for removing the prophets also seemed ample. Quite apart from the recent rebellion, prophets appeared to be persecuting the people through 'witchcraft'. The most notorious 'kujur' in this respect was Tiep Kolang. He had been driven from the Gaawar because of his use of the magic root NAI, and he was held responsible for a number of deaths among the southern Nyuong. Typical of the amoral and haphazard behaviour of the lower Powers, NAI had also killed off most of Tiep's own children, over twenty in number. Fergusson did not distinguish between this 'kujur' and the prophets, though in fact it was at the behest of Wuon Kuoth, the prophet of DIU, that Tiep was banished back to the Gaawar.[55] 'Kujurs' seemed dangerous to internal and external security alike.

More proof of this danger was provided during the rains of 1925, within a few months of Kolang Ket's death. His main bard, Dak Dhon, claimed to be seized by MAANI when a bolt of lightning struck his herd without doing any damage. Dak was already one of Kolang's *dayiemni*; he was already a *guan kuoth*. The thunderbolt was taken as a sign of direct transmission of MAANI, a transmission already in dispute, as Kolang's daughter Nyaruac was even then claiming to be seized by her father's divinity. Dak, the closest of Kolang's male confidants, tried to establish himself as Kolang's spiritual successor, the natural heir to his following. In competing with Nyaruac Kolang he even seems to have announced that he was also seized by a stronger divinity than MAANI. He was able to raise only a small force to raid the Dinka. In November 1925 he attacked an unsuspecting Rek camp who were herding with the Nuer, running off with several prisoners and some 1,200 head of cattle, and even killing and dismembering two Dinka boys. Back in Jagei territory he appropriated all the cattle for himself and even killed three of his own following. To punish him and prevent him from raiding other Nuer Fergusson was sent out on another patrol. In the brief battle which ensued on

54 Caath: [Wedderburn-Maxwell], 'The Nyuong'; Fergusson (1930: photo opposite p. 126); 'Patrol S.1, Intelligence Report No. 4', NRO Intel 2/27/217. Kolang's death: *SMIR* 372 (July 1925), 5; not 1926 as in Crazzolara (1953: 167). Cak Riang: Intelligence Dept. 4 June 1923, NRO Intel 2/27/217; 'Nuer Chiefs and Persons of Note: Bahr el Ghazal Province (1927)'.

55 Fergusson to governor Wau, 29 May 1923, SRO UNP 66.D.11; 'Bahr El Ghazal Province Intelligence Report, March 1923', NRO Intel 2/2/217 and Civsec 1/2/5.

29 December Dak Dhon, a new prophet of DENG, and another prophet or *dayiem* were killed.[56]

Dak Dhon's blood-lust is an aberration in the accounts we have of Nuer prophets. His behaviour was quite unlike anything the Western Nuer had experienced under Kolang Ket and the various prophets of TENY and DENG. His challenge to Nyaruac may have spurred him on to this extremity of action. His defeat served to emphasize the distance between his violent behaviour and the ideals of a higher divinity: his divinity is said to have deserted him.[57] With such dramatic proof before them the Western Nuer prophets in future had to emphasize the more peaceful attributes of their divinities rather than the more warlike.

It was in fact the prophets' interest in order which won Fergusson's admiration after their collective defeat. The prophets he held in captivity seemed, on the whole, to be more able and effective leaders than the 'hereditary chiefs' they overshadowed. Fergusson was clearly disappointed in his chiefs. Dor Dak had little control over his people; Wea Neen, whose legitimate authority Buom Diu was supposed to have usurped, was 'weak and brainless'. Some of the prophets, on the other hand, understood the government's insistence on public order. Buom Diu, returned from exile, became 'a rattling good and staunch friend' who proved 'a very valuable Govt servant and is a man with great control over his people'. Kom Tudel, a Bul Nuer who had been one of Kolang's *dayiemni* and had joined Dak Dhon, was found to be 'a man of possessing character' and the ideal agent for introducing administration to the Bul. Even Gaaluak Nyagh appeared to be 'a rather nice fellow'. Gaaluak imparted the surprising information that he had been dissuaded from submitting to the government on the advice of outwardly 'loyal' government chiefs, perhaps the very ones who had complained to Fergusson that Gaaluak undermined their authority. Gaaluak was recognized as chief of the northern Nyuong in 1925. We hear no more of Bakkam after this.[58]

Fergusson found prophets to be 'very fair in their dealings with the people and ready to take extreme trouble over cases',[59] qualities which were appreciated by an understaffed administration committed to maintaining public order. Prophets were no longer special targets for dismissal. Administrative efficiency and keeping the peace were the two main criteria by which all Western Nuer leaders were evaluated. In August 1925, for instance,

[56] *SMIR* 376 (Nov. 1925), 7; 377 (Dec. 1925), 6; 380 (Mar. 1926), 5; Fergusson (1930: 212–13, 220–2); Crazzolara (1953: 167).

[57] Crazzolara (1953: 166).

[58] 'Nuer Chiefs and Persons of Note: Bahr el Ghazal Province (1927)'; Fergusson (1930: 243–5, 276, 318); 'Extract from the Bahr El Ghazal Province Intelligence Report, April 1925', NRO Intel 2/27/217.

[59] Fergusson, quoted in Jackson (1923: 107).

two chiefs were dismissed for unfairness in hearing cases: Wuon Kuoth, the Nyuong prophet of DIU, and Caath Obang, Fergusson's old friend from Adok.[60] After Wuon Kuoth had been deposed Gaaluak Nyagh was appointed head chief of all the Nyuong, and with Caath Obang out of the way Buom Diu soon proved his worth to government.

The Western Nuer chiefs were largely unsupervised, as there was no permanent inland government office. The district headquarters was the SGS *Kerreri*, a government boat which steamed up and down the rivers, setting the district commissioner down at specific landing places from whence he trekked inland to meet the chiefs and inspect their work. The chiefs were responsible for hearing cases, collecting fines, and organizing labour for making landing places. Fergusson's contact with chiefs and people was necessarily circumscribed, but there were additional limitations. First, Fergusson never learned to speak Nuer. He spoke a mixture of Dinka and Arabic through interpreters, who were mainly Dinka or Atuot, though two Nuer were later enlisted. Thus there was no easy communitcation between himself and the people set under his charge. Second, Fergusson's main base was Rumbek, and his caravans were recruited from the Azande and Dinka living there. Fergusson's letters to his mother, reprinted in his memorial biography, give the impression of a solitary heroic figure endlessly trekking with only a few companions. The list of his entourage during his last trek tells a different story. There were at least thirty-six Dinka carriers, cotton overseers, and other hangers-on; twenty-seven Zande porters and servants; three Nuer; and one Atuot or Dinka interpreter.[61] Fergusson is still remembered by Nuer as travelling with a formidable company of foreigners. He also had a Dinka wife and two children, and this only added to the impression that his Dinka retinue were personally close to him. The only Nuer who could regularly penetrate this daunting human *zariba* were the chiefs. The rest of the people had to rely on them for knowledge of Fergusson's intentions. Few could tell if what the chiefs relayed was coloured by their own anxieties, resentment, or ambition, and even fewer could appeal to Fergusson for redress against the chiefs. Such abuses of chiefly power during Fergusson's regime as did come to light were either uncovered by his own agents, or revealed in denunciations by rival chiefs.

Fergusson was considered progressive by his colleagues because he included medical work and economic development among his administrative priorities. Medicine was part propaganda to demonstrate quickly the physical benefits of government, and Fergusson often undertook some of the simpler treatments himself. He delayed the introduction of a tax until the Nuer had

[60] *SMIR* 373 (Aug. 1925), 6.

[61] W. A. Porter, 'Facts Relating to the Death of Capt. V. H. Fergusson, Andrea, two Merchants and Several Natives at Lake Jorr 11 am. on 14.12.27', PRO FO 371/13128.

cash with which to pay it, rather than extract tribute in cattle as was done across the river in Upper Nile Province. Cattle were collected in court fines, but otherwise they were not touched. Fergusson injected cash into Western Nuer through a system of compulsory cotton cultivation under the supervision of imported Dinka overseers. This became his most unpopular policy.[62] By 1927 he judged that there was enough regular income from cotton sales to justify introducing a tax, and a census of taxpayers was begun that year.

In 1927 Fergusson's district looked secure, but underlying the apparent tranquillity many streams of instability were converging. Fergusson's insulation, the rivalries and abuses of government-backed chiefs, compulsory cotton-growing under Dinka overseers, the beginning of a tax census, the return of captured Dinka cattle, have all been recalled as contributing to the collapse of Fergusson's final year. Of these the most important were the rivalries in local politics and Fergusson's inability to communicate directly with the Nuer.

Fergusson appointed as chiefs those men who had shown themselves willing to enforce government policies. This included some who had attached themselves to him for personal advancement, and government patronage soon became a sure avenue to power. Government chiefs were able to get rich, taking cattle in court from each successful litigant. Because they were appointed by Fergusson people assumed that government backed all their actions. When chiefly abuses were late investigated in the 1930s, it emerged that the worst period was the later 1920s, especially 1927–9. This was also the time that the Dinka cotton overseers were levying their own fines on Nuer who failed to grow cotton.[63]

Rivalries flourished among the Nyuong, as we have already seen, and Gaaluak Nyagh counted both Buom Diu and Cak Riang as personal rivals. Towards the end of 1927 Fergusson learned from his 'Intelligence fellows' that Gaaluak had been levying cattle fines on his own and had appropriated captured Dinka cattle which should have been returned after the 1922 raids. He was charged with distributing the cattle among his own relatives and marrying thirteen wives in one year. Fergusson descended on Gaaluak twice in November and forced him to produce the appropriated cattle and various rifles which should have been surrendered in 1925. In the presence of both Buom Diu and Cak Riang Fergusson stripped Gaaluak of half his 'command', demoted him to chief of the Nyadong area only, and elevated Cak Riang to chief of the larger and more populous Dur area. He also had Gaaluak turn out all his people for the tax census.[64]

[62] [Romilly], 'Report Western Nuer 1929–1934', Nasir END 66.A.1.

[63] Ibid.

[64] 'Extracts from Private Letters of the late Capt. V. H. Fergus[s]on O.B.E.', NRO Civsec 5/3/12; Fergusson (1930: 317–20). Riel Gaaluak Nyagh (Ny1) acknowledged that his father ultimately married as many as eighteen wives.

The return of captured Dinka cattle was naturally unpopular, but so was the demotion of Gaaluak and the elevation of Cak, who was 'of no great importance in Nuer eyes'. Just as he had earlier relied on the patronage of Wuon Kuoth, he now relied entirely on the patronage of the government. The Nyuong sections did not see the logic of the territorial division of chieftainship which Fergusson proposed, and those living in Dur objected to having to obey Cak merely because Dur was where they chose to live. Gaaluak had established his claim to authority through his recognized qualities of leadership; Cak Riang had not.[65]

There was, then, a growing Nyuong resentment towards government policies, which appeared increasingly arbitrary and authoritarian. This dissatisfaction crystallized around a rumour that Fergusson intended to castrate all Nuer men. The origin of this rumour still puzzles modern Nyuong. It is explained in the following way:

> The Nuer version of the story is that Captain Fergusson in explaining the government policy, stressed the government's intention to combat diseases by establishing a hospital where the sick would be provided with medicines and also where operations would be performed, like eye operation and the operation of hernia. The interpreter translated the latter as castration of men. The translator used the practice by the Nuers in castrating their bulls as a way of explaining hernia operation so that he could be better understood. The Nuers were annoyed by this. It also appeared that someone with hernia was indeed operated on. He later claimed he was indeed castrated. This was used as proof that the 'Turk' was bent on castrating Nuer men, and so he had to be eliminated.[66]

This rumour by itself does not explain Fergusson's subsequent murder. A simple mistranslation could have been put right, but by whom? Fergusson was unapproachable except through interpreters and members of his entourage. There are some today who even suggest that the castration rumour originated with his Dinka retinue. Certainly the Dinka appeared to be in favour, with the appointment of Dinka cotton overseers and Fergusson's insistence that Dinka cattle be returned. The rumour, fantastic in its nature even to Nuer ears, was symptomatic of a wider, more generalized feeling of dissatisfaction and unease which Fergusson's method of administration had produced, and paralleled the rumours then spreading across the river concerning the impending confrontation between Guek Ngundeng and Percy Coriat.

The rumour, seen in those terms, is less surprising than the identities of those who propagated it. Cak Riang, who owed his position to Fergusson, not only spread this rumour but planned Fergusson's murder. He met with a number of other Dur headmen at the cattle byre of one of them, Dang Dung Jiak, and emerged from that meeting to warn a young man, Gatkek Jiek, that

[65] [Wedderburn-Maxwell], 'The Nyuong', PPH MSS.
[66] Stephen Abraham Yar, personal communication.

Fergusson planned to castrate him. Cak told other young men to bring their spears to meet Fergusson when he visited Lake Jor to supervise the clearing of a new landing place. When Fergusson's boat arrived on 14 December about half of those present knew of the castration rumour and that two, Col Weng and Gatkek Jiek, planned to kill him. Fergusson landed, going out 'on a carrier, borne on the shoulders of four porters, sitting upright with a note book and a pencil in his hand'. Once on shore he was attacked and stabbed to death by Gatkek and Col Weng. Then the crowd joined in, killing one Greek and two Danaqla merchants, a number of servants and carriers, and a Nuer interpreter. Most of the carriers and servants fled or swam to the safety of the *Kerreri*. One of those who climbed aboard was Cak Riang.[67]

If Cak Riang's involvement in the plot to murder Fergusson seems irrational, his motive emerges from his behaviour once on board the *Kerreri*. The first British official to learn of the murder was the agricultural inspector, W. A. Porter. On board the *Kerreri* Cak 'stated to PORTER he had never heard slightest rumour of proposed attack which he was of opinion was engineered by Chief Garluark's headmen who inflamed this section on account of FERGUSSONS taking them from Garluark week previously owing to Garluarks misbehaviour'.[68]

Cak was unpopular in Dur. He had only recently been appointed chief over headmen who still preferred Gaaluak. His statement, which was the first to reach the government, implicated not just Gaaluak but all his former headmen. It thus seems that the plot against Fergusson was intended to remove Cak's rivals from Nyuong, and elevate his standing both with the Nyuong (for removing Fergusson when he appeared dangerous) and the government (for identifying Fergusson's murderers). In the subsequent operations against the Nyuong Cak took an active part in apprehending the murderers, even trying to kill one before his capture. To reward his loyalty the governor of Bahr el-Ghazal Province recommended Cak for the British Empire Medal.[69]

Cak was not alone in using Fergusson's death to denounce a rival. Rundial, who had complained of the prophets as early as 1921, also accused Gaaluak of instigating the murder. Even Crazzolara's friend Twil Ran denounced Gaaluak. In fact, most of the early denunciations came from chiefs, and the governor of Bahr el-Ghazal, persuaded by their testimony, wired to

[67] 'Statement of Garkek Jeik', 5 Aug. 1930, and 'Corporal Ding Makaoi's Statement Regarding Arrest of Garkek Gir', 30 June 1930, both in NRO Civsec 5/4/15; 'Statement by Dwal Diu taken on February 3rd. 1930', SRO UNP 5.A.3/43; 'Details of the Death of Late Fergusson Bey, by Abdel Salem, Engineer Steamer "Kerreri"', NRO Civsec 5/3/13; Porter, 'Facts Relating to the Death of Capt. V. H. Fergusson'.

[68] Governor Wau to civil secretary, 16 Dec. 1927, NRO Civsec 5/3/13.

[69] 'Political Report Patrol S.9', and 'Trial of Shoul Weng', both in NRO Civsec 5/4/14; Willis to Bell, 17 Aug. 1930, and R. K. W[inter], 'Note on Gaaluak Nyal [*sic*] and Gaaluak Buth', 26 Nov. 1930, both in NRO Civsec 5/4/15.

Khartoum, 'All Nuer Chiefs are fully convinced as indisputable fact that Garluark is behind trouble.' It came as something of a surprise, then, when Gaaluak, protesting his innocence and accompanied by Fergusson's remaining Nuer interpreter, surrendered at Adok within a few days of the murder.[70]

The government anticipated a widespread rising among the Western Nuer. All previous assassinations of British officials in the Sudan had presaged rebellion, and Gaaluak's alleged involvement seemed to parallel the problems of neighbouring Upper Nile Province, where the government was already gathering its forces to attack the Lou prophet Guek Ngundeng. In fact, no rising occurred. There were reports of restlessness throughout the district as the news of Fergusson's death spread, but there were no serious acts of lawlessness beyond the Nyuong area. Buom Diu set his own men to guard government property in Adok. A few Dinka in Nyuong territory for court cases were killed and some Cic Dinka were raided. A number of Gaaluak's own people in Nyadong left him to join those in Dur, but when government troops entered the territory in January 1928 they found little active opposition. Only small groups attacked the armed columns advancing on Lake Jor. The Nyuong fled the approach of the soldiers and hid in the swamps in great numbers, but 'as a precaution and from fright and not because they were implicated in murders or have decided to throw in their lot with murderers'. Once in the swamps they were bombed and machine-gunned by the RAF. The ferocity of the government's attack was not dictated by the strength of Nuer resistance; rather it was a measure of government anger at the murder of a district officer. The crime merited severe punishment and retribution, however few were actually involved in the murders at Lake Jor. In some respects the Nyuong got off lightly. The governor of Bahr el-Ghazal seriously proposed that they be deported *en masse* and permanently exiled to the cotton fields of the Gezira scheme. Government actions no doubt limited the ultimate spread of active defiance, but giving even the most alarmist interpretation to the evidence contained in government reports, it is incorrect to claim that there was a general rising among the Western Nuer, or even among the Nyuong.[71]

It was some three years before the facts surrounding Fergusson's death were compiled and examined. Throughout that time Gaaluak was imprisoned in Malakal, where the government was convinced of his guilt. The evidence was 'overwhelming' and 'ample', there was 'no shadow of a doubt' about it, it

[70] 'Political Report Patrol S.9', NRO Civsec 5/4/14; Wheatley to civil secretary, 26 Dec. 1927, and governor Rumbek to HQ Sudan Defence Force, 29 Dec. 1927, both in NRO Civsec 5/3/13. See also Fergusson (1930: 335–9).

[71] Governor Wau, 22 Dec. 1927, Wheatley to civil secretary, 25 Dec. 1927, governor Rumbek to HQ Sudan Defence Force, 29 Dec. 1927, and Wheatley to civil secretary, 30 Dec. 1927, all NRO Civsec 5/3/13; quotation from civil secretary to Wheatley, 11 Jan. 1928, NRO Civsec 5/3/13; 'Political Report Patrol S.9', NRO Civsec 5/4/14. Documents relating to the punitive operations against the Nyuong can be found in NRO Civsec 5/3/12. See also Kingdon (1945).

was an 'indisputable fact', and later, when it was clear there was no legal evidence to link him with the murder, there was still 'no moral doubt' about his complicity.[72] Col Weng, the first murderer, was arrested in April 1929, and he both implicated Cak Riang and exonerated Gaaluak Nyagh before he was executed. Percy Coriat, who spoke Nuer, was assigned to the district later that year and reported that the only evidence he could find pointed to Cak Riang. Gatkek Jiek was finally captured in 1930, and he, too, implicated Cak and a number of other Dur headmen. In the end Cak was acquitted on the technicality that the most damning evidence came from Col Weng, who had been executed before Cak was brought to trial, and therefore could not be cross-examined in Cak's defence. No evidence was produced in any of these trials linking Gaaluak with the murders.[73]

Cak could not be imprisoned, but he was deposed. Gaaluak was somewhat grudgingly reinstated. Caath Obang, the Dok chief responsible for Kolang Ket's death, had been made chief of the northern Nyuong in Gaaluak's absence. Coriat, who approved of hard men and tough chiefs, thought him 'remarkably able', but the Nyuong found him to be a tyrant and oppressive. He was killed by an elephant while hunting in August 1930.[74] His death is now attributed to MAANI's revenge. Before Kolang Ket died, as the earth was being shovelled into his grave, he is supposed to have cursed Caath saying, 'The next time you meet me, I will come as an elephant.' Gaaluak was returned to Nyadong in December 1930. 'All nas [people] en route very pleased at news of Garluak's return', recorded one district commissioner; 'interview Nuong chiefs who appoint Garluak head chief. Quite satisfactory.'[75] In the same month Wuon Kuoth was reinstated as chief of the Dur. The prophets had returned.

Reinstatement, surveillance, and survival, 1930–1973

At the end of 1930 three prophets who had been prominent before the arrival of government—Gaaluak Nyagh, Wuon Kuoth, and Buom Diu—were still actively involved in local administration. The return of the prophets was not a reversal of government policy, but a concession to the individuals concerned. Prophets had just been suppressed across the river in the Gaawar and Lou territories, and the administration of all Nuer districts had, since 1929, been brought within one province. There was a uniform policy towards Nuer

[72] Wheatley to civil secretary, 26 Dec. 1927, and civil secretary to Sudan Agent Cairo, 26 Dec. 1927, both in NRO Civsec 5/3/13; governor UNP to civil secretary, 12 Apr. 1928, SRO UNP 66.E.2.

[73] Papers relating to the trial of Col Weng are found in NRO Civsec 5/4/14, and of Gatkek Jiek in NRO Civsec 5/4/15.

[74] Coriat (1931*a*); [Wedderburn-Maxwell], 'The Nyuong', PPH MSS.

[75] Romilly Diary 1930, SAD.

religious figures, and 'kujurs' were to be discouraged. As Captain Romilly, veteran of the campaigns against Guek and Dual, wrote of the Western Nuer in 1934, 'in addition to being feared by the hereditary chiefs [the 'kujur'] is also hated. This constitutes one of our main safeguards nowadays as the presence of a Kujur is immediately reported to Government, it being well known that Government is opposed to Kujurs generally.'[76] If individual prophets were retained in local administration it was as a local compromise, a marriage of convenience which could end in divorce.

Gaaluak Nyagh was released warily. It was recognized that he had 'complete and unquestioned authority over the Clan', but that his years in prison 'may also have embittered him and it is probable he will require some years of restraint before he can be given a freer rein'. He was thus confined to the small section around Nyadong, though there seemed no doubt about his popularity throughout the Nyuong area. One source of his influence was his efficacy over cattle, and he was considered the greatest man of cattle in Western Nuer. His enforced propinquity with the government in Malakal, where he had learned Arabic, had given him an insight into official attitudes which few Nuer shared. 'He had great personality and dominated any meeting which he attended, even in areas other than his own.' His capacity was 'wasted' in the narrow confines of his own section.[77]

Gaaluak's potential embitterment was only one factor in the decision to confine him to northern Nyuong. Another was the arrangement with Wuon Kuoth. Wuon had been deposed for maladministration in 1924. When Fergusson was murdered Wuon offered his services to the government. Gatkek Jiek was the son of Wuon's paternal uncle (*gatguanlen*); they lived in the same village. It is now widely understood that Wuon offered to capture his paternal cousin on the condition that he was reinstated as chief once Gatkek had been brought to justice. Wuon sought Gatkek out in his hiding place among the Gaawar and persuaded him to return to Nyuong, assuring him that the 'Turuk' had left. Once back in their village Wuon arrested Gatkek and handed him over to the government. Wuon was reinstated as chief of the Dur a few days before Gatkek's execution.[78]

Wuon's reappointment as chief of the Dur was welcomed by his immediate section only. His betrayal of Gatkek was known. He also, unusually for a prophet, trafficked in magic roots. The administrative assessment of Wuon at that time depicts a personality quite different from Gaaluak's. Wuon was 'slow in action, peculiarly unexcitable[,] ambitious and appears now to realise something of the meaning of government'. As long as strict efficiency was not expected it was thought that Wuon might be able to 'maintain a balance among

[76] [Romilly], 'Report Western Nuer 1929–1934', Nasir END 66.A.1.

[77] Coriat (1931*a*); [Wedderburn-Maxwell], 'The Nyuong', PPH MSS.

[78] Fergusson (1930: 348); 'Statement of Won Kuoth, ex-headman of Dur Nuong (Nuer)', 17 Feb. 1930, NRO Civsec 5/4/15; Stephen Abraham Yar, personal communication.

his heterogeneous collection of Sub-Chiefs', but the jealousies which existed between the disparate groups of the Dur Nyuong were still strong. Wuon appeared to prefer his own Luac section against the Thak, and was detested by the Thak for it.[79]

If the Thak and the Luac could not agree with each other, each could agree with Gaaluak. In February 1935 Gaaluak Nyagh was recognized as chief of all the Nyuong, and Wuon Kuoth was made a subchief of the Luac-Nyuong section under him. This appointment was reported to be immensely popular at the time. It was not, however, popular with Wuon, who by now was better known as a magician than as a prophet. Gaaluak's tenure lasted only three years. He died of a fever on 12 June 1938. During the last year of his life he had to cope with spiritual challenges from some of the young men of Dur and was physically threatened by one of Wuon Kuoth's men. When Gaaluak died somewhat unexpectedly his family accused Wuon's follower of killing Gaaluak with magic. It was really Wuon Kuoth, the dealer in magic roots, whom they suspected, but their case ended inconclusively. The man they accused was made to swear on Gaaluak's grave that he had not killed him. With Gaaluak's death there was no one to keep the two sections of Nyuong together. Wuon Kuoth was reappointed chief of all Dur in 1941.[80]

Gaaluak's divinity, DAPIR, is said to have passed immediately on Gaaluak's death to his young son Danhier. Danhier was still a boy and was initiated within a year or two of his father's death. When he grew up he was reported to have gained considerable influence as Gaaluak's son. The administration treated him cautiously, placing him unofficially on the court in 1951, and allowing his election as Nyuong court president (as distinct from Dur) in 1953. He served in rural administration until his recent death, still bedevilled by rivalry with Wuon Kuoth's family.[81]

Buom Diu's fate was perhaps the hardest of all those Western Nuer prophets allied with the government. Buom's loyalty at the time of Fergusson's assassination was never in doubt. Not only did he guard government and merchant property at his own initiative, he confiscated Nyuong cattle, and even arrested Gaawar fugitives who fled to Dok after being bombed by the RAF. He was awarded a 'Spear of Honour', designed by Governor Willis and manufactured specially by Wilkinson Sword in England. Coriat, the first Nuer-speaking district commissioner to administer Western Nuer, admired Buom's firmness and efficiency. Buom disciplined subchiefs who allowed fighting to get out of hand; collected and paid poll tax in cash;

[79] Coriat (1931*a*); [Wedderburn-Maxwell], 'The Nyuong', PPH MSS; 'Upper Nile Province Personality Report No. 49', NRO UNP 1/34/276.

[80] [Wedderburn-Maxwell], 'The Nyuong', PPH MSS; Maxwell to governor UNP, 1 July 1938 and 7 Aug. 1938, and Maxwell to Thesiger, 1 July 1938, all in SRO UNP 66.D.3; *SMR* 75 (Mar.–Apr. 1935), 5; 111 (July–Aug. 1938), 2.

[81] Riel Gaaluak Nyagh Ny1; 'Upper Nile Province "Who's Who"', Malakal UNP SCR 66.D.4.

heard and settled cases and collected cattle in fines; enforced cotton cultivation and road-clearing; all without the aid of government police or the supervision of the district commissioner. That Buom was 'autocratic' and 'little liked' Coriat recognized, but he thought Buom's harshness was tempered by fairness.[82]

In return for such manifest efficiency and loyalty to government, Coriat overlooked the occasional expropriation of cattle, since a chief's salary was only £E1.50 per month. Coriat's successors were not inclined to such charity. By 1936 Buom was said to have accumulated a number of cattle and wives through unpopular court decisions and was no longer controlling inter-sectional fighting. He was deposed, exiled to Akobo, and over 100 head of cattle were confiscated from him and returned to their owners. In Akobo Buom's contact with other persons was regulated. Visitors who came to see him were also taken to see 'Kotnyangdor', Captain Alban, the district commissioner. Alban invariably tried to shock his visitors by offering them Guek's brass pipe to smoke. Buom was once taken to an intertribal meeting to help mediate a dispute between the Lou Nuer and the Murle, but he had lost interest in administration. The meeting came to an abrupt and embarrassed close when 'Buom, leaning back and puffing at his pipe, was heard to opine that "as all Murle are born liars, there is no possibility of getting them to admit anything against themselves"'.[83]

Buom was allowed to return to Dok in January 1940. The newly appointed chief of Dok died three days later and Buom was insensitive enough to host a dance to mark his own return. Buom was ordered back into exile, this time to Yirol. He held another dance near the Adok police post, apparently in protest, and the police dispersed this dance by firing over the heads of the dancers. In Yirol Buom's cattle died, and he lived chiefly by begging. Unlike that other prophet in exile, Dual Diu, no one sought Buom's blessing or cures in Yirol. He himself claimed that his divinity had stayed behind at his home.[84] By the time Buom was finally allowed back to Adok in 1948, he had ceased to function actively as a prophet.

The reputation for prophecy declined in all three prophets who acted as government chiefs. Gaaluak Nyagh was more sought after as a man of cattle than as a prophet; Wuon Kuoth turned to magic; Buom relied more on the strength of the government than on his curse to enforce his orders,[85] and his

[82] 'Political Report Patrol S.9', NRO Civsec 5/4/14; Fergusson (1930: 343); Governor Rumbek to HQ Sudan Defence Force, NRO Civsec 5/3/13; [Wedderburn-Maxwell], 'Dok and Aak Nuer', PPH MSS; UNPMD Feb. 1931, SRO BD 57.C.1; Coriat to governor UNP, 12 Feb. 1930, NRO Civsec 1/4/9; Coriat (1931*a*, 1931*b*).

[83] Coriat (1931*b*); UNPMD Jan. 1936, SRO BD 57.C.1; *SMR* 85 (Jan.–Feb. 1936), 7; Biel Teny Dk4; Nyadak Cilieny Dk3; J. W[inder], 'John Wicjaal Buom'.

[84] [Wedderburn-Maxwell], 'Dok and Aak Nuer', PPH MSS; B. J. Chatterton, DC Lakes to, DC Western Nuer, 23 July 1947, SRO UNP 66.D.1; Nyadak Cilieny Dk3.

[85] Evans-Pritchard (1935: 56).

divinity TENY grew so distant that it almost ceased to be associated with him. There is more to a prophet's role than keeping internal peace, and the inactivity of the prophets' divinities seems to be the main reason why there was a sudden flourishing of seizures among the Nyuong and Dok between 1935–8. Known to the Nuer as *cieng nyajiok* (family of the dog's daughter), and to the British as the 'dog-eating Kujurs', it was the nearest the Nuer have come to a self-induced spirit-possession cult.

During the rains of 1935 a Dok Nuer named Lia Wel ate a dog, an unnatural food for a Nuer believed to cause illness or even death. Lia did not die, but instead announced himself seized by a new divinity named TILING. Drought had killed crops along the Bahr el-Jebel in 1934, but 1935 was an unexceptional year; there was no general 'crisis' of flood, crop failure, cattle plague, or any other affliction. Lia attracted a good deal of attention in Dok. He was given cattle and sacrificed for a good harvest. Buom Diu saw Lia as a direct threat and tried to persuade the district commissioner, Captain Romilly, to suppress the new activity with troops. Romilly went to Dok and was met by Lia 'with a following of some hundreds, all carrying durra stalks instead of spears, as a sign of peace and to show that the spirit which possessed Liar only called on God for good crops etc.' Since it was still government policy to discourage 'kujurs', Lia 'became a guest of the Government' for a few months.[86]

Lia's exile was never intended to be permanent, and his return to Dok took place shortly after Buom was deposed. This added immensely to Lia's prestige. The Dok attributed both these events to TILING, who 'had made the Government depose a powerful and disliked Government Chief and had also brought Liar safely out of the hands of the Government'. Lia continued to hold large sacrifices, and dances, for good crops. He began to attract *dayiemni*, as all successful prophets do, but these *dayiemni* imitated him by inducing seizures through eating dogs. The bumper harvest of 1937 was attributed to Lia's divinity, and the cult of the 'dog-eaters', now called *cieng nyajiok*, spread throughout the youngest age-set of the Dok. There were some thirty *dayiemni* in all, each wearing the skin of the dog he had eaten, letting their beards grow 'if they have any', and meeting at Lia's house to clap hands (*pat*) and pray for rain and other things.

An efflorescence of prophetic activity followed in the Dur Nyuong area, centred around Teng Joak, about 25 years old, who first came to note in early 1936 by predicting good fortune in hunting, much as Deng Laka and Dual Diu had done before him in Gaawar. He appears to have eaten 'unnatural things' such as dogs and kites. The year 1935 had been a time of scarcity

[86] UNPMD Sept. 1934, SRO BD 57.C.1; 'Extract from Periodical Report Bahr El Jebel Area—Western Nuer District', 17 Oct. 1937, SRO UNP 66.E.2, also quoted in [Wedderburn-Maxwell], 'Dok and Aak Nuer', PPH MSS; Biel Tip Gai Dk1.

among the Nyuong, with many Nuer exchanging sheep and goats for grain with the Dinka, but the sorghum crop in 1936 was appreciably better, and this was attributed to Teng Joak's activities. In 1937 he became known for additional successes in curing barren women and protecting cattle from lions. He also held sacrifices to bless cultivation, and the 1937 harvest in Nyuong, as in Dok, produced great surpluses. It was only after these manifestations of Teng Joak's divinity that he began to attract imitators among the Nyuong. Some of them may have eaten dogs to induce seizure, but in general Teng's group of thirteen *dayiemni* ate no dogs and held no dances, but confined themselves to the occasional public sacrifice.[87]

The areas where *cieng nyajiok* was most active were those where the old prophets had virtually abandoned their divinities. Buom Diu was hardly regarded as a prophet by the time he was deposed,[88] and Wuon Kuoth had become an active magician. Teng Joak masked his implicit challenge to Gaaluak by showing deference to Gaaluak's divinity DAPIR. In the old days Gaaluak used to mutilate bulls in a rite to open the way to Dinka country prior to a raid. In 1938 Teng sent a mutilated bull to Gaaluak as a gift to DAPIR, in order to reverse the flow of cattle, to stop Nuer sending cattle to the Dinka for grain.[89] It was a development of Teng's own role in protecting Nuer herds, whether from the threat of lions or trade, but the gesture was a finely balanced mixture of deference, challenge, and co-optation. The gift was an acknowledgement of Gaaluak's established reputation for protecting cattle, but it also suggested that he was neglecting his duties; Teng Joak was now taking the initiative in identifying the dangers to cattle. In associating himself with DAPIR he not only made an explicit comparison between himself and an established prophet, he was co-opting an established divinity.

There seemed to be some sort of solidarity among the Dok and Nyuong *dayiemni* of *cieng nyajiok*, perhaps because of the similarity of technique in inducing seizure, but there were also rivalries among them and between the new and the old prophets. As Lia Wel's successes grew his imitators multiplied. After the 1937 harvest they began to show more independence of action, holding dances and prayer-meetings on their own. They appeared 'generally unruly to the chiefs', and both Lia and the chiefs tried to rein them in, forbidding any dances or seances except at Lia's homestead. Lia renounced the eating of dog meat and forbade it to his *dayiemni*. When some of his 'presumptuous disciples' continued to meet on their own he denounced them to the government and ten were imprisoned and fined for disobeying their chiefs. Similarly, when one of Teng Joak's *dayiemni*, Yier Puot, held a

87 'Investigation into Nyuong "Kujur" Outbreak', SRO UNP 66.E.2; [Wedderburn-Maxwell], 'The Nyuong', PPH MSS; Wedderburn-Maxwell, DC Western Nuer, to governor UNP, 7 Aug. 1938, SRO UNP 66.D.3.

88 Evans-Pritchard (1935: 56; 1940*a*: 186; 1956: 307).

89 Wedderburn-Maxwell to governor UNP, 7 Aug. 1938, SRO UNP 66.D.3.

dance in Dok country and proposed to raid the Dinka, he was denounced by Teng and arrested at the request of Gaaluak. Gaaluak showed more open hostility to Lia Wel than to Teng Joak, perhaps because of the latter's diplomatic deference, but some of Teng's other *dayiemni* were openly contemptuous of Gaaluak. Early in 1938 they began singing sarcastic songs about him, even foretelling his death, which followed soon after. Teng denied any responsibility for their actions.[90]

The unruliness of many of the *dayiemni* associated with *cieng nyajiok*, and the fact that some of them were reported to have suggested raiding the Dinka, did cause concern. Yet by 1937 government was well enough established through its hierarchy of appointed chiefs to be both cautious and tolerant in its approach to the 'dog-eaters'. There was no panicked reaction, no general suppression. The district commissioner was reassured that *cieng nyajiok* was in some ways a 'source of amusement', and that elders had told individual *dayiemni* not to be fools. The ten Dok *dayiemni* were arrested for disobedience, not for being seized by divinities. When Teng Joak, 'eater of dogs, sacrificer of bulls and singer of provocative songs', too, was deported to Malakal in 1938, this was done merely to reassure the Nyuong chiefs and their police after Gaaluak Nyagh's death. Five more 'kujurs', including two 'dog-eaters', were arrested in 1940 after they advocated raiding the Dinka. The government was concerned mainly that new prophets should not interfere with the functioning of chiefs' courts or try to organize raids. As long as a prophet was content to confine himself to sacrifices in aid of human beings and livestock he was allowed to practise. The religious and curative roles of the prophet were to be strictly divorced from political activity. Thus the government issued guidelines to the Western Nuer prophets in 1937 forbidding 'unnatural' practices, the advocacy of anti-Dinka activities, and the holding of dances and assemblies without the consent of local chiefs. Only sacrifices benefiting crops, barren women, cattle, and hunting were sanctioned. For good measure the eating of dogs was also prohibited, as this seemed to contribute to the proliferation of prophets and their *dayiemni*.[91]

The distinction between the things of government and the things of divinity which administrators formally declared in 1937 was already being made by the Nuer themselves. As one of Buom Diu's sons, who became a civil administrator himself, later explained, once a prophet became a government chief his

[90] 'Remarks on Dok Kujurs 1937', and 'Investigation into Nyuong "Kujur" Outbreak', both in SRO UNP 66.E.2; Wedderburn-Maxwell to governor UNP, 7 Aug. 1938, SRO UNP 66.D.3; [Wedderburn-Maxwell], 'The Nyuong', PPH MSS.

[91] 'Investigation into Nyuong "Kujur" Outbreak', 'Extract from Western Nuer District Periodical Report January 6th–February 6th, 1940', DC Western Nuer to governor UNP, 7 Jan. 1940, all in SRO UNP 66.E.2; 'Extract from Periodical Report Bahr El Jebel Area—Western Nuer District', 17 Oct. 1937, SRO UNP 66.E.2, also quoted in [Wedderburn-Maxwell], 'Dok and Aak Nuer', PPH MSS; Wedderburn-Maxwell to governor UNP, 7 Aug. 1938, SRO UNP 66.D.3; *SMR* 111 (July–Aug. 1938), 2.

divinity became inactive. The prophet was too busy hearing cases, collecting fines and cattle, and arresting persons to attend adequately to the affairs and admonitions of his divinity.[92] The secular powers of the chief, backed by the government's strength, gave the modern chief a certain amount of authoritarian force which was incompatible with some of the requirements of a divinity. This distinction was implicit in the activities of the *cieng nyajiok* prophets who revived the services of divinities which the Dok and Nyuong prophets were neglecting as government chiefs. The distinction also lay behind the success of Nyaruac Kolang, the prophetess of MAANI who, after the death of her father Kolang Ket, achieved far greater spiritual influence among the Western Nuer than any contemporary male prophet.

Nyaruac ('daughter of speech') was a married woman at the time of her father's captivity. She was without children and left her husband to tend her father in detention in Adok. After Kolang died his divinity went to Nyaruac rather than to one of his three surviving sons. 'When the divinity caught her people at once knew that it was MAANI', her brother Kuol Kolang later recalled, 'so she did as her father did. She said, "I will not go to raid people."'[93] This was the time when Dak Dhon, Kolang's bard and closest companion, was also laying claim to the divinity MAANI, but there could scarcely be a greater contrast in style between her announcement of her seizure and his almost frantic and indiscriminate slaughter of cattle, captives, and even his own followers.

The transmission of MAANI to Nyaruac did have a precedent in Jagei, in Nyapuka, the first prophetess of DENG. This may be one reason why the Jagei accepted her claims. In doing so they were providentially able to retain their divinity in their own territory at a time when the government was discouraging and limiting the activities of prophets in the administrative field. Nyaruac, as a woman, was almost completely overlooked by the government. After Kolang's death an earth-master, Thiei Poc, was appointed head chief of the Jagei, and Nyaruac's full brother Kuol was appointed headman of their section, but Nyaruac herself is not mentioned in government reports until 1934, nine years after her seizure.

With the political and religious authority in Jagei thus fortuitously divided according to gender, Nyaruac established her position as prophetess without government surveillance or supervision. The violent deaths of both her father and Dak Dhon while in opposition to the government, and the government's active suppression of raids, certainly directed her exclusively towards those beneficent services which the Nuer had come to expect of divinities, but which were no longer being provided by the prophets further south. As her father had done before her, she sacrificed against cattle diseases and human

[92] John Wicjaal Buom A1.2.
[93] Kuol Kolang Ket Jg3.

epidemics such as smallpox and chicken pox. She herself did not spear the sacrificial animals; this was done by her 'children', her *dayiemni*. Individuals would approach her with gifts (especially cattle) in return for blessings on their own crops and herds. There were also larger gatherings providing more general blessings, in which vast numbers of persons converged on her byre bearing butter and beer. Numerous oxen were sacrificed, and such beer as was not drunk was thrown in the air as an offering to Divinity. On some occasions Kolang Ket's spear would be brought out to kill an ox and was then polished (it was not allowed to get rusty). This sacrifice was made to ensure general public health and plentiful harvests of grain.[94]

By 1934 her fame was such that it could no longer go undetected by government. A rumour circulated that she had told the Jagei to uproot their cotton plants because they brought locusts. When this report was investigated Nyaruac denied it and planted cotton herself the next year. There was another scare in December 1936 when great numbers of Nuer converged on her cattle byre after the harvest. Kolang Ket's spear was brought out for the sacrifices, followed by very large dances. The Dinka of Bahr el-Ghazal Province claimed that she was going to raid them, just as Nyapuka and Kolang Ket had done before her. The panic was all on the Bahr el-Ghazal side of the border; the Upper Nile district commissioner sent to investigate found that only drinking and 'an orgy of meat killing bulls to God' had taken place, and would have joined in the dances himself, in place of the Christmas celebration he missed, had he arrived sooner.[95]

Administrative impressions of Nyaruac from that time on were generally favourable. She was judged 'a good influence on the Nuers is sensible and pleasant to talk to'. She was known to have used her influence to prevent fighting. It was not that, as a woman, she represented peaceful pursuits. Women could fight in wars, and both Nyapuka and Nyacan Ruea before her had died in battle. It was that in the context of colonial administration she did not represent a political challenge. Native administration was firmly in the hands of men, whether district commissioners or the chiefs whose elections they confirmed. When in 1937 Thiei Poc suggested that he would be willing to hand over the office of head chief to Nyaruac if she wanted it, because he felt she had more influence among the Jagei than he had, the government never seriously considered the proposition. She experienced none of the conflict between serving her divinity and serving the government felt by other prophets.[96]

[94] Kuol Kolang Ket Jg3; 'Upper Nile Province Personality Sheet No. 14', NRO UNP 1/34/276; Anon., 'Jagei Nuer'.

[95] UNPMD Sept. 1934, SRO BD 57.C.1; [Wedderburn-Maxwell], 'The Jagei Nuer'; 'Upper Nile Province Personality Sheet, No. 14'; Chapter III, 'Western Nuer', NRO UNP 1/44/328; B. J. Chatterton to his mother, 23 Mar. 1937, Chatterton MSS.

[96] 'Upper Nile Province Personality Sheet, No. 14'. Kuol Kolang Ket (Jg3) confirmed that she intervened in intersectional fights. 'Upper Nile Province Personality Sheet, No. 15', NRO UNP 1/34/276.

Nyaruac died in 1973, having been an active prophetess for nearly fifty years. During that time she established a spiritual primacy in Western Nuer much as her father had done before her. Other Western Nuer prophets visited her; she did not visit them. She faced only one serious challenge, by a Bul Nuer named Tang Kuainy (or Tong Kuei) who visited the Mahdi's son, Sayyid Abd al-Rahman al-Mahdi, in the 1950s and returned home to recruit Nuer labour for the Sayyid's estates in the north. Though circumcised, and said to advocate conversion to Islam, Tang behaved like a Nuer prophet and attracted large crowds, whom he exhorted to confess their evil deeds. He went to Nyaruac around 1956 to take her to the real Mahdi, but she ignored him and invoked the duties owed the government—road work and taxes—as an argument against exodus to the north. Tang was arrested when local chiefs and Nuer politicians complained, and he was taken to Malakal, where he died. Throughout the 1950s and 1960s Nyaruac co-opted other appearances of divinity outside of Western Nuer by reference to a related divinity, JIAR WAN, a younger brother to her own divinity MAANI WAN. When divinities appeared on the Zeraf Island in 1957 and 1968 she announced that they were manifestations of JIAR WAN (both cases will be discussed in Chapter 8). The Lak prophet Ruei Kuic acquiesced and sent emissaries to Nyaruac, who gave them tobacco for Ruei to use in sacrifices, and singers to teach him MAANI's songs. Ruei's divinity sometimes complained of the stinginess of its 'elder brother' in sending only a lump of tobacco, but his own seizure was validated in part by accepting this junior position. Nyaruac's prestige extended as far as Lak, but Lak was still far enough away from Jagei for Ruei to maintain his independence of action.[97]

Contrasts

This survey of the history of prophets among the Western Nuer serves as a contrast to the better-documented occurrences of prophecy among the Lou and Gaawar in the east. Prophets in the east drew heavily on the religious idiom and experience of divinity in the Dinka communities into which the Nuer intruded. Such experiences were absent in the west. Prophets in both regions were innovative, but their originality still had to refer to what was known and familiar. Prophecy in the west was incorporated into an active set of ideas about the manipulation of spiritual powers, and this accounts for its different development from prophecy in the east.

Discussing the attributes of divinities and powers with Nuer cannot be done entirely in the abstract. The personalities of divinities are established by those who are seized by them. Thus to ask questions about a divinity as a

[97] 'Remarks on Dok Kujurs 1937'; Dr Sharon Hutchinson, personal communication (for Tang Kuainy); Kuol Kolang Ket Jg3, Thomas Riek Nguot A13, Peter Rir A11.

disembodied spirit is to limit the scope of inquiry and is answered ultimately by reference to past or current representatives of that divinity. To inquire about DENG leads to Ngundeng and Guek in Lou but to Nyapuka in Jagei. Questions about DIU will be answered with reference to Deng Laka and Dual Diu in Gaawar and to Wuon Kuoth in Dok. This is not to deny that certain general attributes of a divinity or Power may be widely known. It does explain the contradictions Nuer themselves acknowledge and are aware of when trying to establish the characteristic of a divinity or Power through its many different human representatives.

Paradoxically, Fr. Crazzolara, whose work was based exclusively on investigations undertaken among Western Nuer, acknowledges the existence of discrepancies and contradictions[98] far more readily than Evans-Pritchard does in his later writing. Evans-Pritchard had a greater variety of examples, drawn from a wider range of observations, having spent time among the Lou, Eastern Jikany, Dok, and Jagei, as well as the Leek (to whom Crazzolara was mainly confined). He tried to identify what was common to Nuer religious experience and practice, and in the process of generalization he tended to underplay the regional differences. New divinities and Powers were introduced, accepted, and described in a great variety of ways in different parts of Western Nuer. Whereas Evans-Pritchard had to accommodate the diversity of the west within the more uniform experience of the Eastern Nuer, Crazzolara merely recorded the confusion he found among the Western Nuer.

The first area of confusion arises in the terminology used to describe prophets and other mantic persons in the west. In the east prophets are regularly referred to as the 'sacks' or 'vessels' of their divinities, as in *guk DEANG* (Ngundeng). The term *guk kuoth* is known in the west but it is less commonly used. Crazzolara reported that all owners of divinities or Powers can be called *guk kuoth*.[99] This may be so, but the more usual term in the west is the older one, *guan kuoth*, which is qualified by the type of *kuoth*. *Guan kuoth* is also used for prophet in Eastern Nuer, but the two cannot always be transposed. All *guk kuoth* may be *guan kuoth*, but not all *guan kuoth* are *guk kuoth*. A *guk* is one who is seized by a divinity and then speaks directly for that divinity. Not all *guan kuoth* speak on behalf of their divinities. Thus when Evans-Pritchard translates *guan kuoth* as prophet he overlooks distinctions Nuer themselves make.

The abilities of a *guan kuoth* are defined by the type of *kuoth* which he (or she) possesses. A tutelary divinity such as *kuoth biedh*, *kuoth juaini*, or even *kuoth rieng* will manifest itself in one way, while one of the lower Powers, a *kuoth piny*, will manifest itself in the magic used by a magician (*guan wal*). In both types the idea of manipulation of spiritual power by its owner is explicit.

98 Crazzolara (1953: 133, 136, 162).
99 Ibid. 137–8.

The element of manipulation is still evident in the activities of many Western Nuer prophets, more so than in the east. In the west prophets were seized by an air divinity, *kuoth duanga* (a term still used along with *kuoth nhial*), which is often approached like the other *kuuth*.

Both Evans-Pritchard and Crazzolara claim that the divinity seizing a person is induced to reveal itself and speak through a ceremony at which people sing and clap (*pat*). This is done for a person made ill by an earthly Power as well as for an air divinity. Both provide examples from cases of seizure by NAI.[100] We have already described cases where such clapping ceremonies have been held in the seizures associated with *cieng nyajiok*. It may be true that in Western Nuer the air divinities were initially summoned to reveal themselves in this way, but I do not believe this is the case in other parts of Nuerland. For Ngundeng and Deng Laka the singing of hymns and the sacrifice of cattle induced their divinities to speak for the first time. Throughout the Nuer singing is often associated with the revelation of a sky divinity, but rattles and clapping are associated with the talking fetishes of the *kulangni*. In Western Nuer, too, I am sceptical that the clapping ceremony described by Crazzolara and Evans-Pritchard is always associated with the utterances of the owner of an air divinity. Crazzolara cited no example other than NAI. The account we have of seizure by TENY suggests that sacrifice of cattle alone induced this divinity to speak (though we must not argue too much from the silences in our sources). Gaaluak Yuac Liem, the blind singer and *dayiem* to Nyaruac Kolang, began to tremble as if seized when singing MAANI songs in my presence, but neither rattles nor clapping were involved.

The fact that some air divinities in the Western Nuer resemble the lower Powers more than they do the sky divinities of the east is evidence that prophets of the air divinities in the west were first assimilated into the existing idiom of affliction by lower Powers, and only gradually, and perhaps by conscious imitation of the east, established their pre-eminent position. We have already seen in the divinity DAPIR that its origins place it closer to the lower Powers than to the sky divinities. It was only through the claims of Gaaluak Nyagh that it is now classed with MAANI and TENY, the well-known sky divinities who preceded it, but even one of Gaaluak's sons seemed uncertain whether DAPIR was a *kuoth nhial* or not.[101] The divinity TILING, the first to emerge from *cieng nyajiok*, did not fall on its prophet from the sky, but was revealed after eating a dog. Now, however, it behaves like any second-generation sky divinity, and passed to Maadni Lia on the death of his father Lia Wel. The career of NAI, after it was introduced to the Western Nuer by Tiep Kolang, shows another gradual transformation.

There is no doubt from the contemporary record of the early 1920s that

100 Evans-Pritchard (1956: 35–6); Crazzolara (1953: 143–5, 163).
101 Riel Gaaluak Nyagh Ny1.

NAI was a lower Power associated with magic. It was first bought as a root. It was activated by the killing of a goat, whose rectum was enlarged with a knife and whose intestines were pulled out. It killed indiscriminately, turning on the family of Tiep Kolang himself, as often happens in the case of Powers. It entered the southern Nyuong territory before 1920. By 1930 it was reported by both Crazzolara and Evans-Pritchard to be active among the Leek, far to the north along the Bahr el-Ghazal. Its origin was unknown there, and it was associated with the ostrich, a flightless bird who lays its eggs on the ground in the bush. Crazzolara described it as a category of earth spirit, not as the name of an individual divinity with its own personality and characteristics. It was activated in clapping ceremonies with the use of rattles, and spoke through the mouth of those it afflicted. Evans-Pritchard claimed that, on the contrary, NAI, too, was regarded as one of the spirits of the above, even if a very inferior one. It seized persons and made them ill; goats were sacrificed to it; it could be induced to speak at clapping ceremonies where rattles were used, though it would speak through someone else, not through the person it afflicted. When it revealed itself through its medium it first barked like a dog, and then demanded presents. The *guan NAI*, the expert who induced NAI to speak, was called 'a NAI priest' by Crazzolara, and 'a prophet of NAI' by Evans-Pritchard.[102]

In all these actions NAI clearly behaves like the *kulangni* of the east, even though Crazzolara reported that NAI was in competition with the *kulangni* in the west. The point of interest in these two conflicting descriptions of NAI is that they show some difference in interpretation of NAI by the Nuer themselves. We know from the contemporary record what neither Crazzolara nor Evans-Pritchard knew at the time: where and when NAI was introduced into Western Nuer. We also know that it was introduced as magic. Nearly a decade after the first Western Nuer *guan NAI* was banished from the district, NAI had taken on a life of its own through other practitioners well removed from southern Nyuong. If some described it as a lower Power and others claimed it was an inferior sky divinity, this is consistent with the way in which the attributes of other divinities were being developed and redefined at the same time. An ambiguous Power, NAI cannot be presented as typical of Nuer 'spirit possession' and prophecy.

Consistency in the apprehension of a divinity is perhaps only possible where the representatives of that divinity are few and blessed with longevity. The prophetic careers of Kolang Ket and Nyaruac Kolang between them spanned over seventy years. The one Western Nuer divinity who operates unambiguously as a sky divinity, and whose prophets most resemble the eastern prophets, is MAANI, and this is very largely due to the efforts of Nyaruac. As the only active prophet who was not part of the administrative

[102] Crazzolara (1953: 136, 143, 157); Evans-Pritchard (1956: 30–7).

system, she was not directly involved in sectional politics. She could more easily assert the universal appeal of her divinity and attract visitors from beyond Jagei. Rivalries between chiefs in the administrative hierarchy limited the influence of other prophets. Chiefly rivalries were also an impetus to the spread of magic, since chiefs tried to protect themselves from the envy and jealousy of others by buying magic. Even one former prophet, Wuon Kuoth, did so: in distinct contrast with Ngundeng, who buried magic, or Deng Laka and Dual Diu, who smashed fetish gourds, or Kolong Ket, who is credited with killing magicians. But Nyaruac was able to maintain a clearer division between the above and below. As Western Nuer compare her with the well-known prophets of the past in the east, their expectations of what a prophet should do, and how a divinity should behave, have become more sharply defined. The activities of prophets have helped to change the context of religious experience and expectation.

PART III
PROPHECY

But however he was misunderstood at the time, the question for us is, What is the burden of the prophecy, however strangely delivered? what is the drift of his teaching?

(W. G. Collingwood, *The Life and Work of John Ruskin*)

The artist must prophesy not in the sense that he foretells things to come, but in the sense that he tells his audience, at risk of their displeasure, the secrets of their own hearts. His business as an artist is to speak out, to make a clean breast. But what he has to utter is not, as the individualist theory of art would have us think, his own secrets. As spokesman of his community, the secrets he must utter are theirs. The reason why they need him is that no community altogether knows its own heart; and by failing in this knowledge a community deceives itself on the one subject concerning which ignorance means death. For the evils which come from that ignorance the poet as prophet suggests no remedy, because he has already given one. The remedy is the poem itself. Art is the community's medicine for the worst disease of mind, the corruption of consciousness.

(R. G. Collingwood, *The Principles of Art*)

8

Prophetic Traditions in Peace and War

Modern patterns—surveillance and control: prophets at the end of the colonial period—the realignment of divinity: independence and the first civil war—the Addis Ababa peace, Divinity, and the renewal of civil war

Modern patterns

The chapters in the preceding section have described in detail the development of a prophetic idiom involving seizure, speaking with the voice of a divinity, and the powers of healing, life, and death as they related to the moral community. Within that idiom different prophetic traditions arose around the dominant divinities DENG, DIU, MAANI and their most prominent prophets. The early prophets established the character of the divinities which inspired them, and through their actions helped to create an expectation among their own communities of what a specific divinity was capable of and how the prophet of that divinity should behave. Later prophecy worked within the framework of these prophetic traditions. The traditions themselves further developed within a context created by the presence of government. This meant the further desacralizing of power and authority, and alternations between periods of peace and periods of war.

The events of the 1920s produced a clear division between the work of the prophets and the work of the government, with government asserting full responsibility for the mediation of disputes and the maintenance of public order. In so far as it extended medical and veterinary facilities to the people it also co-opted a responsibility for public health. Thus prophets were progressively excluded from those roles which they had claimed, and which had been expected of them. In those few cases where prophets continued in government service they did so without reference to their divinities. Government demands were incompatible with the demands of a divinity, the Nuer began to say. A prophet could listen to one, but not the other. Yet the irony is that where prophets were well and truly suppressed, as among the Lou, the analogy was drawn between the work of the old prophets and the work of the new government. The prophets had done just what the government was doing in keeping the peace and looking after the health and well-being of the people. Despite the fact that the results were seen to be the same, the incompatibility of the two was fixed—at the insistence of the government. The trend of Nuer administration in the 1930s and 1940s further secularized the office of the chief and the work of the courts.

The government administered the Nuer through courts composed of sectional heads, representing political units which decreased in size as the number of recognized headmen grew. A few earth-masters and men of cattle were appointed as chiefs, but only in so far as they commanded a wide following and could perform their administrative duties efficiently, not out of respect for their hereditary spiritual position. Some administrators predicted the 'natural death' of the master's 'occult' powers, looking forward to the time when his status would decline to that of the ceremonial, but largely ineffectual, Anglican clergyman, merely a necessary figure at a wedding or a funeral.[1]

A growing toleration of prophets is recorded in administrative documents after 1930, and this is a direct consequence of government confidence in its hierarchy of chiefs. The accelerated recognition of sectional heads, which took place everywhere in Nuerland at this time, was one reason for this confidence. The district commissioner now had direct and regular contact with smaller and smaller units in the Nuer political structure. No one chief was strong enough to coalesce these representatives of local interests or overcome their checks to his own power. In the 1940s administrators came to regret the absence of a paramount chief with strong executive powers, but that absence ensured that they were free from any serious challenge to their own paramount position. They no longer reacted so nervously to those figures who once appeared to threaten them.

With the independence of the Sudan there was a discontinuity in Southern Sudanese administration. Those Northern Sudanese administrators who were mainly responsible for the Nuer after Sudanization in 1954 were effectively divorced from administrative history, since they had had no part in its past. The widely publicized images and stereotypes associated with an earlier period began to return, especially in religious matters. The pejorative Arabic term *kujur*, once briefly banished under the influence of Evans-Pritchard's ethnography, returned to administrative vocabulary. All post-independence Sudanese governments retained the colonial division between secular and religious duties in Nuer administration. They have preferred to exclude prophets from the administrative structure even if, as their colonial predecessors did, they tried to co-opt particularly influential prophets from time to time; and even when the Southern Regional government of 1972–83 actively celebrated the earlier prophets as national heroes. There has thus

[1] Johnson (1986*a*: 71–3); A. H. A. Alban, 'Note on the Indigenous Basis of the Present Administrative System', 26 June 1935, SRO UNP 32.B.1; J. D. Tiernay to governor Malakal, 21 Mar. 1932, NRO Dakhlia I 1/2/6. For a more ambiguous separation of religious from secular authority among the Dinka of Bahr el-Ghazal, see Mawson (1989: 178–87).

been continuity as well as discontinuity in Nuer relations with government since 1954.

Since the late 1940s Nuer society has experienced accelerated change and exposure to a variety of new influences, only some of which have been the direct result of policies of successive provincial administrations. The anthropologist Sharon Hutchinson has examined many ways in which social relationships and ideas have been affected by the growing acceptance of money and its use in the cattle trade, by the expansion of long distance migrant labour immediately before and following the first civil war in the Nuer districts (1964–72), and by the way in which customary courts have continued to redefine individual rights and obligations. Her research among the Western Leek and the Eastern Jikany suggests that the Western ('Homeland') and Eastern ('Frontier') Nuer have continued to diverge since the period of Evans-Pritchard's field-work. In many Nuer communities kin obligations appear to be contracting, and this contraction sometimes has been encouraged by the decisions of the courts. In addition to this Christian conversion, originally confined mainly to schools and towns, has increased in the rural Nuer areas since the end of the first civil war. These growing Christian communities have become a new force involved in the search for internal peace among the Nuer, while at the same time they have been propelled into the vanguard defending Nuer society from external political and legal assaults by militant Sudanese Muslims.[2]

The frequent eruption of civil war since 1955 has meant that relations between government and the Nuer have been unstable. New prophets and other spiritual figures have taken on different roles as they are thrust upon them or as opportunities arise. Precedents set by earlier prophets are there to guide the later ones, but the lives and words of the first prophets are reassessed in the light of new circumstances. We can examine this continuing development of prophetic traditions through the lives of a few of the prophets who have influenced the Nuer in recent times.

Surveillance and control: prophets at the end of the colonial period

Government maintained its guard against prophets throughout the 1920s and 1930s, but it shied away from becoming the 'Hammer of the Kujurs', and not all prophets or *dayiemni* were harried, detained, or shot. The government set the limits of its own reaction by defining the constraints within which a prophet or an owner of a divinity would be allowed to function. It did this through a series of pastoral visits—what the Quakers would call eldering.

[2] Hutchinson (1985; 1988: ch. 3 (esp. pp. 128–38, 147–80), pp. 236–59; 1990). For migrant labour see El Wathig Kameir (1980). For changes in Jonglei Province see Howell, Lock, and Cobb (1988: ch. 11) and Mohamed Osman el Sammani (1984).

District commissioners were frequently informed of the activities of new prophets because the government's anti-prophet bias was well known. They would then visit or summon the prophet in question to determine if they were extorting cattle, interfering in court cases, obstructing government orders, or preaching anti-Dinka propaganda. If innocent of these 'obnoxious practices' the prophet would be given clear instructions on how to behave and allowed to continue his prayers and sacrifices. Sometimes a set of guidelines would be issued, as with the 'dog-eaters' in Western Nuer. An example of a district commissioner's eldering was the meeting between Macar Teny and John Winder in December 1939.

Macar Teny was a Bar Gaawar water-master (*kuaar thoi*) from a small lineage of Anuak descent, living on the southern tip of the Zeraf Island. He was seized by the divinity BUK,[3] the mother of DENG, who is also associated with rivers and streams. He achieved a reputation for curing barren women and praying for crops around Adok, but he came to prominence during the early rains of 1939 when he returned to his original home on the Zeraf Island. The preceding few years had been years of food shortage, and there was a new threat of locusts with the prospect of famine. Macar toured the western Gaawar area and other parts of the Zeraf Island, calling on people to stop holding public dances and to bring him cattle for sacrifice. He even went to Luang Deng, demanding a beast of the shrine-master. The shrine-master refused, insisting that DENG was the greater divinity, and in the end Macar offered an animal to DENG. During his tour people brought him cattle, which he dedicated and sacrificed. Wherever he went, and wherever his instructions were followed, the harvest was good (though some areas not visited also prospered). When the district commissioner, John Winder, heard of Macar's activities, he arranged to meet him on tour at the beginning of the dry season. He described Macar as 'rather good looking' but unshaven. Macar explained the extent of his activities.

> He insisted that his Kwoth detested discord and blood shed and that he always endeavoured to prevent anything of that sort. I have not heard any suggestion to the contrary and in fact, when he came to Fangak last rains, he told the Government that he wished to see me as there was a matter in the south end of the Island which required looking into as the Chiefs had not properly settled it, and blood shed was likely to ensue. . . . He wished me to understand that he did not want any recompence [*sic*] for his good works. He required cattle etc for sacrifice but he did not want these for himself and always dealt with them in situ.

There might be some complaints against him, he admitted, as he still owed marriage cattle, but 'he was often urged by parents to marry their daughters, as Kwoth men were generally regarded as rich and it was often difficult to get out of marrying them'.

[3] Biel Tip Gai Dk1.

Winder assured him that none of these activities concerned the government. The government had no quarrel with him or his kind, 'as long as they kept themselves to curing barren[n]ess in women or to ensuring good crops—everyone wanted the country to prosper'. The difficulty came when 'Kwoth men' began extorting cattle and intimidating people.

I told Macar that if he looked where he was going and kept to his right sphere and did not put people in fear, and kept in touch with the Government, so that gossip against him could be investigated, there was no reason why we should fall foul of each other. If his influence seemed to be for the bad he must know what to expect. It was up to him to establish that his work was benificient [*sic*] rather than the contrary.[4]

From that time until independence district commissioners kept in regular contact with Macar and reported nothing irregular about his activities. He appeared to have little influence outside his immediate area, but he was still active in the early 1960s.[5]

It is clear from this reported exchange that by the end of the 1930s the Nuer knew precisely what the government did not like, as well as what type of activities might generate rumours against a prophet. Because prophets had a reputation for being wealthy in livestock and regularly sacrificed other persons' animals, envy or resentment could inspire accusations that they were extorting cattle.

The distinction between the work of the government and the work of a divinity was even more clearly delineated in the case of Nyin Nguen, a man of cattle who was the main chief of the Bang section of the Bar Gaawar in the 1930s, and a contender for the presidency of the Bar Gaawar court after Guer Wiu died in 1937. Nyin had considerable support among the neighbouring Dinka, and the government was inclined to favour him, the only reservation being that Nyin was 'of an excitable disposition'. In 1938 he fell ill and was absent from court work, so the position of court president remained vacant.[6]

Nyin's illness was diagnosed as caused by a family *kuoth* (whether Power or divinity will be discussed later) which had killed his elder brother. The *kuoth* demanded cattle sacrifices, and early in 1939 Nyin sacrificed some of his own, as well as his section's, cattle for his 'personal health and safety'. With the appearance of the same locust swarm to which Macar Teny responded, Nyin's *kuoth* went public. The locusts descended on the Gaawar crops just as they were about to be harvested, and since the previous lean years had left no reserve there was great fear of imminent famine. It was then that Nyin announced to the Bar that they should send him cattle to sacrifice on behalf of

[4] John Winder to governor UNP, 12 Feb. 1940, SRO UNP 66.E.2.

[5] 'Personality Report Upper Nile Province: Zeraf District', SRO ZVD 66.K.1; 'Upper Nile Province "Who's Who"', Malakal UNP SCR 66.D.4; Howell (1954: 214–15).

[6] John Winder to governor UNP, 12 Feb. 1940, SRO UNP 66.E.2; 'Nin Nguen', and P. P. Howell, ADC ZD to governor UNP, 18 Jan. 1944, both in SRO ZVD 66.K.1.

his *kuoth*. He sent three beasts to Luang Deng and three others to lesser shrines in Bor District. Nyin began sacrificing cattle, and the locust swarm left after doing only one night's damage.

Not all Gaawar were willing to give up their cattle, and Nyin's rivals in the court hierarchy refused. It was his main competitor for the court presidency, Diu Bang, who informed Winder of Nyin's activities. On the grounds that Nyin 'had taken off and laid down his Government cloth of office' Winder placed Nyin under restraint so that anyone with a grievance could come forward. No one did. No one even complained of being intimidated into giving up their cattle. Rather, most seemed pleased with the results of Nyin's sacrifice.

Nyin argued that he had preserved the distinction between government and spiritual duties and

> protested that he had not meant any lack of loyalty to Government in laying aside his cloth; he had felt himself as one possessed by the Spirit and that this was incompatible with his carrying on as a Government Chief. He had, therefore, taken his clothes off, folded them up and laid them in his box. They were there and now that he felt no longer possessed he was quite prepared to don them again.

Winder was still sceptical and wondered aloud whether Nyin had a 'higher loyalty' than that owed to the government.

> While I might be prepared to agree that his actions in this instance had been above-board and unharmful to the community, it did not follow that they would always be; he might think his Kwoth told him to do things which might be distinctly harmful to Gaweir in the same way as had the Kwoths of Deng Lika, Dwal Diu and Kurbiel not to mention Gwek and other Kwoth men. This was the signal for all the best elements in Bar to say that they knew all about the old Kwoths, that they disliked the idea of that kind of thing, that Nin's Kwoth was of quite a different order and that they would see to it that it remained so.

Dual Diu's own brother Gau Bang offered to guarantee Nyin's good behaviour. Nyin was reinstated as chief of the Bang section, with Gau as his deputy. There was no question of Nyin being made court president.[7]

Nyin resumed his administrative work, and also his rivalry with Diu Bang. He was seized by his *kuoth* again in 1941 (when there was a challenge to his leadership), but returned to normal. During the annual road repair in December 1943 he got into an argument with the police corporal in charge and ordered his headmen to stop work, threatening them with punishment from his *kuoth* if they disobeyed. For attempting to use his spiritual powers to assert authority over his headmen he was briefly imprisoned, 'to emphasise on his mind here and now, that the Government will not tolerate the intervention

[7] John Winder to Armstrong, Awoi, 12 Jan. 1940, SAD 541/1/30; John Winder, DC ZD, to governor UNP, 12 Feb. 1940, SRO UNP 66.E.2.

of a Kwoth in matters which concern either the material work of the District or the well-being and peace of mind of the people'. His work after reinstatement was satisfactory, but he was no longer considered entirely reliable. He was thought to be an epileptic and was 'clearly a neurotic'.[8]

Nyin Nguen's case illustrates how the government repeatedly enforced its restrictions on spiritual activity, and how the Nuer themselves assimilated that separation between government and spiritual work. There was the danger that any spiritual manifestation might be used in political confrontations: Diu Bang tried to get his rival removed for sacrificing to his divinity, and Nyin was tempted to use that power to reinforce his authority over his juniors. As in the case of Macar Teny prophetic activity was directed into clearly defined paths by the steady exertion of government pressure. Just as the aftermath of the 1896–7 risings in Southern Rhodesia influenced the Mwari shrines 'into steering a safer course',[9] so the Nuer divinities now restricted their pursuits. Healing, prayers, and sacrifices were legitimate activities, as long as the prophets did not attract too large a following. Government surveillance ensured that they did not.

There is another aspect of this case which distinguishes it from others. Nyin began sacrificing to his *kuoth* to cure himself. On recovery he was able to sacrifice on behalf of others to avert the catastrophe they faced by the arrival of locusts. He transformed a purely personal *kuoth* into a public one, but another transformation was involved. Nyin Nguen was the grandson of Puol Bidiit, the man who used magic to kill Buogh Kerpeil (described in Chapter 4). The *kuoth* that afflicted him was the Power of his grandfather's magic. It had all the traits of an earthly Power re-emerging in a later generation: it had killed Nyin's brother; it made Nyin ill and demanded cattle for itself; Nyin first sacrificed for his 'personal safety and health'. A magician can use his relationship with an earthly Power to protect those related to him, as Nyin began to do, but such Powers are dangerous and unreliable, as the death of Nyin's brother showed. We can now understand why 'all the best elements in Bar' answered Winder's objections by insisting that 'Nin's Kwoth was of quite a different order' from Deng Laka's, Dual Diu's, or Guek's, but also why Winder did not realize that there was a distinction between Nyin's lower Power (*kuoth piny*) and Dual's divinity of the above (*kuoth nhial*). In this and other cases the government appeared willing to tolerate the activities of earthly Powers more than those of free-divinities.

Magic spread throughout the Nilotic peoples during the colonial period, partly because communication was made easier, partly because chiefs began to rely on it in lineage politics, and partly because prophetic control over magic

[8] 'Nin Nguen', P. P. Howell to governor UNP, 18 Jan. 1944, and 'Personality Report Upper Nile Province: Zeraf District', all in SRO ZVD 66.K.1.

[9] Daneel (1970: 73).

had been removed.[10] Prophets had represented and supported the moral community. Magicians (especially fetish owners—*guan kulang*) imitated prophets in their outward appearance, but not in their support for the moral community. In the absence of prophets there was a demand for medicines with healing and protective powers, and there were owners of such medicines who echoed the prophets in what they offered. But fetishes (*kulangni*) were rarely benign. They are really known mainly for consuming food.[11] The fetish owners did not so much imitate the prophets as parody them, and the fetishes themselves are a parody on the free-divinities. In the fetish owner the prophet's spiritual danger and desire for cattle is recreated without providing any of the benefits in return.

The 1930s saw a trend towards a fragmentation of the moral community. The new court system insisted on the full payment of obligations, and this began to place strains on the older ideals of communal responsibility by increasingly emphasizing the theoretical rights and obligations of individuals.[12] The administrative system further encouraged the recognition of leaders of small political units. Similarly, under government surveillance and secularization 'ritual experts' of all types tended to confine their activities to small groups of kin. This resembled more the restricted social radius of the magicians than the broad moral appeal of the prophets. In this way, too, spiritual figures and magicians came to resemble each other.

Free-divinities continued to be active, but in a contracted arena. Names and characters of divinities and Powers are usually announced and defined by those who claim them. Prophets had exerted some control over spiritual manifestations in their territories and had provided a point of reference for each new mantic person. With the removal of the prophets such definitions were provided mainly by the individuals claiming seizure, and there was some confusion as divinities and earthly Powers appeared haphazardly in different districts. Not only were some fetishes known only in some places and entirely unknown in others, but so were divinities. There were competing claims of efficacy as between divinities, and as between divinities and Powers. Through the inconsistencies of its response to all religious figures the government further encouraged a blurring of distinctions.[13]

During the latter half of the Anglo-Egyptian Condominium in the Sudan the government tolerated most religious activity (Christian, Muslim, or pagan) as long as it did not interfere with administration and was not overtly political. Thus religious figures among the Nuer who stayed out of the administrative structure and avoided involvement in lineage politics tended to have a freer

[10] Johnson (1992*a*).
[11] Ruot Diu G10.2; Evans-Pritchard (1935: 73).
[12] Johnson (1986*a*: 73–4). See Hutchinson (1988, 1990) for detailed analyses of the effect of courts on Nuer social relations.
[13] Johnson (1992*a*).

hand than those chiefs whose seizure by a divinity or ownership of magic became known. The divinities of Car Koryom and Pok Kerjiok passed to their sons when they died without attracting much official notice. The sons of Ngundeng were kept under closer observation. There was some concern when Lel Ngundeng showed signs of inheriting his father's divinity: he sang Ngundeng's songs and reported predictions through dreams. He was disciplined each time he showed this tendency, and the family claim that DENG never descended on Lel; they firmly insist that DENG will never return to them, nor to anyone else.[14] Through this combination of restriction and benign neglect the government and the Nuer finally agreed, for their own reasons, that the prophets and government could work on parallel courses, but not together. Each finally accepted that the other had a sphere of its own in which to operate. This divorce did mean that by the time the Sudan was granted independence in 1956 prophets were beginning to re-emerge as persons of extended spiritual influence. It also meant that prophets as such were not immediate political targets when civil war entered Nuerland. This allowed some to re-enter the political field, but even as they did so the old divinities imposed a pattern which the others tried to follow.

The realignment of divinity: independence and the first civil war

By 1954 it was reported that a new Lou prophet, Yuot Guoguok of the Biliu-Mor, had gained considerable popularity, placing Lel Ngundeng's dreams and songs in the shade. He had enough of a reputation by 1957 that, when the first Northern Sudanese governor of the province met the Lou chiefs and was given an ox-name, the administration invited Yuot Guoguok to officiate at the sacrifices in the governor's honour.[15] Yuot operated as a prophet very much in the shadow of the ruins of Ngundeng's Mound. He performed ceremonies there, once gathering a large number of children and blessing them by placing a small piece of tobacco in each one's mouth. Yuot did not claim to be seized by DENG, but he did claim that whenever he visited the Mound his divinity left him and entered it, just as the divinities of the *dayiemni* did in Ngundeng's day. He thus accepted the primacy of DENG by submitting, fifty years after Ngundeng's death, to the authority of Ngundeng. With no nearby prophet of DENG to challenge him, he helped to establish and strengthen his own reputation by asserting this continuity with Ngundeng.

Any prophet in the early 1950s treading Ngundeng's path found new detours on the way to peace. Britain had decided in 1946 to prepare the

[14] Gany Car L26, Riei Pok Kerjiok L25; 'Chiefs and Headmen Lau Nuer District', n.d. [*c.*1936], SRO LND 66.B.3; Alban (1940: 202); 'Upper Nile Province "Who's Who"', Malakal UNP SCR 66.D.4.

[15] 'Upper Nile Province "Who's Who"', Malakal UNP SCR 66.D.4; *UNP Diary*, Mar. 1957, p. 1.

Sudan for independence, and in 1947 it firmly excluded any possibility of a different process towards self-administration for the three southern provinces. The combination of tribal administration, limited educational facilities, and restricted economic development provided the Southern Sudan with neither the resources nor the institutions to guarantee equitable incorporation into the new nation state. Only a small number of Southern Sudanese had enough education to qualify as clerical staff or junior administrators. After 1947 almost all of these found themselves co-opted into the legislative and elective politics of Sudan; thus they were removed from daily contact with the peoples they were supposed to represent.[16]

The Nuer had an even smaller stake in the institutions of the new state than most Southern peoples. Out of an estimated population of nearly half a million, the Nuer had only one college-level graduate, no more than half a dozen secondary school-level graduates employed in local administration; almost no one in the police or the army; and only a handful of secondary school students approaching completion of their education. The 'Sudanization' of administration prior to independence meant the appointment of Northern Sudanese with no previous experience in the South, rather than the elevation of the Nuer to self-government. A colonial form of administration continued.

Many Nuer in the rural areas were anxious about the future,[17] but the mutiny of the Equatorial Corps and Southern police in August 1955 did not involve them, as few Nuer were represented in those bodies. The first Northern Sudanese officials in the province seemed willing, and even eager, to respect religious figures. During the first few years of independence Dual Diu, Nyaruac Kolang, Macar Teny, and Yuot Guoguok were able to operate normally without attracting much official attention or arousing suspicion. The appearance of a new divinity, and the political attempt to co-opt the symbols of an old one did, however, reawaken mild alarm.

In 1954, shortly before independence, a Lak chief's policeman named Ruac Col left government service, claiming that he was troubled by a divinity which had burned down his cattle byre several times before he sacrificed to it. Two years later Ruac announced that a new divinity was revealed in a *thou* (higlig) tree twenty-five miles north of Fangak. It was called MARPINY ('strikes the ground'), and appeared to persons in dreams, which only Ruai could interpret. The tree first came to the attention of the authorities after the 1957 harvest, when it was reported that thousands of Nuer and Dinka visited it, bringing their children and their sick to be blessed, and that hundreds of cattle were being slaughtered to feed the visitors. The divinity in the tree was also

[16] On educational policy see Sanderson and Sanderson (1981); for pre-independence politics see Collins (1983).

[17] Roussel (1955: 1016).

reported to have advised the Nuer to store their grain reserves and not sell them to the merchants. This last was prudent advice in an area of chronic overall grain shortages with a history of large grain imports, but it could have anti-Northern Sudanese overtones. For this reason the tree was 'kept under the close Satanical observation of the District Commissioner'.[18]

Early in 1959 the governor of Upper Nile received an enquiry from Khartoum about a report of a 'new creed' among the Nuer, Dinka, and Shilluk which the province medical officer had forwarded directly to his superiors. The new 'kujur' was said to have power over health, birth, death, cultivation, and animals, and had amassed over 2,000 head of cattle in fees for interpreting dreams and praying. The provincial government, resenting Khartoum's interference, compiled a report drawing on a number of sources, including Dual Diu and Ruac Col himself. This was not a new religion, the district commissioner insisted. It did attract a number of Shilluk, Dinka, and Nuer, who come mostly after the harvest to brew beer, kill cattle, and enjoy themselves. Ruac Col sacrificed on behalf of visitors, the divinity MARPINY was thought to influence birth and death, and it was approached for blessings on children and sick persons. Ruac Col had less than 400 beasts, not over 2,000, and he was not even a meat-eater, which seemed to clear him of personal greed for cattle. All the same, Ruac impressed the district commissioner as 'a sinister clever sort of person'. With a threat to cut down and burn the tree should Ruac turn nasty, the matter was dropped.[19]

In the same year that MARPINY was officially noticed, and just prior to the first post-independence elections, a group of Nuer politicians requested the central government to return the pipe and drum of Ngundeng, taken from the field of battle in 1929, and then residing in the ethnological museum in Khartoum. The political motivation of the parliamentarians—to gain influence before the election—was enough to give the authorities pause. 'All these antiquities were kept by the British in safe custody in Khartoum,' the district commissioner of the Gaawar acutely observed, 'not for their historical value but for a bigger and more important purpose centred in diminishing the power of Kujur Leaders and evading any rival influence to that of the Government among the Nilotics'.[20] The governor agreed and advised the Ministry of Interior not to release the relics. There was peace now in the province but, he warned, 'this action is like striking a match near barrels of high explosives, once started cannot be controlled and will set ablaze the whole

[18] S. Freigoun, DC Fangak, to governor UNP, 7 Mar. 1959, and 'Extracts from Zeraf District Monthly Reports for Oct. Nov. and December 1957', both in NRO UNP 1/33/270. See SDIT 1954, table 49, for grain imports to Wath Kech and Dyel, 1930–53.

[19] Ahmed Saleem for governor UNP to DC ZD, 19 Feb. 1959, and S. Freigoun to governor UNP, 7 Mar. 1959, both in NRO UNP 1/33/270.

[20] Hassan Dafa'allah, DC Zeraf, to governor UNP, 17 Apr. 1957, Nasir unnumbered file (originally ZD 66.E.2).

area of Low Nuer—a difficult people—with definite consequences of the fire expanding to neighbouring Nuer Districts'.[21]

The mild excitement over MARPINY and Ngundeng's relics showed that the national government was clearly willing to follow the policy of its colonial predecessors towards tribal leaders, but there is no indication that the civil administration at this time feared a pagan rising led by 'kujurs'. Regional politics were more threatening, especially when the civil war, dormant since 1955, intruded into the province in the mid-1960s. This had a direct impact on the careers of prophets who had arisen before the war, as well as those who appeared after hostilities began, disrupting relations with the government as well as internal relations between sections. Prophets had to balance local needs with external demands, the expectations of established divinities with the exigencies of war.

Two prophets who became active in the Zeraf area during the 1960s, Gony Yut of the Gaawar and Ruei Kuic of the Lak, illustrate the effect of war on modern prophecy. In their early years they both attempted to define their roles in relation to existing prophets and shrines. The war brought them into direct conflict, though they were not originally in competition for followers or spiritual influence. The outcome of the war destroyed Gony Yut's career, while Ruei Kuic consolidated his spiritual position among his neighbours.

Gony Yut is descended from a Rut Dinka who came to live with the Nyang-Radh Gaawar during Nuaar Mer's time. As a Gaawar he still claimed a connection with the Luang Deng shrine-masters, whom he called his paternal uncles (*guanlen*).[22] Before his seizure Gony had few cattle, was known as a good cultivator, but was not considered attractive by girls because of his weak eyes (which troubled him all his life).[23] According to Gony he was seized by divinity in 1953: 'When it first came to me I was a young man. I was having guests at my cattle byre, and when I went to the garden to get food for them, suddenly the sky opened up and I fell down. There were clouds in the sky [emblematic of DENG].'[24]

Gony's reputation as a healer after his seizure did not extend much beyond the Radh Gaawar. He gained a small following from his own section through blessing cultivation and curing the sick. His usual technique of curing was to chew some tobacco which the supplicant brought, then rub the tobacco all over the supplicant's body; thus associating tobacco, a common object offered for sacrifice when no animal is available, with spittle and its life-giving symbolism.

Gony Yut's divinity is often referred to by the honorific name *Gatdonga*, but

[21] K. M. Sabir, governor UNP, to permanent under-secretary, Ministry of Interior, 22 May 1957, Nasir unnumbered file (originally UNP SCR/36).

[22] Gony Yut G15.

[23] Peter Rir and David Keak A11.

[24] Gony Yut G15.

he claimed to be seized by DENG, specifically by DENG LUAK, the divinity of Luang Deng. After the death of the shrine-master Raak Yaak in the 1960s, Gony appeared at the shrine and claimed to be the prophet of DENG. Any new shrine-master must prove his acceptance by the divinity by spending the night in the main byre of the shrine, but Gony did not. Rather he slept in a camp some distance away, surrounded by a bodyguard of armed followers. His behaviour did not conform to what was expected of a prophet of DENG, and his claim was thus disputed by the people of the shrine. Gony seemed to be careful to avoid contact with other established living representatives of Divinity. He visited Dual Diu's homestead only after the latter's death. Thus, whenever he associated himself with an accepted manifestation of Divinity, he did so in a way which avoided either confrontation or direct contradiction.[25]

Ruei Kuic was seized by a divinity later than Gony, and he had to accommodate his claims with those of MARPINY and Nyaruac Kolang. Ruei had an early experience with Divinity when, as a boy, he was badly burned while cooking fish. The fire he built got out of control, swept through the grass and killed a number of cattle. The owners of the cattle demanded compensation but withdrew their claim when the death of more of their cattle was attributed to Divinity's displeasure.[26] After Ruac Col's death Ruei Kuic announced that he was seized by MARPINY. Nyaruac Kolang had already claimed MARPINY to be MAANI's younger brother JIAR WAN, and Ruei accepted this. Among the Western Nuer it is said that Nyaruac initially recognized Ruei when those who lost cattle in his fire came to her for help. Apparently, shortly after Ruei's seizure their cattle byres burned down. They moved to Gaawar, and then to Lou, hoping to be protected by DIU and DENG, but each time they built a new byre, it burned down. Nyaruac explained to them that their affliction stemmed from their quarrel with JIAR WAN, who had now seized Ruei Kuic. She offered a lump of tobacco as a sacrifice to JIAR, after which the persons were able to settle in peace.[27]

This was a *post hoc* attribution by both Ruei and Nyaruac. Ruei associated himself with MARPINY after he had already claimed to be seized by the divinity TUT IN KUR (the white bull with black eyes). A ram of the *kur* configuration (black spots around its eyes) had been found walking on the river (some say it fell overboard from a passing steamer and was able to clamber ashore by walking on the *sudd* and water hyacinth). It came to Ruei's village and stopped in front of Ruei's byre. When Ruei slaughtered this ram he was then seized and announced his new name, TUT IN KUR.[28] By later co-opting MARPINY,

[25] Gony Yut G15, David Keak A11.

[26] Thomas Riek Nguot A13. John Winder (personal communication) remembered this incident. The persons whose cattle died were Shilluk.

[27] Kuol Kolang Ket Jg3, Thomas Riek Nguot A13, Peter Gatkuoth Gual, Stephen Ciec Lam, Gabriel Yoal Dok A6.

[28] Thomas Riek Nguot A13.

Ruei attached himself to an established prophetic tradition through an established prophet, Nyaruac Kolang.

In their efforts to build their prophetic reputations Gony and Ruei faced in opposite directions. Gony looked east to Luang Deng, while Ruei looked west to Nyaruac. This was not to last. In the mid-1960s Gony Yut allied himself with the army in its war against guerrillas, and the expanding radius of his own raids brought him into conflict with Ruei Kuic and the Lak.

During the final years of the Abboud regime (1958–64) civil war spread throughout the three southern provinces. The remnants of the old Equatorial Corps mutineers were joined by secondary school students and others to form a new guerrilla movement known as 'Anyanya' (a type of poison). The organization spread slowly out of Equatoria, recruiting locally in the other provinces, reaching Upper Nile and the Nuer in 1964. Throughout its history the guerrilla movement was frequently split along social lines, and the fact that the first Anyanya units in Upper Nile Province were recruited mainly from Dinka kept them apart from the Nuer. The province government tried to restrict the influence of the Anyanya by arming local groups hostile to them; thus increasing intertribal strife. Public opinion began to shift towards the Anyanya when the army, too, began to attack civilians indiscriminately as potential, or probable, supporters of the 'outlaws'. The war intensified throughout the South during the first Umma party government (1965–7), and the worst time for the people of Upper Nile Province was the years 1970–1, shortly after Nimeiri's May 1969 coup. It was only in the later stages of the war (which ended in 1972) that significant numbers of Jikany, Lou, Gaawar, and Lak joined the Anyanya. For some of these Nuer Gony Yut's collaboration with the army propelled them into the guerrilla forces.

In the mid-1960s Gony Yut was known as a healer and, claiming connection with Luang Deng, was not hostile to the Dinka. It is said that Gony first came in contact with the Anyanya when a group of mainly Luac Dinka guerrillas came into his area and asked him to look after their wounded soldiers. While convalescing the soldiers allegedly raped some women. Relations between Gony and the Anyanya deteriorated after that. Fighting between the two began in the rainy season of 1965, and intensified throughout the rains of 1966. At the end of 1966 Gony began to receive army support. His followers were styled 'National Guards' and were supplied with rifles, ammunition, clothes, insignia, and salaries.

Gony's National Guards first attacked the Dinka of Khor Atar in 1966 and 1967, and Gony denounced a Rueng chief for fomenting discord. As early as December 1966 Gony also denounced the Lou for harbouring 'outlaws', and his men fought the Lou in 1969 and 1971. Very early in his career as the leader of a government-backed militia Gony complained about other Gaawar chiefs, urging the appointment of his own supporters. He also denounced those Southern Sudanese administrators who had refused to recognize his candidates or had tried to restrain his raids. The man who was the main target of Gony's denunciations was Philip Reath Kuer, court president of the Bar Gaawar court. Gony's National Guard were reported to have beaten and killed various Bar Gaawar and to have seized Bar cattle. But even Radh Gaawar chiefs complained of some of Gony's activities, especially when a murderer received sanctuary in Gony's byre. It is clear from the contemporary government record that Gony used the backing of the military to involve himself in the lineage politics of the Gaawar, much to the dismay of the civil administrators.[29]

Gony collected large numbers of cattle in his raids on the Anyanya and their suspected supporters, and it was with these (plus the weapons and salaries provided to his National Guard) that he was able to attract a much larger following than he had had when he first became a prophet. He married perhaps as many as ninety wives from the daughters and sisters of his supporters, sometimes paying full bridewealth, sometimes not. Just as Deng Laka had before him, he allowed many of his wives to choose consorts from among his entourage. As his power and the size of his following increased, Gony became more aggressive, ordering the assassination of his personal enemies and directing attacks against persons who were not necessarily associated with the Anyanya. Ruei Kuic was one of them.[30]

Fighting between Gony and Ruei began early in 1968, and there is, naturally, some disagreement about who initiated raiding. Gony first denounced Ruei as harbouring the 'outlaws' and capturing Gony's own people at the end of May 1968. This followed a battle between Gony and Ruei in April. But there may also have been an earlier raid on the Lak, when Gony attacked Ruei's village, killing four of Ruei's sisters and capturing most of Ruei's cattle. In retaliation, it is said, Ruei captured some Gaawar women in a counter-attack against Gony, and gave these women as wives to his own followers. It is further alleged that in response to Gony's raids Ruei sought the support of the local Anyanya and received some arms from them, though he was never as well supplied as Gony. The army continued to support Gony, giving him one of Ruei's drums which they captured, and entrusting Gony with cattle taken from the Lak and Thiang, allegedly stolen from the Gaawar.[31]

This new conflict between the Gaawar and Lak prophets split the Gaawar. Tension had been growing between the Bar and the Radh because of Gony's National Guards stealing Bar cattle. This lay behind Gony's complaints against Philip Reath Kuer, which led to the chief's brief imprisonment in

[29] Based on correspondence in 'Magic & Religion' file, New Fangak ZVR 66.E.1/2/1.

[30] David Keak and Peter Rir A11.

[31] Gony Yut to commissioner UNP, 31 May 1968, New Fangak ZVR 66.E.1/2/1; Louis Umodo, LGI ZVR, to commissioner UNP, 8 Feb. 1972, Malakal UNP SCR 66.A.1/2. Bullen Alier Buttic (1975) gives the date of Gony's first raid as 1971, but this is too late.

Fangak in February 1968. In April 1968 Philip Reath prevented the Bar from joining Gony's Nyang-Radh against Ruei's Lak. Early in 1969 a Gaawar named Mathot Yieth Cung, said to be a new 'kujur', organized a party of some 500 Bar to attack Gony and retrieve Bar cattle, but his following was disbanded by the police of the court presidents of both the Radh and Bar, Ruot Yuot and Philip Reath. Philip Reath's actions were consistent with those of a chief entrusted with preventing intersectional and intertribal feuds. Despite this, or perhaps because of it, some Radh chiefs complained that he had encouraged Mathot. His intervention when Gony was fighting Ruei the previous year was recalled to his detriment. In March 1969 Philip Reath was arrested by the army, accused of supporting Ruei Kuic against Gony Yut, taken to Mogogh (the Radh court centre), and shot out of hand.[32]

The fighting along the Zeraf Valley is one example of the internal disorder generated by the civil war. The civil and military branches of the state were often at odds with each other; chiefs could be killed by that same government whose law they were supposed to uphold; the surrogate militias could use their own criteria to define the state's enemies. Yet not all parts of Nuerland were visited with equal devastation as the war expanded. Most of Western Nuer District remained out of the battle zone, buffered as it was by the rising river and expanding swamp in the mid-1960s. Nyaruac Kolang was not drawn into the conflict. Dual Diu also tried to remain above the war, and it may be only coincidence that fighting intensified in the Gaawar area after he died. Yuot Guoguok was killed unintentionally by the Anyanya, caught in a crossfire during a fight in his village. His death was attributed to the Mound. After the Tree of Bad Things had fallen down, he used some of its wood to construct his byre. It was thus the tree which killed him.

With so many prophets falling victim to the war it seemed impossible for any of them to aspire to peace, but one, at least, tried, in direct imitation of Ngundeng. The complex story of the career of Bangong Diau, a Gaajak of the Reng section from near the Ethiopian border, shows just how difficult it was to attempt to follow Ngundeng's model during this war. Bangong Diau was the son of a chief's policeman. He served as a houseboy to John Wicjaal Buom, the son of Buom Diu, then a junior administrator in Nasir. Bangong was a quiet boy, rarely speaking to anyone, a childhood trait shared with many other prophets. He accompanied John Wicjaal on his administrative postings to the north. He then joined the growing number of Nuer migrant workers and eventually sought work outside the Sudan.[33]

It is indicative of the changing world of the Nuer that two different, but not incompatible, accounts of Bangong's seizure take as their reference points two

[32] 'Information about new kujur Mathot Yieth', New Fangak ZVR 66.E.1.2/1–2/3; Ring (1969: 3–8).

[33] John Wicjaal Buom A12; Bullen Alier Buttic (1975).

contrasting aspects of modern Nuer society: the new experience of migrant labour, and the continuity represented by the Mound. One states that Bangong was seized after a vulture landed on his head while he was working in Libya, and that the divinity which originally troubled him was the 'Fallata divinity', after the West African Muslim immigrants found throughout North Africa and the Sudan. Bangong could have been troubled by seizures during his wanderings (recreating the experience of many nineteenth-century Nilotes), but his associates in the Sudan claim that he was not finally seized until after his return to Upper Nile Province. He joined the Anyanya, and when his unit was stationed in Lou country in about 1968 Bangong visited Ngundeng's Mound. There, it is said, he found a metal ring and went mad on picking it up. He was taken home and left the Anyanya. He eventually announced he was seized by a divinity with the ox-name TUT IN KUAC (the spotted bull).[34]

Bangong reinforced his association with Ngundeng by also referring to his divinity as DENGKUR, Ngundeng's personal ox-name. The metal ring might almost have been a summons to DENG and, as Ngundeng used to do before him, Bangong sent his own metal rings to persons accused of various crimes. Bangong is reputed to have proved his power over life by sacrificing and then resurrecting a bull. He gained a reputation as a healer, curing the sick and making barren women fruitful. He denounced adultery and was able to expose the guilty parties. He also tried to suppress magic. As the influence of local government became increasingly confined to the towns in the final years of the war, Bangong came more in demand to settle disputes in the rural areas. By 1969 the local government inspector in Nasir reported that he was credited with dealing 'with things that can't be proved in the court'.[35]

Bangong was noted for attempting to create peace within a wider community at a time when there was very little peace. Jikany society was experiencing intense internal and external strife. The war between the Anyanya and the government generated a number of intersectional feuds along the border, as it had in the Zeraf Valley. Bangong's own Reng section was feuding with the neighbouring Nyajani section, as well as with the court president of Gaajak, Duop Biciuk. There was increased fighting between Jikany, Anuak, and Meban. Bangong settled the feud between Reng and Nyajani; he forbade fighting between Gaajak sections generally; and he prevented two Gaajak sections from raiding the Meban. It is perhaps for this reason that he was visited by Anuak and Meban, as well as by Nuer from the

[34] Samuel Ater Dak and Moses Cuol Juac A12, David Keak (who was a companion of Bangong Diau's in the Anyanya before his seizure) A11. For the date of Bangong's leaving the Anyanya see Samuel Ater Dak to commissioner UNP, 20 May 1969, and David C. Cotper to commissioner UNP, 16 July 1969, both in Malakal UNP SCR 36.M.1/8.

[35] David Keak A11, Samuel Ater Dak A12; Samuel Ater Dak to commissioner UNP, 16 July 1969, Malakal UNP SCR 36.M.1/8.

Sudan and Ethiopia, all coming to offer sacrifices and receive his blessing. These tangible proofs of his peaceful inclinations temporarily overcame administrative suspicions aroused by his having been in the Anyanya. Southerners in the Northern-dominated civil administration urged toleration. The local government inspector at Nasir, a man of mixed Nuer and Dinka parentage, advised, 'He should not be touched as long as he sticks to his heavenly mission,' and referred to the violence along the Zeraf Valley as an example of what to expect from driving a prophet into opposition.[36]

Bangong's relations with both the government and the Anyanya were delicately balanced. The government sent him gifts of cattle, and he replied with assurances of peace. He sent his emissaries to government courts, but he refused to meet any official or visit any government centre, pleading the prohibition of his divinity. He received groups of Anyanya who came to his camp for food and fed them out of his herd (which by 1972 was estimated at 1,500). He explained this to the government as an attempt at getting the guerrillas to settle down. He gave one Anyanya lieutenant a leopard-skin as a 'sign of peace', and he prevented the Anyanya from indiscriminately raiding villages, as they were in the habit of doing in other parts of the province. But his continued association with rebels could not be tolerated forever. In 1970 the army accused him of collaborating with the guerrillas and raided his cattle camp. Bangong is reported to have defeated the army in two battles before withdrawing when his camp was attacked from the air.[37] His attempt to survive between the opposing political systems of the guerrillas and the government, to carve out a small niche of peace between them, failed. Like the prophets of the 1920s he could not avoid being drawn into disputes with the government.

The Nuer desire for a peace which was at once compatible with the demands of government, yet grounded on the prescriptions of Divinity, is suggested by the experience of the Uduk *arum* man Jang, who incorporated the modes of Nuer prayer in his own rites. The Uduk live in the northern province of Blue Nile, on the border with the Meban of Upper Nile. In about 1964, just before the civil war reached the Eastern Nuer area, Jang was visited by a Nuer who taught him how to pray. The man wore a leopard-skin, which merely suggests an association with Divinity. He may have been peddling medicines and magic, but he instructed Jang to set up a forked shrine-stick made of higlig wood (a tree associated with DENG), and told him what to say in the invocation (*lam*), before sacrificing a beast, using language typical of Nuer prayers:

[36] David Cotper to commissioner UNP, 16 July 1969, and Samuel Ater Dak to commissioner UNP, 20 and 26 May 1969, all in Malakal UNP SCR 36.M.1/8.

[37] Samuel Ater Dak to commissioner UNP, 20 May 1969, Malakal UNP SCR 36.M.1/8; Leith (1970: 13).

'Let the people be well, let the earth be well, let the children remain cool and peaceful. Let there be no anger among them.' For if sacrifices are to be made to Arum, there should be no quarrelling. This would make Arum angry. . . . If there is fighting, Jang should gather the people and ask what is the cause. He should take animals from the people and sacrifice them . . . if the people give him animals, he need not pass the case on to the Government. The work of the Government (*hakuma*, Arabic) and the work of Arum, he explained, 'is the same' . . . If there were no Turuk, then it would not be possible to do the work of God (Arum), for there would be no peace—people would be running about killing each other all the time.[38]

This was about the last time such an equation between the government, Divinity, and peace could be made, as the government soon subtracted itself from that equation. Because of the violence perpetrated by the government and by the guerrilla movement which aspired to be a government, those prophets who tried to create peace were thwarted in their efforts. When peace finally came with the Addis Agreement of March 1972 there had to be a readjustment of political authority, prophets, and Divinity to each other. With a new peace came a new government which included many Nuer and Dinka at all levels.

The Addis Ababa peace, Divinity, and the renewal of civil war

By 1972 the violence generated by the civil war had penetrated deeply into Nuer society, affecting many aspects of daily life. During my first visit to Ayod in 1975 children openly sang Anyanya victory songs. The spear imagery of an earlier era had given way to the rifle, as illustrated in this improvisational song recorded in the late 1970s, where a young man compares his rifle-owning companions with the armed men the Nuer have known this century—from the cavalry of the 1920s, to the Congolese soldiers of World War II, to the Anyanya of the civil war:

> We carry our rifles like those of Waldeth,
> like the cavalry, like the Congolese army,
> like the Anyanya guerrillas. Girls run away,
> smoking like cigarettes when we fire.[39]

The first task of the new Southern Regional government created by the Addis Ababa Agreement was to oversee the implementation of the cease-fire between the government and guerrilla forces and the absorption of former guerrillas into the national army and local police.[40] In asserting its new authority it had to reconstitute provincial administration, reaffirm the jurisdiction of local courts, and disarm the rural areas. Where prophets had

38 James (1988: 179–81).
39 Svoboda (1985: 19).
40 Alier (1990: ch. 9).

their own armed followings, and where they had heard and settled disputes on their own in competition with existing chiefs' courts, they presented a challenge to the new regional authorities. 'Authority is indivisible', declared the province commissioner (himself a Lou Nuer) who had the task of taming the prophets. 'Law and order have no alternatives and as such anything or anybody tending to disrupt it will be severely dealt with.'[41] Behind this bold language was a desire to end the insecurity of the civil war, not to prolong it. The regional government insisted just as adamantly as all its predecessors that it was the ultimate legal authority, but it tried to co-opt the prophets, not overwhelm them. Underlying this pragmatic approach was also a greater respect for prophets than found in previous administrations. Most of the officials entrusted with the task of bringing in the prophets were themselves Nuer. Many shared the attitude publicly expressed by the regional assemblyman Stephen Ciec Lam (son of Lam Liew), when he explained to a Southern Sudanese journalist, 'I think that Kujurs should be understood and respected as laid down by the [1973] constitution, and the administration should only come in . . . when they seem not to comply with local administration.'[42]

There were considerable difficulties in creating the atmosphere which would encourage the prophets to meet officials. The terms of the 1972 Amnesty Act, which followed the ratification of the peace treaty, prohibited prosecution of war-related crimes. Almost all of the prophets were involved in disputes of some sort or another which fell within the terms of the Amnesty Act. The government therefore could not redress old grievances. Most of the major prophets (and some minor ones) were in conflict with government-appointed chiefs and refused to recognize the decisions of their courts. But the real problem lay in cattle captured during the war. Amnesty Act or no Amnesty Act, few pastoralists were willing to see their abducted cattle in someone else's herd. Raiding in the Zeraf Valley had been at its worst during the last two years of the war. Not only did Gony Yut and Ruei Kuic raid each other, but Gony raided the Dinka, Lou, and independent Anyanya groups. Gony had even raided his brother-in-law in the Anyanya, who then proclaimed himself seized by a divinity and raided Gony, the Dinka, and the Shilluk. The new administration found that it was almost impossible to untangle the different claims to cattle held in various herds at the end of the war. As in the days of Nuer–Dinka raiding during World War I, it was also very difficult to arrive at a reasonable figure of cattle stolen. Gony was accused of having taken 8,090 head of cattle from the Lou, but only 959 were verified.[43]

41 Interview with Peter Gatkuoth (1974) in Bullen Alier Buttic (1975).

42 Interview with Stephen Lam (1974) in Bullen Alier Buttic (1975).

43 Correspondence and reports in Malakal UNP SCR 36.M.1/8 and UNP SCR 36.M.1/3 Fangak; Bullen Alier Buttic (1975).

The province commissioner of Upper Nile at the beginning of the Addis Ababa peace was Moses Cuol Juac, a Gaajak Nuer, and he used this common bond to try to bring Bangong Diau in. Bangong was considered the most 'politically aware' of the modern prophets because of his service in the Anyanya. He was recognized as actively striving to maintain peace along the border by forbidding intersectional fights, but he was at enmity with the court president Duop Biciuk, and refused to meet the province commissioner until November 1973. He proclaimed his desire to be a 'good citizen', but continued to be evasive about coming into Malakal himself, giving up his weapons, or enlisting his men in the province police. He was not brought to Malakal until 1974.[44]

The other two major prophets, Gony Yut and Ruei Kuic, were also reluctant to disarm their followers or be taken to Malakal. An unsuccessful peace meeting was held at Fangak in July 1972, which both Gony and Ruei attended. Gony was unsure about his future since the province administration now included a number of ex-Anyanya soldiers and administrators. Having allied with government, he found it no longer sympathetic to him. He avoided visiting Malakal as long as he could until he was personally escorted there by the deputy commissioner. Ruei Kuic was more elusive, more suspicious of the old army behind the new government. He met the local government inspector at his own village in September 1973, but his disputes with Gony and the Lak court president prevented him from coming to Malakal. Finally a government delegation, which included a Nuer Catholic priest and Lili Goak Ruot, one of Kolang Ket's old associates, tracked him down in 1974. The priest appealed to him, as one man of religion and peace to another, to come to the government. Ruei finally agreed, partially because a new prophet among the Western Nuer, a successor to Nyaruac, had recently been killed attacking the army, and he feared the same fate.[45]

Once assembled in Malakal the prophets tried to maintain a distance between themselves and the government, refusing, at first, to accept items associated with government, such as clothes, shoes, chairs, tea, metal cooking pots, medicine, and cars. But the government insisted that they become integrated into town life, and provided them with oxen for sacrifice to appease their individual divinities for changing their lives. Chickens were sacrificed to allow them to take medicine (*wal*). The prophets were brought to Juba to become acquainted with the regional government as part of their orientation. After a year they were returned to their homes.[46] Gony, Ruei, and others were

[44] Correspondence and reports in Malakal SCR 36.M.1/8.

[45] 'Note on Fangak Tribal Conference 31.7.1972 to 1.8.1972 which Resulted in Peace between Kujur Roy and Kujur Gony', and Charles Mobile, LGI to commissioner UNP, 1 Oct. 1973, both in Malakal SCR 66.A.1/2; Venansio Loro, John Wicjaal Buom, Peter Rir A10; Bullen Alier Buttic (1975).

[46] Bullen Alier Buttic (1975).

FIG. 14. Gony Yut (2nd from r.), in leopard-skin, Mogogh Conference, 1975 (Garretson)

brought back together in March 1975 for a conference at Mogogh to settle outstanding cattle disputes, a conference which I attended on my first visit to the Nuer (Fig. 14).

A security committee had been formed to investigate cases of disputed cattle. It verified some 4,009 head of cattle taken by Gony: 959 from the Lou and 3,050 from the Gaawar (most of the latter originally coming from the Shilluk and Dinka). The committee allowed for a deduction of 1,509 cattle dead, sold, eaten, stolen, or otherwise untraceable, leaving 2,500 head of cattle still in Gony's possession. Because of the Amnesty Act the government could not force Gony to return any, but it was clear that peace would not return to the area as long as he retained the cattle. A compromise was proposed by the Gaawar and Lou chiefs, whereby the cattle in question would be handed over to the government for sale. It was understood, though perhaps not strictly enforceable, that the money from the sale would be used to develop the districts involved. Gony complained that, as Deng Laka, Dual Diu, and Kolang Ket had all raided for cattle and had kept their spoils, he did not see why he should be forced to give up his cattle. He even appealed to one of the administrators present, John Wicjaal Buom, the son of a prophet, for support. He thus revealed his ambivalence as a prophet of DENG who modelled himself after the prophets of DIU and MAANI. Gony was told that there had been no government in those days, but there was one now. In the end he had to agree.[47]

The prophets' enforced residence in Malakal and their attendance at the Mogogh conference were the final phases in the local implementation of the Addis Ababa peace agreement, a settling of accounts left over from the war. The war had profoundly affected the careers of Bangong, Gony, and Ruei, involving all three in fighting. They were required now to adjust to peace and to the strictures of government. Two were able to make the transition, but Gony's influence was permanently impaired.

Bangong Diau, a prophet of DENG, was most consistently spoken of as a man of peace. During the war he participated with other chiefs in settling cases, including murder. Because of his influence the government tried to appoint him court president of his own area. Bangong had to choose between the government and his divinity, and eventually declined the appointment, saying that his divinity would leave him if he became too involved in government matters. He maintained his reputation as a man of peace throughout the 1970s. Some Nuer even made a pun on the adopted ox-name of his divinity, DENGKUR (describing a particular configuration of black and white ox), saying that the divinity was no longer DENG *Kor* ('DENG of war') but DENG *Bel* ('DENG of sorghum').[48]

Gony Yut was unable to separate himself convincingly from the government, as during the war he had frequently petitioned it for increases in material support (guns, ammunition, batteries for his radio, etc.). Perhaps for this reason he tried publicly to maintain the fiction of not wanting to touch government things. All three prophets at the Mogogh conference appeared wearing clothes, but Gony insisted on wearing a leopard-skin as well. He sent his wives to get water from wells some distance from Mogogh, rather than drink the water provided by the government donkey pump. When he came down with malaria during the conference he would not ask any official for medicine, but approached me, as a neutral person. Paradoxically the decision of the conference forced him into a closer association with places and things of the government. In his attempt to appeal against the loss of his cattle he spent considerable time in Malakal and Khartoum lobbying the government and trying to get the assistance of Nuer politicians (including the venerable Buth Diu). Gony's influence declined, his eyesight deteriorated until he went blind, and he used to complain bitterly of how he had been abandoned by the government he had supported; 'government' representing a continuing, almost autonomous, entity, even when there was a radical change of personnel.

[47] 'Report of the Committee Meeting held at Mogok between Lou Nuer, Gawer, Dinka and Shilluk of Atar and Khor Fulus and the 3 Kujurs Ruei Kuic, Gony Yuot and Matai Gatluak on 27.3.1975 to 2.4.1975', Malakal UNP SCR 36.M.1/3 Fangak, and my own notes made at the Mogogh Conference.

[48] Moses Cuol Juac and Samuel Ater Dak A12, Thomas Riek Nguot A13.

In the first years of peace Ruei Kuic consolidated his position as a prophet in a way he had been unable to do during the war. Living on the northern end of the Zeraf Island he broadened his appeal not only among the Western Nuer, but among the southern Shilluk of Tonga district. He did so by combining and co-opting emblems of divinity specific to both, especially after the deaths of Nyaruac Kolang and the Shilluk king.

Nyaruac Kolang, the prophetess of MAANI, died in 1973. Shortly after her death a young man from the Leek Nuer, Kai Riek, claimed to be seized by the divinities MAANI and NYAKOLANG (Kolang Ket had announced his seizure while in Leek country). His divinity reverted to the nineteenth-century idiom, and in 1974 he raised some 3,000 warriors to repel the Missiriya Arab nomads who had recently tried to seize Nuer grazing areas. Failing to find any nomads his force returned to Bentiu district and took cattle belonging to some who had rejected the new prophet, including those of the head chief of the district. There were rumours that Kai intended to attack Bentiu town itself, and he did attack the local government inspector, John Wicjaal Buom, when the latter tried to visit him with a police escort. The army quickly intervened, and Kai was last seen standing in front of his men, dressed in a leopard-skin, waving his baton, shouting, according to one journalist's report, 'My people stand firm. Face the enemies. Their bullets will not penetrate your bodies. The spirits of Nyakulang and gods of our great grand ancestors are with us. They will protect you.' But they did not. Kai Riek was killed along with many of his followers.[49]

Ruei Kuic, who had already accepted a junior position as MAANI's younger brother JIAR WAN, now quickly presented himself as the successor to and representative of MAANI. Not only did Ruei incorporate MAANI's songs among his own, but in March 1974 he crossed over to Western Nuer District with 300 armed followers (partly to evade a summons to Malakal) and visited Koat-Liec in Jagei area, the site of the tree where, according to myth, the Nuer were born. His description of his visit illustrates a readjustment of the older Nuer world-view:

> I went there to pay homage to the original birth place of my great-grand-fathers (Liic)—in Jagei area of Western Nuer in Bentiu District. Liic is the cradle of the human race. Mohammed El Rasul (Prophet Mohammed), Kerek (Kerec tribe [the Baggara]), Bel (Jur Bel tribe), Kutet (Shilluk tribe), Kunuar (Nuer) and Jang (Dinka tribe) were born and dispersed at 'Liic'. Their father was and is the Sudan. At Liic I built a hut within three days from the shelter of my great ancestors and their spirits who had been for a long time without a shelter. About 3,000 people gathered for the occasion. They offered a variety of sacrifices during that occasion; also, I sacrificed two bulls of my own which I brought with me from my village on the Zeraf Island. The

[49] Bullen Alier Buttic (1975); Stephen Abraham Yar, personal communication.

Jagei Nuers offered four bulls. All these animals were sacrificed for the blessing of living Nuer generations.[50]

Ruei temporarily appropriated one of the oldest Nuer shrines. The year before this he reproduced one of the central Shilluk shrines. During the civil war the Shilluk king was forced to abandon the royal capital of Fashoda for Malakal, and it fell into disrepair. The old king had not been active in parts of his country for many years before his death in 1974, and the southern Shilluk area in particular had been neglected. Ruei attracted a number of Shilluk, and he seems to have consciously adopted regalia familiar to them. Whereas Gony Yut and other prophets wore leopard-skins, Ruei wore the skin of a Mrs Gray antelope, as worn by the Shilluk king during his installation ceremony. In 1973 Ruei ordered the building of a large mound out of mud, ashes, and tree trunks at his own village. On top of the mound he built a hut. His mound no doubt incorporated the examples of Puom Aiwel and Ngundeng's Mound, but it resembles most closely Atur Wic, the mound at Fashoda which bears the royal huts used at each installation of a new king. Ruei further controlled the use of a number of *thou* (higlig) trees growing in the Tonga district, saying that these trees belong to DENG. The local Shilluk were in the habit of coming to pray at Ruei's village every year to get permission to harvest the trees. Ruei also performed sacrifices to a number of Shilluk and Dinka divinities.[51]

Bangong Diau and Ruei Kuic flourished as prophets after the 1955–72 war because they successfully represented their efforts as being in the interests of peace: peace for their followers and peace in the wider context for the Southern Region. They did this in part by maintaining that distance between government and prophets which evolved by mutual agreement before the Sudan's independence, but they also successfully attached themselves to, and evolved within the prophetic traditions associated with, DENG and MAANI. Gony Yut, on the other hand, was too compromised by his previous association with government to survive the peace. At the end of the war both he and Ruei were better known for raiding than for their divinities. Ruei changed that perception; Gony did not. Ruei offered himself to the Western Nuer and the southern Shilluk at a time when both peoples were bereft of the spiritual figures they had relied on in the past (Nyaruac and the king). Gony was too tainted by fighting to convince completely the Gaawar that he represented the DENG of Luang Deng.

The prophetic traditions of DIU and DENG among the Gaawar and Lou were continued by Jok Wol Diu and Babuny Kir during and after the war. In so far as they were successful, they also avoided direct involvement in lineage or regional politics.

[50] Interview with Ruei Kuic (1974) in Bullen Alier Buttic (1975).

[51] Venansio Loro, John Wicjaal Buom, Peter Rir A10, Maria Nyadhok; Johnson (1990).

The divinity DIU did not settle easily after Dual Diu's death in 1968. Jok Wol Diu, son of one of Dual's brothers killed fighting the Dinka in 1914, presented a plausible claim based in part on similarities between himself and his uncle. Jok was the only child of his mother, as was Dual. He was also a quiet person, and for this reason Dual took a liking to him. It is said that, as a boy, Jok used to attend Dual's guests, serving them milk and tobacco. One day Dual told the boy to bring milk, but he returned with a gourd only partially full, explaining when asked that he had no cow and had had to beg the milk from others. Dual then anointed Jok's mouth with the milk, saying, 'You, boy, you will be rich. You are poor now, but you will be rich.' That DIU later came to Jok seemed entirely in keeping with that divinity's known character. Ruot Diu, one of Dual's brothers (who was present when Dual blessed Jok), explained it this way:

> This divinity we have, the divinity that seized our father, if it sees you are poor or suffering, if you have nothing to eat, if you have no sister and no brother and you are alone, it can come to you. It can give you something to eat. It will bring you things, you will eat; just as it did for Dual and Deng Laka . . . This boy's father, Wol, who was killed by the Dinka, left him behind without a sister and without a brother. He and his mother were alone.[52]

Throughout the 1970s Jok's divinity was described as 'small' even by his supporters. He followed the pattern his uncle adopted in later life, especially in reaffirming his acceptance of the 1925 boundary between the Gaawar and Ghol when there were tensions along that border in 1976. But as war again engulfed the Gaawar after 1983, doubts arose, even among those closest to him, when they compared Jok's performance against the prophetic tradition established by Dual and his father. His cousin Puot Dual Diu enumerated these differences between Jok and Dual in 1990: Jok was unable to call many elephants and buffaloes to be hunted as Dual used to do; Jok failed to protect cattle against predators; he was powerless to prevent the theft of the Diu family's own cattle (unthinkable in Dual's day); and his divinity has not been healing people, the visible evidence being the recent demise of the elder generations, contrasted with the longevity of Dual Diu's generation during his own long lifetime. Jok was at the family home at Kuaideng, sometimes performing sacrifices. Perhaps he had another divinity than DIU, or perhaps he had no divinity at all. Jok's failure to measure up to the expectations of a prophet of DIU is a direct consequence of the current war with its effect on the decline of game, the increase in insecurity and stock thefts, and the high mortality among older generations due to food scarcity and lack of medicines. The nature of the current civil war has undermined Jok's credibility, and any prophet of DIU would find it hard going to recreate the successes of his

[52] Ruot Diu G10.2, also Kulang Majok G6.7.

predecessors. Now other members of the Diu family are setting up shrines, perhaps hoping that DIU will come to them.[53] Desperate to regain his reputation as a life-giver, Jok petitioned the UN Operation Lifeline Sudan in 1990 to use his village as a base for the distribution of food, medicine, and cattle vaccines. Scarcely any of these items reached the Gaawar, and Jok was disappointed in his quest.

Babuny Kir Nyak, from the same section of the Nyajikany-Rumjok Lou as Pok Kerjiok and Lam Liew, became a prophet during the first civil war. He was an uneducated ex-Anyanya soldier who claimed that his father was blessed by Ngundeng in the same way that Pok's and Car's fathers were blessed, with the promise of some gift which would descend to their children. Babuny's divinity, he said, is Ngundeng's gift. His divinity is DENG, and he calls himself YONG (fool, madman) in commemoration of the abuse hurled at Ngundeng when he first went mad. Not all Lou agree that he is seized by DENG. Ngundeng's family recognize Babuny as a prophet, but they claim he is seized by the divinity YONG, not DENG. Babuny is frequently referred to as *guk YONG*, the prophet of YONG. He tried to link himself to Ngundeng in other ways, and, just as Yuot Guoguok did, Babuny officiated at sacrifices at the Mound.

Babuny mixed old and new images in representing Divinity to the Lou. Stephen Ciec Lam once heard him tell people that Divinity was like *peth*, because no one could look at him directly (recalling, perhaps, the *peth* of WIU and Ngundeng). Divinity will also judge all people. Sitting on his stool he will call out names; if two men have the same name, he will call out their fathers' names; if their fathers have the same name, he will call out their grandfathers' names. He will know all the wrongs everyone has committed. If they are small, he will forgive them. If they are big, he will not. Stephen, delighted by this similarity with the Christian day of judgement, told Babuny this was what Christians believed. Babuny claimed not to know this.[54]

Many Nuer have drawn parallels between the teachings of Jesus and the teachings of their own prophets, Ngundeng especially. There were few Nuer Christians before the 1960s, as Christianity was confined to three mission schools which few Nuer attended even after the government began to encourage education in 1947. At least one early Nuer Christian, a Lou veterinary officer in the 1940s and 1950s, used to make explicit comparisons between Ngundeng's songs and passages from Kings and Leviticus (including Ngundeng's condemnation of the eating of 'dirty' animals, such as the ostrich). The expulsion of foreign missionaries in 1963–4 by the military government was intended to bring an end to Christian proselytization in the

[53] Stephen Ciec Lam L24.2, John Wicjaal Buom and Stephen Ciec Lam A1.3, Puot Dual Diu G14.

[54] Stephen Ciec Lam L24.2.

Southern Sudan, but it had the reverse effect. Sudanese churches ceased to be run and organized exclusively by Europeans and Americans but were directed mainly by Southern Sudanese. Nuer living in rural areas were now exposed to Christianity by other Nuer, and the Christian teachings so presented seemed less exotic than the teachings of the missionaries. Conversion to Christianity grew rapidly after 1972, both in the rural areas and among Nuer migrant workers in Khartoum. Hutchinson has described how rural Christian communities have echoed the work of the old prophets in a number of ways, vigorously campaigning against the use of magic and becoming actively involved in ending and preventing feuds.[55]

It is the parallel of the divine sanction against fighting which most impresses modern Nuer. I was often told by Lou in the 1970s, 'When we heard about Jesus we were surprised, because Ngundeng had said it all before.' In this respect Christian Nuer can see their past prophets as modern John the Baptists, preparing the way for the word of Christ. This was certainly how the Lou politician Stephen Ciec Lam accommodated his belief in the prophets with his Christianity. Related to Pok Kerjiok, Stephen had a partisan attachment to the prophets of GÄR. Born after Dual Diu blessed his mother, he also had a personal attachment to Dual, regarding him as a father. Stephen would readily, and quite happily, quote from the Bible or the songs of Ngundeng to prove a point. A convinced rather than pious Christian, he did not reject the sacrifice of animals accompanying prayers, as did many of his co-religionists, but he was no less certain that Ngundeng, Dual Diu, and others had pointed the way towards his own faith. It could not be said that he was typical in the way that he combined these religious traditions, but neither was he unique.

Throughout and following the first civil war there were frequent references back to Ngundeng's songs and prophecies. The reinterpretations of his prophecies of peace and war will be analysed in detail in the final chapter. They are evidence of popular anxiety over the instability of the peace after 1972, and doubts about the ability of those in government to maintain it. Tension developed between the people and the officials over interpretations of the fulfilment of Ngundeng's words. This is further illustrated by the initial reception of the Addis Ababa peace, the struggle for possession of Ngundeng's relics, and the resurrection of compensation claims for Guek's death.

The leader of the government negotiating team at Addis Ababa was the Minister for Southern Affairs, Abel Alier, a Bor Dinka. One of his deputies was Peter Gatkuoth Gual, a Lou Nuer. After the agreement was reached Peter Gatkuoth met with chiefs of the Lou who told him that Ngundeng had

[55] Hutchinson (1985; 1988: 254–8, 319–24). For the parallel spread of Christianity among the Dinka during the current war see Nikkel (1992).

predicted that peace would be brought from the east (the direction of Ethiopia) by two men: a Nuer born of a left-handed woman (as Gatkuoth's mother was known to be), and a thin left-handed stranger (a description which fitted Abel Alier). The peace had been presaged by a singular incident involving an earth-master of the Nyakong family living around Akobo. In the early stages of the war Gik Cam Jok, who had been born at the end of Ngundeng's lifetime, appeared to die. Just before he was buried his corpse sneezed and Gik came back to life. After he revived he claimed that Ngundeng had told him that he was not to die just yet. He would die later, 'when things are finished', and come to Ngundeng as a young man. Consequently Gik was re-initiated in a new age-set. A few months after the Addis Ababa Agreement was signed he finally died. The end of the war seemed to fulfil the phrase, 'when things are finished'.[56] There was a symmetry in this. Yuot Nyakong and his brother were associated with bringing the 'Turuk' to the Lou in the nineteenth century, and Yuot was said to have foretold Ngundeng's emergence as a prophet just before his own death. Now one of Yuot's family was bringing to Ngundeng word of a peace which seemed to mean the end of the 'Turuk' in Nuer country as well. There was hope for the future.

The coming of peace was further marked by the return of some of Ngundeng's personal property, lost nearly half a century before when Guek was killed. The most important items lost were Ngundeng's baton, his brass pipe, his small drum, and his large drum (*jok luala*). The first three were taken off Guek by the British (see Fig. 15). The baton was taken back to England, but the pipe and drum were eventually deposited in the ethnological museum in Khartoum. *Jok luala*, a drum said to be almost as tall as a man, may in fact have been burned as long ago as the campaign of 1902. Many Nuer claim, however, to have sighted it stored in the basement of the National Museum. Requests for the return of all of these items, were resisted, as we have already seen, during the period of the first independence government.

Bangong Diau made a bid for the relics soon after the end of the war, in an attempt to secure a tangible demonstration of the transfer of Ngundeng's divinity to himself. A translated request sent to the province commissioner in 1973 reads, 'I want this year, let it be a good year, for all Nuer, to pray their God Deng Kur. I am not going anywhere I have to be here till the big drum & Dang [baton] come from Khartoum, and I want you to be very strong, to get them back to our people.' Senior officials in the new regional government had already appealed to President Nimeiri for the return of the relics to the Lou, just as the spear of Lirpiou had been returned to the Bor shortly before the end of the war. The commissioner informed Bangong that the pipe and drum

[56] Peter Gatkuoth Gual A3.1.

FIG. 15. Wyld, Coriat, and Tunnicliffe (OC police) with Ngundeng's relics (spear, pipe, drum, sack, shrine-stick, and barbless fish-spear), 1929 (Coriat)

would be returned to their home in May 1974, perhaps intending to make them part of local annual May Revolution celebrations.[57]

The pipe and drum rested in the province storeroom in Malakal for several years while the politicans manœuvred to receive the credit. Peter Gatkuoth, a Mor Lou, had been appointed commissioner of the province in 1974 and was responsible for arranging the ceremony to hand over the relics at the Mound. Biel Lel Ngundeng, who represented Nasir in the National Assembly, felt that the relics should be given to him, as a grandson of the prophet. Nothing had been done by the end of 1975, when Peter Gatkuoth was appointed Minister of Finance in the regional government in Juba. When the former Anyanya leader Joseph Lagu was elected president of the regional High Executive Council in 1978, replacing all ministers appointed by Alier, the politicking moved to another level. Lagu (an Equatorian) appeared to want to present the pipe and drum to the Nuer as his personal gift. He was a party to the Addis

[57] Tungkuac Bangaong [*sic*] to Sayed Mosses [*sic*] Chol Juac, 7 Dec. 1973, and Moses Chuol to Tungkuac Bangoang, 15 Dec. 1973, both in Malakal UNP SCR 36.M.1/8.

Ababa Agreement for which Peter Gatkuoth and Abel Alier received local credit. A large ceremony was planned, to which the Shilluk, Anuak, Dinka, and other Nuer would be invited, as in the days of Ngundeng. But this required contributions in the form of cattle and food which the Lou were expected to provide, and a number of cattle were officially gathered at Waat. The pipe and drum were transported by steamer to Bor (the capital of the new Jonglei Province which included the Lou), but they got no further. Politicking in Juba caused the cancellation of the ceremony.

The Lou were naturally angry. Their cattle, they felt, had been extracted by force, and they were not mollified even after the cattle were returned. When the 1978 sorghum crop failed they said that DENG, too, was angry and was punishing the people. Then in 1979 Lagu brought into his government a number of Alier's former allies, and Peter Gatkuoth was made regional vice-president. He immediately authorized the return of the relics without a formal ceremony. Two officials (one Shilluk, one Dinka) from the commissioner's office in Bor took the pipe and drum by vehicle to Waat where they were given to the local government inspector, who then gave them to Ngundeng's family. The family took them to the Mound, and only then invited the people to receive them.

The progress of the pipe and drum from Malakal to the Mound via Bor was marked by singular events and many sacrifices. The celebration at the Mound on 26 December 1979 was organized by the Lou and not by government officials. Peter Gatkuoth was there, as was the new commissioner of Jonglei Province, Jonathan Malual Leek, but as guests and onlookers, not as central participants. All the sections of Lou came with cattle, and sacrificed them at the same sites at and around the Mound where they had sacrificed in Ngundeng's time. The Lou slaughtered seven oxen in honour of the province commissioner, who was also the grandson of the late Nyareweng chief Deng Malual. In the public speeches accompanying these sacrifices the Lou referred to the commissioner as their sister's son; thus underlining the relations of peace that they hoped would prevail between the Lou and Nyareweng, and between the Lou and the province government. Those Ngundeng songs sung at the Mound all emphasized Ngundeng's teachings of peace. The crowd was so large and dense that observers were unable to make any realistic estimate of the numbers, but placed them in the thousands. One of those conducting sacrifices at the Mound was the prophet Babuny Kir. When the pipe and drum were displayed some of the Lou representatives raised the question of Ngundeng's baton, recently located in England, and impressed upon those present that it should be returned as soon as possible. Otherwise there would be no lasting peace.[58]

58 The above is based on Peter Gatkuoth Gual and Biel Lel Ngundeng A3.2, Jonathan Malual Leek A16, and other participants.

Peace was beginning to look fragile by this time. The first five years after the Agreement had been marred by a number of mutinies of ex-Anyanya soldiers who refused to hand in their weapons and be fully integrated into the national army. One of the most serious mutinies occurred at Akobo in March 1975.[59] In the dry season of 1975 and 1976 soldiers were frequently in the Lou area looking for escaped mutineers. In addition to this the Lou and their southern Dinka neighbours were annually raided by the Murle, who had been given rifles by the army during the civil war but who had never surrendered them. The Lou and Dinka, outgunned by the Murle, began buying semi-automatic rifles to defend themselves, as the army and regional government were unable to disarm the Murle or curb their raids. Along the Ethiopian border itself the easy availability of weapons increased the number of fatalities in feuds, which intensified the feuds themselves. The army and police were often outgunned and were, in any case, unable to control fighting on the Ethiopian side of the border. The government tried to transcend the border itself by appointing as chiefs local prophets, such as Bangong Diau and Kun Thoan, a Gaaguang earth-master on the Baro River who was also a prophet.[60] But they withdrew from government service, sometimes crossing back into Ethiopia, saying that their divinities remained distant from them while they did government work.

Local government was not matching the euphoric expectations which had greeted the peace and the establishment of the regional government in 1972. Attempts by different politicians, representing different interests, to make political capital of Ngundeng's relics while not providing the security and services the government had promised only added to public disenchantment. This was articulated by a new Lou prophet who appeared pressing claims against the government's local agents, the chiefs and chiefs' policemen, for their part in the death of Guek.

In the late rains of 1981 (a year of increased insecurity in Jonglei Province) a young man named Kuaijien, from Pieri in Rumjok, arrived at Waat with three small bulls, demanding to see the six major chiefs of Lou. He claimed to be seized by DENG. One of the Lou chiefs, Kom Joar (a man renowned for his knowledge of Ngundeng songs), asked Kuaijien sceptically, 'You people who get mad (*yong*) and claim to be caught by a divinity, what divinity is it that you claim has seized you?' '*DENG jaangni*' (DENG of the Dinka), Kuaijien replied, then elaborated, '*DENG nuera DENG jaangni, DENG kelo*' (DENG of the Nuer, DENG of the Dinka, it is all one DENG). His claim to be caught by *DENG jaangni* was later explained by the fact that his grandparents were Nyareweng who had been captured and brought into Lou, an explanation which is similar to those used for tutelary divinities.

59 Alier (1990: 154–7).

60 Dr Sharon Hutchinson, personal communication.

Kuaijien then announced that it was time that the blood-money for Guek's death be paid, and that as his death in 1929 was caused by his betrayal by the government chiefs and chiefs' policemen of the day, the current chiefs and chiefs' police were responsible for paying compensation. He made no accusation against any single chief, living or dead. Instead he treated government chiefs as if they formed a separate section against which such claims could be made. The present chiefs were treated as the younger generation of that section, bearing collective responsibility to pay off a long-standing debt, and so end a feud.

He itemized the number of cattle each chief, subchief, and policeman was personally responsible for, according to their position in the administrative hierarchy. He told the Ngundeng family that when all necessary cattle were collected in the vicinity of the Mound, then the family itself should preside over the sacrifices: a child from either Guek's eldest or youngest wife should officiate. Kuaijien then instructed Deng Bor Ngundeng, Ngundeng's oldest living descendant, that Guek should be treated as a *col wic*, the spirit of a person who had died in the bush. Deng Bor protested, saying that Guek's body was not lost, but had been found hanging from the Tree of Bad Things and had been buried. Kuaijien asked if it had been buried intact. Deng Bor admitted what all Lou already knew, that part of Guek's beard and his testicles had been cut off. Kuaijien replied that since parts of his body were never found, he must be treated as a *col wic*, and the appropriate ceremony for laying a *col wic* to rest should be made at the same time as the sacrifices of cattle at the Mound. Another shrine (*yik*) should simultaneously be made at the border between the Lou and Murle, for all those Lou recently killed by the Murle whose bodies had been left in the bush and never recovered.

Kuaijien had one notable peculiarity. He was supposed to be very sensitive to the sound of a bullet, and would start up from his sleep on hearing a rifle fired, even at so great a distance that no one else heard it. He once predicted that his own brother would return from Juba with a rifle and announced that he would not let the gun enter the homestead. It had to be kept away at a great distance.[61]

Kuaijien's startling demands and pronouncements were not welcomed by the Lou chiefs, but they were made at a crucial time in the history of the Southern Region, and they represented a logical application of the prophetic tradition of DENG to the current situation. Kuaijien adopted the persona of a prophet of DENG with a modern twist, an abhorrence of firearms. As a prophet of DENG he confronted not just the government, but the local representatives of government among the Nuer, and presented them with a specific reason for their failure to secure real peace, rooted in the history of the government's relations with the Lou, and with the Nuer in general. If the

[61] Cuol Rambang A7.

government wished to demonstrate finally and unambiguously its commitment to peace in partnership with the Nuer, it must put an end to the feud between itself and the prophet of DENG; a feud which was legally unrecognized, but which by their own logic all Nuer must admit existed. If the internal bitterness Guek's betrayal caused the Lou was to be set aside, then Guek must surely be laid to rest. By treating Guek as a *col wic*, Kuaijien suggested not only a reason why Guek's shade might still be disturbed, but a means by which it could be pacified. He also linked Guek's death, over fifty years previously, with the recent deaths among the Lou which the government had failed to prevent. It brought the past responsibility of 'government' full circle to its current responsibility.

National events overtook Kuaijien's unique proposal. Even if the chiefs, and the government behind them, had agreed to take responsibility for Guek's death, the Addis Ababa peace was rapidly coming to an end. The overthrow of Haile Selassie in 1974 broke the personal link which had bound Ethiopia to the agreement, but it also released the Sudan from any inhibitions concerning support for the Eritrean guerrillas. As early as 1976 the revolutionary Ethiopian government warned the Sudan that it would renew support for Sudanese dissidents if the Sudan did not cut its own ties with the Eritreans. Many of Eritrea's backers in the Arab world were also the Sudan's creditors, and even had the Sudan wished to make the break, it would have been difficult to do so. One of those who benefited from Ethiopian support was Sadiq al-Mahdi, who made anti-Nimeiri broadcasts from Ethiopia after the failure of his 1976 coup attempt. Other beneficiaries were the remnants of the Anyanya who had either refused to accept the Addis Ababa Agreement and had been living in camps inside Ethiopia since 1972, or who had mutinied after 1972 and sought refuge across the border. By 1980 new guerrilla groups, some of them Nuer and all eventually styled 'Anyanya II', began returning to the Sudan and became active in many of the Nuer areas.

Guerrillas were active in Nasir, Bentiu, and Fangak districts by 1981; they attacked isolated and weakly defended police posts in other parts of Jonglei Province during the rains of that same year; by 1982 they were also active in Aiwel, Rumbek, and other largely Dinka districts in Bahr al-Ghazal and Lakes provinces. Their reappearance worried many Nuer, who feared that they were going to find themselves squeezed once again between the army and the *ji-doar*, 'people of the bush'. By late 1982 and early 1983 guerrilla tactics had changed. Their targets were more selective, as they tried in many areas to avoid civilians and to persuade ex-Anyanya and other Southerners among the police and army to join them. By the end of 1982 the army had also changed tactics, becoming more indiscriminate in its intimidation. Townspeople in Nasir and Bentiu were subjected to regular house-to-house searches; civilians were arrested in Bentiu and sometimes shot out of hand; the army sweep through Aiwel, reputed to be the most populous Dinka district, disrupted the 1983 national census there.

The gradual shift of popular opinion away from the government and towards the amorphous guerrilla groups was motivated by more than dissatisfaction with the bickering of regional politicians in Juba, though their failure to run an effective government was no small part of public disillusionment. There had been a major change in national politics. Prior to 1977 President Nimeiri enjoyed widespread popularity throughout the Southern Region as the one Sudanese national leader who had brought peace to the area, and as virtually the only Northern Sudanese the South could trust. His reputation as a peacemaker was so high that some Dinka even speculated that his father (like Aiwel's) must have been a divinity.[62] Southerners in politics and in the army often saw their role as protecting Nimeiri from the conspiracies of Northern Sudanese, especially those committed to an Arab identity for the Sudan and an Islamic state. Southerners did play a substantial role in defeating Sadiq al-Mahdi's attempted coup in Khartoum in 1976, the first really bloody uprising in Khartoum itself. But 'National Reconciliation' in 1977 brought Sadiq al-Mahdi back into the Sudan, and briefly into the government. Hassan al-Turabi, Sadiq's brother-in-law and leader of the Muslim Brothers (later the National Islamic Front), was also brought into the government and exerted steady pressure for the Islamic reform of the national legal system. Both men, and the parties they represented, were known to be hostile to the Addis Ababa Agreement as giving too much autonomy to the South and compromising the nation's integrity. Southerners saw themselves as helping Nimeiri fight the enemies from within, but their own lack of unity and purpose undermined their effectiveness. By 1981 it was clear that Nimeiri, responding to pressures in Khartoum, was no longer committed to the Addis Ababa Agreement, to the autonomous Southern Region, or to the secular state enshrined in his own constitution. He would abandon them all in order to survive.

The period between 1981 and 1983 was one of rising political instability which made itself felt in the provinces by frequent changes of administrative personnel. The issues at stake for the future of the Southern Region were widely discussed in the rural areas during the elections to the national assembly at the end of 1981 and to the regional assembly in early 1982. Throughout this period a number of senior and well-known Southern Sudanese leaders were imprisoned for political reasons, facts which were widely broadcast over national and regional radio, not to mention the BBC World Service. The experiences of the previous civil war were such that anyone over the age of 16 had a clear idea of what to expect with a new war, and personal decisions about the future were made accordingly. In May 1983 the garrison of ex-Anyanya at Bor mutinied and escaped with their equipment to the camps of the new guerrillas. The president announced the abolition of the Southern Region a few days later. Other mutinies and desertions followed,

[62] Deng (1980: 97).

especially in garrisons in Nuer districts. The rapidity with which the Sudan People's Liberation Army and the new civil war developed after the initial uprising took most external observers by surprise. It should not have done. The scale of the disaffection was already clear. It had all, as we shall see in the final chapter, been foretold by Ngundeng anyway.

The context in which prophetic traditions developed through most of this century has never been one in which it has been possible to take the continuation of peace for granted. While successive provincial administrations after 1930 refined the definition of their administrative duties, and by doing so managed to decrease the areas of potential conflict between themselves and religious leaders among the Nuer, the continuity of peace depended on the attitude of the national government. The local compromise allowed prophets to function in Nuer religious life, some becoming major focuses of religious activity. The *modus vivendi* struck between government and the Nuer encouraged new generations of prophets to voice a concern for social harmony and public health, but they did so by referring back to the words of past prophets and adopting the personae of well-known divinities. Prophets were seen to be most successful when they emphasized these peaceful pursuits. They were seen to fail when they became involved in the strife generated by national politics. 'Government' proved itself an unreliable, even a treacherous, ally.

The current war has brought about an ambiguous presence of competing 'governments'. From 1986 onwards the SPLA brought large areas of the Southern Sudan under its control, until by the beginning of 1989 it had liberated the whole of Jonglei Province and large parts of Bahr el-Ghazal, Lakes, and Upper Nile, including most of Bentiu District, where the main oilfields are. Civil administration, however, followed slowly, and in many areas was impossible to institute because of the presence of large groups of Nuer in the government-backed Anyanya II militia, formed in 1984. One of the most comprehensive civil administrations was established by Dr Riek Mashar, the SPLA commander in Western Nuer, long before the Lou area and the Ethiopian border were considered secure. Prophets have played different roles in establishing peace, and the SPLA has gone to great lengths to secure their assistance. Bangong Diau was brought to Addis Ababa in 1985 and spent a month in SPLA headquarters there. On returning home, however, he was confronted by the stark reality of a continuing and brutal war between the Gaajak and the SPLA. He sided with his own section and was killed in battle. Kun Thoan, the Gaaguang prophet, on the other hand, helped to keep his side of the border quiet. Ruei Kuic was very influential in maintaining peace in his area of the Zeraf Island and was actively involved in negotiating a reconciliation between the SPLA and local Anyanya II in 1987–8. Later in 1988 he collapsed and died while addressing a rally in his village, perhaps a victim of the now endemic disease Kala Azar. His death was announced on

Radio SPLA. Western Nuer prophets, however, have tried to revive those nineteenth-century prophetic traditions which include organized violence. Prior to the arrival of the SPLA a Western Jikany man named Jiaar claimed to be seized by yet another brother of MAANI. He ruthlessly suppressed magic, having his armed bodyguard shoot anyone accused of owning it. In a grisly twist to the Aiwel myth he tried to build a *luak* out of the bones of sacrificed animals and executed men. His excesses are reminiscent of Dak Dhon. He flourished for only a year, dying suddenly in 1985, possibly of Kala Azar. After SPLA administration was established one of Kolang Ket's grandsons in Jagei announced he was seized by MAANI and tried to organize a raid on the Dinka. He was prevented by Commander Riek Mashar, a member of the family of the original prophet of TENY, who, referring to Nyaruac as a model, explained that raiding was no longer the way of MAANI. Riek's own brother later proclaimed himself the new prophet of TENY and had to be similarly restrained from raiding.[63]

Modern prophets have behaved very much as the nineteenth-century prophets did. They have gathered around themselves a variety of divinities and other spiritual manifestations; they are eclectic in their choices but also build on established traditions. The personalities of existing divinities, as defined by previous prophets, serve as clear models of behaviour. The most successful prophets have extended their influence across social, political, and even linguistic divisions. The range of prophetic influence is more often limited by rivalries with other prophets or established religious centres. In some cases potential rivalries are avoided by the creation of a spiritual order of seniority, as with Nyaruac and Ruei Kuic. It is significant that a number of new prophets have a family connection with a divinity, or a childhood experience attributable to Divinity which made them vulnerable or susceptible to seizure later on. Jok Wol Diu was singled out by his prophet uncle for special attention; Gony Yut was related to the caretakers of Luang Deng; the hand of Divinity was seen in the fire which scarred Ruei Kuic as a boy; Macar Teny was the owner of a tutelary divinity before being seized by BUK; Nyin Nguen inherited an ancestral Power; the divinities of Kolang Ket, Car Koryom, and Pok Kerjiok all passed to their children. In the Lou and Jikany areas new prophets tried to link themselves in some way to Ngundeng.

The alternations between war and peace have been the most serious challenges to the prophets since 1930, especially as government, too, has oscillated between reinforcing peace and waging war. War in the 1960s and 1980s found prophets already active. Towards the end of the first civil war some men who became prophets, such as Bangong Diau and Babuny Kir, tried to withdraw from it. War ultimately destroyed the prophetic careers of Gony Yuot, Jok Wol Diu, and Bangong Diau—Gony and Bangong because

[63] Cmdr. Riek Mashar A18, Dr Sharon Hutchinson, personal communication.

they became actively involved in fighting, Jok because war undermined the prophetic character he tried to project. Among the Western Nuer, where a raiding tradition is stronger, Nyaruac Kolang maintained her role as a prophetess of peace partly because the first civil war passed her by. Others revived warrior attributes when confronted by Arab Missiriya raids in 1974 or the full force of war in the 1980s. War did not create the new prophets. It did not call them into being, but it was a challenge to which all tried to respond according to the specific prophetic tradition of which they were a part.

9

The Life of Prophecy

In Part II I have described in detail the activities of Nuer prophets, trying to identify their conscious goals, the adaptations and changes they made, as well as the continuities they represented. In the pre-existing figures of DENG and Aiwel, in the activities centred around major shrines, in the experiences of various types of masters, the prophets of the nineteenth century had models of inspiration on which to draw. They did not create an entirely new religious language, but they did alter the application of the religious idiom, they did represent a new form of religious experience and expectation. In the details of the prophets' lives, in the examples of their songs, we must revise what has been generally accepted about Nuer prophets, and to some extent Nuer religion. It will be useful here to summarize what we now know to be different about the prophets' lives, before turning to the life of prophecy itself.

The distinguishing feature of the major prophets, according to 'Evans-Pritchard, 'was their hermeneutic role in warfare' against the Dinka, the slavers, and the administration. Other activities such as healing and controlling spirits, which they shared with lesser religious figures, were subsidiary to this main political function.[1] This emphasis on the prophets' political role in response to external threats has, I suggest, obscured their very important contribution to Nuer religious life and thought. It equates protection exclusively with defence, and divorces the prophets' 'subsidiary' activities in the preservation of life from their attempts to create and maintain a moral community. Their entire careers are thus defined by the outcome of colonial conflicts.

Similarly the role of 'crisis' in the development of prophecy has been emphasized, partly because prophets and crisis have long been equated with each other. The composition and organization of Nuer society, especially Nuer society east of the Nile, was changing throughout the nineteenth century as a result of resettlement and the assimilation of other peoples. But change is a constant fact of life and does not by itself constitute a 'crisis'. Prophets first arose in the east where these changes were most marked, and their example was subsequently followed in the old homeland in the west. Individual prophets did respond to a variety of challenges: the Dinka assault at Pading, the tyranny of Nuaar Mer, the floods and epidemics of the 1890s. The careers

[1] Evans-Pritchard (1956: 308).

of the prophets were affected by these challenges, their individual responses did influence the way they were received by others. Such challenges tested the validity of prophetic claims, but they were not the initial or sole motivation of prophetic careers; rather they were episodes in the prophets' lives. The real test of the prophets' appeal and durability came, not in the momentary hope they may have offered during a 'crisis', but in their ability to enunciate a coherent set of ideas which helped the members of contemporary Nuer society comprehend their own time and situation, but which ultimately was not restricted to any one period or condition.

The time in which the first prophets lived and flourished was a time in which the individual experience of divinities and Powers was multiplying throughout Nilotic society, whether because of the dislocation caused by movement and raiding, or because of the very success of the prophetic idiom of 'seizure' itself. The more active presence of clan- and tutelary divinities, the reference to Powers as the explanation for the potency of new foreign magic, attribution of spiritual causes to illness, all formed the background to the emergence of prophecy through seizure by a divinity. Seizure by a free-divinity involves social recognition and may not be as much the product of individual whim as has been presented in the ethnography. The seizure and apparent madness of an incipient prophet is resolved by sacrifice initiated by his relatives or age-mates. It is then up to the afflicted person to speak the name of the divinity and establish its personality; but what name is spoken, and the personality displayed, has increasingly been a response to public expectation.

The most successful prophets tried to regulate the appearance and activity of divinity in society. Their own success inspired further appearances; for not only did other prophets seek the established prophets' recognition, but magicians adopted the outward appearance and manner of prophets as well. Prophets attempted to co-opt other free-divinities and control their proliferation. They often tried to gather such divinities around them, Ngundeng especially by 'burying' them in his Mound. The homesteads of prophets, and later their graves, were sites for the accumulation of divinities: through reserving small shrines for individual divinities, through dedicating cattle, and even through marrying wives to divinities. Deng Laka was particularly known for this, and went to extraordinary lengths, even inventing divinities to co-opt. He was almost like a modern composer who copyrights song titles before writing the songs, merely to pre-empt anyone else's inspiration. The prophets' opposition to the earthly Powers was a rejection of the private use of a supernatural power for individual and personal gain, or for evil ends. It was a rejection inherent in their own claims to seizure by transcendent divinities, but the definition of evil was also determined by whether spiritual power was used publicly or privately, for the community at large or for the individual or small group alone. The prophets did not invent this definition of evil; it is inherent in Nilotic notions of the moral community. By condemning magic and actively trying to suppress it, the prophets drew attention to the differences between their free-divinities and the earthly Powers not only in the spiritual hierarchy, but in the social order.

Where prophets attempted to establish their spiritual dominance, regulating the appearance of other free-divinities and opposing the private use of magic, they could do so only by attempting to overcome internal political and social divisions. In claiming seizure by transcendent, rather than personal or family divinities, the major prophets created new focuses of religious and social activity which included peoples outside of, but related to, these newly established communities. The more they emphasized the transcendent character of their divinities, the more their efforts were directed towards establishing a community which embraced distant as well as near relatives, potential members of that community as well as its current members. This was more extensive in the east than in the western homeland, where communities were smaller and had fewer ties beyond other Nuer groups; but even in the west prophets appealed beyond their own groups and competed for a broad audience.

The peace the prophets offered and represented was the peace which combats death. It came in the fertility of crops, human beings, and animals; in the bringing of rain; in the controlling of epidemics and curing the sick; in the prohibition against fighting and settling feuds; and it came in the unity of all humanity in relation to Divinity. Prohibition of intersectional fighting, and then the prohibition of fighting among all those who responded to the prophets' words, was part of this unity. The claim to make peace is a claim to political authority,[2] and it was this assertion and this unity which the colonial authorities who confronted the prophets in the twentieth century most feared. The colonial government established a rival claim to political authority in its own demand that people make peace on its terms. It feared the potential unity of the people it tried to rule, because unity meant the possibility of united action, which meant incipient rebellion. Thus the clash between government and the prophets was in part a conflict over who had the right to make peace.

It was not that the Nuer prophets, such as Guek, were arrogating to themselves a previously unheld right to settle disputes, as Guek's administrative competitors claimed. The government was, quite self-consciously, arrogating that right to itself. It was not the prophets who upset tradition, it was the government which was creating a new machinery for administration. The government attempted to 'bureaucratize charisma' as it tried to establish new offices and procedures of succession, or as it tried to govern through established sacral figures such as the Shilluk king, priestly leaders, and other 'ritual experts'. It was the government who also chose which charismata to make routine, and the charisma of the prophets was not one.

[2] Lienhardt (1961: 179 n. 2).

Of the main Nuer prophets who flourished during the first third of this century, only Ngundeng and Deng Laka died quiet deaths in the fullness of age. Of the rest, Guek Ngundeng and Dak Dhon were shot dead by government troops; Kolang Ket and Pok Kerjiok died in captivity; Dual Diu, Car Koryom, Gaaluak Nyagh, and Buom Diu all spent long periods in prison and exile. Those who were allowed to operate after 1930, such as Macar Teny and the woman prophet Nyaruac Kolang, did so under the scrutiny of a government which imposed constraints, constraints which continued under independent Sudanese governments. These conditions shaped modern Nuer prophetic traditions, accentuating the importance of the words and actions of dead prophets. There are still prophets in Nuer society, but they have yet to establish a spiritual authority independent of their predecessors. They claim links with the divinities who spoke through the prophets of the past. Those prophets are still more widely known, and their prophetic utterances are given more weight than those of the present.

The pre-eminent position of the old prophets has been a product of continual assessment and re-evaluation, just as the Nuer experience under colonial rule has been reassessed in the light of later events. There is no great evidence that the vast majority of Nuer were completely reconciled to the British administration which ruled them. Individual administrators won respect and acceptance through their learning to speak Nuer and sometimes integrating themselves into Nuer society rather more than their superiors approved. The Nuer chiefs, and many others, valued the system of customary courts the British created for the settlement of disputes through customary law. But it is only now, after suffering from the civil war which followed soon after the Sudan's independence in 1956, that the Nuer look back on the days of their British overlords with anything akin to nostalgia. It is only by comparison with their most recent trials that the British-run administration appears in its most favourable light; for despite the restrictions it imposed on Nuer sovereignty, it also, in its own time, and after its own fashion, brought peace.

So it was with the prophets. During their lives the demands of their divinities were frequently irksome, and the retribution of Divinity channelled through them could arouse fear, anxiety, and resentment. But after their deaths the calamities of the wars which followed—between Nuer and Dinka, Nuer and Anuak, Nuer and Nuer, and the Nuer and government—made the prophets' message, especially Ngundeng's, all the dearer for the very absence of that peace they tried to attain. Perhaps prophets of peace never succeed so well as when they fail. That Ngundeng did not achieve complete peace in Eastern Nuer society in his lifetime, that he could not prevent the outbreak of war after his death, only confirms the rightness of his attempts to do so. The Nuer learned to their cost what the price of the absence of peace was. This lesson was relearned during the last decade of the first Sudanese civil war, and it is not surprising that as the war intensified Ngundeng's teachings and fame spread both within Nuer society and beyond it. Perhaps also Ngundeng's real achievements have become magnified in the comparison between his time and the present.

The Southern Sudanese, and those who write about them, are still living with the effects of the suppression of the prophets in the early part of this century. We have already seen some ways in which the anti-prophet propaganda which accompanied that suppression was either incorporated into the ethnographic record or used to direct scholarly inquiry.[3] In another way government action resulted in a suppression of evidence about the prophets among the Nuer themselves. Evans-Pritchard drew our attention to the reluctance with which Nuer spoke to him about their prophets and divinities because of government hostility. He frankly admitted the difficulty of his inquiry,[4] and the incompleteness of his data which resulted from it. In trying to describe the Nuer belief in their divinities he gave only tentative explanations. His list of free-divinities is obviously an amalgamation from various sources, but without identifying what distinguished the activities of different prophets of the same divinity in different regions. He often assumed that if the name of one divinity was mentioned to him in one place and not another it was known in only one place. This is a distortion of the Nuer description of the character of their divinities, and therefore of their understanding of them. Such is particularly the case in his presentation of the divinities DENG, DIU, and MAANI.

DENG was the first divinity known to the Nuer, Evans-Pritchard says. This is probably true: DENG seems to have been known in the Nuer homeland before the migrations, the Lou remember DENG as their first divinity, the first prophet among the Western Nuer was the prophetess of DENG, and even the Gaawar now claim not only that DIU and all other divinities came from Luang Deng, but that DIU is DENG. The names that Evans-Pritchard then gives for DENG—DENG JUR (DENG of the foreigners) and DENG JAANGNI (DENG of the Dinka)—may be 'refractions' of DENG known to some Nuer, but it is not how DENG is universally described. Certainly this is not the way the DENG of Ngundeng is described among the Lou. Evans-Pritchard also states that the divinities DHOL and DAYIM are said to be sons of DENG, and as such are Dinka conceptions.[5] This conclusion can only come from a misunderstanding of Lou statements. As we have seen in Chapter 3, DHOL was a divinity which seized one of Ngundeng's *dayiemni*. All of the divinities of the prophet's *dayiemni* were lesser divinities and were described as children of DENG; the *dayiemni* themselves are sometimes described as the prophet's children.

[3] See esp. Johnson (1981, 1985*a*).

[4] Evans-Pritchard (1956: 28–9, 305, 307).

[5] Ibid. 29.

Expressions of the primacy of DENG say nothing about the 'ethnic' origins of other, lesser, divinities.

Evans-Pritchard also claims that DIU is a Dinka divinity, and that it was better known in the west than in the east.[6] He did not visit the Gaawar, where the prophets of DIU were well known. Dual Diu had just been arrested in Eastern Jikany country, so few Eastern Nuer would have been willing to speak to a European about an outlawed prophet. It is possible that DIU is a Dinka divinity, but we have yet to find any convincing evidence of this from the Dinka. Any statements the Lou may have made to Evans-Pritchard about DIU would have referred to Deng Laka, who was a Dinka, but the Lou would have also been expressing their disregard for the Gaawar prophets (a disregard stated in some of Ngundeng's songs). At the time Evans-Pritchard was doing his research there was a prophet of DIU, Wuon Kuoth, who was still active among the Western Nuer as a government chief, and who had even helped arrest one of Fergusson's murderers. It is not surprising that Evans-Pritchard would have heard DIU mentioned more openly and freely in the west than in the east, and this led him to the conclusion that DIU there, who was only a minor divinity, was better known than the DIU of the Gaawar.

The most striking misattribution concerns the divinity MAANI. Because the Western Nuer claimed that MAANI came from the north Evans-Pritchard tentatively connected it with the *mani* magic of Darfur, with some possible association with the *Mani* society of the Azande.[7] MAANI, as Crazzolara points out, is a form of *Madni*, where the 'd' is elided, and it is the divinity of Kolang Ket.[8] It is a loan word, as Evans-Pritchard suggested, but it is derived from the Arabic 'Mahdi'. When the Jagei say that MAANI came from the north, they are referring indirectly to the Mahdi of the Northern Sudan and specifically to Kolang Ket's sojourn in the north at the end of the last century.

Nuer divinities are historical figures because they are associated with, and known through, historical persons, the prophets. The Nuer belief in their divinities can only really be described through their historical experiences. Evans-Pritchard never met an active major prophet. Because of this his Nuer spirits appear to be disembodied and ethereal. This is not how Nuer experienced them. The Nuer knew their divinities through their prophets and their earthly Powers through their magicians. When they imagined a divinity they associated it with a face, a body, a voice, and physical actions: the face and body of the prophet, the divinity's voice as it spoke through the prophet's mouth, and the prophet's actions when seized. The Nuer also knew their divinities at fixed places. By Evans-Pritchard's time Ngundeng's Mound, Luang Deng, Deng Laka's grave, and Nyaruac's homestead were all active

[6] Ibid. 29–30.

[7] Ibid. 30 n. 2.

[8] Crazzolara (1953: 162, where MAANI is spelled both MÄÄNÄ and MÄÄDI).

centres of worship. The physical presence of divinities was well established, their individual personalities were well defined.

But in one way the divinities are detached from the physical presence of their prophets, and this is in their words, transmitted through hymns and sayings. As the body of hymns and sayings grew, so they took on a life of their own, especially in the absence of a prophet who could apply and interpret their meaning. The sayings, songs, and stories of a prophet have a specific application to his own time and can be explained by reference to his own experience; but they can also be applied to future time, to the present of later generations. In this sense, as in all prophecies—whether those of Isaiah, St John the Divine, Muhammad, or Nostradamus—the truth of a prophet is continuously tested in the present.

Belief requires credulity, but credulity (in its original sense) does not preclude scepticism. In fact, scepticism can be, and often must be, a component of active belief, part of the recurrent testing which confirms belief. This is as true in the so-called 'traditional' or 'primitive' religions as in the 'revealed' or 'historic' religions. Believers of 'traditional' religions can display, as Godfrey Lienhardt pointed out long ago, 'scepticism and an ironical recognition of the ambiguities of human experience and knowledge'.[9] Even the central figures of 'traditional' religion will express an awareness 'of the difference between what men can *know* and what they have been brought up to believe', recognizing 'that experience sometimes contradicts belief' and that contradiction must be resolved. Beliefs, Lienhardt explained,

> are not simply the result of ignoring blandly the experience which contradicts them at times; nor are they arrived at by a kind of reasoning, though they may be defended by a kind of reasoning; nor are they just taken over, quite unthinkingly, from social tradition. They are supported by all three of these—by the will, by the reason, and by traditional teaching.[10]

So, too, we find the Nuer testing their prophets through scepticism. Ngundeng, Deng Laka, Dual Diu, Buom Diu, and probably all others, were frequently denounced as liars by their contemporaries. When I asked Tut Jiak Gai, a man who bore witness to the effects of Ngundeng's curses and blessings, why Ngundeng and so many other prophets were disbelieved when they announced their seizure by a divinity, he explained: 'It was said, "Perhaps no divinity has caught him, he is a lair. . . . perhaps he will solve nothing. If a [sick] person is brought to him, perhaps he will not be healed. If he calls for something as a divinity, something like rain, perhaps it will not fall."'[11]

There were always some during a prophet's time who were never convinced, but scepticism often seems to have diminished, rather than

[9] Lienhardt (1954: 103).
[10] Lienhardt (1956: 321–2).
[11] Tut Jiak Gai L21.2.

increased, in those generations following a prophet's death. Belief was founded on events within the prophet's life, but the prophet's words remained after his death, and these words were constantly tested against the experience of the living. The family of the Lou magician Lam Tutthiang, for instance, now accept Ngundeng's prediction about their being swallowed up by the 'Turuk', though it would be fair to assume that during his own life Lam Tutthiang did not. When I used to ask for examples of the proof of Ngundeng's prophecies, most of the proofs I was given, aside from the victory at Pading, were predictions which were fulfilled *after* Ngundeng's death. Individuals would apply phrases of songs to themselves and would say that Ngundeng had foretold what they were now doing or had done. Other songs, sayings, or even gestures would be applied to events of wider importance. In this way 'the burden of the prophecy' and 'the drift of his teaching' (to use W. G. Collingwood's phrase) were elucidated by later generations.

The complex and ambivalent relations which developed between the Nuer and the colonial and national state have also been frequently explained by reference back to Ngundeng's words. Ngundeng did not create these relations, but he is believed to have explained them. The validity of his explanations is thought to have been demonstrated over and over again. It is to those repeated demonstrations that we now turn: to describe how Ngundeng's words have been applied to a number of situations (especially to alternations between peace and war), and to suggest how this autonomous life of prophecy has reinforced the core of Ngundeng's teachings, first addressed to his contemporaries and to the situations of his own time.

According to the Lou the whole process of their relations with external governmental authority was predicted by Ngundeng, usually in a way that made no sense, and therefore was not understood by his contemporaries. He was supposed to have foretold the coming of the road as a thing which was like a river, but not a river; with things like canoes, elephants, and buffaloes which were not canoes, elephants, or buffaloes passing along it. Naturally, not knowing what Ngundeng meant until after the fact, the Lou resisted the building of the road in 1927, despite this forewarning. The recollection of these predictions after the occurrence of the events which fulfilled them has helped to reconcile the Nuer to new situations, but in recollecting earlier disbelief in the prophecies they also express deep ambivalence. The Lou assessment of the British administrators who used to reside among them is exemplified by this story of one of Ngundeng's predictions told by Tut Jiak Gai, who claimed to have heard it when it was first made. It involves Dok Kuok, the man whom Garang Ngundeng mentioned as refusing to attend Ngundeng's mourning ceremony.

Ngundeng said that the 'Turuk' would come one day and mix with us and that we would marry them. A man named Dok Kuok said that what Ngundeng said was a lie, there could be no marriage with the 'Turuk'. [Ngundeng] told him, 'It will begin with your daughter.' Nyanjiek Dok later married Kotnyangdor [A. H. A. Alban].[12]

The way this story is sometimes told, the marriage of Dok Kuok's daughter to Captain Alban (DC Lou 1929–41) was not so much a prediction as a curse, Ngundeng's punishment for Dok Kuok's scepticism. Some also say that Ngundeng added that Dok's family would derive no benefit from this union. This was supposed to be fulfilled by the fact that Alban's son by Nyanjiek (a man who died in 1981) was never sent to school and took no interest in education. There is a neat balancing of feeling for the British in this story. Individual representatives of the administration, those who learned to speak Nuer and entered into a variety of relationships with the Nuer, were accepted and even liked. But the benefits the Nuer received in turn were disappointingly small, compared to what it is now thought these men (and the administration they represented) could have bequeathed. The marriage may have been satisfactory at the time, but it was not fruitful in a lasting sense.

The ultimate dominance of the 'Turuk' might have been something an experienced and reflective Nuer could have foreseen at the beginning of this century; as indeed Deng Laka and Kolang Ket were supposed to have done, and as official records suggest that many of Ngundeng's other contemporaries (such as Kuony Gol) also did. It would have taken more prescience to have anticipated the destruction of the Mound and the extirpation of the prophets but this, according to modern Lou, is what Ngundeng did. The Mound's demolition and Guek's death should have shaken the people's faith in Ngundeng and DENG. Guek's death seemed senseless, yet it was later reconciled with Ngundeng's words. 'Guek Ngundeng did nothing bad', his younger brother Macar explained nearly forty years after his death. 'We did not know the reason why the "Turuk" killed him, but when people began to remember what Ngundeng said before, they knew why Guek was killed.' When they recalled that Ngundeng had said his speech would end with Nyaduong, Guek's mother, this was interpreted to mean the death of Guek and the silencing of his words.[13] Guek's death became the proof of prophecy, rather than the proof of its falseness.

The way in which Ngundeng's predictions were 'recollected' after the event gives us some idea both of the elasticity of Ngundeng's words, at least as they are remembered, and the flexibility of Nuer interpretation. After the top of the Mound had been blown off and Guek's body hung from a fig-tree, a song (already quoted in Chapter 3, pp. 119–20) was recalled and applied to both events, declaring, 'I will lay down the point of the mound; the fig-tree will bend in the middle.' We know from the rest of the verses already cited that

[12] Tut Jiak Gai L21.1, also told by Deng Bor Ngundeng L5.1, Dhieyier Bol Ngundeng L6.2, Simon Mayan Tut L17.

[13] Macar Ngundeng L2.

the song referred to events at the beginning of this century, yet this line certainly does aptly describe the circumstances of Guek's death. But it did not end there. After the 1964 race riots in Khartoum North, in which many Southern Sudanese, including Nuer, were killed, this song was recalled yet again, and applied to that event. So, too, was the song which states, 'Khartoum Bahri belongs to *rol mayok* | My eyes are filled with blood'; again a reference perfectly comprehensible in its original nineteenth-century context (see Chapter 3, p. 119).

The first Sudanese civil war produced a host of interpretations of Ngundeng's words and remembered actions. Some of his songs, which had previously seemed mysterious, suddenly appeared to describe recent events. Other songs which had previously been applied to earlier events were reinterpreted. The song quoted in Chapter 3 (p. 98), ridiculing the 'leaders of the ants' for their weakness, once denounced the Jikany supporters of Nyakong Bar during the 1890s. It was applied in the late 1960s to the plight of chiefs caught between the government and the guerrillas; specifically to Hoth Nuaar, a Jikany chief killed by the army because his son was in the Anyanya.[14]

We can cite another song and compare its nineteenth-century references with those subsequently attributed to it during the first civil war:[15]

Jipinyɛ thieca yɛ Dol Gɛŋ bɛ cuɛk? Mi wa rɛk jɔɔk dial bia guic ni dɔr	People of the earth I ask you, Will Dol Geng bear twins? If he enters the fence, all the ghosts will watch from the bush
Cia luak bi nyak kɛ neen Jɔɔk me te gat tɔŋɛ luak be guic dɔr	You will not see the byre again Ghosts will watch from the bush as their child builds the byre
Cɛ be ränh luak	He will never reach the byre
Ba ruacda cieŋ kɛ wɛal jok Laata ruac teke gatboŋ ka ci naathɛ ŋac	They keep turning their backs to my words I speak the word of life with Bong's son but the people do not know
Jin lɔu yene kany mi waa kɛ duoth ne yak-yak gaakɔ ghɔk ɛ tör-tör Pal gaawar yene thiaŋ kam yɛ wic ruac kame gik ŋundeaŋ	You, Lou and [Ji]kany, I will leave you only a few seeds and you will quarrel and wrestle with cattle I leave Gaawar and Thiang and give you the beginning of the word and give the truth to Ngundeng
Wec thɔn nyaŋ ba rɔda dhil ci gaawarɛ duɔr be kɛ thiec	The camp of the crocodile-marked ox I will come before the Gaawar become something and I will ask them

[14] Nyang Kuac Agok L15.5.
[15] Nyang Kuac Agok L15.2.

The first line has been interpreted two ways: as a reference to an ox Ngundeng sacrificed for the fertility of women, or as the bull Dol Pajok which Kulang Majok claims his father killed when it was rampaging among the Gaawar (see Chapter 4, pp. 149–50). Other references have been taken to mean an invitation to the Gaawar and Thiang to come to pray at the Mound, or criticism of the Gaawar for disputing Ngundeng's word and listening to Deng Laka instead. This is consistent with the restrained rivalry we know from other sources existed between the prophets. Now, however, other allusions in the song are used to fix it to the time of the civil war. The lines mentioning 'all the ghosts' predict the devastation of the first war, when bodies of the dead were left unburied in the bush. The final line is now interpreted as predicting the alliance between the Gaawar prophet Gony Yut and the government; or, as the singer of this song explained it, when Gony Yut became a 'CID' (Criminal Investigation Department)—a spy.

The attribution of obscure and well-known phrases from Ngundeng's songs to specific, even minor, events in the civil war became common. Some of his songs have a descriptive quality which invites such comparisons. The following song is now represented as a prediction of the general dilemma the civilian population faced during the war. If they stayed in the town (*rek*—'fence', an old allusion to a *zariba*), or went to the bush, they would be killed either by the government troops or by the Anyanya. The milk of the white-brown cow will no longer be drunk by children, as first the soldiers and then the Anyanya would come and capture cattle.

Gaati, cäŋ tayɛ rɛɛk	Children, even if you are in town
cɛ bi gɔa	it will be no good
Kä mi waa rar kä cia kor	And if you rebel, it will be war
Jokthiaŋlual ci gaat cakɛ	The children will not drink the white-brown cow's milk
bi cam cia yaŋ kor	it has become the cow of war[16]

This song, too, can be understood as a description of the state of war that radiated out from the nineteenth-century *zara'ib*, but by the 1960s there was scarcely anyone left alive who had lived through that earlier period of intermittent insecurity. The song spoke directly to the experience of the living. The modern interpretations of Ngundeng's words became known over a wide area during the civil war. Not only did the Lou and Jikany prophets Yuot Guoguok, Bangong Diau, and Babuny Kir model themselves after Ngundeng and sing his songs, but a large number of Nuer and Dinka from other places joined the Anyanya or fled to Ethiopia for refuge. There they heard both Ngundeng's songs and the modern interpretations of them and sometimes witnessed events later attributed to prophecy. By the end of the war in 1972

[16] Nyang Kuac Agok L15.1 and L15.5.

Ngundeng and his songs were better known throughout the Nilotic heartland than at the time of his death.

Peace, as we have already noted in the previous chapter, was heralded (or followed) by Ngundeng prophecies. In keeping with the tendency during the war to apply Ngundeng's songs to recent events, so one story of Ngundeng's meeting with an Ethiopian at the end of the last century was recast to incorporate one of the principal figures behind the Addis Ababa Agreement. Ngundeng is supposed to have given succour to an Ethiopian, who internal evidence suggests was one of *ras* Tesemma's soldiers separated from the main band after failing to meet Marchand at Fashoda in 1898. Ngundeng gave him cattle and helped him return home because, as the prophet explained to the Lou, the Nuer would follow those cattle one day. As the story is now told, the Ethiopian was none other than Haile Selassie, who hosted the negotiations which finally led to peace in 1972. It is also sometimes said that Ngundeng gave Haile Selassie refuge when he was fleeing from the Italians. The fact that Haile Selassie was still only a boy when Ngundeng died, and that both Ngundeng and Guek were dead by the time of the Emperor's flight from his own country, has not proved strong enough evidence to dissuade many educated Nuer from believing this story.[17]

The reattribution of Ngundeng's words to modern times was not an exercise in fortune-telling. The central theme of Ngundeng's prophency remains a concern for the moral behaviour of individuals and the entire community. The retold prophecies demonstrate that Ngundeng foresaw all the bad things people would do, not just the bad things done in his own time. If he knew the bad which was coming, he also knew what had to be done to avoid it. His prophecies sometimes merged into curses, as if he were condemning people to a bleak future, when they can also be understood as conditional, telling people what they must do on their own behalf. In the mid-1970s, when dissatisfaction with the Addis Ababa peace was beginning to emerge, this story was told to me, explaining why the Nuer remained divided, backward, and were missing out on development. When the Lou refused Ngundeng's suggestion to move to Buongjak, Ngundeng slaughtered a white and brown ox and slit its tongue into many strips. He then addressed the people, saying:

> My maternal uncle's sons, you are like the tongue of your white and brown ox. You will not meet in one place, you will always be scattered. You will always doubt Divinity and you will be scattered. You will remain behind. You will be split like the tongue of your white and brown ox. You will be divided. You will not taste the first good thing that comes, you will only taste the second thing that follows. This will be until the distrust within you comes to an end.[18]

[17] Johnson (1986*b*: 242–4).
[18] Gatkek Bol Ngundeng L7.2.

The curse was originally aimed at the Lou, but it now seems to embrace all Nuer. It would come to an end when the people changed and rid themselves of that scepticism and argumentativeness which was so characteristic of them. Until that change comes, there are more bad things in store for the Nuer.

There was one prophecy which seemed to outline what the immediate future was about to bring. Unlike other prophecies discussed above, which involve a certain amount of 'post-diction', this has a long pedigree that can be studied in some detail. It represents a continuing re-evaluation of the moral relations which exist between the Nuer and external authority. The prophecy concerns the arrival of 'government', the subjugation of the Nuer, the participation of Nuer in government, and the final erosion of that government. It was first reported in 1927; it was recorded again in 1954; I first heard it in 1975; it appeared to be fulfilled in 1983; it was partially reinterpreted in 1991.[19]

In 1927, as rumours of Guek's resistance to the road began to circulate, Coriat was told of a prophecy which seemed to refer to a number of recent events, and which also appeared to be guiding the Nuer in their response to the quickening confrontation between Guek and the government.

> Two Chiefs Police from Mor came in to see me and corroborated the news that Gwek was attempting to disaffect the tribe. I was told that he had given out a prophesy [*sic*] said to have been foretold by his father that the 'Turk' (Government) would defeat the Lau Nuer and take over their country (i.e. 1917 Patrol), there would then be a period under the 'Turk' and Chiefs and tribesmen would be compelled to meet at Courts regardless of inter-section feuds, young men would be made into 'Turks' (this would appear to allude to Chiefs Police) finally a road would be started in the direction of the Lau country and on that road reaching a certain point (Gwek obviously meant the Dinka boundary), a small root would be found to have grown at the apex of the Dengkur pyramid. This would be the signal for the Lau to rise and throw off the Turk power and the tribes would then amalgamate and revert to the days of Dinka raiding.[20]

The prophecy was fulfilled only in part, but Guek was killed and the Lou came under government administration. Another form of the prophecy resurfaced, or at least came to administrative attention, just before the departure of the British. P. L. Roussel, the last British district commissioner of the Lou, reported for the benefit of his Northern Sudanese successor in 1954:

> Ngundeng is reputed to have performed many wonders in the cure of both men and cattle, but to history his greatest achievement was in uniting so many Nuer in a common and peaceful cause that promised no rewards in plunder. He also made one startling prophesy [*sic*] namely that white people would come and make a great road through Lou (he called it a 'river') and that they would rule the Lou and that the Lou

[19] For an earlier discussion of this prophecy see Johnson (1985*b*).
[20] Coriat (1928).

'Kwoth' would go away. After a time, however, the white people would go away and a small portion of the Lou would go with them. After this the Lou would go back to being as they were before.[21]

There are recognizable elements from Coriat's version and other prophecies and sayings we have already discussed above. There is the road, there is an oblique reference to Lou being assimilated with the 'Turuk', there is an allusion to Ngundeng's divinity going away after the 'Turuk' come, and there is a promise of the Lou being finally freed from external restraint. There was no hint, at least no hint admitted to the district commissioner, that Ngundeng had foretold the coming of civil war.

When I first visited the Southern Sudan in 1972, just a few months after the Addis Ababa Agreement, I was told by a Nuer politician that Ngundeng had foretold a civil war of eight year's duration, which it had been from the Nuer point of view, taking 1964 as the starting-point. I was not told then what later became current, that Ngundeng predicted *two* wars, the first of eight years and the second of one year. By the time I visited Nuerland for the first time in 1975, the two-war prediction was already being discussed.

Between 1975 and 1976 I was told several times that Ngundeng had foretold the coming of the 'Turuk', but he also said that the 'Turuk' would leave and be replaced by people from the north called *DENG pake*, or *DENG faki*, using the Nuer form of the Arabic *faqi* which in the nineteenth century referred to itinerant Arab pedlars (*jallaba*). There would be war between the Nuer and the *DENG pake*, but the *DENG pake* would leave, not having stayed as long as the 'Turuk'. They would be replaced by the *Turuk col*, the 'black Turuk', or the marked 'Turuk' (referring to the *gar*, or parallel lines marked on Nuer boys' foreheads on reaching manhood). These black 'Turuk' would rule for a short time, but the *DENG pake* would return and there would be a second, shorter, but more terrible war than the first. This would end with the foreigners' expulsion, a lasting peace, and, some said or hoped, the return of Ngundeng himself.

The *DENG pake* were of course the Northern Sudanese, and the use of the archaic term for *faqi* in conjunction with the divinity DENG does evoke the element of religious struggle in the first civil war, when Christian churches were suppressed and people were encouraged to convert to Islam. The black 'Turuk' were the Nuer and other Southern Sudanese employed in the regional administration after 1972, 'Turuk' referring to anyone in the modern sector who is educated and wears clothes. This prophecy of Ngundeng's was discussed against the background of growing disquiet about the stability of the peace brought by the 1972 agreement. It was already felt that the autonomy of the Southern Regional government was repeatedly circumscribed by the power of the central government in Khartoum: Northern Sudanese soldiers

[21] 'Lou District Handing Over Notes of Mr. P. L. Roussel', SRO LND 48.A.2.

still made up the majority of the army in the South; the integration of ex-Anyanya units was not proceeding smoothly; the president of the regional High Executive Council was thought to compromise too readily with the government in Khartoum.

The elements of this new version entered Nuer popular culture very quickly. One modern singer, Moses Cot (who died in 1978), composed songs to tunes suitable for playing on the guitar or *oud*. His compositions drew on Nuer folk themes, but they could also be highly political comments on contemporary society. He sometimes sang on radio and at the National Theatre in Omdurman. One song of his referred obliquely to the anticipated second war:

> Our problem arose with red people.
> We have no forgiveness.
> They kill us day by day,
> Yet they say we are brothers.
> We have no forgiveness.
> If you come for the second time,
> We shall fall together,
> And it will be the end.

During the eleven years of peace there were growing divisions within the Southern Sudanese political leadership at the same time that politics in Khartoum and the North were increasingly dominated by militant Islam. The retelling of Ngundeng's prophecies during this time was a reflection of the escalating disappointment with the outcome of the peace, dissatisfaction with the performance of the regional government in Juba, and an anticipation of betrayal by the central government in Khartoum. The prophecies struck a resonant chord in many Southern Sudanese, and not just the Lou or the Nuer. I was first told this prophecy by a man from Equatoria Province, who exclaimed, 'If it is going to happen, let it happen soon, so that we can get it over with!'

By 1983 it was clear that the peace agreement, under assault from both Khartoum and Juba, was going to fail.[22] In the early part of 1983 I was told by Nuer living in Juba that the old people of Jonglei Province were beginning to speak of Ngundeng's prophecy, and that they were applying it to the construction of the Jonglei Canal. They claimed that Ngundeng had foretold that the canal would reach a certain tree roughly parallel to Ayod and would then stop, never to be finished. By mid-1983 rumours began circulating that the canal dredger had reached the tree and had come to a halt. In fact, digging continued until November, but the civil war which began in earnest with the Bor mutiny of May 1983 did bring construction to a complete halt later that year. The dredger was fought over by the guerrillas and the army

[22] Johnson (1988*c*).

and abandoned. It was not just the Nuer who were anticipating this. The Dinka of Bor District also interpreted the halt to the canal as a fulfilment of Ngundeng's prophecy, adding that Ngundeng foretold the war would start in the place of trees (i.e. Bor). Thus the elements of the prophecy as reported by Coriat have once again come to the fore: a great construction project cutting across the land is stopped at (or by) a plant. The halting of that project immediately precedes the beginning of a war.

Ngundeng's songs became very popular with the soldiers of the Sudan People's Liberation Army (SPLA), who were originally recruited mainly from the Dinka and Nuer of Bahr el-Ghazal and Upper Nile regions. The ultimate retreat of the *DENG pake* was confidently (perhaps all too confidently) expected; songs mentioning *Kartum bari* were interpreted as predicting both political and military victory in Khartoum. But anticipating Ngundeng's prophecies is never a straightforward matter. The unity of the guerrilla movement was fragmented at its very inception, and anti-SPLA guerrillas used Ngundeng's songs against them.

After the 1983 Bor mutiny various groups of mutineers and the original Anyanya II guerrillas met in Ethiopia, and with the backing of the Ethiopian government formed a new political movement and a new army, the Sudan People's Liberation Movement and the Sudan People's Liberation Army (SPLM/SPLA). One of the mutineers, Colonel Dr John Garang, had Ethiopian support over the senior veterans of the old Anyanya days, Samuel Gai Tut and Akuot Atem, and became the leader of both the political and military wings of the movement. Some say that Akuot Atem repudiated this arrangement when he returned to the Sudan; others say that the Ethiopians engineered an SPLA attack on Samuel Gai Tut's men. Akuot Atem (a Twic Dinka) and Samuel Gai Tut (a Lou Nuer) rallied the dissident elements of the Anyanya II and continued to fight on their own, mainly against the SPLA, not the government. Eventually both Akuot Atem and Samuel Gai Tut were killed. The new Anyanya II leader, William Abdallah Col, was brought into an alliance with the government before the fall of Nimeiri in April 1985, and his men continued as a Nuer militia for the government of Sadiq al-Mahdi. They drew their support from Lou (mainly Mor), Gaajak, and Lak as well as some Dok and Bul Nuer from the west. Since John Garang is a Dinka, this gave rise to the assertion that the SPLA was a Dinka-dominated force opposed by the Nuer. In fact the Anyanya II never had substantial support throughout the Nuer, many of its recruits being motivated by outstanding feuds with those Nuer recruited by the SPLA. Reconciliation between the two guerrilla groups followed the assassination of William Abdallah Col by one of his own men. Early in 1988 a battlefield merger was announced over SPLA radio. While an Anyanya II 'politburo' continued to reside in Khartoum, and some Nuer militiamen around Bentiu, Malakal, New Fangak, and Abyei continued to be supported by the government, the main force of the Anyanya II was absorbed into the SPLA.

The various stages in the Anyanya II–SPLA confrontation and reconciliation were marked by reinterpreted, or rediscovered, Ngundeng songs. Samuel Gai Tut took great interest in the Ngundeng songs he had on home-recorded cassettes. He claimed that one referred to him, though he did not tell his friends what it said. Now it is thought that he must have had a forewarning of his death from Ngundeng, because before he went into the bush to join the guerrillas he used to say that he did not have long to live. In October 1985 the SPLA attacked William Abdallah Col's Anyanya II at Riim, not far from Weideang, the site of Ngundeng's Mound in Lou Nuer country. William Abdallah had only about 800 men (mostly Lou and Lak), but the SPLA units attacked in uncoordinated waves over a period of fifteen days and were decisively defeated, losing some 2,000 men, whose bodies were left out in the open at Riim (where their skeletons still lie). The SPLA soldiers were Nuer (mainly Gun Lou) and Dinka. The SPLA commander of this assault was William Nyuon Bany, one of their most successful leaders and then the most senior Nuer officer in the SPLA. After his defeat a Ngundeng song was revived and sung against him, declaring, 'tell the son of Bany that you will walk alone, you have refused unity (*mal*)'.[23] Another song which became popular at this time mentioned bones lying exposed at Riim. During the battle there was a downpour in the area around Weideang, in which a rainbow appeared. The SPLA said they could not see their enemies, and this is why they themselves were killed in such large numbers.

The import of these songs and stories was that the SPLA—both its leadership and its soldiers—were responsible for creating the division between the two guerrilla armies and alienating local Nuer. Attempts at reconciling the two forces allegedly foundered on William Abdallah's implacable hostility to the SPLA and John Garang. As William Abdallah was a lame man, songs referring to Ngundeng's *dayiem* Rambang Thiciot, who was known as *ngol rietni* (the lame man of words), began to be applied to him. One in particular which identified the lame man as stubbornly insistent (*magil ngol emo*) was thought to sum up William Abdallah's character. He seems to have taken Ngundeng's songs to heart, and he began imitating the prophets in his appearance.[24]

When the two forces finally did merge to fight the common enemy in the Khartoum government, this reconciliation was also announced by a Ngundeng song, which went in part:

Nuaar yɛn jaŋ	Nuer and Dinka,
caŋ lokɛ rɔ ba	even if you hate yourselves
bɛ ŋoaŋ bɛ dhil agurun	There will come a time when you will recognize me as your father

[23] *Mal* means peace, but my source for this song gave 'unity' as the gloss.
[24] Alier (1990: 253).

It was originally aimed at Nuaar Mer, but the younger generation understand his name to be their own modern self-name, and have applied it to themselves.

The reconciliation agreement was broadcast over SPLM radio early in 1988. It was discussed in the weekly Nuer language programme by reference to Ngundeng's prophecies, and it is reported that the Nuer in Khartoum listened very attentively to this. Radio SPLM continued to reinforce the message in its Friday afternoon Nuer broadcasts which began with a mixture of Ngundeng songs and songs composed by the late Moses Cot, who, as we have already seen, incorporated themes from Ngundeng's songs. One frequently repeated asked, 'Why do I hate myself? Some call me Nuer, some call me Dinka. Let us leave that behind.' Younger Nuer, less familiar with the old core of Ngundeng songs, have assumed that Moses Cot's songs were also composed by Ngundeng. As these refer specifically to problems of recent times, this has only reinforced the general opinion that Ngundeng knew and predicted the future.

With most of the Jikany and Lou reunited in the SPLA under William Nyuon Bany and Gordon Kong (the Jikany Anyanya II leader) the remaining government forces in the Nuer country rapidly became isolated. Another prediction attributed to Ngundeng circulated concerning the ultimate flight of the 'Turuk' from Nasir and Waat. Nasir fell to the SPLA after heavy fighting on 28 January 1989, Akobo on 4 April, and Waat on 2 May. Shortly after the fall of Waat Gordon Kong sent word to the Lou to prepare the Mound to receive elephant tusks which he had collected in Ethiopia. Some eighty tusks sent from Nasir were placed in a double row around the Mound, with six small tusks placed on the top. For the first time since the 1920s there was no government presence among the Lou and Jikany, and for the first time since 1902 ivory returned to Ngundeng's Mound (see Fig. 16).

In May 1990 I visited the Lou after an absence of eight years. Only one man, Bil Peat, was left alive of my earlier informants. His father Pet Nyakur had been one of Ngundeng's bards. His brother Kueth Peat had been involved in the events leading to Guek's confrontation with the government and had died with Guek at the Mound. Talking at his homestead within sight of the Mound Bil Peat reflected on the events which had transpired since Ngundeng's time.

Back then Ngundeng thought the world was his. 'It is in my hand, I, Ngundeng.' When the 'Turuk' came he said that is not the one. Ngundeng said, 'I want my own government [*kume*], too. I will have my own government like you.' They disagreed about this. The 'Turuk' rejected it and Ngundeng refused also. They did not agree on this, they quarrelled. That was the cause of the dispute. They separated until he caught [Guek?] Ngundeng. When he caught Ngundeng, authority [*ruai*] became the government's authority. What Ngundeng had to say was little. This is what brought death up to today.

FIG. 16. Ngundeng's Mound, 1990; see also Figure 1

This is what is taken up by these children, this is what has taken people to the bush. It was the problem of Ngundeng back then. He left the war with us, and he said, 'My mother's brothers' sons, you are rejecting my word. I will rescue you only when you come to one hand.' He was asked, 'If we are in one hand, won't we be finished?' He said, 'No. That is Divinity's hand, not your hand.' When he said, 'I will rescue you when you come to one hand', it was this unnecessary death which is happening now. This was Ngundeng's doing. He spoke and it is true. Because Ngundeng was rejected by the people [*nei ti nath*] he cursed the people with bad things. All his truth was rejected. People told Ngundeng that 'We refuse what you said.' Because of this he cursed the people with death, because those people then were very proud, up until Ngundeng died.

Then, summarizing Guek's dispute with the government, ending in Guek's death, he concluded,

This remains with us now but nobody cares about it. Each generation comes and says, 'We will claim our own government.' We then believe we can expect death. . . . Back then he said that a black 'Turuk' will come. This black 'Turuk' will rule you, and if you oppose him, he will kill you. We did not learn from Ngundeng when the war will end. As people are dying, when it is going to end, nobody knows. It is known only by Ngundeng alone.[25]

The troubles of the Nuer stemmed not just from the government, but from rejecting Ngundeng's words. If it looked as if Ngundeng's prophecies were

[25] Bil Peat L12.3.

about to be fulfilled and the bad times he foretold and inflicted on the people were about to end, there was still some cautious scepticism from a man who has seen it all and heard it all before.

The military momentum which had brought the SPLA very close to victory by the end of 1990 was halted in 1991. The collapse of the Mengistu government in Ethiopia in May 1991 deprived the movement of its closest ally. Not only did this end a source of supply, but SPLA bases and Sudanese refugee camps inside Ethiopia had to be evacuated. This precipitated a crisis within the movement. The three SPLA commanders then based in Nasir—Dr Riek Mashar, Dr Lam Akol ('the two doctors'), and Gordon Kong (a former Anyanya II leader)—had already been critical of John Garang's leadership. Now exposed to a Sudanese government military build-up in Malakal and Kurmuk, and having to receive the majority of Sudanese returnees, the commanders declared a coup in August, proclaiming themselves in favour of an independent Southern Sudan. This not only appealed to a strong separatist sentiment among the returnees from Ethiopia and the former Anyanya II forces in the Upper Nile command, the call was intended to test the commitment of the new military government in Khartoum, who had already stated a willingness to consider separation between North and South in order to safeguard the gains of its Islamic revolution. The Khartoum government exploited the split, manipulating the delivery of relief food to the Sobat, engaging in a variety of talks with the Nasir faction, and even allowing some shipments of arms to reach the separatist guerrillas in their fight against the main faction of the SPLA under Garang. The weakening of the SPLA allowed the Sudanese army to retake large parts of Upper Nile and Equatoria in 1992. For some months prior to this, however, there was an anticipation among many Nuer that peace was at last on its way. This anticipation was reflected in yet further interpretations of Ngundeng's prophecy, and the more serious consequences of fighting within the SPLA ranks were addressed by a new prophet of DENG.

The Nasir coup was supported mainly by Nuer in Riek Mashar's command. By the end of the 1991 dry season many Nuer civilians along the Sobat were openly stating that this was the year Riek would bring peace. Riek Mashar is a lineal descendant of the first prophet of TENY; he is also a left-handed man. There is no evidence that he himself used these facts to generate a belief in divine sanction for his acts (he denied that he was a 'Nuer messiah'), yet there were clearly those among his supporters who either believed, or wanted others to believe, that Riek had prophetic authority behind him. When Riek's forces advanced from Ayod to engage Garang's troops at Bor in November 1991, some officials in Nasir put about their own version of Ngundeng's prophecy. It was no longer that war would start in Bor, but that once the war reached Bor there would be peace. Other Nuer who rallied to Riek placed a further burden of interpretation on this prophecy, which was that Ngundeng had foretold that now the Nuer would rule. On a more practical level, many of the people in Nasir felt that once they defeated Garang on his home territory the rest of the SPLA would come off the fence and join them.

The appeal to Ngundeng was not an exclusive right of the Nuer, however. The Dinka, too, had their own memories of the prophet. One Twic woman, recently returned from Ethiopia to her home at Wangolei, composed this song in defence of Garang which, in rebutting the accusations of the Nasir faction, presented Ngundeng's prediction of bad times to come in terms very similar to those given by Bil Peat of the Lou Nuer the year before:

> Your word is yours alone, yours alone,
> Like the coughing of a goat
> You who hate the Doctor, saying he has spoiled the land,
> How does he spoil it when he has the *wei* [life]?
> The destruction of the land was foretold by Ngundeng, who said,
> 'The youth who will come will have bad times.'[26]

The fighting between the two SPLA factions had disastrous consequences for the civilian population. When William Nyuon Bany led a force against Riek's troops in the Kuaideng area, the Nuer there (mainly recently converted Anyanya II, but including some Gaawar civilians) retaliated by raiding as far south as Kongor. When William Nyuon Bany diverted his attention to Riek's home area around Adok, Riek's forces retaliated by briefly taking Bor. The destruction was considerable, as the ex-Anyanya II continued to employ the despoiling tactics they had used when on the government side. Villages were destroyed, cattle stolen, women and children abducted, and civilians of both sexes and all ages killed. The commanders from Nasir were not in control of their followers in the field, and they were clearly shaken by the massacres.

The fighting around Kongor and Bor was a turning-point in the fortunes of the coup of 'the two doctors'. It undermined their claim to represent all of the South in a new humanitarian movement; it brought an end to any possible reconciliation between the two factions before the government's dry season offensive began; and it scared off potential international backing for the Nasir group. The failure to knock Garang out with one blow aimed at Bor also demonstrated the danger of trying to use Ngundeng's words as an almanac for future action.

From this point on the split in the SPLA was generally represented by outsiders as a tribal fight between Nuer and Dinka, yet not all Nuer welcomed these developments. The Lou were especially reluctant to give credence to the reinterpretations of Ngundeng. The rainy season of 1991 had been particularly long and heavy, and almost all Lou cultivations had been washed away. Having suffered poor harvests from drought for several preceding years,

[26] My grateful thanks to the Revd Marc Nikkel for drawing my attention to this song and providing this translation for publication. For *wei* (life), see Lienhardt (1961: 206–7).

the Lou faced a very serious general famine. Their only neighbours who had any surplus grain to sell or exchange were Dinka along Khor Fulluth or in the Duk Fayuil area. The latter were devastated during the attack on Kongor and Bor. Very few Lou joined that raid, and by November they were already receiving Dinka refugees, though they had nothing but sanctuary to offer. While Nuer along the Sobat were confidently citing Ngundeng in anticipation of military victory, the Lou were holding small gatherings at Ngundeng's grave praying for the survival of their crops and cattle, for some relief to their desperate situation.

The old character of the divinity DENG was soon forcefully reasserted by a new prophet, Wut Nyang, a Lak Nuer. He had recently come to prominence as a prophet of DENG on the Zeraf Island, where, disturbed by fighting between Nuer, he had moved between government and SPLA lines encouraging the soldiers to stop fighting. The government at Malakal hoped to co-opt him, much as the previous government had done with Gony Yut, by supplying his immediate following with food and other items. Despite this Wut Nyang was later instrumental in persuading the last garrisons of the Anyanya II (who were mainly Lak) to join the SPLA. During the early months of the split within the SPLA it was rumoured first that Wut Nyang was on his way to Nasir with a message to the commanders there to stop fighting; and then that he had been recruited by the ex-Anyanya II for their attack on the Dinka. It appears that in fact he was continuing his mission of trying to prevent Nuer soldiers from fighting each other, and he seems to have gone to Kuaideng (the home of Jok Wol Diu) to persuade William Nyuon Bany to call off his attack. The Nasir-faction troops at Ayod even put him on their military radio to speak directly to William Nyuon. When William later attacked Adok, Wut Nyang was again put on the radio to take the veteran commander to task—a modern twist to the old idiom of divinities of the air.

In the aftermath of the Kongor and Bor fighting Wut Nyang took the initiative to reconstitute peace. The Dinka communities bordering the Nuer had been severely disrupted. The Dinka chiefs who fled to Bor could not see how they could restore peace along the border. One Kongor chief explained to me that he was surprised the Nuer had attacked, as there were so many intermarriages with them. The fighting was now beyond the level of the chiefs, it was nothing they could control, it could only be controlled by the people higher up who had organized it. Many of the Nuer also began to fear retaliation when the Dinka returned, backed by the main SPLA. The hostility between the commanders of the two factions was pronounced and attempts at political mediation across the split were having no success. It was Wut Nyang who circumvented the obstacle created by those higher up, and personally contacted the Dinka chiefs to persuade them to meet with Nuer leaders in Ayod. It was Wut Nyang, more than anyone else, who mediated a temporary local truce between the Nuer and Dinka communities. In a year when educated Nuer were proclaiming Ngundeng the prophet of military victory, an uneducated prophet recalled that DENG did not like fighting between people who were related.

As the original promise of the Nasir coup faded and the prospects for peace receded throughout 1992, Wut Nyang's reputation grew, and he became increasingly occupied with attempts to guarantee the security of the people along the Sobat. He followed precedents established by earlier prophets. Like Bangong Diau before him, he would gather large crowds together to expose publicly adulterers and thieves. As he moved between Malakal and Ethiopia he attracted several hundreds—perhaps thousands—of people to his entourage: women, children, old people, and even soldiers. Yet Wut Nyang's peacemaking activities reflected an understandable ambiguity during a time of unresolved war, when a truce is called between old adversaries and former allies are suddenly declared enemies. Defining that circle of people with whom one must be at peace can define, by exclusion, those on whom one can wage war.

After the evacuation of the main refugee camp at Itang two pressing needs faced the people of the Sobat and the border: obtaining enough food to feed the vastly increased population, and securing some immunity from attack by the two hostile forces that bracketed them—the Sudanese army at Malakal and the Ethiopian People's Revolutionary Democratic Front (EPRDF) forces at Gambela. The two issues were connected, for UN relief food could be delivered in sufficient quantities only via Malakal or Gambela. Sudan government control over the river route made continued deliveries very uncertain. Fighting between Anuak and the Gaajak Nuer inside Ethiopia, which had gone on intermittently since May 1991, blocked the overland route. With the Nasir commanders entirely dependent on the Sudan government's goodwill to keep the river route open, and unable—or unwilling—to impose some order on their part of the Sudan–Ethiopia border, Wut Nyang enlarged his role as mediator. He was able to do this partly because he had already shown that he could cross battle lines, and partly because he had demonstrated his success in negotiating for food directly with the government.

Early in 1992, it is said, Wut Nyang entered Malakal and announced to the authorities there that the Southern Sudan must be allowed to separate peacefully from the North (he probably also obtained food for his following at the same time). He then declared that he would go to Ethiopia to make peace between the Gaajak Nuer and the Anuak. The Nasir commanders gratefully devolved that responsibility to him. In July he led his 'White Army' of civilians and soldiers to Itang. His followers appear to have had mixed expectations, but all seem to have believed that Itang was still a centre for relief distributions. It had, in fact, been officially closed since February, following a major incursion into Gambela region by Nuer and Nasir-SPLA soldiers from Jokau and Akobo in January. Some of the armed Nuer with Wut Nyang evicted Uduk refugees from their houses, declaring that they were 'the government' and had come to get food.

Wut Nyang gathered the Anuak, some highland Ethiopians, and his own Nuer at Itang. The Anuak sat in a group to the east, and the Nuer and highlanders sat to the west. Wut Nyang addressed the Anuak and Nuer, telling them that they were all black people and brothers together, and that there should be no more fighting between them. He then sacrificed a white and a black ox, declaring that the oxen would fall facing whoever was at fault for starting the fighting. Both oxen fell facing the Nuer and the highlanders. Wut Nyang then announced to the Nuer that, as the fault lay with them, he was leaving. It was shortly after his departure that some armed Nuer, singing Ngundeng songs, began looting lorries loaded with grain. They then rampaged through Itang killing highland Ethiopian traders as well as EPRDF soldiers. Bound by Wut Nyang's sacrifice, however, they did not attack the Anuak. Despite this, both the Anuak and the Uduk refugees (who fled Itang because of the fighting) quite understandably remain suspicious of the Nuer and sceptical of Wut Nyang.

Wut Nyang returned to the Sudan and announced another march on Malakal. It is reported from a number of sources that he arrived outside Malakal in October and again demanded food for his followers. This time, against expectations, it was refused, and Wut Nyang appears to have taken offence at the way he was treated. It was after this that he initiated a full-scale surprise assault on Malakal town, which was carried out not only by his 'White Army', but by local SPLA and ex-Anyanya II, and was even joined by some Southern soldiers of the Malakal garrison. One of their main targets of attack was the new Islamic Mujahidin volunteers. Reports from Malakal said that Wut Nyang reassured his people that the army's shells would not explode—a clear recreation of Guek's pronouncement to the Lou before the RAF bombed his Mound. It is also said that Wut Nyang demonstrated his control over life and death by killing and then resurrecting a goat, another act attributed to prophets in the past.

The attack on Malakal, which was later presented by the Nasir-SPLA as premeditated, with clear military and political objectives, seems from subsequent reports to have been little more than organized looting. In the government's counter-attack which regained control of the town it was Wut Nyang's personal following, the people dressed in white or covered in white ash, who were mown down by the score. Wut Nyang's reputation seems enhanced by the fact of the attack (the first time that forces of the Nasir faction were seen to be fighting Khartoum) but damaged by its outcome. The Nasir-SPLA have tried to make political capital out of their close association with the prophet, even, apparently, granting him the rank of commander. Yet there is evidence that Wut Nyang's involvement in the fighting was precipitated by a split between the Lou and Zeraf Nuer, following arrests of

Anyanya II soldiers ordered by the Nasir commanders. Wut Nyang's assault forcibly reunited the Nuer by aborting a reconciliation between the government and the Anyanya II.[27]

Wut Nyang's intervention came when the political and moral authority of the SPLA was fragmented and weakened, but when local expectations of peace had been raised beyond the ability of any faction to deliver. The SPLA's original commitment to a united, non-sectarian Sudan was being abandoned in favour of separatism. Wut Nyang's activities must be seen as taking place within this contracting sphere. The moral community to which he responded and which he tried to sustain was inclusive of many former adversaries—Nuer, Dinka, Anuak, SPLA, Anyanya-II, and the Southern soldiers of the Sudanese army—and perhaps for this reason it also had a very ambivalent attitude towards the governments of the Sudan and Ethiopia. The expectations of this highly volatile community have also changed. Wut Nyang's life-giving abilities may be expressed in stories of his resurrecting sacrificed animals, but he must also demonstrate an ability to manipulate the new politics of food aid which have become so much a part of the war. He has had to reinforce his general appeal by continually negotiating access to external sources of supplies, just as Gony Yut did through the government in the 1960s, and as Jok Wol Diu tried to do through the UN in 1990. Wut Nyang attempted a precarious balance in his dealings with several different actors in the regional conflict; but their continued hostility to each other, his own close identification with one political faction, and the heightened anticipations of a significant section of his following all combined to limit his scope of action and undermine the possibility of sustained success. Wut Nyang has adapted old idioms to new circumstances to a surprising degree. Like the prophets before him, Ngundeng especially, he arouses contrasting feelings of awe, hostility, expectation, and suspicion among those most directly affected by him. Like those early prophets, also, he is being judged as much by what the people around him have done invoking his inspiration as by what they have done under his direction. Whatever Wut Nyang does in the future, up to now he has followed the main trajectory of Nuer prophecy.

The autonomous life of Ngundeng's prophecies helps us to understand the historical trajectory of prophecy, placing both the role of prediction and the politics of prophecy in perspective. In any society with a developed, or developing, prophetic tradition prophecy does take on a life of its own because its meaning and truth are of lasting concern for the society to which it refers.

In Ngundeng's lifetime his sayings and songs were applied, quite naturally, to the lives of his contemporaries. After his death his words were recalled

[27] The above is based on personal observations in 1991 and various reports from the field. I am especially grateful to Dr Wendy James (1992: 21–2, 37) and Eisei Kurimoto (personal communication) for descriptions of Wut Nyang's activities in Ethiopia as seen by Uduk refugees and local Anuak.

whenever a new event brought them to mind. But the historical circumstances of Ngundeng's life have not been forgotten or completely subsumed within later events. The historical circumstances of most of Ngundeng's prophecies are remembered as contributing to what he said, and as elucidating his meaning. They are part of the prophecy itself, part of the remembered truth of Ngundeng's words. Ngundeng may have applied the Aiwel myth to himself, but he has not become a mythological figure in the same sense. Ngundeng's words are not used, as myth is used, to explain the origin of things, to explain how things came to be 'long ago'. He brought the myth out of timelessness and the beginning of time into his own time. His words are tested historically. Prophecy is repeatedly validated by events: not only current events, but current understandings of what are seen as past events. As the past is contained in the present, so the present is contained in the future, and the prophet makes his own and succeeding generations aware of that continuum. In this way prophecy can be seen as a form of historical discourse, both about history and within history.

Ngundeng's time is related to the present, and this is one reason why his prophecies are still alive. The moral relations he spoke of are crucial to the survival not only of the Nuer, but of the entire nation in which they now find themselves. Ngundeng and other prophets repeatedly addressed themselves to the divisions which still drive Nuer society apart. In so far as they were community spokesmen they were like R. G. Collingwood's artist. To speak truly the prophets did have to see into the hearts of their contemporaries, utter their secrets, expose that 'corruption of consciousness' ignorance about which meant death. They did have to combat those frictions in Nuer society which threatened the moral community, and by extension threatened the political community. In this respect Evans-Pritchard was correct to emphasize the political importance of the prophets, and to suggest that they 'emerged in answer to changes in the social order'.[28] The threats the prophets identified and confronted were not, however, mainly external; the defence they organized went beyond war; the interpretation of the divine will was applied to fields other than military tactics. The Nuer never did live in complete isolation; external influences did affect moral relations within Nuer society and did command the prophets' attention. They were concerned—Ngundeng more than most—with the tensions which then existed, and still exist, between the Nuer and their neighbours. The time in which they lived was also a time of intrusive commercial activity and advancing centralizing states from the north. This brought the moral relations between the Nuer and other strangers into sharp focus. So today it is remembered as important that in Ngundeng's time there was an aggressive state centred in the north trying to subjugate the Nuer, and that there were people called Danaqla who cut off

[28] Evans-Pritchard (1956: 308).

other people's hands. These images are still potent, because the experiences they describe have their counterparts in the Sudan today.

Ngundeng began his prophetic career before that of Muhammad Ahmad al-Mahdi (fl. 1881–5). His words are receiving renewed interest in the Sudan even at a time when latter-day Mahdism and militant Islam have seized the centre of Sudanese state politics. It is not just this parallel which is important. Ngundeng stood on the fringe of the nineteenth-century state during a time when that state passed from Turco-Egyptian to Mahdist to Anglo-Egyptian control. He was unaware of the distinctions between the three powers, but he did perceive the intrinsic values of that state in its relations to the peoples beyond its direct control: essentially exploitative of what it classed as its own periphery. Ngundeng observed detached, but not isolated; touched, but not overwhelmed by the state. In moral terms he described its essential character. Because that essential character remains the same today, his prophetic message is still considered relevant and is valued beyond his original audience.

The specific prophecy of war we have analysed above seems to have circulated at times of tension, suspicion, and uncertainty in Nuer relations with the wider nation, at times when the Nuer themselves faced both the present and the future with great ambivalence. But it refers directly back to the core of Ngundeng's prophetic message—that people should live in peace. It is a reminder that people failed to achieve that peace in Ngundeng's lifetime. But it also provides some hope for surviving each subsequent failure. The old people who discussed this specific prophecy and thought they saw it come true in 1927–9 could be convinced that they were living through the time of trouble Ngundeng foresaw, but that they might also survive into the era of peace he tried to create, and which he tried to bring about through his prediction. Those born after 1929 had only their elders' word to go by, but since 1954 they, too, have felt that they are seeing the truth demonstrated in their own time. Ngundeng had a vision of the Nuer living in internal peace, but even in his day this could be achieved only by living at peace with those neighbours with whom the Nuer were most intimately connected. As the Nuer became progressively integrated into the Sudanese nation in this century, that circle of neighbours with whom there must be peace if internal peace is to be achieved has expanded. What Ngundeng and many other prophets understood was that peace is not just the absence of fighting: peace has to be constructed. It is a lesson all can apprehend intellectually, but which can be taught only by experience. It has yet to be demonstrated that those modern Sudanese leaders who follow other prophets have understood the lesson half so well as Ngundeng did.

Evans-Pritchard's explanation of the appearance of new spirits and prophets among the Nuer influenced models developed by later anthropologists, especially those working in East Africa. Externally induced 'radical social change' in 'traditional' society has become a standard explanation for spirit possession and spirit mediumship. Anthropologists writing from the perspective of field-work undertaken in the late colonial period tended to describe pre-colonial African societies as 'closed systems', essentially conservative and viewing change of any sort as unwanted, dangerous, or evil. The colonial era was seen as opening up such societies, making them less bounded, introducing them to a series of unprecedented changes which were accompanied by afflicting spirits and the growth of spirit possession cults. Such spirits are sometimes explicitly identified in the ethnography as 'spirits of social change', and spirit possession itself described as a 'metaphorical representation of fundamental changes' in society. The role of spirit mediums (including prophets) has been to preserve the unchanging appearance of traditional society, while incorporating and accommodating change or legitimizing new patterns of power and authority. The psychological crisis of spirit possession and ecstatic seizures has also been linked with social deprivation and social upheaval generally.[29]

This model of response to change within 'traditional' societies is now widely accepted and has been applied to earlier periods of European political ferment and social upheaval as well as to a variety of anti-colonial protests.[30] Studies of ancient and modern millenarianism rely implicitly on the crisis model associated with prophets and charismatic figures, and prophecy in millenarianism has even been described in semi-anthropological terms as a 'validating myth' or a 'founding charter', disguising radical breaks with the past.[31] This style of analysis has frequently provided valuable insights. It often assumes, however, a static model for 'traditional' society and, as applied to Africa at least, stresses discontinuities between the pre-colonial and colonial periods at the expense of investigating continuities. Invoking unprecedented change is always a doubtful explanation if there has been no search for precedents. The presumption of a static and changeless time period is a mythological concept as well as a historical fallacy.[32]

The general theory has often been supported by specific reference to the Nuer prophets as described by Evans-Pritchard. The historical data we now have require a re-evaluation of the dynamics of 'traditional' society and thought. We can no longer assume that the pre-colonial period in the Upper Nile was a period of static isolation.[33] That most Southern Sudanese peoples were not incorporated into or subjugated by neighbouring states and kingdoms does not mean that they were insulated from change. The very

[29] See Beattie and Middleton (1969: esp. pp. xx–xxiii, xxviii–xxix); Middleton (1969: esp. 221, 227–9; 1971); Southall (1969: 258–9, 265–6); Lewis (1989). For a critique see Johnson and Anderson (1994).

[30] See esp. Hobsbawm (1965); Ranger (1967); Thomas (1973); Adas (1987).

[31] Thomas (1973: 176, 505).

[32] For a critique of ideas about 'tradition' see Hobsbawm and Ranger (1983).

[33] Johnson (1982*d*).

nature of the environment, the periodicity of the rivers especially, meant that alterations in the ecology could, and did, have a substantial impact on social and political life. The movement of peoples in response to the environment in itself was a regular impetus to change. As groups of people moved there were internal developments as they spread and incorporated others, or contracted and lost population. Changes in the composition of society and in social relationships, even perhaps 'radical social change', were thus regular features of the pre-colonial period.

There has been constant alternation between periods of relative stability and instability, and this has an effect on religious experience. Religious leaders must 'assess and express the ideals and values' of their people, as Michael Bourdillon suggests in his study of Shona spirit mediums. 'In more stable situations the ideals and values of the people are easier to assess, and include an emphasis on stability and order, which successful mediums must accordingly exercise.' In unsettled times this assessment is more difficult to make; ideologies cease to be widely accepted, 'and the symbols they contain lose their moral force'. The spirit mediums must adjust their ideologies in different ways in order to gain or retain acceptance. There are thus times in any society when reference to 'tradition' may mask subtle developments, and other times when greater variation is more in evidence.[34]

The composition of Nuer society was changing throughout the nineteenth century. The assessment and expression of the ideals and values of such a society was a complex undertaking; doubly complex because of the multiplicity of ideals to assess. Those prophets who appeared on the frontier addressed not just 'Nuer society', but Dinka, Anuak, and other societies as well. Through their efforts the mythologies and symbols of the Dinka, in particular, became part of the religious imagery and symbolic armoury of the Nuer. The activities of the prophets were new in this respect, and are acknowledged as new by the Nuer. What distinguishes them from other mantic persons is the idiom of their inspiration and the resonance of their explanation of the truth. In so far as masters and diviners contribute to promoting moral behaviour and serving the moral community, their abilities are related to those of the prophets. The prophets revealed greater accepted truths along with lesser secrets, and by such revelation established them for their own and later generations.

The careers of individual prophets have been little studied in the context of 'traditional' religion in Africa. The focus has usually been on belief systems or on the history of cults, where the founding figures have been analysed mythologically. Studies of the lives of specific, historical, mantic persons and their religious, as well as social and political, contributions should help us to understand that African religions have a dynamic character hitherto denied

[34] Bourdillon (1982: 188; 1978: 239).

them and reserved only for the 'revealed' or 'historical' religions. Where this dynamism has been recognized in 'traditional' religion its appearance has often been attributed to contact with world religions. The example of the Nuer suggests that no society is so bounded as to be incapable of producing its own prophets; that where religion incorporates the visions of a prophet, it can be said to be a revealed religion; and where there is prophecy, there is also history.

APPENDIX 1
Nilotic Populations

There are no reliable demographic data for the Sudan from which we might calculate trends in Nilotic population growth or distribution. Nineteenth-century travellers' estimates were mainly extrapolated from casual hut counts along the river or around armed trading centres. Twentieth-century figures before the first national census in 1955/6 were based on taxpayers' lists (introduced in the 1920s), which counted only adult males. The very large increases registered in some taxpayers' lists (as much as 25 per cent over a ten-year period) indicated only 'administrative progress and a more efficient system of listing' rather than any real measure of population growth.[1] The 1955/6 national census was the first systematic count of all peoples in the Sudan employing a uniform methodology. The results showed considerable variation from previous estimates, but the methods of the census itself have since been criticized as inaccurate, inconsistent, 'and of limited usefulness for demographic analysis'.[2] The 1973 census has proven even less satisfactory, as it was undertaken before resettlement following the first civil war was complete, and it was never officially released. The 1983 national census was also incomplete, being conducted during a period of growing rural unrest and guerrilla activity in the Nilotic districts of the Southern Region. Any numbers for Nilotic peoples based on this census therefore must be treated as conjecture. Even so, the 1983 figures are further evidence that the population of the Southern Sudan was underestimated in 1955/6.

Having made this caveat, we must use such figures as we have. The 1955/6 census at least gives some idea of proportion. The enumeration by tribal court centres (*omodias*) corresponds roughly to internal political divisions and gives some indication of *relative* population size throughout the Nilotic region. The 1983 figures, which do not indicate tribal sections, can at least suggest a pre-war minimum. It would be difficult to extrapolate backward from the 1955/6 figures. The growth and decline of different tribal groups was affected as much by immigration and emigration as by natural increase. Between *c.*1850 and 1930 the population of the Nilotic regions was reduced by mass exportation of slaves, intertribal and externally provoked warfare, war-induced famine, and epidemics of imported diseases. It was only during the last twenty-five years of British rule that famine relief efforts, control of warfare, and occasional mass vaccination campaigns had any impact on population growth.

Population density is another difficult statistic to assess, and is largely misleading. Because of seasonal inundation, most of the territory under consideration is unsuitable for permanent settlement and is uninhabited for most of the year. Population density calculated on the total area of an administrative district gives the impression of a uniform scattering of small settlements, when in fact the habitable areas are limited

[1] JIT 1954: i. 229.

[2] Jonglei Social and Economic Research Team, *An Interim Report* (Khartoum: Jonglei Executive Organ, 1976), 21.

TABLE 1

District	Group	Population 1955/6	1983
Renk and Malakal			
[Meban RC]	Meban	31,192	47,986
[Renk RC]	Abialang Dinka	8,846	38,824
[Melut RC]	Paloic Dinka	13,124	21,474
[Baliet RC]	Dungjol Dinka	9,554	57,552
	Ngok Dinka	19,943	
Shilluk	Shilluk	90,738	116,817
[W. Cent. AC, UNP]			
Eastern Nuer	E. Jikany Nuer[a]	102,089	203,029
[Eastern AC, UNP]	Koma	6,313	
Lou Nuer	Lou Nuer	102,982	192,434
[Akobo AC[b]]			
Zeraf Valley	Lak Nuer	31,763	
[Fangak AC]	Thiang Nuer	16,374	
	Gaawar Nuer	42,490	144,527
	Atar Dinka	16,175	
Western Nuer	Rueng Dinka	31,641	
[Western AC, UNP]	Bul Nuer	33,893	
	Leek Nuer	24,552	
	W. Jikany Nuer	32,248	292,091
	Jagei	20,539	
	Dok and Aak	31,296	
	Nyuong and Dur	16,111	
Bor [Bor AC]			
[Kongor RC]	Nyareweng Dinka	12,447	
	Ghol Dinka	11,058	134,325
	Twic Dinka	43,399	
[Bor RC]	Bor Dinka	62,231	158,815
Lakes			
[Central AC, Lakes]	Agar Dinka	93,064	258,628
	Gok Dinka	37,389	
[Eastern AC, Lakes]	Cic Dinka	31,087	
	Aliab Dinka	12,408	
	Atuot	58,147	214,137
	Jur Beli	5,115	
Jur River			
[Gogrial RC]	Rek Dinka (Gogrial)	107,337	329,009
[Twic RC]	Twic Dinka	70,986	187,397
	Rek Dinka (Tonj)	100,611	
[West. AC, Lakes]	Luac Dinka	22,111	270,390
	Bongo (Tonj)	2,911	
Aweil [Aweil AC]	Malual Dinka	71,340	
	Abiem Dinka	139,789	
	Palyopiny Dinka	67,365	662,356
	Paliet Dinka	40,736	

Note: Administrative districts are given for 1955, with the 1983 Area Councils (AC) and Rural Councils (RC) indicated in brackets wherever clarification is necessary. The 1955/6 figures are given for each tribe or tribal group, whereas the 1983 figures are for Area and Rural Councils as a whole (less Town Councils).

[a] Excluding Gaajak Nuer permanently resident in Ethiopia.

[b] Including some Anuak of Akobo.

TABLE 2

District and people	Region	Sq. miles	Density 1955/6	1983
Northern AC (Dinka and Meban)	rainlands;[a] rainlands and flood	12,475	4.2	8.6
Baliet RC (Dinka)	flood	4,425	6.6	11.6
W. Central AC (Shilluk)	rainlands and flood	5,850	15.5	19.9
Eastern AC (E. Nuer and Koma)	flood	7,430	14.5	27.3
Akobo[b] and Fangak (Nuer and Dinka)	flood	17,750	11.8	18.9
Western AC (W. Nuer and Dinka)	flood; rainlands and flood	14,000	13.5	20.8
Bor AC (Dinka)	flood	9,860	13.0	29.7
Central and Eastern AC, Lakes (Dinka, Atuot, and Jur)	ironstone and flood	16,593	14.2	28.4
Western AC, Lakes and Gogrial AC (Dinka and Bongo)	ironstone and flood	16,087	18.8	48.3
Aweil AC (Dinka)	ironstone and flood	11,706	27.2	56.5

[a] Includes large stretch of uninhabited land between Dinka and Meban.
[b] Includes some Anuak around Akobo.

Sources: Compiled from SDIT 1954, tables 13 and 14, recalculated according to 1955/6 census (less town and special category figures) and 1983 census (less town councils).

and more densely populated. A recent survey of the Jonglei area (from Bor to the White Nile) gave an overall population density of ten persons per square mile. It noted, however, that only about one quarter of the region was permanently settled, and that the largest areas of settlement in fact had densities of as high as 100 persons per square mile. The rest of the region was either totally uninhabited or inhabited only intermittently.[3] Such figures impose caution on inferring population pressure from figures alone. Land types must be considered. Any long-term alteration in flooding patterns will affect both population distribution and density.

Table 2 indicates that the most densely populated areas are those which combine significant areas of flood-free land with seasonally inundated territory suitable for dry season grazing. The territories are classified according to the SDIT 1954 report as containing land types from the central rainlands region (rainlands), flood region (flood), or the ironstone plateau (ironstone). Those areas containing both flood and ironstone plateau form part of the flood plain transition belt. Population densities for 1955/6 and 1983 are calculated according to the figures given in Table 1. Territorial units are listed according to the 1983 Area and Rural Council names but are calculated according to the 1954 district boundaries. In some cases the boundaries of the administrative units may have changed since 1954, but not to such a degree as to alter drastically the population density figures.

[3] Jonglei Social and Economic Research Team, *Interim Report*, 22, 24. See also Mohammed Osman el Sammani, (1984: fig. 6, p. 59).

Appendix 2

Nuer Divisions

The following chart of Nuer divisions is intended to show the relationships of only those groups mentioned in the text. It is not a complete list of Nuer political and territorial divisions in any one period. Some of the more prominent persons mentioned in the text are also listed, prophets' names being italicized.

Tribe	Major divisions	Secondary and minor sections	Prominent persons and *prophets*
Bul			*Kom Tudel, Tang Kuainy*
Leek			Twil Ran
Western Jikany			
Jagei	Bur		*Nyapuka Dan*
	Rengyan		*Kolang Ket, Nyaruac Kolang*
Dok	Tigjiek		*Macot Nyuon, Puot Nyuon*
	Dogwar		*Buom Diu,* Caath Obang
Nyuong	Nyawar	Gamuk	
		Galieth	*Gaaluak Nyagh*
	Nyal	Luac	Tiep Kolang, *Wuon Kuoth*, Cak Riang
		Thak	
		Leik	
Lak			*Ruei Kuic, Wut Nyang*
Thiang			
Gaawar	Radh	Kerpeil	Buogh Kerpeil
		Teny	Mer Teny, Nuaar Mer, Cany Reth
		Nyang	*Gony Yut*
		Nyadikuony	
		Jithep	
	Bar	Jamogh	*Deng Laka*, Macar Diu, *Dual Diu*
		Bang	Puol Bidiit, Nyin Nguen
		Cam	
		Dol	
		Gaakuar	
		Long	Guer Wiu, *Gatbuogh Yoal*
Lou	Gun	Gaadbal	
		Nyarkuac (Yoal)	
		Ciec	Thie Ruea, Guet Thie
		Manthiep	Dhiew Dieng
		Leng	
		Puol	*Ngundeng Bong, Guek Ngundeng*
		Thiang	
		Rumjok	
		Dak	
		Dung	*Thijok Dul*
		Nyajikany	*Pok Kerjiok, Babuny Kir*

Tribe	Major divisions	Secondary and minor sections	Prominent persons and *prophets*
		Palker	
		Lang	
		Jak	
		Maiker	Lam Tutthiang, *Car Koryom*
	Mor	Gaaliek	
		Nyabor	
		Bul	
		Buth	Weituor Begh
		Jimac	
		Biliu	*Yuot Guoguok*
Eastern Jikany	Gaajak	Thiang	
		Reng	*Bangong Diau*
		Gaaguong*	
		Cany	
		Nyaayan	
		Nyajani	
	Gaajok	Laang	
		Thiur	
		Guandong	
		Wangkeac	
		Biciuk	Yioi Binie
		Minyal	
		Yol	
		Gaaguang	

* By the end of the 1930s the individual sections of Gaaguong were recognized as administratively autonomous units.

Appendix 3
Nuer Age-Sets

Table 3, of Western Nuer (Dok and Jagei), Gaawar, Eastern Jikany and Lou age-sets, is drawn from several previously published lists (Stigand 1918*a*, Coriat 1923, Huffman 1931, Crazzolara 1932, Evans-Pritchard 1936*a* and 1940, Howell 1948*a*, Johnson 1980, Jal 1987) in addition to my research among the Gaawar in 1981–2. The most thorough reconstruction and dating of any age-set series is that of Gabriel Jal for the Eastern Jikany (Jal 1987: 382–4). As the Jikany and Lou age-sets are usually the same he provides a rough guide for the Lou as well, and I retain his dates here, with only minor alterations, placing age-set names exclusive to the Lou in brackets.

Evans-Pritchard's calculation of an interval of about ten years between the opening of one age-set and the opening of the next has been generally accepted. A longer interval in the past of some fifteen years, in order to guarantee that all initiated men would be old enough to be fit warriors, has also been suggested, but no firm evidence has been cited. In recent years the interval between the opening and closing of age-sets has been reduced considerably. We know from studies of age-sets elsewhere that demographic and environmental factors often affected the initiation of age-sets, so no exact regularity can be assumed. The whole process of dating from the 'opening' of age-sets is complicated by the initiation of a series of subsets who are only later grouped together under one name. The Gaawar sets Pilual, Cayat, and Paduom were initiated in about 1922, 1924, and 1927; it was only after the initiation of the latter that the prophet Dual Diu separated Paduom from the other two, which then went under the single name of Pilual. Paduom later became a subset of Rialmai, which was initiated after Dual's capture in 1930. The following dates refer only to the opening of the initiation period. Recorded or verifiable dates (those linked to a datable event) are given in roman type, while estimated dates are given in italics.

The first reported date for initiation of a Jikany age-set is 1915 for Lithgai (Stigand 1918*a*: 118), opened by Gai Jang, after whom it was named. As his death in 1913 is also recorded, we must assume that he in fact opened the set in 1913, and that it was still being initiated in 1915, shortly before Stigand arrived in the district. It is from that date that we are able to work backwards in calculating earlier age-sets. I have estimated the dates of the Gaawar age-sets according to their known relationship to floods and other datable events. The dates of the floods have been calculated from contemporary Nile flood records (see Johnson 1992*b*). The names given here are commonly used by the Bar Gaawar on the Duk ridge. Where these differ from names collected by Howell on the Zeraf Island I have given Howell's names in parenthesis.

The Western Nuer list gives the Dok names first (recorded by me in 1976), with Jagei names (taken from Evans-Pritchard) given in brackets. I am not certain of exact correlations and have no Jagei names earlier than Wea. The order of the Dok names before Thut is a matter of conjecture. The list is incomplete and is produced for comparative purposes only.

TABLE 3

Western Nuer	Gaawar	Date	Eastern Jikany/Lou	Date
	Guk	1957	Litjang:	
			Jagai/Sudan	1957
			Thok-Thok	1955
Beljuong (*c.*1949)			Litjang	1945
Tunjuok	Guoluong	1937	Reang-gai:	1940
			Dengyan	
			[Kuek]	
Wat	Rialmai:		Rialmai	1929
	Rialmai	1930		
Jur	Paduom	1927		
Pilual [Pilual]	Pilual:		Cayat [Pilual][a]	1925
	Cayat	1924		
	Pilual	1922		
Lieth [Karam]	Karam	1913–14	Lithgai	1913
			[Luac[b]	*1908*]
			Carboi[c]	*1903*
Cuol	Yaal	*1900–5*		
Lier [Lier]	Lier	*1896*	Dang-gonga	*1895*
	(Kiec)			
Dang [Wangdeal]	Dang	*1879–80*	Maker	*1877*
Guoluong [Ruob]	(Gwulung)			
Nyapec	Lailek	*1870*		
Wur [Boiloc]	Wuor	*1860*	Boiloc	*1865*
	(Boiloc)			
Thut [Thut]	Thut	*1850*	Thut	*1855*
Wea [Wea]	Wea	*1840*	Lajak	*1845*
Kuoiy			Cuet-cuor	*1830*
Tharpi	Tharpi[d]	*1838*	[Tharpi	*1830*]
Dangdeal				
Kunjuoc			Ngompiny	*1825*
Yilbith	Yilbith	*1815*	Yilbith	*1815*
Yuai			Yoac-nuac	*1805*

[a] Sometimes given as a subset of Lithgai.

[b] Luac (meaning gum) is a Lou nickname for Carboi, but the set was initiated later among the Lou; it includes the subset Karam.

[c] Sometimes given as a subset of Dang-gonga.

[d] In Coriat's list only (with his estimated date); not mentioned by recent Gaawar sources.

SOURCES AND REFERENCES

ARCHIVAL AND MANUSCRIPT SOURCES

Sudan

The main collections of official records for the Sudan are the National Records Office, Khartoum (NRO), and the Southern Records Office, Juba (SRO). The NRO contains the records of central government departments, plus some provincial files transferred to Khartoum in the early 1960s. The main classes consulted in the NRO were Intelligence Department (Intel), Civil Secretary (Civsec), Interior Department (Dakhlia), and the provincial files Upper Nile Province (UNP), Bahr el-Ghazal Province (BGP), and Mongalla Province (MP).

Provincial and district records were transferred to the Southern Records Office in Juba in 1981–3. The dissolution of the Southern Regional government brought the region-wide collection to an end, but files transferred from Upper Nile Province remained in Juba. As the files were not reclassified, their original numbers are retained here. Classes of files consulted included the province headquarters files from Malakal, Upper Nile Province (UNP), Bor District (BD), Lou Nuer District (LND), Zeraf Valley or Central Nuer District (ZV, ZVD, CND), Torit District (TD). Files consulted in their original offices which were not transferred to Juba are prefixed by the name of the office (Nasir, New Fangak, Malakal, etc.), followed by the file reference number.

The chaos which followed the dissolution of the Southern Regional government and the outbreak of civil war in 1983 has meant that many records transferred to Juba have not been preserved. I am unable to say at this time what records listed as part of the SRO holdings have survived.

Britain

The Library of the University of Durham houses a large collection of private papers of former Sudan government officials. These are prefixed by SAD (Sudan Archive Durham). Many of the collections contain official records not currently found in the Sudan. Papers consulted include those of F. R. Wingate, H. C. Jackson, C. A. Willis, J. Winder, J. Longe, P. P. Howell, and H. A. Romilly.

There are smaller collections of personal papers in Oxford: the Coriat papers at Rhodes House (MSS Afr. s.1685), and the B. A. Lewis papers in the ethnographic archive of the Institute of Social and Cultural Anthropology.

Some reports of internal conditions of the Sudan were forwarded to the Foreign Office, and these can be found under the FO 371 listing at the Public Records Office, Kew (PRO).

I have also been able to consult some papers in private hands, in particular those of B. J. Chatterton, G. A. Heinekey, and Brigadier G. A. Eastwood.

Italy

The Comboni Fathers began a mission among the Western Nuer in the 1920s. Papers relating to that mission, as well as notes by Fr. Crazzolara and others who worked among the Nuer, can be found in the Archivio Storico della Congregazione dei Missionari Comboniani, Rome (AMC).

ORAL SOURCES AND INTERVIEWS

The following is a list of interviews, either taped at the time and later transcribed, or taken down in note form. Interviewing was done in 1975–6 (among the Gaawar, Lou, Jikany, Dok and Jagei Nuer, and Nyareweng Dinka), in 1977 (among officials and friends in Juba), 1980 (on a short visit to Khartoum), and 1980–2 (while employed as Assistant Director for Archives in the Regional Ministry of Culture and Information, Juba). Informants' names are given, followed by their sections, age-sets (where known), other relevant information, date and place of interview. There are two groups of interviews: those undertaken by me in 1975–6 (with supplementary interviews in 1977 and 1980), and those undertaken by Philip Diu Deng and me as part of the Ecology and History of Jonglei Province project (funded by a Fulbright Senior Research Grant) in 1981–2. The former set of interviews were transcribed with preliminary translations by Gabriel Gai Riam, Simon Kuny Puoc, Timothy Tot, and Timothy Tap. The latter set of interviews are listed separately with the prefix EHJP. The Nuer interviews were transcribed with preliminary translations by Stephen Tut Puol. For the Dinka interviews I have used a provisional translation provided by Philip Diu Deng. All tapes and some completed transcripts of the EHJP series were deposited in the Southern Records Office, Juba. In addition to the main body of interviews I have added some extracts from notes made while working with Operation Lifeline Sudan in 1990. Other persons who provided information informally are listed here, or are given full references in the footnotes when they are referred to.

Gaawar

G1: Malual Mayom: Teny-Radh Gaawar; former court president, 27 Mar. 1975, Mogogh (with Ruot Rom (Teny-Radh Gaawar; Guoluong age-set; court president); and others present).

G2: Ruot Yuot: Jithep-Radh Gaawar; *c.*75 years old; ex-court president. G2.1: 12 Apr. 1975 Mogogh; G2.2: 13 Apr. 1975 Mogogh.

G3: Gel Pakur Mer: Teny-Radh Gaawar; grandson of Mer Teny (mother a Rut Dinka), 4 May 1976, Mogogh.

G4: Diu Garadin: Jamogh-Bar Gaawar; Yaal age-set, 28 Apr. 1975, Dhuarweang.

G5: Mar Kutien: Jamogh-Bar Gaawar; Karam age-set, 16 Apr. 1976, Ayod.

G6: Kulang Majok: Bang-Bar Gaawar; Pilual age-set (both his father and grandfather were companions of Deng Laka; he was a companion of Dual Diu and a former chief's policeman). G6.1: 29 Mar. 1975, Mogogh; G6.2: 24 Apr. 1975, Gung; G6.3: 28 Apr. 1975, Ayod; G6.4: 7 June 1975, Ayod; G6.5: 13 June 1975, Ayod; G6.6: 28 Mar 1976, Ayod; G6.7: 31 May–1 June 1976, Malakal.

G7: Dongor Diu and Tuny Diu: sons of Deng Laka; Younger brothers of Dual Diu, 22 Apr. 1975 Ayod (not taped).

G8: Nyanyai Kal: daughter of Deng Laka (mother was sister of Nuang Lol, government interpreter, and was married for the divinity KAL), 12 June 1975, Dor.

G9: Matit Kal: son of Deng Laka (younger full brother to Nyanyai Kal, G8). G9.1: 12 June 1975, Dor; G9.2 (with Cuol Macar, see G12 below): 14 Apr. 1976, Ayod; G9.3 (with Cuol Macar): 15 Apr. 1976, Ayod; G9.4 (with Cuol Macar): 1 May 1976, Ayod (not taped); G9.5: 5 May 1976, Ayod.

G10: Ruot Diu: son of Deng Laka (mother was a sister to Nuaar Mer); Pilual age-set. G10.1 (with other sons of Deng Laka: Kuac Diu (Lieth age-set), Tuny Diu (Rialmai age-set)): 16 Apr. 1976, Ayod; G10.2: 19 Apr. 1976, Ayod; G10.3: 4 May 1976, Mogogh.

G11: Pöc Nap Laka: posthumous son of Deng Laka (mother a Nyang-Radh Gaawar, married for the divinity NAP); Guoluong age-set; singer of songs learned from his mother, 4 May 1976, Ayod.

G12: Cuol Macar: son of Macar Diu; Rialmai (Paduom) age-set. G12.1: 5 June 1975, Ayod (not taped); G12.2: 10 June 1975, Ayod.

G13: Cuol Dual: son of Dual Diu; Guoluong age-set. G13.1: 17 Apr. 1976, Ayod; G13.2: 3 May 1976, Ayod.

G14: Puot Dual Diu: son of Dual Diu, 3 May 1990, Ayod (not taped).

G15: Gony Yut: Rut Dinka/Radh Gaawar; prophet of DENG, 2 Apr. 1975, Mogogh.

Lou

L1: Garang Ngundeng: son of Ngundeng; Luac age-set. L1.1: 26 June 1975, Lun; L1.2: 1 Apr. 1976, Walgak; L1.3: 14 May 1976, Lun.

L2: Macar Ngundeng: posthumous son of Ngundeng; Rialmai age-set, 28 June 1975, Waat.

L3: Gatkal Ngundeng: posthumous son of Ngundeng (by son Reath); Gelmai age-set. L3.1: 23 June 1975, Waat (not taped); L3.2: 31 Mar. 1976, Weideang; L3.3: 23 Apr. 1976, Waat.

L4: Cuol Ngundeng: posthumous daughter of Ngundeng (by son Reath). L4.1: 11 July 1975, Weideang (not taped); L4.2: 15 May 1976, Weideang.

L5: Deng Bor Ngundeng: grandson of Ngundeng; Lithgai age-set. L5.1: 25 June 1975, Waat; L5.2: 12 July 1975, Waat.

L6: Dhieyier Bol Ngundeng: grandson of Ngundeng; Thok-Thok age-set; medical dresser. L6.1: 24 June 1975, Waat; L6.2: 26 June 1975, Waat; L6.3: 27 June 1975, Waat (not taped); L6.4: 13 July 1975, Waat (not taped).

L7: Gatkek Bol Ngundeng: grandson of Ngundeng; Thok-Thok age-set (half-brother to Dhieyier Bol, L6). L7.1: 31 Mar. 1976, Waat; L7.2: 25 Apr. 1976, Malakal.

L8: Nyakuil Tuel [Mangai]: youngest wife of Guek; Palker-Rumjok-Gun Lou, 16 May 1976 (Gatkal Ngundeng (L3) present).

L9: Dang Guek: posthumous son of Guek (mother Nyakuil, L8); Thok-Thok age-set, 16 May 1976, Waat (with Cuol Guek, son of Guek, Litjang age-set).

L10: Cuol Thijoak: Dul-Rumjok-Gun Lou (son of Thijok Dul; married Ngundeng's granddaughter; Guek married his sister). L10.1: 1 July 1975, Waat; L10.2: 15 July 1975, Waat.

L11: Marieu Thijoak: Dul-Rumjok-Gun Lou (son of Thijok Dul; mother a Luac Dinka; younger brother to Guol Thijoak, L10); Rialmai age-set, 28 Mar. 1976, Ayod.

L12: Bil Peat: Lak-Gaadbal-Gun Lou (son of Pet Nyakur, one of Ngundeng's singers; mother a Twic Dinka); Rialmai age-set. L12.1: 11 July 1975, Weideang; L12.2: 14 July 1975, Waat; L12.3: 5 May 1990, Weideang.
L13: Puot Gai: Lak-Gaadbal-Gun Lou (singer of songs; learned songs from Guek, Deng Peat, and others around the Mound); Rialmai age-set, 11 July 1975, Weideang.
L14: Nguth Kuny: Thiang-Gaadbal-Gun Lou; (family closely connected with Guek; former subchief); Luac age-set, 9 July 1975, Wunbil.
L15: Nyang Kuac Agok: Thiang-Gaadbal-Gun Lou (singer of songs; learned songs from uncle Nguth Kuny, L14); Kuek age-set. L15.1: 1 July 1975, Waat; L15.2: 2 July 1975, Waat; L15.3: 4 July 1975, Waat; L15.4: 11 May 1976, Waat; L15.5: 12–13 May 1976, Waat.
L16: Cuol Pathot: Thiang-Gaadbal-Gun Lou (singer of songs); Kuek age-set, 30 June 1975, Waat.
L17: Simon Mayan Tut: Gun Lou (veterinary officer), 24 Mar. 1975, Malakal.
L18: Wor Tiäp: Ciec-Gaadbal-Gun Lou; Dang-gonga age-set, 28 July 1975, Pul Turuk (not taped).
L19: Lok Jabä: Thai-Gaadbal-Gun Lou; Lithgai age-set, 17 May 1976, Pul Turuk.
L20: Madhir Lam: Maiker-Rumjok-Gun Lou (son of Lam Tutthiang; mother an adopted Dinka); Lithgai age-set, 6 July 1975, Waat.
L21: Tut Jiak Gai: Bul-Mor Lou (former subchief); Dang-gonga age-set. L21.1: 3 July 1975, Paddoi; L21.2: 14 May 1976, Paddoi.
L22: Cuol Puyu: Manweituor-Mor Lou (singer of songs; learned songs from Thiciot Ngundeng and Nyar Kueth Rundial of Gaajak). L22.1: 27 June 1975, Waat; L22.2: 6 July 1975, Waat; L22.3: 23 Apr. 1976, Waat; L22.4: 7 May 1976, Waat.
L23: Bibak Lam: Nyajikany-Rumjok-Gun Lou (son of Lam Liew; composer and singer of songs); Guoluong age-set, 27 Mar. 1976, Ayod (with Gatwic Wie Gak, Kulang Majok (G6), and Stephen Ciec Lam (L24)).
L24: Stephen Ciec Lam: Nyajikany-Rumjok-Gun Lou (son of Lam Liew; cousin of Riei Pok (L25); Nuer politician); Sudani age-set. L24.1: 29 Mar. 1976, Ayod (not taped); L24.2: 11 and 13 Nov. 1976, Malakal (not taped); L24.3: 23 July 1977, Juba (not taped); L24.4: 23 Feb. 1980, Khartoum (not taped).
L25: Riei Pok Kerjiok: Nyajikany-Rumjok-Gun Lou (son of Pok Kerjiok; prophet of GÄR), 29 Mar. 1976, Ayod (with Bibak Lam (L23); interview conducted by Stephen Ciec Lam (L24)).
L26: Gany Car: Maiker-Rumjok-Gun Lou (son of Car Koryom); Jagai age-set, 12 July 1975, Waat.

Jikany

Jk1: Jok Jang (Minyal-Gaajok; Lithgai age-set) and Gai Ruea (Minyal-Gaajok; Cayat age-set). Jk1.1: Jok Jang and Gai Ruea, 10 June 1976, Nasir; Jk1.2: Jok Jang, 20 June 1976, Nasir; Jk1.3: Gai Ruea, 1 July 1976, Nasir.
Jk2: Duop Biciuk: Nyajaani-Gaajak (court president Gaajak); Dengyan age-set, 20 Oct. 1976, Khartoum.
Jk3: Dhoal Kikwe: Ketbel-Gaajak; Cayat age-set, 6 July 1976, Nasir (with Wal Lual Puka, Nyathol-Gaajak, Dengyan age-set).
Jk4: Chiefs of *cieng* Yol-Gaajok, 16 May 1990, Nasir (not taped).

Western Nuer

Dk1: Biel Tip Gai: Tigjiek-Dok (a *tiet*); Jur-Teny age-set, 26 July 1976, Ler.

Dk2: Riei Kuong: Dok, 26 July 1976, Ler (not taped).

Dk3: Nyadak Cilieny: Begh-Dok (wife of Buom Diu); and Nyakieneu Teny: Maleak-Dok (daughter of Puot Nyuon), 5 Aug. 1976, Ler.

Dk4: Jior Cuol: Begh-Dok (paternal cousin of Buom Diu); Pilual age-set; and Biel Teny: Nyuon-Dok; Lith age-set, 5 Aug. 1976, Ler.

Jg1: Lili Goak Ruot: Jabany-Jagei (former chief and companion of Kolang Ket); Karam age-set, 1 Aug. 1976, Ngong.

Jg2: Tutjiok Malieth: Jagei (led group singing of MAANI songs), 1 Aug. 1976, Ngong.

Jg3: Kuol Kolang Ket: Jagei (son of Kolang Ket: full brother to Nyaruac), 2 Aug. 1976, Lingpuot.

Jg4: Gaaluak Yac Liem: Jabany-Jagei (singer to Nyakolang); Tunjuok age-set, 6 Aug. 1976, Ler.

Nyl: Riel Gaaluak: Nyuong (son of Gaaluak Nyagh). 8 Aug. 1976, Adok (not taped).

Dinka

D1: Wan Deng: Rut Dinka living with *cieng* Gany (Jamogh-Bar Gaawar) (son of Deng Aguer, late caretaker of Luang Deng; paternal uncle of current caretaker); Paduom age-set, 13 June 1975, Ayod.

D2: Mier Deng Reng: Nyareweng Dinka (nephew to Car Koryom), 28 Apr. 1976, Duk Fayuil

D3: Nyareweng Dinka elders: Leek Deng Ajok (*beny nhialic*); Leek Deng Malual (son of Deng Malual and court president); Deng Macot (Palual-Abiok section); Anyang Goc Kuol (Lok section); Nhial Jok Lual; Tiop Alum; Rueben Riak Cuol; Malual Amol Gol; Makor Guot Ruel (Lok section); Deng Jok Abot (Bikar section), 29 Apr. 1976, Duk Fayuil (translated by Lazarus Leek Mawut).

Administrators and officials (ranks and positions at time of interview)

A1: John Wicjaal Buom: Dok Nuer (son of Buom Diu); assistant commissioner, Western Nuer. A1.1: 28 May 1976, Malakal (not taped); A1.2: 9 and 13 June 1976, Malakal (not taped); A1.3: 22 Aug. 1977, Juba (with Stephen Ciec Lam) (not taped).

A2: David Koak: Lou Nuer; assistant commissioner, Akobo, 22 Sept. 1976, Malakal (not taped).

A3: Peter Gatkuoth Gual: Gaaliek-Mor Lou; commissioner UNP, then Regional Minister of Finance, Juba. A3.1: 8 Sept. 1977, Juba (not taped); A3.2: 5 Feb. 1980, Khartoum (with Biel Lel Ngundeng) (not taped).

A4: Gabriel Yoal Dok: Rumjok-Gun Lou (paternal nephew of Car Koryom); captain in office of state security, 18 Mar. 1981, Juba (not taped).

A5: Gabriel Yoal Dok (A4) and Stephen Ciec Lam (L24), 14 Nov. 1980, Juba (not taped).

A6: Cuol Kai: Thiang Nuer; Peter Gatkuoth Gual (A3); Stephen Ciec Lam (L24); Gabriel Yoal Dok (A4); 16 Nov. 1980, Juba (not taped).

A7: Cuol Rambang: Mor Lou; ex-Anyanya; local government inspector, Waat, 22 Oct. 1981, Khartoum (not taped).

A8: Philip Diu Deng: Luac Dinka (grandson of Akuei Biel); department of information, Malakal, then department of religious affairs, Bor (bilingual in Dinka and Nuer). A8.1: 23 Sept. 1976, Malakal (not taped); A8.2: 22 May 1982, Ayod (not taped).

A9: Moses Cot Dak: Rumjok-Gun Lou; executive officer, Waat, 26 Mar. 1981, Waat (not taped).

A10: Venansio Loro: deputy commissioner UNP; John Wicjaal Buom (A1); Peter Rir: local government inspector, Fangak, 28 Mar. 1975 (not taped).

A11: Peter Rir (A10); David Keak: Gaajok, ex-Anyanya; executive officer; Fangak, 1–2 Apr. 1975, Mogogh (not taped).

A12: Moses Cuol Juac: Gaajak, former commissioner UNP, Regional Minister of Interior; Samuel Ater Dak: deputy commissioner UNP; John Wicjaal Buom (A1); 12 July 1976, Malakal (not taped).

A13: Thomas Riek Nguot: Dok Nuer (cattle-master family); ex-Anyanya; executive officer, Ler, 29 July and Aug. 1976, Ler (not taped).

A14: Clement Gatut Ngundeng: Dok Nuer, headmaster, Ler; James Cany Rer: Dok Nuer, schoolmaster, Ler; 26 July 1976, Ler (not taped).

A15: Alier Mariel: Bor Dinka; nephew of *beny jok* of Lirpiou, 16 June 1976, Juba (not taped).

A16: Jonathan Malual Leek: Nyareweng Dinka (grandson of Deng Malual); commissioner of Jonglei Province, 18 Feb. 1980, Khartoum (not taped).

A17: John Kaan Wuawu: Lak Nuer, 8 Apr. 1982, Ayod (not taped).

A18: Dr Riek Mashar: Dok Nuer; Zonal Commander, Northern Upper Nile, Sudan People's Liberation Army, 12 Oct. 1989, Liverpool (not taped).

Ecology and history of Jonglei Province (Southern Records Office)

EHJP-1: Rut, Thoi, Luac Dinka elders: Piot Yak (Ator-Rut; court president of Rut and Thoi); Thon Marol (executive chief, Thoi); Rut Deng Akol (Thoi); Thuar Djok (Rut); Cuol Yoal Abiel (Luac; Malek age-set); 20 May 1982, Malual Ajing.

EHJP-2: Lueth Ayong Yor: Duor Dinka (son of Ayong Yor); Thonading age-set (with Malok Lam: Duor subchief; Ayau age-set), 21 May 1982, Ninadung.

EHJP-3: Luac Dinka elders: Diu Angok, Dau Kur, Kon Awer, Man Ajer, 21 May 1982, Wunalam.

EHJP-4: Cuol Macar (G12), Ruot Rom (G1), Gai Thung (Radh Gaawar; Pilual age-set), 12 Apr. 1981, Ayod.

EHJP-5: Ruot Diu (G10), 22–3 May 1982, Ayod.

EHJP-6: Cuol Cany Bul (Dol-Bar Gaawar; Pilual age-set); Pok Tuot (Per-Radh Gaawar; Pilual age-set); Jal Wang (Jamogh-Bar Gaawar, Guoluong age-set); 23 May 1982, Ayod.

EHJP-7: Kulang Majok (G6), 13 Apr. 1981, cattle camp.

EHJP-8: Kulang Majok, 24 May 1982, Gung.

EHJP-9: Wan Deng (D1) and Ater Deng (Rut Dinka; Paduom age-set; brother to Wan Deng), 24 May 1982, Ayod.

EHJP-10: Ghol Dinka elders: Marol Ater (Pilual age-set); Macol Dier (Paduom age-set); Deng Mawaak (Malek age-set); Jany Awan Mabur (Mabior age-set); Man Awol Akwoc (Duor Dinka; Koryom age-set); Aguek Dak (Ric Dinka; Rialmai age-set); 24 May 1982, Duk Fadiat.

EHJP-11: Family of Mabur Ajuot (Ghol Dinka): Jany Awan Mabur (Mabior age-set); Mabur Malual Mabur (Agok age-set); Marol Ater (Pilual age-set); Franco Manyok Moinkuer; 25 May 1982, Duk Fadiat.

EHJP-12: Twic Dinka elders: Bior Aguer Bior (Marol age-set; former court president, Kongor); Cornelio Duot Bior (Nyinriel age-set; court president, Kongor); Thon Deng Yong (Thuar age-set; executive chief); Abraham Cany Awol (Nyinriel age-set; executive chief); 25 May 1982, Kongor.

Other Sudanese

Atem Yaak Atem: Twic Dinka; journalist and colleague in the Regional Ministry of Culture and Information, Juba.

Bullen Alier Buttic: Bor Dinka; journalist and colleague in the Regional Ministry of Culture and Information, Juba.

Dak Dei: Lou Nuer; early Southern Sudanese politician.

Francis Gai: Western Jikany Nuer; merchant and regional assemblyman.

James Gaaluak Kuny: Lou Nuer; graduate of Makerere College; early Southern Sudanese politician.

Joseph Banak Riak: Dok Nuer; retired executive officer, Ler.

Maria Nyadhok: Shilluk; tape and transcript of interview (Mar. 1979) in Institute of Social and Cultural Anthropology, Oxford.

Moses Cot: Lou Nuer; composer and singer of songs.

Philip Obang: Anuak; commissioner UNP, 1976.

British personnel

Former British administrators with whom I have corresponded or whom I have interviewed. Only relevant dates of service and postings are given.

Edward Aglen: DC Eastern Nuer (Nasir), 1936–9.

B. J. Chatterton: DC Western Nuer, 1932–7.

Mrs K. Coriat: widow of Percy Coriat; she was in UNP 1928–30.

E. G. Coryton: deputy governor UNP, 1925–7, 1930–2, 1935–6; governor UNP, 1936–9.

Dr P. P. Howell, CMG, OBE: ADC Central Nuer, 1941–6; chairman Jonglei Investigation Team, 1948–53; chairman Southern Development Investigation Team, 1953–5.

Martin W. Parr, CBE: governor UNP, 1934–6.

A. Guy Pawson, CMG: inspector UNP, 1916–17; governor UNP, 1931–4.

Philip H. C. Pawson, MBE: (son of above) ADC Central Nuer, 1946–9.

Philip Lyon Roussel: ADC and DC Central Nuer, 1951–5.

Adrian Struvé: son of K. C. P. Struvé (inspector UNP 1906–10, governor UNP 1920–6).

John Winder: ADC Pibor, 1936–7; DC Zeraf 1937–42; member, Jonglei Investigation Team, 1946–8; deputy governor UNP, 1948–51; governor UNP, 1953–5.

PRINTED SOURCES

ADAS, M. (1987), *Prophets of Rebellion: Millenarian Protest Movements against the European Colonial Order*, Cambridge.

Alban, A. H. (1940), 'Gwek's Pipe and Pyramid', *SNR* 23/1.

Alier, A. (1990), *The Southern Sudan: Too Many Agreements Dishonoured*, Exeter.

American Mission: (1932), 'Some Nuer Diseases and their Remedies', Nasir (mimeo).

—— (1938), 'Nasir District Sub-divisions and Native Nuer Chiefs', Nasir (mimeo).

Anon. (1900), 'List of Shilluk, Dinka, Nuer and A[n]yuak Shiek[h]s', *SIR* 74 (9 Sept.–9 Oct.), appendix B.

Asad, T. (1970), *The Kababish Arabs: Power, Authority and Consent in a Nomadic Tribe*, London.

Aumont et de Villequier, Duc d' (1883), 'Du Caire à Gondokoro et au Mont Redjaif, 1855', *Bull. de la Soc. Khédiviale de Géog.* 2.

Bacon, C. R. K. (1917), 'The Lau Nuers', 4. Feb. 1917 (mimeo) (NRO Dakhlia I 112/13/87 and SAD).

Baker, S. W. (1875), *Ismailïa*, 2 vols., London.

Bartoli (1970), 'A History of the Sudan, 1822–1841', in Hill (1970).

Beattie, J., and Middleton, J. (1969) (eds.), *Spirit Mediumship and Society in Africa*, London.

Beltrame, G. (1974), 'On the White Nile from Khartoum to Gondokoro, 1859–1860', in Toniolo and Hill (1974).

Ben Assher [C. Borradaile] (1928), *A Nomad in the South Sudan*, London.

Blewitt, A. (1902), 'Diary and Report of Expedition against Nuer Sheikh Denkur', *SIR* 94 (May), appendix B.

Bourdillon, M. F. C. (1978), 'The Cults of Dzivaguru and Karuva amongst the North-Eastern Shona Peoples', in J. M. Schoffeleers (ed.), *Guardians of the Land: Essays on Central African Territorial Cults*, Gwelo.

—— (1982), 'Freedom and Constraint among Shona Spirit Mediums', in J. Davis (ed.), *Religious Organization and Religious Experience*, ASA Monograph 21, London.

Brun-Rollet, A. (1852), 'Excursion de M.—— dans la région supérieure du Nil', *Bull. de la Soc. de Géog. de Paris*, ser. 4, 4.

—— (1855), *Le Nil Blanc et le Soudan*, Paris.

Bullen Alier Buttic (1975), manuscript on modern Nuer prophets.

—— (1982), 'The Cult of Lirpiou Spear', *Heritage: A Journal of Southern Sudanese Cultures*, 1/1.

Burton, J. W. (1981), *God's Ants: A Study of Atuot Religion*, St Augustin.

—— (1987), *A Nilotic World: The Atuot-Speaking Peoples of the Southern Sudan*, Westport, Conn.

Cameron, A. (1905), 'Extract from a Private Letter from Angus Cameron Bey to Wilson Bey, Dealing with his Tour in the Dengkur District', *SIR* 130 (May), appendix B.

Chadwick, N. (1952) [1942], *Poetry and Prophecy*, Cambridge.

Chaillé-Long, C. (1877), *Central Africa: Naked Truths of Naked People*, New York.

Collins, R. O. (1962), *The Southern Sudan 1883–1898: A Struggle for Control*, New Haven, Conn.

—— (1971), *Land beyond the Rivers: The Southern Sudan, 1898–1918*, New Haven, Conn.

—— (1975), *The Southern Sudan in Historical Perspective*, Tel Aviv.

—— (1983), *Shadows in the Grass: Britain in the Southern Sudan, 1918–1956*, New Haven, Conn.

COOKE, D. K. (1935), 'Native Administration in Practice: Historical Outline', in J. A. deC. Hamilton (ed.), *The Anglo-Egyptian Sudan from within*, London.

CORFIELD, F. D. (1938), 'The Koma', *SNR* 21/1.

CORIAT, P. (1923), 'The Gaweir Nuers', document 1.2 in Coriat (1993).

—— (1925), 'Settlement of Ol Dinka–Gaweir Nuer Boundary Dispute', document 2.1 in Coriat (1993).

—— (1926*a*), 'Transfer of Barr Gaweir to Zeraf Valley District', document 1.3 in Coriat (1993).

—— (1926*b*), 'Bloodwealth Payments', document 1.4 in Coriat (1993).

—— (1927), 'Gwek Diary', document 3.1 in Coriat (1993).

—— (1928), 'General Report: Patrol S8 (Lau Nuer) 1928', document 3.2 in Coriat (1993).

—— (1929*a*), 'Nuer Settlement—Gun Lau (Guncol) Area', document 3.3 in Coriat (1993).

—— (1929*b*), 'Southern (Abwong) District: Handing Over Notes', document 1.4 in Coriat (1993).

—— (1931*a*), 'Western Nuer District', document 4.1 in Coriat (1993).

—— (1931*b*), 'Administration—Western Nuer', document 4.2 in Coriat (1993).

—— (1931*c*), 'Notes on Political Prisoners in Malakal', document 3.4 in Coriat (1993).

—— (1939), 'Gwek the Witch-Doctor and the Pyramid of Dengkur', *SNR* 22/2.

—— (1993), *Governing the Nuer: Documents in Nuer History and Ethnography, 1922–31*, ed. D. H. Johnson, JASO Occasional Papers No. 9, Oxford.

CRAZZOLARA, J. P. (1932), 'Die Gar Zeremonie bei den Nuer', *Africa*, 5/1.

—— (1933), *Outlines of a Nuer Grammar*, Vienna.

—— (1951), *The Lwoo: Part II Lwoo Traditions*, Verona.

—— (1953), *Zur Gesellschaft und Religion der Nueer*, Vienna.

CRUIKSHANK, A. (1962), *The Kindling Fire: Medical Adventures in the Southern Sudan*, London.

CUDSI, A. S. (1969), 'Sudanese Resistance to British Rule, 1900–1920', M.Sc. thesis, University of Khartoum.

DALY, W. M. (1980), *British Administration and the Northern Sudan, 1917–1924*, Leiden.

—— (1986), *Empire on the Nile: The Anglo-Egyptian Sudan, 1898–1934*, Cambridge.

DANEEL, M. L. (1970), *The God of the Matopo Hills: An Essay on the Mwari Cult in Rhodesia*, The Hague.

DAVID, N. (1982), 'Prehistory and Historical Linguistics in Central Africa: Points of Contact', in C. Ehret and M. Posnansky (eds.), *The Archaeological and Linguistic Reconstruction of African History*, Los Angeles.

DEBONO, A. (1860), 'Fragment d'un voyage au Saubat (affluent du Nil)', *Le Tour du monde*, 2.

DENG, F. M. (1973), *The Dinka and their Songs*, Oxford.

—— (1974), *Dinka Folktales: African Stories from the Sudan*, New York.

—— (1980), *Dinka Cosmology*, London.

—— (1986), *The Man Called Deng Majok: A Biography of Power, Polygyny, and Change*, New Haven, Conn.

—— and DALY, M. W. (1989), *Bonds of Silk: The Human Factor in the British Administration of the Sudan*, East Lansing, Mich.

DIGERNES, O. (1978), 'Appearance and Reality in the Southern Sudan: A Study in the British Administration of the Nuer 1900–1930', Major thesis, University of Bergen.
DRIBERG, J. (1931), 'Yakan', *JRAI* 61.
EHRET, C. (1974), *Ethiopians and East Africans: The Problem of Contacts*, Nairobi.
—— (1982), 'Population Movement and Culture Contact in the Southern Sudan, *c.*3000 BC to AD 1000: A Preliminary Linguistic Overview', in J. Mack and P. Robertshaw (eds.), *Culture History in the Southern Sudan*, Nairobi.
—— *et al.* (1975), 'Some Thoughts on the Early History of the Nile–Congo Watershed', *Ufahamo*, 5/2.
EL WATHIG KAMEIR (1980), 'Nuer Migrants in the Building Industry in Khartoum: A Case of the Concentration and Circulation of Labour', in V. Pons (ed.), *Urbanization and Urban Life in the Sudan*, Department of Sociology and Social Anthropology, University of Hull.
EVANS-PRITCHARD, E. E. (1933), 'The Nuer: Tribe and Clan', *SNR* 16/1.
—— (1934), 'The Nuer: Tribe and Clan', *SNR* 17/1.
—— (1935), 'The Nuer: Tribe and Clan', *SNR* 18/1.
—— (1936*a*), 'The Nuer: Age-Sets', *SNR* 19/2.
—— (1936*b*), 'Customs and Beliefs Relating to Twins among the Nilotic Nuer', *Uganda Journal*, 3/3.
—— (1937), 'Economic Life of the Nuer: Cattle', *SNR* 20/2.
—— (1938*a*), 'Economic Life of the Nuer: Cattle', *SNR* 21/1.
—— (1938*b*), 'Some Administrative Problems in the Southern Sudan', *Oxford University Summer School on Colonial Administration*, Oxford.
—— (1940*a*), *The Nuer: A Description of the Modes of Livelihood and Political Institutions of a Nilotic People*, Oxford.
—— (1940*b*), *The Political System of the Anuak of the Anglo-Egyptian Sudan*, London (repr. New York, 1971).
—— (1947), 'A Note on Courtship among the Nuer', *SNR* 28.
—— (1949), 'Burial and Mortuary Rites of the Nuer', *African Affairs*, 48/190.
—— (1950), 'Kinship and Local Community among the Nuer', in A. R. Radcliffe-Brown and D. Forde (eds.), *African Systems of Kinship and Marriage*, London.
—— (1951), *Kinship and Marriage among the Nuer*, Oxford.
—— (1953), 'The Nuer Spirits of the Air', *Annali Lateranensi*, 17.
—— (1956), *Nuer Religion*, Oxford.
FAKHOURI, H. (1968), 'The Zar Cult in an Egyptian Village', *Anthropological Quarterly*, 41/2.
FAUSSET, M. (1939), *Pilate Pasha*, London.
FERGUSSON, V. H. (1921*a*), 'Summary of Information on the Nuong Nuer in the Northern Bahr-el-Ghazal extracted from a Report by Capt. V. H. Fergusson, O.B.E. (The Cameronians) on a Tour in the Nuer Country, February and March 1921', *SMIR* 323 (June), appendix A.
—— (1921*b*), 'The Nuong Nuer', *SNR* 4/2.
—— (1922), 'The Holy Lake of the Dinka', *SNR* 5/3.
—— (1923*a*), 'Mattiang Goh Witchcraft', *SNR* 6/1.
—— (1923*b*), 'Nuer: Ba[h]r el Ghazel', *SMIR* 350 (Sept.), appendix.
—— (1930), *The Story of Fergie Bey, Told by Himself and Some of his Friends*, London.
GESSI, R. (1892), *Seven Years in the Soudan* (London).

GHAWI, J. B. (1924), 'Notes on the Law and Custom of the Jur Tribe in the Bahr el Ghazal', *SNR* 7/2.

GLEICHEN, Count EDWARD (1898), *Handbook of the Sudan*, London.

GORDON, C. G. (1881), *Colonel Gordon in Central Africa, 1874–1879*, ed. G. B. Hill, London.

—— (1953), *Equatoria under Egyptian Rule: Unpublished Correspondence of Col. C. G. Gordon with Ismail, Khedive of Egypt and the Sudan during the Years 1874–1876*, ed. M. F. Shukry, Cairo.

GORDON, H. (1903), 'Report on the Nuers of the Sobat River', *SIR* 107 (June), appendix D.

GOWLETT, J. A. J. (1988), 'Human Adaptation and Long-Term Climatic Change in Northeast Africa: An Archaeological Perspective', in Johnson and Anderson (1988).

HASSAN AHMED IBRAHIM (1985*a*), 'African Initiatives and Resistance in North-East Africa', in A. Adu Boahen (ed.), *General History of Africa*, vii: *Africa under Colonial Domination 1880–1935*, London.

—— (1985*b*), 'Politics and Nationalism in the Maghrib and the Sahara, 1919–35', in A. Adu Boahen (ed.), *General History of Africa*, vii: *Africa under Colonial Domination 1880–1935*, London.

HAWKER, C. L. (1902), 'Information Procured about the Present Condition of the Nuer Tribe', *SIR* 98 (Sept.), appendix B.

HEASTY, J. A. (1937), *English–Shilluk, Shilluk–English Dictionary*, Doleib Hill (repr. 1974).

HERRING, R. S. (1979), 'Hydrology and Chronology: The Rodah Nilometer as an Aid to Dating Interlacustrine History', in J. B. Webster (ed.), *Chronology, Migration and Drought in Interlacustrine Africa*, London.

HEUGLIN, T. VON (1941), 'Travels in the Sudan in the Sixties', *SNR* 24.

HILL, R. L. (1959), *Egypt in the Sudan 1820–1881*, London.

—— (1970), *On the Frontiers of Islam: The Sudan under Turco-Egyptian Rule, 1822–1845*, Oxford.

HOBSBAWM, E. J. (1965), *Primitive Rebels, Studies in Archaic Forms of Social Movement in the 19th and 20th Centuries*, New York.

—— and RANGER, Terence (1983) (eds.), *The Invention of Tradition*, Cambridge.

HOFMAYR, F. (1925), *Die Schilluk*, Vienna.

HOLT, P. M. (1970), *The Mahdist State in the Sudan 1881–1898*, 2nd edn., Oxford.

HOWELL, P. P. (1941), 'The Shilluk Settlement', *SNR* 24.

—— (1945*a*), 'A Note on Elephants and Elephant Hunting among the Nuer', *SNR* 26/1.

—— (1945*b*), 'The Zeraf Hills', *SNR* 26/2.

—— (1948*a*), 'The Age-Set System and the Institution of "Nak" among the Nuer', *SNR* 26/2.

—— (1948*b*), '"Pyramids" in the Upper Nile Region', *Man*, 48/56.

—— (1953), 'Some Observations on "Earthly Spirits" among the Nuer', *Man*, 53/126.

—— (1954), *A Manual of Nuer Law*, London (repr. 1970).

—— (1961), 'Appendix to Chapter II', in Lienhardt (1961).

—— LOCK, M., and COBB, S. (1988) (eds.), *The Jonglei Canal: Impact and Opportunity*, Cambridge.

HUFFMAN, R. (1931), *Nuer Customs and Folklore*, London.

HUTCHINSON, S. (1985), 'Changing Concepts of Incest among the Nuer', *American Ethnologist*, 12.

—— (1988), 'The Nuer in Crisis: Coping with Money, War, and the State', Ph.D. dissertation, University of Chicago.

—— (1990), 'Rising Divorce among the Nuer, 1936–1983', *Man*, 25/3.

IBRAHIM BEDRI (1939), 'Dinka Beliefs in their Chiefs and Rainmakers', *SNR* 22/1.

—— (1948), 'More Notes on the Padang Dinka', *SNR* 29/1.

JACKSON, H. C. (1923), 'The Nuer of the Upper Nile Province', *SNR* 6/1 and 2.

—— (1954), *Sudan Days and Ways*, London.

JAL, GABRIEL GIET (1987), 'The History of the Jikany Nuer before 1920', Ph.D. thesis, SOAS, London University.

JAMES, W. (1979), *'Kwanim Pa: The Making of the Uduk People: An Ethnographic Study of Survival in the Sudan–Ethiopian Borderlands*, Oxford.

—— (1988), *The Listening Ebony: Moral Knowledge, Religion, and Power among the Uduk of Sudan*, Oxford.

—— (1990*a*), Introd. to the paperback edition of E. E. Evans-Pritchard, *Kinship and Marriage among the Nuer*, Oxford.

—— (1990*b*), 'Kings, Commoners, and the Ethnographic Imagination in Sudan and Ethiopia', in R. Fardon (ed.), *Localizing Strategies: Regional Traditions of Ethnographic Writing*, Edinburgh.

—— (1992), *Uduk Asylum Seekers in Gambela, 1992: Community Report and Options for Resettlement*, Addis Ababa: UNHCR.

JOHNSON, D. H. (1979), 'Colonial Policy and Prophets: the "Nuer Settlement", 1929–30', *JASO* 10/1.

—— (1980), 'History and Prophecy among the Nuer of the Southern Sudan', Ph.D. dissertation, University of California, Los Angeles.

—— (1981), 'The Fighting Nuer: Primary Sources and the Origins of a Stereotype', *Africa*, 51/1.

—— (1982*a*), 'Tribal Boundaries and Border Wars: Nuer–Dinka Relations in the Sobat and Zaraf Valleys, *c*.1860–1976', *JAH* 23/2.

—— (1982*b*), 'Ngundeng and the "Turuk": Two Narratives Compared', *History in Africa*, 9.

—— (1982*c*), 'Evans-Pritchard, the Nuer and the Sudan Political Service', *African Affairs*, 81/323.

—— (1982*d*), 'The Isolation of the Southern Sudan: A Re-examination of the Evidence', *Heritage: A Journal of Southern Sudanese Cultures*, 1/2–3.

—— (1985*a*), 'C. A. Willis and the "Cult of Deng": A Falsification of the Ethnographic Record', *History in Africa*, 12.

—— (1985*b*), 'Foretelling Peace and War: Modern Interpretations of Ngundeng's Prophecies in the Southern Sudan', in M. W. Daly (ed.), *Modernization in the Sudan: Essays in Honor of Richard Hill*, New York.

—— (1986*a*), 'Judicial Regulation and Administrative Control: Customary Law and the Nuer, 1898–1954', *JAH* 27/1.

—— (1986*b*), 'On the Nilotic Frontier: Imperial Ethiopia in the Southern Sudan, 1898–1936', in D. Donham and W. James (eds.), *The Southern Marches of Imperial Ethiopia: Essays in History and Social Anthropology*, Cambridge.

—— (1986*c*), 'The Historical Approach to the Study of Societies and their Environment in the Eastern Upper Nile Plains', *Cahiers d'études africaines*, 26/1–2.

JOHNSON, D. H. (1988*a*), 'Adaptation to Floods in the Jonglei Area: An Historical Analysis', in Johnson and Anderson (1988).

—— (1988*b*), 'Divinity Abroad: Dinka Missionaries in Foreign Lands', in Wendy James and D. H. Johnson (eds.), *Vernacular Christianity: Essays on the Social Anthropology of Religion Presented to Godfrey Lienhardt*, JASO Occasional Papers No. 7, Oxford.

—— (1988*c*), *The Southern Sudan*, Minority Rights Group Report No. 78, London.

—— (1988*d*), 'Environment and the History of the Jonglei Area', ch. 9 in Howell, Lock, and Cobb (1988).

—— (1989*a*), 'The Structure of a Legacy: Military Slavery in Northeast Africa', *Ethnohistory*, 36/1.

—— (1989*b*), 'Enforcing Separate Identities in the Southern Sudan: The Case of the Nilotes of the Upper Nile', in J.-P. Chrétien and G. Prunier (eds.), *Les Ethnies ont une histoire*, Paris.

—— (1989*c*), 'Political Ecology in the Upper Nile: The Twentieth Century Expansion of the Pastoral "Common Economy"', *JAH* 30/3.

—— (1990), 'Fixed Shrines and Spiritual Centres in the Upper Nile', *Azania*, 25.

—— (1991*a*), 'Criminal Secrecy: The Case of the Zande "Secret Societies"', *Past and Present*, 130.

—— (1991*b*), 'From Military to Tribal Police: Policing the Upper Nile Province in the Sudan', in D. Anderson and D. Killingray (eds.), *Policing the Empire: Government, Authority and Control, 1780–1940*, Manchester.

—— (1992*a*), 'On Disciples and Magicians: The Diversification of Divinity among the Nuer during the Colonial Era', *Journal of Religion in Africa*, 22/1.

—— (1992*b*), 'Reconstructing a History of Local Floods in the Upper Nile Region of the Sudan', *International Journal of African Historical Studies*, 25/3.

—— (1993*a*), 'Percy Coriat's Life and the Importance of his Work', in Coriat (1993).

—— (1993*b*), 'Deng Laka and *Mut Roal*: Fixing the Date of an Unknown Battle', *History in Africa*, 20.

—— (1993*c*), 'Prophecy and Mahdism in the Upper Nile: An Examination of Local Experiences of the Mahdiyya in the Southern Sudan', *British Journal of Middle Eastern Studies*, 20/1.

—— (1994), 'The Prophet Ngundeng and the Battle of Pading: Prophecy, Symbolism and Historical Evidence', in D. M. Anderson and D. H. Johnson (eds.), *Revealing Prophets: Prophecy in Eastern African History*, London.

—— and ANDERSON, DAVID, M. (1988) (eds.), *The Ecology of Survival: Case Studies from Northeast African History*, London.

—— —— (1994), 'Revealing Prophets', in D. M. Anderson and D. H. Johnson (eds.), *Revealing Prophets: Prophecy in Eastern African History*, London.

—— and PANKHURST, RICHARD (1988), 'The Great Drought and Famine of 1888–92 in Northeast Africa', in Johnson and Anderson (1988).

Jonglei Investigation Team [JIT] (1954), *The Equatorial Nile Project and its Effects on the Anglo-Egyptian Sudan*, 4 vols., Khartoum.

KIGGEN, J. (1948), *Nuer–English Dictionary*, London.

KILLINGRAY, D. (1984), '"A Swift Agent of Government": Air Power in British Colonial Africa, 1916–1939', *JAH* 25/4.

KINGDON, F. D. (1945), 'The Western Nuer Patrol, 1927–1928', *SNR* 26/1.

LEITH, P. P. (1970), 'The War Scene', *Grass Curtain*, 1/2.

LEJEAN, G. M. (1865), *Voyage aux deux Nils*, Paris.

LESSER, A. (1978) [1933], *The Pawnee Ghost Dance Hand Game: Ghost Dance Revival and Ethnic Identity*, Madison, Wis.

LEWIS, B. A. (1951), 'Nuer Spokesmen: A Note on the Institution of the *Ruic*', *SNR* 32/1.

LEWIS, I. M. (1971), 'Spirit Possession in North-East Africa', in Y. F. Hassan (ed.), *The Sudan in Africa*, Khartoum.

—— (1989), *Ecstatic Religion: A Study of Spirit Possession and Shamanism*, 2nd edn., London.

LIDDELL, J. S. (1904), 'Report on March from Taufikia to Twi and Visit to Twi by Steamer', *SIR* 119 (June), appendix A.

LIENHARDT, P. A. (1975), 'The Interpretation of Rumour', in J. H. M. Beattie and R. G. Lienhardt (eds.), *Studies in Social Anthropology: Essays in Memory of E. E. Evans-Pritchard by his Former Oxford Colleagues*, Oxford.

LIENHARDT, R. G. (1951), 'Some Notions of Witchcraft among the Dinka', *Africa*, 21/4.

—— (1954), 'Modes of Thought', in E. E. Evans-Pritchard *et al.*, *The Institutions of Primitive Society*, Oxford.

—— (1955), 'Nilotic Kings and their Mother's Kin', *Africa*, 25.

—— (1956), 'Religion', in H. L. Shapiro (ed.), *Man, Culture, and Society*, New York.

—— (1958), 'The Western Dinka', in J. Middleton and D. Tait (eds.), *Tribes without Rulers*, London.

—— (1961), *Divinity and Experience: The Religion of the Dinka*, Oxford.

—— (1975), 'Getting your Own Back: Themes in Nilotic Myth', in J. H. M. Beattie and R. G. Lienhardt (eds.), *Studies in Social Anthropology: Essays in Memory of Evans-Pritchard by his Former Oxford Colleagues*, Oxford.

MACHELL, P. [Ali Effendi Gifoon] (1986), 'Memoirs of a Sudanese Soldier', *Cornhill Magazine*, ser. 3, 1/439.

MCLAUGHLIN, J. (1967), 'Tentative Time Depths in Nuer, Dinka and Anuak', *Journal of Ethiopian Studies*, 5/1.

MCMEEKAN, G. R. (1929), 'The Demolition of a Pyramid', *Royal Engineers Journal*, 43.

MACMICHAEL, Sir H. (1934), *The Anglo-Egyptian Sudan*, London.

MAJOK, D. D. (1984), 'Resistance and Co-operation in Bahr El-Ghazal 1920[*sic*]–1922', in Mohamed Omer Beshir (ed.), *Southern Sudan: Regionalism & Religion: Selected Essays*, Khartoum.

MAKEC, J. W. (1988), *The Customary Law of the Dinka People of Sudan in Comparison with Aspects of Western & Islamic Laws*, London.

MARNO, E. (1873), 'Der Bahr Seraf', *Petermann's Mitteilungen*, 19.

—— (1874), *Reisen im Gebiete des Blauen und Weissen Nil, im egyptischen Sudan, 1869–1873*, Vienna.

MASSAIA, L. G. (1974), 'Khartoum to the Gold Workings of Fazughli, 1851', in Toniolo and Hill (1974).

MATTHEWS, G. E. (1902), 'Annual Report: Upper Nile Province 1902', GGR 1902.

—— (1904), 'Note on the Nuer Question', *SIR* 120 (July), appendix C.

MATTHEWS, G. E. (1905), 'Annual Report: Upper Nile Province 1905', GGR 1905.

—— (1906), 'Annual Report: Upper Nile Province 1906', GGR 1906.

—— (1907), 'Report on Journey up the Zeraf Valley to Visit Nuer Chief Diu, and thence across to the Khor Filus and Sobat River', *SIR* 152 (Mar.), appendix A.

MAWSON, A. N. M. (1989), 'The Triumph of Life: Political Dispute and Religious Ceremonial among the Agar Dinka of the Southern Sudan', Ph.D. dissertation, Cambridge University.

MAWUT, L. L. (1983), *Dinka Resistance to Condominium Rule, 1902–1932*, Khartoum.

MERCER, P. (1971), 'Shilluk Trade and Politics, from the Mid-Seventeenth Century to 1861', *JAH* 12/3.

MESSING, S. D. (1958), 'Group Therapy and Social Status in the Zar Cult in Ethiopia', *American Anthropologist*, 60.

MICHEL, C. (1901), *Vers Fachoda*, Paris.

MIDDLETON, J. (1963), 'The Yakan or Allah Water Cult among the Lugbara', *JRAI* 93/1.

—— (1969), 'Spirit Possession among the Lugbara', in Beattie and Middleton (1969).

—— (1971), 'Prophets and Rainmakers', in T. O. Beidelman (ed.), *The Translation of Culture*, London.

MOHAMED OSMAN EL SAMMANI (1984), *Jonglei Canal: Dynamics of Planned Change in the Twic Area*, Khartoum.

NEBEL, A. (1979), *Dinka–English, English–Dinka Dictionary*, Bologna.

NIKKEL, M. (1992), 'Aspects of Contemporary Religious Change among the Dinka', *Journal of Religion in Africa*, 22/1.

OCHOLLA-AYAYO, A. B. C. (1976), *Traditional Ideology and Ethics among the Southern Luo*, Uppsala.

O'FAHEY, R. S., and SPAULDING, J. L. (1974), *Kingdoms of the Sudan*, London.

O'SULLIVAN, H. D. E. (1908), 'Dinka Customs and Laws', *SIR* 162 (Jan.), appendix D (later published as 'Dinka Laws and Customs', *JRAI* 40 (1910)).

—— (1910), 'Annual Report, Upper Nile Province 1910', GGR 1910.

OWEN, R. C. R. (1910), 'Annual Report: Mongalla Province 1910', GGR 1910.

P'BITEK, O. (1971), *Religion of the Central Luo*, Nairobi.

PEAKE, M. (1898), 'The Second Reconnaissance of the Bahr el Zeraf', *SIR* 60 (25 May–31 Dec.), appendix 67.

PETHERICK, J. (1861), *Egypt, the Soudan and Central Africa*, Edinburgh.

—— and PETHERICK, Mrs (1869), *Travels in Africa*, 2 vols., Edinburgh.

PONCET, J. and A. (1937), *Le Fleuve blanc: Notes géographiques et ethnologiques, et les chasses à l'éléphant dans le pays des Dinka et des Djour*, Alexandria.

Population Census Office, Ministry of Social Affairs (1958–61), *First Population Census of Sudan 1955/1956, Final Report*, vols. i, ii, iii, and *Notes on Omodia Map*, Khartoum.

RANGER, T. O. (1967), *Revolt in Southern Rhodesia, 1896–7. A Study in African Resistance*, London.

Report of the Commission of Enquiry, Southern Sudan Disturbances 1955 (1956), Khartoum.

Reports on the Finance, Administration, and Condition of the Sudan (1902–14), Cairo and Khartoum (abbreviated as GGR).

RING, B. M. M. (1969), 'The Death of Philip and its Implications', *Vigilant*, 6 Apr. (repr. in *Sudan informazione*, 41 (10 May 1969), 3–8).
ROBERTSHAW, P. (1987), 'Prehistory in the Upper Nile Basin', *JAH* 28/2.
ROBERTSON SMITH, W. (1978), *The Prophets of Israel and their Place in History*, London.
ROUSSEL, P. L. (1955), 'Last Days in the Sudan', *Time and Tide*, 6 Aug.
RUAY, P. B. (1981), Letter to the editor, *Southern Sudan Magazine*, 5/3.
SANDERSON, G. N. (1965), *England, Europe, and the Upper Nile, 1882–1899*, Edinburgh.
SANDERSON, L. M. Passmore, and SANDERSON, G. N. (1981), *Education, Religion & Politics in Southern Sudan, 1899–1964*, London.
SANDES, E. W. C. (1937), *The Royal Engineers in Egypt and the Sudan*, Chatham.
SANTANDREA, S. (1948), 'The Luo of the Bahr el Ghazal (Part III)', *Annali Lateranensi*, 12.
—— (1968), *The Luo of the Bahr el Ghazal*, Bologna.
SCHOFFELEERS, J. M. (1974), 'Crisis, Criticism and Critique: An Interpretive Model of Territorial Mediumship among the Chewa', *Journal of Social Science*, 3.
SCHUVER, J. M. (1883), *Reisen im Oberen Nilgebiet*, Gotha.
SCHWEINFURTH, G. (1874), *The Heart of Africa*, 2 vols., New York.
SELIGMAN, C. G. and B. Z. (1932), *Pagan Tribes of the Nilotic Sudan*, London.
SELIM BIMBACHI (1842), 'Premier Voyage à la recherche des sources du Nil-Blanc', ed. E.-F., Jomard, *Bull. de la Soc. Géog. de Paris*, ser. 2, 18.
SHAW, A. (1915), 'Dinka Songs', *Man*, 15/3.
SIMEONI, A. (1978), *Päri: A Luo Language of Southern Sudan*, Bologna.
SOUTHALL, A. (1969), 'Spirit Possession and Mediumship among the Alur', in Beattie and Middleton (1969).
Southern Development Investigation Team [SDIT] (1954), *Natural Resources and Development Potential in the Southern Provinces of the Sudan*, London.
SPARKES, W. W. (1899), 'Extracts from the Diary of Kaimakam Sparkes Bey during his Patrol from Fashoda to the Bahr Ez Zeraf in the "Hafir", 10th March to 12th April 1899', *SIR* 62 (16 Feb.–30 Apr.), appendix E.
STEVENSON-HAMILTON, J. (1920), 'The Dinka Country East of the Bahr-el-Jebel', *Geographical Journal*, 56/5.
STIGAND, C. H. (1918*a*), 'Warrior Classes of the Nuers', *SNR* 1/2.
—— (1918*b*), 'Dengkur Earth Pyramid', *SNR* 1/3.
—— (1919), 'The Story of Kir and the White Spear', *SNR* 2/3.
STRUVÉ, K. C. P. (1907), 'Report on the Khor Atar District', *SIR* 153 (Apr.), appendix B.
—— (1908*a*), 'Report on a Tour in the Nuer Country with the Object of Visiting Wol Deng Laka, Diu's Successor', *SIR* 163 (Feb.), appendix A.
—— (1908*b*), 'Annual Report: Upper Nile Province 1908', GGR 1908.
—— (1909), 'Report on Administrative Boundaries between the Twi Dinka and Nuers (Mongalla and Upper Nile Province)', *SIR* 177 (Apr.), appendix C.
—— (1926), 'Annual Report: Upper Nile Province 1925', *Reports of Governors of Provinces for the Year 1925*, Khartoum.
STUBBS, J. M., and MORRISON, C. G. T. (1938), 'The Western Dinkas, their Land and their Agriculture', *SNR* 21/2.
SVOBODA, T. (1985), *Cleaned the Crocodile's Teeth: Nuer Song*, New York.

TANGYE, H. L. (1910), *In the Torrid Sudan*, London.
THESSIGER, W. (1986), *The Life of my Choice*, London.
THIBAUT, G. (1856), *Journal de l'expédition à la recherche des sources du Nil, 1839–1840*, Paris.
THOMAS, K. (1973), *Religion and the Decline of Magic*, Harmondsworth.
TITHERINGTON, G. W. (1927), 'The Raik Dinka of Bahr el Ghazal Province', *SNR* 10.
TONIOLO, E., and HILL, R. (1974) (eds.), *The Opening of the Nile Basin*, London.
TRIMINGHAM, J. S. (1949), *Islam in the Sudan*, Oxford.
TRIULZI, A. (1975), 'Trade, Islam, and the Mahdia in Northwestern Wallagga', *JAH* 16/1.
TUNNICLIFFE, G. W. (1932), 'Anuak Vocabulary', typescript in the Tylor Library, Institute of Social and Cultural Anthropology, Oxford University.
WALLER, R. (1988), 'Emutai: Crisis and Response in Maasailand 1883–1902', in Johnson and Anderson (1988).
WARBURG, G. (1971), *The Sudan under Wingate*, London.
WERNE, F. (1849), *Expedition to Discover the Sources of the White Nile*, 2 vols., London.
WILLIS, C. A. (1928), 'The Cult of Deng', *SNR* 11.
WILSON, H. H. (1902), 'Letter from Administrator, Fashoda, *re* Sheikh Diu', *SIR* 99 (Oct.), appendix B.
—— (1903*a*), 'Report by Bimbashi H. Wilson on the Dinkas of the White Nile', *SIR* 104 (Mar.), appendix C.
—— (1903*b*), 'Notes on the Nuer Districts of Bahr el Zeraf and their Sheikhs', *SIR* 106 (May), appendix B.
—— (1903*c*), 'El Kaimakam Wilson Bey's Trip up the Bahr El Zeraf', *SIR* 112 (Nov.), appendix A.
—— (1904), 'Report on the Situation along the Sobat Valley', *SIR* 117 (Apr.), appendix A.
—— (1905), 'Report by El Kaimakam H. H. Wilson Bey on March from the Sobat (Mouth of the Filus) to Bor', *SIR* 128 (Mar.), appendix A.
WILSON, S. C. (n.d.) [*c.*1939], *I Was a Slave*, London.
WOODWARD, F. W. (1907), 'Report on Patrol in the Nuer Country', *SIR* 153 (Apr.), appendix A.
—— (1911), 'Annual Report: Upper Nile Province 1911', GGR 1911, vol. ii.
—— (1912), 'Annual Report: Upper Nile Province 1912', GGR 1912, vol. i.
ZENKOVSKY, S. (1950), 'Zar and Tamboura in Omdurman', *SNR* 31/1.

INDEX

Aak (Nuer ancestor) 45, 50
Abboud regime (1958–64) 302
Abdallah Col. William 342, 343
Abiel (earthly Power) 62
above and below, Powers of 60–2
ABUK (divinity) 40, 41, 67
Abwong outpost 172, 178, 179, 180, 188, 191
aciek (creators, men of divinity) 64
acuk (black ant) 60
Addis Ababa Agreement (1972) 113, 237, 307, 316, 317, 323, 338
administration, *see* British administration; native administration; Sudanese government
Adok 252, 253, 254, 255, 259, 265, 271, 292, 347
  Dual Diu 231, 232, 233
  floods 16, 49, 252
adoption of strangers 53, 54, 57, 111
  accumulation of divinities 63
  by Gaawar 67, 83–4, 126, 128, 131, 132, 142, 167
  Deng Laka 126, 128, 132, 142
  Nuer mythology 45, 51
  social and religious idioms 55
Agar Dinka 27, 28, 47, 69, 244
  conflicts with Nuer 245, 247, 248, 254, 256, 257, 258
age-set system 83, 147, 174, 175, 362–3
  Deng Laka 141, 144–5, 147
  Dual Diu 215, 216, 217, 220, 222
agnatic kinship 56, 57, 63
Aguer Ayuel 160
Aguer Wiu 160
air divinity (*kuoth duanga*) 283
  see also sky divinities
Air Force (RAF), Royal 21, 33, 192, 193, 195, 350
Aiwel Longar myth 41–3, 58, 59, 64, 325, 327
  Gaawar prophets 152, 204, 239
  Lou prophets 73, 74, 75, 76, 85, 94, 95, 112, 124, 199, 352
  Nuaar Mer 140
  spear of Aiwel Longar 94
  see also under spear-masters
Aiwel Longar shrine 40, 42, 43–4, 93–4, 313
Ajak government post 32, 170
ajuogo (Shilluk diviners) 64
Ajuong 48, 49, 132, 138, 144, 157
Akobo 179, 184, 275, 320, 344
Akuei Biel (Dinka medicine man) 97
Akuot Atem 342
Alban, Capt. A. H. A. 32, 275, 335
Aliab Dinka 47–8
Ali al-Tom 23
Ali Dinar's sultanate 28
Alier, Abel 113, 316, 317, 319
Ali Nasir and Ali wad Rahma 131
Allah Water cult 27
Al-Zaki Tamal 92, 115
Amnesty Act (1972) 308, 309
ancestor myths 41, 48, 51, 65, 66
  Gee 45, 50, 58
ancestral divinities 40, 41, 325
ancestral ghosts (*jok* or *juok*) 60
Angai Dinka 47, 49, 158, 244
Anglo-Egyptian army, 5, 116
Anglo-Egyptian government 7
  see also British administration
ansar, see Mahdist wars
ant, black (*acuk*) 60
anthropologists 353–4
  see also Bourdillon; Chadwick; Crazzolara; Evans-Pritchard; Howell; Hutchinson; James; Lienhardt
Anuak people 38, 46, 57, 93, 355
  conflicts, Jikany Nuer 12, 53, 54, 77–8, 124, 305, 349, 350
  conflicts, Lou Nuer 12, 53, 54, 77–8, 124, 165–6, 167, 168, 173, 221
  conflicts, Mahdist 115
  conflicts, Meban 305
  intermarriage 51, 57, 165
  links with Jikany Nuer 51, 53–4, 77
Anyanya *vii*, 204–41, 302, 304, 307, 336, 337, 341
  Babuny Kir Nyak 315
  Bangong Diau 305, 306
  Gony Yut 301, 302, 303, 308
  Joseph Lagu 318
  mutinies 320
Anyanya II *vii*, 323, 324–5, 342, 343, 344, 346, 347, 350, 351
Arabi Dafaʿallah 158
Arab peoples 23, 28, 46, 312, 323, 326
AREK (divinity) 40
Arianhdit 27, 28, 256, 257
Ariath the Great (divinity) 28
arms trade 220–2
Armstrong, C. H. 230
Army, Sudan People's Liberation, *see* SPLA
army, *see* Anglo-Egyptian army; French army; guerrilla warfare; Mahdist wars; military administration; Sudanese army
arum man Jang (Uduk) 306
Atuot people 27, 28, 69, 256, 257

Atuot people (*cont.*):
similarities with other Nilotes 56, 58, 59, 60, 62, 64
Atur Wic royal enclosure 40, 313
authority, *see* power
Aweil, guerrilla warfare (1982) 322
Awin, King of the Shilluk 52
Awin Wut 67
Ayod 130, 157, 307
administrative post 15, 16, 179, 211, 215
Ayong Yor 117, 156, 160
Azande people 23, 27, 69, 332

Babuny Kir Nyak (Lou prophet) 313, 315, 319, 325, 337, 360
Bad Things (*jiak jiathni*), Tree of 106, 107, 200, 304, 335–6
Bad Things (*pul jiakni*), Pool of 98, 106, 107
Bahr el-Ghazal region 12, 18, 27, 28, 43, 69, 324
Captain Fergusson 22
Dinka/Nuer conflicts 45, 47, 245
floods 37, 45–6, 52
guerrilla warfare 322, 342–3
missionaries 264
Bahr el-Jebel region 7, 68, 115
Dinka/Nuer conflicts 45, 48, 51
floods 45–6, 49, 52, 245, 247
Bahr el-Zeraf region 49, 128, 144
Dinka/Nuer conflicts 47, 49
famine (1904) 121
floods 49, 126, 131, 133, 139, 143, 145, 157
trade 114, 130
see also Zeraf area
Bakkam (man of cattle) 260, 261, 265, 266
Balang Ngundeng 70
BANG (divinity) 144, 152
Bangong Diau (E. Jikany prophet) 304–6, 325–6, 337, 349, 361
appointed as chief 320
brought to Malakal (1974) 309
death of 324
Ngundeng's relics 317–18
as peacemaker 304–6, 309, 311, 313
Bang section (Bar Gaawar) 227, 293, 294
bany, *see* spear-masters
barbless spear of Aiwel Longar 199
Bar Column troops 229
Bar Gaawar 48, 49, 50, 133, 231
age sets 215, 216, 217, 220, 222
Dinka/Nuer conflicts 49, 158, 208–9, 213, 226–7, 249
dominant lineage 142
floods (1878) 133
prophets *see* Deng Laka; Dual Diu
Radh/Bar conflicts 127, 139, 142–3, 163, 303
Baro river, 46, 320
barren women, *see* infertility cures
baton, prophet's 141, 154, 251
Ngundeng Bong's 86, 109, 113, 118, 190, 317, 318
Battle of the Foreigners (Mut Roal 1890s) 158
Battle of the Grandmother (Mut Mandong *c.*1900) 155, 158, 159
Battle of Juac (Mut Juaca 1890s) 158
Battle of Mogogh (1879) 140, 156
Battle of Muot Tot (1917) 171, 172
Battle of Omdurman (1898) 7, 258, 261
Battle of Pading, *see* Pading Battle
Battle of Pakuem (1830s) 49, 51, 127
Bayak Bior 168
Beac Colieth 78, 83
bieli 61
belief and scepticism 333–4
below and above, Powers of 60–2
Bentiu District 323, 324
beny bith, see spear-master
beny and *kuaar* 59
beny yath (clan-divinity master) 40
bie 88, 89
biel 61–2
BIEL (divinity) 96, 253
Biel Lel Ngundeng 318
Biem Jiak (failed Gaawar prophet) 133–4, 137, 141
Bilieu Wayu 253
Biliu section (Lou Mor) 297
Bil Peat 344–5
biographers and prophecy *ix*
biri (secret societies) 29, 256, 257
black ant (*cuk, acuk*) 60
blessings 66, 128, 277, 280, 297, 299, 300, 306
Dual Diu 233, 241, 316
earth-masters 83
let 128
Ngundeng Bong 87, 109, 122, 124, 315
Blewitt, Major Arthur 4, 9, 10, 13, 117, 125, 160
blood-money 112, 316, 321–2
Blood (*riem*) 58
Board of Ulema 24
Boiloc age-set 175, 363
Bol (Deng Laka's mother) 132
Bol Ngundeng 178, 192
Bol Toang (Lou elder) 4
Bol Yol (Arianhdit) 27, 28, 256, 257
Bong Can 74, 75, 77, 83
Bor 7, 68, 159, 161, 234, 319
garrison mutiny (1983) 323, 341, 342
raids (1991) 346, 347, 348
transferred to Upper Nile Province 222
border conflicts, Anglo-Egyptian government/Nuer 6, 12, 166, 208–9, 227, 228

see also border settlement; Gaawar/Anglo-Egyptian government conflicts; Lou/Anglo-Egyptian government conflict; Nuer settlement
border conflicts, Dinka/Nuer 12–13, 16, 167, 168, 209–13, 225, 234, 314, 347
administrative changes (1920s) 18, 166, 167, 177, 182, 213, 222, 272
Lou prophets 203
border conflicts, Sudan/Ethiopian border 320, 349
border settlement (1909–11) 12, 20, 30, 166, 169, 183
Bor Dinka 41–2, 48, 54, 67, 100
Dinka/Nuer conflicts 13, 159, 167, 168, 169, 170–1, 172
Both Diet 134
boundaries, *see* border conflicts
Bourdillon, Michael 355
bridewealth 52, 144
British administration 7, 9, 12, 15, 144, 164, 176, 234
administration of borders 18, 177, 182, 213, 222, 273; *see also* border conflicts, Anglo-Egyptian government/Nuer; border settlement, Nuer Settlement
conflict with Nuer prophets 12, 24–9, 31, 32, 122, 183, 189, 203, 215, 272, 278, 292, 322, 329; *see also* suppression of prophets, British administration and *under* Buom Diu; Car Koryom; Dual Diu; Gaaluak Nyagh; Guek Ngundeng; Kolang Ket; *kujur*; military force; Ngundeng Bong, Pok Kerjiok, Wuon Kuoth
Deng Laka 11, 25, 26, 121, 141, 156, 160–3
decentralization 15–16
discontinuity 7–8, 9, 22, 183–4, 222
magicians 200, 202, 295–6
Nuer people 5, 21, 22, 30, 44, 121, 256, 321
official records 32, 33, 93
religion 24, 29, 296
and security 9, 11, 14–15, 21, 121
tolerance of prophets *see* tolerance
Western Nuer (1921–23) 256–63
see also Dinka/Anglo-Egyptian government relations; Gaawar/Anglo-Egyptian government relations; Lou/Anglo-Egyptian government relations; military administration; native administration
British Empire Medal proposed for Cak Riang 270
BUK (divinity) 94, 103, 292, 325
Buk (*let*) 127
Bul Kan (magician) 98, 117, 177, 191
Bul Nuer 52, 74, 250, 266, 281, 342
Bul section (Mor Lou) 109
Buogh Kerpeil (Gatnyal) 49, 50, 51, 66, 127, 128, 360
Buom Diu (Dok prophet) 248, 251–2, 254, 333, 360
conflict with government 257–67 *passim*, 271–7 *passim*, 330
Gaaluak Nyagh 263, 268
buom (strength) 76
Buongjak 53, 54, 77–8, 124
bush, people of '*jidoar*' 240
Buth Diu 311

Caath Obang 260, 264–5, 267, 272, 360
CAK (divinity) 96, 152, 239
Cak Riang 260, 265, 268–70, 271, 360
Camel Corps 235
Cam section (Bar Gaawar) 227
canal construction, Jonglei 341–2
Cany Reth 161, 216–18, 219, 360
car for Ayod 15
careers of prophets:
effects of ecology 113, 244, 327, 327–8, 329
effects of war 300, 304, 307, 311, 313, 314, 324, 325–6, 327, 328, 352, 353
Car Koryom (Lou prophet) 166, 167–9, 172, 173, 178, 201–2, 227, 360
cattle raids 197–8
conflict with government 179, 195–7, 201, 330
divinity passed to son 297, 325
castration rumour and Fergusson 269–70
Catholic Verona Fathers 264
cattle:
as compensation 104, 217–268
Nuaar Mer's 133, 141
tribute 11, 12, 13, 14, 15, 84, 259
see also cattle disease: cattle-master; cattle-pegs; cattle, prophet's; men of cattle; sacrifice
cattle disease 78, 137
cures 87–8, 90, 95, 113, 124, 250, 279
motive for moving 48, 143
motive for raids 133–4, 247
cattle-masters (*kuar ghok*) 73
cattle-pegs 61, 63, 151, 239
cattle, prophets' 111, 255, 277
Buom Diu 251, 275
dedicated to divinities 151, 152, 154, 219, 239, 328
dispute after civil war 308, 309–10
Gaaluak Nyagh 273, 277
minor prophets 172, 249, 250, 292, 302
see also under Deng Laka: Ngundeng Bong
cattle raids 12, 52, 157, 169, 197–8, 207, 210, 265
after 1st civil war 308, 309–10, 311
Arianhdit as Dinka peacemaker 28

cattle raids (*cont.*):
  Dinka/Nuer 52, 167, 170, 171, 197, 209–13, 225, 234, 247, 253, 268, 269
  Gony Yut 303, 308, 310
  Nuaar Mer 133–4
cattle trade 50, 84, 291
Cayat age-set 220, 362–3
central government of Khartoum 340, 341, 343, 346
Central Nuer, *see* Gaawar Nuer; Lak Nuer; Thiang Nuer
Chadwick, N. (*Poetry and Prophecy*) 35
change, radical social 353, 355
chicken pox 280
chiefly lineage (Dinka) 161
chiefs (goverment appointed), *see* Dinka people, chiefs; Nuer chiefs
childlessness, *see* infertility cures
children of the white ox, *see* Dang-gonga
children of women (spear-masters) 113
Christianity 29, 296, 315–16, 340
  see also missions
Church Missionary Society at Lau 347
Cic Dinka 47, 159, 244, 247, 255–62 *passim*, 271
Ciec Lam, Stephen *viii*, 308, 315, 316
Ciec section (Gun Lou) 79–81, 122
cieng (agnatic lineages) 56, 57, 63
cieng nyajiok (family of the dog's daughter) 276–8, 279, 283
civil administration, British 8, 9, 10, 11–12, 14–15, 16, 21
civil war, Shilluk (1827–30) 52, 54
civil war, Sudan 330
  (1956–72) 237, 298, 300–7 *passim*, 325, 336, 337
  (1983 onwards) 323–6 *passim*, 339, 341–51 *passim*
  cause of feuds 302, 303, 304, 305, 308
  dead prophets' messages 330
  influence on Nuer prophets 240–1, 291, 297–307, 311, 313, 314, 320–6
  Ngundeng's predictions 340–53 *passim*
  Ngundeng's songs (1954–72) 336–8
clan ancestors (Nuer myth) 45, 50
clan-divinities 28, 59, 60, 63, 328
  Aiwel 41, 42
  proliferation 63, 64–5
  see also Flesh; WIU
clan-divinity master (*beny yath*) 40
clans, Nuer 45, 360, 361
clan spears 52, 63, 67, 74, 100, 103
clapping ceremonies 276, 283, 284
Closed Districts policy 29
'closed systems', African 354
clouds, symbol of DENG 28, 300
CMS mission station at Lau 247
Collingwood, R. G. 287, 352
Collingwood, W. G. ix, 287, 334
colonial government, *see* British Administration
Col Weng 270, 271
col wic spirits 61, 321, 322
commerce, *see* trade
communication problems (language) 267, 268
communications, *see* canal; river transport; road building; road transport; telegraph
compensation 104, 217–18, 268
  blood money 112, 316, 321–2
competition, *see* ecology, competition; magicians, rivalries; Nuer chiefs, rivalries; prophet rivalries
conference, Mogogh (1975) 309–10, 311
Corfield, F. D. (*quoted*) 31
Coriat, Percy 16, 21, 147, 181, 215
  Buom Diu 274–5
  Dual Diu 26, 214, 215, 218, 230
  Gaaluak Nyagh 272
  Gaweir March 222, 224, 225, 226, 228
  Guek Ngundeng 174–5, 178, 184–5, 186–95 *passim*, 339, 340
  knowledge of Nuer feuds 123, 198
  Ngundeng Bong 90–1, 93, 119
  oxname Girkuai 214
  Willis 18, 184
costs, *see* finance
Cotrial (Nyang Macar) 139, 141
cotton cultivation 267, 268, 269, 274–5
coups:
  Nimeiri (1969) 302
  'two doctors' (1991) 346, 347, 349
  attempt by Sadiq al-Mahdi (1976) 322, 323
courts, *see* judicial systems; native courts
Crazzolara, J. P. xi, 58, 95, 104, 243, 264
  divinities and powers 282, 283, 284, 332
creators (*aciek*, men of divinity) 64
crisis and prophets 31–2, 252
  crisis theory *ix*, 114–16, 123, 124, 327–8, 354
crocodile divinity, owner of 62
Cromer, Lord 24
crops, *see* cultivation
cuk (black ant) 60
cultivation 38, 110, 268, 269, 275
  mantic activities, 41, 83, 277
  see also fertility
CUOL NYALJOK (divinity) 119
Cuol Juac, Moses 309
Cuor Dinka 157, 158, 159
cuor (Vulture) sacrifice 106
cures, *see* cattle disease, cures; healing; infertility cures; medicine
curse(s) 41, 48, 65, 83, 275
  earth-master 58–9, 65
  Guek Ngundeng 202, 335

Kolang Ket 249, 272
Ngundeng Bong 98, 109–10, 112, 338–9
power of prophets' 85–6
custodian of the shrine, *see* shrine-master
customary law and British administration 10, 17
see also judicial systems

Dag Mer 142, 146, 197, 211, 219, 232
Dak Dhon (Jagei: Prophet) 250, 265–6, 279, 325, 330
Danaqla 115, 116
dances 275, 277–8, 280
Dang age-set 141, 144–5, 147, 363
Dang Dung Jiak 269
Dang-gonga age-set (children of the white ox) 87, 95, 111, 175, 363
dang, see baton
Danhier Gaaluak 274
DAPIR (divinity) 248, 253–4, 274, 277, 283
Darfur, *mani* magic of 332
dayiemni 148, 291
Deng Laka's 140, 145, 149, 152, 154–5
Dual Diu's 220, 222
Guek Ngundeng's 200
Kolang Ket's 250, 265–6, 266
Lia Wel's 276, 277, 278
Nyaruac Kolang's 280, 283
see also Ngundeng Bong's *dayiemni*
DAYIM (divinity) 331
Debono, A. 77
decentralization 15–16
Deng Aguer (shrine-master) 95, 148
Deng Bor Ngundeng 199, 321
Deng Cier 85, 139
DENG CIERKOAR and DENG COTKUAI (divinities) 99
Deng cult 29
DENG (divinity) 55, 63, 282, 289, 327
Car Koryom 166, 167, 168, 198–9
DIU as 148
emblems and symbols 28, 87, 112, 113, 168, 300, 313, 321, 349
as free-divinity 67, 70
Guek Ngundeng 173–4, 179, 190, 198–9, 322
minor prophets 85, 249, 266, 279, 301, 310, 315, 320, 348
myths 40, 41, 43
Ngundeng Bong 73, 75, 83–8, 94–101, 102, 103–4, 110, 124, 297, 319
powers 75, 85, 86–7, 112, 113, 148, 168, 190, 321–2, 349
primacy 85, 94–101, 103–4, 110, 154, 297, 332
rivalry with BUK 292
variations 28, 99, 148, 152, 219, 300–1, 305, 311, 331
Deng, Frances M. 145
DENG GIL (divinity) 152
DENGKUR (divinity) 219, 305, 311
Dengkur, *see* Ngundeng Bong
'Dengkur Patrol' 117–18, 121
Deng Laka (Gaawar prophet) x, 51, 126–63, 283, 284, 332, 360
adoption 126, 128, 132, 142
ancestor shared with Pok Kerjiok 169
and Car Koryom's father, 167
cattle 144, 151, 152, 154, 157, 239
comparisons 126–7, 133–41, 151, 154, 163
death of (1907) 162, 330
Dinka/Nuer conflicts 85, 111, 127, 148, 155, 158, 156–60 *passim*, 162
DIU 100, 135–7, 138, 141–7, 152–3, 154
legacy 219, 220
myths 51
opposed magic 155, 163, 285
as peacemaker 142–3, 146, 163
power of resurrection 86
predictions 138, 150, 155, 276, 335
rivalries 132, 138, 140, 141, 147–55, 163, 285
seizures 100, 135–7, 138, 151–2, 154
shrines 126, 138, 143, 151, 154, 328
social network 126, 141–7
songs 95, 148, 152–5, 159
see also under British administration
DENG LUAK (divinity) 148, 300–1
Deng Majok (Ngok Dinka chief) 23, 145
Deng Malual (Nyareweng Dinka leader) 182, 189, 225, 227–8, 231, 232, 233
DENG MAROAL (divinity) 152
DENG NYANGEAR (divinity) 99
DENG pake 340, 342
DENG PALOI (divinity) 152
DENG PIOL (divinity) 28
deng (rain) 41, 60, 87, 172, 329
desacralization of power and authority 32, 278–9, 289–90, 292, 293, 294, 295, 297, 313
dessication, *see* drought
devolutionary policy 182–3
see also native administration
Dhiew Dieng 188, 192, 197, 202–3, 360
DHOL (divinity) 96, 111, 331
diel, see dominant lineage
din dyor 43
see also spear-master
Ding Tuil (Nuer chief) 197
Dinka/Anglo-Egyptian government relations 12, 16, 18, 20, 24, 115, 267
conflict with Arianhdit 27, 28, 256, 257
Dinka allies 10, 13, 22, 116, 118, 160, 162, 167, 170, 182, 231

Dinka Anglo-Egyptian (*cont.*):
  government as mediator 16, 268, 269
Dinka chiefs, *see under* Dinka people
Dinka language 110, 141
Dinka/Nuer conflicts 6, 10, 12–13, 56, 57
  Bahr el-Ghazal region 45, 47, 245
  Bahr el-Jebel region 45, 48, 51
  Bahr el-Zeraf region 47, 49
  Bor Dinka 13, 159, 167, 168, 169, 170–1, 172
  Cic Dinka 159, 247, 255–61 *passim*, 271
  Dinka as government allies 10, 13, 22, 116, 118, 160, 162–3, 167, 170, 182, 231
  Dok Nuer 245, 247, 248
  environment as a cause 163, 169, 210, 212, 241, 247
  Fergusson's death 242–3
  Gaweir March 227–8
  Jagei Nuer 245, 247, 258
  Jikany Nuer 46, 47, 52, 245
  Ngok Dinka 48, 49
  Nyareweng Dinka 12, 33, 84, 148, 156–60 *passim*, 167, 170, 227, 228
  Nyuong Nuer 48, 49, 156–60 *passim*, 245, 247–8, 255–63 *passim*, 271
  Padang Dinka 53
  Rek Dinka 247, 248, 252, 257, 258, 265–6
  Rut Dinka 49, 156, 157
  Sudan civil war 302, 303, 304, 305, 308, 323, 346, 347–8
  Twic Dinka 149, 158, 207, 167, 168, 169, 117, 156–9 *passim*
  Western Nuer 47, 244–5, 247–8, 254, 256–64, 265
  see also border conflicts; cattle raids; Gaawar/Dinka conflicts; Lou/Dinka conflicts
Dinka/Nuer relations 49, 51, 157–63
  appropriation of Dinka land 55, 57, 148–9
  Car Koryom 168
  chiefs' meeting (1947) 234
  conflicts, *see* Dinka/Nuer conflicts
  friendly 47, 52, 54, 85, 148, 149, 156, 157, 229, 244, 244–5, 319, 348
  government influences 118, 160, 162–3, 167, 170, 182, 231
  influences on each other 55, 67, 74, 243, 250, 281, 355
  Ngundeng Bong 110, 111, 112, 121, 342
  Nuer assimilation 47, 53, 55, 57, 66, 84, 104, 112, 126, 128, 142, 144, 149, 165, 168, 222, 348
  Nuer expansion 38–55 *passim*
  Ruac Col 299
  see also adoption of strangers; Gaawar/Dinka relations; intermarriage
Dinka people 44, 46–7, 56, 244–5
  Arianhdit 27, 28, 256, 257
  chiefly lineage 161
  chiefs 156, 182, 231, 234; *see also* Ayong Yor; Deng Malual; Monykuer Mabur
  conflicts: guerrilla warfare 302, 322, 342–3; internal 16, 160, 167; Mahdist 115, 158–9; Murle 54, 158, 320; Nuer *see* Dinka/Nuer conflicts; Turco-Egyptians/Shilluk 46; Zeraf merchants 130
  cotton cultivation 267, 268
  earth-master lineage 67, 83–4, 128, 131, 142
  environmental pressures 128
  migrations 47, 48
  mythology 355; *see also* Aiwel Longar
  Nuaar Mer 133, 156
  as original settlers 128, 131, 148–9
  prophets 27, 28, 256, 257
  religious and social traditions 40, 57, 59, 95, 222–13, 243, 253, 331, 332, 355; *see also* Aiwel Longar; spear-master
  settlements 40, 43, 46, 49, 128, 156, 182, 197
  shrines 40–1; *see also* Luang Deng
  similarities with other Nilotes 56, 57, 58, 59, 60, 64
  slavery 9, 52, 68, 157
  as warriors 244–5
  see also Agar; Aliab; Angai; Bor; Cic; Cuor; Dinka/Anglo-Egyptian government relations; Dinka/Nuer conflicts; Dinka/Nuer relations; Eastern Dinka; Ghol; Kuil; Luac; Ngok; Nyareweng; Nyiel; Padang; Rek; Ric; Rueng; Rut; Thoi; Twic; Western Dinka
Diop (Dual Diu's brother) 228
disasters, *see* crisis
disciples, *see dayiemni*
discontinuity of British administration 7–8, 9, 16, 22, 183–4, 222
discontinuity of Sudanese government 290–1, 323–4
disease, *see* cattle disease; chickenpox; epidemics; Kala Azar; seizure; illness; smallpox
district commissioners' duties 16, 292
Diu Bang 294
DIU (divinity) 111, 148, 155, 220, 283, 289, 331, 332
  Car Koryom 167
  Dual Diu 205, 206, 209, 239, 241
  Gony Yut 310
  powers 148
  primacy 154
  prophetic traditions 313–15

Wuon Kuoth 253, 254
see also under Deng Laka
Diu Garadin relates Nuer myth 50
divergence of East and West Nuer 291
diversity of Sudanese Society 16
diviners 52, 62, 64, 96
divinities 28, 148, 331–3
above and below 249
Aiwel Longar 40
annunciation 563, 100
cattle dedicated to 151, 152, 154, 219, 239, 328
descent 76, 100, 142, 325, 346
Fallata divinity 305
Kolang's satellite 250
peace brought by 112, 113, 168, 252, 276, 321–2, 349
power of 148; 154; *see also* DENG (divinity), powers; spiritual power
proliferation 328; *see also* DENG (divinity), variations
reassigned by Deng Laka 154
rivalries 258, 292, 296
as social bonds 100, 124, 136, 138, 142
spiritual attributes 281–5
symbols, *see* emblems and symbols
vessel of divinity 73, 282
see also ancestral divinities; clan-divinities; DENG; DIU; Divinity; Flesh; free-divinities; *quan kuoth*; MAANI; seizure; tutelary divinities
Divinity 59, 60, 102, 152, 315
national divinity (NYIKANG) 40
terminology 59, 60–5
transcends political fragmentation 70, 100, 329
see also divinities; men of Divinity
DOANG, *see* Nyacan Ruea
documentation 32, 33, 93, 247
primary sources *xii*
see also oral testimony
'dog-eating Kujurs' 276–8, 279
dogs, divinities found in 248
Dogwar section (Dok Nuer) 251
Dok 48, 51, 251, 275
Dok Kuok (Lou elder) 4, 334
Dok Nuer 252, 282, 342
conflict, Agar Dinka 245, 247, 248
conflict, British administration 258–9
Kolang Ket's influence 250, 252, 263
prophets 249, 276, 277, 278, 283; *see also* Buom Diu; Caath Obang
Dol Pajok 149–50, 337
Dol section (Bar Gaawar) 143, 227
dominant lineage (*diel*) 65–7, 83, 84, 128, 131, 142, 144
Dor 144, 146–7
Dor Dak 260, 265, 266, 625
Dor (*let*) 127
dreams 40, 298
drought 77, 90, 113, 169, 247
Nuer migrations 37, 53
drums, return of Ngundeng's 317–19
Dual Diu (Gaawar prophet) x, 204–41, 282, 301, 304, 316, 332, 360
cattle 151, 219, 239
conflict with British 13, 19, 22, 27, 170–1, 195, 197, 200, 208, 209–15 *passim*, 218, 222–33 *passim*, 330
Coriat 26, 214, 215, 218, 230
dayiemni 220, 222
Dinka/Nuer conflicts 33, 170, 182, 197, 208–9, 227, 228, 232, 234, 235–6, 241
DIU 205, 206, 209, 239, 241
elephant hunting 220–1, 222, 276
healing powers 233, 241
opposed magicians 218–19, 222, 239–40, 285
paramount chief 184, 204, 217
peacemaker 215, 217–18, 222, 238, 241
regulation of Gaawar society 215–22
relations with Sudanese government 234, 235–6, 237, 238, 240
sceptics 333
shrines 239, 240, 315
tolerated by British administration 164, 205, 215, 216, 218, 221, 222
wives 219–20
see also under blessings; seizure; sacrifice; predictions; prophet rivalries
Duk Fadiat 54, 179, 182, 238
police post 6, 12, 166, 208–9, 227, 228
transferred to Upper Nile 18, 213
Duk Fayuil 182, 197
police post 18, 32, 184, 226, 227, 228
transferred to Upper Nile 18, 213
Duk ridge 51, 131
Dinka settlement 43, 49, 54, 157
Gaawar 143–4, 149, 209, 213
Gaawar/Ghol land dispute 210, 213
let befriended by Puot Bidiet 127–8
Dungjol Dinka 52, 54
Dung-Rumjok section (Gun Lou) 111
Duop Biciuk 305, 309
Duop Thar 98, 99–100, 121
Duor Dinka 54, 139, 156, 157, 228
dura-bird, owner of the 62
Dur area 268, 269, 270
Nyuong Nuer settlement 253, 254–5
Dur Nyuong section 247, 272, 273–4, 276–8
durra stalks as sign of peace 276
Dut section (Ngok Dinka) 132

Dwal Diu, *see* Dual Diu
dynamic character of African religions 355–6

earthly Powers 59, 60–1, 62, 328
  Dual Diu 219
  men of cattle 253
  reside in magical substances 69, 282, 295, 332
  and sky-divinities 249, 283, 284, 296, 329
earth-master lineage:
  Dinka 67, 83–4, 128, 131, 142
  Jimem 45, 84
  Western Nuer 66
earth-master(s) 73, 83, 131, 142, 290, 317
  curse of 58–9, 65
  demise due to magic 127
  Maleak lineage 66, 74
Eastern Dinka 40, 41, 55, 58
Eastern Jikany 51, 52, 282, 291
  Ngundeng Bong 77, 102, 124
  resist payment of tribute 12, 13, 15
  see also Bangong Diau; Gaajak; Gaajok; Jikany Nuer
Eastern Nuer 252, 282–3, 291, 327
  prophets 281, 328, 329
  relations with Dinka 54, 224–5
  see also Bangong Diau; Eastern Jikany; Lou Nuer; Lou prophets
ecology:
  competition 45, 133–4, 143, 163, 169, 210, 212, 241, 244, 247, 327
  effect on prophets' careers 113, 244, 327, 327–8, 329
  Fergusson's murder 242–3
  impact on social organization 36, 37–8, 48, 54, 143, 354
  induces change 355
  see also drought; epidemics; famine; floods; Nuer expansion, environmental influences
economic development 298
education 298, 315–16
Egyptians 9, 114–15, 245, 247, 249
  see also Anglo-Egyptian
eldering 291–2
elephant hunting 220–1, 276
  see also ivory
emblems and symbols 59, 60–3, 64, 108, 137–8, 138, 248, 253
  female 58, 112–13
  light and lightening 61, 254, 265
  NAI 284
  Nuer adopt Dinka's 243, 355
  peace 112–13, 276
  rain, see *deng*
  red cobra 61, 152
  rifle imagery replaces spear 307
  rivers 61, 292
  spiritual power 41, 75–6, 141
  strength 154
  see also baton; fishing spear; leopard skin; pipe of Ngundeng Bong; social and religious idioms; trees and *under* DENG (divinity)
emergency leaders, *see* crisis
environment, *see* ecology
epidemics 113, 327–8, 329
  see also rinderpest; smallpox; tse-tse
EPRDF (Ethiopian People's Revolutionary Democratic Front) 349
Equatoria 27, 346
Equatorial Corps, mutiny (1955) 237, 298, 302
Equatoria retaken (1992) 346
Eritrean guerrillas 322
Ethiopia 53, 320, 323, 342, 346, 349
Ethiopian People's Revolutionary Democratic Front (EPRDF) 349
Evans-Pritchard, Sir Edward E. *viii*, *ix*, *xi*, 8, 44, 64, 90, 114, 244, 264
  on age-sets 147, 362
  on divinities and powers 55, 69, 174, 243, 282, 283, 284, 332, 353
  Nuer religion vii
  on prophets 31, 32, 100, 138, 327, 352, 353
  study of terminology 30, 56, 59, 60, 61, 332
  theory of structural opposition 141
'evil eye' (*peth*) 64, 86, 100, 150–1, 219, 314
evil, Nuer definition of 328

fakirs (*faqis*) 24
Fallata divinity 305
Famenkwai killings 229
family of the dog's daughter (*cieng nyajiok*) 276–8, 279, 283
family of Ngundeng Bong *see* Ngundeng Bong's family
famine 53, 121, 128, 249, 348
fanaticism 24
  see also militant Islam
Fangak 22, 223, 241, 309
  district 322
Faragalla Buluk Amin *see* Cany Reth
Farag Osman (Nuang Lol) 161
Fashoda 7, 40, 115, 116, 160, 313
Faussett, M. (*Pilate Pasha*) 24–5
female symbols 58, 112–13
Fergusson, Captain V. H. 264, 18
  assassination (1927) 22, 32, 222, 223, 242–3, 268–9, 270–2
  method of administration 26, 256, 256–65 *passim*, 266, 267–8
  sent to Western Nuer 245, 248, 256
fertility 85, 113, 148, 292, 329
  mantic activities 41, 83, 277
  see also infertility cures (women)

fetishes 60–1, 97, 155, 283, 285, 296
owner of a fetish (*guan kulang*) 69
feud(s),
aggravated due to civil war 302, 303, 304, 305, 308
Gony Yut 302, 303, 308, 310
Kolang Ket 247, 248, 252, 257, 258, 262, 265–6
Nuaar Mer 85, 130–2, 133, 138, 139, 140, 141, 142, 163
Western Dinka migrations 47, 48
see also Anuak people, conflicts; border conflicts; British administration, conflict; cattle raids; Dinka people, conflicts; magicians, rivalries; Nuer chiefs, rivalries; Nuer people, conflicts; prophet rivalries; war
fighting expert (*ngul*) 63
finance for administration 11, 17, 20, 22
Finance Minister (Juba regional government) 318
fines 267, 268, 274
see also compensation
Fire (*mac*) 58
fishing-spear 94, 118, 140, 199, 251
fishing-spear, master of *see* spear-masters
fishing-spear, owner of 63
fishing-trap, owner of 62–3
Flesh (RING) 41, 58–9, 62, 83, 103, 282
floods 7, 55, 144, 252, 254
ABUK 41
affect prophet's careers 327–8
Ajuong 48, 49, 157
Bahr el-Ghazal 37, 45–6, 52
Bahr el-Jebel 45–6, 49, 52, 245, 247
Bahr el-Zeraf 49, 126, 131, 133, 139, 143, 145, 157
DENG LUAK's powers 148, 159
disputes 45, 143, 247–8
Lou territory (1917) 173, 210
Nuer expansion 37–8, 46, 48–9, 143, 210
'Pilual' (1916–18) 247–8, 252
spiritual centres 38–44
food relief 346, 351
food to attract followers 110, 111
foreigners:
and Deng Laka 156
expulsion of missionaries 315–16
'foreign' influences 24, 29
made masters 'by hand' 66
and Ngundeng Bong 114–22
see also adoption of strangers; Turuk
Foreigners, Battle of the (*c.*1890) 158
Fox, Robin Lane *x*
free-divinities 40, 59, 61, 67, 296, 329, 331
invoked by Ngundeng's songs 103–4
new idiom 254
proliferation 65–9, 203, 239, 276, 277, 278; *see also* DENG (divinity), variations
social recognition 138, 328
French Army at Fashoda 7
'frontier' Nuer, *see* Eastern Nuer
frontier, *see* border conflicts
funds, administration 11, 17, 20, 22

Gaadbal section (Gun Lou) 106, 110, 165, 184, 202
Ciec 79–81, 122
feuds 79, 105, 113, 123
Gaaguang earth-master 320
Gaajak section (E. Jikany) 53, 66, 74, 221, 304
conflicts 53, 77, 79, 305, 324, 342, 349, 350
Gaajok section (E. Jikany) 53, 74, 77, 79, 105, 115
Gaaleak clan 103
Gaaleak earth-masters 74
Gaaliek section (Mor Lou) 105, 168
Gaaluak Nyagh (Nyuong prophet) 248, 254, 255, 262, 275, 283, 360
conflict with British 6, 22, 26, 242, 260, 263–8 *passim*, 330
raids on Agar Dinka 257, 258
Gaaluak Yuac Liem 283
Gaatgankir clan 52, 53, 66, 74, 77, 103
Gaawar/Anglo-Egyptian government relations 12, 29, 32, 183, 259
border conflicts 22, 30, 167, 198, 209, 213, 228
discontinuity 222
military force 6, 13–14, 22, 171, 195, 208, 223, 224, 195
prophets 11, 22, 25, 26, 121, 141, 156, 160–3, 231; *see also under* Dual Diu
tribute 12, 207–8
Gaawar/Dinka conflicts 32, 156–63, 166, 167, 209–10
Bar Gaawar 49, 149, 158, 208–9, 213, 226–7, 249; *see also under* Deng Laka, Dual Diu
border conflicts 12, 167, 209–13, 225, 234, 314
cattle disputes 157, 170, 171, 210
Cuor Dinka 158, 159
Ghol Dinka 12, 148, 156–60, 170, 210 *passim*, 213, 227, 228
Gony Yut 302, 308
Guek Ngundeng 197–8
Luac Dinka 48, 49, 155, 157, 160
Macar Diu 207
Nyareweng Dinka 12, 33, 148, 156–60 *passim*, 167, 170, 227, 228
Pakuem battle 49, 51, 127
Twic Dinka 117, 148, 156–9 *passim*, 167, 207

Gaawar/Dinka relations 49, 157–63 *passim*
 adoption of Dinka, *see under* adoption of strangers
 alliances 85, 148, 238
 appropriation of Dinka territory 148–9
 assimilation of Dinka 66, 84, 126, 128, 142, 144
 intermarriage 149, 163, 165
 see also Gaawar/Dinka conflicts
Gaawar Nuer 127, 161, 221, 240–1, 255, 292
 age-sets 362, 363; *see also* Boiloc; Dang; Lier
 chiefs 141, 231, 293–5, 325
 conflicts: Dinka *see* Gaawar/Dinka conflicts; guerrilla warfare 302; internal 123, 143, 207, 241, 302, 303, 310; intertribal 167, 229, 302, 303, 308, 310; tribute collecting patrols 207–8; Zeraf merchants 130
 DENG and DIU 331, 332
 floods 126, 143
 friendship, Lou Nuer 149, 165, 222, 332
 kinship with Nyuong Nuer 254
 Lak/Gaawar Nuer alliance 158
 migrations 44, 48–51, 127–8
 mythology 45, 48, 50–1
 Nuaar Mer 126, 131–2, 133
 Pok Kerjiok 169, 170
 relations with Western Nuer 50, 127
 see also Bar Gaawar; Gaawar/Dinka relations; Gaawar prophets; Radh Gaawar
Gaawar prophets 282, 332
 British administration 11, 22, 25, 26, 121, 141, 156, 160–3
 see also Deng Laka; Dual Diu; Gatbuogh Yoal; Gony Yut
Gai Diu 145
Gai Jang 362
Gai Mot 89–90
Gai Tut, Samuel 342, 343
Galieth section (Nyawar Nyuong) 253, 254
Gambela 349
Gamuk section (Nyawar Nyuong) 253
Gang Wan 3
Ganwar clan 45, 50, 52
GÄR (divinity) 169, 316
GARANG (divinity) 40, 67
Garang, Col. Dr John 342, 343, 346, 347
Garang Ngundeng (oral testimonies) 3, 33–4, 90, 94, 116, 117–18, 334
Garjak, *see* Gaajak
Garluark, *see* Gaaluak Nyagh
Gatbuogh Yoal (Gaawar prophet) 223–4, 228, 229, 230, 231, 360
gatdonga (honorific name of divinity) 300–1
Gatkek Jiek 223, 269, 270, 272, 273
gatkuoth 61
Gatkuoth Dual 233
Gatkuoth Gual, Peter 113, 316–17, 318, 319
Gatnyal, *see* Buogh Kerpeil
Gau Bang 220, 228, 229, 231–2, 233, 294
Gaweir, *see* Gaawar Nuer
Gaweir March 222–9 *passim*
Gee (Nuer ancestor) 45, 50, 58
Gessi Pasha 245
Ghattas trading company 130
Ghol Dinka 47, 49, 54, 238
 British administration 30, 182
 chiefs *see* Monykuer Mabur
 Nuer/Dinka conflicts 12, 149, 156–60 *passim*, 170, 210, 213, 227, 228
 Nyareweng/Ghol alliance 12, 32, 156–60 *passim*, 167, 170, 227, 228
ghoro (shrine-stick) 63
ghosts, ancestral (*jok* or *Juok*) 60
Giet Majok 230
Gift of DENG 75
gift of life 83, 86–7, 113, 169–70, 230, 241
Gik Cam Jok 317
Gir Kuai (Peicy Loriat) 214
GOG (divinity) 216
Gok Dinka 247
Gony Yut (Gaawar prophet) 300–4, 328, 337, 349, 351, 360
 effects of war 311, 313, 325–6
 Mogogh conference 309–10
Good Things (*jiak leak*), Tree of 106, 107
Good Things (*pul leak*), Pool of 106, 107
Gordon, General C. G. 28, 131
GÖT (divinity) 100, 103, 119, 120, 121
gourds, fetish 155, 285
government chiefs, *see* Dinka people, chiefs; Nuer chiefs
government records *xi*, 32, 33, 93
government(s):
 discontinuity of Sudanese 290–1, 323–4
 Ethiopian 323, 342, 346
 influence prophetic traditions 289
 Ngundeng's songs 334
 Nuer's opposition 243
 see also British administration; Sudanese government(s); Turco-Egyptian regime
Grandmother, Battle of the (Mut Mandong *c*.1900) 155, 158, 159
grass and divinities 61, 248, 253
grasslands and grazing 37–8, 45, 47, 225, 234, 236, 237
grass, owner of (*guan juani*) 63
graves of prophets 200, 239, 328, 332, 348
guan biedh (owner of the fishing-spear) 63
guan bila (owner of *biel*) 61
guan juani (owner of grass) 63
guan kulang (owner of a fetish) 69
guan kuoth 61, 62, 73, 137, 248, 282
 see also *guk kuoth*

guan kuoth keca (owner of the dura-bird) 62
guan kuoth nyanga (owner of the crocodile) 62
guan muot or *guan tang* (owner of the spear-shaft) 63
guan thoi (owner of the fishing-trap) 62–3
guan wal (owner of magic) 69, 283
guan yiika (owner of the woman's sleeping mat) 63
guardians of the clan spear of WIU 52, 74, 103
Guek Ngundeng (Lou prophet) *x*, 98, 150, 166, 174, 175, 179, 282, 360
  conflict with British 21, 26, 27, 32, 33, 122, 125, 176–9, 182, 184–200, 202, 222, 329, 339, 340, 345, 350
  death 199, 200–3, 316, 321, 322, 330, 335
  Gaweir March 227
  Ngundeng Bong's teaching 125, 198, 199, 335
  peacemaker 105, 329
  rivalries *see under* prophet rivalries
guerrilla warfare 307, 322, 323, 342
  see also Anyanya; Anyanya II; SPLA; SPLM/SPLA
Guer Wiu 214, 218, 224, 231, 232, 360
Guet Thie 165, 175, 179, 360
  false rumours 190–1
  favoured by government 172, 176, 180
  rivalries 81, 166, 180, 189, 192, 202
GUIC-GUIC (divinity) 96
guk 30
guk kuoth 40, 73, 248, 282
  see also *guan kuoth*
Gun Lou section 53, 165, 172, 343
  feuds 105, 113, 114, 165, 173, 180–2
  prophets, *see* Babuny Kir; Car Koryom; Guek Ngundeng; Ngundeng Bong; Pok Kerjiok; Thijok Dul
  see also Gaadbal; Rumjok
gun traders 220–2
gwan nhial 62
Gwan riang (owner of Flesh) 58
Gwek Wendeng, *see* Guek Ngundeng

Haile Selassie I (1930–1974) 322, 338
'Hammer of the kujurs' 29
  see also Willis, C. A.
Hassan al-Turabi 323
Hassan Dafaʿallah 234, 235–6
healing 64, 85, 250, 289, 327, 329
  Gaawar prophets 155, 233, 241, 300, 302
  legitimate practice 295
  Lou prophets 87–8, 90, 95, 106, 113, 114, 175, 181
  miscarriage (childbirth) 63
  Ruac Col 299
  see also cattle disease, cures; infertility cures; medicine; sacrifice, for healing
health, public 17
heavenly, *see* sky
High Executive Council 318, 341
higlig tree 298, 306, 313
history and prophecy *ix*, 351, 352, 356
holy lake 27, 28, 256, 257
holy men (*sufi faqis*) 24
'homeland' Nuer, *see* Western Nuer
Honour, spear of 274
Hoth Can 75, 76
Hoth Nuaar 336
Howell, P. P. 31, 59, 64, 147
hunting 155, 220–1, 276
Hutchinson, S. 281, 291, 316
Hyena (*kor luny yak*), War of the 114
hymns, *see* songs

idioms, *see* social and religous idioms
illness, *see* chickenpox; epidemics; Kala Azar; seizure, illness; smallpox
immigrants, *see* migrant workers; migrations
imperial rule, *see* British Administration
independence, Southern Sudan 346
  see also Southern Sudan Regional Government
independence, Sudan (1956) 297
indirect rule, *see* native administration
individual rights 291
infertility cures (women) 85, 97, 113, 292, 329, 337
  Bangong Diau 304
  divinities 58, 75, 87, 96, 148
  Dual Diu 233
  Lou prophets 87, 95, 169–70
  Nyuong prophets 254, 277
  Tiep Kolang 255
inspectors renamed 16
intermarriage:
  Anglo/Dinka 267
  Anglo/Nuer 214, 335
  Anuak/Nuer 57, 165
  Lou/Gaawar 165, 184–5, 222
  Lou/Jikany 100, 165
  Nuer/Dinka 24, 45, 54, 64, 66, 112, 244–5; additional divinities 63; Gaawar Nuer 149, 163, 165; Jikany Nuer 47, 51, 52, 53, 244; Lou Nuer 112, 165, 168; maternal kinship 43, 57, 66, 70, 104; Nyuong Nuer 47; social and religious idioms 55; wives of Deng Laka 132–3, 160; wives of Ngundeng Bong 110
  Nyuong-Gaawar 222, 254
internal Nuer feuds 45–6
  Gaawar Nuer 123, 127, 139, 142–3, 143, 163, 167, 207, 229, 241, 302, 303
  Jikany Nuer 48, 53, 77, 79, 105, 305

internal Nuer feuds (*cont.*):
  Lak Nuer 49, 130, 139, 302–4, 303
  Lou Nuer 105, 113, 114, 123, 130, 164, 165, 173, 180–1, 229, 302, 308, 310
  Nyuong Nuer 253, 262, 263, 268, 274
invocation, *see* prayer
Islam 24, 29, 291, 296, 323, 340, 346
  immigrants 305
  militants 323, 340, 341, 346, 350, 353
  Mujahidin volunteers 350
  Tang Kuainy 281
Israel, prophets of 31, 32, 114
Itang 349, 350
ivory 93, 114, 130, 220–1, 344, 345

jaang (Dinka) 54
Jackson, H. C. 26, 177–8
Jagei Nuer 45, 52, 245, 247, 258–9
  Evans-Pritchard 282
  prophets, *see* Kolang Ket; Nyapuka Dan; Nyaruac Kolang
  see also Rengyan
Jakar clan 45, 52
Jal, Gabriel 44, 52, 53, 362
Jaloh clan 50, 51
Jambiel 131
James, Wendy *xiii*, 307, 351
Jamogh section 132, 143, 156, 227
Jang (Uduk *arum* man) 306
Jesus, parallels with 315–16
Jiaar (Western Jikany prophet) 325
JIAR WAN (divinity) 281, 301, 312
jiath jiakni (Tree of Bad Things) 106, 107, 200
jiath leak (Tree of Good Things) 106, 107
jidoar people of the bush 240
Jikany Nuer 51, 90, 103, 115, 144, 176
  age-sets 47, 362, 363
  anthropological studies 44, 282, 291
  conflicts: Anuak 12, 53, 54, 77–8, 124, 305; Dinka 46, 47, 52, 245; guerrilla warfare 302, 345; internal and Meban 305
  friendship: with Anuak 51, 53–4. 77; with Lou 53, 54, 77–8, 165, 173
  intermarriage, Dinka 47, 52, 244
  lineage structure 66, 74
  migrations 48, 51–5, 74, 244
  see also Eastern Jikany; Western Jikany
Jimem clan 52
Jimem earth-master lineage 45, 84
Jinaca clan 48, 66, 103, 104
Jok Diet 134
JOK (divinity) 138, 144, 152
jokpading (ox sacrificed at Pading) 108
jok (Power) 41, 60, 64
Jok Wol Diu (Gaawar prophet) 313, 314–15, 325, 326, 351
Jonglei canal 341–2
Jonglei Investigation Team 32–3, 242
Jonglei Province 319, 323, 324
jong piny (earth Powers) 60
Jor, Lake attack 271
Juac Battle of (Mut Juaca 1890s) 158
Juba 309, 318, 323
judicial systems:
  British administration and security 9, 11, 14–15
  Guek Ngundeng's 176, 177–8
  Ngundeng Bong's 104, 305
  see also native courts; Sudan Penal Code
Juet 81, 84, 89, 113
jujumen 27
Jul Luak 132
juok, see *jok*
Jur-Beli 27, 28, 69

Kababish Arabs 23
Kai Riek (Leek Nuer prophet) 312
Kala Azar disease 324, 325
KAL (divinity) 144, 152
Kan Boi 207, 210–11
Karam age-set 217, 363
Kar (Nuer myth) 50–1
Keij 90
KERBIEL (divinity) 223, 224
KERCIEK (divinity) 40
Kerjiok Dieu 169
Kerjiok Laka 132
Kerpeil section (Radh Gaawar) 142, 217, 227
  Nuaar Mer 130, 131, 132, 133, 142
Kerreri, SGS 267, 270
Khandak 130
Khartoum 316, 336, 350
  attempted coup (1976) 322, 323
  British administration 7, 15
  central government 340, 341, 343, 346
  fall of (1885) 115
  mutiny (1924) 17, 18
Khor Atar Dinka 32
Khor Fulluth Dinka 10, 13, 54, 156, 165
  conflicts with Nuer 111, 160, 169
Khor Yirkou column 263–4, 265
kic clans 66
king (*reth*) 40
kinship 56–7, 100, 104, 185, 291
  see also agnatic kinship; intermarriage; maternal kinship
Kir, (Jikany ancestor) 51, 53, 66
Koat-Liec 45, 50, 312
koat (tamarind tree) 45, 90
Kolang Ket (Jagei Prophet) 243, 249–51, 285, 325, 360
  Buom Diu 248, 263
  conflicts: with British 257, 258–9, 261–2, 263, 264, 265, 330; with Rek Dinka 247,

248, 252, 257, 258, 262, 265–6
curse of 249, 272
grandson's seizure 325
Kai Riek 312
predictions 249, 335
Kom Joar 320
Kom Tudel 266, 360
Kong, Gordon 344, 346
Kongor 160, 347, 348
Kong Pan 181
kor luny yak 114, 165, 173
kor rialbeagh 170–1, 172
Koryom Bidiet 167
'Kotnyangdor', (Capt. A. H. A. Alban) 32, 275, 335
kuaar, definition of 59
kuaar muon, see earth-master
kuaar rieng (master of the Flesh) 83
kuaar thoi (water master) 293
kuaar yiika 63
Kuacdeng (*let*) 127
Kuaideng area 347
Kuaijien (Lou prophet) 320–2
KUAIJOK DENG (divinity) 152
Kuanylualthoan 115
kuar ghok (cattle-masters) 73
kuar see earth-masters
kuar tuac (earth-masters) 73
Kuçuk Ali 130
Kuec clan ancestors 50, 51
kueijiok (ox-name for DENG) 103
Kuei (*let*) 127
Kuerjak shrine 143
Kueth Peat 192, 202, 344
Kuil Dinka 245
kujur 30
as British term 6, 21, 22, 25, 29, 265
'hammer of the kujurs' 29
as Northern Sudanese term 290
'*kujur* conspiracy' 21, 22
kulang (pl. *kulangni*) 69, 97, 155, 284
talking Powers 60–1, 218, 283
see also magic, fetishes
Kulang Majok (oral testimonies) 134, 136, 139, 145, 150, 156, 337
Kun Thoan (Gaaguang earth-master and prophet) 320
Kuny Nyang (Lou chief) 229
Kuol Kolang 279
Kuony Gol 118–19, 164, 335
kuoth biedh (tutelary divinity) 282
kuoth (Divinity) 60, 61, 102, 282
kuoth duanga 283
see also sky divinities
kuoth dit (great Divinity) 73
kuoth juaini (tutelary divinity) 63, 282
kuoth nhial 60, 283, 295
kuoth, Nyin Nguen's 293–4, 295
KUOTH PINY (divinity) 240
kuoth piny (lower power) 282, 295
kuoth rieng (tutelary divinity) 282
kuoth yiika 63
Kurmuk 346
kuuth nhial, see free-divinities
kuuth piny (magical substances) 61
'Kwoin medicine man' 247, 256
kwoth (rain) 60

Laang Gaajok (E. Jikany) 53–4, 77, 79
Lagu, Joseph 318, 319
Lake Jor attack 271
Lakes Province 324
Lak Nuer 12, 48, 49, 66
conflicts: Gaawar 49, 303; guerrilla warfare 302, 342, 348; Ruei Kuic 302–4
Deng Laka 144, 147, 158
Nuaar Mer 130, 133, 139
prophets, *see* Ruac Col; Ruei Kuic; Wut Nyang
Lam Akol, Dr 346
Lam Liew 170, 173, 222, 227
lam, see prayer
Lam Tutthiang (Rumjok man-of-cattle) 98, 119, 166–7, 177, 361
as government chief 172, 175–6
Ngundeng Bong's rival 98, 179, 202, 334
land, pasturage 45, 47
land rights 128, 253
Dinka land appropriated 46, 55, 57, 148–9
Ghol Dinka/Gaawar dispute 210, 213
Lang section (Gun Lou) 3
language:
'linguistic parallax' *x*
Nuer/Dinka similarities 140
problems of communication 267, 268
see also Dinka language; Lwo language; Nuer language; social and religious idioms; terminology
Latjor Dingyang (Jikany leader) 52, 53, 77
'Latjor Dingyan' (C. H. Armstrong) 230
Lau, *see* Lou Nuer
Lau mission station 247, 256
Lau river 245
law, *see* judicial systems; native administration; Sudan Penal Code
leadership, Nuer concept of 185
Leak section 103
Lee, John 16
Leek, Jonathan Malual 319
Leek Nuer 52, 250, 284, 312
anthropological studies 243, 244, 282, 291
left-handedness 76, 112, 113, 345
legal system, *see* judicial systems
legitimacy of Nuer chiefs, *see under* Nuer chiefs,

legitimacy of Nuer chiefs (*cont.*):
British administration
Leik section (Nyal Nyuong) 253
Lek Jiel 132
Lel Lublub 218
Lel Ngundeng 297
leopard-skin (*tuac*) 58, 108, 141, 142
Ler 259
let 127–8, 160
Lia Wel (Dok Prophet) 276, 277, 278
Lienhardt, Godfrey *x*, 42, 56, 57–8, 59–60, 68, 333
Lier, age-set 145, 147, 363
life, *see* gift of life
light and lightening 61, 254, 265
Lili Goak Ruot 309
lineage 56, 57, 63, 161
divinities 100, 142, 325, 346
see also dominant lineage; earth-master lineage
lion (*let*) 160
Lirpiou, spear of 67, 317
Lithgai age-set 362–3
local courts, *see* judicial systems; native courts
local police 9, 16, 17, 184, 186, 307
locust swarm dispersed 293–4, 295
Loh 50
Loic-Rek Dinka 248
Longar, *see* Aiwel Longar; Puom Longar
Lou/Anglo-Egyptian government relations 13, 32, 170, 176, 183, 321–2
border conflicts 12, 22, 30, 167, 198
Lou hostages taken 201
military force 4, 6, 10, 13, 15, 21, 117, 125, 160, 171–2, 195, 209, 223
prophets 22, 23, 166–8, 200; *see also under* Ngundeng Bong; Guek Ngundeng
tribute 12
'witch doctors' conspiracy 21
Lou/Dinka conflicts 12–13, 85, 111, 189, 197–8
Bor Dinka 13, 167, 168, 169, 170–1, 172
Ngok Dinka 49, 112
Ngundeng Bong's lifetime 112, 123
Nyareweng 84, 112, 167
Rumjok Gun Lou 169, 227
Twic Dinka 167, 168, 169
see also Pading Battle
Lou Nuer 45, 110, 130, 144, 320, 360–1, 363
chiefs 185, 187–8, 189, 229
conflicts: with Anuak 12, 53, 54, 77–8, 124, 165–6, 167, 168, 173, 221; with Dinka, *see* Lou/Dinka conflicts; with Gaawar 167, 229, 302, 308, 310; guerrilla warfare 302, 342, 343, 345; internal 105, 113, 123, 165, 179; with Mahdists 114, 116
Dinka/Lou relations 66, 67, 83–4, 112, 128, 131, 165, 229, 319, 348; *see also* Lou/Dinka conflicts
earth-masters 74
environmental pressures 49, 173, 210, 348
Evans-Pritchard 283
friendship, Gaawar 32, 149, 165, 222, 332
Jikany/Lou relations 53, 77–8, 103, 105, 325
migrations 48, 52, 169
Ngundeng's relics 319
sacrificial sites, *see* Ngundeng's Mound
slavery 114
Zeraf Nuer, split with 350
see also Gun Lou: Lou/Anglo-Egyptian government relations; Lou prophets; Mor Lou
Lou prophets 22, 23, 125, 331, 332, 337
intimidated 200
as peacemakers 203
reappearance 166–78
rivalries 166, 178–85, 198–9, 203
see also Babuny Kir Nyak; Car Koryom; Guek Ngundeng; Kuaijien; Ngundeng Bong; Pok Kerjiok; Thijok Dul; Yuot Guoguok *and also* under Lou/Anglo-Egyptian government relations
lower Powers, *see* earthly Powers
'loyal' contenders, appointment of 23
Luac age-set 174, 175, 363
Luac Dinka 30, 41–2, 47
Nuaar Mer 133, 156
Nuer/Luac conflicts 48, 49, 155, 156, 157, 160, 302
Luac section (Nyal Nyuong) 253, 254, 274
Luak Deng 89
Luak Kuoth, *see* Luang Deng and Ngundeng's Mound
Luang Deng shrine 40, 87, 113, 156, 331, 332
abandoned 49, 67
Car Koryom 168
Dinka songs 95
Dual Diu 219
mythology 51
prophet rivalries 147–8, 292
Luang Deng shrine-master 40, 300, 301, 302, 325
Luang (Puom) Aiwel shrine 40, 42, 43–4, 93–4, 313
Lueth Ayong (oral testimony) 156
Luo people, *see* Shilluk-Luo
Lwo language 55
Lwo-speaking peoples 38, 56, 60, 64

Maadni Lia (Dok prophet) 283
MAANI (divinity) 219, 258, 272, 289, 310, 313, 331, 332
Kolang Ket 243, 248, 249, 325

Nyaruac Kolang 279, 284–5
seizure 265, 312, 325
songs 257, 283, 312
Wol Athiang 247, 250
Mabur Ajuot 158, 159, 160, 207
Macar Diu 142, 146, 205, 241, 360
conflict with government 12, 207–8
feud with Dual Diu 206–7, 211
Macar Teny 292–3, 294, 298, 325, 330
mac (Fire) 58
MacMichael, Sir Harold 6, 17, 28, 29, 183
Macot Nyuon (Dok Nuer prophet) 249, 360
Madhir Lam 193
Madi, *see* MAANI
Madni 332
Maffey, Sir John 21, 29
magic 58, 152, 253, 256, 316, 328
Azande 69
Azande *mani* society 27, 332
earthly Powers 60, 69, 282, 295, 332
fetishes 60–1, 97, 155, 283, 285, 296
magical substances 60, 61, 69
owner of (*guan wal*) 69, 283
prophets' opposition 97, 155, 163, 250, 285, 304, 325, 328–9
spread of 295–6
see also kulang; magicians; magic roots; *wal*; witchcraft
magicians 65, 117, 282, 332
Bul Kan as 98, 117
Cany Reth as 217–18
government opposition 200, 202, 295–6
guan wal (owner of magic) 69, 283
Guet Thie as 179, 180
Lam Tutthiang as 98
opposed by prophets 96–8, 155, 218–19, 222, 239–40, 249, 284, 285
rivalries 127, 216–17, 261, 262
spiritual figures 296, 328
Tiep Kolang as 248, 260
Wuon Kuoth as 274, 275, 277, 285
see also magic; witchcraft
magic roots 255, 265, 273, 283–4
Mahdi 24, 25, 281, 332, 353
Mahdist wars 5, 24, 65
Deng Laka 158–9, 162
Ngundeng Bong 114, 115, 116
Maiker-Jak section (Gun Lou) 168
Majok Juc 134, 136, 139, 140, 149–50
Majok Kolang 258, 261, 262, 263
Maker age-set 53, 363
Malakal 346, 348, 349
attack on 350–1
prophets detained 201, 230, 231, 233, 237–8, 271, 273, 309, 311
Maleak earth-masters 66, 74
Malou Nuer settlement 52–3, 54, 77
Malual Leek, Jonathan 319
Malual section (Gun Lou) 81
ma'mur and sub-*ma'mur* 9
Mandari people 250
MANDIU (divinity) 155, 254
MANDONG, *see* Nyacan Ruea
mani society 332
mantic activity 173, 327
Nilotes 35
predating Nuer prophets 61–4
prophetic activity redefined *xi*
prophetic idiom 248, 254
see also blessings; curse(s); desacralization; healing; prayer; predictions; rainmaking; resurrection; sacrifice
mantic figures 62
see also dayiemni; Dinka people, prophets; magicians; master; masters; mediums; men of cattle; men of Divinity; Nuer prophets; owner of
Marno, E. 114
MARPINY (divinity) 298, 299, 300, 301–2
marriage, *see* intermarriage; kinship; wives
master of the clan-divinity 40
master of the fishing spear, *see* spear-master
master of Flesh 83
masters, *see* earth-masters; master of; shrine-master; water-master
maternal kinship 57, 79, 113, 184–5
Dinka/Nuer 43, 57, 66, 70, 104
maternal uncles 66, 70, 79
maternal transmission of divinity 76
Mathot Yieth Cung 304
Matit Kal 150, 219
Matthews, Maj. G. E.:
administrative method 9, 10, 11, 12, 118
Deng Laka 25, 121, 161–2
Ngundeng Bong 121–2
matthiang goh magic 256
MAYAN DENG (divinity) 152
Mayan Lam 98, 180, 191–2
MAYAN YIETH TUT (divinity) 134, 154
Mayom Kuai (earth-master) 142
Meban people 13, 305
mediators 57, 59, 83, 105
see also peacemakers
medicine 68–9, 97, 120, 120–1, 289
co-opted by government 267
see also healing; *wal*
'medicine man' attacked Lau mission 247, 256
mediums, Shona spirit 355
meeting at Fangak (1972) 309
men of cattle 58, 61, 83, 253, 254, 290
see also Bakkam; Gaaluak Nyagh; Lam Tutthiang; Nyin Nguen
men of Divinity (*ran nhialic*) 59, 64, 70

men of Divinity (*ran nhialic*) (*cont.*):
see also Arianhdit
men dyor 43
see also spear master
Mengistu government of Ethiopia 346
merchant companies, Zeraf 84, 130–1
Mer Teny 128, 130, 360
Meshra el-Rek 68, 245, 247, 248
message of prophets *ix*, *x*
see also predictions
metal rings for judicial system 104, 176, 305
Michel, Charles 46
migrant workers 231, 291, 305, 316
migrations 36–8, 47, 48, 244
see also Nuer expansion
militant Islam 323, 340, 341, 346, 350, 353
military administration, Anglo-Egyptian 7, 17
security before justice 9, 11, 14–15
tribute collecting patrols 11–12, 14–15, 16, 169, 207–8, 209
versus civil administration 8, 9, 10, 11–12, 14–15, 16, 21
see also military force
military force, Anglo-Egyptian:
against Guek Ngundeng 192, 193, 194–5, 199
against Macar Diu 207–8
against Ngundeng Bong 101, 116, 117–18, 121, 160
against Nuer prophets (1917) 13, 171–2, 175, 195
against Nuer prophets (1922–3) 258–9, 260–1, 263
against Nuer prophets (1924–7) 263–4, 265–6, 271
against Nuer prophets (1926–34) 4, 6, 10, 13, 14, 15, 22, 195, 222–6
Buom Diu's dance 275
Fergusson's death 242
Nuer settlement 198, 229
Royal Air Force 21, 33, 192, 193, 195, 350
military force, Sudanese army 312
military, *see* Anglo-Egyptian army; French army; guerrilla warfare; Mahdist wars; military administration; military force; Sudanese army
Milner Commission (1919–20) 15–16
Minister of Finance, Peter Gatkuoth as 318
Minister for Southern affairs 316
miscarriage (childbirth) 63
missions and missionaries 29, 243, 256, 264, 315–16
see also Christianity
Missiriya Arab nomads 312, 326
Mogogh 131, 133, 139
Mogogh Battle (1879) 140, 156
Mogogh conference (1975) 309–10, 311
money and social relationships 291
Mongalla Province 18, 20, 166, 167, 170
border disputes 12–13, 209, 210
Monykuer Mabur (Ghol Dinka chief) 182, 213, 225, 231, 232, 237, 238
moral community:
divinities and social bonds 100, 124, 136, 138, 142, 329
fragmentation 296
Nilotic communities *x*, 56, 57
peacemakers 57–8, 70, 104
prophetic idiom 289, 328
reaffirmed and redefined 43, 57, 70, 107, 124
supported by prophets *ix*, 35, 36, 104, 105, 106, 111, 163, 296, 327, 351, 352
see also social networks; social order
Mor Lou 53, 106, 110, 119, 198, 342
feuds 105, 109, 113, 114, 123, 165, 168, 173, 180–2
intermarriage, Anuak and Jikany 165
see also Gaaliek
Moses Cot 341, 344
Moses Cuol Juac 309
mother's brother relationship 66, 79, 113, 184–5
motor car for Ayod 15
Muhammed Ahmad al-Mahdi 24, 353
Mujahidin volunteers, Islamic 350
muok 76
Muot Dit 149, 201
muot sacrifice 65, 172
Muot Tot 169
Muot Tot Battle (1917) 171, 172
Murle people 54, 93, 158, 320
Muslim Brothers 323
muslims, *see* Islam
Mut Dung 4
mut ghama (spear of Jinaca) 103
mutinies:
Akobo (1975) 320
Bor garrison (1983) 323, 341, 342
Equatorial Corps. (1955) 237, 298, 302
Khartoum (1924) 17, 18
Mut Juaca (Juac Battle 1890s) 158
Mut Mandong (Battle of the Grandmother *c.*1900) 155, 158, 159
Mut Roal (Battle of the Foreigners 1890s) 158
mut WIU (spear of Gaatgankir) 103
Mwari shrines 295
mythology 40, 41, 43, 45–6, 143, 355–6
see also Aiwel Longar; ancestor myths

nabi 'isas (prophet Jesuses) 24
NAI (magic root) 255, 265, 283–4
Nasir 323, 344, 350

British administration 7, 14, 16, 114–15
coup (1991) 346, 347, 349
Nasir Muhammed 131
national army, *see* Sudanese army
National Guards, Gony Yut's 302, 303
National Islamic Front 323
National Reconciliation (1977) 323
native administration, British 21, 23, 28, 29, 182–3, 280
customary law 10, 17, 330
decline of Flesh 59
Dual Diu 204, 241
structure 16, 231
see also Dinka people, chiefs; native courts; Nuer chiefs, British administration; Nuer chiefs, rivalries
native courts, British administration 7, 16, 181–2, 184, 330
Buom Diu 274, 275
Dual Diu's exile 232
Fergusson's administration 257, 267
fines 267, 268, 274
fragmentation of moral community 296
sectional heads 290
see also native administration; Nuer chiefs, British administration; Nuer chiefs, rivalries
native courts, Sudanese administration 291, 307
see also Nuer chiefs, rivalries; Nuer chiefs, Sudanese administration
nature sprites (*biel*) 61
Ngok Dinka 23, 51, 54, 132, 144
Ngundeng Bong 90, 111, 112, 121
Nuer/Ngok conflicts 48, 49, 112
ngol rietni (Rambang Thiciot) 102, 343
Ngony 261
ngul (fighting expert) 63
Ngundeng Bong (Lou prophet) *vii*, *x*, 70, 73–125, 282, 283, 360
Aiwel Longar 73, 74, 75, 76, 85, 94, 95, 112, 124, 352
baton 86, 109, 113, 118, 190, 317, 318
birth and early years 74–6, 77
blessings 87, 109, 122, 124, 315
comparison with Deng Laka 126–7, 151, 154, 163
conflict with British 4, 10, 11, 13, 26, 101, 119, 122, 124–5, 126, 164; *see also under* military force
crisis and 31–2, 124
curses 98, 109–10, 112, 338–9
death 3–5, 121–2, 330
as earth-master 74, 78, 83–4, 119, 124
friendship with Dinka 110, 111, 121
healing powers 87–8, 90, 95, 113, 124
legacy 122–5, 164, 166, 203, 351
model for other prophets 73, 166, 169, 297, 305, 315, 325, 337
oral testimonies 73–4, 122
overcame problem of legitimate authority over land 128
parallels with Jesus 315–16
peacemaker 82, 83, 85, 95, 104–14, 123, 125, 330
prayers 103–4, 348
relics 299, 300, 317–19, 320
sacrifices 82, 85, 88, 90, 95, 113, 117, 122, 124
sceptics 333
shrines 10, 32, 89, 94; *see also* Ngundeng's Mound
teachings in relation to Guek Ngundeng 125, 199, 198, 335
Thut age-set 70, 77
wives 110, 222
see also Ngundeng Bong's *dayiemni*; Ngundeng Bong's family; Ngundeng Bong's predictions; Ngundeng Bong's songs; pipe, Ngundeng Bong's; *and also under* cattle, prophet's: DENG (divinity); prophet rivalries; seizure
Ngundeng Bong's *dayiemni* 95–6, 98, 99, 100, 297, 331
after his death 164, 165–6
duties 104, 106, 108, 109, 110
modern Lou views on 122
songs 101, 102, 119, 120, 343
Ngundeng Bong's family 164–6, 173, 297
blood-money for Guek 321
Ngundeng's relics 319
see also Guek Ngundeng
Ngundeng Bong's predictions 81, 100, 113, 149, 202
his own death 3, 5, 151
his son Guek 150, 174
Pading Battle 334
reinterpretations *vii*, *viii*, 166, 316, 317, 324, 330–1, 334–53
Ngundeng Bong's songs 82, 86, 92, 95, 98, 99, 125, 283, 332
arabic words 115, 116
conflict with government 122
dayiemni 101, 102, 119, 120, 343
decline of Mound 119
Deng Laka 149, 151
Dol Pajok 150
for peace 105, 117
propaganda 101–4, 124
reinterpretations 316, 334, 336–8, 343–4
sung by Lel Ngundeng 297
to invoke clan-divinities 103–4
Ngundeng's Mound 43, 109, 119, 122, 124, 305, 328, 332

Ngundeng's Mound (*cont.*):
comparisons with other shrines 126, 151, 313
construction 88–101
Guek Ngundeng 175, 190, 193, 198–200, 335
ivory 93, 344, 345
raided by government 32, 93, 116, 117, 175, 194–5
return of relics 318, 319
sacrificial site 106, 315
spiritual and political centre 90, 99, 100, 105, 106, 126, 151, 154
Yuot Guoguok 297, 304
nhialic (Divinity) 60
see also Divinity
nhial (sky) 60
Nile river, *see* Upper Nile
Nilotic communities:
constant change 35–6, 327
mantic activity 35
populations 357–9
social and religious idioms 55–65
Nimeiri, President Gaafar Mohammed El 302, 317, 323, 342
Northern Dinka 58
Northern Sudanese 290, 298, 299, 323, 332, 340, 341, 342
see also Sudanese governments (1956–72)
Nuaar Mer 51, 67, 84, 156, 327, 345, 360
adopted by Nuer 128, 142
compared with Deng Laka 126, 128–41
feuds 85, 130–2, 133, 138, 139, 140, 141, 142, 163
Nuang Lol ('Farag Osman') 161
Nuba Mountain Province 12, 257
Nuer chiefs, British administration 9, 59, 229, 234
Cany and Dual 217–18
Dual Diu as paramount chief 184, 204, 217
Fergusson 266, 267, 268, 269
Gaawar 141, 231, 293–5
Guek Ngundeng and Lou chief meetings 187–8, 189
legitimacy and loyalty 23, 25, 26, 141, 177, 185, 215, 223, 263
new class of 20, 23, 25, 26, 27, 172, 329
paramount chiefs abolished 190
power controlled 16, 183, 231, 272, 273–4, 275, 290
tribal chiefs incorporated 16, 17, 178, 181, 182, 189, 215, 273, 290
Western Nuer prophets reinstated 272–6
see also native administration; Nuer chiefs, rivalries; Nuer chiefs, Sudanese administration
Nuer chiefs, rivalries 127, 141, 259, 263, 268, 294, 309, 329
Nuer chiefs, Sudanese administration 320
Nuer expansion 44–55
conflicts 46, 124, 127, 143
environmental influences 37, 37–8, 46, 47, 48, 54, 143, 210, 244
growth in free-divinities 65, 328
Jikany Nuer 48, 51–5, 74, 244
men-of-cattle 83, 253
Nuer language 55, 110, 141
Nuer people 45, 243, 244, 291
Anglo-Egyptian administration, *see* British administration; conflicts: with Anuak, *see* Anuak people, conflicts; with British administration, *see under* British administration; with Dinka, *see* Dinka/Nuer conflicts; guerrilla warfare 302, 342–3; internal, *see* internal Nuer feuds; with Meban 13, 305; with Shilluk 53; with Zeraf merchants 130
Dinka/Nuer relationships, *see* Dinka/Nuer conflicts; Dinka/Nuer relations
friendships with Anuak 46, 53–4, 57, 77, 93, 165, 355
section (*cieng*) 56, 360–1
similarities with other Nilotes 56, 57, 58–9, 60, 64, 68
slavery 9, 52
Sudan government 334
as warrior race 5–6, 13, 21, 22, 30, 44, 56, 256
see also adoption of strangers; age-set system; Bul; Dok; Eastern Nuer; Gaawar; Jagei; Jikany; kinship; Lak; Leek; Lou; Nuer chiefs, British administration; Nuer chiefs, British administration; Nuer chiefs, rivalries; Nuer chiefs, Sudanese administration; Nuer expansion; Nuer prophets; Nyuong; social order; Thiang; Western Nuer
Nuer prophets 327–34, 355, 360, 361
Evans-Pritchard on power of 30–1
graves of 200, 239, 328, 332, 348
misconceptions 5, 29, 242, 243
oppose magic 97, 155, 163, 250, 285, 304, 325, 328–9
parallels with Jesus 315–16
'priest' and prophet dichotomy 59, 141
religious idioms 243, 248, 254, 327, 328
Sudanese governments (1956–72) 234, 235–6, 237, 238, 240, 241, 291, 297–307
war *xi*, *xii*, 173, 240–1, 243, 289, 297–307, 300, 311, 320, 324, 353
see also careers of prophets; cattle, prophets'; crisis; Gaawar prophets; Lou prophets; mantic activities; message of prophets; moral community, and prophets;

peacemakers, Nuer prophets; prophet rivalries; suppression; tolerance; Western Nuer prophets; *and also under* British administration; Eastern Nuer; Southern Sudan Regional Government
Nuer religion (Evans-Pritchard E. E.) *vii*
Nuer Settlement (1928–9) 6, 22, 30, 33, 98, 231
armed assistance 198, 229
Guek's involvement 186–200
Nyabor section (Mor Lou) 119
Nyacan Ruea 155, 159, 254
Nyadong 254, 272, 273
Nyaduong (Ngundeng's wife) 97, 174
Nyai Car cattle disease 252
Nyajani section (E. Jikany Gaajak) 305
Nyajikany-Rumjok section (Gun Lou) 171, 193, 227, 315
Nyak Kuic 192
Nyak Nguol (Lou elder) 4
NYAKOLANG (divinity) 312
Nyakong Bar (Gaajak prophetess) 98–9
Nyal Nyuong Nuer 253
NYANCAR (divinity) 40
nyangaat medicine 120–1
Nyang Kuac Agok, *quoted* 151
Nyang Macar (Cotrial) 139, 141
Nyang Yuot 98
Nyanhial 229
Nyanjiek (Captain Alban's wife) 335
NYANWIR (divinity) 239
Nyanyai Kal, oral testimony 145
Nyapuka Dan 249, 279, 282, 360
Nyareweng Dinka 30, 41–2, 54
chiefs, *see* Deng Malual
Ghol/Nyareweng alliance 12, 32, 156–60 *passim*, 167, 170, 227, 228
Lou Nuer friendships 111, 112, 121, 165, 168, 319
Nuer/Dinka conflicts, 12, 33, 84, 148, 156–60 *passim*, 167, 170, 227, 228
Nyarkuac section (Gaadbal Gun Lou) 105
Nyaruac Kolang (Jagei prophetess) 283, 284–5, 304, 312, 326, 332–3, 360
British administration 279, 280–1
rivalries 265, 266, 281
Ruei Kuic 301, 302, 325
Sudanese government 298
Nyatot Kun (Ngundeng's wife) 81
Nyawang Lul (Deng Laka's wife) 150
Nyawar Nyuong Nuer 253
Nyayiel (Ngundeng's mother) 75–6
Nyerol, British administration 172, 176, 177, 179, 193
Nyiel Dinka 52
NYIKANG (divinity) 40, 55
Nyin Nguen 293–5, 325, 360
Nyok Biciuk (Maiker chief) 168
Nyot 51
Nyuon Bany, William 343, 344, 347, 348
Nyuong Nuer 50, 284
conflicts with British 32, 223, 276–8; *see also under* Gaaluak Nyagh; Wuon Kuoth
conflicts with Dinka 48, 49, 156–60 *passim*, 245, 247–8, 255–63 *passim*, 271
conflicts, internal 253, 262–3, 268, 274
friendships with Dinka 47, 244
Gaawar kinship 222, 254
Kolang Ket 250, 263
prophets 248, 253–6; *see also* Gaaluak Nyagh; Teng Joak; Wuon Kuoth

official records xi 32, 33, 93
Old Testament prophets *ix*, 31, 32, 114
Omdurman 249
Omdurman Battle (1898) 7, 258, 261
Operation Lifeline Sudan, UN *xii*, 315
opposition theory, structural 141
oral testimony *x*, 34
original settlers 128, 131, 148–9
dominant lineages of 65–7, 83, 131
ostrich associated with NAI 284
O'Sullivan, Capt. H. D. E. 4, 9, 11, 25, 122, 123, 165
Owen, R. C. R. 12
owner:
of *biel* (*guan bila*) 61
of a divinity *see guan kuoth*
of the dura-bird (*guan kuoth keca*) 62
of a fetish (*guan kulang*) 69
of the fishing-spear (*guan biedh*) 63
of the fishing-trap (*guan thos*) 62–3
of Flesh (*gwan riang*) 58
of grass (*guan juani*) 63
of magic (*guan wal*) 69, 283
of the spear-shaft (*guan tang*) 63
of the woman's sleeping mat (*guan yiika*) 63
ox and oxen 102, 225, 251
see also Dang-gonga age-set; sacrifice, oxen

Pacier 49, 51, 144, 157
Padang Dinka 52, 53, 54, 165
Paddoi 149
Padiak 168
Padicier 143
Pading Battle (1878) 86, 95, 96, 118, 124, 125
aftermath 156
crisis theory 327
Lou stories 149
Ngundeng's baton 113, 190
Ngundeng's predictions 334
Nuaar Mer followers 139
ox sacrifice 85, 108
precedent for Guek 190, 199

paduil see Ngundeng's Mound
Paduom age-set 220, 362–3
Paguir (*let*) 127
PAJOK (divinity) 40, 67, 96, 152, 239
Pakol Nyakong 83, 84
Pakuem battle (1830s) 49, 51, 127
Palker-Rumjok section (Gun Lou) 193, 227
pal see prayer-meeting
Pan Bior Twic chiefly lineage 161
Panyang 79
paramount chiefs abolished 290
Pariath clan, Abiem Dinka 27
pastoralists 37
pastoral visits 291–2
pasturage 37–8, 45, 47, 225, 234, 236, 237
paternal kinship 57
Pawarjak 51
Pawson, A. G. 230
peace:
  after Addis Ababa agreement 307–19
  brought by divinity 112, 113, 168, 252, 276, 321–2, 349
  brought by President Nimeiri 323
  sacrifices and ceremonies for 104, 234, 238, 319
  symbols of 112, 113, 276
peacemakers 28, 59, 66, 142, 316
  moral community 57–8, 70, 104
  see also mediators; peacemakers, Nuer prophets
peacemakers, Nuer prophets *xi*, 260, 266, 324, 330, 353
  Bangong Diau 304–6, 309, 311, 313
  British administration as rival 329
  Car Koryom 168
  Deng Laka 142–3, 146, 163
  Dual Diu 215, 217–18, 222, 238, 241
  Guek Ngundeng 105, 329
  Kolang Ket 250, 258
  Lou prophets as 203
  Nyaruac Kolang 280, 326
  Ruei Kuic 313, 324
  Thijok Dul 165–6
  Wut Nyang 348, 349, 350
  see also under Ngundeng Bong
Penal Code, Sudan 10
people of the bush (*jidoar*) 240
person of the king (*reth*) 40, 43
peth, *see* 'evil eye'
peth (witchcraft) 58, 150–1, 155
Pet Juol 109
Pibor river *vii*, 77
Pieri 320
Pilate Pasha (Faussett, M) 24–5
Pilual age-set 216, 220, 362–3
'pilual' (flood 1918–19) 247–8, 252
pipe, Ngundeng Bong's 120, 121, 166, 175, 199
  return of 299, 300, 317–19
plagues, *see* epidemics
Poetry and Prophecy (Nora Chadwick) 35
Pok Kerjiok (Lou prophet) 166, 169–72, 175, 178, 223, 316, 360
  conflict with government 170–3, 195, 197, 201, 230, 231, 330
  divinity passed to son 297, 325
  Gaweir March 227
  Guek Ngundeng 198
police, local 9, 16, 17, 184, 186, 307
political fragmentation of society 63, 70
political networks, Ngundeng's Mound 90, 99, 100, 105, 106, 126
political power, *see* power (political)
political units altered by kinship 57
Pool of Bad Things (*pul jiakni*) 98, 106, 107
Pool of Good Things (*pul leak*) 106, 107
population changes, *see* migrations
Porter, W. A. 270
possession by spirits, *see* seizure
power (political):
  after Addis Ababa Agreement 307–19
  desacralized 32, 278–9, 289–90, 292, 293, 294, 295, 297, 313
  Evans-Pritchard on Nuer prophets' 31, 327 ff
  Nuer chiefs controlled 16, 183, 231, 272, 273–4, 275, 290
  peacemaking 329
  seizure and manipulation 283
  suppression of Nuer prophets, *see* suppression
Powers (spiritual) 58, 60, 138, 148, 281–5
  above and below Powers 60–2
  illness 68–9
  Nilotic proliferation 328
  Nuer religion 61, 328
  rivalry between Powers and divinities 258, 296
  see also DENG (divinity), powers of; divinities; earthly Powers; spiritual power; talking powers
prayer 65, 155, 241, 306, 316, 348
  legitimate practice 295
  for peace and welfare 113
  power granted by Aiwel 41
  for rain 172
  Thiang spear invocation 100
  to invoke Dinka divinities 67
  to invoke Flesh 58
prayer meetings 82, 138, 276, 277
predictions:
  Deng Laka's 138, 150, 155, 276, 335

Dual Diu's 206, 276, 314
Kolang Ket's 249, 335
Pok Kerjiok's 172
see also Ngundeng Bong's predictions
'priests' 59, 141
primacy of DENG 75, 85, 94–101, 103–4, 110, 154, 297, 332
primacy of DIU 154
primary sources *xii*
see also oral testimony
procreation and Flesh 58
propaganda:
British medicine 267
Ngundeng Bongs' songs 101–4, 124
prophecy as a historical discourse *viii*, *ix*, 351, 352, 356
prophetic idioms *x*
see also social and religious idioms
prophetic traditions:
evolution of 313, 315, 321, 324
new and old prophets 330
organised violence 325
prophet rivalries 203, 325
Deng Laka 132, 138, 140, 141, 147–55, 163, 285
Dual Diu 33, 170, 175, 201–2, 206–7, 210–11, 216–18, 218, 222, 227, 228, 232, 285
Guek Ngundeng 81, 97, 166, 175, 180, 189, 192, 198–9, 202, 222
influenced by war 300, 303
Lou Nuer 166, 178–85, 198–9, 203
Luang Deng shrine 147–8, 292
magicians 96–8, 155, 163, 218–19, 222, 239–40, 249, 250, 284, 285, 304, 325, 328–9
Ngundeng Bong 4, 79, 98–100, 105, 147, 149–51, 164, 166, 179, 202, 285, 334, 337
Nyin Nguen 294, 295
Nyuong Nuer 253–6
prophets versus government chiefs (1970s) 141, 259, 263, 309, 329
Ruei Kuic 302–4
Western Nuer 164, 243, 248–63 *passim*, 265–72, 274, 277, 281, 285
prophets, *see* Dinka people, prophets; message of prophets; Nuer prophets
prosperity brought by TENY 259
public health proposal rejected 17
puc cattle disease 133, 137
pul jiakni (Pool of Bad Things) 98, 106, 107
pul leak (Pool of Good Things) 106, 107
Pul Turuk 79
Puol Bidiit 127–8, 295, 360
Puol subsection (Gun Lou) 81
Puom Longar shrine 89, 94
Puom (Luang) Aiwel shrine 40, 42, 43–4, 93–4, 313
Puot Dual Diu 314
Puot Nyuon (Dok Nuer prophet) 249, 360
PUP (divinity) 240

race riots in Khartoum (1964) 336
Radh Gaawar 48, 217
Bar/Radh coflicts 127, 139, 142–3, 163, 303
Deng Laka 144, 147, 158
Dinka/Radh conflicts 49, 158, 208–9, 227
Nuaar Mer 128, 139, 142
see also Kerpeil section; Teny section
'radical social change' 353, 355
RAF (Royal Air Force) 21, 33, 192, 193, 195, 350
raids, *see* cattle raids; slave raids
rain (*deng*) 41, 60, 87, 172, 329
rainfall reduction, *see* drought
rainlands zone 37
rainmaking 24, 27, 172
Rajaf 159
Rambang Thiciot 102, 343
ran nhialic (man of Divinity) 59, 64, 70
see also Arianhdit
Ran Pinyien 82
Ranger, T.O. *xiii*, 354
rattles used in ceremonies 283
Reath Kuer, Phillip 303, 304
Reath Ngundeng 81, 173–4
Reath Yac 98, 99
Reconciliation, National (1977) 323
reconciliation agreement (1988) 344
records, official *xi*, 32, 33, 93
red cobra 61, 152
refugees 346, 348, 349, 349–50
regional government, *see* Southern Sudan Regional Government
Rek Dinka 28, 247, 248, 252, 257, 258, 262, 265–6
relics of Ngundeng Bong 299, 300, 317–19, 320
relief food to the Sobat 346, 347
religion:
'African traditional' 355
British administration 24, 29, 296
organized, *see* Christianity; Islam
religious change *x*
religious idioms, *see* social and religious idioms
Reng section (Gaajak Jikany) 304, 305
Rengyan Jagei 48, 52
resistance leaders, prophets seen as 5
resurrection 86, 169, 172, 251, 305, 350
reth (Shilluk king) 40, 43

revolution, Islamic 346
revolutionary government of Ethiopia 323, 342
Rhodesia uprisings (1896–7) 295
Riak Cany 263, 264
Rialbeagh (Saʿid Nur) 170
Rial Mai (Nyajikany chief) 190–1
Rialmai age-set 362–3
Riam Ngundeng 97
riek (shrine-stick) 63
riem (Blood) 58
Ric Dinka 49, 156
Riek Dol 96
Riek Mashar, Dr 324, 325, 346, 347
riek (shrine-stick) 63
RIEM (divinity) 144
rifle imagery replaces spear 307
rifle trade 220–1
Riim 343
rinderpest 87–8, 90, 95, 113, 124
RING, *see* Flesh
rites, clan-divinity 63
rivalries, *see* feud(s); magicians, rivalries; Nuer chiefs, rivalries; powers (spiritual), rivalries; prophet rivalries
river, associations and symbols 61, 292
river transport 267
road building 17, 183–4, 185, 275
  Ngundeng's predictions 334, 339–40
  Nuer opposition 186, 188–9, 190, 194
road transport 15
Robertson Smith, W. 31
Romilly, Captain H.A. 223, 224, 225, 226, 273, 276
Roussel, P. L. 339–40
Royal Air Force (RAF) 21, 33, 192, 193, 195, 350
Ruac Col (Lak prophet) 298–9, 300
Ruea Kerjiok 79, 84
Ruei Kuic (Lak prophet) 281, 300, 303, 304, 325, 360
  after civil war 309, 312–13
  career affected by war 311, 324
  Mogogh conference 309–10
  Nyaruac Kolang 301, 302, 325
  sacrifice 313
Rueng Dinka 47, 51, 52, 67, 244
ruic (spokesman) 58
Rumbek 27, 28, 68, 267, 322
  Egyptian garrison, fall of, (1883) 245, 247, 249
Rumbek district 252–3, 256, 257
Rumjok section (Gun Lou) 3, 106, 110, 111, 165, 166
  feuds 105, 113, 169, 171, 227
  Nyajikany 170, 193, 227, 315
  prophets, *see* Babuny Kir; Car Koryom; Pok Kerjiok; Thijok Dul
rumours:
  castration of men 269–70
  downfall of Guek 189–93
Rundial (Gamuk-Nyuong chief) 260
Ruop Jiak (Gaawar policeman) 229
Ruot Diu, oral testimony 140
Ruot Yuot (Gaawar court president) 304
Rupciengdol 51, 143
Rut Dinka 41–2, 67
  Nuaar Mer 133, 156
  Nuer/Rut: conflicts 49, 156, 157, 158; friendships 144, 148, 149, 157

sacks of divinity (*guk kuoth*) 73, 282
sacred spear of Lirpiou 67, 317
sacrifice 45, 118, 283, 284
  after seizure 328
  clan-divinities 63
  for cultivation 41, 277
  cuor (Vulture) 106
  Dual Diu 233, 234, 238, 239, 241
  for healing 82, 87–8, 90, 95, 113, 117, 122, 124, 279, 337
  for health and well being 280, 293
  Kolang Ket 250
  Luang Deng shrine 40, 148
  minor prophets 276, 277, 299, 313, 315, 350
  muot sacrifice 65, 172
  Nyaruac Kolang 279–80
  oxen sacrifice 85, 108, 199, 234, 238, 280, 319, 337, 350
  for peace 104, 234, 238, 319
  for social recognition of divinity 136, 138
  universal effect 105, 106
  views on 278, 295, 316
sacrificial sites, *see* shrines
Saddle-bill stork War 170–1, 172
Sadiq al-Mahdi 322, 323, 342
Saʿid Nur (Rialbeagh) 170
Sayyid Abd al-Rahman al-Mahdi 281
scepticism and belief 333–4
schools 298, 315–16
Schweinfurth, G. 24
seasonal migrations 37–8, 244
secret societies 28, 29, 256, 257, 332
sectional heads 290, 296
sections (*cieng*) 56, 260–1
security and British administration 9, 11, 14–15, 21, 121
seizure 61, 63, 67, 283, 289, 329, 354
  after removal of prophets 296, 297
  Bangong Diau 304–5
  Buom Diu 248, 251, 252
  Car Koryom 167, 168, 169
  cieng nyajiok 276–8
  dayiemni 96, 250

Deng Laka, *see under* Deng Laka
Dual Diu 205, 206, 209, 215–16, 217, 241
Evans-Pritchard's studies 174, 243
Gaalak Nyagh 248, 253–4
Guek Ngundeng 174
Guet Thie 180
illness 81, 82, 135–6, 167, 174, 293
Kolang Ket 249, 250, 325
minor prophets 67, 100, 133–4, 155, 169, 248, 249, 250, 251, 252, 254, 265, 276, 281, 292, 293, 300–1, 312, 325
NAI magic 284
Ngundeng Bong 73, 74–5, 76, 78, 79, 81, 82, 85, 92, 101, 116, 126
Nyaruac Kolang 279
shrine-masters 40
slave camps 68
social recognition 136, 138, 328
transcendent 329
Sennar Kingdom 46
separation of Dinka and Nuer *xi*, 20, 30
separatist movement (1990s) 346, 349, 351
SGS *Kerreri* 267
shamans 24
Shaw, Archdeacon A. 247
Shilluk-Luo people 28
Shilluk people 9, 29, 52, 54, 70, 93
conflict: with Al-Zaki Tamal 92, 115; with Dinka 46; with Nuer 53
Fashoda 40, 313
historical traditions 38
King (*reth*) 40, 43, 125, 313, 329
maternal kinship 57
native administration 23
Ruac Col 299
Ruei Kuic 312, 313
similarities with other Nilotes 57, 64, 65–6
Shona spirit mediums 355
shrine-master, Luang Deng 40, 95, 148, 300, 301, 302, 325
shrines 24, 33, 36, 40–1, 117, 327
accumulation of divinities 63, 328
cattle-pegs 63, 151, 239
Dual Diu 239, 240, 315
moral community 43, 124
Mwari 295
Nuaar Mer 141
prophets' graves 239, 328
Shilluk people 313
spiritual power 42–3
to PAJOK 96, 239
see also Aiwel Longar shrine; Luang Deng; Ngundeng's Mound; *and also under* Deng Laka; Ngundeng Bong
shrine-stick *ghoro* 63
shrine-stick *riek* 63
sister's son and mother's brother relationship 66, 104, 113
sky divinities 60–21, 86, 128
and earthly Powers 249, 283, 284, 285, 329
songs 153, 283
sky (*nhial*) 60
slave raids 52, 116, 132, 157, 162, 251
Nuaar Mer 126–7
slaving wars (1870s) 245
slaves 9, 14, 52, 114, 157
growth of free-divinities 65, 68
slave trade 68, 84, 156
sleeping mat (*guan yiika*), owner of the woman's 63
smallpox 78, 175, 181, 280
Ngundeng's cure 87–8, 90, 95, 113
Smith, W. Robertson *viii*, *ix*, 31
Sobat 54, 114–15, 346, 347, 349
Sobat river 7
Sobat Valley 11–12, 14, 169
social bonds, *see* moral community
social groups and divinities 64, 70, 329
see also spiritual networks
social idioms, *see* social and religious idioms
social networks:
Deng Laka 126
Dual Diu 215–22
social recognition of seizure 136, 138, 328
see also moral community; spiritual networks
social order:
change 352, 353, 355
Deng Laka 141–7
impact of money 290
political fragmentation 63, 70
see also ecology, impact on social organization; moral community
social and religious idioms 282–3
changed 37, 55–6, 289, 351
Nilotic peoples 55–65
Nuer prophets 243, 248, 254, 281, 327, 328
see also terminology
society, *see* moral community; social networks; social order
soldiers, *see* Anglo-Egyptian army; French army; guerrilla warfare; Mahdist wars; military administration; military force; Sudanese army
songs:
Deng Laka's 95, 148, 152–5, 159
Dinka 95, 112
MAANI 257, 283, 312
Ngundeng Bong's, *see* Ngundeng Bong's songs
sources, *see* documentation; oral testimony
Southern Rhodesia uprisings (1896–7) 295
Southern Sudan:
civil war, *see* civil war, Sudan
diversity of societies 16

Southern Sudan (*cont.*):
economic development 298
independence 346
Southern Sudan Regional Government (1972–83) 307–23 *passim*
High Executive Council 318, 341
Northern Sudanese 323, 340–1
Nuer prophets 290, 307–13, 316–19 *passim*, 320, 321, 322, 340
see also Sudanese army, (1972–83)
spear of Aiwel Longar 94
see also under spear-masters
spear of Gaatgankir clan 52, 74, 103
Spear of Honour for Buom Diu 274
spear imagery replaced by rifle 307
spear of Lirpiou 67, 317
spear-masters (*beny bith*) 27, 44, 52, 58, 113, 243
Aiwel Longar 41, 42, 43, 58
curse 65
Dinka shrines 40
Ngundeng Bong's kinship 104
as original settlers 66
spears, clan 52, 63, 67, 74, 100, 103
spear-shaft, owner of 63
spear of Thiang 100
spear of the thigh 103, 104, 105
spear of WIU, guardian of 52, 74, 103
spirit cults, growth of 68
spirit mediums, Shona 355
spirit possession, *see* seizure
spirits *colwic* 61
spiritual activity, *see* mantic activity
spiritual attributes of divinities 281–5
spiritual networks:
Deng Laka's collective 147–55
Dual Diu 215, 216
flood region centres 38–44
Guek Ngundeng 185
Ngundeng's Mound as centre 90, 99, 100, 105, 106, 126, 151, 154
spiritual pollution medicine 68–9
spiritual power 41, 148, 254, 297, 329
control of 42–3, 281–2, 296, 327, 328
Kolang Ket's 249–50
Ngundeng Bong's monopoly 154
order of seniority 324, 329
primacy of DIU 154
primacy of Nyaruac 281
rivalries between leaders 141, 262
shrines 40, 42–3
women as moderators 43, 52
see also DENG (divinity), power; DENG (divinity), primacy; divinities, power; powers (spiritual)
spiritual reward 110
spiritual strength, Deng Laka's 155
spiritual work, *see* mantic activity
SPLA (Sudan People's Liberation Army) *vii*, 324–5, 342, 343, 346–51 *passim*
SPLM/SPLA (Sudan Peoples' Liberation) Army and Sudan Peoples Liberation (Movement) 342
SPLM radio 344
spokesman (*ruic*) 58
Stigand, Major C. H. 9, 14
stones associated with *biel* 61
Strength (*buom*) 76
structural opposition theory 141
Struvé, K. C. P. 18, 25, 161–2, 177–8
border negotiations 12, 20, 183
method of administration 9, 11, 15, 16, 17, 20, 26, 182–3, 189
sub-*maʿmur* and *maʿmur* 9
Sudan:
Independence 297
reconquest (1989) 5, 7
see also Southern Sudan; Sudanese government(s)
Sudanese army:
(1956–72) 302, 306
(1972–83) 307, 312, 322, 323, 340, 341
(1990s) 346, 349
Sudanese government (1899–55), *see* British administration
Sudanese government (1972–83), *see* Southern Sudan Regional Government
Sudanese governments (1956–72) 290, 298
Umma party government and Nimeiri coup 302
see also Sudanese army, (1956–72) *and also under* Nuer prophets
Sudanese governments (1983 onwards) 324
Kharthoum 343, 346, 350
Northern Sudanese 342
see also SPLA; Sudanese army (1990s)
Sudanese refugee camps in Ethiopia *vii*, 346, 349
Sudan Notes and Records (Evans-Pritchard) 8, 30
Sudan Penal Code 10
Sudan People's Liberation Army, *see* SPLA
Sudan People's Liberation Movement and Sudan Peoples' Liberation Army (SPLM/SPLA) 342
Sudan reconquest (1898) 5, 7
sufi faqis (holy men) 24
Sulaiman Zubair revolt (1878) 245
suppression of prophets, British administration 23, 25, 29, 30, 203, 230, 271, 272, 330, 331
(1930s) 273, 276, 278, 291–3, 295, 296, 297
desacralization 32, 278–9, 289–90, 292,

293, 294, 295, 297, 313
Ngundeng Bóng 10, 13, 101
Nyuong Nuer 263–4, 265–6, 268–9
surveillance 32, 273, 276, 278, 291–3
suppression of prophets, Sudanese administration 299
symbols, *see* emblems and symbols

talking powers 60–1, 218, 283
see also *kulang*
tamarind tree (*koat*) 45, 51, 90
Tang Kuainy (Bul Nuer prophet) 281, 360
taxes, *see* tribute and taxes
teeth, full set at birth 41, 75–6
Tek Macot 250
telegraph line to Bor 161
Teng, *see* TENY
Teng Joak (Nyuong Nuer prophet) 276–8
TENY (divinity) 103, 152, 258
Buom Diu 248, 251, 252, 276
lineal descent 325, 346
powers 86, 252, 259
seizures 248, 249, 250, 251, 252, 283
Teny Kerpeil 128
Teny section (Radh Gaawar) 133, 142, 144
terminology:
confusion amongst Nuer 282–3
Evans-Pritchard's study 30, 56, 59, 60, 61, 332
see also language; social and religious idioms
termite mounds 137–8
territorial rights, *see* land rights
testimony, importance of oral 34
tetde ('by hand') 66
Thak section (Nyal Nyuong) 253, 256, 274
theory of structural opposition 141
Thiang Nuer 12, 48, 49, 66, 100, 147, 161
Nuaar Mer 130, 133, 139
Thiang spear invocation 100
Thiei Poc (Jagei chief) 279, 280
Thie Ruea 4, 123, 164–5, 360
thigh, spear of the 103, 104, 105
Thijok Dul (Lou Prophet) 96, 111, 125, 165–6
Thoi Dinka 49, 128, 129, 133, 156
Thoi Thiep (Thiang Nuer chief) 161
Thorow 78
thou (higlig tree) 298–9, 306
Thut age-set 70, 77, 132, 363
Tiep Kolang (Western Nuer magician) 248, 253, 254–6, 283, 284, 360
dealings with government 257, 260, 262, 265
tiet (diviner) 52, 64
Tigjiek section (Dok Nuer) 251
tiit (diviners) 64
TILING (divinity) 276, 283
Tip Gai 251
toic (river-flooded grasslands) 37–8, 225, 234, 236, 237
tuac (leopard-skin) 58, 108, 136, 141, 142
tolerance of prophets, British administration 278, 290, 296
Dual Diu 164, 205, 215, 216, 218, 221, 222
Nyaruac Kolang 279, 280–1
tolerance of prophets, Sudanese government 298, 299
Tonga mission 264
Tonga district (Shilluk) 312, 313
Tong Kuei, *see* Tang Kuainy
Torit mutiny 237
totems, *see* emblems
trade 50, 65, 84, 220–1, 244, 291
Zeraf merchant companies 84, 114, 130–1
'traditional' religion in Africa 355
transcendent seizure 329
transport, *see* canal; river transport; road transport
trees as symbols 45, 51, 61, 90, 298, 306, 313
Tree of Bad Things (*jiath jiakni*) 106, 107, 200, 304, 335–6
Tree of Good Things (*jiath leak*) 106, 107
tribute and taxes 9, 167
cattle as tribute 11, 12, 13, 14, 15, 84, 259
Fergusson's administration 267–8
tribute collecting patrols 11–12, 14–15, 16, 169, 207–8, 209
tse-tse fly 78
Tung Diu 146
tuok cattle disease 143
Turco-Egyptian regime 24, 46, 52, 54, 65, 114, 259, 353
Turu 229, 241
Turuk 4, 115, 340
tutelary divinities 61–4, 103–4, 253, 282, 325, 328
TUT GAR (Divinity) 102
TUT IN KUAC (divinity) 305
TUT IN KUR (divinity) 301
Tut Jiak Gai (oral testimony) 77, 90, 94, 96, 109–10, 181, 333, 334–5
Twic Dinka 47, 67, 161
Nuer/Twic conflicts 117, 148, 156–9 *passim*, 167, 168, 169, 170, 207
Twil Ran (government chief) 243, 270, 360
'two doctors' coup (1991) 346, 347, 349
tyet (diviner) 64

Uduk people 306, 349, 350
Ugandan Allah Water Cult 27
Ulema, Board of 24
Umma party government (1965–7) 302
United Nations Operation Lifeline Sudan 315

Unlawful Societies and Witchcraft Ordinance (1919) 27
unorthodox Muslims 24
UN relief food 315, 346, 347
Upper Nile Basin 7, 36–8
Upper Nile Province 299, 346
  British administration 7–8, 9, 14, 16, 18, 22, 26, 166, 182–4, 222
  Dinka settlements 38–44
  guerrilla warfare 302, 324, 343
  Nuer settlements 12, 209, 214

vessel of divinity (*guk kuoth*) 40, 73, 248, 282
  see also *guan kuoth*
visits, pastoral 291–2
Vulture (*cuor*) sacrifices 106

Waat 320, 344
Wal Atiang, *see* Wol Athiang
wal (magical substances) 60, 155
  see also medicine
Wan Deng (oral evidence) 148
Wang Guet 202
Wangkeac Gaajok (E. Jikany) 53, 77, 79
war:
  effect on prophets, *see* Nuer prophets, war
  growth of free divinities 65
  Mut Mandong 155
  Nuer as warrior race 5–6, 13, 21, 22, 30, 44, 56, 244–5, 256
  World War II 232
  see also Anuak people, conflicts; border conflicts; civil war; Dinka people, conflicts; guerrilla warfare; Mahdist wars; military force; Nuer people, conflicts; Shilluk people, conflict
War of the Hyena (*kor luny yak*) 114
War of the Saddle-bill stork (*kor rialbeagh*) (1916) 170–1, 172
War and Kar myth 45, 50–1
War Nyigol 120, 166
Water Cult, Allah 27
water master (*kuaar thoi*) 61, 293
Wau 51, 68, 231
Wea Neen 266
Wedderburn-Maxwell, H. G. 223, 224, 226, 229, 230, 232
Weibel 78, 89, 90, 177
Weideang 78, 89, 90, 177
Weituor Begh (Lou chief) 191, 361
West African Muslim immigrants 305
Western Dinka 42, 43, 47, 48, 63, 66, 67
Western Jikany 51, 325
  see also Jikany Nuer
Western Nuer *xi*, 45, 61, 66, 69, 77, 144, 244
  age-sets 362, 363
  British administration *xi*, 12, 18, 27, 32, 245, 248, 266, 271, 272–6
  conflicts with Dinka 47, 244–5, 247–8, 254, 256–64, 265
  Eastern Nuer divergence 291
  men of cattle 253, 254
  religious traditions 70, 253, 282–3, 331
  Ruei Kuic 312
  see also Bul Nuer; Dok Nuer; Jagei Nuer; Leek Nuer; Tiep Kolang; Western Jikany; Western Nuer prophets
Western Nuer prophets 312, 325
  chiefs reinstated 272–6
  as peacemakers 260, 266
  religious idioms 243, 248, 254, 327
  rivalries 164, 243
  see also Dok Nuer, prophets; Kolang Ket; Nyapuka Dan; Nyaruac Kolang; Nyuong Nuer, prophets; prophet rivalries; Wuon Kuoth
White Nile Dinka 46
White Nile Region 7, 43, 46, 54, 115, 249
white ox, children of the 87, 95, 111, 175
Wicjaal Buom, John 310, 312
Willis, C. A. 22, 29, 186, 274
  Dual Diu 222, 226, 227, 230
  military force 21, 29, 193, 198
  Nuer as security threat 22, 189, 193, 198
  method of administration 9, 17, 18, 20, 26–7, 183, 184
Wilson, H. H. 121, 156, 161
Wilson, Salim 68
Winder, John 32, 233, 234, 236, 292–3
Wingate, Sir Reginald 242
winnowing-tray, woman's 112
witchcraft (*peth*) 27, 58, 64, 150–1, 155, 163
witch-doctors 21, 22, 24, 26, 29, 30
WIU 98, 170, 222
  guardian of the clan spear 52, 74, 103
  Ngundeng's songs 100, 103
  peth 86, 315
wives:
  Deng Laka's 126, 132–3, 144–7, 154–5, 204
  divinities' 144–7
  Dual Diu's 219–20
  Gony Yut's 302
  Kulang Ket's 250
  the 'lion' 160
  Ngundeng Bong's 110, 222
  see also intermarriage
Woi 51, 209
Wol Athiang 247, 248, 249, 250, 257, 259
Wol Diu 146, 205
Wol Kan 207
woman's sleeping mat, owner of 63
woman's winnowing tray 112
women:
  barren, *see* infertility cures
  as *dayiemni* 155

as diviners (*tiet*) 52
female symbols 58, 112–13
focus of Dor village 146–7
moderators of spiritual power 43, 52
prophetess, government tolerance 279
Woodward, Captain F. W. 9, 11–12
World War II 232
Wulnyang 143
Wundeng, *see* Ngundeng Bong
Wuol Kor 192
Wuon Kuoth (Nyuong prophet) 248, 252–3, 253, 254, 262, 360
conflict with British administration 260, 265, 267, 332
as a magician 274, 275, 277, 285
raids on Cic Dinka 257–8
reinstatement as Dur chief 272, 273–4, 275
Wuor Yiec 134, 135, 138
wut ghok, *see* men of cattle
Wut Nyang (Lak Prophet) *viii*, 348–51, 360
Wyld, Major J. W. G. 20, 184, 230
administrative methods 18, 20, 22, 183
Gaweir march 222, 223, 224, 225, 226
Nuer as security threat 21, 27, 184, 189, 193

Yaal age-set 50, 147, 205, 220, 363
Yakan cult 27
yath 60, 67
yeeth (clan- and free-divinities) 60
YIAN DENG (divinity) 152
Yiek Jok (Lou elder) 4
Yier Puot (Teng Joak's *dayiem*) 277–8
Yilbith age-set 49, 363
Yioi Binie (Wangkeac leader) 109, 361
Yirkuo column attacked at Khor 263–4
Yirol 275
Yoac-nuac age-set 46, 52, 363
Yoal-Gaadbal section (Gun Lou) 79
Yod (*let*) 127
Yoinyang mission 243, 264
YONG (divinity) 315
YUOL (divinity) 152
Yuot Guoguok (Lou prophet) 297, 304, 337, 361
Yuot Nyakong (Lou leader) 67, 83, 84, 114, 128, 317

Zande secret societies (*biri*) 29, 256, 257
zar spirit cult 68
Zeraf area 14, 300
merchant companies 84, 114, 130–1
Zeraf island 48, 49, 51, 127–8, 131, 281, 292, 312, 324, 348
Zeraf Nuer, split with Lou Nuer 350
Zeraf valley 16, 156, 220, 241, 304–6, 308
see also Bahr el-Zeraf region